BOOKS BY CARL BRIDENBAUGH

VEXED AND TROUBLED ENGLISHMEN

MITRE AND SCEPTRE

CITIES IN REVOLT:
> Urban Life in America, 1743–1776

CITIES IN THE WILDERNESS:
> The First Century of Urban Life
> in America, 1625–1742

MYTHS AND REALITIES:
> Societies of the Colonial South

THE COLONIAL CRAFTSMAN

SEAT OF EMPIRE:
> The Political Role of Eighteenth-
> Century Williamsburg

PETER HARRISON, FIRST AMERICAN ARCHITECT

REBELS AND GENTLEMEN (co-author)

CITIES IN THE WILDERNESS

CITIES IN THE WILDERNESS

The First Century of Urban Life in America 1625-1742

by

CARL BRIDENBAUGH

New York: ALFRED·A·KNOPF

1968

C.1

L. C. catalog card number: 55–8593

THIS IS A BORZOI BOOK,
PUBLISHED BY ALFRED A. KNOPF, INC.

FIRST BORZOI EDITION SEPTEMBER 1955

SECOND PRINTING, AUGUST 1968

Originally published in 1938 by The Ronald Press

To
JESSICA

PREFACE

TO THE SECOND EDITION

Cities in the Wilderness has been out of print for several years, and it now seems appropriate to reissue it in conjunction with *Cities in Revolt: Urban Life in America, 1743–1776,* which continues the history of colonial cities to the outbreak of the American Revolution. Errors that have been called to my attention have, for the most part, been corrected in the text; and I hope that I have caught them all. Mr. Lawrence C. Wroth has pointed out that the broadside opposing markets at Boston (page 194), of which I said no copy exists, can be found in the John Carter Brown Library at Providence. The statement on page 441 that there was a Jockey Club at Charles Town in 1735 turns out to be an error, though the York Race Course was laid out at that date; there was no jockey club until 1754. It is to me a matter both of satisfaction and of gratitude that Mr. Alfred A. Knopf has so generously undertaken to bring out my book under the distinguished imprint of his house.

C. B.

Berkeley
November 15, 1954

PREFACE

Today more than half of all Americans make their homes in cities, and the ease of modern transportation causes the lives of many more to be affected by town conditions. Our national history has been that of transition from a predominantly rural and agricultural way of living to one in which the city plays a major role. Both materially and psychologically urban factors govern much of American life. Their origins are therefore of more than passing interest. I do not believe them to have been solely the product of nineteenth century industrialism, but rather to have germinated with the earliest settlement on American soil. Surviving evidence justifies the temerity of my conclusion that a full-fledged urban society existed well before the close of our first century of history.

In these pages I have undertaken to describe the life of colonial America from 1625 to 1742 as it developed under urban conditions. In an attempt to secure a fully rounded treatment, the examination of this emerging urban society is concerned with its physical, economic, social and cultural aspects. For the purposes of a complete picture five representative towns have been selected, — Boston, Newport, New York, Philadelphia, and Charles Town. These five towns were the largest on the continent at the eve of the American Revolution, and all fall well within the census definition of a city. They are further representative in respect to geographic position and political institutions, and illustrate the influence of such factors on urban development. To emphasize the course of historical change in town life the work is divided into three chronological periods, each bearing a title suggestive of its predominant characteristics. The year 1742 is selected as a stopping point because in many respects it seems definitely to mark the end of an era in colonial town life. Under each of these periods four chapters deal with the physical aspects, economic development, urban problems, and social life in the five towns. Thus the book may be read as a whole, or any one of the four topics followed through by itself.

The selection of sub-topics for discussion within each of the four major categories may seem to some capricious. I must urge in my own defense the words of a writer from the period with which I deal, that "Whoso desireth to discourse in a proper manner concerning Corporated Towns and communities must take in a great variety of matter, and should be allowed a great deal of time and preparation." The fac-

PREFACE

tor of "variety" has made it necessary to limit investigation to those problems, physical and social, upon the solution of which urban development was entirely dependent. Hence, the omission of some subjects intrinsically interesting, or important from an antiquarian, romantic or literary point of view, yet hardly vital to or characteristic of the growth of colonial towns into present day cities. And both the "variety of matter" and the element of time have made exhaustive treatment of any one topic impossible. I should like to see definitive studies on any one of a number of subjects covered cursorily in these pages. For myself, I have tried to create a picture of colonial town society as a composite of all the evidence has led me to believe it must have been.

Emerging from forty years' preoccupation with the significance of the frontier in early American history, historians are now beginning to realize that much that was characteristic of life in the colonies did not necessarily bear the stamp of frontier democracy and individualism. Commercial as well as agrarian interests dictated political if not also social revolution; most of the intellectual activity and much of the social and political advance of the eighteenth century depended upon an urban rather than a rural environment; certainly a large part of our radical thought came neither from farm nor forest but from the seaboard towns. I believe the colonial city, though it never embraced more than ten percent of the population of the colonies, exercised a far more important influence on the life of early America than historians have previously recognized. Here a type of society and a way of life developed which stood in marked contrast to that of the rural regions or of the frontier. Being mainly interested in the emergence of this society, I have tried throughout for a comparative treatment of the towns. I have sought to portray the characteristics of this society in the large rather than to achieve an antiquarian completeness. I have endeavored, furthermore, always to view the development of colonial urban society not only in relation to the colonies as a whole but also in a world setting. I have tried to describe the historical change in these towns as part of a great period of transition affecting all of western Europe. One of the most important aspects of this study I believe to be the role played by the towns in the transit of civilization from Europe to America.

In any description of past conditions the author must ask of the reader this cooperation, that he attempt for a time to live vicariously in the age under consideration. Colonial towns should be viewed as they appeared in relation to the civilization and developments of the seventeenth and early eighteenth centuries, not in comparison with the great aggregations of population and industry that constitute pres-

PREFACE

ent day cities. It must be remembered that the rise of large cities is a phenomenon of the years since about 1760. For the purposes of this study we must ignore later developments, and consider only the period, 1625–1742. Hence certain expressions used throughout the work must be divorced from their present connotations and considered with the meaning they held for the age that used them. For example, phrases such as "congestion" and "urban maturity" must be read not in the light of twentieth century developments, but with reference to the conditions and psychology of the times. Where long usage has endowed a word with new and different associations, the *New Oxford Dictionary* has served me for a guide. In a further effort to recreate the atmosphere of the period I have indulged in frequent quotation and in detailed pictures of certain events. Where the documents of an age preserve its thought and flavor it is well to let them speak for it. Also, I believe that one should never lose sight of the individual, even in the chronicle of social forces.

I also firmly believe that the story of any period is more than the sum of the written records it leaves behind. The feeling for an age which long association with its physical and documentary remains imparts leads to conclusions and generalizations which are logically sound and intuitively certain but for which no specific references may be cited. This is especially necessary in any study dealing with the pre-statistical period of history. Particularly in the seventeenth century men were not statistically-minded, and in very few cases can complete reliance be placed upon contemporary figures.

Certain friends, old and new, have unselfishly shared with me their materials and advice, and it is with pleasure that I acknowledge their generosity. In particular I wish to thank Miss Ellen Fitz Simons and Samuel Gaillard Stoney of Charleston, Alexander S. Salley of Columbia, Dr. Bruce M. Bigelow and Howard M. Chapin of Providence, Albert Cook Myers of Philadelphia, Dr. Clifford K. Shipton and Dr. Dirk J. Struik of Cambridge. To Dr. Raymond P. Stearns of Urbana I am especially indebted for materials from the Royal Society of London. A grant from the Social Science Research Council made possible study in Charleston during the summer of 1936. Finally, to the stimulating experience of friendship with Arthur Meier Schlesinger I wish to pay tribute, the extent of which only other equally fortunate scholars can appreciate.

CARL BRIDENBAUGH

Providence, Rhode Island,
　　November, 1938.

CONTENTS

PRINCIPAL ABBREVIATIONS USED IN THE REFERENCES

AAS *Trans.* — American Antiquarian Society, *Transactions.*

Bos. Rec. Com. — *Report of the Record Commissioners of the City of Boston.*

Cal. St. Pap. — *Calendar of State Papers. Colonial Series, America and West Indies.*

Col. Soc. Mass. *Trans.* — Colonial Society of Massachusetts, *Transactions.*

Courant. — *The New England Courant.*

Edwards, *New York.* — Edwards, *New York as an Eighteenth Century Municipality.*

Eve. Post. — *Boston Evening Post.*

Mass. Acts and Resolves. — *Acts and Resolves of the Province of Massachusetts Bay.*

Mass. Col. Recs. — *Records of the Governor and Company of Massachusetts Bay.*

MHS *Colls.; Procs.* — Massachusetts Historical Society, *Collections; Proceedings.*

Mercury. — *American Weekly Mercury.*

N. E. Journal. — *The New England Weekly Journal.*

Newport T. C. Recs.; T. M. Procs.; T. M. Recs. — Newport Town Meeting: *Town Council Records; Town Meeting Proceedings; Town Meeting Records.*

N. Y. Col. Laws. — *Colonial Laws of the State of New York.*

N. Y. Hist. Soc., *Colls.* — New York Historical Society, *Collections.*

N. Y. Journal. — *The New York Weekly Journal.*

N. Y. M. C. C. — *Minutes of the Common Council of the City of New York.*

News Letter. — *Boston News Letter.*

Pa. Col. Recs. — *Minutes of the Provincial Council of Pennsylvania.*

Pa. Mag. — *Pennsylvania Magazine of History and Biography.*

Pa. Statutes. — *Statutes at Large of the State of Pennsylvania.*

Peterson, *New York.* — Peterson, *New York as an Eighteenth Century Municipality.*

P. M. C. C. — *Minutes of the Common Council of the City of Philadelphia.*

Recs. N. Am. — *Records of New Amsterdam.*

Rehearsal. — *Boston Weekly Rehearsal.*

R. I. Acts. — *Acts and Laws of the Colony of Rhode Island and Providence Plantations.*

R. I. Col. Recs. — *Rhode Island Colonial Records.*

R. I. Hist. Soc., *Colls.; Pubs.* — Rhode Island Historical Society, *Collections; Publications.*

S. C. Hist. & Gen. Mag. — *South Carolina Historical and Genealogical Magazine.*

S. C. Pub. Recs. — Public Records of South Carolina.

S. C. Statutes. — *Statutes at Large of South Carolina.*

Stokes, *Iconography.* — Stokes, *The Iconography of Manhattan Island.*

Votes Pa. Assembly. — *Votes and Proceedings of the House of Representatives of the Province of Pennsylvania.*

PART I

THE PLANTING OF THE VILLAGES,
1625-1690

I

THE VILLAGE PHYSIOGNOMY

I

Cities rise and flourish in proportion as their natural advantages correspond with the demands of a particular age. This correspondence may be either accidental or the result of preconceived purpose, but history provides many instances of towns which, lacking this harmony between physical and economic environment, have despite artificial efforts of founders or promoters remained condemned to comparative unimportance, outdistanced by more fortunate rivals. In the seventeenth century material greatness was commercial, not industrial. Those towns prospered, therefore, whose sites commanded certain vital trading advantages — the possession of good natural harbors, the control of avenues of trade and communication, or the domination of a productive countryside. When in this period the Old World began to plant its colonial settlements on the North American continent, commercial considerations such as these largely dictated their locations. Design rather than accident endowed the principal offspring of seventeenth century colonizing impulses with situations favoring the pursuit of trade and navigation.

First in point of time, New Amsterdam on Manhattan Island enjoyed the finest harbor on the continent. Its site was the deliberate choice in 1625 of the engineer, Cryn Fredericksen, for the New World trading post of the Dutch West India Company. Five years its junior, Boston, at the mouth of the Charles, possessed a natural landlocked port open for most of the year, so that the capital of John Winthrop's Bible commonwealth was destined too to reap prosperity from its seaborne trade. Similarly, when William Coddington and his friends separated from the Portsmouth, Rhode Island, settlement in 1639, they chose an excellent year-round harbor, the best on Narragansett Bay, as setting for the town of Newport; not liberal politics so much as maritime adventure guaranteed its future increase.[1] Nature thus formed the destiny of these island villages;[2] good

[1] Wieder, F. C., *De Stichting van New York in Juli 1625* (*Linschoten-Vereeniging*, XXVI, 1925); Col. Soc. Mass., *Trans.*, XXVII, 272–285; Richman, *Rhode Island: Its Making and Its Meaning*, I, 117–134.
[2] Boston, too, originally was almost an island; "Invironed . . . with the Brinish flouds," Boston Neck was frequently under water during heavy storms.

harbors and a command of prevailing trade routes characterized all three.

Another burst of colonizing activity a generation later produced two settlements of slightly different character but equally conditioned by considerations of commercial advantage. Proprietary interests, ever watchful for returns from an investment not yet proved profitless, dictated the founding of a settlement at Albemarle Point in South Carolina in 1670, but fear of the Spaniard and the "sickliness of the coast" led ten years later to its transfer to the tongue of land between the Ashley and Cooper Rivers, where it received the royal name of Charles Town. Here a fine harbor behind Sullivan's Island fostered exportation of the exotic produce of this semi-tropical land. Shortly after this another proprietor appropriated a protected site which promised security for the domestic and commercial development of an emigrating people. Philadelphia never knew the savage warfare of a wild frontier, for Dutch and Swedish settlers as well as many Englishmen had already established homes on the banks of the Delaware when Thomas Holme first surveyed the city's bounds for William Penn in 1682. Though one hundred miles from the sea, the Quaker town found in the placid Schuylkill and the broad Delaware ready highways to world markets and their profitable trade.[3]

Coeval with the founding of these five settlements appeared certain factors and influences which in large measure conditioned their future growth and development. All were situated in the temperate zone and enjoyed its advantages of climate, although the semi-tropical location of Charles Town in a swampy region made it less healthy than the four northern ports. Moreover, the early villages were all similarly and strikingly isolated. From Boston on the north to Charles Town on the south stretched eleven hundred miles of wilderness, broken only by rare and occasional settlements. The four northern towns lay comparatively close together. The distance overland from Boston to Newport was seventy miles, from thence to New Amsterdam, one hundred and eighty, and from Manhattan to Philadelphia, ninety-five miles; but, seven hundred and fifty miles separated Charles Town from the Quaker village. This element of distance was multiplied many times by the difficulty of communication in a new country, and the villages were thus denied any great interchange of experience during most of the seventeenth century. The one notable exception was Newport, which as an offshoot from Boston and with easy access to it by land and sea developed in many ways similar to the Bay town. The

[3] S. C. Hist. & Gen. Mag., IX, 12–27; Records in the British Public Records Office Relating to South Carolina, I, 95; Westcott, History of Philadelphia, chapters XX–XXI.

factor of distance diminished in importance as the villages progressed. Although overland connections were practically non-existent, the fact that each village was a seaport made possible communication by water, and the presence of the ocean highway was a circumstance that tended with the passage of years to link the villages together economically and culturally, and thus to give them an advantage over the more isolated settlements of the interior.

The geographic position of the villages largely determined the form of their economic life. As seaports they became the focal points for trade between Europe and the colonies, and life within them was in consequence strongly commercial. But the character of the commercial development in each settlement depended chiefly upon the nature of its hinterland. The Appalachian mountain chain, which lies close to the sea in New England, extends in a south-westerly direction, forming an ever widening coastal plain to the south. The back country of Boston and Newport was consequently very limited. Such, too, would have been the case at New Amsterdam had not the Hudson and Mohawk Rivers provided an avenue through the barrier to the interior. Philadelphia and Charles Town, on the other hand, possessed seemingly unlimited hinterlands, which, when settled and connected with these centers by roads, promised wide territory for economic exploitation. Considerable diversity in the agricultural and industrial produce of the regions served by each of the five settlements resulted as the century passed in a coastwise exchange of goods, and the merchants of these villages became the agencies through which the first intercolonial contacts were effected. Seaborne trade made for the first intercourse between port and port.

The distantly separated villages were further united by the common national origins of the early settlers. The Dutch of New Amsterdam constituted the only non-English group of any size, and by 1690 this strain was becoming diluted by the steady infiltration of Englishmen. In like manner, the religious beliefs of the villagers, heterogeneous as they were, exhibited more common elements than divergencies. All were Protestant; nearly all, save the ruling class of Charles Town, radically so. The social complexion of each town was further fashioned by persons whose economic and cultural roots, whether English or Dutch, lay for the most part in the rising middle class of the Old World.

The political institutions of the colonial villages derived from common European sources, and despite varying applications in the New World, their similarities were more striking than their differences. English and Dutch local institutions had much in common, and after 1664, when New Amsterdam became New York, the last vestiges of non-English political life all but disappeared from the American urban scene.

These various influences, geographic, economic, social and political, conditioned the early development of the five villages. Save for the factor of distance they made in general for the formation of a uniform type of society. Just as rural regions and colonial frontier developed their distinguishing characteristics, so also did the urban centers. By 1690 a distinct village society was appearing in the American colonies. The five settlements had by that time outgrown most of the crudities of their village state and were emerging on the American scene as prosperous provincial towns. Collectively they harbored nine per cent of the colonial population.[4] Boston, with seven thousand inhabitants, had attained a size which made it comparable with some of the cities of the Mother Country. In 1680 there were only four cities in England whose populations exceeded ten thousand; Bristol, the second city, contained only about twenty thousand inhabitants in 1690. Boston was about as large as Gloucester at this time; Philadelphia and New York, with populations of approximately four thousand, paralleled Derby.[5] The New World towns had thus passed well beyond the stages of colonial experiment or frontier outpost, and an examination of their physical properties reveals much that was to characterize urban America throughout its early history.

II

During this period some form of local government to meet the special needs of village populations was established in every settle-

[4] J. T. Adams estimates the entire colonial population of 1690 to have been about 206,000. *Provincial Society*, 2.
[5] Van Rensselaer, *New York in the Seventeenth Century*, II, 210; Latimer, *Bristol in the Seventeenth Century*, 5.

The comparative growth of the villages in these years may be seen from the following table:

Population of the Colonial Towns, 1630–1690

	New Amsterdam (New York)	Boston	Newport	Philadelphia	Charles Town
1630......	300				
1640......	400	1,200	96		
1650......	1,000	2,000	300		
1660......	2,400	3,000	700		
1680......	3,200	4,500	2,500		700
1685......				2,500	900
1690......	3,900	7,000	2,600	4,000	1,100

These figures are estimates, based upon data in Greene and Harrington, *American Population before the Federal Census of 1790*, 19, 22, 65, 66, 117, and some dozen other references. Population statistics for this period are bound to be mere approximations, as contemporary reports are contradictory. The same holds true for England.

ment except Charles Town. Originally what powers of government the colonists possessed inhered in the provincial governments, and authority for dealing with local situations had to be coaxed or wrung from governors, proprietors or assemblies. The ability of each village to cope with its own particular problems depended to a considerable extent upon the measure of self-government accorded it. Police powers and the right of taxation were vital to the solution of incipient urban problems. In general the privileges granted to the villages were similar to those possessed by English boroughs and parishes. Boston and Newport, with their town meeting systems, enjoyed considerable local autonomy in the seventeenth century, and the Selectmen or Town Councils of these villages were relatively successful in their attempts to secure needed powers from provincial authorities. Especially was this true of the Rhode Island community, for it was the customary policy of that province to allow its towns wide freedom in dealing with their local affairs.[6]

On four occasions between 1650 and 1677 the inhabitants of Boston petitioned that "they might become a corporation," but, though the General Court repeatedly signified its willingness to accede to the request, nothing came of the matter.[7] We are denied an explanation for the failure of these attempts, and can only conjecture that the people of the town could not agree among themselves, or that the proposed charters did not meet with the complete satisfaction of the Court, or perhaps that the interest represented by the petitioners was not sufficiently vital or widespread. At all events, the town did not become an incorporated municipality in this period, although it frequently compared itself to the "City of London," and the General Court continued to allow the Selectmen and the Town Meeting more and more liberty in settling town affairs.

A director, appointed and sent out by the Dutch West India Company, governed New Amsterdam as a trading post in its earliest years. The inhabitants waged a long and bitter struggle with successive directors for some measure of home rule, and finally in 1653 received a charter providing for government by Burgomasters and Schepens. This corporation was quietly transformed into the Mayor and Common Council of New York in 1664 merely by changing the titles of its members, and its privileges were enlarged by Governor Thomas Dongan's charter of 1685.[8]

The county judges, grand jury, and Provincial Council of Pennsylvania controlled the local affairs of Philadelphia until 1684, when it

---

[6] Foster, *Town Government in Rhode Island* (Johns Hopkins *Studies*, 1884), 10.
[7] *Mass. Col. Recs.*, III, 207; IV, i, 368; IV, ii, 26; 7 *Bos. Rec. Com.*, 111.
[8] This government is carefully analyzed in Peterson's *New York*, chapter I.

became a borough. The rapid growth of the village, however, made the need for a separate government early apparent, and it received its charter of incorporation from the proprietor in 1691.[9]

Although the Carolina charter of 1665 authorized the Proprietors "to erect . . . cities, burroughs, towns, villages, . . . and to grant letters or charters of incorporation," Charles Town had no municipal government in this period. The Assembly of the Province made all rules for town, church and colony. In the case of legislation specifically affecting the village a number of members of the Assembly known as "Commissioners" were named in the act to put it into execution.[10] In the first decade of Charles Town's development this means of control seems to have been adequate to its needs, but the system was weak and clumsy, and the failure of Charles Town to meet its problems as promptly as the northern towns may be in large measure attributed to the absence of any effective and unified local government.

III

The villages advanced in this period from the crudest of frontier settlements to the dignity and comparative comfort of established towns. Because of peculiar local conditions and varying degrees of age the rate of growth, especially at Charles Town and Philadelphia, was uneven. By 1690, however, the village physiognomy was easily distinguishable from that of the countryside. As in all pioneer countries the erection of temporary shelters had been the first concern of the colonial townsfolk, but soon these "hovels and holes, in which . . . they huddled rather than dwelt," gave way to more permanent abodes.[11] The bark houses of Manhattan, the wattle huts of Boston and Newport, and the famous caves in the banks of the Delaware were rapidly replaced by substantial homes of wood, brick or stone.[12] The character of the buildings erected in each village was largely determined by the Old World traditions of the inhabitants and by the nature of the materials at hand. The features of the terrain whereon it was located further conditioned the appearance of each community. Thus by the close of the period each little seaport exhibited its own already perceptible individuality, while a suggestion of urban compactness was common to them all.

With the exception of New Amsterdam all the towns were decidedly English in appearance. The local stone of Massachusetts was unfit for

---

[9] *Pa. Col. Recs.*, I, 117; *Pa. Mag.*, XVIII, 504–509.
[10] Carroll, *Historical Collections of South Carolina*, II, 52; *S. C. Statutes*, VII.
[11] Versteeg, ed., *Manhattan in 1628*, 64–69.
[12] Watson, *Annals of Philadelphia*, I, 171–172; Winthrop, *History of New England*, I, 44–45; Richman, *Rhode Island: Its Making and Its Meaning*, I, 129–130; Kimball, *Domestic Architecture of the American Colonies*, 4, 12–13.

building purposes, and since Boston Neck was almost entirely devoid of timber, the inhabitants were forced to procure their building materials by water from islands in the harbor. Their early homes were one-story structures, covered with thatch, and flung at random over the peninsula.[13] By mid-century larger abodes were being raised; built around a single chimney, they had high-pitched, shingled roofs, and were lighted by small windows with leaded casements and diamond panes. In 1663 Josselyn noted that "the houses were for the most part . . . close together on each side of the streets as in London."[14] The Paul Revere house, built in 1676, with its unlighted side walls, indicates that domestic architecture was already beginning to conform to town conditions. The prevailing architecture of Boston, like that of medieval England which it so greatly resembled, was still essentially Gothic. Buildings of brick and stone, like Richard Wharton's triangular warehouse, became more common after the disastrous fire of 1679.[15] Boston, wrote a nameless Huguenot refugee near the end of the period, "is built on the slope of a little Hill, and is as large as La Rochelle. . . . The Town is almost wholly built of Wooden Houses; but since there have been some ravages by Fire, building of Wood is no longer allowed, so that at this present writing very handsome Houses of Brick are going up."[16]

The early buildings of Newport did not differ greatly from those of Boston, though the Rhode Islanders were more fortunate in finding a ready supply of timber in the woods surrounding their town. The relative security of life on the island led many of the more wealthy citizens to lay out large estates on which they built fine mansions,[17] and although some maintained town houses as well, the result was the slow development of any thickly settled district in Newport. By 1670 the old one-room, end-chimney pioneer home had been supplanted by the central chimney type with either two or four rooms on a floor. Of such construction was the large town house built in 1641 by the founder, William Coddington; the Wanton-Lyman-Hazard house, erected in 1675 and still standing, is another example of this more developed style.[18] Newport was reported to contain four hundred houses in 1675; probably two thirds of these were located within the

[13] Winthrop, I, 48; Dow, *Everyday Life in the Massachusetts Bay Colony*, 16–17, 39. The use of thatch persisted in Bristol, England, until at least 1665. Latimer, *Bristol in the Seventeenth Century*, 336.

[14] 3 MHS *Colls.*, III, 319.

[15] Dow, *Everyday Life*, 22, 232–234; Kimball, *Domestic Architecture*, 23–24.

[16] Shurtleff, *Topographical and Historical Description of Boston*, 47. In 1675 there were over twenty houses of ten rooms apiece in Boston. Drake, *History and Antiquities of Boston*, 395–396.

[17] Kimball, *Domestic Architecture*, 12–13; Richman, *Rhode Island: Its Making and Its Meaning*, II, 45.

[18] Chapin, *Documentary History of Rhode Island*, II, 44–64; *Cal. St. Pap.*, 1675–1676, 321; *Historic Newport*, 34–35.

village proper, and represented the limits to which the town was to expand for several decades.[19]

The other two English towns were founded late in the century and experienced a more mushroom growth. The problem of adequate housing for the vast numbers of immigrants who crowded over with William Penn confronted the town of Philadelphia from the beginning. It was solved with great rapidity; in ten years' time the Quaker city was as large as its oldest neighbor, New York. Penn wrote in July, 1683, that "within less than a Year" there had been erected "about four score Houses and Cottages," while in December he noted an increase of seventy more. The next year saw the total rise to 357 dwellings, sheltering a population of about twenty-five hundred. In 1685 the number doubled, brick construction was said to be as cheap as wood, and the Proprietor was boasting of the great rise in the value of town lots — four times the original price, "and over!" "As to the Town," reported Robert Turner in 1686, "Building goeth on. Now many brave Brick houses are going up, with good Cellars. . . . We build most Houses with Balconies." Construction had so far progressed by April, 1687, that the Provincial Council ordered the remaining denizens of the caves within a month "to provide for themselves other habitations, in order to have the said Caves Distroy'd."[20] In 1690 most of the inhabitants were well housed, and John Goodson was finding "rents towards the river high." Penn's dream of a "great town" had become a reality, and there seems reason in the enthusiasm of William Rodeney's review of the eight years' progress: "Philadelphia is mightily improved, (for its famous Buildings, Stone-Brick and Timber-Houses of very great Value, . . .) the most of any settlement in the World for its time."[21]

At Charles Town over a hundred houses were built in 1680 in the small area which had been "regularly laid out," with places reserved for a church, town house, and other "publick structures." Two years later Thomas Newe was able to write proudly that "The Town which two years since had but 3 or 4 houses, hath now about a hundred houses, all of which are wholly built of wood, tho there is excellent Brick made, but little of it."[22] Unfortunately, after this auspicious beginning, there is little record of the early progress of building at Charles Town.

[19] *N. E. Hist. & Gen. Reg.*, XXXVIII, 380.
[20] *Narratives of Early Pennsylvania*, 239–240, 261, 263, 269–272, 290–291; *Pa. Mag.*, XLIX, 116; *Pa. Col. Recs.*, I, 120.
[21] "They Build all with Stone and Brick now, except the very meanest sort of People, which Build Framed Houses with Timber, . . . two stories high," like those in Southwark, London. *Pa. Mag.*, IV, 195–196, 198.
[22] *Historical Collections of South Carolina*, II, 24–82; cf. *Cal. St. Pap.*, 1681–1685, 17; *Narratives of Early Carolina*, 181.

By 1636 the Dutch West India Company had constructed five large
stone houses to be used as shops, and numerous other buildings outside
the Fort, which added to private dwelling houses thus early gave to
New Amsterdam, as it nestled complacently in the shadow of Fort and
windmill, the appearance of a Dutch town.[23] Prior to 1650 most houses
were built of wood and covered with thatch, like that provided for the
town schoolmaster in 1642, but by the time of the first English occupation Dutch brick "alla moderna" had largely supplanted wood as
a building material. New Amsterdam was then a "brave place" containing about three hundred and fifty houses, "the meanest house
therein being valued at one hundred pounds," and an ordinary dwelling
yielding an annual rent of 120 to 180 guilders.[24] English rule in the
seventeenth century wrought little visible change in the Dutch town.
More houses were erected, some of wood, but the majority as in the
past "built of brick and stone and covered with red and black tile."
Placed gable-end to the street, and surrounded by gardens and fruit
trees, these homes were indeed "after the manner of Holland."[25]

After the first desperate shortage townsfolk in the seventeenth
century succeeded in providing themselves with shelter sufficient for
their immediate needs. Constant building had by 1690 begun to invest
the villages with an urban appearance. Save at Newport the houses of
each community were set close together and usually directly upon the
streets. A Massachusetts law of 1684, allowing half of a party wall
to be placed upon the adjoining property, is evidence of the growing
compactness of Boston.[26] Since the first necessity of the colonists was
for shelter, and their means limited, we cannot look for much architectural distinction prior to 1690. Most buildings were small, one- or
two-story dwellings, but here and there appeared an occasional fine
residence with its gardens and fruit trees. The severe, unpainted frame
structures, grayed by the weather, that were the rule in Boston, Newport and Charles Town, gave to these settlements a more somber
aspect than the colorful brick and stone houses with stepped gables
and tiled roofs at New York, or the sightly Flemish bond of the
balconied homes of the Philadelphians. Yet, despite the considerable
progress of this period the problem of housing in the colonial villages
was a continuous one, which grew rather than diminished as they
expanded into towns and their enlarged populations came to include
the poor and indigent as well as the enterprising and self-sufficient.

An adequate and inexpensive supply of firewood was indispensable

[23] *New York Colonial Documents*, XIV, 16–17; Stokes, *Iconography*, I, cf. Plates
Ib and VIIa.
[24] Stokes, *Iconography*, I, 27; IV, 95; 3 MHS *Colls.*, III, 314; Van Rensselaer,
New York in the Seventeenth Century, I, 454.
[25] *Documentary History of New York*, I, 90, 160. Cf. *N. Y. M. C. C.*, I, 14.
[26] *Mass. Col. Recs.*, V, 432.

to the life of the towns. Wood was the only fuel used for heating, and in the homes of the poor pine knots and "lightwood" were often also the sole means of illumination. The country was so well forested in the early years that there was seldom any necessity for townsfolk to go far afield for this commodity; an ample supply could be cut in the nearby woods and brought into the villages to be sold. The only town threatened with a fuel shortage in this period was Boston, for though the shores of Massachusetts Bay were well wooded no timber grew on the peninsula itself. During the winter of 1637 this scarcity became so acute that the inhabitants considered for a time abandoning the settlement. Wood was brought by sledge from the mainland in wintertime, and by boat from islands in the harbor during the rest of the year. As roads were opened up fuel from Muddy River and Roxbury could be carted into Boston, but the poor, who multiplied as time passed, annually suffered from its scarcity and high cost.[27] Manhattan Island furnished sufficient firewood for New Amsterdam in its early years. When the supply began to fail, about 1680, a space was set aside on the Strand, near Smith's Fly, for the measurement and sale of cordwood brought by water from Long Island and New Jersey. In 1684 the General Assembly of New York, to protect people from "great abuses . . . by them that make their profession to sell firewood," ordered that no wood should be sold until officially corded by the standard measure.[28]

IV

Town planning is generally regarded as a development of recent years, yet the two villages founded late in the period within the proprietary governments were carefully laid out prior to settlement according to the checkerboard plan proposed by Hooke and Wren for the city of London after the great fire of 1666.[29] As early as 1672 Lord Ashley instructed Sir John Yeamans to lay out Charles Town "into regular streets, for be the buildings never so mean and thin at first, yet as the town increases in riches and people, the void places will be filled up and the buildings will grow more beautiful." When completed, the town, "so famous for the regularity of its streets," formed a narrow trapezoid four squares long by two squares wide, fronting on the Cooper River. Charles Town was enclosed on three sides by a line of

[27] Drake, *History and Antiquities of Boston*, 181n.; 5 MHS *Colls.*, V, 163; Winthrop, *New England*, I, 393; 2 *Bos. Rec. Com.*, 4.
[28] Stokes, *Iconography*, I, 175; *N. Y. M. C. C.*, I, 138; *N. Y. Col. Laws.*, I, 164.
[29] The geometric plan for city streets well illustrates the seventeenth century passion for universal order and symmetry. Robert Hooke's model provided for "all the chief streets . . . to lie in an exact strait line; and all the other cross streets turning out of them at right angles; all the churches, public buildings, market-places, and the like, in proper and convenient places." Birch, *History of the Royal Society*, I, 115.

fortifications, and was "laid out into large and capacious streets, which to Buildings is a great ornament and Beauty." [30] Similarly, the "great Town" of Philadelphia was surveyed in the summer of 1682 by Captain Thomas Holme, according to the plans of the founder. Like Charles Town it conformed to the gridiron pattern which has set the fashion for most of our American cities, and with few minor changes remains today as its founder designed it. [31]

Only in Charles Town and Philadelphia did the laying out of streets precede the erection of dwellings; elsewhere the evolution of a highway system was largely fortuitous. Paths appeared from house to house as they were needed, and an occasional road pushed to a nearby settlement. The first paths tended naturally to follow the configuration of the terrain with little thought of symmetry; ease of travel was the prime consideration. In time such paths, developing into lanes and streets, came to demand the attention and care of village authorities, and deliberations over highway problems claimed a lion's share of space in town records.

Early in the life of the villages it was discovered that the control of streets and highways was a problem that transcended private initiative and demanded the serious attention of municipal authorities. By 1690 all of the towns had recognized this fact, and some provision, varying with each locality but everywhere based largely upon the transplanted institutions of the Mother Country, had been made to place so important an urban function under public authority. [32]

In 1634/5 a petition to the General Court of Massachusetts, complaining "that many highways in the country are inconveniently layde out," led to the first official regulations of this nature in any of the new communities. Acting upon this protest the Court placed the surveillance of highways in the hands of the Assistants. The next year Boston began to follow the English precedent of appointing annually four "Surveyors of ye Highways." [33] The village of Newport pursued a similar policy, and in 1639 its chosen surveyors laid out the lane "which ran to the harbor." [34] Prior to 1653, when New Amsterdam received municipal privileges, the director and council of the West India Company supervised the opening up of highways there. Under Peter Minuit (1628–1632) two lanes were constructed and a wagon road built from the Fort to the bouweries outside the settlement. In 1644

[30] Cal. St. Pap., 1677–1680, 455; S. C. Hist. & Gen. Mag., IX, 12–27; Crisp's Map of Charles Town (1704).
[31] Pa. Mag., XIX, 413–427; Westcott, History of Philadelphia, Chapters XX–XXI.
[32] For the English background see Sidney and Beatrice Webb, English Local Government: The King's Highway, 14–61; and Toulmin Smith, The Parish, 88–92.
[33] Mass. Col. Recs., I, 141; 2 Bos. Rec. Com., 10, 16; Webb, The King's Highway, 14–51.
[34] R. I. Col. Recs., I, 89; Doc. Hist. R. I., II, 70.

a "good stiff Fence" was built across Manhattan for protection against the Indians, and the lane on its southern side became the renowned Waal or Wall Street. The burgomasters of New Amsterdam were slow to yield their control of highways to a special group, as had the authorities of Boston and Newport. Not until 1666 did they request "Mr. Tho: Hall and other farmers" to nominate six persons as "Overseers of the Roads and Fences." [35] In the absence of local government in South Carolina the provincial parliament exercised supervision over all streets within the line of fortifications at Charles Town. At Philadelphia in the early years there was much discussion as to what body should enjoy jurisdiction over the streets of the town. The provincial council settled the controversy by decreeing on May 7, 1686, that "ye County Court, . . . its presumed has power to appoint Roads to Landing places, to Court, & to Market." [36]

As town populations increased and the number of houses was augmented, local or provincial authorities provided for the construction of further highways. Few of the lanes so built deserve the dignity of the name street before the end of the period. As a result of the labors of director and council it was reported in 1648 that there were "whole streets full of houses close under *Fort New Amsterdam.*" Under the burgher government, instituted in 1653, the work of constructing highways continued, and in 1656 a survey of existing streets was laid down on a map made with further growth in view. Another survey, made for Governor Nicolls in 1665, indicated seven principal lanes in the area between the Fort and the Wall. The meager evidence seems to indicate that New York enjoyed more success than Boston or Newport in its first dealings with the highway problem. Most of its streets were about thirty feet wide and made a good impression upon strangers: "The Town is compact and oval, with very fair Streets and several good houses." [37]

On October 17, 1636, the Selectmen of Boston ordered the construction of two "street ways" and three "laynes" ranging from "a pole breadth" to "1 Rod and halfe broad." Where expansion was rapid authorities often failed to keep pace with the demands of the community, and the Selectmen frequently granted "liberty" to individuals to open highways on their own initiative, and at their own "proper expense." [38] By mid-century a crude street system had been evolved at Boston, which was probably adequate for the needs of the town.

[35] Flick, *History of the State of New York,* I, 246, 292, 328; *Recs. N. Am.,* V, 342; Peterson, *New York,* 76–79.
[36] *S. C. Statutes,* VII, 1–2; *Pa. Col. Recs.,* I, 190; *Votes Pa. Assembly,* I, i, 41.
[37] *N. Y. Col. Docs.,* XIV, 94–96; *Recs. N. Am.,* II, 43; V, 221–225; *N. Y. M. C. C.,* I, 203; Stokes, *Iconography,* IV, 277.
[38] 2 *Bos. Rec. Com.,* 13, 52, 94, 100, Maps in Appendix; 7 *Bos. Rec. Com.,* 22, 31.

The Royal Commissioners of 1665 were, however, unimpressed; "Their houses are generally wooden, their streets crooked, with little decency and no uniformity." The rapid growth of the village after 1660 led to a demand for wider and better thoroughfares. The main highway across the Neck to Muddy River and Roxbury was widened in 1671, and after the destructive fire of 1676 the Selectmen secured a ruling from the General Court forbidding rebuilding in the burned area until the Overseers had remedied "the Inconvenience of ye straightnesse of ye streets," and made them "wider and more accommodable to the publicke." [39]

The settled portion of Newport grew slowly and highway construction lagged. The village tended to spread out along the Narragansett shore and the road to Portsmouth. It thus became a "scattered" town of two streets, Thames and Marlborough, both of which had been carefully laid off by 1654. With growing commerce and an expanding population the town needed improved highways, and in the decade from 1680 to 1690 the surveyors were kept busy by continuous demands from the Town Meeting for new roads. [40]

Provisions for highways had been made in the original plans for both Charles Town and Philadelphia. There were very few houses built at the former town outside the fortifications until after 1717, and streets within the lines had been laid off at the time of the town's founding. The Parliament of South Carolina was slow to make highway regulations in these early years, contenting itself with an order in 1685 requiring abutters to "clear out, stubb upp and remove all bushes, stumpes, young pines, and weeds . . . out of one halfe of the breadth of the street." The thoroughfares of Philadelphia had been carefully surveyed by Thomas Holme before colonists arrived. Nine broad streets ran from the Delaware to the Schuylkill, and twenty-one crossed them at right angles. This system provided ample communication for the town of two square miles. The problem confronting Quaker villagers was one of maintenance and improvement rather than of opening up new highways. [41]

With the increase in the number of streets, distinction by name became a necessity. At an early date New Amsterdam seems to have given names to the streets below the Wall; on the "Duke's Plan" of 1664 we find about twenty streets, lanes and alleys vaguely designated. Boston was more tardy in christening its thoroughfares, such labels

[39] Winsor, *Memorial History of Boston*, I, 231 n.; Hutchinson, *Papers relative to the History of the Colony of Massachusetts*, 421; 7 *Bos. Rec. Com.*, 61, 105, 164; *Mass. Col. Recs.*, V, 139–140.

[40] *Newport Hist. Mag.*, I, 182–185; *Newport T. M. Recs.*, I, 5; *R. I. Col. Recs.*, III, 235.

[41] *S. C. Statutes*, VII, 1–2; *Cal. St. Pap.*, 1677–1680, 455; Westcott, *History of Philadelphia*, Chapter XXI.

as "the street leading to the Neck" and "John Thwings land to the lane by Houghton's house" serving until well after the turn of the century. Newport was apparently the first village to provide methodically for the naming of its streets. The Town Meeting ordered the surveyors in September, 1679, "to consider of making foure equall divisions of this Towne . . . [which] will be useful about ye naming of ye highways." Holme had called the streets of Philadelphia by the names of eminent personages, but Penn, wishing to avoid all appearance of "man-worship," redesignated them, giving numbers to north and south thoroughfares, and names of trees and fruits indigenous to Pennsylvania to those that intersected them.[42] This nomenclature gave rise to an old rhyme the writer learned in his childhood:

> High, Mulberry, Sassafras, Vine;
> Chestnut, Walnut, Spruce, and Pine.

Encroachment on the highways was a misdemeanor which village authorities continually took steps to prevent. In 1636 the Boston Selectmen forbade the erection of any buildings "neere unto any of the streets or laynes" without their consent, and eleven years later the prohibition was extended specifically to include the digging of cellars. Peter Stuyvesant issued a similar ordinance for New Amsterdam in 1647, and provided for three Roymeesters with power to stop the construction of all "unsightly and irregular buildings." Newport and Charles Town both took steps to check encroachments on their streets. Traffic was frequently obstructed by materials lying in the roadways, and both Boston (1641) and New Amsterdam (1650) found it necessary to make stringent regulations and levy heavy fines on builders and others guilty of "crowding the streetes" with "stones, clay, firewood, boards or clapboards, or any other thinge that may annoy the towne's streets." Another source of annoyance to Bostonians was the need to open the streets for the laying of drains. So frequently did inhabitants fail to fill in and repair these excavations that the Selectmen decided in 1660 to require the taking out of a permit by anyone wishing to install a drain.[43] Despite continued regulations such misdemeanors tended to increase with the size of the villages and remained to plague authorities for generations.

In Boston and Newport, as in the English parishes, roads were built by the inhabitants, who were required either to labor on the highways or to employ substitutes. The town of Boston decided in 1641 that "for the maintenance of the high wayes, the Richer sort of

[42] *Recs. N. Am.*, V, 221–225; *N. Y. M. C. C.*, I, 112; *Newport T. M. Recs.*, 5; *Narratives of Pennsylvania*, 317.

[43] *2 Bos. Rec. Com.*, 12, 60, 90, 98, 157; *7 Bos. Rec. Com.*, 31–32, 141, 146, 179; *Laws of New Netherland*, 74, 114; *N. Y. M. C. C.*, I, 7, 224, 247; *Newport T. M. Recs.*, 21; *Cal. St. Pap.*, 1677–1680, 455.

Inhabitants shall afford three daye's worke of one man (except such as have Teames) ; the men of middle estate, two daye's worke ; and the poorer sort one day, . . . and every Teame in the Towne is to afford one daye's worke." The other English villages followed a similar method, and after the English occupation the scheme was much the same for New York. In addition to the labor of citizens, the villages levied "rates" to pay for materials and other costs. Sums thus raised were very small, and the streets accordingly poor.[44]

The first roads were mere open spaces from which the tree stumps had been removed, but as they grew more useful and necessary two of the towns made efforts to pave them. Residents of Brouwer Street in New Amsterdam petitioned the Burgomasters in 1658 for permission to pave their street with cobblestones. Their prayer was granted, but no financial aid was forthcoming. The Mayor and Common Council of New York were more progressive and in 1684 made a fair beginning when they ordered "Smith's Street" and the "Beuer Gracht" to be paved on each side "Eight foot in Breadth from the Houses." [45] The "lane which goeth to the Cove," paved as early as 1652, was Boston's first real thoroughfare, and it is significant that this improvement was accomplished by private initiative rather than "by order of the Selectmen," who contributed only forty shillings to this laudable enterprise. Although the Town Meeting frequently discussed the question of paving, lack of public funds for any such undertaking proved an insurmountable obstacle, and Boston streets were inferior to those of New York in this respect. The belief that those who used the roads should care for them led the Selectmen in the 1670's to regulate the width of cart wheels and to arrange with the carters for repairing the streets. Most attempts in this period to improve the thoroughfares were abortive, and the laying of a few cobblestones or the spreading of an occasional load of gravel was more usually the result of some townsman's public spirit or regard for his personal convenience than of any municipal enterprise.[46] In 1690 the streets of all the villages remained, for the most part, unpaved and badly drained. In wet weather they became miry and dangerous; when Samuel Sewall, after venturing forth on the 6th of March, 1684/5, reported to his *Diary*, "wayes extream bad," he was undoubtedly describing

[44] In 1649 Boston spent £33.1. on its streets. *2 Bos. Rec. Com.*, 62, 96; Webb, *King's Highway*, 27–42.
[45] *Recs. N. Am.*, II, 289; VII, 166; *N. Y. M. C. C.*, I, 151, 179.
[46] *2 Bos. Rec. Com.*, 113, 139; *7 Bos. Rec. Com.*, 53, 66, 85, 107. Boston's failure to pave its streets must not redound greatly to its discredit, for on July 31, 1662, John Evelyn "sat with the commissioners about reforming the buildings and streets of London, and we ordered the paving of the way from St. Jame's North, which was a quagmire, and also of the Haymarket about Piquidillo, and agreed upon instructions for the better keeping the streets clean." Traill, *Social England*, IV, 493.

with great restraint the frightful conditions to which spring rains and thaws gave rise.

In the dirtiness of their thoroughfares colonial villages vied with, but never equalled, the filthiness prevalent in contemporary English towns.[47] Casting rubbish and refuse of all kinds into the streets without let or hindrance was a confirmed habit of both English and American town-dwellers. The burghers of New Amsterdam, with their inherited traditions of cleanliness, were the first to tackle this problem. In 1657 the authorities forbade the throwing of "any rubbish, filth, oyster shells, dead animal or anything like it" into either streets or inlet. Responsibility for the condition of the street before his dwelling was placed upon the individual householder, and this plan was continued under the English regime. The prevailing absence of what would today be termed a sense of civic responsibility led to frequent violations of these laws; in 1671 one John Sharp was haled into Court for gathering his rubbish and casting it in the street before a neighbor's house. It was arranged in 1670 that the city's carmen should take turns weekly in collecting the rubbish gathered up in the streets, "provyded the dirt be throwne & Loaden uppon the Cart by the owners or tenneants of the howses in the said streets."[48] Such regulations proved ineffectual to prevent dumping of refuse in the lanes of New York; progress in dealing with this problem was to wait for a later period.

Boston first took action against the dirtiness of its thoroughfares in 1662, when the Selectmen hired Thomas Willsheer as a scavenger to clear the streets of "all Carrinon & matters of offenciue natuer." Four years later orders were issued against casting any filth or dirt into the streets, directing inhabitants to "bury ye same," while "all garbidge, beast entralls &c." were to be thrown from the drawbridge into the Mill Creek. Consistent disregard of these "good rules" led to the annual appointment of four scavengers beginning in 1684, and somewhat cleaner thoroughfares were the result.[49] In general, however, save in these two older towns, little effort was made by the villagers to tidy up their streets, and throughout the seventeenth century rain storms and similar acts of God were far more effective than any human agency in clearing the highways of filth.

[47] In 1641 Bristol, with a population of about fourteen thousand, hired a "Raker" to clean the streets at £30 per annum. The office was vacated during the Civil Wars, and the Corporation made no effort before 1700 to clean up the streets, which by its own admission were "full of dirt, soil, filth, and very dangerous." Latimer, *Bristol in the Seventeenth Century*, 64, 212.

[48] *Recs. N. Am.*, I, 31; VI, 349; VII, 273, 360; *N. Y. M. C. C.*, I, 28, 137; Peterson, *New York*, 93, 99.

[49] 2 *Bos. Rec. Com.*, 112; 7 *Bos. Rec. Com.*, 8, 31, 54, 85, 166, 179; *Mass. Col. Recs.*, V, 438. There is no record of the care of the streets in early Newport, Charles Town or Philadelphia.

In every village in the colonies, as in those of England, hogs roamed the streets at will, serving a useful purpose as scavengers, but making passage of the thoroughfares dangerous for man and horse. Constant attempts were made to abolish this nuisance. In 1634 Bostonians voted that swine should not be allowed to run at large, but should be "kept up in yards," and two years later chose Richard Fairbanks as hogreeve with power to impound all strays. The frequency with which the hog appears in town records is mute proof that despite many "good and sufficient" measures the problem was never solved, and the bicameral legislature of Massachusetts remains a monument to its persistence. In like manner the village of Newport resolved in 1639 that no man might keep swine about the town except within his own enclosure, and in 1663 the General Assembly ordered the erection of a "sofitient pound," which does not, however, seem to have been built for over twenty years. But it was at New Amsterdam that roving swine proved most obnoxious. From the days of Peter Stuyvesant's "great grief" over damages done to the walls of the Fort the ubiquitous hog succeeded in continually vexing the city fathers. Ordinance after ordinance, as in Boston, was issued to restrain this nuisance, always with little or no success. There were many bitter complaints of damages, such as those of Henry Van Dyke, who in 1674 told the Mayor's Court that he was "greatly damnified," cattle and hogs belonging to Sheriff Anthony having destroyed his orchard. The failure of village authorities to banish swine from their streets was owing in large part to the obstinacy of many townsmen, who preferred their hogs should forage for themselves and thus spare them the cost of providing feed; also, regarding their hogs as good scavengers, they refused to go to the trouble and expense of building pens for them.[50]

As the villages developed their inhabitants were confronted with certain importunate engineering problems. Marshes and swamps needed draining and filling in to insure solid ground for buildings and streets, streams and brooks required bridging, and in some localities there was a demand for canals for drainage and transportation. These problems were not confined solely to village settlements, but here the need for solution was more pressing than in rural districts. It was prerequisite to any town expansion. When Newport was laid out there was a large swamp along the waterfront where Marlborough Street now runs, and this, as well as the marsh along the Strand, was gradually filled in by the populace. In Boston, lands in the North End near the Mill Creek and marshes at the heads of the several coves required filling in, and the ravages made by the tides on Boston Neck had re-

[50] 2 Bos. Rec. Com., 3, 5, 32; Doc. Hist. R. I., II, 80; Newport T. M. Recs., 13, 45; Peterson, New York, 91-98; Pa. Col. Recs., I, 327, 329.

peatedly to be repaired. Most of these reclamation projects were consummated by private persons with the "liberty" of the Selectmen; the infant villages in their corporate capacities were too poor to finance large public works, and the inherited conception of the medieval town with its limited charter acted as a brake on municipal enterprise. The largest project of this nature undertaken in the seventeenth century was at New York, and, contrary to the general rule, was accomplished by the civic authority. The "great Graft," an inlet from the East River, was lined with sheet piling in 1664, the abutters on the "ditch" being assessed forty guilders each to meet the expense. In 1671 Governor Lovelace urged the city to renew the piling and to regulate the casting of filth into the Graft, but not until four years later did the Common Council order the residents of Heeregraft "forthwith & without delay" to fill in the ditch level with the street and "then to pave & pitch the Same before there dores with stones." Thus did this foul inlet give way to the present Broad Street.[51]

The building of bridges bore a close relation to the evolution and extension of highways. As in the case of land reclamation, they were usually the result of private enterprise, although authorities insisted upon their maintenance as part of the highway system. As early as 1643, under Director Van Twiller, a bridge was thrown across the creek which flowed through the center of New Amsterdam. One of the most interesting projects of the period was the drawbridge over the Mill Creek in Boston, built in the same year. Ten years later the Selectmen authorized Joshua Scotto and William Franklin "to alter the drawe bridge, . . . to make it rise in two leaves; provided they make it suffityent as when the towns Men First accepted it." The crowds returning from witnessing the execution of the Quakers in 1659 were so great that this bridge collapsed under their weight, and the new one which replaced it was, like all moving structures, constantly in need of repairs.[52]

In Philadelphia, Benjamin Chambers and Francis Rawle were granted permission by the Provincial Council in 1690 to undertake a remarkably ambitious piece of highway engineering. Mulberry Street was extended to the water's edge by means of an "Arch" cut under Front Street, and town carts thus afforded more easy access to the wharves and docks. When this project was within a short space of time completed, the inhabitants were so pleased with the improvement that Mulberry became henceforth popularly known as Arch Street.[53]

[51] Peterson, *History of the Island of Rhode Island*, 29; Shurtleff, *Topographical and Historical Description of Boston*, 106–112; *N. Y. M. C. C.*, I, 19.
[52] Van Rensselaer, *New York in the Seventeenth Century*, I, 144; 2 *Bos. Rec. Com.*, 98, 117, 153; *Mass. Col. Recs.*, II, 263.
[53] *Pa. Col. Recs.*, I, 330.

The building up of the towns led naturally to increased care for the open spaces that remained. At a Town Meeting held in Boston, March 30, 1640, it was agreed that henceforth there should be no land granted either for houseplot or garden out of "the open ground or Comon Feild." This order, carefully observed, reserved to the town the famous Boston Common as a public park. The land was used for pasturing the town's cows, and at certain times of the year as a drill ground for the train bands. Here on this "small but pleasant Common . . . ," wrote Josselyn in 1663, "the Gallants a little before Sunset walk with their Marmalet-Madams, as we do in the Morefields. &c. till the nine a clock Bell rings them home to their respective habitations." Not until 1682 was another provision of this sort made, and then not by the town but by the proprietor. William Penn, foreseeing the rapid growth of his city, ordered five squares laid off and set aside for the permanent use of its people. Also in Philadelphia a wide area in High Street near Second served for many years as a grassy common for the pasturing of sheep.[54] These early efforts constituted the beginnings of the American park system of which our city-dwellers are today so proud.

Through the streets and lanes of the colonial villages there daily passed an ever-increasing concourse of townsmen; some on foot and some on horseback; apprentices and laborers carrying burdens or pushing wheelbarrows; and a growing number of horse and ox sledges, carts and wagons, supplanting the pack horse traffic. In addition, the public ways served as the principal playground for village children. By mid-century this congestion had reached such proportions in the three villages of Boston, Newport and New Amsterdam that accidents were frequent and inevitable. In Boston in 1655/6 the Town Meeting moved to protect pedestrians, especially children playing in the thoroughfares, against "persons irregular riding through the streets of the towne and galloping" by levying a fine of 2s. 6d. for such a misdemeanor. Three years later the Selectmen ordered all carters to lead their horses through the highways of the town "with a rayne," and forbade them to leave their animals alone in the streets unless securely "tyed to some place." Apparently these ordinances proved difficult to enforce, for in 1662 the General Court found it necessary to add its weight to their execution since "many take the liberty & boldness to gallop frequently, . . . to the great endaingering the bodies and liues of many persons, especially children, who are ordinarily abroad in the streets, & not of age or discretion suddainly to escape such danger." Accordingly, the Court sustained the Town's action, and

[54] 2 *Bos. Rec. Com.*, 52; 3 MHS *Colls.*, III, 319; Scharf and Westcott, *History of Philadelphia*, I, 122.

levied an additional fine of 3s. 4d. on any "galloper" within Boston Neck, "unlesse it appears on extreme necessity." This "drive" was more successful. In 1663 the General Assembly of Rhode Island passed an act to prevent "excessive riding" in the streets of Newport, which placed the heavy fine of five shillings on the offense. In reenacting this law in 1678 the Assembly gave as its principal justification the fact that recently in Newport there had been "a very great hurt done to a small childe, by reason of exceeding fast and hard ridinge of horses." Over twenty years before, in 1652, Director Stuyvesant had had to issue an order against the fast driving of wagons and carts through the streets of New Amsterdam.[55]

Among the novelties of Restoration England were wicker and spring carriages, "glass coaches," and the Hackney coach. Introduced first in London, the fashion soon spread to provincial towns. But it is interesting to discover that there were in Boston as early as 1669 persons of sufficient affluence to be able to maintain coaches, among them the Reverend Mr. Thomas Thatcher of the Old South Meeting. In 1674 the last Dutch governor of New York made a present of his coach and three horses, the only equipage in the colony in the seventeenth century, to Sir Edmund Andros.[56] Thus early did two American villages strive to emulate the splendors of metropolitan cities. Towards the end of the period a Hackney coach was available for public hire in Boston. A glimpse into Samuel Sewall's diary reveals him a constant patron of this new vehicle: "Oct. 17, 1688. Ride in the Hackney-Coach with Govr Bradstreet, his Lady, Mrs. Willard, Mrs. Mercy Bradstreet, Josiah Willard, to Roxbury the ordination of Mr. Nehemiah Walter." On another occasion Sewall hired "Ems Coach" and drove Hezekiah Usher and their two wives to Roxbury to dine at the Greyhound Tavern, returning home between ten and eleven in the evening, "in the brave moonshine."

V

Provision of adequate landing places for shipping followed close on the erection of homes in all the villages; attraction of trade was necessary, first for comfort, and later for prosperity. In the beginning ships were unladed by lighters which conveyed the cargoes to a convenient cove or natural landing place at the water's edge. Thus the "Coves" at Boston and Newport, and the "Strand" at New Amster-

[55] 2 *Bos. Rec. Com.*, 129, 147, 158; *Mass. Col. Recs.*, IV, ii, 59; 7 *Bos. Rec. Com.*, 44, 63, 126; *R. I. Acts (1744)*, 12; (1705), 20; *R. I. Col. Recs.*, III, 12; *Laws of New Netherland*, 128; *N. Y. M. C. C.*, I, 136.
[56] Latimer, *Bristol in the Seventeenth Century*, 230; Van Rensselaer, *New York in the Seventeenth Century*, II, 212.

dam became the early shipping centers of those villages. The need for wharves and docks was soon felt, however, and townsfolk set about their construction. As in the case of other public improvements, the first work was undertaken by substantial private citizens, singly or in association, who alone could finance such expensive projects. By 1639 there were at Boston a "Wharfe and Crayne" built by a group of merchants to whom the town granted for their maintenance and repair a hundred acres of land at Mount Wollaston. At Newport wharves were built into the Cove in 1639 by well-to-do citizens like Nicholas Easton and William Brenton. As late as 1667 Brenton's wharf was the principal docking place for vessels from the West Indies. There was no wharf at New Amsterdam until 1648/9, when a little pier with a crane nearby was erected by the Company, after townspeople had twice petitioned for this improvement. At Philadelphia there was a fine natural landing place known as the Blue Anchor, from a tavern located near there before the city was founded. This served for docking small boats and lighters for many years after the construction of large wharves.[57]

During the seventeenth century Boston was the largest and most important colonial port and it is natural to find the greatest activity along its waterfront. By 1645 fifteen private wharves had been built, the smaller by individuals, and the larger by joint enterprise. The town granted a large tract of land along the harbor to Valentine Hill and several associates in 1641, with liberty to erect wharves thereon and to charge tonnage and wharfage for a period of eighty-five years. Largest and finest of these private projects were the wharves built by Samuel Scarlet and Thomas Clark, on which were erected warehouses and cranes for the handling of cargoes.[58] The "Dock" at the head of the Cove was improved by the town authorities, and maintained as a public landing place for smaller boats. Great care was exercised to prevent encroachment on the land around the Dock; in 1661 Francis Smith paid a fine of twenty shillings for erecting a building at the head of the dock without a license. An effort was made to keep the waterfront clean by the appointment of water

[57] 2 Bos. Rec. Com., 37; Doc. Hist. R. I., II, 70; Stokes, Iconography, I (Plates); IV, 112; Recs. N. Am., VII, 219, 225, 230; Westcott, History of Philadelphia, chapter XXVIII.

[58] Between 1645 and 1690 over thirty "liberties" were granted to construct wharves. 2 Bos. Rec. Com., 63, 106, appendix; 7 Bos. Rec. Com., passim.

In 1673 provincial authorities recommended the construction of a sea-wall to run before the town from the Sconce to Scarlet's Wharf to protect vessels from French fireships. Proving too expensive for the town, the project was turned over to a group of public-spirited citizens. This sea-wall, completed in 1687, was twenty-two hundred feet long, twenty-two feet wide at the bottom, twenty-two inches at the top. Never needed, it gradually fell into decay. That forty-one townspeople could subscribe enough money to complete 1,872 feet indicates the growing prosperity of Boston. Mass. Col. Recs., V, 310; 7 Bos. Rec. Com., 79–82, 84.

bailiffs in 1636, "to see that noe annoying things be left or layd about the sea shore," and in 1658 the town erected two privies at the dock "for the accommodation of strangers and others." [59]

The growing commerce of Newport after the mid-century led to a demand for better docking facilities. Some time after 1680 a group of merchants styling themselves "the Proprietors" built the Long Wharf, probably the finest structure of its kind then existing in the colonies; and in 1685 another large wharf was erected by six prominent citizens.[60]

Philadelphia was fortunate in having citizens of sufficient wealth to undertake the construction of large wharves as soon as the village was founded. In 1684 Penn granted land along the Delaware waterfront to Samuel Carpenter, "in order to erect a wharf or key, and to build [ware]houses thereon for the better improvement of the place as well as for his own particular profit." The completed wharf, which ran out into the River near the foot of Walnut Street, was two hundred and four feet in width, and supported several "stores," or warehouses, and a flour mill. Penn could thus report in 1685 that "There is . . . a fair Key of about three hundred foot square, Built by Samuel Carpenter, to which a ship of five hundred Tuns may lay her broadside, and others intend to follow his example." [61]

When the English reoccupied New York in 1676 they found the old pier unserviceable, and soon made provision for a new "wharfe." This was built by the Corporation and financed by an assessment on the merchants of New York in proportion to their "Estates." The Dock, as it was called, was substantially built, it being estimated that eighteen thousand cartloads of stone at two shillings a load went into its construction. At its completion the Corporation made elaborate regulations for its care and appointed a "haven-master" to take charge of it. He was to collect wharfage money and render yearly accounts to the Mayor and Common Council. Successive havenmasters appear to have been guilty either of mismanagement or of peculation, and in 1685 the Corporation decided to farm out the collection of the Dock money to the highest bidder. This "great Dock" remained the only public wharf at New York until 1750. Although its harbor teemed with shipping, vessels docking at Manhattan were less adequately served than at any other village save Charles Town, where there were no wharves at all in this period.[62]

[59] At this time there were no public privies in the city of London. 2 Bos. Rec. Com., II, 98, 148; 7 Bos. Rec. Com., 4, 16; Bryant, The England of Charles II, 17.
[60] Newport T. M. Recs., 44; Peterson, History of the Island of Rhode Island, 61.
[61] Westcott, History of Philadelphia, chapter XXVIII; Narratives of Pennsylvania, 261, 268 n.; Pa. Mag., IV, 200.
[62] N. Y. M. C. C., I, 9; Peterson, New York, 108–113; Stokes, Iconography, IV, 311; Cal. St. Pap., 1689–1692, 187.

VI

In the seventeenth century settlers in the five colonial villages succeeded in housing themselves and their manifold activities as town-dwellers. They built their homes of timber or brick for the most part close together, both for protection against the dangers of an unfriendly back country and because of their gregarious habits as town-dwellers in the Old World. They laid out streets which, however primitive in surface and extent, were to determine the lines of future growth. They attacked the more pressing problems of clearing and drainage, built bridges, and erected wharves and docks to attract ocean commerce, the basis for their future prosperity. By the end of the period these compact villages, their streets active with the life of pedestrian, pack horse, cart and occasional carriage, their waterfronts busy with the reception and distribution of firewood and other necessary commodities, presented a distinct contrast to the more sporadic settlement of the interior countryside. They had by no means achieved an equal growth; Boston, even by the standards of today, might rank as a large town; Philadelphia, though founded late, and New York had attained the status of small towns, while Newport on its beautiful island and Charles Town behind its walls were still mere villages, which the commercial prosperity of the next century would render comparable with their larger neighbors.

II

ECONOMIC LIFE IN THE VILLAGES

I

Pursuit of trade and commerce was the all-embracing activity of the early colonial villages — the very basis for their existence. These little seaports served as the focal points at which immigrants and manufactured articles from the mother country converged for redistribution in the New World, while through them the produce of rural and frontier settlements found its way to distant markets. The colonial town was primarily a commercial community with its daily exchange of goods, — a community of market places, warehouses, wharves and shops. This fact, more than any other, tended to weld these five widely scattered villages into a uniform type of society, differing radically from that of farming community or wilderness outpost.

The villages were planted just at the time when European towns were undergoing their transition from medieval to modern economy. With truth, wrote Edward Eggleston, "The seventeenth century lay in the penumbra of the Middle Ages." The colonists brought with them certain institutions which bore strong traces of their medieval origins, and the tenacity with which they clung to outmoded customs, often impracticable of application in a new world, is eloquent tribute to the force of conservatism. On the other hand, the breakdown of ancient institutions was easier to effect in the colonial towns, as yet unhampered by restraints of tradition, than in the older cities of Europe. Nowhere can this metamorphosis be more readily observed than in the economic life of the villagers.

Town governments in the Middle Ages always kept certain trades wholly or in part under their own direct supervision. They carefully regulated the distribution of corn, meat, salt and wines, — commodities so necessary in times of war or famine — in order to secure to the consumer the benefit of a "just price." Thus, the first concern of colonial authorities was to provide their villages with an adequate food supply when provisions brought by sea had become exhausted. Some inhabitants kept cows and pigs, and cultivated little gardens, but a settled community must soon be fed from sources outside itself. William Wood described the problem of Boston in 1634: "Those that live here upon their Cattle, must be constrayned to take Farmes in the Countrey, or else they cannot subsist; they [sic] place being too small to contain many, and fittest for such as can Trade into England, for such commodities as the Countrey wants." [1] Medieval towns met this problem by erecting markets and fairs to be held at stated intervals, and their colonial children quite naturally followed their example. Every village had by 1690 made some provision for the holding of regular markets, occurring generally on a stated day each week at a place designated by provincial or village authorities, and in the northern towns the custom of yearly fairs had become well established.

The Dutch West India Company arranged, with indifferent success, for the food supply of its servants during the first years at New Amsterdam. "Food here is scanty and poor," wrote Dominie Michaelius in 1628. "Fresh butter and milk are difficult to obtain, owing to the large number of people and the small number of cattle and farmers. These articles are dear." Not until 1648 was a weekly market opened on the Strand, where "strangers" as well as burghers could set up their booths. Here, on Saturdays, meat, pork, butter, cheese, turnips, carrots, cabbage and other country produce were brought and exposed for sale "on the beach." In 1662 the Court designated Tuesdays and Saturdays as the days on which "country people" might offer their wares to the townsfolk. [2] Market day in New Amsterdam, when farmers from Brooklyn, Gowanus and Bergen haggled over the sale of their produce to wary Knickerbockers from their boats in the "great Graft," was a reenactment in the New World village of scenes from the life of old Holland. Transition from Dutch to English rule apparently dislocated existing market arrangements. Governor Andros in 1677 ordered a weekly market to be held on Saturdays, for which there was "a fit house beinge now built" at the waterside. Three years later the Mayor and Common Council provided for an additional market on Wednesdays at the same place "for ye Better Supply of ye Cytie." The Dongan charter of 1683 introduced English market custom into New York, and from then on the Mayor and Aldermen appointed a clerk, or clerks, of the market. In 1684 the Corporation published elaborate market regulations which closely resemble those of English market towns. [3]

Although the most complete development of markets occurred at New York, the institution had first appeared at Boston. On March 4, 1633/4, the Court of Assistants ordered the erection of a "mercate"

[1] Shurtleff, *Topographical and Historical Description of Boston*, 41.
[2] *Narratives of New Netherland*, 64; *Laws of New Netherland*, 86; *Recs. N. Am.*, I, 23; II, 169.
[3] *N. Y. M. C. C.*, I, 40, 139–140. For market regulations of Bristol, England, see Latimer, *Bristol in the Seventeenth Century*, 365.

in the Bay town, "to be kept upon Thursday, the fifth day of the week, being lecture day," when the country people all came into town. This market was held in an open space at the head of King Street until 1658, when funds left by Robert Keayne made possible the building of a town house, concerning which the General Court decreed that "the place underneath shall be free for all inhabitants in this jurisdiction to make use of as a market place forever." Increased trading at the Boston market led the Town Meeting in 1649 to follow the old English custom of appointing "Clarkes of the market" to supervise its business, a method of regulation that continued in use for nearly two hundred years.[4]

The essentially rural character of life in early Newport made it possible for inhabitants to supply themselves with foodstuffs throughout most of the period. By 1672, however, conditions had so greatly changed that George Fox, after a visit to Rhode Island, wrote to the Governor earnestly advising "that you have a market once a week in your town and a house built for that purpose." His wise counsel soon bore fruit in the setting apart of Saturday as market day. In 1677 the Governor humored the religious scruples of the Sabbatarians by naming Wednesday an additional day for the holding of markets.[5] No market building was erected in Newport until well into the eighteenth century.

The intentions of William Penn for the development of Philadelphia included a market inaugurated shortly after the colonists arrived. Two weekly markets were in operation in 1685, and the next year James Claypoole, in a letter to the Proprietor, mentioned that "Provisions [are] very cheap . . . in our market."[6] Alone of the five villages, Charles Town enjoyed no market facilities in this period, although in 1690 the Parliament of South Carolina did set aside land for a "market place" in the town.[7]

Like their European fathers colonial town-dwellers instituted annual or semi-annual fairs in addition to their regular market days. Governor Kieft of New Amsterdam in 1641 appointed annual cattle and hog fairs to be held in the "open spaces" before the Fort. The cattle fair was a "free market"; that is, strangers as well as burghers might retail goods and enjoy exemption from arrest while there. To encourage trading, proclamations were issued in English as well as

[4] Winthrop, *New England*, I, 124; *Mass. Col. Recs.*, I, 112; IV, i, 327; 2 *Bos. Rec. Com.*, 94, 154.

[5] Jones, *Quakers in the American Colonies*, 113; Richardson Collection (Newport Hist. Soc.), 972: 161.

[6] *Narratives of Pennsylvania*, 262, 292.

[7] In 1682 Thomas Newe wrote, "All things are very dear in the Town; milk 2d a quart, beefe, 4d a pound, pork 3d, but far better than our English." *Narratives of Carolina*, 181; *S. C. Statutes*, II, 73.

Dutch, and farmers with their herds and flocks came from points as distant as Milford, Connecticut, and Southampton, Long Island. In 1659 the Burgomasters designated the space before the Fort a "market for fat and lean cattle" to be held continuously for forty days each autumn, and for this purpose erected a building with a tiled roof, later called the "Broadway Shambles." Governor Andros ordered an annual fair to run for three days in November, 1677, for cattle, grain and other country produce, "att the market house & Plaine afore the Forte." Boston was granted "two faires in the yeare" in 1648, but here the custom soon fell into disuse.[8]

At Philadelphia a yearly fair seems to have been held from shortly after the beginning of settlement. Not confined to livestock, it more resembled English fairs where all manner of merchandise changed hands. The handiwork of the Mennonite weavers of Germantown, to the dismay of Francis Daniel Pastorius, brought only ten thalers at the fair of 1684. Quaker merchants and farmers valued their fair, and the various districts of Philadelphia county contended eagerly for the privilege of holding it. In the year 1688 the Provincial Council granted the petitions of the residents at "ye Center of Philadelphia," requesting that the fair be kept there. This decision in favor of the "metropolis" angered some country people, who issued "a Contemptuous Printing paper" on the subject. The Council, standing upon its dignity, summoned the subscribers for contempt, and the hapless offenders obtained pardon only after humbly apologizing for their presumption. The Council then reiterated that the fair should be held regularly on May 20 and August 20 at "ye Center."[9] There is no evidence of fairs held in the seventeenth century in either Newport or Charles Town.

II

Medieval towns grew in proportion to their success in catering to their own needs and those of nearby villages. They cultivated enough purely local trade to meet their daily requirements and to supply them with commodities for exchange in the world market, where their chief interests lay in the exploitation of the most profitable portions of distant international commerce. They made little effort to realize the rich possibilities in the economic subjugation of a wide hinterland. The colonial villages were modelled after the economic pattern of medieval towns, and colonial commerce became chiefly an "ocean-

---

[8] *Laws of New Netherland*, 29; *Recs. N. Am.*, VII, 215; V, 312; *N. Y. M. C. C.*, I, 40; *Mass. Col. Recs.*, II, 257; III, 138. For English fairs, see Jusserand, *English Wayfaring Life*, 248–253.
[9] Westcott, *History of Philadelphia*, chapter XXXV; *Pa. Col. Recs.*, I, 218, 224.

borne, out-going commerce, rather than a continental, inland traffic." [10]
By 1650, however, Boston had begun to extend its control into the
back country, and to develop a metropolitan form of economy that was
essentially modern. Towards the close of the century a similar tendency
to become the economic center of its province became noticeable at
New York. This process was simultaneous with like developments
all over Europe, but was speeded and facilitated in the case of colonial
towns by the pioneer nature of the countryside. The frontiers of the
New World were far more dependent upon districts of earlier settlement than were corresponding geographic areas in the Old, and there
was here no need to break down any prearranged economy of little
towns with their local interests and jealousies before the larger town
could become "the economic centre for a very large number of
goods and services."

For over a decade after its founding Boston remained primarily a
farming community. But in 1642 came the outbreak of the civil wars
in England, which cut off the flow of emigrants and exports. "All
foreign commodities grew scarce," wrote John Winthrop sadly, "and
our own of no price. These straits set our people on work to provide
fish, clapboards, plank &c, . . . and to look out to the W. Indies for
a trade." Transforming necessity into opportunity, the town slowly
drew to itself a lion's share of the traffic of the English colonies, beginning with the coastwise carrying trade. From the north the lumber
and cattle of New Hampshire and the "sacred cod" of the Grand Banks
found their way to West Indian or European markets through the
little port of Boston. To the same place came, overland or by sea,
cattle from central and western Massachusetts, horses, sheep and dairy
produce from Rhode Island, grain from Connecticut and provisions and
furs from New York. In like manner the "Bostoners" absorbed most
of the carrying trade of Pennsylvania, Maryland, Virginia and the
Carolinas.[11]

The mariners of the Bay next extended their traffic to the West
Indies, the Portuguese Islands, England, and the continent of Europe,
where, in the famous triangular trade, they exchanged colonial fish,
lumber, and cereals for "European goods," wines, salt, bills of exchange, and occasional "pieces of eight." From 1642 to 1690 the

[10] "There was no effective large-scale organization of the commerce of a wide
compact area or hinterland. The essence of town economy was the subordination of
villages, not of towns. The growth of London, Paris and Berlin, and of Manchester,
Liverpool, Hamburg and Marseilles, as towering economic centres for the exploitation
of a vast area at home as well as for the carrying on of commerce in distant parts,
is a modern growth." Gras, in *Legacy of the Middle Ages*, 460–462; Nettels, *Money
Supply of the American Colonies*, 101.
[11] Winthrop, *New England*, I, 307; II, 31; Bidwell and Falconer, *History of Agriculture*, 24, 27, 43; Weeden, *Economic and Social History of New England*, I, 136–
139, 155, 244, 333; *Cal. St. Pap.*, 1661–1664, 328; *R. I. Col. Recs.*, I, 337; Nettels,
Money Supply, 100–101; *Letter Book of Peleg Sanford*, 36.

seaborne trade of Boston flourished and grew; after the mid-century Boston ships could be found in almost every port known to English mariners. In 1676 Edward Randolph described the town as a thriving seaport: "It is the great care of the merchants to keep their ships in constant employ, which makes them *trye all ports to force a trade,* whereby they abound with all sorts of commodities, and *Boston may be esteemed the mart town of the West Indies.*" [12]

None of the four other colonial villages approached Boston in commercial importance in the seventeenth century, although all save Charles Town sought with some success to capture a share of maritime trade. Until 1653 New Amsterdam was not a municipality, but a trading post of the Dutch West India Company. As such it became in 1629 the staple for New Netherland, where all vessels touching at the colony were required to discharge their cargoes and pay duties. To explain why trade languished at New Amsterdam burghers often advanced the argument of this economic subordination to the Company. Furs and liquors were the principal articles of commerce; after 1650 meats, dairy produce and provisions became equally important. All of these were drawn from the immediate vicinity — the Hudson valley, Long Island, and adjacent parts of Connecticut. The coming of English rule set New York free to seek a trade with the West Indies and other colonies, but expansion was slow, because, as Governor Nicolls said, "The whole trade is lost for want of shipping." New Yorkers recognized the value of their port, however, and dreamed not only of freeing themselves from dependence upon Boston, of whose mercantile success they were heartily jealous, but even of surpassing the Bay town in traffic.[13]

Absence of a surplus of marketable commodities and lack of large sums of capital for investment precluded Newport for several decades from engaging in any extended commercial activity. "The trade and business of the town at the first," recorded the Reverend Mr. Callender, "was but very little and inconsiderable, consisting only of a little corn, and pork and tobacco, sent to Boston for a few European goods they could not subsist without, and *all at the mercy of the traders there too.*" By 1650 a few men of wealth and ability who lived in Newport realized that "Nanhygansett Bay is the largest and safest port in New England, and fittest for trade," and began to look abroad to Barbados and Nevis for an outlet for their sheep, pork, garden produce, butter and cheese, which hitherto they had sent to market via Boston. From

[12] Morison, *Maritime History of Massachusetts,* 11–18; Col. Soc. Mass. *Trans.,* XXIX, 317, 452, 661; Johnson, *Wonder-Working Providence,* 71; Hutchinson, *Papers relative to the History of Massachusetts,* II, 231–232, 239.
[13] *Laws of New Netherland,* 4; *N. Y. Col. Docs.,* I, 259, 270; *Recs. N. Am.,* VII, 215, 219; *N. Y. M. C. C.,* I, 80; *Narratives of New Netherland,* 423; *Cal. St. Pap.,* 1661–1669, 337; Stokes, *Iconography,* IV, 343.

the first their efforts met with success, and by the outbreak of the Anglo-French wars shipping interests of Rhode Island were well equipped to reap rich dividends from the opportunities offered by privateering and traffic with the enemy.[14] The volume of this trade can the better be appreciated when it is remembered that nearly all the colony's shipping issued from behind Conanicut Island; commercially Newport *was* Rhode Island for over a century.

Even while the town of Philadelphia was building, its inhabitants began to cut into Boston's monopoly of the carrying trade for the Delaware region. The Free Society of Traders, a joint stock company chartered by the Proprietor, early commenced whaling in Delaware Bay and importing English goods for sale in the town. Individual merchants soon engaged in "a smart trade" with the West Indies, consisting largely of provisions and horses. In the summer of 1690 at least ten ships sailed from Philadelphia to the Caribbean. "We now begin to have a Trade abroad as well as at home," wrote John Goodson to Friends in England. "Here be several Merchants that Transport several Ship-loads of Bread, Flower, Beef and Pork to Barbados and Jamaica; a fine trade here is in the Town." A few years later Gabriel Thomas ascribed the growing prosperity of the Philadelphians to "their great and extended Traffique and Commerce both by Sea and Land." [15]

Not until South Carolina began to produce staple crops in the second decade of the eighteenth century did Charles Town rival the four northern ports. Prior to 1710 the produce of the colony was considerably diversified, the principal exports being deerskins to England, and pork, corn, a few naval stores and lumber to Barbados. As late as 1687 Carolinians had "hardly overcome ye Want of Victuals & not as yett produced any Commodities fitt for ye Markett of Europe, butt a few Skins . . . and a little Cedar." [16]

The only town to extend its economic control beyond nearby hamlets to the hinterland in the seventeenth century was Boston.[17] By 1680 Newfoundland, Maine, New Hampshire, Massachusetts, Rhode Island, and the River towns of Connecticut all paid tribute to the Bay

[14] R. I. Hist. Soc. *Colls.*, (1839), 95; XXV, 73–91; *Cal. St. Pap.*, 1661–1669, 343; Richman, *Rhode Island*, 84–87, 107, 109; *R. I. Col. Recs.*, I, 337; III, 32, 110; *Letter Book of Peleg Sanford;* Weeden, *Economic and Social History*, I, 259. *Cf.* Bigelow, Commerce between Rhode Island and the West Indies before the Revolution (Ms.), chapter I.

[15] *Narratives of Pennsylvania*, 241–242, 325; *Pa. Mag.*, IV, 4–5, 199.

[16] *S. C. Statutes*, II, 55–57; Gray, *History of Agriculture in the Southern United States*, I, 57–58; *Narratives of Carolina*, 158; Latimer, *Bristol in the Seventeenth Century*, 318.

[17] This study omits discussion of the fur trade, by means of which New York and Charles Town, especially, drew profits from large areas to the west. The early fur trade was a peculiar and short-lived activity, essentially a pioneer traffic, never at any time engaging the energies of a large proportion of the citizenry of any town, and exercising, in general, no permanent influence on the economic structure of any of the communities under consideration.

town's commercial leadership. In 1640 cattle began to move overland from the Piscataqua, and after 1660 Hampshire County, Massachusetts, specialized in grass-fed cattle for the Boston market. Newport was throughout the period the commercial satellite of Boston. Thither Peleg Sanford sent overland his flocks of sheep in 1667, and received in exchange clothing and dry goods by pack horse. The "mart town" assiduously drained Connecticut of its surplus produce, occasionally taking more than that region could spare. From Milford came beaver pelts and grain; peas and pork were shipped from the River towns to Boston, whence they went to feed the fishermen of Salem and Marblehead. An overland route from Windham County was opened after 1686, when people from Muddy River, Massachusetts, settled there. Clement Corbin of Woodstock carried produce by oxcart over the hills into Boston, and returned with dry goods, liquor, ammunition, and "other necessaries" for his general store. Connecticut authorities tried in vain to stem the flow of produce into Massachusetts. Their order of 1650 that "no Foreigners . . . shall retaile any goods, by themselves in any place within this Jurisdiction, nor shall any Inhabitant retayle any goods wch belongs to any foreigner," was fruitlessly directed against the ubiquitous Bay traders. With a predominantly agricultural population and inadequate harbors, it was inevitable that Connecticut should be subordinated to Boston, as it later was to New York. In 1683 the Governor and Council of New Hampshire proposed to forbid lumber ships from Boston to enter the ports of the province without a permit from the Governor, in an effort to prevent their more aggressive neighbors from absorbing their entire trade, "drawing all ye Shipps to Boston, & thereby supplying all ye neighboring Colonies." The Assembly rejected the bill, because, as Cranford explained, "some interested & ill tempered persons" blocked it.[18]

The coastal towns of Massachusetts also came under the aegis of Boston, and apart from Salem they did not venture much into distant trade. They suffered the fate of Ipswich, where there were some merchants, "but Boston being the chiefest place of resort of Shipping, carries all the Trade." Randolph reported in 1676 that about three hundred small vessels, ranging from six to ten tons burthen, were employed in carrying goods between Boston and surrounding towns.[19]

[18] Bidwell and Falconer, *History of Agriculture*, 24, 27; Weeden, *Economic and Social History*, I, 190, 197, 208, 245; *Letter Book of Peleg Sanford*, 36, 52; 2 MHS Procs., I, 243; Lawson, *Descendants of Clement Corbin*, 17–18, 23–24; *Conn. Col. Recs.*, I, 562; Nettels, *Money Supply*, 106.

[19] Ipswich supplied Boston with beef; Malden, Hingham, and Weymouth provided timber, planks and masts; Woburn, Concord, Sudbury, Duxbury and Hingham sent provisions to the mart town; Dedham "Bisquett makers and Butchers" (of whom there were many) had "Vent enough for their Commodities at Boston" by 1660. A flourishing trade went on at Taunton and Rehoboth; the latter was "not above 40 miles from Boston, betweene which there is a Comone trade, carrying and recarrying goods by land

At the same time that Boston was draining produce from the hinterland settlements she acted as the agent by whom they were in return supplied with the European and West Indian commodities they believed necessary for their existence and comfort. By means of crude but improving roads the little metropolis maintained a growing trade, not only with the seventy-odd coastal and inland settlements of Massachusetts, but also with the neighboring colonies of New Hampshire, Rhode Island and Connecticut.[20] Boston, Sir Robert Carr summarized tersely, had "engrossed the whole trade of New England."[21]

As the staple for New Netherland, New Amsterdam until 1664 was the port of both entry and departure for all commerce of the province, but after that date, especially with its loss of the fur trade to Albany, the business of the town, like the radius of its economic influence, greatly contracted. It now had to regain by slow penetration the control over its hinterland which once it had enjoyed by statute, and from this time on, though on a much smaller scale, its economy developed similarly to that of Boston. With its admirable location it found in the Hudson River a ready avenue by which it drew to itself provisions from Esopus and even furs from Fort Orange. A packet service of some regularity for carrying freight and passengers up the Hudson had been begun by Cornelius Van Tienhoven in 1633. By way of Long Island Sound the Dutch and English at Manhattan drew within their orbit the villages of Connecticut as far east as Milford; while on Long Island they gradually weaned Southold and other eastern towns from their New England connections.[22]

The other villages had perforce to be content to act as marketing

in Cart and on Horseback, and they have a very fayre conveyance of goods by water also." In 1650 Johnson reported an absence of artisans in Maine, "shopkeepers there are none, being supplied by Massachusetts Merchants with all things." Johnson, *Wonder-Working Providence*, 96, 117, 348; 2 MHS *Procs.*, I, 236-244; 3 MHS *Colls.*, III, 348; Nettels, *Money Supply*, 103; Weeden, *Economic and Social History*, I, 310.

[20] The "great Eastern road" through Newbury was opened as far as Cape Porpoise, Maine, in 1664, and improved in 1687. It was reported that often in winter twenty horsemen and as many drovers with twenty or thirty cattle would pass over a certain bridge in one day on their way to Boston. The "Bay Road" to the west reached Hadley by 1674, and the way to Connecticut was changed and vastly improved in 1682. Judged by modern standards these roads were crude indeed, but heavily freighted carts could pass along them in favorable weather, and they were at least equal to contemporary highways in England or France, which were notoriously "bad for the rider, good for the abider." Weeden, *Economic and Social History*, I, 310-312; Parkes, *Travel in England in the Seventeenth Century*, 5-18, 28; Clark, *The Seventeenth Century*, 51-53.

[21] *Cal. St. Pap.*, 1661-1669, 346. One gathers from Latimer's *Bristol in the Seventeenth Century* that Boston by 1690 enjoyed a wider trade into its hinterland than did the metropolis of the West Country.

[22] Van Rensselaer, *New York in the Seventeenth Century*, I, 210; II, 328; *Recs. N. Am.*, V, 124, 152; *Narratives of New Netherland*, 205; Bidwell and Falconer, *History of Agriculture*, 47.

and distributing centers for hamlets and rural districts within their immediate vicinity. Newport had almost no inland territory to serve, a fact of no little importance in explaining its slow commercial development. After the destruction of the Indian power in King Philip's War the Narragansett country and northeastern Connecticut could be tapped, but it was many years before the town's inland trade assumed any large proportions. Carolina Indian traders pushed many hundreds of miles into the interior of the southwest in search of deerskins; supplies for their little posts and caches were served out of Charles Town by means of perriaugers and canoes, winding up the numerous rivers to their headwaters, and thence overland by pack horse.[23] But this was a peculiar traffic, and Charles Town in this period developed no staple of trade to support her economic life when the supply of furs should become depleted. Philadelphia in 1690 had not yet exhausted the rich possibilities of the Delaware valley, and Quaker merchants had only just begun to probe the back country of the Schuylkill. They had as yet no opportunity to realize the broad and fertile hinterland that was to enable them in the course of the next century to outstrip their New England rivals.

III

These little seaports pulsed with lively enterprise. The absorbing business of making a living occupied townspeople of all classes. The shipping, which increasingly crowded their waterfronts, engaged in one capacity or another the bulk of the inhabitants. Preparation of commodities for export employed some; recruiting of ship's crews from among villagers took many more. Artisans and mechanics pursued their trades with industry, and shopkeepers diligently supplied burgher and countryman with the necessities of life. All this activity was in a sense controlled and managed by a few wealthy merchants, who constantly made it their function to extend and superintend the traffic of their towns. From the simple manorial village organization of the earliest settlements there gradually emerged a more complex town life, increasingly differentiating town from country.

In keeping with European tradition there soon sprang up in the colonial villages all the appurtenances of a medieval manor, introduced largely by individual enterprise, though often stimulated by official inducement. Grist and saw mills, breweries, bakeries, cooperages and tanneries appeared in all settlements almost as soon as they were planted. As trade swelled in the villages these occupations

[23] Peterson, *History of the Island of Rhode Island,* 61; Crane, *Southern Frontier,* 22–24.

expanded into industries and engaged the labor of many of the "poorer sort" of people.

By 1637 two windmills were in operation at New Amsterdam, and millers there were soon grinding Esopus, Long Island and some Connecticut flour for export. In 1672 the village bakers petitioned the governor that they might send their grain to Milford, Connecticut, to be ground, giving as their reason the inadequacy of the two mills in the town. Governor Andros in 1680 granted New York a monopoly of making, bolting and packing all flour for export from the province, a favor the town enjoyed until 1694. Special privilege, as always, bred resentment, and the city soon found itself the object of hearty dislike from country districts on account of such actions as the seizure of 148 barrels of flour from the brigantine *Hopewell* of Albany and other confiscations for violation of the bolting act.[24] In other colonial towns the "mistery" of milling did not attain as great proportions as at New York, but in the early decades of the century it prospered in both Boston and Newport, while towards the end of the period Philadelphia was seriously threatening the supremacy of New York in the flour export trade.[25]

The baker played an important role in the early villages, supplying inhabitants with one of their principal articles of diet, and preparing large quantities of bread and biscuit for the West Indies and for use on shipboard. In New Amsterdam at the time of its surrender to the English ten bakers plied their trade. That same year the Boston Selectmen refused to permit John Waite to "set up the Trade of a Baker," probably because of the great number already so engaged in the town; in 1679 the craft had grown to the extent that its members petitioned the General Court "to consider & make an experiment" of regulating the bakers of Boston. In 1690 Philadelphians furnished employment for "seven Master-Bakers, some of them bake and send away many Thousand Bushels in a Year of Bread and Flower, this is Truth." [26]

Among the busiest of village artisans were the coopers, who made barrels, hogsheads, pipes, kegs, and other "caske" for packing flour, salted meats, fish, beer, and provisions for merchant exporters. Coopers were especially numerous in Boston where their services were greatly in demand for making barrels and casks for fish and salt pork. In 1648 they joined with their brethren of Charlestown (Massa-

[24] Stokes, *Iconography*, IV, 78; *N. Y. M. C. C.*, I, 80, 152; II, 37; Peterson, *New York*, 45.
[25] 2 *Bos. Rec. Com.*, 74, 97; Kimball, *Providence*, 43, 227; *Narratives of Pennsylvania*, 261.
[26] *Recs. N. Am.*, V, 107; 7 *Bos. Rec. Com.*, 49; *Pa. Mag.*, IV, 194; *Narratives of Pennsylvania*, 267–268.

chusetts) in a petition to the General Court "about being a company" with power to set standards for their trade. They were incorporated as a guild for three years "& no longer." [27] In 1680, when New York received the bolting monopoly, the coopers of that village, instead of seeking incorporation, employed the ancient device of a cartel to raise the price of their wares. The Court, on finding them guilty, fined them £2. 10. each. The four "Master Coopers" of Philadelphia, who made "an abundance of Caske for the Sea," and those of Newport and Charles Town, where the principal commodities for export were also grain, beef and pork, while without the spectacular history of their fellows in Boston and New York, were equally active in the "mistery of cooperage." [28]

As we have seen, the whole economic life of the villages depended upon their shipping. In the earliest days English and Dutch vessels served as carriers for colonial commerce. Before long, however, colonists were felling the nearby forests, and carpenters, smiths, joiners, shipwrights, and other artisans united in the building of tall ships from their lumber. Boston and Newport led the five towns in shipbuilding. From 1643 to 1690 the shipwrights of Boston and Charlestown (Massachusetts) were especially active. "Many a fair ship," reported Edward Johnson in 1650, "had her framing and finishing here, besides larger vessels, barques and Ketches." Newport entered the industry in 1646 with the building of a small vessel for New Haven; inexpensive craft could be easily constructed when Ralph Earle and his partner Wilbore were able to deliver "Good sufficient Stuff" at the water side on short notice. In 1690 the trade was flourishing on the Narragansett shore. New Amsterdam, prior to the Navigation Act of 1651, had been a growing competitor of the Bay Colony, but soon fell behind in the race, so that her plight immediately concerned the first English governors. Philadelphia and Charles Town, founded so late in the period that their greatest need was still "to provide in the first place for the belly," were both too much occupied with the work of building up their towns to engage before 1690 in so extensive an industry as shipbuilding. [29]

A corps of artisans and laborers cared for the ships riding in each colonial harbor. Rope walks were set up, and sailmakers' lofts erected; carpenters, smiths, caulkers and braziers joined in the bustling activity of the waterfronts. Although a French visitor to Boston in 1687 reported that "there are here Craftsmen of every kind, and particularly

[27] *Mass. Col. Recs.*, II, 250; *7 Bos. Rec. Com.*, 22.
[28] Stokes, *Iconography*, IV, 319; *Pa. Mag.*, IV, 195; Austin, *Journal of William Jefferay*, 28; *S. C. Statutes*, II, 55-57.
[29] Johnson, *Wonder-Working Providence*, 247; Weeden, *Economic and Social History*, I, 143, 154; Stokes, *Iconography*, IV, 343.

Carpenters for the building of ships," yet merchants of the town had to purchase additional vessels from the surrounding villages of Charlestown, Dorchester and Salem to satisfy their ever-expanding needs.[30]

All this activity, this far-flung trade, these ships which were built, equipped and kept in repair, and whose holds were filled with commodities for exchange by a small army of laborers, presupposed capital, imagination and direction. These the little towns were not slow in developing. In each community a small group of men arose, some of them "damnable rich," who gathered into their hands the control of colonial commerce, and with it political power and social prestige. Active, ambitious and venturesome, these merchants made it possible for the five little villages to grow up into sizable towns. It was their accomplishment from the untouched resources of a new continent to create a traffic that penetrated every corner, and a fleet that found its way into nearly every harbor of the western world.

At the time of the founding of the villages there came over a few men possessed of sufficient funds to set up as merchants in a small way. In Boston such men as John Coggan, Anthony Stoddard and William Brenton early took the lead in mercantile pursuits. By 1640 the principal, or at least the most notorious of this group was Robert Keayne, who, though his commercial operations did not invariably meet with the approval of church and state, was one of the first to exhibit that civic pride and interest for which colonial merchants as a class later became famous. In answer to the increased demands of trade at Boston the Selectmen in 1664 ordered a bell rung at eleven o'clock in the morning of each working day to summon merchants to meet "for the space of one hower" in the room under the Town House, "For the more convenient and expeditious dispatch of Merchants Affayres." This merchants' exchange continued under the Town House until the fire of 1711. The number and importance of Boston merchants increased with the trade of the port until by 1690 they had attained the dignity of an economic and social class that challenged the supremacy of the Puritan priesthood. William Harris told English authorities in 1675 that Boston "merchants seem to be rich men, and their houses are handsomely furnished as most in London." Five years later Governor Bradstreet summed up the growth of this group in a report to the Privy Council: "There may bee neer twenty English merchants within our Government bred up to that calling, and neer as many others that do trade and merchandise more or less; but Foreign merchants of other Nations we have none." [31]

[30] Shurtleff, *Topographical and Historical Description of Boston*, 49.
[31] 7 *Bos. Rec. Com.*, 22; *Cal. St. Pap.*, 1675–1676, 221.

John Hull, "captain of militia, and owner of ships; business man and magistrate, master of the mint, and deacon of the church, first in a long line of master goldsmiths," was perhaps the most interesting figure among the merchants of seventeenth century Boston. Hull engaged mostly in coastwise trade, but occasionally he ventured a cargo to Europe. He exported furs, Piscataqua lumber and Rhode Island horses, and imported European goods, especially clothing — "for, as yet [1657] our chief supply, in respect to clothes, is from England." [32] Unlike most of his fellow merchants he lived some distance from the business center in Dock Square, and probably maintained his stores and shop apart from his dwelling.

Newport was founded by several men of substance, and gradually attracted to itself other possessors of wealth. William Brenton and William Coddington, accounted the richest men of early Boston, were among the planters of Newport, and immediately assumed a leading position in the merchant group, which included Thomas Owen, John Strettin, Nicholas Easton, and others. Brenton, in addition to his general trading, built a large wharf and engaged in shipbuilding. After 1650 a new group, more nearly approaching the importance of the Boston merchants, entered upon the scene. Peleg Sanford, Walter Newbury, Benedict Arnold, Caleb Carr, the Cranston and Wanton families laid the solid foundations of Newport's commercial greatness, and richly merited the sobriquet, "Quaker grandees of Rhode Island," bestowed on them by Sir Edmund Andros. [33] Peleg Sanford's *Letter-Book* records the operations of a typical seventeenth century merchant. In 1667 Sanford purchased "European Goods" of William Pate in London, for which he paid by sending horses and provisions to William Sanford in Barbados, who in turn shipped sugar to London to be credited against Peleg's account. He received Pate's shipment by way of Boston through his kinsman, Elisha Hutchinson. The medieval habit of maintaining trade relations by means of family ties could not be better illustrated.

The Dutch West India Company occupied the place of the merchant in the life of New Amsterdam for several decades, but even before the coming of English rule a few Dutch and English merchants had begun to develop an independent trade. There was sufficient traffic at New York in 1670 to impel Governor Lovelace to issue a proclamation about keeping a "Punctuall tyme for meeting at ye Exchange," for which he designated a "fitt place" where "Merchants (whether Strangers as well as Townsmen) & other artificers may resort & discourse of their seuerall affaires according to ye universall custome of all marytime

---

[32] AAS *Trans.*, III, 158, 180; Morison, *Builders of the Bay Colony*, 135.
[33] *Doc. Hist. R. I.*, II, 147, 149; *R. I. Col. Recs.*, III, 255.

Corporations." The iron rule of the Company had stunted the commercial growth of New York, and as late as 1678 Andros reported that "Our Merchts are not so many, . . . [and] a mercht worth 1000 lb or 500 lb is accompted a good substantiall merchant." A few New Yorkers, like John Winder and Cornelius Steenwyck, possessed considerable fortunes, but the concentration of wealth there before 1690 was not so great as in Boston or even Newport.[34] The era of New York's commercial importance was yet to come.

A few wealthy Quakers directed the commercial life of Philadelphia from its earliest days. William Frampton operated as a merchant on a fairly large scale in 1685. He engaged in an importing and exporting trade, built a wharf and warehouse, opened a retail shop for merchandise, directed a bake-house, and set up "a large Brew House . . . to furnish the People with good Drink." Another enterprising merchant was James Claypoole, agent for the Free Society of Traders, who, with the aid of his wife and children, operated several businesses as side lines to his work for the Society.[35] These early Quaker merchants pursued trade and commerce with an avidity and a success that soon merited the envy of their neighbors at New York.

Village merchants either owned or took shares in the ships that carried their ventures. In addition they built wharves and erected warehouses in which to store their goods. Frequently, also, they kept shops in their homes for retail trade. Thus the seventeenth century merchant conducted a general business which aimed to supply the diverse needs of people in both town and country. Peleg Sanford's dealings were probably those of the average merchant. He imported sugar, molasses, rum and cotton from Barbados, and dry goods and hardware from England. These he disposed of in Newport at both wholesale and retail. In 1666–1667 he sold at his shop five thousand pins, £20 worth of haberdashery, brass kettles worth £5, a quantity of Barbados brooms, and some English hats and furniture. In exchange he accepted pork, beef, peas, butter and cheese, which he marketed in the West Indies.[36]

Bostonians conducted business on a larger scale, frequently acting as agents for merchants of other villages. Sanford made his English purchases through Elisha Hutchinson and Peter Oliver of Boston. Much of the town's business consisted in the transshipment of European goods destined for small coastal villages or for inland shopkeepers. In addition to utilitarian dry goods and hardware Boston merchants imported considerable quantities of wines and spirits, and

[34] Stokes, *Iconography*, IV, 93, 275; *Doc. Hist. N. Y.*, I, 91; Valentine, *Manual of the Corporation of New York* (1858), 511; *Recs. N. Am.*, II, 93.
[35] *Narratives of Pennsylvania*, 267–268; *Pa. Mag.*, X, 275.
[36] *Letter-Book*, v, 11, 14–16, 24, 46.

luxuries such as spices, chocolate, raisins, figs and oranges. For the towns especially butter and cheese had to be imported, as the countryside did not yet produce a sufficient surplus to meet the demand.[37]

Country storekeepers and "petty traders," who purchased goods in quantity, dealt directly with the merchants at their warehouses, but townsfolk who made small individual purchases resorted to the increasing number of little shops in the towns.[38] There were two classes of shops: those conducted by persons "who buy to sell again," and those kept by various artisans for disposal of their handiwork. Of the first class there were but few in the seventeenth century, and the absence of evidence circumscribes our knowledge of their activities, but it is certain that a shop trade of this type was flourishing in the villages by 1690.

The first shopkeepers of whom we have any record were John Coggan and Solomon Stoddard of Boston, both merchants, who conducted retail shops as well; Stoddard, a "linen-draper," was in business for over half a century. Merchants of Newport, Philadelphia and Charles Town, and the West India Company at New Amsterdam maintained similar shops, and probably transacted the bulk of the retailing in these towns.[39]

Sometime prior to 1645 the Widow Howin kept a tiny shop at Boston, and the following year "Wm Davice, the apothecary," was conducting a small retail business there. Most shops sold dry goods and groceries, occasionally offering other "European" items for sale. "For rayment, our cloth hath not been cut short," wrote Johnson in 1650, "as but of late years the traders that way have encreased to such a number, that their shops have continued full all the year long, all one [the same as] England." "The town is full of good Shopps well furnished with all kinds of Merchandize," reported Maverick in 1660, and by 1675 Bostonians were beginning to complain bitterly of "*Shopkeepers* and merchants who set excessive prizes on their goods."[40] The journal of a Boston shopkeeper for the years 1685 to 1689, recording hundreds of small purchases by a large number of persons, yields unmistakable evidence of the existence of a retail trade. Though the shopkeeper's town custom exceeded his country trade by about ten to one, it is interesting to note among his customers Joseph Parker of Chelmsford, John Taylor, Preserved Clapp and Samuel Bartlett

[37] 64 MHS *Procs.*, 193; Bidwell and Falconer, *History of Agriculture*, 27.
[38] In the seventeenth and eighteenth centuries a *store* was a warehouse, not a *shop* as the present meaning has it.
[39] 5 MHS *Colls.*, V, 170; Austin, *Journal of William Jefferay*, 28; Van Rensselaer, *New York in the Seventeenth Century*, I, 186; Leiding, *Charleston*, 34; *Pa. Mag.*, XI, 275.
[40] 2 *Bos. Rec. Com.*, 83, 89; Johnson, *Wonder-Working Providence*, 211; 2 MHS *Procs.*, I, 238; *Mass. Col. Recs.*, V, 62–63.

of Northampton, and Edward Taylor of Westfield. The last named purchased goods worth £5 in the spring of 1686, on credit, "to pay next autumn." Some sales were very small, as on occasions when "Joseph Wheeler, Taylor," dropped in to buy "6 yds cloth at 1s." Most transactions were by barter; the word "cash" occurs but seldom in the record.[41]

In none of the other towns did the retail shop trade develop so early as at Boston. The Director and Council of New Netherland made regulations in March, 1648, regarding persons who "kept a public or private shop . . . in cellar or garret, or . . . carry on any Trade by the small weight and measure," and in September forbade "Scottish Merchants and small traders" from Holland, who undersold the burghers "in wholesale and retail," to do business in New Amsterdam. In a petition from inhabitants of New Amsterdam to Peter Stuyvesant in 1657, protesting the high prices of necessary commodities and household supplies, distinction is carefully made between "Merchants, . . . Shop-keepers, Tradesmen, Brewers, Bakers, Tapsters and Grocers."[42] At Newport in 1668 Peleg Sanford did business with Mahershallalhashbaz Dyer, who kept a tobacconist's shop, and probably purchased his medical supplies of Thomas Rodman, to whom the town in 1677 granted a lot "whilst he lived & practiced the [trade of] an Apothecarie." As early as 1685 Cornelius Born opened a notion shop in Philadelphia, and by 1690 the town sheltered "twenty-nine Shop-Keepers, great and small."[43]

Among shopkeepers, only apothecaries and tobacconists approached the specialization of modern retailing. Most little shops resembled the general store of today, and their stocks included such diverse articles as looking-glasses, candlesticks, gloves, tin lanterns, rat traps, woodenware, fishing tackle, bottles and trays. They carried an assortment of dry goods and imported groceries for sailors, laborers, and the "poorer sort of people," who could not afford to buy in bulk, to purchase in small quantities.

As the villages grew in population, an increasing number of artisans and "Tradesmen" were needed to satisfy the varied demands for their

[41] Much of the stock was purchased from Solomon Stoddard, aforementioned Boston merchant. At no time do these purchases exceed £50, and more frequently they consist of single items, like a dozen pairs of men's gloves, at £1. 7. Dealings with customers at Chelmsford, Plymouth, Salem, Eastham and Rowley in Massachusetts, and Killingworth in Connecticut appear. Journal of a General Store in Boston, 1685–1689 (MS). For retail shops in London, of which there were nearly 100,000 in 1686, see *Early English Tracts on Commerce*, 454.

[42] Some retailing was conducted by auctioneers. Timothy Gabry became official "vendue master" in 1662, although the practice dated back to 1652. However, auctions became a generally popular method of merchandising only in the eighteenth century. *Laws of New Netherland*, 87, 109, 289; *Recs. N. Am.*, I, 10; II, 12, 54; IV, 85.

[43] *Letter-Book of Peleg Sanford*, 3; *Newport T. M. Recs.*, 17, 37; 5 MHS *Colls.*, V, 103; *Pa. Mag.*, IV, 194.

handiwork. Almost from the beginning the complexities of village life made for some specialization of activity, and village artisans could thus devote themselves more entirely to their trades, with a consequent higher degree of craftsmanship, than could their country brethren, some of whose time had of necessity to be given to farming. Craftsmen generally worked in their homes, frequently keeping small shops, tended by their wives or children, for the disposal of their products. There were enough shoemakers in Boston by 1648 to enable the General Court to incorporate them as a guild like the Coopers' Company previously mentioned.[44] The West India Company before 1633 had provided five stone houses at New Amsterdam, with shops for the artisans — "coopers, armorers, tailors, hatters, shoemakers" — sent over to supply the needs of the village. Thomas Applegate, weaver, of Newport, assured himself a place in the memory of posterity by getting into legal difficulties in 1643, and within the next ten years his town was well supplied with smiths, joiners, masons, and cordwainers.[45]

After the mid-century the number of "misteries" represented in the villages greatly increased. Boston, as the largest town, was amply supplied from artisans' shops with the necessities of life and some of its luxuries. Samuel Sewall mentions many of these craftsmen: "Wm Harrison, the Bodies Maker," Smith, the "joiner," "Hill, Shoemaker," an "Upholsterer," and "Wm Clendon, the Barber and Perriwigmaker," — who died a drunkard in the watch-house before a gaping crowd. When 129 "Handycraftsmen" petitioned the General Court about trade conditions in 1677, they claimed to be "a very considerable part of the town of Boston." A sign of the growing wealth and trade of the place was its ability to support the work of twenty-four silversmiths in 1680. These skilled craftsmen fashioned the artistic plate we prize so much today, not only for the town, but for all New England. Peleg Sanford wrote from Newport in 1668 to his relative in Boston, "Cosen, I pray send my wine Cupp from Mr. Hull." [46]

Hundreds of artisans came over to Philadelphia at the time of the first settlement. In 1685, according to William Penn, "There inhabits most sorts of useful Tradesmen, as Carpenters, Joyners, Bricklayers, Masons, Plumers, Smiths, Glaziers, Taylors, Shoemakers, Butchers, Bakers, Brewers, Glovers, Tanners, Felmongers, Wheelwrights, Millrights, Shiprights, Boatrights, Ropemakers, Saylmakers, Blockmakers, Turners, etc." [47]

[44] Mass. Col. Recs., II, 249; III, 132; Johnson, Wonder-Working Providence, 247.
[45] N. Y. Col. Docs., XIV, 16; Van Rensselaer, New York in the Seventeenth Century, I, 186; Doc. Hist. R. I., II, 141; Newport T. M. Recs., 21.
[46] Mass. Col. Recs., V, 143; Letter-Book of Peleg Sanford, 52.
[47] Narratives of Pennsylvania, 261; Pa. Mag., IV, 194.

Fewer skilled craftsmen were to be found in the other three villages, though there is no evidence of lack of workers wherever there was demand for their produce. Among the artisans and tradesmen who served Manhattan were several tanners, twelve butchers, many brewers (including Isaac and Joannes Verveelen, with their famous Red Lion Brewery), Evart Duycinck, glazier, and three silversmiths. At Charles Town, too, "Tradesmen" plied their crafts in much the same manner as in the northern towns, though here, as at Newport during the seventeenth century, a simpler society created a smaller demand for the products of their specialized workmanship.[48]

The problem of transportation arose early in each settlement. Merchants had goods to send to shops, artisans needed conveyance for their raw materials, and the heavy loads of builders had constantly to be carried from one part of the village to another. In each little seaport carters or carmen, with their "Draughts & teams & the like," served this need, playing a vital part in the conduct of trade and well aware of their importance. At New Amsterdam in 1667 the authorities recognized eight carters as forming an exclusive guild, "until more carters are required." They were a rough lot, and so addicted to the use of "ill and bad Language to the Burghers" that they had to be threatened with dismissal if they did not in the future treat people more "Civilly." In 1670 "Karmen" were ordered to charge a set price of "ten Stivers in Seawant & No more" for any load carried within the gates. On March 15, 1684, the number of carters was increased to twenty, and ordinances were passed regulating the charges for carting firewood, and establishing precedence of transport for goods arriving by ferry. About ten days later fifteen of the twenty carmen went out on strike. The authorities acted with swiftness, "Suspended and Discharged" the strikers, and notified townspeople that all "persons within this Citty have hereby free Lyberty and Lycence to Serve for hyre or Wages as Carmen." When a week later the penitent carters pleaded to be returned to their jobs, they were required to conform to certain "Laws and Orders Establisht," and to pay a fine of six shillings each. Only three of them appear to have been reinstated. Thus ended America's first transportation strike.[49]

The functions of the carters were much the same in all the villages, and their activities occasioned considerable legislation by town or provincial authorities. As early as 1637/8 the General Court of Massachusetts regulated the rates which carmen might charge, because of complaints of their "excessive prizes for . . . work."

[48] *Recs. N. Am.*, II, 183; V, 184; Stokes, *Iconography*, IV, 207, 960, 962; *S. C. Statutes*, VII, 2–3.

[49] *Recs. N. Am.*, VI, 70, 217, 273, 360; VII, 51; *N. Y. M. C. C.*, I, 135.

Bridges had to be made "sufficient for Cart and horse," and wear and tear on the streets led to frequent regulation of the size of cart wheels. The growing traffic of Philadelphia demanded in 1690 the services of "six carters that have Teams daily imployed to carry and fetch Timber and Bricks, Stone and Lime for Building," and about twenty-four others with four and six horse carts to bring merchandise from the wharves through the Arch into the town. New York merchants and shopkeepers could also be served by "Porters," available at the Bridge and Weighhouse for carrying parcels and light burdens during specified hours at rates set by the Corporation. In Boston, too, porters played an important part in the daily traffic of the town after 1660.[50]

IV

Certain economic ideals of medieval England came with the colonists to America. These included the beliefs that the prime function of merchant, craftsman, artisan and laborer was the service of the community, and that careful and minute regulation of all phases of commercial life was the proper responsibility of municipal authority. Hence municipal provision for a "fair customary price" for goods and labor, for wares of a standard quality, for strict supervision of food supply and regulation of weights and measures, for payment of debts when due, and for protection of the community's trade by the exclusion of strangers and interlopers, — all these were medieval legacies to America. By 1690 these inherited institutions had become adjusted to their new locale. Some had been discarded as useless in a frontier society; others, though obviously outmoded, were still retained; and many had been successfully transplanted to the new soil.

In the beginning village inhabitants trafficked gladly enough with any merchant or trader that appeared, but as soon as they had completed the first business of pioneering the authorities followed the Old World custom of protecting their local business men against intruders. In 1648 the Director and Council of New Netherland ordered "That no person shall henceforward be allowed to keep a public or private Shop on shore, in cellar or garret, or to carry on any Trade by the small weight and measure . . . except our good and dear Inhabitants," while in 1657 the Selectmen provided that only admitted inhabitants might keep shop or set up business in Boston. In the latter year the Burgomasters of New Amsterdam likewise forbade anyone

[50] *Mass. Col. Recs.*, I, 223; 2 *Bos. Rec. Com.*, 82, 99, 144; *Pa. Mag.*, IV, 195; *Narratives of Pennsylvania*, 331; *N. Y. M. C. C.*, I, 174–180. For use of porters in Bristol, England, see Latimer, *Bristol in the Seventeenth Century*, 58, 214, 230.

to do business there before he had received the "Burgher-right" of the city. Some time prior to 1680 the village of Newport also prohibited all save inhabitants, who had "liberty," from opening shops there. So far as is known only New Amsterdam, and later New York, set any fee for the burgher-right; here, in 1675, a shopkeeper had to pay six beavers, and a "Handi Craft man," two, for the coveted privilege.[51]

The towns very carefully enforced their regulations against the intrusion of strangers within their precincts. The New Amsterdam ordinance of 1648 was directed against certain "Scottish merchants and small traders," who undersold Dutch burghers in "wholesale and retail," and in 1662 the town of Boston fined Nathaniel Milles and Thomas Alline twenty shillings each for having opened shops in the town before becoming admitted inhabitants. In 1675 nine Bostonians took the law into their own hands, "forcibly taking John Langworthy upon a pole & by violence carrying him from the North end of Boston as far as the Town dock; which occasioned a great tumult of people." When the constables finally rescued Langworthy they found that he was an "interloper and had never served his time to the trade of a Ship carpenter." Not always did the towns have the support of provincial authorities in their attempts to protect their infant industries. A petition from craftsmen of Boston to the General Court, complaining of the "frequent intruding of strangers from all parts, especially such as are not desirably qualified," who set up as tradesmen when they could not even pay their taxes, and desiring a grant of power to the Selectmen for the regulation of this evil, came to nothing in 1677.[52]

Within the towns, merchants, artisans and shopkeepers secured their supply of skilled labor by means of the transplanted English system of apprenticeship. The custom of apprenticing both boys and girls for a given term of years to some master workman who would teach them a trade began in Boston as early as 1631. In that year, for example, Lucy Smith was apprenticed to Mr. Roger Ludlowe for seven years, and in 1632 John Smithe was bound over to Mr. John Wilson for five years, during which time he was to have meat, drink, apparel, and "the some of fforty shillings." William Boreman, a servant, indentured himself in 1639 to William Townsend as "Apprentice of the crafte of thatcher." Many a Boston lad was bound out to learn "the art and mistry of navigation and of a mariner."

[51] *Laws of New Netherland*, 87; *2 Bos. Rec. Com.*, 135; *Recs. N. Am.*, VII, 147; *Newport T. M. Recs.*, 17, 21; Peterson, *New York*, 46; Latimer, *Bristol in the Seventeenth Century*, 4, 96, 259.
[52] *Recs. N. Am.*, I, 10; III, 143; *7 Bos. Rec. Com.*, 11, 16; *N. Y. M. C. C.*, I, 153; *Records of the Suffolk County Court*, 602; *Mass. Col. Recs.*, V, 143.

Indentures of apprenticeship were made before the county courts, but after 1645 the Boston Selectmen occasionally aided the magistrates in putting out children as apprentices, especially when their parents, through either poverty or neglect, failed to make provision for them. In 1646 they bound out John Berry as "an apprentice to Edward Heyly for seaven yeares," and in 1656/7 notified Goodwife Sammon, as her son was "living withoutt a calling, that if she dispose not of him in some way of employ," the Selectmen "will dispose of him to some service according to the law." The parents of twelve children were notified in 1672 that unless they bound out their children "to serue by Indentures" within a month the town would be forced to provide masters for them. The great need for artisans in the growing towns often led to indentures of only three or four years in length, "Contrary to the Customes of all well governed places," and it was soon evident that youths so inadequately trained proved "by sad experience . . . their unmeetness att the expiration of their Apprentice-ship to take charge of others for government and manual instruction." To remedy this situation Boston voted in 1660 that no person could open a shop who was not twenty-one years of age and could not present evidence from town records of full seven years' service as an apprentice.[53]

The English apprentice system became naturalized in New York after 1675. In 1679 William de Meyer tried to get his son released from his four year contract to Tobias Steenwick. The Court advised that "unless the Plt. and Deft. can agree between themselves the Plt. his sonn is to serve his tyme according to contract." An apprentice whom, because of "unreasonable Correction" by his master, the Court had sent home to his father in 1683, was soon ordered to serve out the period of his indenture, unless "undue or unreasonable Correcon" should be proved in the future. The village of Newport also followed closely the English system. Here, since the Town Council possessed magisterial powers, all apprenticeships were registered in the Town Records. In 1690 William Walton, son of a widow, was bound for eleven years as "apprentis unto John Odlin of Newport, Blacksmith." In addition to instruction in the "Smith's craft," he was to receive meat, drink, lodging, clothing and lessons in reading. In Philadelphia before 1690 provincial authorities handled all indentures of apprenticeship. No rigid system of apprenticeship could exist at Charles Town, for there in the early years labor was so scarce that bounties had to be offered for the attraction of workmen. Yet by the end of the seventeenth century apprenticeship was a part

[53] *Mass. Col. Recs.*, I, 90, 98; AAS *Trans.*, VII, 210; Weeden, *Economic and Social History*, I, 259; 2 *Bos. Rec. Com.*, 87, 132, 156; 7 *Bos. Rec. Com.*, 67.

of the labor system in all of the towns.[54] Though it everywhere presented variants on the practice of the Mother Country, these divergencies were less striking in towns than in rural regions, where it was more difficult to enforce regulations governing the training and practice of specialized crafts. Hence labor trained under the apprentice system in the towns was probably superior in quality to that of the countryside.

The common laborer, a much needed person in the little villages, undoubtedly played an important part in their economic life, but like members of his class in most ages he left few traces behind him. That some laborers of "the inferior sort" dwelt in every village is plainly evident, and that common labor was scarce is a certainty. The argument of the presence of unoccupied land on the frontier, sometimes advanced in explanation of this shortage, would seem to apply more to farm hands than to town labor. Many who had been town-dwellers in the Old World probably preferred life in the villages to that of the frontier. But in the villages varied opportunities confronted the common laborer, and if ambitious he might, because of the continual expansion of the towns, rise in a short time above his station. In early Boston some workmen could earn enough in four days to remain idle the rest of the week, spending their wages for tobacco and liquor.[55] Many found they could do better by working for themselves or by going to sea. The same held true for servants whose time was out.[56] A similar situation existed in the other villages. When a stone church was built at New Amsterdam in 1642 John and Richard Ogden of Stamford, Connecticut, had to be called in to do the mason's work, and whenever common laborers were needed in the town "able Ditchers and Diggers" had to be recruited from among the farmers of outlying districts. The Company tried to maintain a corps of workers, but was generally unsuccessful in holding them to such menial labor, when they could enjoy independence in the villages, or a better living by taking up farms.[57] At Newport, Philadelphia and Charles Town there is no reason to believe that the same conditions did not prevail.

The African Negro constituted another source of common labor in all the villages. Negro slaves appeared in New Amsterdam shortly

[54] Peterson, *New York*, 70; McKee, *Labor in Colonial New York*, 17; *Newport T. M. Recs.*, 51; *Pa. Col. Recs.*, I, 186; Indentures of Apprentices (MS.); *S. C. Hist. & Gen. Mag.*, VI, 114.

[55] Winthrop, *New England*, I, 116; II, 24, 219; Myers, *Irish Quakers*, 106.

[56] The house servant problem at Boston goes back at least to 1687, when Samuel Sewall wrote: "Just now wanted a Maid very much; courted Goodwife Fellows Daughter: she could not come till spring: hard to find a good one." 5 MHS *Colls.*, V, 34.

[57] Flick, *History of the State of New York*, I, 346.

after its settlement, and after the mid-century their numbers made them important in the town's economic life. In 1644 Governor Kieft freed eleven Negroes and their wives, after nineteen years of faithful service to the Company. These became the nucleus of the free Negro laborers of New Amsterdam. Two years later the first cargo of slaves, so far as is known, was sold to the burghers, and by 1690 Negroes formed a considerable element in the population of New York. Boston and Newport also resorted to black slaves for unskilled labor. A traveler in 1687, commenting upon the scarcity of white labor in Boston, reported, "You may also own Negros and Negresses; there is not a house in Boston; however small may be its Means, that has not one or two. There are those that have five or six, and all make a good living." A glance into court records confirms this assertion. The "unflattering inventory" of the estate of John Stoughton in 1661 shows that he possessed along with "5 bbs of stinking beife, . . . 2 firkins of butter, bad, . . . 1 stone horse," and "1 Gelding Lame & Sickly," a "Negro man named John & one Negro boy Peter." Early settlers in South Carolina brought slaves with them from Barbados and employed them within the town as well as on their farms. In 1690 they were made subject to a slave code copied directly from the Barbados act of 1668.[58]

Village authorities sought to dominate the economic life of the townsmen. At almost every point inhabitants found themselves limited in their actions and inspected in their dealings, for prevailing theory held that the individual owed more to the group than did society to him. The measures taken by town fathers thus to circumscribe the activities of the citizen were in all cases adaptations of English or Dutch law and practice. The authorities of Massachusetts Bay made a brave but unsuccessful attempt in 1630 to regulate prices and wages, but after having tried every possible means of securing a "just price" for labor and commodities, repealed their orders in 1635, and placed the burden on the towns, whose freemen were, from time to time, "to agree about the prices, & rates of all workmen, laborers & servants wages." Regulation of wages in a new country where labor was scarce was foredoomed to failure, for many artisans "would remove to other places," or else they would take up farming and "would not be hired at all." [59]

The famous case of Robert Keayne indicates that in spite of this defeat the people of Boston did not discard the ideal of a fair price. Keayne, a merchant rich by the standards of the day, who kept a

---

[58] *Laws of New Netherland*, 36; Stokes, *Iconography*, I, 24; Shurtleff, *Topographical and Historical Description of Boston*, 48; *Suffolk County Court Records*, 47; Schaper, "Sectionalism and Representation in South Carolina," 311.

[59] *Mass. Col. Recs.*, I, 79, 83, 88, 109 ff.; Winthrop, *New England*, I, 161; II, 24.

shop in Boston, was accused in 1639 of "oppression used . . . in the sale of foreign commodities." Though not alone in the offense, he "notoriously above others" took profits in excess of sixpence in the shilling, occasionally as high as "two for one." Keayne used his influence to secure first the halving and then the entire remittance of his fine of £200, and finally escaped with only the censure of the court. The magistrates found Keayne the worst of all offenders, because of his wealth and the fact that he sold "dearer" than most tradesmen. His dealings so outraged community sentiment that some members of the Boston church demanded his excommunication. Aware of his duty as upholder of the social discipline, the Reverend John Cotton took the case as subject for his weekly lecture, and expounded from the pulpit the medieval doctrine of the just price. Winthrop tells us that "although the cry of the country was so great against oppression [profiteering]," and although the deputies voted for Keayne's punishment, the Bostonians, being mostly tradesmen, exerted their influence on the side of leniency.[60] By way of compensation, perhaps, Keayne was later moved to play the Maecenas, and in a will of twenty-nine pages bequeathed a library and town house to the village of Boston.

Fair prices were also a matter of concern to the burghers of New Amsterdam. In 1657 townsmen and strangers petitioned Stuyvesant to remedy the prevailing high prices, especially of "necessary commodities and household supplies." They charged that not only "Merchants, but also, consequently, Shop-keepers, Tradesmen, Brewers, Bakers, Tapsters, and Grocers make a difference of 30, 40 & 50 per cent when they sell their wares." There is no record of any action taken in this case. The West India Company also made strict rules concerning the work of its servants. An ordinance of 1638 decreed that none might leave the village without permission from the Director, and another the next year required them to go to work at the ringing of a bell. A "Commissary of the Workmen" supervised their labors. In 1658 the Burgomasters laid down regulations for village workmen, dictating the length of the working day and the recess period allowed for meals. At Philadelphia complaints of "the Great grevance of Tradesmen's Exaction" led the Council to issue a trade regulating ordinance in 1683. Two years later Penn wrote, "The hours for Work and Meals to Labourers are fixt, and known by Ring of the Bell." [61]

Village authorities maintained a similar surveillance over weights and measures. In 1631 the General Court of Massachusetts ordered all weights and measures used by tradesmen to be "sealed" according

[60] Winthrop, *New England*, I, 313–317.
[61] *Laws of New Netherland*, 18, 289; *Recs. N. Am.*, II, 410; *Pa. Col. Recs.*, I, 91; *Narrat'ves of Pennsylvania*, 262.

to standards proclaimed by the colony, and in 1650 the town of Boston began its annual practice of selecting a "Sealer of weights and measures." New Amsterdam in 1649 required all wholesale and retail merchants to have "old Amsterdam" weights and measures, which had been inspected at the Fort, and in 1675 the Court of Assistants at New York ordered that henceforth Winchester measures should be standard for city and province. Newport adopted the English peck and half-peck measures in 1643, and in 1675 sent to Boston for a set of Winchester measures. English standards were adopted in Philadelphia in 1683, and were probably also in use at Charles Town.[62]

The medieval assize of bread, insuring a fair price and weight for all products of the baker's ovens, soon appeared in the villages. At Boston in 1639 John Stone and his wife were admonished to make "bigger" bread and "to take heed of offending by making too little bread hereafter." The next year the General Court of Massachusetts passed a law providing an assize of bread for all towns. In 1646 every baker was required to mark his products in order that they might be identified if found lacking in weight or quality. All bread so found was to be forfeited to "the use of the poore." In each town the clerks of the market enforced the assize. The bakers of Boston petitioned the Court in 1681 about the set price of bread in times when wheat was high, seeking permission to choose annually three or more "meete persons" familiar with their trade to set the assize. This was granted, but although the Town Meeting the next year chose three inhabitants to make the assize no further regulation appears until 1701. At New Amsterdam the assize of bread was regularly published after 1649. David Provoost, baker, was brought into the Mayor's Court in 1681 "for having bad breed not fitt for Sale." Leniency ruled, and the offender escaped with an admonition to take greater care in the future.[63]

Save at Charles Town colonial authorities everywhere exercised great care to insure fairness in all dealings, and their records teem with accounts of "Corders of Wood," "Cullors of Staves," "Packers of flesh and fish," "Searchers of leather," "Measurers of Salt," and so on. To describe the activities of all these officers would result only in wearisome detail. Their duties were all much the same: the examination of products for quality and the supervision of gauging and measuring to insure fair treatment to both inhabitants and strangers. In Boston and Newport these minor functionaries were gen-

[62] Mass. Col. Recs., I, 87; Laws of New Netherland, 109; Doc. Hist. R. I., II, 142; Votes Pa. Assembly, I, i, 15.
[63] Mass. Col. Recs., I, 278; V, 322, 498; 7 Bos. Rec. Com., 156; Laws of New Netherland. 115; Peterson, New York, 43.

erally tradesmen and artisans elected to their offices at Town Meeting; in New York and Philadelphia they owed their appointments to the local authorities.[64]

V

The history of the colonial villages in the seventeenth century is primarily a tale of commercial expansion. In this period the five towns grew from wilderness settlements to fully developed little seaports challenging comparison with any European centers of the same size. The necessary corollary of this growth was the accumulation of capital, derived not only from the extension of wholesale trade by enterprising merchants but also from the small savings of prosperous tradesmen and artisans. A rise in the standard of living, historically one of the outstanding characteristics of American life, accompanied the increasing prosperity of life in the villages. The infectious winds of trade, blowing through the colonial settlements, everywhere stirred up the commercial spirit. As early as 1650 Edward Johnson noted that the merchants, traders and vintners of Boston "would willingly have had the Commonwealth tolerate divers kinds of sinful opinions to intice men to come and sit down with us, that their purses might be filled with coin." "New England was originally a plantation of Religion, not a plantation of Trade," thundered John Higginson in his election sermon of 1663. "Let Merchants, and such as are increasing Cent per Cent remember this." And John Hull, who, though a merchant, was an ardent theocrat, perceived sadly that "Self-interest is too predominant in many." [65] So soon did dwellers in this City of God find profits in the service of Mammon! This same leaven was quietly at work increasing cent per cent in the other villages, preparing the breakdown of time-worn medieval practices, and facilitating the transition to modern capitalism that was transforming the western world.

Commercial development in both Boston and New Amsterdam quickly outgrew the system of barter, and these years saw many unsuccessful attempts to provide a sufficient medium of exchange. In early New Amsterdam beaver skins and wampum circulated in place of money. From time to time efforts were made to regulate the value of these media, always with small success. In 1657 the burghers petitioned the Director and Council in regard to the decline in the value of beaver and wampum currency, alleging that profiteering by merchants and tradesmen resulted, and declaring that the supply of silver coin from the Fatherland failed to meet the demands of their

[64] See, for instance, 7 *Bos. Rec. Com.*, 182–184.
[65] *Cal. St. Pap.*, 1675–1676, 221; Johnson, *Wonder-Working Providence*, 212, 248; Col. Soc. Mass., *Trans.*, I, 398; AAS *Trans.*, III, 21.

growing trade. The need for a circulating medium in Massachusetts became acute by the mid-century and in 1652 the General Court set up a mint to coin the gold and silver brought into the colony, "bringing it to the sterling standard of fineness, and for weight every shilling to be three pennyweight." John Hull, merchant and silversmith, was made mintmaster, and struck off the famous pine tree shillings, "flatt and square on the sides." The money question, however, grew increasingly complicated and was farther than ever from an answer when the period ended. The events of the 1680's, the closing of the mint, the enforcement of the Navigation Acts and the temporary suppression of piracy effectively dried up the colony's few poor sources of metal coin. "The Labyrinth New-England was in, for want of a Conveniency to mete their Trade with," led to proposals for a medium of exchange based upon real estate, which would eliminate "the mystery of Trucking by sinking Barter." Proposals for a "Bank of Credit Lumbard" were made to the Colony Council in July, 1686, and two tracts were written to defend the new credit schemes. The coming of the Revolution of 1689 prevented any action in this period.[66]

The expansion of trade made communication among the several villages a necessity. At Boston as early as 1639 an office was opened to serve as a clearing house for the town's mail, and in 1652 a similar arrangement was introduced at New Amsterdam. In 1672 Governor Lovelace of New York inaugurated a monthly postal route between New York and Boston, but the service was discontinued after a few trips. Nine years later William Penn's post between Maryland and the Falls of the Delaware, was more successful. Just as the period ended Andrew Hamilton of New Jersey, royal deputy for the King's post in America, established a line of posts from Portsmouth, New Hampshire, to Philadelphia.[67] The villages remained unconnected by stage routes in this period; land communication was undeveloped, and trade was forced to rely almost entirely upon water transportation.

Of the five villages Boston in 1690 enjoyed preeminence in respect to her ocean-borne commerce. Her success was the result of a location most favorable for a center of distribution and of her priority in the field of trade. A highly developed shipbuilding industry, which enabled Boston merchants to monopolize most of the colonial carrying trade, the aggressiveness of her mariners and merchants, and the existence of a relatively large population in the New England hinter-

[66] Peterson, New York, 40; Laws of New Netherland, 289; AAS Trans., III, 145; Davis, Colonial Currency Reprints, I, 113 et passim.
[67] Mass. Col. Recs., I, 281; N. Y. Col. Docs., XIV, 186; Stokes, Iconography, IV, 286, 359; Rich, History of the United States Post Office, 7; Jackson, Cyclopedia of Philadelphia, IV, 1017. Postal service in contemporary Europe was still crude and sporadic. Clark, Seventeenth Century, 54–57.

land also aided this port in her chosen sphere of activity. Rural districts did not always regard her domination of their trade with pleasure. Edward Randolph saw this resentment developing in the political factions of 1686: "There are no small endeavors betwixt the Landed men and the Merchts: how to ease the publick Charges: The Merchts: are for Land Taxes: but . . . others who haue gott very large tracts of Land are for laying all upon the trading party."[68] This divergence of interests was an important factor running through the whole history of the Dominion of New England; an incipient antagonism between town and country, based upon economic differences, was already becoming evident.

At the close of this period the five villages exhibited varying degrees of economic development. Boston stood far in advance of the others in every respect, and her economic superiority made her a cause of jealousy to the other towns; merchants of both New York and Newport covertly resented the control exercised by "Bostoners" in their own villages. Philadelphia and New York approached nearest to Boston in economic development, while Newport and Charles Town lagged behind. But in all five the spirit of economic enterprise created a commercial society definitely contrasted to the agricultural society of the back country. The maritime activity of the villagers brought the mercantile groups of each town increasingly in contact with one another and with Europe as the century progressed. The mutual isolation of the villages was far less in 1690 than in 1640; indeed, it is probable that at the close of the period many townsmen possessed greater familiarity with other villages than with the back country of their own provinces. Commercial and economic factors, more than any others, were making for the development of an early village society.

[68] The break occurred between 1660 and 1670. The farmers, wrote Johnson as early as 1650, accepted the commercial leadership of the towns, because "if the Merchants trade be not kept on foot, they fear greatly their corne and cattel will lye in their hands." Toppan, *Edward Randolph*, VII, 211; Johnson, *Wonder-Working Providence*, 211.

III

THE APPEARANCE OF URBAN PROBLEMS

I

Community living in all ages produces its own peculiar social problems. Many of these are not unknown to country-dwellers, but appear in closely settled areas in more acute and complex forms; others are more directly the results of urban conditions. Protection against the ravages of fire and provision of sufficient water are complicated by the density of the population to be served; maintenance of order and the need for police protection become more vital where crowded settlement and heterogeneous society encourage the growth of moral delinquency and crime; pauperism becomes a community problem with the increase of those unable or unwilling to provide for themselves; and finally, the relative congestion of town living forces upon the inhabitants some consideration of the rudiments of sanitation and public health. From the beginning these problems in varying degrees confronted the colonial town-dweller, and their solution required all his past experience and native ingenuity. In this chapter we shall see what success attended his earliest efforts.

II

The specter of fire has ever haunted the town-dweller. This necessary servant may, amidst crowded town conditions, buildings of inflammable construction and the combustible materials of daily housekeeping and commerce, become his deadly enemy. Even in Europe the means of fighting fire were very crude in the seventeenth century, and only towards its close did the great cities, driven by a series of disasters, begin to evolve a system for combatting it. Though their methods were still rudimentary, their interest in fire protection was rapidly developing in the period of New World colonization. Fortunately in the early years the villages were mere rural communities and relatively free from the menace of general conflagration, but when after the mid-century they gradually became more congested they suffered the same dangers as cities and towns of the Old World.

As soon as the three oldest villages had become built up into compact settlements the authorities introduced measures, borrowed from European practice, for the prevention of accidents by fire. The Massachusetts laws of 1638 and 1646, forbidding smoking "out of dores" or near the Town House in Boston, were not so much dictated by Puritan bigotry as by the fact that "fires have bene often occasioned by taking tobacco." Other safety measures forbade the burning of brush and provided penalties for incendiarism. Boston Selectmen adopted the English curfew in 1649, when they hired Richard Taylor "to ringe the bell" at nine o'clock in the evening and at half past four in the morning. Between these hours all fires were to be either covered over or put out to lessen the hazard of fire during the night. A curfew was ordered for New Amsterdam in 1647, and it seems probable that the custom had been instituted in the other villages before 1690.[1]

Curfew laws were designed to eliminate some of the principal causes of fire. The first building regulations in the colonial towns professed a similar intent. In 1653, when ordering the houses of New Amsterdam placed closer together for protection against Indians, Peter Stuyvesant forbade the use of straw or reeds for roofing. This injunction was not well obeyed, and in 1658 the firewardens found it necessary to enlist the aid of the schout in its enforcement. The General Court of Masachusetts was made aware of the dangers of wooden houses by the great fire of 1679, which destroyed, it was estimated, one hundred and fifty buildings. In October of that year it ordered that all new dwellings be constructed of "stone or bricke, & covered with slate or tyle," upon pain of forfeiting double the value of the building. In this the Court seems to have been following the illustrious precedent of the Proclamation issued by Charles II after the Fire of London thirteen years before. The measure was not well adapted to a locality which afforded no building stone and where brick construction was still expensive. The inability of the poor to comply with its terms led to its frequent suspension and modification, and frame houses continued to be erected in the town for many years.[2]

Defective chimneys occasioned by far the greatest number of village fires. In 1648 Stuyvesant forbade the construction of any more chimneys of "wood or plaister in any house" at New Amsterdam, and levied a fine of twenty-five florins on the poor unfortunate whose house should be "burned either by negligence or his own fire." Four firemasters, appointed by the West India Company, were ordered to collect "immediately without contradiction" three guilders for each chimney "neglected and foul." The English authorities in 1664 also appointed

---

[1] *Mass. Col. Recs.,* I, 241; II, 151, 180; III, 101; 2 *Bos. Rec. Com.,* 96; 7 *Bos. Rec. Com.,* 97; *Laws of New Netherland,* 60.

[2] *Recs. N. Am.,* I, 5, 19; II, 419; VII, 184; Mather, *Magnalia,* I, 104; *Mass. Col. Recs.,* V, 240; Birch, *Historical Charters and Constitutional Documents of the City of London,* 224.

firewardens to inspect the chimneys and fireplaces of New York, levy fines for dirty ones, and remove all wooden or otherwise "improper" chimneys. No fine was actually imposed until 1680, the offender then being William Dervall, a former mayor. In 1686 "Viewers and Searchers of Chimneys" were appointed, and instructed to visit each house once in fourteen days, or oftener if necessary.[3]

The Boston Town Meeting instructed the Selectmen in 1651 to view all chimneys reported defective and order "there repayre upon penalty if not repared." Despite such ordinances inhabitants continued careless about their flues and complaints of delinquency were frequent. After the fire of 1676 it was charged that "ye towne is in great danger of being Fired by ye insufficiencie of Chimneys. & neglect of the Owners seasonablie to cause them to be swept & kept cleane." The Selectmen thereupon appointed eight inspectors, who were to be accompanied on their tours of investigation by bricklayers so that the heavy fine of twenty shillings should not be imposed without the benefit of expert advice. Although two chimney sweeps had been appointed in 1655, they do not seem to have been regularly patronized, for in 1687 the town ordered the Selectmen to name sweepers who alone should have the right to clean chimneys in the town. Responsibility for flaming chimneys thereafter rested upon the sweepers, and upon the overseer selected to superintend their work.[4]

The fragmentary records of the town of Newport indicate that by 1680, at least, inhabitants annually chose three "viewers of Laders & chimneys"; in 1687 the Court of Quarter Sessions set a fine of 2s. 6d. upon any householder whose chimney blazed. William Penn desired that each house in his new town should be placed in the middle of its lot and surrounded by gardens, "so that it may be a greene country towne which may never be burnt." Unfortunately his plans never materialized, and Philadelphia, like the other villages, developed its thickly settled areas. Chimney fires often occurred, but no laws concerning them were passed until 1696.[5]

Villagers took numerous other precautionary measures to prevent the outbreak of fire. At both Boston (1653) and New York (1679) crews were forbidden to keep fires on board vessels lying at the docks and wharves. In 1680 a skipper paid a fine of twenty shillings in New York for violation of this order. Bostonians proceeded against "careless persons" who carried fire from house to house in open pans; in 1658 this offense was made liable to a ten shilling fine, half of which

[3] *Laws of New Netherland*, 82; *Recs. N. Am.*, I, 11, 304; V, 298; VII, 146; Stokes, *Iconography*, IV, 113; *N. Y. M. C. C.*, I, 42, 184; Peterson, *New York*, 179.
[4] *2 Bos. Rec. Com.*, 106, 121, 127; *7 Bos. Rec. Com.*, 12, 18, 40, 56, 80, 104, 191.
[5] *Newport T. M. Recs.*, 19; *R. I. Col. Recs.*, III, 233; Westcott, *History of Philadelphia Fire Department*, I, chapter I.

went to the informer. Ten years later coopers were forbidden to fire "caske" in any shop or warehouse without a chimney sufficient for that purpose. In 1671, to forestall fires and explosions, all gunpowder landed at Boston was ordered deposited in Robert Gibbs' warehouse on Fort Hill, and shops were forbidden to carry more than twenty pounds of this dangerous commodity in stock. The large fine of forty shillings was the penalty for violations of the powder ordinance.[6]

In spite of all efforts fires, often disastrous in extent, became more frequent with the building up of the towns. By the mid-century it was evident that mere precautions against the outbreak of fire were insufficient, and villagers began to devise what means they could for combatting conflagrations. The provisions of our forefathers, though feeble enough, easily challenged comparison with the best contemporary arrangements in the great cities of Europe.

The steadily increasing number of frame houses at Boston made protection against fire there a question of great public interest, and hardly a Town Meeting convened without prolonged discussions of this subject. On March 14, 1653, occurred the first of the "Great" fires of Boston, the locality and extent of which are unknown. This disaster led to the promulgation of the town's first fire code. Every householder was ordered to provide at his own expense a ladder "that shall rech to the ridg of the house" and a "pole of about 12 feet long, with a good large swob at the end of it, to rech to the rofe . . . to quench fire in case of such danger." In addition, the town purchased six long ladders and "fower strong Iron Crooks" for pulling down houses, which were to be kept at the meeting house ready for any emergency. Provision was made that no house should be demolished without the consent of a majority of the public officials present at the fire, and "that noe person whoos house shall be so pulled down . . . shall . . . recover any satisfacktion by law." In 1658 Ralph Marshall was chosen inspector of ladders, with orders to return to the Selectmen the names of all delinquents. At the same time the town ordered six more ladders and the repairing of its leather fire buckets.[7]

In 1659 the town resolved that when the authorities ordered the pulling down of a house to check the spread of a fire, it should "againe be repayred and made good by the towne." The more efficacious method of blowing up houses was soon adopted; in 1671 the Selectmen awarded to John Anderson £120 for "his house and goods lost in ye great fire blowne up with gun powder." Blowing up houses

[6] 2 Bos. Rec. Com., 116, 147; 7 Bos. Rec. Com., 10, 40, 62; N. Y. M. C. C., I, 73; Peterson, New York, 178.

[7] 2 Bos. Rec. Com., 114, 122, 150; Latimer, Bristol in the Seventeenth Century, 216; 7 Bos. Rec. Com., 56.

was a dangerous business, and accidents frequent: Jeremiah Mather suffered severe bruises as a result of an explosion at a blaze in 1681.[8]

Two great and terrifying conflagrations, in 1676 and 1679, brought before the people of Boston the necessity for more heroic public measures to defend the city from fire. Samuel Sewall was present on November 27, 1676, when "Boston's greatest Fire breake forth at Mr. Moors, through the default of a Taylour Boy, who arising alone and early to work, fell asleep and let his light fire the House, which gave fire to the next, so that about fifty Landlords were despoyled of their Housing." After this disaster a fire engine was ordered from England, and Thomas Atkins, carpenter, and twelve assistants hired to manage it when it arrived in 1679. Boston now possessed the most up-to-date fire fighting equipment available, — twenty years before the city of Paris secured its first fire engine.[9]

Even more terrible than the destruction wrought in 1676 were the ravages of the fire of August 7–8, 1679. "About midnight," wrote John Hull, "began a fire in Boston, [in] an ale-house [the Sign of the Three Mariners near the Dock], which, by sunrise, consumed the body of the trading part of the town; from the Mill Creek to Mr. Oliver's Dock, not one house or warehouse left." The greatest disaster yet experienced in the colonies, it was probably, in proportion to the size and wealth of the town, as frightful as the Fire of London. "Fourscore of thy dwelling-houses and seventy of thy warehouses in a ruinous heap," wailed Cotton Mather. Inhabitants believed the fire to have been of incendiary origin, and a wave of hysteria ensued, though little came of the many investigations save discomfort to Baptists and Frenchmen, who because of the unpopularity of their religion or nationality were "under vehement suspition" of having attempted to burn the town. But the catastrophe had consequences more constructive and lasting. In August the town chose a committee of six prominent men who joined with the town officers in the formulation of new fire regulations. They divided the town into quarters, and placed each under the supervision of a militia officer, who had custody of additional powder, swabs, axes, buckets, scoops and ladders. Likewise they enjoined each householder to provide himself with buckets, swabs and scoops according to his estate. Each successive fire produced new plans for dealing with the danger. In 1682, after the destruction of twenty-eight warehouses and ten dwellings, the Selectmen hired Ralph

[8] 2 Bos. Rec. Com., 150; 7 Bos. Rec. Com., 57, 111, 141. This method was first used on the third day of the Fire of London (Everybody's Pepys, 365), and Boston practice closely follows the new London regulations of 1667. Young, Fires, Fire Engines and Fire Brigades, 29.
[9] Bristol had only one hand engine in 1672. 5 MHS Colls., V, 28. For European fire engines, see Fuller, Worthies of England, II, 334; Young, Fire Brigades, 70, 78, 86; 7 Bos. Rec. Com., 70; Latimer, Bristol in the Seventeenth Century, 344, 363.

Carter and seven members of the train-bands as an engine company to "take the care and charge of the water Engine," to keep it in good order and ready for use whenever an alarm of fire should arise in any quarter of the town. Carter and his "Company" continued in the employ of the town until August, 1686, when they were discharged and the engine turned over to two of the Selectmen "vntill further Ordr." [10]

Panic-stricken Bostonians prayed fervently to Jehovah, and bravely sought to arrest the progress of each fire when it broke out, but with the methods then known there was little they could do beyond saving their movable property. On such occasions, to revive their flagging courage, they depended upon other than heavenly stimulants, as in 1672 when Nathaniel Bishop, innkeeper, supplied £3. 6 worth of "beere" at Mrs. Oliver's fire, "by Ordr of the Deputy Gouernr & some of the select men." Contemporary opinion clearly endorsed the theory that,

> There's naught no doubt so much the spirit cheers,
> As rum and true religion.

The destruction of so much property brought great hardship to the townsfolk. A petition of the Selectmen to the General Court in 1683/4 presented the inability of many Bostonians to meet their taxes because "by the prouidence of God many of the habitations & much of the Estate of sundry persons to the value of several thousand pounds hath beene consumed by the late fire." The Selectmen were permitted to abate the rates of fire victims, but "not exceedinge" £25. [11]

The fact that Boston alone of the five villages suffered devastation by fire in the seventeenth century probably accounts for the advanced state of its fire defenses. The Burgomasters of New Amsterdam made their first attempt to provide fire fighting apparatus for their town in 1658, when they summoned four cordwainers to examine sample buckets from Holland and "give their opinion thereon and the lowest price they will make them for." After some haggling one hundred and fifty buckets were ordered, and paid for by means of a special tax which was with great difficulty collected from the burghers. The town acquired ladders and fire-hooks in 1659, and the next year arranged with a carpenter to make a "shed to keep the ladders under," after he had discovered where they were. In 1665 the firewardens, in addition to inspecting chimneys, took charge of the maintenance and repair of the village equipment. The Common Council of New York, finding the old Dutch fire regulations wofully inadequate, issued new orders in 1687. These required the inmates of each two-chimney house

[10] AAS *Trans.*, I, 245; Mather, *Magnalia*, I, 104; *Mass. Col. Recs.*, V, 250; 7 *Bos. Rec. Com.*, 130, 132, 162, 188; *N. E. Hist. & Gen. Reg.*, VII, 59.
[11] 7 *Bos. Rec. Com.*, 71, 164, 168.

to keep one bucket on hand, two buckets being required where there were more hearths. Each baker had to have three, and every brewer, six. Two men were appointed in 1689 "to make a view . . . of all Bucketts & other Materialle against fyre"; they were to be assisted in the performance of their duty by the constables of each ward, and were to report to the Corporation all violations of the fire laws. Sometime prior to 1680 "viewers of Laders & chimneys" were appointed by the Town Meeting at Newport, and in 1687 the Court of Quarter Sessions ordered every householder to provide himself with a ladder "that shall reach up to or near the ridg of the . . . house." [12] During this period Philadelphia was spared any large fires, largely by reason of its brick houses, and inhabitants both there and at Charles Town were still too busy with the work of actual pioneering to give much thought to the possible prevention of fire in the future.

III

Of the other elements, water, too, was of such vital concern to the villagers as to constitute a community problem. As a beverage it did not particularly interest the colonist; after the earliest years he seldom drank any in its pristine form save as a last resort. Among the first works of the new villages was the erection of breweries to supply townsfolk with their customary table drink. Water, however, was a necessity not to be dispensed with, and consistent efforts were made to secure an ample supply both for domestic uses and for protection against fire. The site of Boston was chosen largely because there were good springs at "Trimountaine," and in 1684 the Proprietors of Carolina, on being generally misinformed that Charles Town had no good water, urged shifting the settlement to a new location.

Springs furnished most of the water used in the earliest years, but in each village wells were soon sunk. At Boston by 1643 an inhabitant had to secure permission from the Selectmen when he wished to dig a well or set up a pump. Most wells and pumps were constructed by private initiative, neighbors who made use of them being obliged by law to contribute to their support. In 1657 Mr. Bushnell and Mr. Glover were granted liberty to "sett up a pump and to repayre the well," and the Selectmen ordered that the use of this pump should be denied any neighbors who refused to contribute to the charge. A few wells were dug from time to time at public expense, and maintained for the use of the poor; very soon after the settling of Boston the one which became famous as the "Town Pump" was by the authorities sunk

[12] *Recs., N. Am.,* VI, 67; VII, 191, 201, 206, 220, 228; *N. Y. M. C. C.,* I, 144, 211; *Newport T. M. Recs.,* 19; *R. I. Col. Recs.,* III, 233, 245.

at the market place. By 1678 the village was abundantly supplied with pumps and wells, and complaints were beginning to be heard in Town Meeting of the "Abuse of streets by wast water comeinge from ye pumps." Six years later, when one of the town pumps overflowed and damaged the streets near the home of Thomas Brattle, a group of residents secured permission from the authorities to "lay pipes from sd well through the streets to the head of the Dock . . . at their own charge." [13]

New Amsterdam was the only village not favored with good well water. There was, so far as we know, no public well on Manhattan before 1666, when Governor Nicolls caused one to be dug within the Fort. In 1671 another was sunk in the Stadt House yard. Water from these wells was so brackish that it could not be used for drinking or cooking, and burghers had to secure their supply for these purposes from a spring outside the village limits. The island of Rhode Island contained many "fair" springs, and Newport enjoyed an extraordinarily good water supply. In 1686 Caleb Carr's spring was the place to which nearly all inhabitants resorted for their water. Philadelphia had two pumps in 1682, one in Walnut Street, and the other in Norris' Alley, from both of which pure and wholesome water, especially "for boiling greens," could be procured. At Charles Town, also, excellent water was available. Here, because of the geological formation of the land, wells needed only to be sunk twelve or fifteen feet to tap a pure and unfailing supply.[14]

The importance of an adequate water supply in case of fire was first demonstrated at Boston, and here between 1649 and 1652 the earliest colonial attempt to provide for such emergencies was made, when "James Everill and the Neighbours . . . set up the Cunditt." This conduit was a reservoir about twelve feet square fed by pipes leading from nearby wells and springs, and was situated in the square formed by the junction of Union and Ann Streets. The General Court incorporated the "inhabitants of the Conduit Street" for the purpose of providing a ready supply of water for their families, especially in case of fire. This project never came up to the expectations of its promoters, although it was of considerable use in the fire of 1679, undoubtedly doing much to save property in the vicinity. Its chief function seems to have been to supply water to neighboring housewives on washdays. In 1643 William Franklin and his neighbors had been permitted to build a "sistern of 12 foot or greater, . . . at the pumpe" in the highway near the State Arms Tavern, "to howld water

[13] 2 Bos. Rec. Com., 76, 101, 141; 7 Bos. Rec. Com., 27, 117, 172.
[14] Recs. N. Am., VII, 190; Stokes, Iconography, IV, 262; Newport T. M. Recs., 48; Repplier, Philadelphia, 26; Charleston Year Book, 1881, 258.

for to be helpful in case of fier." Notwithstanding these measures, the experience of Boston had shown by 1670 that in times of fire its welfare was gravely threatened "for want of a speedy supply of water," and every householder was therefore ordered to keep a filled pipe or hogshead always ready by the door of his dwelling.[15]

The Common Council of New York, considering the problems of fire protection in 1677, found the two wells then in use insufficient to meet an emergency demand for water. They provided for the digging of six wells in the middle of the public ways "for the Publique good of the Cytie, by the inhabitants of each street." Again in 1686 the question of water supply was raised, and ten more wells ordered. They were to be made of stone, and the charge divided equally between the city and the users of the wells. To each of the six which were actually built the Corporation assigned a caretaker. It is evident that by the close of the period the authorities of New York, like those of Boston, were deeply engaged in the problem of securing to the village a water supply sufficient and speedily obtainable for the fighting of fire.[16]

IV

The problem of defense was coeval with the founding of the towns. In the seventeenth century each little colonial community was constantly threatened from without, on land by Indians, from the sea by pirates and foreign enemies. Military activities of a sort were, therefore, familiar to them from the beginning. More significant for their development as future cities were the measures they took to maintain the laws within their bounds and to protect themselves against disorderly, law-breaking and criminal inhabitants. In any urban community police power is soon needed. In the early villages with their simple conditions of life and uniform public sentiment it could be vested in some semi-official agency sufficient to preserve order, but it had to be strengthened and augmented as the towns grew larger, their life more complex and their populations more diverse.

Almost immediately village authorities found it necessary to select persons to serve as guardians of the peace. The titles and functions of their first police officers were of European origin: English constable and Dutch schout were both petty officers in whose hands the enforcement of law and order was placed. The range of their duties may be seen from a typical Massachusetts law of 1646:

> Evry cunstable . . . hath, by virtue of his office, full powr to make, signe, & put forth pursuits, or hues & cries, after murthrers, man-

[15] Col. Soc. Mass. *Trans.*, I, 199; 2 *Bos. Rec. Com.*, 108, 138, 158; 7 *Bos. Rec. Com.*, 20, 56, 67.
[16] *N. Y. M. C. C.*, I, 46, 179, 185.

slayrs, peace breakrs, theeves, robers, burglarers, where no ma[gis]trate is at hand; also to apphend without warrant such as are ovr taken with drinke, swearing, breaking ye Saboth, lying, vagrant psons, night walkers, or any other yt shall break o[u]r lawes; . . . also to make search for all such psons . . . in all houses licensed to sell either beare or wine, or in any othr suspected or disordered places, & those to apphend, & keepe in safe custody. . . .

Constables appeared in all of the towns as soon as local government was organized. The job was a thankless one and the duties so onerous and distasteful that men persistently endeavored to avoid the office. Complaints at Boston in 1653 that many able-bodied men were trying to escape constabulary duty led the town to authorize the Selectmen to levy the enormous fine of £20 on anyone refusing to serve. In 1690/91 Jacob Moline and John Boreland paid fines of £10 each rather than undertake the office.[17]

In the performance of their unpleasant duties the constables too often found their authority flouted. In 1643, when Job Tyler of Newport was summoned to court by the constable, "he sd he car'd not a fart [or] turd for all their warrants." Job paid for his insolence, however, and was "adjudged to be whipt till his back be bloody." At New Amsterdam the schout did not always receive the full cooperation of the magistrates. The Suffolk County Court found it necessary in 1671 to admonish Richard Barnum, who had been presented for "disorders in his house & reflective speeches to the constable that made inquiry about it." [18] Assuredly, the constable's lot was not a happy one!

Throughout the century the constables were the sole officers of the law on duty in the daytime. There were five of these functionaries at Charles Town in 1685; the Corporation of New York assigned one or more to each of the six wards of the city in 1686; Newport elected two in 1688; and Boston chose eight in 1690. This personage, parading daily through the streets upon the town's business, armed with a long black staff, his badge of office, was a familiar sight in all the villages.[19]

The first efforts to assure the nocturnal security of town-dwellers were the "military watches" set up by provincial authorities. In 1631 the Court of Assistants ordered a "court of guard upon the neck" between Roxbury and Boston, consisting of an officer and six men. A similar provision was made at New Amsterdam in 1643 when Director

[17] *Mass. Col. Recs.*, II, 150; IV, i, 327; Peterson, *New York*, 151–160. For English background, see Webb, *English Local Government: The Parish and the County*, 25–29.
[18] *Doc. Hist. R. I.*, II, 142; *Recs. N. Am.*, I, 309; IV, 55; *Recs. Suffolk County Court*, 22, 26.
[19] *N. Y. M. C. C.*, I, 134; *R. I. Col. Recs.*, III, 241; 7 *Bos. Rec. Com.*, 199; *S. C. Statutes*, VII, 2.

Stuyvesant formed a "Burgher Guard," which served "in full squads" as a military watch on nights when the island was believed in danger.[20]

Fear of Indian outrages under cover of darkness led to the establishment of a "rattle watch" in New Amsterdam in 1658. A captain and eight men received twenty stivers a night for walking the rounds of the town. But only the threat of immediate danger could have induced the burghers to consent to a tax for such a purpose. After the Indian scare had passed the watch was allowed to lapse because of the expense, although it was revived in 1661 and continued its useful duty until 1682. By this year so much friction had developed between the English constable and the Dutch members of the watch that, when further dangers from Indians and slaves threatened the peace and security of the village, the governor replaced the citizen Dogberrys by a military patrol. Upon the arrival of Governor Dongan in 1684 the "military Officers and Troopers" were withdrawn, leaving the citizen's watch to preside once more over the nocturnal destinies of New York. Each night the constables of the five wards hired eight men at twelve pence each to serve as watchmen. With forty-five paid officers on duty nightly the people of New York probably enjoyed better police protection than the residents of any contemporary town, colonial or English.[21] The new watch continued to function until the outbreak of the revolution of 1689, when the Leislerian troubles made it necessary again to place the city in the hands of a military "Night Guard."

Boston had been the first village to form a citizen's watch, but unwillingness or inability of inhabitants to provide the necessary financial support resulted in a far less efficient patrol than that of New York. In February, 1635/6, the Town Meeting ordered a "Watch taken up and gone round" after sunset during the summer months. A constable set the watch each night, and province law required every male inhabitant to take his turn therein or provide a substitute. Bostonians soon felt the need for protection in winter as well, and in 1653 directed the Selectmen to hire a "bellman" to go round the town by night at such times in "Winter as there is noe watch kept." Two men were hired in 1654 at ten shillings a week to serve as bellmen from 11 P.M. to 4 A.M. In 1677, as a result of the bad fire of the previous year, the town approved the appointment of four or six more men, to "walke priuatelie about the towne euery night to prevent fire," until the constable's watch should begin.[22]

[20] *Mass. Col. Recs.*, I, 190; *Laws of New Netherland*, 35.
[21] With a population perhaps four times that of New York, Bristol employed only two constables, twenty-six watchmen and two bellmen in 1674. *Recs. N. Am.*, VII, 195, 198, 265; *N. Y. M. C. C.*, I, 90, 147, 266, 390; Latimer, *Bristol in the Seventeenth Century*, 366.
[22] 2 *Bos. Rec. Com.*, 8, 115, 118; *Mass. Col. Recs.*, II, 151; III, 265; 7 *Bos. Rec. Com.*, 2, 11, 108.

Prior to 1663 the night watch at Boston had been made up of a constable or his deputy and eight citizens drafted for each night. Watching being both unpleasant and comfortless, the Selectmen decided in that year to dispense with the services of the public, and hired seven men as a "standing watch"; they were each paid eighteen pence a night from a "voluntary gift" subscribed by the townsmen and supplemented by the Selectmen from the town rates. This innovation proved too costly for the town to bear, and after a year the old watch was restored. As one of its chief duties was to prevent the outbreak of fire, its numbers were increased to twelve following the conflagration of 1676. A "police investigation" by local and provincial authorities after the disastrous fire of 1679 found existing arrangements insufficient for the safety of the town, and a military watch was ordered. The civilian watch thus disappeared in Boston, and did not again emerge until 1698.[23]

The isolated location of Charles Town made necessary protection against surprise attacks by Spaniards or Indians as well as from local disorders, and authorities there inaugurated a "Constable's Watch" in April, 1685. A constable and six armed men made the rounds nightly from ten o'clock until sunrise, and the village was divided into four "precincts" for the purpose of listing persons liable for such service. At about the same time the Provincial Council of Pennsylvania ordered a watch for Philadelphia, and Penn was shortly able to report that "After nine at Night, Officers go the Rounds, and no Person, without a very good cause [is] suffered to be at any Public House that is not a Lodger." In 1690 further strengthening of the authority of the watch was approved by the Council, and given "due Countinuance . . . vpon all occasions."[24]

The services of a single constable seem to have been sufficient for Newport until about 1676, when, during the Indian War, the town began to fill up with refugees from the mainland. In 1681 the General Assembly of Rhode Island empowered the towns to choose a "Constable or more than formerly" for "suppressing of disorder," and Newport added another of these officers to the one already in the town's employ. During the disturbances of King Philip's War train-bands protected the growing village, but in 1681 the Town Meeting provided for its own security at night by hiring Richard Barnes bellman "to walke up and down ye Streets of this Town in ye nights . . . for one whole year."[25]

The duties of the night watches were much the same in all the vil-

[23] 7 Bos. Rec. Com., 16, 21, 23, 119, 128, 131, 136, 231.
[24] S. C. Statutes, VII, 2; Narratives of Pennsylvania, 262; Pa. Mag., IV, 196.
[25] R. I. Col. Recs., III, 102, 241; Newport T. M. Recs., June 7, 1682.

lages, since they drew their inspiration from a common European source and all adhered rather closely to the Old World model. Typical are the seventeen "Items" of the orders for the paid "Rattle Watch" of 1658 at New Amsterdam. Watchmen were to report promptly each night; they were to be sober, to refrain from "opposition, insolence or impiety," and were forbidden to "blaspheme the name of God." Sleeping or fighting while on duty were punishable by heavy fines. After these careful admonitions, watchmen were instructed "on going the rounds to call out how late it is, at all corners of the streets from nine O'Clock in the evening untill the *reveille* beat in the morning." In 1661 the watch was especially enjoined to aid in the discovery and putting out of fires, while in 1674 the city gate was ordered closed at nine o'clock and the watch directed to make at least three rounds of the village during the night. To prevent their disturbing the slumbers of the burghers watchmen were ordered in 1682 to be "Still and quiett and not Suffer any Laughing or Loud talking in the Streets." At Boston, where curfew rang at nine, the watch made their rounds from then till five in the morning. The constable was cautioned against selecting a watch made up entirely of youths or of "any that are of notorious euill life & manners & likewise such as would watch two nights togeather, not haueing sufficient sleepe betweene." The watch itself was to have especial care for the waterfront, the Town House and the fortifications. It was to suppress nocturnal disturbances such as "danceing, drinckeing, Singinge vainlie, &c." and was to see that no one was abroad without good cause after 10 P.M. Above all,[26]

> For as much as the watch is to see to the regulateinge of other men actions & manners, that theirfore they may be exemplary themselues neither vseing any vncleane or corrupt language, nor vnmannerlye or vnbeseming tearmes vnto any, but that they behaue themselues soe that any person of quallitye, ore strangers yt ar vppon occation abroad late, may acknowledge that or watch neglects not due examination, nor offers any iust cause of prouocation.

While the problem of public safety was not confined to thickly settled communities, it was there intensified by the peculiarities of urban conditions, and there demanded a more immediate solution. By 1690, therefore, each colonial village had made some provision for the nocturnal security of its inhabitants. Citizens were required to serve their turns in the watches of Boston, New York, Philadelphia and Charles Town, although New York alone paid for these services. At Newport one bellman was the only watch. In Boston the civil authority broke down as a result of a series of disastrous fires and was forced to

---

[26] *Recs. N. Am.,* VII, 196, 264; *N. Y. M. C. C.,* I, 8, 93; 7 *Bos. Rec. Com.,* 8, 110.

admit its incompetence in providing for the public security; the general uncertainty of the period of the Revolution, the threat of foreign invasion and civil strife, undoubtedly contributed to the delay in reestablishing the constable's watch. Yet, however inadequate by modern standards, police protection in the colonial villages was at least as efficient as in towns and cities of old England; in the case of New York the system was well in advance of the times.

v

In the rural neighborliness of the early villages disorder was rare and violence relatively unknown, so that the age-old problems of crime and punishment troubled the first settlers but little; but as the villages grew into towns and became active seaports the amount of crime steadily increased, until by 1690 it had in several of them become a civic problem of first magnitude. In proportion to the number of inhabitants crime was probably no more prevalent in the towns than throughout the countryside, but it requires no hypothesis of the urban origins of wrong-doing to demonstrate that in areas of greater concentration of population and of wealth offenses against society are certainly more evident, and their punishment more vitally necessary.

New Amsterdam included restless elements from the beginning. The servants of the Dutch West India Company were "an unruly, rebellious lot," who showed slight respect for the Company's officers, but lazy and disorderly as they were, there is still little evidence of criminality in the early years. Increased traffic subjected the Dutch village to the common plague of seaports, — sailors on shore leave. To guard against nocturnal disturbances and possible burglaries a law of 1638 forbade the crews of vessels riding in the harbor to remain on shore over night. An added cause for uneasiness lay in the fact that New Amsterdam had become a haven for runaway servants from the English settlements in New England and Virginia, who constituted the first truly criminal element in the little village. By 1652 the stern rule of Peter Stuyvesant had succeeded in controlling this incipient criminality at Manhattan; although street fighting and tavern brawls were not uncommon, robbery was almost unknown. While Hendrick van Duyck was schout (1645–1650), there occurred only two cases requiring corporal punishment.[27]

This peaceful state of affairs could not last, for the increasing population, especially of Negroes and mulattoes, included many elements of danger and unrest. Hendrick Jansen Claarbout van ter Goos, a convicted felon, was banished from the colony in 1660, and four years

[27] *Laws of New Netherland,* 10, 15; *Recs. N. Am.,* I, 31.

later a Negress who confessed to setting her master's house on fire was condemned to be burned at the stake. In 1662 Reyer Cornelissen, a miller, confessed after torture that he had been guilty of stealing grain; some years later the city hangman was convicted of a series of thefts, but "scaped his neck through want of another hangman to truss him up," the authorities exacting only thirty-nine lashes and an ear before they banished him. After English occupation the amount of crime increased, — horse-stealing, assaults by slaves, and the reception of stolen goods being prominent among the offenses. Mary, wife of John Henries, was convicted before the Mayor's Court in 1680 of reselling stolen goods, fined £10, and threatened with being whipped out of town if the offense were repeated. Less serious, but more informing, was the case of a man convicted of stealing bed-sheets from a tavern in 1672. To curb the frequent misdemeanors of slaves the Corporation enacted strict regulations concerning them in October, 1682. Increasing disorders and a growing tendency towards mob violence led Governor Dongan in 1687 to advocate a strengthening of the forts on the island; "the people growing every day more numerous a[nd] they generally of a turbulent disposition." [28]

The highly religious character of the Boston settlement, and the fact that most of the wage-earning class lived "proportionally better than the rich" proved definite deterrents to the emergence of crime in the years of the Puritan migration to New England. After 1640, however, when this ideal community began to look out to the West Indies for a trade, John Winthrop recorded sadly that "as people increased, so sin abounded." The General Court, too, found a reason for the prevalence of crime at Boston in the great concourse of trade there, and by 1651 felt compelled to take steps to deal with the situation. A commission of seven, chosen annually by the freemen, was to handle breaches of the law that did not exceed £10. The next year, for the better prevention of theft, "a crime of late much growing vppon us," the penalty demanding restitution to the aggrieved party was augmented by the addition of whipping or a heavy fine upon the offender. The rapid increase of strangers, many of them persons of "ill behaviour," threatened "further mischiefe and chardge" to the town, and in 1662 householders were forbidden to entertain such people without license from the authorities.[29]

The records of the Suffolk County Court give ample evidence of the prevalence of crime at Boston. Cases of assault, arson, breaking and entering, embezzlement, fighting and brawling, manslaughter, theft,

[28] *Recs. N. Am.*, III, 110, 328; IV, 70; Peterson, *New York*, 198; Stokes, *Iconography*, IV, 313–319; *Doc. Hist. N. Y.*, I, 150.
[29] *Mass. Col. Recs.*, III, 244, 293; IV, i, 82; 7 *Bos. Rec. Com.*, 7.

and the reception of stolen goods appear in mounting numbers as the years go by. In 1671/2 John Hull recorded, "This County Court, three or four young men were convicted of several burglaries in breaking open warehouses, ketches, and cellars. . . . The good Lord give check to such wickedness." In 1673 the Court convicted Joseph Pollee, Stephen Hoppin and Anthony Grinnings of the theft of "severall parcells of Linnen," and sentenced each to make threefold restitution of goods, to be severely whipped, and to be detained in prison until the performance of the sentence. At the same session Hannah Hoppin, after her own confession of "receiving severall of the stoln goods abouesd of her Son & others," was ordered whipped with fifteen lashes. The year before the Court had pronounced sentence in the case of Gillian Knight, convicted of "Enticing Danll Herring to her house & there Embracing him pick't his pocket and Stole Seven Shillings from him." The ancient English "Art of Cony-Catching" was also practiced in the New World, and the innocent and unsuspecting countryman who came to town to shop occasionally met the fate supposed to await his kind in all ages. Samuel Sewall noted in 1687 that "One Wm Sargent of Almsbury [Amesbury] is trapaned into a Tipling house" at nine o'clock at night, and there robbed of some money, a ring and his papers.[30]

The increase in theft after 1676 may be in part attributed to the infiltration of refugees during the Indian troubles. Rapidly growing as a seaport and trading center, Boston had become the "continual resort of all sorts of persons from all ptes"; the town now included the rowdy elements common to a waterfront society, which when added to the floating population of refugee strangers formed a ground swell that might upon occasion break forth in waves of mob action. The opening of the Anglican Church in 1689 provided one such occasion; the populace, both genteel and vulgar, vented its spleen upon members of the strange communion. The church edifice was an especial object of the mob's fury, "receiving marks of their indignation and scorn by having the Windows broke to pieces and the Dores and Walls daubed and defiled with dung and other filth in the rudest and basest manner imaginable." [31]

No evidence concerning crime is available for early Charles Town, but with the lax and spasmodic control exercised over the affairs of the town by the Parliament of South Carolina the assumption seems justified that here as at Boston and New York a certain amount of lawlessness existed. At Philadelphia the unchallenged Quaker discipline still made for peace and order. As for Newport, Bostonians

[30] *Recs. Suffolk County Court*, 94, 113, 334; 5 MHS *Colls.*, V, 172.
[31] 7 *Bos. Rec. Com.*, 135; *Andros Tracts*, I, 53.

continually regarded it as a sink for all varieties of iniquity, but the evidence does not warrant such an indictment. On the contrary, the Rhode Island village seems to have been in all respects the most orderly of the settlements. The only reference to a crime in the history of early Newport is the discharging of Richard Caines from his office of constable and his removal from the freeman's list in 1662 for the commission of a felony.[32]

With Boston and New York, however, the case was otherwise. Both towns by 1690 faced the problem of growing disorder. Their developing activities, diverse populations and increasingly complex social structures provided opportunity and material for criminals of all sorts. As compared with English towns of the same size, crime here was not so widespread, nor were the penalties meted out so severe. The comparative youth of New World towns rendered them free from the organized shame of such districts as London's Whitechapel, the accretion of generations of outlawry and vice. But they could not escape the penalties of their growth, and the significant fact is that as the colonial villages emerged as towns they were forced to meet the same social problems as the cities of the Old World.

Coincident with the growth of crime in the villages came an increase in moral delinquencies and vice. Before Boston became a thriving seaport the morals of the townsfolk were relatively pure and unsullied. Severe penalties existed for offenses of a sexual nature, and the few cases that arose seem to have been largely among servants and the very lowest strata of village population. Neither can any distinction be made between the moral rectitude of country districts and that of the little village on the Bay. Of some thirty cases of fornication and adultery coming before the Court of Assistants between 1630 and 1643, only four or five were from Boston. But when the inhabitants took to the sea, their town inevitably suffered from the vices of the waterfront. Notwithstanding all magisterial efforts, sailors from foreign lands could not be controlled while on shore. As early as 1646 a mariner brought the "lues venerea" to the village, and other signs of sexual laxity began to appear.[33] Governor Winthrop saw clearly the reason for the growing immorality of Boston: "As people increased, so sin abounded, and especially the sin of uncleanness" among the lower classes. Then, too, lack of normal outlets for the exuberant spirits of the common man forced him to take refuge in the only

---

[32] *Newport T. M. Recs.*, 34.

[33] Although "about sixteen persons, men, women and children were infected" it must not be thought that this reflects greatly upon the morals of the whole community; Winthrop clearly shows the extenuating circumstances. I cite this merely as an example of the dangers to which a seaport is exposed. Winthrop, *New England*, II, 257–258.

diversions available. Excessive drinking and vice were bound to prevail among the less austere elements of a population denied even the most harmless amusements. There is no doubt of the growth of sexual irregularity in Boston toward the close of the seventeenth century. It was the result of the natural increase of urban population, of the flooding of the town with fugitives from the frontiers during King Philip's War, and most of all of the growing cosmopolitanism of the seaport. Many of the "Rabble" were "like Watermen, that look one way and row another." One observer noted that hardly a court day passed without its share of cases of immorality: "How agreeable is the sweet sin of Lechery . . . to them!" [34]

More serious than the occasional moral lapses of the townsfolk was the growth of commercialized vice. As early as 1663 Josselyn noted that in Boston "there are many strange women too (in Solomon's sence) more the pity." The Widow Alice Thomas, tavern-keeper, was tried before the Suffolk County Court, January 30, 1671/2, upon charges of receiving stolen goods, selling liquors without license, entertaining children and servants unseasonably, "Profanation of the Lord's day," and giving "frequent secret and vnseasonable Entertainment in her house to Lewd Lascivious & notorious persons of both Sexes, giving them opportunity to commit carnall wickedness, & that by common fame she is a common Baud." Convicted upon all counts, the Widow was forced to make threefold restitution of the stolen goods, fined £50, ordered whipped at the cart's tail with thirty-nine stripes, and imprisoned during the pleasure of the court. Aroused by this case, the General Court on May 15 enacted its first law against erecting "a stews, whore house or brothel house," providing barbarous penalties for such offenses. In April Alice Thomas was permitted to leave the prison daily after giving bond to return at night, and was discharged by order of the General Court in October but forbidden to live in Boston. In September, 1673, she subscribed a considerable sum of money to build thirty feet of the great sea-wall in Boston harbor, and — the sequence of events invites suspicion — was the same year readmitted as an inhabitant. In the decade 1670 to 1680 eleven other cases of prostitution appeared before the Suffolk County Court, and the "Whores of Boston" became notorious throughout the colonies.[35]

The conclusion to be drawn from a study of the seamy side of Boston life is not that the inhabitants lived, as one observer believed, in "a continual course of Debauchery," but rather that as the village grew it merely took on the normal aspects of any urban community.

[34] *Recs. Court of Assistants*, II; Winship, *Boston in 1682 and 1695*, 4.
[35] 3 MHS *Colls.*, III, 332; *Mass. Col. Recs.*, IV, ii, 513; *Recs. Suffolk County Court*, 82, *et passim*; 7 *Bos. Rec. Com.*, 83; Winship, *Boston in 1682 and 1695*, 5.

That vice was developing among the rougher elements in no way impugns the virtue of the major portion of inhabitants who continued, as before, to lead a sober and moral existence.[36]

Early New Amsterdam was not conspicuous for its virtue. The "improper conduct" of its women was frequently observed, even Annetje Jans, the dominie's wife, being charged "with lifting one's petticoats too high in crossing the streets." To safeguard the morals of the village sailors were forbidden in 1638 to remain on shore over night, and strict regulations to prevent immorality were enacted. As contrasted with Boston, sexual laxity ran vertically through all classes. In 1653 Schout Allard Anthony was proved to have had illicit relations with the wife of Jan Gooderis, and a considerable scandal broke out in 1673 when it was found that Peter Smith, "alias Groenendyke," had seduced Annetie Blanck and Marie de la Noy, daughters of two prominent families, under promise of marriage. Between 1662 and 1667 at least four women were convicted as prostitutes and banished from the village precincts. Margaret Anthony, proven a thief as well as a bad woman, was banished for a year and a day, after having been whipped with thirty-nine lashes on the bare back.[37]

At Philadelphia the Friends' Meeting exercised rigid control over the morals of its members, but "the number of sailors of every nationality, [and] of foreign merchants and tradesmen come to buy and sell," had already by 1685, greatly to the distress of quiet Quakers, led to the introduction of many of the sorts of debauchery which naturally attach to active seaport towns. Much of the "lewdness and all manner of wickedness" prevalent in the village could be traced to the presence of the caves, such notorious dens of iniquity by 1685 that Penn ordered them vacated for "ye reputation of the Government." Newport, despite all scandalous tales gratuitously disseminated by the people of the Bay colony and their descendants, was easily the quietest and most moral of the early villages. This may be attributed in part to the Quaker influence predominant there, but also to the fact that not until about 1675 did the village engage widely in shipping, and was thus spared the presence of sailors on shore leave.[38]

[36] Boston's population, 1670–1680, was about forty-five hundred. An analysis of cases of moral laxity during this decade is interesting: illicit relations before marriage, eighteen; adultery, twelve; fornication, fifty; women bearing bastards, forty-eight; prostitution, eleven (not proved in all cases); seduction, two; bigamy, one; miscegenation, one; attempted rape, three; lasciviousness by men, eleven; wanton carriage by women, four. The close correspondence between the number convicted of fornication and the number of bastards is significant; in the absence of evidence many cases of the former must have escaped detection. *Recs. Suffolk County Court, passim.*

[37] *Laws of New Netherland,* 10; *Recs. N. Am.,* I, 51, 192, 238, 298, 317; II, 201; IV, 163; V, 272; VI, 35, 101, 114; VII, 38; *Minutes of the Mayor's Court of New York,* 741, 744.

[38] Westcott, *History of Philadelphia,* chapter XXX; *Pa. Col. Recs.,* I, 116, 156, 176, 188; *R. I. Col. Recs.,* III, 44. There is no evidence for Charles Town in this period.

Despite valiant efforts on the part of authorities, vice was creeping slowly into the little colonial ports. The bulk of the people lived honestly and morally in their homes, but down by the waterfronts, in caves or mariners' groggeries, "Lewdness, whoredom and wickedness" took root, furnishing a distinctly urban problem of some proportions.

In each colonial village a variety of penalties awaited the wrongdoer, whether criminal or moral delinquent. Fines, whippings, and restitution of stolen goods, often two or threefold, constituted the more usual punishments. Less use was made of the stocks and pillory than is generally believed; in New York these instruments of punishment were unknown before 1690. Two generalizations emerge from study of the court records of the period: first, that sort of punishment was in greatest favor which was speedy and least expensive to the community; and second, that colonial practice tended to be more humane than contemporary European codes, which exacted the death penalty for many trivial offenses.[39]

A place of confinement for those whom society felt it unsafe to allow at large was an early necessity in each community. Nothing better indicates the comparative absence of vicious or dangerous criminals from the seventeenth century villages than the haphazard fashion in which all alike dealt with this problem. Moreover, imprisonment as a punishment for crime was still unusual. It was far cheaper to the community to impose fines or floggings on offenders, so that the chief function of our early prisons was to serve as places of detention for those under arrest and awaiting trial.

Massachusetts authorities ordered the erection of a colony prison, or "howse of correccon," in 1632, but the building was not ready for occupancy until 1637, when Richard Brackett was appointed keeper. The prison at Boston was left in a state of consistent neglect, and attempts to prevent its falling into utter dilapidation generally proved abortive. In spite of orders to repair the building in 1647, the Court was informed a year later that the ground sills and studs of the structure were "very rotten," and the partitions "weake," that new clapboarding was needed to replace disintegrating planks, and that the "pales" around the prison yard were about to fall. Similar reports in 1649, 1650, 1679 and 1680 indicate that at no time in the period under review was the Boston prison sufficiently staunch to prevent the escape of a vigorous inmate who thought to throw his whole weight against its door.[40]

To prevent "many misdemeanors and evill practizes dayly increasing," the General Court in 1655 directed each county to provide

[39] Peterson, *New York*, 198; *Recs. Suffolk County Court*, index.
[40] *Mass. Col. Recs.*, I, 100, 337; II, 196, 230, 288; V, 237.

a house of correction, and the next year ordered that county prisons be temporarily employed for this purpose. Boston did not comply with the terms of this law for thirty years, and then only by employing the new Alms House, built in 1685, rather as a convenient dumping place for unruly servants and slaves than as a refuge for the poor.[41]

In 1640 offenders against the law at Newport were detained at the home of Sergeant Bull, but sometime before 1648 a gaol was there erected for the use of the entire colony. In 1655 an order of the General Assembly directed the town to build a new prison at a cost of £80, a quarter of the expense being allotted the town of Portsmouth, which was to share the use of the building. Opened three years later, this structure enjoyed much the same official neglect as did the one at Boston.[42]

At New Amsterdam the Stadt Huys, built in 1642 by the Company for a tavern, served as a place of confinement for offenders, and was so used by the English until the completion of the city hall in 1700. Shortly after the Pennsylvania Assembly had required each county to provide a house of correction in 1683, William Clayton built a "Cage" at Philadelphia for the reception of minor criminals. Despite repeated Grand Jury presentations of the need for a strong brick prison, a most unsatisfactory log structure was erected in 1687 at the corner of High and Second Streets; so inadequate did it prove that a house for confinement of offenders had to be rented instead from Patrick Robinson. Little progress was made in the seventeenth century toward providing adequate prisons for the villages. It should be noted, however, that Bristol, the second city of England, had no permanent prison until the eighteenth century, being served only by a small "cage" erected in 1647, and that Norwich used as a combination bridewell, house of correction and prison a squalid and ancient building which dated from the fourteenth century.[43]

In addition to legal restrictions and penalties for their violation similar to those that govern the life of a citizen today, colonial townsfolk found themselves limited on all sides by regulations of a moral and ethical character. Village fathers, in keeping with the tradition of their homelands and the psychology of their times, regarded themselves as rightfully their brothers' keepers, and exercised a continuous and strict supervision over the daily lives of all inhabitants.

[41] *Mass. Col. Recs.*, IV, i, 222; V, 237; 7 *Bos. Rec. Com.*, 157, 174, 186.
[42] *Journal of William Jefferay*, 18; *R. I. Col. Recs.*, I, 209, 391.
[43] Peterson, *New York*, 192; *Votes Pa. Assembly*, I, i, 11; *Pa. Col. Recs.*, I, 61; Latimer, *Bristol in the Seventeenth Century*, 218; Bayne, *History of Norwich*, 277.

In all communities rigid observance of the Sabbath was the rule. In Massachusetts there had been little need to protect by law the sacred character of the Lord's Day prior to 1653, but beginning in that year the General Court laid down a series of regulations for the observance of the Sabbath, placing enforcement thereof in the hands of the several towns. No person might travel, cook, clean house, or make beds on the Lord's Day, which began at sundown Saturday and lasted until Monday morning. In 1656 the town of Boston had to order the constabulary to bring before authority "any young person or others" found "idling or playing" outside either meeting house during the time of public worship. Frontiersmen seeking refuge from Indians in the town in 1676 greatly disrupted the quiet of the Boston Sabbath. Boston deputies urged upon the General Court the necessity for measures to stop the profanation of that day, which was "growing more & more amonge" them, and the Court responded by placing greater powers of enforcement in the hands of the Selectmen. Two years later, to prevent Saturday night disorders, such as "horses and carts passing late out of ye towne of Boston," the Court ordered the keeping of a ward on Boston Neck to stop the passage of any cart out of town after sunset, and that of any man, whether on horse or foot, "without . . . good account of the necessity of his business." By 1680 the tendency to disregard the strict Sabbath was on the increase, although great efforts were still made in the enforcement of the laws.[44]

Authorities at New Amsterdam were less severe. But in 1641 complaints that some of the inhabitants made a practice of tapping beer during divine service, "which tends to the dishonor of religion," led the Director to forbid tapping during church time or after 10 P.M. Jan Peecq, tapster, was merely one of many who disregarded this order. In 1654 Sheriff van Tienhoven accused him before the Court of selling beer "during Preaching," and testified that "there was a great noise made by drunkards especially yesterday, Sunday, in this house so that he was obliged to remove one to jail in a cart." Peecq lost his license in consequence. In the English city more rigid Sabbath observance prevailed. In 1676 the Common Council forbade business or trading on Sunday, and frowned upon "Playinge att Cards Dice Tables or . . . Games . . . in Sermon Time," while in 1684 they promulgated what was perhaps the most rigorous Sabbath code in any of the colonies. Rhode Islanders enacted no Sabbath legislation until 1679, when an act prohibiting "Sports and Labours on the First Day of the Week" was passed. The presence of a congregation of

[44] *Mass. Col. Recs.*, IV, i, 150, 347, 395; V, 239, 469; 2 *Bos. Rec. Com.*, 131, 151; 7 *Bos. Rec. Com.*, 8, 111.

Seventh Day Baptists undoubtedly contributed to a more liberal attitude toward the Sabbath at Newport. The very first law passed by the South Carolina Parliament established the Church of England throughout the colony, and provided for the careful observance of the Sabbath in the single parish of St. Philip's, Charles Town. Because all breaches of the Sabbath in Philadelphia came before the Monthly Meeting for discipline, the Quakers apparently felt no need for legal restraints before 1690. Thus either through political enactments or control by a dominant religious group, strict observance of the Lord's Day was required in every village, and everywhere severe penalties awaited the Sabbath breaker.[45]

The principal moral problem demanding solution in every village was the curbing of drunkenness. New Amsterdam was notorious for the sottishness of its burghers. In 1648 the Reverend Johannes Backerus wrote to the Classis of Amsterdam that the hundred and seventy members of his congregation were ignorant of religion and much given to drink: "To this they are led by seventeen tap-houses, here." Temperance education begun in early youth was the only solution he could suggest. Intoxicated Indians were especially troublesome, and persons furnishing thirsty savages with firewater suffered heavy penalties. The reputation established by the Dutch survived in the English city throughout this period.[46]

Intemperance, according to Thomas Lechford, was almost unknown at Boston in the early years. At a great training day in 1641, although twelve hundred men were present, he was amazed at the absence of "profane swearing, drunkenness, and beggars." But conditions changed after the mid-century, and we find the town in 1670/1 forbidding Samuel Howard, John Matson, and Joseph Sowter to frequent public houses "vpon the penaltie of a law lately published for that purpose," and again in 1676 conducting a further campaign against inebriates. Though a quiet and moral little village, Newport had its troubles with town drunkards who annoyed inhabitants and neglected their families. In 1672 George Fox wrote to the Governor of Rhode Island urging the enactment of a law against the drunkenness he had observed while in Newport, but nothing seems to have come of his recommendation.[47]

Although Philadelphia Quakers later became noted for their tem-

[45] *Laws of New Netherland*, 25, 60; *Recs. N. Am.*, I, 255; *N. Y. M. C. C.*, I, 27, 28; *R. I. Acts (1744)*, 18; *S. C. Statutes*, I, 1; Sharpless, *Quaker Experiment in Government*, 23. See Latimer, *Bristol in the Seventeenth Century*, 266, 353, 396, for the rigorous Sabbath of that city, and Smith, *History of Modern Culture*, I, 488–500, for conditions on the continent.

[46] *N. Y. Eccles. Recs.*, I, 236; Peterson, *New York*, 51–54.

[47] 3 *MHS Colls.*, III, 86; 7 *Bos. Rec. Com.*, 58, 204; *R. I. Col. Recs.*, I, 94; *Doc. Hist. R. I.*, II, 79; Jones, *Quakers in the American Colonies*, 113.

perance, such was not always the case in the early days. The caves
in the banks of the Delaware, transformed into grog shops catering to
the loose elements of the waterfront, necessitated the passage of a law
against drunkenness in 1682/3, which was strictly enforced. Heavy
drinking among Friends themselves was not exceptional.[48]

In all the northern villages gambling and card playing were absolutely forbidden, and idleness regarded as a vice. Pious Bostonians
lamented in 1675 that "the sin of idleness (wch is the sin of Sodom)
doeth greatly increase," and in 1683 the Selectmen banished to the
West Indies William Batt, "an idle person yt refuseth to worke." [49]

Whether or not the result of stringent codes and official meddling,
the village populace was on the whole virtuous and law-abiding.
Thomas Lloyd, Increase Mather, Governor Dongan or George Fox
might complain of looseness of morals, the Boston Town Meeting
might be frightened into asking greater powers to defend the town
from the profaneness "too much growinge upon" it — and with some
justice. But on the other hand, the Reverend Charles Wooley in 1678
found the inhabitants of New York "both English and Dutch, very
civil and courteous. . . . I cannot say I observed any swearing or
quarrelling but what was easily reconciled and recanted by a mild re-
buke," while a Huguenot visiting Boston in 1687 reported that "the
English who inhabit these Countrees are as elsewhere, good and bad."
Perhaps the words of Alexander Beardsley, written from Philadelphia
in 1690, best describe the true state of all the villages: "Here is good
government, and the Magistrates are Careful to keep good Order, to
suppress Vice and encourage Vertuous Living." [50]

VI

American villages, like settled communities in any age, soon found
themselves faced with the problem of society's dependents. Despite
favorable opportunities for gaining a living in the new country, each
community was early confronted with the necessity of providing for
its poor, whose numbers steadily increased with the growth of the villages into towns. In this respect village society presented a notable
antithesis to that of more rural communities, where pauperism was
almost non-existent and newcomers usually most welcome. The townsfolk who migrated to the New World had behind them a fund of experience in the care of the poor and indigent, and naturally enough
the Elizabethan Statute of Artificers (1562) and the Poor Law of

[48] Pa. Col. Recs., I, 198; Votes Pa. Assembly, I, i, 17.
[49] Westcott, History of Philadelphia, chapter LI; Mass. Col. Recs., IV, i, 366; V,
62, 373; Priestly, Coming of the White Man, 340.
[50] 7 Bos. Rec. Com., 135; Stokes, Iconography, IV, 315; Shurtleff, Description of
Boston, 51; Pa. Mag., IV, 196.

1601 supplied the framework for colonial legislation on public poor relief. This Elizabethan experience had shown that the care of the poor was a responsibility of society, and had given rise to certain conceptions : that dependent classes should be maintained by general taxation, that the local group should provide for its own poor through its own officers, that "sturdy and valiant beggars" were a species of criminal, and that workhouses should be set up wherein paupers might be segregated in groups from the rest of society. All found expression in the social legislation of the colonies.

The exclusive policy of the villages with regard to the admission of strangers did not arise solely from the fancied necessity of protecting local trade. In England at this time social changes were causing a perceptible migration of countryfolk into the towns, where they tended to become charges upon the rates, and the colonists feared to encounter a similar burden in the new communities. They therefore scrutinized very carefully the qualifications of "strangers," especially their means of livelihood, before admitting them as inhabitants. In regard to commercial considerations, they further argued that any disturbance to local manufactures or unrestricted competition with established merchants from an influx of foreign artisans and shopkeepers would add to the public burden by decreasing the prosperity of stranger and burgher alike.

Boston established the pattern for the exclusion of poor and undesirable strangers in May, 1636, when the Selectmen forbade any inhabitant to entertain a stranger for more than two weeks without official permission. The frequent reappearance in Boston records of regulations of similar tenor indicates that the authorities had continually to face the problem of caring for intruders who became public charges. After 1639 the custom prevailed of requiring some townsman to provide security for the newcomer, "to save the towne from charge," and in 1647 inhabitants were forbidden to rent or sell either shop or dwelling within the town's limits without permission from the Selectmen. The influx of refugees from frontier settlements during the Indian troubles of the 1670's created an especially stubborn problem for Bostonians. The constables in 1676–1679 reported sixty-two persons as public charges who had recently come to town and should be "warned out"; doubtless many more escaped detection. Boston deputies urged upon the General Court in 1679 that the town be granted power to eject all persons coming to reside there from other towns and counties without due approbation and admission by the Selectmen, and that "those Easterne people & others" who came thither for relief and shelter in time of war and had already proved a great expense to the town, be immediately removed. The Court merely passed a law granting greater power to tithing men for the supervision of public morals, which hardly met the dilemma.[51] Boston was now confronted with a vagrancy problem that was never to be solved.

Peter Stuyvesant ordered in 1642 that no strangers should be harbored in New Amsterdam for more than one night without first having their names recorded. Very little attention was devoted to this problem, however, until 1676, when the Corporation of New York city required all masters of vessels to list their passengers with the Recorder. Eight years later the laws against "forriners" were amplified, codified and published. In 1684 the constables of each ward were instructed frequently to search out all strangers and present a list of them to the Mayor. Tavern keepers who entertained strangers over two days had to register with the constable "the Name Surname Dwelling place, Profession and Trade of Life and Place of Service of all Such . . . Persons, and for what Cause . . . they Came to Reside there." Like New York, Newport was too small to attract many strangers until the events of King Philip's War thrust upon the rates of the little village vast numbers of fugitives from the Narragansett country. The General Assembly of Rhode Island, with more concern than that of the Bay for the welfare of its towns, authorized them in 1682 to reject any person as an inhabitant "unless sufficient bond be tendered," and empowered the town councils to warn any such persons to depart the town within a stated time.[52]

Although provision for public poor relief was made at the time of the founding of the villages, in none of them did the situation become acute before the mid-century. By that time, however, — and this runs counter to current beliefs, — the growing populations of Boston, Newport and New Amsterdam, at the least, included indigent persons in sufficient numbers to make their care a community function and responsibility.

Authorities of both Massachusetts and Rhode Island adopted the main provisions of the Elizabethan poor law. In the Bay Colony, where the old country distinction was carefully retained between "impotent aged psons" and vagrants, the General Court or any two Magistrates were empowered to order the care of the poor. From 1637 to 1659 the province administered the poor relief; in the latter year it shifted the responsibility to the towns. The government of Rhode Island adopted the English poor laws *in toto* merely by enacting in 1647 "that each Towne shall provide carefully for the reliefe of the poore, to maintayne the impotent, and to employ the able, and shall

[51] Over two hundred persons were excluded from Boston, 1660–1684. *2 Bos. Rec. Com.*, 10, 37, 130, 142; *7 Bos. Rec. Com.*, 62, 102–130, 135; *Mass. Col. Recs.*, V, 240.
[52] *Laws of New Netherland*, 32; *N. Y. M. C. C.*, I, 10, 18, 135; *R. I. Col. Recs.*, II, 394; III, 116.

appoint an overseer for the same purpose. *See 43 Eliz., 2."* The Pennsylvania Assembly in 1682 passed a poor law also based on the Elizabethan model, and in 1688 authorized county courts to levy taxes for the support of paupers.[53] In New Netherland, too, the burden of the poor rested upon local authorities, although here it was the church rather than the town which was particularly responsible for the poor relief.

Boston's first important encounter with pauperism occurred in 1658, when it was found that servants whose time was served out "either through Idleness or sickness become unable to help themselves," and hence an expense to the town. The Selectmen directed inhabitants henceforth, in order to secure the town from charge, to look after the employment of any persons they should so "sett att Liberty." That pauperism was rapidly increasing is further revealed by the fact that certain philanthropic citizens of Boston began at this time to make bequests to the town for charitable purposes. Between 1658 and 1660 William Paddy, Robert Keayne and Henry Webb left funds amounting to £235 to be employed for the amelioration of the lot of village dependents. The legacies of Keayne and Webb, along with "severall other gifts," were used to build a frame almshouse, which, though completed in 1662, remained unoccupied until 1665, when the Selectmen admitted Mrs. Jane Woodcock, widow, "duringe the Towne pleasure." This building burned down in 1682, and was replaced three years later at a cost of £1,000 by a brick structure which served both as almshouse and workhouse.[54]

Unique among the agencies of the seventeenth century for the aid of society's unfortunates was the "Scot's Charitable Society," instituted in 1657 by twenty-seven of that nation resident at Boston. Founded for the "releefe of our selves or any other for which wee may see cause," the society pursued an uneven existence until about 1667, when it died out, because, through the "Smallness of their Number, Lowness of their Stock, & Mismanagement of some private Trustees, it had not the desired Success and Effect." It was revived in 1684, when the Scots found "their Number and Abilities, being considerably increased, & particularly encouraged thereto by the Success of a Scot's Society in London of the same Nature, established by Charter of King Charles 2d." Since that time the organization has had a continuous existence. A hundred and eighty Scots joined the Society between 1684 and 1690, among whom were several wealthy merchants resident in other American colonies and in Scotland. The society provided for

[53] *Mass. Col. Recs.,* I, 264; III, 15; IV, i, 365; *R. I. Col. Recs.,* I, 184; *R. I. Acts* (1705), 11; *Votes Pa. Assembly,* I, i, 6; *Pa. Col. Recs.,* I, 216.
[54] *2 Bos. Rec. Com.,* 141, 148, 154; *7 Bos. Rec. Com.,* 7, 24, 157, 174, 186.

its sick countrymen, maintained its poor and buried its dead. It undoubtedly reduced the number of that nation dependent on the town to
a minimum at a time when public relief agencies were severely over-
taxed. This Scot's Society of Boston holds additional interest in that
it became the model for similar organizations in nearly all of the
colonial towns in the eighteenth century.[55]

Refugees of King Philip's War left their mark indelibly upon the
town of Boston. The Town Meeting in December, 1682, deplored the
great cost of relief, arising not only from the care of the sick and aged,
and those who though willing to work could find no employment in
the crowded village, but also from "persons & Families yt misspend
their time, in idlenesse & tipplinge with great neglect of their callings
and suffer ye Children shamefully to spend their time in ye Streetes."
The erection of a workhouse and the provision of employment for
such persons at the town's charge, it was thought, might prove a partial solution. Unfortunately this workhouse, completed three years
later, served also as a house of correction (Boston, it will be remembered, had never complied with its obligations in this respect), where
all sorts of indigent and vicious persons were thrust together, a situation which prevented many "Honest Poor Peoples" from seeking
there the relief and support for which the place was designed.[56]

Throughout the seventeenth century the usual method of aiding the
poor was by boarding them in private houses at the public charge. The
Selectmen allowed £6 to Edward Weeddine in 1663 for a year's
"dyete and lodging" for Elizabeth Ward, and in 1684 the Widow
Blore agreed with the Selectmen to board Mary Chelsam for five shillings a week "in mony & one Load of Wood for the winter." The town
also provided charity in cases of temporary distress. In 1662 William
Ockenton was given twenty-five shillings relief money, and Elizabeth
Pickett was aided in "her present straite." The Widow Harden, "being blinde," was given three shillings a week and allowed to live in her
own home, while Elizabeth Harbell was supported in the "time of her
sickness outt of ye Townes stock." After 1676 the General Court
placed the care of the insane in the hands of local authorities, who paid
the charges from the estate of the distracted person, or, if there were
no estate, from the public funds.[57]

Fugitives from the frontiers, pouring into Boston in the 1670's,
found the little town totally unprepared either to receive them or to
provide for their sustenance, and soon exhausted its meager facilities
for charity. In January and July of 1677 the provincial government

[55] *Records of the Scot's Charitable Society of Boston,* 27, 29, 73, 105.
[56] 7 *Bos. Rec. Com.,* 157; 8 *Bos. Rec. Com.,* 93.
[57] 7 *Bos. Rec. Com.,* 4, 11, 15, 171; *Mass. Col. Recs.,* V, 80.

procured some provisions from Ireland which they turned over to the Selectmen for distribution among the town poor and "such as came hither from the Easterne ptes & other places." But with the close of the war when colony support was withdrawn, the paupers remained to be constantly augmented by many more who availed themselves of the peace to make their way into Boston. Desperate townsmen addressed the General Court with frequent petitions for aid. As late as 1687 that august body was receiving pleas for assistance in dealing with the increasing numbers of poor, based on reverses the town had suffered from Indian warfare, fire and declining trade.[58] Though sympathetic to these appeals, the Court was powerless to come to the aid of Boston. The devastating effects of war were everywhere evident in the colony, and the "mart Town," with all its burdens, was probably better off than its inland neighbors. The metropolis of the American colonies was becoming a town, and as such was acquiring all the appurtenances of urban life, — the bad along with the good.

Newport had had almost no paupers before the Indian War, but in 1675–1676 the little village took care of so many refugees that the Quaker authorities cited the expense of maintaining them when criticized for not doing their full share in the prosecution of hostilities. Indeed, their policy throughout the war was to make a safe haven of the island and to encourage the resort thither of people from outlying and exposed districts. More than five hundred fugitives from Providence and many others from Warwick and Westerly fled to Newport in 1675, necessitating an expenditure of £800 in that one year; after the danger had passed many of them remained in the town where they became permanent public charges. Under the law of 1647 overseers of the poor were annually chosen by the town, and it appears that a regular yearly poor rate was levied after 1685. Here, too, out-relief was the usual method: in 1679 the Town Meeting directed Nathaniel Coddington and Jonathan Holmes to investigate the circumstances of Walter Congreaves and see that the overseers cared for him.[59]

The poor of New Amsterdam during the early years were cared for both by the Company and by the Reformed Dutch Church. One of the first acts of the new burgomaster government in 1653 was the appointment of orphan masters. Director Stuyvesant declared that such agencies were unnecessary in so small a city, and that the deacons of the Church could still "keep their eyes open" and look after destitute widows and children. The Indian raids of 1655 brought about an increase in the number of widows and orphans and the erection of the

[58] 7 Bos. Rec. Com., 106, 111, 190.
[59] Jones, Quakers in the American Colonies, 184–185; Newport T. M. Recs., 7, 55; R. I. Col. Recs., III, 77, 116, 232; Kimball, Providence, 95, 118; Dennison, Westerly, 53.

Orphan Masters' Court. The deaconry in 1653 built a house for the poor, and in 1655 purchased a bouwerie near Hellgate, which they called the "poor farm." Its support derived from voluntary contributions deposited in church poor boxes. Occasionally an appeal for aid came before the Burgomasters, who generally referred such cases to the deacons.

In 1661, after the deacons had demonstrated to the Company that many needy from outlying districts were drifting into the town for help, a poor code was enacted, which required every village to maintain its own poor and specifically relieved New Amsterdam from the care of those not resident there. A decade later, after Lutherans and other sects had established flourishing congregations, the Burgomasters ordered that henceforth each church should be responsible for the poor among its membership, the deacons of each denomination to render yearly accounts of their use of the poor money.[60]

English poor relief was introduced into New York in 1683. Two years later the Common Council ordered the aldermen of each ward to submit to the Mayor a list of those in need of relief from the public treasury; later still aldermen were allowed to draw directly on the city funds for the benefit of the poor in their precincts. The sum demanded for this purpose was £20 in 1688, but by 1690 the expenses of the relief had created a deficit, to meet which the constables were ordered to take up a "free gift" from the residents of their respective wards. "Noe Beggars," reported Governor Andros, summing up the charity situation at New York, "but all poore cared ffor." [61]

In early Philadelphia as at New Amsterdam the church was the dispenser of charity, and public authorities were not taxed with the problem of the poor before 1690. The Society of Friends found itself in 1685 "greatly burthened and oppressed by the increase of the poor, more than any other place in the province by reason of people's general landing here," and a committee of the Philadelphia Monthly Meeting was charged with looking after the needs of penniless newcomers. Yet in comparison with the older and more exposed communities to the north the Quaker city was little troubled by the problems of poverty, and the needy immigrant was practically the only pauper requiring charity at this time.[62]

Well before 1690 it had become evident that pauperism was a necessary concomitant of urban growth, but in general, with the

[60] *Recs. N. Am.*, I, 56; III, 143; VI, 352; VII, 242; Stokes, *Iconography*, IV, 132; *N. Y. Col. Docs.*, XIV, 326; *Laws of New Netherland*, 411.
[61] *N. Y. Col. Laws*, IV, 131; *N. Y. M. C. C.*, I, 172, 194, 205, 212; *Doc. Hist. N. Y.*, I, 92.
[62] Myers, *Irish Quakers*, 45; Sharpless, *Quaker Experiment in Government*, 33; Woody, *Quaker Education in Pennsylvania*, 45.

exception of Boston, its burden rested lightly on the seventeenth century villages. On the few occasions that arose these New World communities seem to have made adequate provision for their poor, either through the town as in Boston or Newport, or through the church as at New Amsterdam and Philadelphia. Charles Town alone failed to take any official cognizance of its pauper problem in this period. In the story of the rise of poverty in colonial villages the effect of the contracting of the frontiers as a result of Indian wars and the consequent dislocation of population in New England can scarcely be overemphasized. By the close of the period Boston, emerging as a sizeable town, was definitely menaced by a growing dependent class, and both Newport and New York had been made uncomfortably aware of the developing problem.

VII

The general health of the community is of necessity an important consideration in urban centers. At the time of the founding of the villages ideas of sanitation prevailing in Europe were exceedingly crude, and methods of combatting disease still a compound of superstition, "kitchen-physic" and common-sense palliatives. These the colonists immediately applied in the treatment of sickness in their new homes. But the location of the villages, Charles Town excepted, in a temperate and healthful climate probably contributed more to the longevity and well-being of the townsfolk than all the medical lore of the Old World.

The sanitary regulations passed by some of the village authorities constitute an interesting aspect of seventeenth century urban development. In enacting these ordinances villagers probably thought most of eliminating obvious public nuisances, yet the current belief in the dangers to health from malignant vapors might upon occasion, quite as much as the germ theory of disease, lead to the better disposal of garbage or the cleaning up of dumps, and therefore to the safeguarding of the public health.

To prevent annoyance to citizens from the indiscriminate disposal of garbage, the Boston Selectmen in 1634 prohibited the depositing of fish or garbage near the town dock. In 1652 a fine was levied upon anyone who cast "any intralls of beast or fowles or stinkeing thing, in any hie way or dich or Common": henceforth all refuse had to be buried. A similar ordinance for New Amsterdam in 1657 provided for the disposal of refuse at five specified places only. Hitherto the most convenient spot, generally the great Graft, had served as a community dump. Especially obnoxious and lacking in public consideration were the village butchers, and after repeated admonitions concerning the "noisome smell" caused by members of this trade throwing garbage into the streets, both towns set about the regulation of slaughterhouses. In 1656 Boston set aside a place near the Mill Creek where butchers were ordered to dispose of their refuse, "and in no other place." The Common Council of New York solved the problem by banishing slaughterhouses from the city in 1676, and for several years all slaughtering was conducted at Smith's Fly on the East River just beyond the wall. Tanneries and tan-pits, by reason of the stench arising from the water in which leather was soaked, proved most offensive to town residents, and were the subject of repeated regulation in both Boston and New York.[63]

Town-dwellers made other efforts at public sanitation. After 1652 no inhabitant of Boston was allowed to build or maintain a "house of office" within twelve feet of a street or house, "unless it be vaeted [vaulted] 6 foot deep." At New Amsterdam, where the noisome activities of the village swine complicated the problem, the authorities in 1657 condemned all privies opening on the street and ordered their removal within eight days. In the interests of public welfare the Selectmen of Boston in 1646 ordered that all graves be dug at least five feet deep, while in 1687 William Penn forbade the cutting of timber on his lands near the city, lest the resultant growth of underbrush should breed vermin and "tramps." [64] The absence of a closely settled community at Newport doubtless rendered such sanitary regulations relatively unnecessary, while Charles Town and Philadelphia were established too late in the period for much development of this sort to take place.

Infectious disease proved by all odds the most serious threat to the health of town-dwellers. Entering by way of the sea, it gave rise to the earliest genuine public health measures. In 1647 reports of an epidemic at St. Christopher's impelled Massachusetts authorities to require all ships coming from the Caribbean to undergo strict inspection before landing passengers or cargo. A quarantine station was established at Castle Island in Boston harbor, and no one without a license was permitted to board any of the suspected ships. While plague was raging in London in 1665 these rules were again put into effect, and the Corporation of New York took similar precautions in 1689.[65]

The dreaded smallpox visited Boston in 1666 and claimed forty victims. Brought again by the crew of an English vessel in 1678, it

[63] 2 *Bos. Rec. Com.*, I, 70, 91, 97, 110, 118, 131, 148; *Recs. N. Am.*, I, 31; *N. Y. M. C. C.*, I, 20, 217; Peterson, *New York*, 61.
[64] 2 *Bos. Rec. Com.*, 86, 109; *Recs. N. Am.*, I, 38; VII, 187; Scharf and Westcott, *History of Philadelphia*, I, 122.
[65] *Mass. Col. Recs.*, II, 237; III, 169; Green, *Medicine in Massachusetts*, 36; *N. Y. M. C. C.*, I, 208; Latimer, *Bristol in the Seventeenth Century, passim.*

ran through the town like the plagues of the Middle Ages. Fifteen-year-old Cotton Mather, unaware of the service he was one day to perform in the long battle with the disease, watched its fatal progress and confided his horrified impressions in a letter to John Cotton, his maternal grandfather:

> Never was it such a time in Boston. Boston burying-places never filled so fast. It is easy to tell the time when we did not use to have the bells tolling for burials on a Sabbath morning by sunrise; to have 7 buried on a Sabbath day night, after Meeting. To have coffins crossing each other as they have been carried in the street; — To have, I know not how many corpses following each other close at their heels, — to have 38 dye in one week, — 6, 7, 8, or 9 in a day. Above 340 have died of the Small Pox in Boston since it first assaulted this place.

It has been estimated that eight hundred persons died during this visitation. The townsfolk ordered fasts, but "God's elected" though they were, they also sought for earthly means to lessen the scourge. The Council ordered the Selectmen to see that inhabitants did not air infected clothes or bedding within the town "to the offence or prejudice of theire neighbrs.," or permit persons recovering from the disease to "goe abroad too soone." Five remote places were set aside where bedding and clothes from infected houses might be brought and aired "in ye dead time of ye night," and three men were appointed inspectors to enforce the law.[66] As if forewarned of the epidemic the Reverend Thomas Thatcher had printed in 1677 a broadside giving *Brief Rules to Guide the Common People of New England: How to Order themselves and Theirs in the Small Pox, or Measles.* This timely little publication undoubtedly enjoyed wide currency during the next dreadful year.

New York's severest calamity in this period was an epidemic of "an unusuall sicknesse" (dysentery), under which Governor Dongan found the village "groaning" when he arrived in 1683. The governor ordered a fast day — prompt application of the customary remedy. A "general sickness" beset Charles Town in 1685, which the Proprietors blamed upon the "unhealthy situation of Charlestown and the bringing down of the people of the country to keep guard there in the unhealthy months." They concluded, in view of its unhealthy and exposed location, "We do not think Charlestown a proper place for a seat of government." In a sense they were right, for no locality could be less healthful than the fever-infested swamps of the Carolina tidewater region, but ere long planters would be trooping into Charles

    [66] AAS *Trans.,* III, 223, 243; 4 MHS *Colls.,* VIII, 383; Drake, *Antiquities of Boston,* 429; 2 *Bos. Rec. Com.,* 119.

Town in the summer months to avoid the fevers, as they came to believe it the healthiest spot in the colony. Newport and Philadelphia were uniquely fortunate in escaping serious consequences from infectious diseases before 1690.[67]

With the exception of these dreaded epidemics, townsfolk generally enjoyed good health. Save at Charles Town they were favored with healthy locations for their villages and spared the evil effects of recurrent country fevers. In comparison with European city folk their lot in this respect was enviable. Occasional "fevers, agues and fluxes" proved exceptions to this rule, but on the whole, as phrased by Adrian van der Donck, "Galens had [but] meager soup" in the villages. Nevertheless, the colonists required the services of a physician or "chirurgion" in cases of accident, ordinary sickness, or chronic visitations of infectious disease. In small hamlets and country districts few physicians were available, and the clergyman, if there were one, generally ministered to body as well as soul. In the little seaports, on the other hand, it was possible for professional practitioners to eke out a modest existence by fees received from patients. As the villages grew, the gulf between the medical facilities available in town and country continually widened.

The people of Boston enjoyed the best medical facilities in the colonies. Yet, it being the perverse fate of professions often to be known for their unworthiest practitioners, the first Boston doctor of whom we have record was a quack, Nicholas Knopp, who in 1630 was fined £5 "for takeing vpon him to cure the scurvy by a water of no worth nor value, which he solde att a very deare rate." Even so, there is soon evidence of that dependence of rural districts upon the settlements for medical aid which was always to continue. In the winter of 1639 a certain "Barber-Chirurgion" froze to death on Boston Neck while en route to Roxbury to draw a tooth. There were several physicians at work in Boston in 1643, for whom the General Court resolved, "We conceive it very necessary that such studies as physick, or chirurgery may have liberty to reade anatomy & to anatomize once in four years some malefactor in case there be such." Two years later the Court made an effort to regulate the medical profession by forbidding anyone to perform the office of practitioner "without the advice & consent of such as are skillful in the same art, if such may be had, or at least the wisest & gravest then present." The consent of the patient was also required. This wise measure, which attempted to confine the profession to skilled persons, was voted against by seven deputies, three of them from Boston. Certain indication of the early importance of Bos-

[67] N. Y. Eccles. Recs., I, 597; Stokes, Iconography, IV, 375; Cal. St. Pap., 1681-1685, 647; S. C. Statutes, VII, 1.

ton as a medical center is the regulation made by the Town Meeting in 1659 to secure the town from charge by "sojourners, inmates, hyred servants, journeymen, or other persons that come for help in physick or chyrurgery." [68]

Between 1675 and 1680 at least seventeen physicians and surgeons lived and practiced at Boston, all but one of whom had learned his profession in the colony. Of these Dr. William Avery was reported a man of "pretty ingenuity: who from the Ars Veterinaria fell into some notable skill in physick and midwifery & invented some usefull instruments for that case." According to Samuel Lee, in 1690 no Boston doctor held any degree or practiced under any license "but by their patients." Yet several of these practitioners were skilled in their profession and learned in its literature; their libraries after 1660 contained the works of Étienne La Rivière, Van Helmont, Paré and Boyle, and most important of all, Harvey's *De Motu Cordis et Sanguinis*. Book knowledge of latest scientific developments undoubtedly served Boston physicians better than the crude medical education offered by most English schools of the day. Moreover, some restriction upon the free practice of the art of healing did prevail. In 1672 the Suffolk County Court granted Dr. Avery's petition to "practice physick & Chirurgery," and the next year fined Walter Barefoote of Portsmouth £10 for unauthorized practice of medicine within its jurisdiction. The same year also the Court received testimonials of several persons "of the benefit they have received by William Snelling in his administring of Physick," and accordingly granted him leave to practice in the town. Even the critical Samuel Lee admitted that some improvement had been made over earlier days, for barbering was now a "trade by itself," although "tooth drawing . . . [is still] used at pleasure." [69]

For treatment of the "poorer sort" of people who could not meet the doctors' fees, the Selectmen employed various physicians, not always those with the best qualifications. In 1644 they paid Elder Thomas Oliver of the Boston church £5 "for seaven months attendance upon the Cure" of a servant of Thomas Hawkins, and thirteen years before receiving his license from the General Court William Snelling collected from the same source fifty-four shillings "for physick administered to Robt. Higgins." However, as qualified practitioners multiplied in the town they were more and more called upon for services to the poor. The Selectmen abated the rates of "Henry

[68] *Mass. Col. Recs.*, I, 67; II, 175, 278; Johnson, *Wonder-Working Providence*, 191; 2 *Bos. Rec. Com.*, 152.
[69] Col. Soc. Mass. *Trans.*, XIV, 146–164; *Recs. Suffolk County Court, passim;* Green, *Medicine in Massachusetts*, 40; 7 *Bos. Rec. Com.*, 191; Morison, *Harvard College in the Seventeenth Century*, I, 283–284; and *Puritan Pronaos*, 133-134.

Taylor Chirurgion" in 1669, "in consideration of a cure upon good wife Franklin . . . & his promise of attendance for the year ensuing vpon any poore, sick or hurt of this towne." In 1671 Dr. Daniel Stone, who had been practicing medicine in Boston for a decade, applied for remuneration for medical services rendered to "seuerall poore" in past years. The Selectmen not only rewarded him by remission of his taxes, but requested him to continue his attendance upon the town poor for the ensuing year, for which they allowed him twenty shillings and freedom from the rates. Dr. Stone, one of the best physicians of the community, thus became official practitioner to the Boston poor, and continued in municipal employ as late as 1687.[70]

Obstetrics in early Boston, as in Europe, was the prerogative of the midwives. Anne Hutchinson was one of the first of these, and her sex retained control of maternity cases throughout this period. It is doubtful if even Dr. Avery competed successfully with them, despite his new instruments. Sewall mentions many midwives in his accounts of the births of his children, and the courts frequently called on these good dames to testify as experts in cases of doubtful pregnancy.[71]

For medicine the Boston physicians and midwives could "make or buy or send to the Potecaries," of whom there were "3 or 4 in that great town." Here again they enjoyed a distinct advantage over the country practitioner. In 1688 Samuel Sewall had to purchase in Boston medicines which a physician had prescribed for his mother at Newbury. Apothecaries were not inspected in their trade as in London. Lee found that they "doe practise what they will. physick & Surgery. . . . Things are very raw here in these cases." The only "punishment" an apothecary ever suffered for dispensing "Venice Treacle" and other quack remedies was a "noli me tangere" if he failed.[72] "Kitchen physick" seems to have been giving way in Boston to the patent medicine already, even though it was to be nearly fifteen years before the newspaper appeared to aid the latter in its conquest of American taste.

Prior to 1664 medical facilities at New Amsterdam surpassed those of Boston, and throughout the period the trained physicians resident in New York outnumbered those of the Bay town. At least five graduates of famous European medical centers, Leyden, Utrecht and Magdeburg, practiced in New York in these years. In addition, many "chirurgions" and apprentice-trained medicos plied their trade in the village. The West India Company encouraged the migration of these men from Holland, usually employing at least one medical man and

[70] 2 Bos. Rec. Com., 81, 156; 7 Bos. Rec. Com., 12, 44, 51, 64, 76, 83, 162.
[71] Green, Medicine in Massachusetts, 53.
[72] 6 MHS Colls., I, 76; Col. Soc. Mass. Trans., XIV, 146.

supplying midwives for the care of its settlers. In 1635 Tyntgen Jones, midwife, applied to the Amsterdam Chamber for an increase in "wages and some necessaries"; Van Twiller ordered a house built for Lisbert Ducken, the midwife, in 1638; and Hildegarde Joris, appointed in 1655, received in 1660 a salary of a hundred guilders for assisting at the lyings-in of the poor. Many of New Amsterdam's early practition-ers were barber-surgeons, and in 1652 they petitioned the Director for the exclusive privilege of shaving all persons in the village. Stuyvesant characteristically replied that "shaving is not properly in the province of surgeons, but is only an appendix to their calling," and forbade their "keeping a shop to do it." If the truth were known, the surgeons were probably seeking to augment their incomes by these tonsorial activities, for as De Sille observed in 1654, "This country is good and healthy, . . . the people are seldom sick." [73]

Numerous doctors appeared in the city after the English conquest. In 1684 the General Assembly enacted a medical code which took over word for word the Massachusetts law of 1649, although there is no evidence of any rigid enforcement of the terms of this good measure. Another Boston precedent was followed in 1687 when the Common Council of New York appointed Dr. Johannes Kerfbyl to serve as physician to the poor for a period of two years. In 1680 all but licensed practitioners were forbidden to practice in New York. [74]

The first settlers at Newport were fortunate in having among their number Dr. John Clarke, a trained physician, who early set a high standard for a long line of Rhode Island practitioners. It was prob-ably under his influence that one of the first medical licenses in the colonies was issued at Newport in 1641, when the Assembly authorized Mr. Robert Jeoffreys "to exercise the functions of chirurgerie." At least seven other doctors and one apothecary served the little village by 1690, and if their prescriptions did not satisfy, townsfolk could turn to Dr. Caleb Arnold, son of Benedict Arnold of Newport, who lived at Portsmouth only ten miles away. Critical Samuel Lee knew Arnold well, and reported that he was "a practitioner of good request." [75] Several physicians, like the Huguenots Peter Ayrault and Norbert Vigneron, and Dr. John Brett from Germany, were European trained, and thus the people of Newport enjoyed the services of a higher class of practitioners than was to be found elsewhere in the colonies with the possible exception of New York.

[73] Bosworth, "The Doctor in Old New York," 286; Stokes, *Iconography*, IV, 83, 91; *Recs. N. Am.*, I, 34; VI, 16; *N. Y. Col. Docs.*, XIV, 155.
[74] Stokes, *Iconography*, IV, 280, 285; *N. Y. Col. Laws.*, I, 146; *N. Y. M. C. C.*, I, 206; II, 68; *Recs. N. Am.*, I, 321; VII, 17; Van Rensselaer, *New York in the Seventeenth Century*, II, 222.
[75] G. H. Richardson Collection, 969: 58, 81, 85; 972: 95; Col. Soc. Mass. *Trans.* XIV, 144, 152; *Doc. Hist. R. I.*, II, 113.

The two youngest communities were from the beginning well served by medical men of European experience. Three trained doctors came over to Philadelphia with William Penn, though only one, Griffith Owen, regularly sought to match his skill against the quacks with whom the colony abounded. By 1690 a dozen physicians were practicing in the Quaker village, while at least four medical men ministered to the wants of the Charlestonians.[76]

By 1690 townsfolk had made a fair beginning toward a public health code; they practiced the rudiments of public sanitation, and at Boston and New York had some understanding of the responsibility of the community for the care of the sick poor and for the control of infectious disease. With the exception of Charles Town, health was the general rule in the villages. Smallpox, which was soon to appear with alarming regularity in each town, had as yet visited only Boston. From the bubonic plague, the scourge of European communities, they were fortunately free. In the field of medical practice, wherein the colonies have been bitterly assailed, it would be well, at least insofar as concerns the villages, to reexamine the known evidence. There were, it is true, no great medical centers in the New World, no traditions of research and discovery. Yet individual physicians were better and more widely read than their average European contemporaries, and very early became familiar with the works of Harvey and his peers. It must be remembered that in Europe the revolutionary discoveries of contemporary scientists were little known and less accepted outside the more important centers, and except in great cities like London daily practice of medicine in England and on the continent probably presented little superiority to that of the better town doctor in colonial America.[77] Moreover, it can be demonstrated that medical practice in the villages had made definite progress by 1690. Residents of New York and Newport enjoyed the services of a number of able physicians, several of whom had received their training in Europe, as had the practitioners of Philadelphia and Charles Town, while Boston and New York had both realized the necessity for some regulation of the medical profession. When we compare the facilities for medical advice and treatment which were available to inhabitants, especially the poor, in town and country, it is clear that the former had acquired a distinct advantage, which was to grow with the towns.

[76] Pa. Mag., XXV, 104; Norris, Medicine in Philadelphia, 10, 13; Henry, Medical Profession of Philadelphia, 21–27; Wallace, South Carolina, I, 408; Annals of Medical History, VII, 311.

[77] For the general conservatism and superstition in European medical practice see Smith, Modern Culture, I, 140–144.

VIII

By 1690 inhabitants of every colonial village had had to face certain problems of urban living which required solution not by individual but by community effort. In the country a man might construct his home, build his fire, dig his well, erect his privy, and dispose of his rubbish without thought for the well-being of his neighbors, but in town these things became objects of community concern and gradually of civic ordinance. In the country a man might be little affected by the poverty or wrong-doing of others, but the towns soon discovered their civic responsibility in the combatting and control of these social evils. Townsmen were guided by European experience in dealing with similar problems, and as new solutions appeared in the Old World they were quickly adopted by the colonists. In the matter of fire protection, for instance, they took over from England ancient practices like the curfew, which they supplemented with more modern methods of fire fighting as soon as they became known. Colonial townsmen adopted and modified means of preserving the public peace that had long been in use in European cities. Their system of poor relief they drew directly from English law, and for their instruments of social discipline, like Sabbath legislation, they found ample precedents in the Mother Country. In these problems of town living, which affected the entire community, lay one of the vast differences between town and country society, and out of the collective efforts to solve these urban problems arose a sense of community responsibility and power that was further to differentiate these two ways of life.

IV

VILLAGE SOCIETY

I

As the physical expansion and economic development of the seventeenth century gradually forged the five villages into one common type of society, existence in these communities assumed some of the social and cultural attributes of urbanization. The life of farmer or frontiersman was relatively much more simple than that of town merchant or artisan. The rudiments of definite class distinctions cut through town society, the presence of various racial elements and of growing religious diversity further complicated it. Here the tavern flourished, and amusements not of his own making offered themselves to the inhabitant. The town-dweller more easily found education for his children, and, especially if he were a cultivated man, the companionship of like minds for himself. Finally, he experienced the variety and gregariousness of a life where people meet frequently in commercial, social or political intercourse, where talk and ideas circulate readily, and where there is some knowledge of the world beyond his own immediate horizon.

II

Except at New York, an overwhelming majority of inhabitants in each village were English. A common tongue and common social characteristics thus linked these widely separated communities. But almost from the beginning of their settlement there could be found in each of them, living together in close neighborliness, representatives of other nations and races. This heterogeneity, growing more marked as the colonial era advanced, increasingly distinguished town from countryside, where national groups tended to settle in areas peopled by others of their kind. The five villages were the first American melting pots.

In early Newport virtually every inhabitant was of English extraction. The addition of a handful of Jews, expelled from New Amsterdam in 1654, and of a few Huguenots towards the close of the period hardly altered the general picture. In 1680 the Governor of Rhode Island reported that "We have lately had few or no new comers, either of English, Scotch, Irish or foreigners; only a few blacks imported."

94

When the period closed Newport had the most homogeneous population of any of the five towns.[1]

Like Newport, Boston contained very few non-English elements. Its founders were English Puritans who sought to work out their peculiar religious theories secure from outside interference. They discouraged settlement by people of other nations and creeds within their village, and gladly granted all such intruders "free liberty to keepe away, . . . and such as will come to be gone as fast as they can, the sooner the better." In 1652 the arrival of 272 Scots, banished from England by Cromwell, provided the first considerable non-English element in Boston, and the advent of a few French Huguenot families in 1685 tended further to break down the town's Anglo-Saxon exclusiveness. Although by 1690 the foreign-born residents included in addition to Scots and Frenchmen some Negroes and a handful of Irish, the population of Boston remained of predominantly English stock.[2]

The other villages nourished more diversified populations. While the majority at Charles Town were Englishmen who had come from Barbados with their slaves, there were in the town by 1690 many Huguenots and some Ulster Scots. At this time Negroes constituted probably one third of the inhabitants. To the Swedes, Dutch and English dwelling in the neighborhood of Philadelphia at the time of its founding were soon added peoples from many other lands. By 1690 the little village numbered among its denizens many Welsh, Irish, Scotch-Irish, Swiss and Germans, lured thither by William Penn's attractive "Accounts" and "Further Accounts."[3] The presence of these different groups endowed the Quaker village with an international flavor from its earliest years, but it is to New York, where they attained far greater proportions, that one must look for the real cosmopolitanism of the period.

In spite of the preponderance of natives of the Netherlands among employees of the Dutch West India Company, many representatives of other countries labored at its New World post. Father Isaac Jogues found "men of eighteen different languages" at New Amsterdam in 1643. The arrival of Jews from Holland and Brazil in 1654 further complicated this mélange. Four years later the number of French Walloons and English had so increased as to necessitate publication in three languages of all official edicts. Eighteen tongues continued to be spoken at the time of the surrender to the English, and although the Dutch were still numerically predominant Governor Lovelace reported

[1] Peterson, *History of the Island of Rhode Island*, 180; Bull, *Memoir of Rhode Island*, II, 29.
[2] *N. E. Hist. & Gen. Reg.*, I, 377; Shurtleff, *Description of Boston*, 50.
[3] *S. C. Hist. Soc. Colls.*, I, 112; Hirsch, *Huguenots in South Carolina*, 14; *Pa. Mag.*, LII, 320; Myers, *Irish Quakers*, 30; Learned, *Pastorius*.

large numbers of English and French living there. Under English rule the Dutch inhabitants, more numerous than their conquerors, frequently became restive, and clashes occasionally ensued. Friction between English constables and their watch has already been noted. In 1679 a street brawl broke out between some Englishmen and the watch, in the course of which a Dutch watchman was heard to cry out, "Slay the English doggs, slay the English doggs!" several persons being severely beaten up before order was restored. New York, though remaining characteristically Dutch in appearance throughout the seventeenth century, was easily the most cosmopolitan village in the colonies.[4]

Before the century closed New York and Philadelphia had acquired the racial heterogeneity that was to characterize the towns and cities of the Atlantic seaboard, and Charles Town, too, exhibited the mixture of elements that would set the tone of its society for over a century. Newport and Boston alone remained almost wholly English in make-up. Seeds of a nativist feeling were already germinating at Boston and Charles Town. Yet, as contrasted with rural districts, where national groups tended to preserve their languages and customs unchanged, the mingling of peoples in the villages was an important factor making for a less provincial outlook.

III

The colonists who came to settle in the villages brought with them the social order then existing in England or Holland, and sought with considerable success to set up a similar system in America. While the English nobility did not migrate, many "gentlemen" of wealth and standing came over prepared to assume the functions of an aristocracy in the New World. With these substantial leaders came artisans, tradesmen and servants, thoroughly indoctrinated with prevailing ideas of social inequality. In this they were all, better, middling and inferior sorts alike, entirely the children of their age:

> The people were not democrats then,
> They did not talk of the rights of men,
> And all that sort of thing,

and they certainly had never heard of a classless society. The subsequent addition of Negro and a few Indian slaves provided all the elements for the development of a caste system, which the settlers recognized and enforced from the beginning.

The leaders of early Boston were gentlemen of considerable wealth who, in association with the clergy, eagerly sought to preserve in America the social arrangements of the Mother Country. By means of their

---

[4] *Narratives of New Netherland*, 259, 392; *Recs. N. Am.*, I, 240, 252; Wilson, *Memorial History of New York*, I, 346; Peterson, *New York*, 160.

control of trade and commerce, by their political domination of the inhabitants through church and Town Meeting, and by careful marriage alliances among themselves, members of this little oligarchy laid the foundations for an aristocratic class in seventeenth century Boston. As the trade of the little port increased, prosperous merchants accumulated wealth and successfully achieved social prominence. By 1663 the town had become "rich and very populous," and Josselyn found that "The grose Goddons [Magistrates], or great masters, as also some of their Merchants are damnable rich; generally all of their judgement, inexplicably covetous and proud." Rich Boston merchants erected fine mansions of stone and brick, luxuriously appointed as many in London or Bristol. "Ministers and other persons of Qualitie" began to travel abroad in coaches, calashes or Sedan chairs, to have their portraits painted, to wear periwigs, to adorn their sideboards with John Hull's silver, and to line their bellies with rich food and good Madeira.[5]

Realization of the economic superiority of their class led Boston aristocrats early to disregard the sumptuary laws prohibiting the wearing of fancy clothes, lace, gold braid, slashed sleeves, etc., enacted in 1634. The Elders seemed powerless to suppress this evil, because "divers of the elders wives, &c, were in some measure partners in this general disorder." The truth was, however, that the gentledame who inquired "what dress the queen is in this week," and her husband, bedecked in "silver laced coate and gold wrought cap," were birds of a feather. After 1639 the Court neatly solved the problem by denying such brilliant plumage to those of the "Middling" and "Inferiour sort" whose yearly incomes were less than £200. In 1676 the Suffolk County Court severely admonished Abigail Roberts, a former servant girl, "for excess in her apparell." John Hull deplored as "a visible evil among us" the "want of subjection of inferiors to superiors." Even the watch had to be cautioned in 1662 to comport themselves "soe that any person of qualitye . . . may acknowledge that o[u]r watch neglects not due examination." Class lines may have broken down in rural regions or on the frontier, but at Boston they seem rather to have tightened as the century progressed.[6]

[5] Winsor prints the Boston social register of this period in *Memorial History of Boston*, I, 574; 3 MHS *Colls.*, III, 319; AAS *Trans.*, IV, 105; *Cal. St. Pap.*, 1675–1676, 221.
[6] Signs of the social and political influence of the aristocracy appear frequently. In 1678 the Court sentenced Dyonisia Savage to be punished and fined for bearing a bastard, but in "Answer to the petition of Major Tho: Savage in behalfe of his daughter," one-third of the fine was remitted. Abigail Merrifield had a bastard by Joseph Belcher, "as she saith," and was punished, but Belcher was never summoned to answer the charge as was usual in such cases. In 1674 Elizabeth Wheeler and Joanna Pierce, gentlewomen, "being married women & found sitting in other mens Laps with their Arms about theire Necks," upon confession, escaped by paying the court fees. *Mass. Col. Recs.*, I, 126; AAS *Trans.*, III, 21; *Recs. Suffolk County Court*, 443, 751, 939, 959, 1018.

The founders of Newport were men whose wealth had given them a preeminent position at Boston. Brentons, Clarkes, Coddingtons, Coggeshalls and Dyers, later joined by Arnolds, Carrs, Newburys, Sanfords and Wantons, formed the basis of an economic aristocracy, which, like that of Boston, was considerably strengthened by inter-marriage. These early "Quaker Grandees" quietly established in the seventeenth century, on the secure foundations of "property and privi-lege," one of the most wealthy and cultivated groups in the colonies. They lived in splendid homes, dressed in the ostentatious finery of the age, and spread sumptuous repasts before their guests upon tables groaning beneath the weight of their fine silver. Although they reaped their fortunes from trade, their situation on Rhode Island kept them from being divorced from the soil, as was the merchant class at Bos-ton; country estates were everywhere to be seen about Newport.[7]

At New Amsterdam the Company's iron rule prevented the early development of class distinctions, but a definite social alignment had become noticeable by 1656. In that year the embarrassed schout asked the burgher court what he should do about confining "persons of qual-ity, or of good name and character," and was instructed to carry them to a tavern if they were willing to pay, otherwise, to the gaol at the Stadt Huys. An evaluation of estates made in 1674 affords evidence of the growth of a ruling class. Sixty-two estates, including those of Cornelius Steenwyck, Nicholas de Meyer, Olof van Courtlandt, J. de Peyster, and Jacob Leisler, were valued at 520,000 Dutch florins. Though "people of figure" at New York had not yet amassed fortunes so large as had the Bostonians, they were even more devoted to finery and display. One has but to view the portrait of Cornelius Steenwyck, painted in Holland by Jan van Gooten, to see that he well merited his reputation as the best-dressed man in New York. Already in this pe-riod this merchant aristocracy was conspicuous for its command of all the social graces. As competent a judge as courtly Governor Francis Lovelace wrote to King Charles in 1668: "I find these people have the breeding of courts, and I cannot conceive how such is acquired."[8]

Among the additions to this incipient aristocracy after 1670 were the English families of Nichols, Smith and Willet, and the Huguenot Bayards and Rambouls. In 1683 Governor Dongan arrived bearing instructions "forthwith to call together Fredericke Phillips, Stephen Cortland and so many more of the most eminent inhabitants of New York" as he should deem necessary. Thus began the alliance of great families with royal officials that was so characteristic of the province

[7] Austin, *Genealogical Dictionary of Rhode Island;* Kimball, *Providence,* 32, 63; 6 MHS *Colls.,* V, 21.

[8] *Recs. N. Am.,* II, 80; Stokes, *Iconography,* IV, 297; *Doc. Hist. N. Y.,* I, 91; Wilson, *Memorial History of New York,* I, 349.

of New York. Here, even more than at early Boston, did economic prestige and political power go hand in hand.[9]

More wealth was available for the founding of Philadelphia than at any of the other villages. The riches of Quakers like Samuel Carpenter, William Frampton and John Wheeler enabled them immediately to erect "brave brick houses" with balconies that overlooked the Delaware from Front Street. These favored few began life at Philadelphia in the grand manner. Robert Turner, his daughter and seventeen indentured servants arrived in 1683 to live in the first brick house built in the town. By 1687 Samuel Carpenter's "Slate Roof House" was the show place of the village, though Joseph Growden's country seat, with its orchards near the town, challenged its supremacy. Well might Judge Thomas Holme exclaim:

> Strangers do wonder, and some may say, —
> What mean these Quakers thus to raise
> These stately fabrics to their praise?
> Since we well know and understand
> When they were in their native land
> They were in prison trodden down,
> And can they now build such a town?

The answer is easily found, — profits from commercial ventures as high as one hundred per cent. The Quakers had not yet assumed their garb of "homespun drab and gray," but dressed as did their neighbors in the other villages. Long hair, wigs, side swords and other frippery were as frequently seen in Philadelphia as elsewhere. Elaborately appointed houses, rich and varied foods, and choice wines were the daily portion of the heavy drinking aristocrats of Front Street.[10]

Emigrant planters from Barbados formed the nucleus for Charles Town's ruling class. The early addition of English colonists and Huguenots to this group produced an oligarchy whose control of the community has never been relaxed. Though living more nearly under pioneer conditions than did members of their class in northern towns, Amorys, Bulls, Harlestons, Manigaults, Mazycks, Pinckneys and Rhetts were all to be found dwelling in the southern capital prior to 1690.[11]

By the end of the period in the villages a small, exclusive class of rich merchants had raised themselves above the level of their fellow townsmen and were assuming the trappings of a commercial aristoc-

[9] N. Y. Col. Docs., III, 331, 369, 685, 819; Becker, Political Parties, chapter I.
[10] Pa. Mag., VIII, 334; XVII, 1; Myers, Irish Quakers, 55, 101, 202, 260; Westcott, Historic Mansions of Philadelphia, 11–37.
[11] Journal of the Grand Council of Carolina, 1692, 10; S. C. Hist. & Gen. Mag., passim; Hirsch, Huguenots in South Carolina, 14.

racy. They differed from the gentry of the countryside in that they drew their wealth not from land but from trade, though later they were to demonstrate the same desire for ownership of real estate that motivated a similar class in England. As yet colonial society was too young to insist upon heredity as the basis for social distinction; with the possible exception of the clerical rule at Boston, wealth was still the measure of all things. This being the case, a humble man, like Sir William Phips, might strike it rich and be elevated to the aristocracy. Colonial society was fluid, but, as always, the ruling class resented interlopers and *nouveaux riches*. Its exclusiveness at Boston brought about its temporary political eclipse, for it was in part the demands of a newly established merchant group to whom political privileges had been denied that led to the recall of the charter in 1684.

The lot of the common man in the villages was not a bad one. Indeed, he fared far better than did members of his group in England, France or Holland. At Charles Town many servants, "being Industrious since they came out of their time . . . have gotten good Stocks . . . and Servants of their own; have here also built Houses. . . . Many . . . are worth several Hundreds of Pounds." John Goodson found that Philadelphia tradesmen were "sufficient House-Keepers; anl live[d] gallantly," and that laboring people were comfortable and happy.[12] But this is not to say that the average man in any one of the five villages enjoyed the opportunity to escape from his class to any such degree as did servants and farmers of the hinterland.

IV

The people who settled these American villages lived in an age when religion was still the most vital factor in men's lives. To an extent hardly conceivable today theology dominated the thought of the seventeenth century. Consequently, throughout the period, the church was the most characteristic institution of the villages and the focal point of their social life. Though apparently enjoying the active cooperation of a smaller proportion of the village population than tradition has taught us to believe, it still touched the average life at countless points from which it has today been excluded by other and more mundane agencies. Sharing political control with the magistracy, entrusted by the Bible with the exercise of moral discipline, and respected by those who directed trade and commerce, the village clergy exerted an influence that is today almost incomprehensible. As representatives of a vested institution in an age

[12] Carroll, *Hist. Colls. S. C.*, II, 23; *Pa. Mag.*, IV, 194. For the dress of the common man, see Dow, *Everyday Life in Massachusetts*, 60, 65.

whose theory admitted of no separation between church and state, or the toleration thereby implied, the clergy could largely be counted upon to wield the spiritual sword on the side of conservatism and stability. Indeed, the power which the church has continually exercised in the past as a force for social discipline is nowhere better illustrated than in the history of the American towns in the seventeenth century.

In many respects, the founding of the American colonies may be viewed as a series of experiments in religion, and in each of the five villages at its inception a different form of religious control was instituted. With minor differences of doctrine or discipline, the ruling denomination was in all cases Protestant; four out of the five were puritan. By the close of the century the towns had seen, or were about to witness, the breakdown of this practical monopoly of a predominant or established church by the intrusion of rival sects. As a consequence, there came a lessening of the authority of the church over the lives of the villagers.

Definite establishment existed in three of the villages. At New Amsterdam only the Reformed Dutch Church received official recognition. But there were present from the start many individuals who did not subscribe to the tenets of the established denomination. When Father Isaac Jogues visited Manhattan in 1643 he found that although there was no religion publicly exercised but the Calvinist, the official policy to admit none save professors of that faith was not observed, and numerous Catholics, English Puritans, Lutherans and Mennonites worshipped privately in the village. Two years later Dominie Backerus admitted to the Classis of Amsterdam that his congregation numbered only a hundred and seventy members, "most of them are very ignorant in regard to true religion and very much given to drink." [13]

The Lutherans petitioned Director Stuyvesant in 1653 for the privilege of calling a minister and forming a congregation, but steadfast opposition from the Reformed ministers initiated a controversy that ended only when Governor Nicolls allowed the sect to call a pastor in 1664. Dominie Megapolensis took vigorous steps to oust the Jews, when some of them appeared in the town in 1654. There were already too many people of divers faiths in the town, he asserted, and "it would create a still greater confusion, if the obstinate and immovable Jews came to settle there." [14]

Upon the overthrow of the Dutch regime in 1664 the English authorities assumed a liberal attitude towards the various sects;

[13] Veersteeg, *Manhattan in 1628*, 71; *Narratives of New Netherland*, 260; N. Y. *Eccles. Recs.*, I, 236.
[14] N. Y. *Eccles. Recs.*, I, 317, 335, 354, 357, 360, 371, 403.

Dutch establishment had, of course, ceased with the revolution in political control. William Edmundson in 1671 conducted the first uninterrupted Friends' Meeting before town leaders in a Dutch tavern, and "very attentive they were." Huguenots formed a congregation in 1674, and in 1678 an army chaplain began to read the liturgy at the Fort for some thirty members of the Church of England. The Jews, however, since they did not profess faith in Christ, were by the Common Council in 1685 denied the exercise of their religion. Governor Dongan thus described the chaotic state of religion in the village near the end of the period: "Here bee not many of the Church of England; few Roman Catholicks; abundance of Quakers preachers men a[nd] Women especially; Singing Quakers, Ranting Quakers; Sabbatarians; Antisabbatarians; Some Anabaptists; some Independents; some Jews; in short of all sorts and opinions there are some, and the most part of none at all. . . . The most prevailing opinion is that of the Dutch Calvinists." [15] New York was as cosmopolitan in creed as in race.

According to the "New England Way," the church and town of Boston were coeval, and Puritanism was there established from the beginning. The first small meeting house was soon outgrown, and a fine new frame structure erected near the market place in 1640. The rapid expansion of Boston in the next decade led to the founding of the Second Church in the North End in 1649, which became the seat of the Mathers — "the unmitred popes of a pope-hating commonwealth" — in 1664, when Increase Mather began his sixty-two years of ministry there.[16]

The determination of the Puritans to work out their peculiar faith in their own way, and the belief that "God do no where in his word tolerate Christian States, to give Toleration," led them to take the short way with dissenters. To insure peace, avoid disharmony, and exterminate heresy they expelled Roger Williams and the Antinomians, treated Anabaptists with great severity, and persecuted members of the Society of Friends. But after the Quaker hysteria had subsided, and the colony was faced with the loss of its charter, established church and dissenters tended to draw closer together against the common enemy threatening both. Even "Orthodoxy" itself was tempered by the adoption of the Half-Way Covenant by the Boston Synod of 1662.

In the summer of 1665 John Hull learned that several Anabaptists had gathered privately in the town to form a congregation. So bold did this sect become that four years later Hull attended "a public

[15] N. Y. Col. Docs., III, 218; Doc. Hist. N. Y., I, 92, 186; N. Y. M. C. C., I, 169.
[16] Winthrop, New England, I, 87, 318; Ellis, First Church, 84.

dispute" between six Puritan ministers and "a company of Anabaptists" in a Boston meeting house. Unconvinced by all clerical
arguments and obstinately true to their own beliefs, the Baptists
not only persisted in their worship but built a small church in 1680,
where they conducted their services without annoyance from authorities. Quakers enjoyed similar immunity after 1677.[17]

Introduction of the Anglican communion at Boston in 1686
aroused in the hearts of Boston saints the twin emotions of fear and
curiosity. The Reverend Robert Ratcliffe first read the liturgy on
May 30th. "It seems many crouded thither," noted Sewall sadly,
"and the Ministers preached forenoon and Afternoon." The church
was organized two weeks later, and soon its supporters claimed four
hundred "daily frequenters." Sewall's Diary records the anger and
resentment caused by the decision of Andros that Episcopal services
should be held in the South Meeting House until a chapel could be
built. One need not seek far for explanation of the fury with which
the mob assailed the newly erected King's Chapel during the uprising of 1689.[18] The reign of the saints was passing: by 1690 most
Christian sects were able to conduct their worship at Boston with a
considerable degree of freedom, and this growing liberty was to be
definitely guaranteed them by the Charter of 1691.

In the south Anglicanism had its stronghold. The early Carolina
settlers recognized the Church of England as the established religion
of the colony, and the first enactment of their new government was a
Sabbath law. In 1682 St. Philip's Church was built at Charles Town,
its parish embracing the entire province. The few Quaker families
living in Charles Town were urged by George Fox to hold regular
meetings, which they commenced in 1682. About two years later an
Independent congregation was formed, and shortly afterwards Charles
Town Huguenots founded a Calvinist church (ca. 1687).[19]

At Philadelphia, though the Society of Friends made no attempt
to establish their religion by law, its predominant influence in the
early years produced the same effect as virtual establishment. Conservative to the core, Philadelphia Quakers regarded ranters and reformers of the Keithian breed with contempt, and Anglicans with
suspicion. By 1685 two meeting houses had been built, and a Yearly
Meeting established with central authority over Pennsylvania, Delaware and West Jersey, its sessions held alternately at Philadelphia
and Burlington. The rapid ascendancy of Quaker influence at Phila-

[17] The Third, or South Congregational Church was formed in 1669. AAS *Trans.*,
III, 219, 227; Winsor, *Memorial History*, I, 172, 565.
[18] 5 MHS *Colls.*, V, 143, 171; Hutchinson, *Papers relating to Massachusetts Bay*,
II, 294.
[19] Dalcho, *Episcopal Church in S. C.*, chapter II; *S. C. Statutes*, I, 1; Wallace,
South Carolina, I, 145, 152; *S. C. Hist. & Gen. Mag.*, XXVIII, 23.

delphia enticed Edward Shippen and several other Friends from Newport in 1689 and 1690.[20] No other denomination sought to set up a
different form of worship in the town before 1690, so that of all
the villages Philadelphia was religiously the most uniform at the close
of the period.

Newport alone of the villages adopted from the beginning a liberal
religious policy. Conservative in that they regarded their churches
as essential for social discipline, members of the ruling class were
yet tolerant of dissenting religious opinions and, shrewd beyond
their times, they realized the superiority of persuasion over compul-
sion. It was a source of amazement and alarm to representatives from
John Winthrop's church in Boston that the Coddington-Coggeshall
group, who had formed a congregation at Newport in 1639, entertained views similar to those later held by Quakers, and further,
that they dwelt in harmony with the despised "Paedobaptists," led by
John Clarke and Robert Lenthall.[21]

The shabby treatment received by Quakers at New Amsterdam
moved them to make Newport their base in the colonies. Since the
vituperative Dominie Megapolensis viewed Rhode Island as "the receptacle of all sorts of riff-raff people, and . . . nothing else than
the sewer of New England," it seemed just the place for such ranters,
and for the Jews as well. The first Friends arrived at Newport in
August, 1657, and soon won over the Coddington group to their
faith. Four years later "The Yearly Meeting for Friends in New
England" was set up by George Rofe at the "island of error," and
in 1672 a small frame meeting house was built. George Fox and
William Edmundson visited Newport at this time, gaining many adherents and planting Quakerism in the Narragansett country. By
1690 the Society of Friends included nearly half the population of
Newport, and Quakers were already exercising a predominant and
conservative influence in the political, commercial and social life
of the colony.[22]

A group of Seventh Day Baptists was organized at Newport
in 1671, and Mordecai Campanall, Moses Pacheco and other Jews
from Curacao began to settle in the village in 1658, where they purchased a burial ground.[23] Also living here were individuals of many
other sects, and some of no faith at all. Episcopalian Samuel Maverick described Newport as "a receptacle for people of severall Sorts

---

[20] *Pa. Col. Recs.*, I, 366, 378; Myers, *Irish Quakers*, 107; Scharf and Westcott,
Philadelphia, I, 121; Jackson, *Cyclopedia of Philadelphia*, IV, 1028.
    [21] A second Baptist church was founded in 1656. *Doc. Hist. R. I.*, II, 166; Backus,
New England Baptists, II, 16.
    [22] *N. Y. Eccles. Recs.*, I, 399; Jones, *Quakers in the American Colonies*, 51, 54, 65,
137 n.
    [23] Gutstein, *Jews of Newport*, 30; Platt, *Seventh Day Baptists*, I, 119, 122–127.

and Opinions." From its earliest days the town was open to all
sects, and since such freedom ran counter to contemporary political
and religious beliefs, naturally became the butt of unfriendly critics,
especially at Boston and New Amsterdam.

To many villagers in the early years the church constituted the
chief source of recreation, and listening to learned and usually lengthy
sermons served in some measure to enliven an otherwise dull and
restricted Sabbath. At Boston a weekly lecture on timely topics was
held on Thursday, and similar meetings took place on other days
in nearby villages. The trial of Anne Hutchinson or the baiting of
Quakers catered to a public appetite for sensationalism that is today
satisfied with quite different fare and furnished matter for lively
conversations over mugs of cider and beer in many a tavern. Large
crowds eagerly attended the much advertised doctrinal debate at
Newport, August 6, 1672, between Roger Williams, who rowed in
a skiff all the way down from Providence for the event, and the
Quaker Edmundson, *vice* George Fox. As Philadelphia and Newport
became the twin centers of American Quakerism, their inhabitants
thoroughly enjoyed the week devoted to the Yearly Meetings. At
Philadelphia Quaker farmers from the country welcomed the excuse
to come to town and brought their produce to sell in the market,
while their wives made needed purchases in village shops. The whole
week passed in a round of generous hospitality. Church-going for
South Carolina planters was truly a social event, and every Sabbath canoes and perriaugers brought people from distant points into
Charles Town for services at St. Philip's.[24]

Several influences, chiefly of an urban nature, tended to under-
mine the power of the church for the enforcement of social discipline
in the villages in the latter half of the period. Dominie Backerus
found in 1648 that his hearers rushed to tap houses as soon as church
was out, for further fortification against evil. At Boston, under
the leadership of a learned and able clergy with the zealous assistance
of their elders, discipline was strict, and the civil authorities thus
found powerful allies, especially before 1670, in the preservation
of good order in the village. But with the expansion of the town,
the disorders resulting from the Indian wars, and the increasing encroachments of secular affairs in the lives of a younger generation
which lacked the primitive piety of their fathers, there came a visible
decline in religious control. In 1675 Mary Wheeler was presented
for "disorderly carriages" in the South Meeting House, "in hunch-
ing Rebecca Bulley in the publique worship of god." There were

[24] Jones, *Quakers in the American Colonies*, 117; Myers, *Irish Quakers*, 221;
Leiding, *Charleston*, 42.

other convictions for similar wanton behavior, which could certainly never have occurred in the austere atmosphere of the meetings of an earlier day. Members of the First Church might resolve in 1691 to prevent "pollution of the *Lords day* by any of ye familie, . . . and keep yr. Children & servants within doores, God assisting," but actually, as even Increase Mather learned, many were "gospel-glutted and growing weary." [25] The ministers themselves, ever awake to the intellectual currents of the age, were in some cases consciously partaking of the spirit of rationalism that was astir in Europe at the time.

In seventeenth century villages, especially Boston, with their strict Sabbatarian codes, it has generally been assumed that nearly everyone attended church on Sunday. Such may well have been the case in the earliest years, but as the villages expanded nothing could have been further from the truth. A consideration of the number and seating capacities of village meeting houses and churches demonstrates the sheer physical impossibility of crowding the entire village populations into their houses of worship. At no time after 1650 does it seem possible for the churches of Boston to have contained anywhere near a majority of the inhabitants; in 1690 little more than a quarter of them could have attended church simultaneously had they been so disposed. In other towns the proportion was probably even smaller.[26] At New Amsterdam in 1655 there were many "Atheists, and various other servants of Baal among the English" [and probably among the Dutch as well], and in 1687, as we have noticed, Dongan found people of all opinions, — "the most part of none at all." Sabbath laws were directed more at preventing "prophanation" of that day than at enforcing church attendance; they were a form of police regulation, enacted in an attempt to control the new complexities of growing village society. The Massachusetts code of 1653 appeared at a time when the town was beginning to expand rapidly; succeeding laws became increasingly strict, evidently as the problem grew more formidable.

Of the large number of people living without the religious pale we know very little. Many of them were probably laborers, artisans, servants and slaves. At New York few masters took much care for the conversion or religious instruction of their blacks. Many of the

---

[25] *N. Y. Eccles. Recs.,* I, 236; *Recs. Suffolk County Court,* 305; Ellis, *First Church,* 148; 4 MHS *Colls.,* VIII, 314.

[26] In 1690 Boston had six church buildings of various sizes. If we assume, somewhat liberally, an average seating capacity of three hundred, then eighteen hundred persons might have attended worship. From the population of seven thousand perhaps one thousand should be deducted, who would not in any case have attended. New York had two large and two tiny buildings for thirty-nine hundred persons; Philadelphia, two fair-sized meetings for four thousand; Newport, three structures for twenty-six hundred; and Charles Town, two for eleven hundred residents and the entire population of the province.

village youth also lived apart from the church. At Boston, one Sabbath day in 1678, young Robert Hill stayed home from church to shave himself. When his landlord's daughter "asked him the reason why hee trimmed himself on the Lords Day his answer was that a pretty wench Invited him to see her in the afternoone." On his return that night she asked him what Meeting he had attended, and he replied "A Church with a Chimney on it." For young people in the towns there were more pleasant diversions than taking notes on sermons or sitting silently in Quaker Meeting. They had not the "Primitive Zeal, Piety and Holy Heat found in the Harts of . . . [their] parents," for which old Joshua Scottow sighed in vain. Nor was it all "metamorphosed into Land and Trade breathings." [27] In some people it had never been present, and never would appear.

v

The tavern was probably the most important social institution in the little seaports. Certainly its supremacy was contested only by the church, whose influence did not reach equally to all classes of people. Much of life centered about the taverns; the common meeting ground for all ranks of society, they were the most democratic places in the villages. Here townsfolk came daily to eat and drink, gossip and traffic, to hear the latest news or to post notices on the walls where all might see and read. Strangers and seafaring men usually lived at the inns, or, if they lodged with private families, frequently took their meals at the "ordinary." Here merchants and mariners bargained over cargoes; here the courts adjourned for dinner; here pious churchgoers took refuge in winter to warm themselves after a frigid two hours in a heatless church. Mine host, with his cry of "Coming, sir," was an important village personage. But, although the tavern performed a vital social service, its very existence raised knotty problems the solution of which sorely taxed the ingenuity of townsfolk. Indeed, the liquor question seems perennial. Some inns and ordinaries became centers of vice and unrestraint, gave poor service and poorer liquor, encouraged idleness and viciousness, and enticed customers into debt. Fortunately the colonial villages were founded shortly after the system of liquor licensing had been introduced into England, and thus possessed a form of regulation for a guide.

In every village the social importance of taverns and the need for them was recognized at an early date. Barely ten years after settlement the General Court of Massachusetts moved to remedy the "great inconvenience that is found for want of fit places of entertainment of

[27] *Doc. Hist. N. Y.,* I, 186; *Recs. Suffolk County Court,* 914; Scottow, *Old Men's Tears.*

people vpon occasion of great assemblies, . . . & arrivall of ships with passengers," by authorizing any townsman to entertain "such people . . . at reasonable rates," and the selection in each town of a "fitt man" to sell wines and liquors. In New Amsterdam Director Kieft suffered such "great annoyance" from English visitors, passing through the town on their way from New England to Virginia, that he was himself forced to open a tavern for their accommodation in 1642.[28]

On March 4, 1634, Samuel Cole opened the first tavern at Boston, which he operated until 1638 when, his sympathy with the Antinomians getting him into trouble with the authorities, he sold out to Robert Sedgwick. Another early innkeeper, William Baulston, whom we shall meet again in Newport, had his career at Boston similarly cut short. It was probably to one of these houses that John Josselyn repaired when on his first visit to Boston he went ashore and refreshed himself at an "ordinary." Between 1633 and 1662 fourteen different persons kept inns, ordinaries, taverns or victualling houses at Boston.[29] With the expansion of the village after the latter date the number of licensed public houses increased rapidly until by 1690 there were fifty-four establishments purveying food, liquor, coffee, tea or chocolate for the Boston appetite; of these twenty-four were conducted by women.

Buildings used for taverns varied greatly with the kind of service offered. Retailers merely sold drink in small quantities from their dingy little houses on side streets and alleys. Along the waterfront were to be found all sorts of taverns, groggeries and pot-houses, catering to the transient population of sailors and sea captains. The Ship Tavern, at the head of Clark's Wharf, which was more than thirteen years old when John Vyall took it over in 1663, was the most famous of these waterfront inns. Nicholas Upshall, stout-hearted Quaker who dared send food to Mary Fisher and Ann Austin, was host at the Red Lion, located in 1654 close to the harbor in North Street. The better taverns were located in the center of town near the market place and Town House, and their hosts were men of considerable importance. Among better known hostelries were the Bunch of Grapes, operated by William Hudson, and Hugh Gunnison's King's Arms at the head of Dock Square, George Monk's Blue Anchor near the South Meeting House, and the Castle Tavern in Dock Square,

[28] *Mass. Col. Recs.*, I, 279; Van Rennselaer, *New York*, I, 188.
[29] No sharp distinction can be made between these terms. Generally speaking, an *inn* was a public house for the lodging and entertainment of travelers; a *tavern* was a public house or tap-room where drink was retailed, a dram shop; and an *ordinary* was a house serving a public meal at a fixed price. *Retailers* sold liquor in small quantities, but provided no food or lodgings. 3 MHS *Colls.*, III, 230; Krout, *Origins of Prohibition*, 4, 8 n.

whose host in 1687 was "Captain" Daniel Wing. The inventory of
the King's Arms, which Hugh Gunnison sold for £200 in 1650, affords a glimpse of one of the better Boston taverns. On the ground
floor were one large "Chamber called the Exchange," kitchen, larder,
hall, a "low p'lor," and a public room near the bar which could be
divided into three small stalls. Upstairs were lodging quarters for the
"better sort of people," consisting of the "chamber called London,"
with a bedstead and two benches, a nursery, the "Court chamber,"
and the "Star Chamber." For ordinary guests there were three
small sleeping compartments in the garret. In the yard were a brew-
house, stable, pump, "with pipes to convey the water to the brew-
house," five hog-sties and "one house of office." The King's Arms
was well appointed for those days, within and without.[30]

In addition to "houses of entertainment" which furnished board
and lodging, the village of Boston was well supplied with "cook's
shops" and "victualling houses," where inhabitants and strangers
could try the "ordinary" or table d'hôte for a reasonable price, or
have food "dressed" to take to their homes as they had done in England. Most of these early restaurants were conducted by men, though
frequently widows, with whom the town abounded, sought a livelihood
by the exercise of their culinary skill. The first of these eating houses
appeared in 1643, when Goody Armitage, William Hudson, Jr., and
"William Knop[']s wife" received licenses to keep "the ordinary,
but not to draw wine." So many of these establishments sprang up
in the town that in 1666 the General Court denied William Kent
license for a cook's shop, even though he had "served an apprenticeship in England." [31]

Always alert to innovations in England, "severall Merchants &
Gentlemen" urged the Selectmen in 1676 to allow some person "to
keepe a publique house for selling of Coffee." Opening in October,
under the management of John Sparry, the first American coffee
house speedily became the center of mercantile Boston. Here in 1689
Sewall betook himself for the latest news from Connecticut, and here
in the following year he arranged with Captain Clark for his passage
to England. There were two coffee houses in the town in 1690, one
of which, the London Coffee House, was conducted by Benjamin Harris, bookseller, and publisher of the first colonial newspaper.[32] Only
at Boston was the economic life sufficiently developed to support so
specialized an institution during this period.

Not every stranger sojourning in Boston stayed at a tavern. Many,
especially seafaring men, took rooms with private families, as did

[30] Drake, *Old Boston Taverns*, 19–32; *N. E. Hist. & Gen. Reg.*, XXXIV, 42.
[31] *Mass. Col. Recs.*, II, 46; IV, ii, 302; 7 *Bos. Rec. Com.*, 60, 68, 139.
[32] 5 MHS *Colls.*, V, 196, 233; 7 *Bos. Rec. Com.*, 104, 110, 156, 204.

often unmarried men of the poorer classes. When the Sieur d'Aulnay and his men came to Boston in 1646 they hired lodgings in the town, and ate their dinners with Winthrop at "the ordinarie, . . . where the magistrates used to dine." Katherine Franklin kept such a lodging house in 1677, and when John Warner, aged twenty-one, went off to sea without settling his bill for thirty-two weeks, the irate goodwife broke open his trunk of linen to satisfy her claims.[33]

Although authorities conceived of taverns primarily as places of "conuenience for travellers and saylors," houses of public entertainment were much frequented by town inhabitants, both "poorer" and "better sort." Until the erection of the Town House the General Court, the Selectmen, and the Commissioners of the United Colonies held their meetings in taverns, and continued to dine there throughout the period. For many years members of the General Court were fed by Elder James Penn, who held a liquor license for his ordinary "so long as he keepes entertainment for ye Courts," and a gratuity of twenty shillings paid his servants for "theire paines this Court" was a regular item of expense in the Treasurer's report. In 1654 the Deputies resolved to dine together at the Ship Tavern, as "most comly, convenient & conduceable to the dispatch" of public business. On July 21, 1685, the "31 Ministers" meeting in Boston to determine the attitude of the colony toward the demands of the Mother Country, dined with George Monk at the Blue Anchor, and "after Diner about 3 or 4 aclock," says Sewall, "they gave their Answer." That it was so uncompromising may be due in part to the excellence of Mr. Monk's "dyet."[34]

Seafaring men resorted to houses like John Vyall's Ship Tavern, in the taproom of which the latest shipping news was daily discussed, and masters of vessels signed Boston lads for voyages to the Caribbean or Mediterranean. Here in 1685, after the drums had beat up a crowd in the streets, were enlisted volunteers to chase the pirates, and here, too, Sir Robert Carr once thrashed a constable who made to arrest him. Boston inns offered good fare, if we may believe Josselyn's savory report. Upon landing in 1663, "We repaired to an Ordinary (for so they call their Taverns there) where we were provided with a liberal cup of burnt Madera-wine, and a store of plum-cake, about ten of the clock" in the morning.

Public houses often afforded scenes of gaiety and merriment, innocent and otherwise. In 1638 Mistress Anne Walker was expelled from the Boston church "for intemperate drinking from one inn to another and for light and wanton behaviour." In less respectable

[33] Winthrop, *New England*, II, 273; *Recs. Suffolk County Court*, 105.
[34] *Mass. Col. Recs.*, II, 139; III, 352.

houses there was a continuous round of disorder, idleness and "immoderate drinking" by sailors whose masters frequently complained of the loss they suffered through "theire men being many times arreasted for debt." Nor were drunkenness and disorder confined to seafarers. Many townsfolk haunted the inns to drink and play shuffleboard, until the game was forbidden, along with bowling and any form of gambling, in 1647. The "younger sort" were by 1664 "taking their opportunity, by meeting together in places of publick entertainment, to corrupt one another by their vnciuill & wanton carriages, rudely singing & making a noyse to the disturbance of the family & other guests." The tavern of the Widow Thomas near the waterfront served as a blind to attract sailors into her bawdy house. In 1687 Samuel Sewall and other town fathers felt it their duty to reprove Captain Wing, proprietor of the Castle Tavern, for "Setting a Room in his House for a man to shew tricks in." Poor Sewall could hardly know in what short time tavern shows would become popular and plentiful in Boston.[35]

Residents and visitors at Manhattan were as well served by taverns and public houses as the Bostonians. The Dutch West India Company, as one of its first works there, erected a brewery, the products of which it sold in wholesale quantities along with imported wines and brandies to its servants from the "Store" at the Fort. As the liquor traffic bulked next largest to the fur trade in its business, the Company encouraged inhabitants to sell by retail in their homes. In 1637 Governor Kieft estimated that fully one quarter of the dwellings in the village were "grog-shops or houses where nothing is to be got but tobacco and beer." After Kieft had caused the first real inn to be opened under the management of Philip Gerritsen, licensed taverns and public houses multiplied rapidly. Under the burgher government, from 1653 to 1664, at least seventeen such establishments catered to the needs of inhabitants and villagers; the number had nearly doubled by 1680. The need for lodging houses was met at Manhattan as at Boston. In 1654 a rooming house for strangers was in operation near the Dock, and the next year Op Dyck rented rooms at his dwelling next to the City Hall. Also, as in Boston, widows opened eating houses to cater to those who disliked tavern fare. Pretence of keeping boarders furnished in New Amsterdam a convenient dodge for the selling of liquors without payment of the usual fee for a tavern license. Indeed, the very general retailing of liquor in homes throughout the town characterized the entire tavern problem of both New Amsterdam and New York. Both Stuyvesant (1648) and Andros

[35] Winthrop, *New England*, II, 349; *Mass. Col. Recs.*, III, 114, 184, 201; IV, ii, 100; 5 MHS *Colls.*, V, 196.

(1680) reiterated the earlier judgment of Governor Kieft that fully a quarter of the houses in the village had been "turned into taverns for the sale of brandy, tobacco and beer." [36]

Social life at New Amsterdam centered even more about the taverns than at Boston. The Director and his Council, the Burgomasters, and the Court of Orphanmasters always dined at a tavern, and frequently held their meetings there. Many commercial transactions took place in exchange rooms, and there Dutchmen heard the latest news of the Fatherland or of English encroachments on the Connecticut. In the evenings jolly burghers liked nothing better than to join their "drinking clubs" at their favorite taverns, and there to spend the night in dancing and song. On the Sabbath after sermon-time, it was the custom of many families "to eat their usual Sunday meal" at an inn. In 1654 Hans Stein was detected selling liquor to some of these people in violation of the Sabbath law. Some publicans sought to attract patronage by providing bowling greens where customers were free to play at ninepins at all times save during divine service. One of New York's most popular taverns was located on the Fresh Water Pond outside the Wall. Jasper Danckaerts went there one Sunday evening in 1679, "on account of its being to some extent a pleasant spot." A favorite Sunday resort for "all sorts of revellers," it had fortunately a lovely little garden, where the shocked Labadist walked to get away from the unholy noise. New Amsterdam and New York had also their dives, which debauched sailors and "Common people" and "still worse, the Youth." Innkeepers like George Dobson (1663) kept disorderly houses so attractive to sailors that their captains could get no work out of them. A pot-house had to be closed in 1660 because of its too frequent brawls, one of which had resulted in a stabbing.[37]

Newport required and enjoyed fewer taverns than its older neighbors. William Baulston, the heretical innkeeper of Boston, opened a tavern at Portsmouth in 1638, which seems to have been the only establishment on the island until 1643, when a "publick house" appeared at Newport. Two more taverners obtained licenses in 1654. These men seem to have confined themselves to the dispensing of liquor "by the small measure," for in 1661 after "great complaynt by reason that there is no places for strangers to be entertained" the Assembly had to order that none might sell "wine or lyckers, but such as shall keepe one bed at least, and victuals for the enterteyning of Strangers." Apparently this act had its effect, for within a short

[36] Wilson, *Memorial History of New York*, I, 224, 379; Stokes, *Iconography*, IV; N. Y. M. C. C., I, 80; *Recs. N. Am.*, I, 5, 280, 317; II, 222; *Laws of New Netherland*, 364.
[37] *Recs. N. Am.*, I, 255, 259, 261; II, 53; IV, 192; Bayles, *Old Taverns of New York*, 35; *Journal of Jasper Danckaerts*, 47; Stokes, *Iconography*, I, 27.

time the peripatetic Baulston had moved his hostelry to Newport, and Henry Palmer had opened an inn there. By 1686 there were in the village six licensed taverns and several victualling houses, offering visitors and townsfolk good "dyett and lodgings." In one of these the General Court sat when in Newport.[38]

The swarming of immigrants into Philadelphia during its early years provided a thriving custom for taverners, and a number of inns, ordinaries and pot-houses soon appeared. William Frampton opened an excellent tavern in 1685. In that year also there were "Seven Ordinaries for the Intertainment of Strangers and Workmen, that are not Housekeepers, and a good meal to be had for six pence, sterl." Within three years at least four more public houses were licensed, and countless illicit "groggeries" had sprung up in the notorious caves and along the waterfront, where rioting sailors and disorderly laborers were nightly scandalizing more sober inhabitants. At Charles Town in 1683 there was a sufficient number of taverns and eating houses to warrant a provincial licensing act, and in 1687 the familiar problem of tippling sailors neglecting their work called for immediate official attention.[39]

In all villages public houses required regulation, and the existence of taverns, necessary though they were, bred abuses with which municipal or provincial authorities had to deal. Few topics claim so much space in the Colony records of Massachusetts as the tavern and liquor questions, and Penn's distress over the disgrace of the caves of the Delaware corresponds with the constant concern of New York governors over the too abundant sale of spirituous liquor in their capital city. In general, village authorities followed English precedent in the careful licensing of taverns, and except in the case of New York, saw to it that their provisions were successfully enforced.

Massachusetts' first licensing law was enacted in 1634, when the General Court forbade any person to operate an unlicensed public house under penalty of twenty shillings fine for every week of violation. The Court retained the licensing power until 1646, when, not wishing any longer to be "hindered in their more weighty affairs," they turned this onerous duty over to the County Courts. Thereafter the Boston Selectmen presented to the Suffolk County Court at its spring session a list of nominees whose application for licenses they approved. Provincial authorities continued, however, to enact legislation designed to control the liquor traffic and the conduct of

[38] *Doc. Hist. R. I.*, II, 123, 146; *R. I. Col. Recs.*, I, 313, 441; II, 371; III, 31; *R. I. Acts* (1705), 31; *Newport T. M. Recs.*, 13.
[39] *Pa. Mag.*, XVIII, 420 n.; XX, 421; Scharf and Westcott, *History of Philadelphia*, I, 107; *Narratives of Pennsylvania*, 262; *Pa. Col. Recs.*, I, 166; *S. C. Statutes*, II, 3, 31, 51.

taverns, rules against disorder, gambling, the sale of liquor on Sundays and the entertainment of youths and Indians, ordinances to prevent innkeepers from trusting sailors for drinks, and forbidding the collection of debts so contracted, and penalties for unlicensed houses and those not closing at curfew time. Prices and quality of food and liquor served were also subject to legislative specification. In 1637, because of complaints "that diverse pore people, who would willingly content themselves wth meane dyot," were forced to buy "ordinary" meals at twelve pence, the Court ordered that every innkeeper should provide his guests only such victuals as they might call for, "& not force them to take more or other than they shall desire, bee it never so meane & small in quantity." All inns were required by law to be furnished with good rooms for travelers, and with ample feed and stables for their horses. Briefly stated, the tavern was conceived as a public institution which should provide all needed services, and which should be carefully regulated by law to prevent all usual sorts of abuses. Said Boston's foremost cleric in 1673, "I know that in such a town as this, there is need of such houses and no sober Minister will speak against the Licensing of them, . . . but see that you keep a vigilant eye over these private, dark Houses, where wicked Persons sell Drink and Destroy Souls to get a little Money; and which do more Mischief, than all the Publick Houses do good." [40]

The public house legislation of the other English villages was similar to that of Boston, since all drew their inspiration from English tavern law. Until 1663 the Rhode Island Assembly issued all licenses for the colony; after that date town councils granted such permits to applicants who produced sureties for their good behavior. In 1647 gambling, idleness and excessive tippling were forbidden at all public houses, and after 1655 inns were closed at nine o'clock at night to all save lodgers. No Sabbath closing law was enacted until 1673, so late as to suggest very little trouble with disorderly taverns during the first thirty-five years of life on the "island of error." Its passage may have resulted from the increasing presence of seafarers, which was also responsible for a law of 1679 forbidding innkeepers to "give creditt unto, and trust any seaman" without an order from the master of his ship. The taverns of Charles Town and Philadelphia came under almost identical legislation in 1683 and 1685. [41]

New Amsterdam reaped a harvest of stubborn problems from the original sowing by the West India Company, when, because of its financial interest in the traffic, it encouraged the sale of beer and

---

[40] *Mass. Col. Recs.*, I, 140, 213, 280; II, 100, 172, 188; III, 427; Wertenbaker, *First Americans*, 196.

[41] *R. I. Acts* (*1705*), 32; *R. I. Col. Recs.*, I, 185; II, 503; III, 31, 237; *S. C. Statutes*, II, 3, 31, 51; *Pa. Col. Recs.*, I, 166.

liquor by inhabitants from the earliest years. Governor Kieft reported in 1637 that "Mischief and perversity is daily occasioned by immoderate drinking," and a year later forbade the sale of liquors anywhere in the village except at the Company's "Store." Little improvement seems to have followed, for in 1648 Peter Stuyvesant reported the presence of so many illicit houses that licensed taverners who honestly paid their excise dues could hardly make a living. He set about to reform the liquor traffic, and thereafter licensed only those who took an oath to observe the law, and who, moreover, met the unanimous approval of Director and Council. As in the English villages, innkeepers had to refuse liquor to Indians, report all brawling to the authorities, and close their establishments at the ringing of an evening bell; they could, however, do business on Sundays after three o'clock. When the city charter went into effect in 1653 the licensing power was placed in the hands of the Burgomasters. In 1676 the Common Council moved to improve the lodging situation at Manhattan inns by requiring all publicans to sell beer as well as stronger liquors and to keep accommodations for strangers. Andros made a survey of taverns in 1679 and found many unlicensed grog-shops, which he endeavored with small success to suppress. Although food and service at the better inns was all that could be desired, the satisfactory regulation of the New York liquor traffic was still in 1690 an unrealized ideal.[42]

Stranger or inhabitant who went to the average village tavern was well served. In general, the somewhat literary descriptions of small and dirty hostelries probably more accurately represent the country than the village inn. In the towns competition incited the taverner to provide beds, food and service of superior quality. Fairly steady and dependable patronage encouraged him to introduce innovations and improvements into his business, and public regulation prevented many abuses for which there was no remedy in the back country. The cost of setting up as an innkeeper in the towns, the expense of license fees and equipment, made it a business enterprise of some magnitude, attracting mainly those with capital and social standing. Furthermore, the varied patronage of town populations fostered the existence of many types of public houses, types to answer the needs, taste, purse and morals of nearly everyone. But the other side of the picture, the vices and disorders that flourish in tavern tap-rooms and grog-shops, were likewise intensified in the towns, where they constituted one of the prominent social problems with which village communities had to deal.

[42] *Laws of New Netherland*, 6, 12; *Recs. N. Am.*, I, 5; II, 263; *N. Y. M. C. C.*, I, 18, 80, 178; Wilson, *Memorial History of New York*, I, 379.

VI

The fundamental necessity of getting a living absorbed the waking hours of virtually every village-dweller. In the new land this was for everyone a rigorous business; breadwinning, either by commerce or by manual labor, and the staggering domestic tasks of a more primitive age than our own left little leisure or opportunity for purely recreational activities. From the wealthy merchant and his women-folk down to servants and slaves, work filled the days of all. There was, to be sure, a certain gregariousness to labor in the villages that was denied the country-dweller. But, wherever one went in the colonies, the practice of the time was busily creating a virtue out of necessity, and hard work was already becoming a part of the American creed.

For a great majority in each village the church supplied the most usual form of entertainment and relaxation. There was a vividness and color to religion in the seventeenth century that was none the less genuine because we find it hard to comprehend today. The lives of these people were truly filled with the beauty of holiness: certainly few men have ever found more satisfaction anywhere than did Samuel Sewall in his church. But there were large elements of the population who found morality and theology alone a savorless diet, and who sought amusement beyond the humdrum of every-day life. Their numbers increased as the towns grew older, and in all villages secular amusements existed by the end of the period. Most of the diversions enjoyed by the people they brought with them from their different homelands; little that was novel was added in these early years.

The Reformation was primarily a middle class movement, and as such it glorified the virtues by which the middle class had raised itself, — diligence, sobriety, and thrift. Idleness being thus a sin, it followed that protestantism regarded many harmless amusements as a waste of precious time. The puritan spirit was strong in the four English villages. As early as 1633 the General Court of Massachusetts decreed that no person "shall spend his time idly." Constables were directed to keep a weather eye on "common coasters vnprofittable fowlers [persons hunting for pleasure] & tobacco takers." Under these conditions less innocent sports would have to be indulged in secret, and so they were. Gaming and card playing prevailed at Boston almost as soon as it was founded, and laws were immediately enacted to suppress them. By 1680 so many people were, like Benjamin Gold, "playing at Cards & keeping bad company," that the Reverend Mr. Increase Mather felt it necessary to preach against such vices at his Thursday lecture. Gaming in its various forms was the favorite diversion of servants and slaves at Boston, when they were not assembled in "tumultuous gatherings . . . Shailing or throwing at Cocks." [43]

Children laid aside their toys at an early age and went to work, although their parents or masters frequently allowed them time for play. Boys and young men played football in the village streets until 1658, when, because of injuries received by several innocent bystanders, the Town Meeting ordered them to desist. Like most young people growing up, these lads and their sisters soon became interested in the forbidden pastime of dancing. A dancing school, opened in Boston in 1672, was shortly suppressed by the authorities, and we know that in 1676 there were there "no musicians by trade." Some persons, who like John Chandler defied the authorities, were punished for disorders in their houses at unreasonable hours, and "suffering people to bee singing & fidling at midnight." [44] Others, with hearts undaunted by the rigorous social code, took to riding from town to town, ostensibly to lectures, "but it appears . . . merly to drinck & reuell in ordinaryes & taverns, which is in itself scandalous." [45] But youth was merely imitating its elders: did not the Sewalls and the Ushers hire Em's coach and drive to the Greyhound in Roxbury to dine "with Boil'd Bacon and rost Fowls," staying until quite late at night? Even within the town occasional wild parties occurred, to be promptly suppressed when discovered. Youth also did not take kindly to rules laid down by its elders for the regulation of courtship. The law requiring the consent of the young lady's parents before an admirer might pay her his attentions had only the imperfect success we might expect. Court records between 1670 and 1680 abound with cases like that of John Loring, who admitted "making Love to & engaging the affections of Mary Willis . . . without her parents consent & after his being forewarned by them." [46]

In 1681 the first of numerous French dancing-masters to make a living from the patronage of the gentry of colonial towns made his appearance in Boston. The Selectmen reported Monsieur Henri Sherlot to be "a person of very insolent & ill fame that Raues & scoffes

[43] *Mass. Col. Recs.*, I, 109; II, 180; III, 102; *Recs. Suffolk County Court*, 5, 7, 131, 184, 259, 263, 1162; 5 MHS *Colls.*, V, 184, 312.

[44] Dow, *Everyday Life*, 110; 2 *Bos. Rec. Com.*, 141; *Cal. St. Pap.*, 1675–1676, 362; *Recs. Suffolk County Court*, 232.

[45] Such practices proved a "notable meanes to debauch our youth and hazard the chastity of such as are drawn thereunto." (1675) *Mass. Col. Recs.*, V, 63.

[46] The unsuccessful lover could, by recourse to a medieval love philter, surmount all obstacles. In 1674 Edward Peggy was haled into Court "for useing by indirect meanes by powders . . . to Engage the affections or desires of women kinde to him & for begetting Ruth Heminway of Roxbury with Childe." He was fined £10. *Recs. Suffolk County Court*, 183, 485, 559.

at Religion," and ordered him out of town. Shortly after this incident Increase Mather let fly his tract, *An Arrow against Profane and Promiscuous Dancing, Drawn out of the Quiver of the Scriptures,* for the guidance of Boston conduct. But in 1685 the ministers complained that Francis Stepney conducted "mixt Dances" on Lecture Day, and were scandalized by his boast that "by one Play he would teach more Divinity than Mr. Willard or the Old Testament. Mr. Moodey said 'twas not a time for N. E. to dance. Mr. Mather struck at the Root speaking against mixt dances." Mr. Stepney was requested to depart from Boston, and Mr. Mather loosed a second arrow against his art by reprinting his now famous pamphlet. For village aristocrats, however, the exercise of the art of self-defense was permitted by Governor Andros. "Sword playing . . . this day openly practised on a Stage in Boston & that immediately after Lecture," lamented Mather on August 27, 1687, "so yt the Devil has begun a Lecture Day in Boston on a Lecture Day wch was set up for Christ." [47]

On the whole there was no distinct line between town and country diversions. Denizens of seventeenth century towns, even of the great metropolis of London, still maintained an intimate contact with the countryside, and in the New World this relationship was of course even closer. Rural excursions enjoyed great popularity, where leisure permitted; Sewall and his wife frequently drove out Dorchester way "to eat Cherries & Rasberries, [but] chiefly to ride and take the Air." Shortly after 1660 a mineral spring at Lynn became "noated" for its qualities in relieving scorbutic and pulmonary afflictions, and was eagerly patronized by Boston gentlefolk. On one occasion Noadiah Russell ascribed an attack of ague to his too liberal indulgence in its sulphuric waters. This famous Red Spring received the puritan accolade from Increase Mather who frequented it regularly from the earliest days of his ministry. Young Cotton accompanied him thither for a fortnight's sojourn in August, 1683, where relief from the heat of Boston and "happy Hours in the countrey" appealed to New World town-dwellers quite as did Bath, Tunbridge Wells and other "spaws" to Samuel Pepys and John Evelyn. [48]

Social life at Newport exhibited even more of a rural character. From 1640 to 1690 village men amused themselves with bowling on the green, ranging the island in search of wild fowl, or fishing in the bay. As at Boston the gentry devoted much of its leisure to the church, though in general with a more understanding attitude for the weaknesses of the common man. "Cards, dice or any other unlaw-

[47] *Recs. Court of Assistants,* I, 197; 5 MHS *Colls.,* V, 103, 112, 121; 2 MHS *Colls.,* XIII, 411; 3 MHS *Colls.,* VII, 157.
[48] Lennard, *Englishmen at Rest and Play,* 18, 39, 46, 73; Lewis and Newhall, *Lynn,* I, 71, 279; Marvin, *Cotton Mather,* 40; 7 MHS *Colls.,* VII, 69.

full game," along with philandering, were strictly denied apprentices and laborers, but at a meeting called in 1654 to discuss abuses of the Sabbath the townsmen debated "what dayes they shall agree uppon for theire men servants and maid servants to recreate themselves, to prevent ye incivilities which are amongst us exercised on that day." With somewhat greater wisdom than their stricter neighbors to the north Newporters early recognized the necessity and value of a "maid's day out." Probably the chief social delight of Newport throughout this period was the gossip freely dispensed at the miller's, the cobbler's, or the village tavern.[49]

The first decade of settlement at Charles Town and Philadelphia was, perforce, devoted to building the villages, and left little time for recreation or entertainment. In the latter town Front Street aristocrats divided their time between Friends' Meetings and great dinners, while the "inferior sort" had to content themselves with a few days' amusement during the yearly fairs held at the Center, gatherings usually characterized by "riots, gambling, [foot] races, and drunkenness." For the remainder of the year an occasional hour stolen from work and spent at a tavern had to suffice. Christmas mumming was frowned upon by the Meeting: in fact, any custom not specifically condoned by the Society of Friends was narrowly regarded as a vice and promptly suppressed.[50]

The Dutch at New Amsterdam did not take life quite so seriously as did the English colonists, and though they, too, had to labor hard for a living they apparently found ample time for amusement and recreation. Near the village was Collect Pond with a little island in its center which by 1631 had become the usual scene for open-air outings of fishing parties and "unprofitable fowlers." Within the Wall the sports and games of the Fatherland soon appeared, especially bowls and dancing. "The women of the neighborhood entertain each other with a pipe and brazier," wrote Nicholas de Sille in 1654. "Young and old, they all smoke."[51] Tobacco and gossip were certainly the least expensive and probably the most generally enjoyed amusements the village afforded.

To Dutch burghers there was nothing sinful about holidays, and they were thoroughly enjoyed at New Amsterdam. The Bacchanalian revelries of country people who thronged the little village at Shrovetide generally ended with the barbarous sport of riding the goose. By 1658 the Director had been forced to put a stop to this cruel

---

[49] *Journal of William Jefferay,* 38, 61; *Newport T. M. Recs.,* 51; *R. I. Col. Recs.,* I, 280.

[50] Myers, *Irish Quakers,* 223; Scharf and Westcott, *History of Philadelphia,* I, 151.

[51] Van Rennselaer, *New York,* I, 75; *Recs. N. Am.,* I, 51; III, 217; IV, 264; *Quarterly Journal N. Y. State Hist. Assn.,* I, 101.

game. New Year's and May Day were celebrated with great drunkenness, frequent accidents, and a waste of precious gunpowder. Accordingly, in 1655 the authorities had to forbid the firing of guns, erection of may-poles and treating with liquor on these fêtes. Christmas was a more sober holiday, its revels being held indoors.[52]

More sophisticated amusements offered themselves to the aristocrats. Boat racing was popular, and an old Dutch game, a sort of midget golf, played with a crooked club, small ball and holes in the turf, was in vogue at Manhattan after 1652. Governor Nicolls appointed annual horse race meetings to be run off at Hempstead on Long Island in 1668, and the custom was encouraged by Governor Lovelace, "not so much for the divertisement of youth alone," as for "bettering the breed of horses." At the Newmarket Course, during the Long Island militia muster, races for a silver trophy were run each May. The Reverend Mr. Charles Wooley found that "the diversion especially . . . used by the Dutch is aurigation, i.e. riding about in Waggons [and sleighs?] which is allowed by Physicians to be very healthful exercise by Land. And upon the Ice its admirable to see Men and Women as it were flying upon their Skates from place to place." Under English rule dancing was somewhat frowned upon, and when Francis Stepney, erstwhile dancing theologian of Boston, appeared in New York in January, 1687, the Governor's Council sent him on further travels. But, as early as 1675, Thomas Smith was licensed by the Governor to teach "the use and exercise of arms" at Manhattan.[53]

Such were the rather simple diversions of seventeenth century villagers. Before 1690 these little communities were so much occupied with business that any elaborate amusements were entirely unknown. The demand for labor was so great that in several villages idleness was regarded as unsocial, and so an economic need was dignified as a moral law. At Boston, as the struggling village developed into a flourishing town, leisure with its accompanying recreation began to appear, and people increasingly sought new forms of diversion. The Dutch of New Amsterdam from the beginning gave amusement a large place in their scheme of life, and their clergy proved powerless to restrict its exercise. The smallness of Newport throughout this period led inhabitants to be satisfied with more bucolic forms of enjoyment, yet they recognized recreation as a part of life necessary to a balanced existence. The other two settlements had barely passed the pioneer stage by 1690. Sophisticated diversions like the theater,

[52] Stokes, *Iconography*, IV, 146; *Laws of New Netherland*, 205; *N. Y. M. C. C.*, I, 7.

[53] Van Rensselaer, *New York*, I, 462; *Recs. N. Am.*, V, 290; Stokes, *Iconography*, IV, 271, 308, 316; *Calendar Council Minutes*, 52.

concerts and assemblies, requiring the patronage of a moneyed leisure class, do not appear in the colonial villages in this period, but at New York or Boston it would have been possible at this time to lead as pleasant and varied a life as in the provincial towns of England.[54]

VII

Colonial town-dwellers had behind them nearly a century of educational upheaval and reform. In that time the schools of England had undergone a general secularization, and education was becoming the particular desire of the Protestant urban middle class, the key to godly life and worldly success, the means of increasing one's estate and enhancing one's prestige. The interest of tradesmen in education had manifested itself in experiments from the Mercers' famous school at St. Paul's to Gresham College. The colonists, then, brought with them a typical burgher view of the importance of schools and a modern belief in popularized and utilitarian learning. These they set about realizing in the New World, incompletely at first, to be sure, but with the result that by 1690 in all villages save Charles Town there was some form of schooling available to village youth.

That Boston possessed the best educational facilities in the colonies may be attributed to the great interest in the subject constantly evinced by the body of its citizenry. In August, 1636, forty-five of the "richer inhabitants" raised a sum of about £40 for the support of Daniel Maud as master of a free school. This, it will be observed, was a school set up by voluntary subscription, not a town supported institution. In January, 1642, the town voted to improve Deer Island for the "maintenance of a free schoole," but not until December, 1644, was the island rented for three years at £7 per annum. About the same time the Selectmen paid Mr. John Woodbridge £8 for services as schoolmaster the preceding year. It is evident, then, that by 1643 the town of Boston had made a land grant to insure a permanent income for public education, and had assumed responsibility for the support of the school known today as the Boston Latin School. A schoolhouse and dwelling for the master were provided in 1652, and three years later a new school building was erected by the town.[55]

One of the principal purposes of the Boston free school had been the training of village youths for entrance into Harvard College. By 1678 augmented population brought a demand for additional estab-

[54] Citizens of Bristol suppressed their theater in 1688. Church-going for those of religious bent, suburban revels, cock fights, and tavern drinking were about all that England's second city offered for diversion at this time. Latimer, *Annals of Bristol in the Seventeenth Century;* Ogg, *England in the Reign of Charles II,* II, 105.

[55] 2 *Bos. Rec. Com.,* 5, 17, 27, 65, 82, 109, 129, 139, 160.

lishments devoted to less lofty objectives, and in 1684 and 1686 the town provided two free schools "for the teaching of Children to write & Cypher." At the close of the period Boston was spending nearly £200 annually upon its three schools, — half the "standing charge" of the town.[56]

Private schools made their appearance in the village after 1660. The Selectmen closed one in 1666 because the master was not an inhabitant, but the next year freely gave "liberty" to Mr. Will Howard to keep a writing school to teach children "to writte and keep accounts." Boston had at least eight private schools before 1690. John Sanford, "a pious Skillfull and prudent Man," opened his establishment to girls, and Hannah Hull attended his classes. Frequently daughters of more wealthy families boarded at their schools, as was the case of Mary Brattle, who had "a hundred pounds bestowed upon [her] . . . at a boardinge Scoole: to learn manner[s] & breeding." [57]

Instruction in the home or at the transplanted English dame schools, where the rudiments of spelling and reading were taught, served in a small way to prepare children for the grammar school. In 1687 the little daughters of Samuel Sewall were attending a school kept by Dame Walker. About the same time John Barnard, aged six, attended a "reading school at Boston," which had sufficient pupils for him to serve as a sort of usher "to teach some children that were older than . . . [himself] as well as some smaller ones." [58]

A long line of excellent masters at the Latin School, most able of whom were Ezekiel Cheever and Benjamin Thompson, assured the town admirable instruction for its children. Yet education in Boston, as elsewhere in the seventeenth century, was largely the monopoly of boys. Save for the rudiments of knowledge gained at dame school, or further study at a private school for the daughters of aristocrats, girls had little opportunity for education; decidedly, woman's place was in the home. Boston schools were the best in New England, and under the school law of 1647 provided excellent training for the town's youth, the results of which may be seen in the considerable increase in the literate population toward 1690. In addition, recognition by successful merchants of the value of education induced men like Robert Keayne and John Coggan to contribute to the support of Harvard College, whither Ezekiel Cheever increasingly sent students from the Latin School.[59]

[56] 7 *Bos. Rec. Com.*, 127, 158, 161, 171, 187.
[57] 7 *Bos. Rec. Com.*, 32, 36; Seybolt, *Private Schools*, 3–5; *Providence Town Records*, XVII, 53; 6 MHS *Colls.*, II, 135.
[58] 5 MHS *Colls.*, V, 164; Seybolt, *Private Schools*, 9.
[59] Morison, *Puritan Pronaos*, chapters III, IV; Earle, *Child Life*, 97; Kilpatrick, *Dutch Schools*, 229 n. (on literacy); Morison, *Harvard College in the Seventeenth Century*, I, 38, 101; II, 449.

Within a year of their arrival the founders of Newport were making provision for the education of their children. The impulse undoubtedly came from William Coddington, John Coggeshall and William Brenton, who had been among the principal contributors to the fund for hiring a schoolmaster at Boston in 1636. In August, 1640, the Town Meeting "laid forth" a hundred acres of land for a school for the "encouragement of the poorer sort to train up their youth in learning," the first large tract to be set apart anywhere in the colonies as a permanent endowment for education. The Reverend Robert Lenthall, B. A. Oxon., formerly of Weymouth, was called to keep this "public school." After his departure for England two years later, there is no further record of it until 1663, when the town ordered the school lands divided into lots for sale or lease, and the proceeds placed in a fund controlled by the Town Council for the education of poor children.[60] In 1665 Robert Williams, brother to Roger, was schoolmaster at Newport. By 1683 a schoolhouse had been built and the town was displaying great interest in the matter of the master's salary. The next year Christopher Lodowick requested from the Friends' Meeting the use of their Newport meeting house for a school; the Quakers consented, being "willing to give him what encouragement they can." This appears to have been a private school, and as such it continued until January, 1686, when Lodowick's petition to the town for aid in his work resulted in his being awarded the income from the town lands and the position of public schoolmaster, which had probably been vacant since 1684.[61] The mutilated town records of Newport yield unmistakable evidence of widespread interest in public education from the days of its founding, and of the existence by 1690 of a schoolmaster teaching in the village schoolhouse and in the town's pay.

Obviously, so far as Newport is concerned, there is little ground for the oft-repeated indictment of Rhode Island education in general.

In the two New England villages education came largely under civic control; at New Amsterdam and Philadelphia it was regarded as the joint concern of church and state. The Society of Friends, while indifferent to higher education, was notably active in furthering elementary schools. Thus in 1683 the Provincial Council appointed Enoch Flower, a teacher of twenty years' experience in England, to board and instruct the children of Philadelphia in reading, writing

---

[60] Callender, *Historical Discourse*, 116; R. I. Hist. Soc. *Procs.* (1873), 78; *Newport Mercury*, Dec. 4, 1875. Town records for this period are lost; the school may well have continued under another master.

[61] *Newport T. M. Recs.*, 40, 43, 45; Savage, *Genealogical Dictionary*, 567; Klain, *Educational Acts of New England Quakers*, 7; *Newport Mercury*, Dec. 4, 1875.

and casting accounts. In 1689 the Monthly Meeting established another elementary school under the mastership of Thomas Makin.[62]

As early as 1683 Penn and his Council had considered the need for a "scool of Arts and Sciences." As a result of widespread interest in the undertaking the Philadelphia Monthly Meeting of the Friends on June 26, 1689, established a public grammar school which should meet the demands of both rich and poor in the village, and for which they provided liberally. They sought out an excellent master, George Keith, whom they hired at £50 a year, giving him a house and the privilege of taking tuition fees upon condition that he teach the children of the poor for nothing. The Friends' School grew so rapidly that in January, 1690, Master Keith complained of the "inconvenience and straightnesse" of the building, with the result that within a month a larger one was procured, and Thomas Makin hired as an usher.[63]

From the beginning Philadelphia schools reflected current interest in educational reform. The first elementary school, particularly, was conducted according to latest European theories, and its reputation was such that Robert Webb could write of it: "Among other things great care is taken for the education of the young, and to this end a large school is erected, to which the children of several English colonies are sent, especial from Barbados. One [Enoch Flower] endeavors to use good methods for the best instruction, wherein the method of [Johannes Andreas] Comenius be freely employed." Under able masters like Flower, Keith and Makin the schools of Philadelphia enjoyed in 1689 instruction equaling, if not surpassing, that given in any other village.[64]

At New Amsterdam, as in Philadelphia, education was largely under the control of the church, a fact which explains much of the village's later educational history. In 1638 Adam Roelantsen, appointed by the Amsterdam Chamber of the Company in response to requests from Director Van Twiller and Dominie Bogardus, became master of the first elementary school in any colonial town. Unfortunately Master Roelantsen proved to be of "immoral character" and had to be replaced by Jan Stevensen in 1642. This "official" school maintained a continuous existence throughout the period of Dutch rule at Manhattan.[65]

Successive masters of the New Amsterdam school taught their pupils in their own dwellings. In 1647 Stuyvesant asked the Nine Men

[62] *Pa. Col. Recs.*, I, 91; Jackson, *Cyclopedia of Philadelphia*, III, 704; Mulhern, *Secondary Education in Pennsylvania*, 28.
[63] *Pa. Col. Recs.*, I, 93; Woody, *Quaker Education*, 45, 46.
[64] Woody, *Quaker Education*, 26–40; *Pa. Mag.*, XLIX, 121. For Comenius, see Smith, *Modern Culture*, I, 348.
[65] Kilpatrick, *Dutch Schools*, 49, 51–70, 93; *N. Y. Eccles. Recs.*, I, 91, 122.

to provide a schoolhouse, and an effort was made to collect funds. But the next year the burghers, in petitioning for better school facilities, observed that "the bowl has been going round a long time for the purpose of erecting a common school and it has been built with words, but as yet the first stone is not laid. . . . As it is now the school is kept very irregularly." [66] Yet even this eloquent plea failed to produce action, and no building was available for the school in the seventeenth century.

A Latin school was opened by Jan de la Montagne in 1652, but lasted only two years. In 1658 the burghers petitioned for its revival on the grounds that the many children who could now read and write needed more advanced instruction, that the nearest grammar school was two hundred and fifty miles away at Boston, and that if New Amsterdam could have a similar institution it might "finally attain an academy" and become a "place of great splendor." Consequently the Company provided in 1659 for a Latin school, conducted by Dominie Curtius, "late professor in Lithuania," and supported by both Company and burgher government. Curtius charged his seventeen pupils eight guilders a quarter, "when six was considered enough"; furthermore, citizens complained "that he does not keep strict discipline over the boys, . . . who fight among themselves and tear the clothes from each other's bodies." His successor, Aegidius Luyck, averaged about twenty students, some of whom came from places as distant as the Delaware regions and Virginia. This school seems to have lasted until the capture of the village by the English in 1664.[67]

Transition to English rule in New York greatly disturbed the educational system. The elementary school continued throughout the period, but ceased after 1664 to be a public institution. It gradually became a parochial school, supported by the Dutch Reformed Church, in which the principal studies were the Dutch tongue and the Reformed religion. There thus existed no school for children of English speaking inhabitants. The Latin school apparently did not survive. In 1676 Ebeneezer Kirtland petitioned the Mayor and Common Council to allow him to conduct a school for "Readinge Writinge Arithmetick Lattin or Greek," but Matthew Hiller, who had been teaching since 1674, asked the authorities to retain him, "notwithstanding Some Complaintes have been made (unmerited)." Hiller was continued, but deprived of his salary of £12 and allowed only a room to teach in. In 1684 a Latin school was opened by a learned Jesuit, but according to Jacob Leisler it was not a success and "the collidge vanished." The

---

[66] *Narratives of New Netherland*, 327.
[67] Kilpatrick, *Dutch Schools*, 95, 99, 105, 109; *Recs. N. Am.*, VII, 257; Stokes. *Iconography*, IV, 210.

following year the Corporation bought the time of David Jamison, a Quaker redemptioner, when it learned of his college education, and set him up as master of a Latin school.[68]

Several private schools existed in New Amsterdam as early as 1649. In fact, even during the Dutch period there seems to have been more private than public instruction. Private teachers had to secure permission from the Director before they could open a school. Probably a majority of the white population could read and write in 1664, and a study of marks and signatures to public papers reveals the fact that literacy was higher in New Amsterdam than in surrounding rural localities. It is also clear that, as in Holland, a larger number of women received education than in the other villages.[69] The importance of private schooling increased as the period advanced, for it was the only source of education for children of non-Dutch parentage. No public school served the English and other nationalities resident in New York after its surrender in 1664.

There is no evidence of the existence of any facilities for public education at Charles Town during its first decade. The northern towns, however, had all gone about providing the framework for an educational system to answer burgher needs and ideals. That both need and ideal were present may be seen in the rapidity with which these village communities became the educational capitals of their provinces. Philadelphia and Boston schools already drew students from a wide radius, not only from the surrounding countryside, but from other English colonies, continental and island, which lacked such urban centers. The same was true of New York so long as any general educational facilities existed there. Also, it may be said of the villages, that the demand for education outran the means for its fulfillment, a challenge that promised well for town schools of the future.

Supplementing the schools, the imported system of apprenticeship constituted an important agency for elementary education in the colonial villages. The English Statute of Artificers and the Poor Law of 1601 furnished the basis of this system. In 1642, because of "the great neglect in many parents and masters," the General Court of Massachusetts passed a law requiring them to train their children "in labor and learning and other employments." By this act towns could apprentice the children of "such as shall not be able and fit to employ and bring them up," and parents and masters were particularly enjoined to provide for the "imployment of their children, especially their ability

[68] Kilpatrick, *Dutch Schools*, 142, 146; *Recs. N. Am.*, V, 137; *N. Y. M. C. C.*, I, 22; Wilson, *Memorial History of New York*, I, 419; *N. Y. Eccles. Recs.*, II, 893.

[69] Mrs. Van Rennselaer says twenty-eight masters and tutors were licensed by 1664. *New York*, I, 442; Kilpatrick, *Dutch Schools*, 117; Flick, *History of the State of New York*. II, 23.

to read." In 1648 an additional act made more definite provisions for compulsory book learning and religious instruction in all indentures of apprenticeship. Twenty years later an enforcing act had to be passed to prevent neglect of these laws. Despite slight evidence, it is probable that within the village of Boston these laws were fairly well observed. In 1677 Peter Goulding sued James Russel in the Suffolk County Court for not teaching his daughter Mary, or having her taught "as Shee should have been by virtue of the . . . Jndenture." [70]

Rhode Island in 1662 adopted the apprentice provisions of the Poor Law of 1601 and empowered towns to "put out to service" all children likely to become a public charge. Although the law specified no sort of instruction other than for a trade, educational clauses frequently appeared in the indentures. William Walton, apprenticed by the town of Newport to John Odlin, blacksmith, in 1690, was to be instructed in the smith's craft and also "in ye reading of English according as hee is capable for to learne." The English at New York adopted the Massachusetts apprentice laws in 1665, although there was no provision guaranteeing the education of apprentices. At his death in 1679 an inhabitant of New York ordered in his will that his "children are to be caused to learn to read & write, and a trade," and by the terms of another will a girl was to be taught "reading and writing, and a trade." In a Harlem indenture of 1690 the master agreed that his apprentice "shall have the privilege of going to the evening school" at New York. The apprentice system thus served the double purpose of providing much needed practical training of the youth in arts and crafts, and of supplying rudiments of reading and sometimes writing to a great majority of village children. [71]

VIII

It has become a commonplace that the battle for a living so absorbed the time and energies of the colonists that they had little left to devote to cultural pursuits. Yet among the first settlers there were men of learning and scholarly interests, and in the last two decades of the period under review there can be found as well signs of an intellectual awakening in the new land. The villages naturally assumed the lead in this movement, for only there was it possible to experience that "constant friction of mind with mind" which is the essence of culture. There existed the curiosity and mental activity bred of social and

[70] *Mass. Col. Recs.*, II, 6; Jernegan, *Laboring and Dependent Classes*, 89–93; *Recs. Suffolk County Court*, 155, 792.

[71] *R. I. Acts (1719)*, 10; *Newport T. M. Recs.*, 51; *Col. Laws N. Y.*, I, 26; N. Y. Hist. Soc. *Colls.*, I, 121, 143, 236; II, 441; Seybolt, *Apprenticeship and Apprenticeship Education*, 94.

competitive living; there first appeared the wealth and leisure necessary to intellectual advance; there, too, the first colonial contacts with new ideas from Europe could be had.

Boston from its earliest beginnings enjoyed the leadership of men of ability and culture. It had a remarkable proportion of learned men, — Winthrop, Cotton, Mather and others, — men trained in European universities, widely read, and accustomed to express themselves in literary form. These accomplishments, with the earnestness that made them fanatics and saints, they constrained to the service of a narrow religious creed and throttled by a rigidly self-imposed censorship of the press. Yet though they thus deliberately cut themselves off from a wide range of literary activity and human experience, they possessed a great reverence for learning and a desire to cherish and perpetuate it. Harvard College, across the Charles, early attained its importance in Boston life as the seminary to train its young men for the ministry or for secular professions. At first Boston probably fared no better in respect to intellectual leadership than did other villages on the Bay, for the township system of settlement that prevailed in New England placed in each Massachusetts community a learned minister well able to serve as a nucleus for its intellectual life. Thus much of the literary output of seventeenth century New England was the work of men not residents of Boston. But as the century marched on, many of the best minds of the colony were drawn to the metropolis, so that the Bay town, as the largest community of a region characterized by love of learning and respect for scholarship, far surpassed other villages of the Atlantic seaboard in intellectual attainments, — an accomplishment of which its citizens were from the first supremely conscious.[72]

Typical and best of this first generation of Boston culture was John Winthrop, the elder. Aware of his high purpose and of the importance of the movement of which he was a part, he began as soon as he had set sail from England to set down in diary form the history of that movement. Pressure of affairs in the New World prevented a full artistic development of that chronicle, but the character and ability of the man reveal themselves in its hurried pages. The careful recording of his speech of self-justification to the General Court in 1645, wherein is contained the famous passage on natural and civil liberty, shows his capacity for nobility and clarity of thought and eloquence and power of expression. The diary habit he inaugurated remained strong in the New England town throughout the period, and

[72] For English backgrounds, see Wright, *Middle Class Culture in Elizabethan England,* and for New England in general, Tyler, *American Literature,* and Morison, *Puritan Pronaos.*

laymen like Judge Sewall, as well as clerics like the Mathers, were accustomed to take time from busy professional lives to set down on paper their activities or meditations.[73]

Throughout the period, 1630 to 1690, able ministers served the town: "for once in the history of the world, the sovereign places were filled by the sovereign men." First as graduates of Cambridge, later of Harvard, the Boston clergy imparted a serious and strongly religious tone to the entire culture of the village. But their learning was not devoted exclusively to theology. John Wilson wrote creditable English and Latin verse; John Cotton gave the colony *Moses: His Judicials,* and rules for the carrying on of business, while for its youth he wrote his famous *Spiritual Milk for Boston Babes.* Increase Mather deluged the press with writings on many subjects, not the least of which were those evincing an enlightened interest in the progress of science. In the spring of 1683 Mather, Samuel Willard and others "promoted a design for a private philosophical society." For at least a decade the members met bi-weekly for a "conference upon improvements in philosophy and additions to the stores of natural history." Among their number were probably men like John Foster, printer and student of comets, Doctors Benjamin Bullivant and William Avery, Hezekiah Usher, who corresponded frequently with the Royal Society of London, and Edward Tyng, known to be an admirer of Robert Boyle. It was the Boston clergy who made contact with contemporary scientific and intellectual developments in Europe, passing them on to friends and parishioners and to the colony at large.[74]

Books have always been associated with Boston. Many of the early settlers, university men and others, brought with them good libraries to which they were "constantly" adding new volumes. Notable among such Bostonians were John Winthrop and Edward Tyng. As early as 1637 one Saunders opened a "Bookebynder" shop in the village, and in 1647 Hezekiah Usher began importing books to sell. That there was an excellent market for books in the town is proved by the fact that from 1669 to 1690 twenty booksellers conducted shops in Boston, most of them clustered about the Town House. These shopkeepers not only served the town itself, but distributed books throughout the New England colonies. Sometimes they ordered large quantities of stock from London for their inland customers, as Samuel Sewall did for people in Newbury, but more frequently, perhaps, like Cotton Mather, they employed "an Old Hawker" to "fill the Country with . . .

---

[73] Though not published until recent times, the *Journal* of Winthrop and the diaries of Sewall and Cotton Mather are products of this period and necessary for a consideration of its intellectual temper and habits.

[74] Murdock, *Handkerchiefs from Paul; Harvard Graduates' Mag.,* XLII, 41; Morison, *Puritan Pronaos,* 247; Royal Society of London (MS).

Books." One of John Usher's invoices for 1685 supplies an idea of the literary diet of Boston Puritans. Of 874 titles there were 391 schoolbooks, 311 works on religious subjects, 55 Bibles, Testaments, etc., 50 books on navigation, 36 on law, while the remaining 21 were distributed about equally among medicine, history, military science and romance.[75] As in most of western Europe at this time, the interests of people in this New World community were in religion, education and practical matters.

While most books sold in shops near the Town House came from London, a fair number issued from the presses of Boston and Cambridge. The first printing press in the American colonies was set up in Cambridge in 1638, and for many years it enjoyed exclusively the "liberty" of printing. The growth of Boston as a commercial center with a need for printing establishments led townsfolk to regard the Cambridge monopoly as a serious grievance. In 1668 the General Court rejected a petition for a press at Boston, but sufficient pressure was applied to break the monopoly in 1674. In that year John Foster became proprietor of the first Boston press, which produced before 1690 editions of such works as *Pilgrim's Progress,* Mrs. Rowlandson's *Narrative,* and Anne Bradstreet's poems. Other printers soon appeared, and sermons, pamphlets and almanacs began to issue in large quantities from their presses. Between 1682 and 1684 over a hundred and thirty books and brochures were printed at Boston, the majority of a religious character.[76]

Throughout this period the press remained under the rigid surveillance of censors who approved all work before publication, and it was on this score that the first colonial attempt at a newspaper ran afoul of authorities. English gazettes were eagerly read by Bostonians as soon as they arrived by ship, but these contained no local news. Enterprising Benjamin Harris, a bookseller recently come from London, conceived the idea of a monthly newspaper for Boston, and induced Richard Pierce to undertake the printing. The initial issue of *Publick Occurrences, Both Foreign and Domestick* appeared on September 25, 1690. It was designed to counteract false reports and to do "something toward the curing, or at least the charming, of the spirit of lying." To the authorities, however, it gave "much distaste because

---

[75] But in Boston shops one might procure *Paradise Lost,* Sidney's *Arcadia,* More's *Utopia,* Hakluyt's *Voiages,* and even Rochester's salacious *Poems on Several Occasions.* Wright, *Literary Culture,* 30, 37, 61; 2 *Bos. Rec. Com.,* 19; Littlefield, *Early Boston Booksellers,* 65, 71, 79; Ford, *Boston Book Market,* 44, 81–140; 6 MHS *Colls.,* I, 88; 7 MHS *Colls.,* VII, 65; Morison, *Puritan Pronaos,* 126.
[76] Duniway, *Freedom of the Press,* 22, 50, 56; Wright, *Literary Culture,* 161. Almanacs enjoyed a wide audience in the country, and as early as 1659 a Boston almanac was prepared according to the views of Copernicus, Galileo and Kepler. Morison, in *N. E. Quarterly,* VII, 8–9, 14; *Puritan Pronaos,* 121.

not Licensed," and was suppressed before another issue could be published.[77] Consequently the latest news continued to be circulated by hand in "newsletters," or by word of mouth as in the past, and Boston had to wait fourteen years more for a regular newspaper.

Only the wealthy could afford the purchase of books; the poor had either to borrow of their friends or do without. In 1656 at his death Captain Robert Keayne expiated his sins of profiteering by leaving funds to build a town hall, and his will provided that one of the rooms therein be fitted up as a library for the use of townsfolk. It is impossible to determine just when this library was started, but it was clearly in existence in 1674, when John Oxenbridge bequeathed his books to "the Public Library in Boston." Sometime later Richard Chiswell of London wrote to Increase Mather: "I have sent a few books to Mr. Vsher without orders. . . . You may see them at his shop, & I hope may help some of them off his hands by recommending them to your publick Library, especially the new ones." [78]

Like Boston, Philadelphia in its early years escaped the intellectual poverty so common to pioneer societies. But in contrast to the Puritan center with its learned clerical group, educated men were here either physicians or men of affairs, and their interest in literary and scientific pursuits was not so tinged with theology. From the first the culture of Penn's city was primarily secular. William Penn, Francis Daniel Pastorius, George Keith, Thomas Makin, Thomas Lloyd and Dr. Griffith Owen formed a group, mostly university trained, whose classical learning was unsurpassed in the colonies. There is no need to catalogue the acomplishments of William Penn, but for sheer force of intellect coupled with sympathetic insight into human nature Pastorius, perhaps the most learned man who ever came to live in America, highly deserves attention. Classicist, philosopher and teacher, his remarkable versatility made of him also the leading poet of seventeenth century America. Yet, if Pastorius represented the best of colonial poetry, the work of Richard Frame, another denizen of early Philadelphia, was incomparably the worst. His *Short Description of Pennsilvania* (1687) was an ill-advised attempt to write real estate "literature" in verse. Judge Thomas Holme's *A True Relation of the Flourishing State of Pennsylvania* (1689) was very nearly as bad; the sole redeeming quality of these paeans was their enthusiasm. Immigrant literature occupies an

[77] Duniway, *Freedom of the Press,* 41–69; 6 MHS *Colls.,* I, 38, 67; 5 MHS *Colls.,* V, 332.
[78] Vague traces of portrait painting at Boston have been found, but are unimportant in this period. Legislative references to unseasonable use of musical instruments indicate a rather general practice of music among Boston Puritans, but of this nothing definite may be said. *N. E. Hist. & Gen. Reg.,* VI, 90; Col. Soc. Mass. *Trans.,* XII, 20; 4 MHS *Colls.,* VIII, 576; 7 *Bos. Rec. Com.,* 162; Morgan, *Early American Painters,* 13; Dow, *Everyday Life,* 64.

important place in the history of colonial letters, and to it Philadelphians made substantial contributions in the first decade of settlement. Many Quakers wrote home describing the growth of their town and the charm of the Pennsylvania countryside, and these glowing accounts make far more pleasant reading today than all the countless sermons of learned Boston divines.[79]

Printing began in the Quaker village in 1685, when William Bradford issued an almanac, *Kalendarium Pennsilvaniense*. In his preface to the reader Bradford announced his intention of introducing "that great Art and Mystery of Printing into this Part of America," and hoped for public support in his enterprise. In this he was not disappointed, for between 1685 and 1690 he issued at least twenty-two almanacs, pamphlets and controversial tracts, a good half of which were of a distinctly secular nature. The most interesting of Bradford's imprints was *The Temple of Wisdom for the Little World*, compiled in 1688 by Daniel Leeds of almanac fame. This volume contained a large chunk of the religious writings of the German mystic, Jacob Boehme, George Wither's satire, *Abuses Stript and Whipt*, a few poems from Francis Quarles, and "Lastly. Essayes and Religious Meditations of Sir Francis Bacon Knight." Here was varied intellectual fodder, to say the least.[80]

Ravages of time and war have deprived us of more than a glimpse of the intellectual life of early Newport. This is indeed a misfortune, for the cultural achievement of the eighteenth century was so rich that we would do well to know its antecedents. There were several well educated men in the Narragansett village. Dr. John Clarke, "both learned and wise," was a friend of John Milton and the Earl of Clarendon. He and his associates possessed "books of value," and their interest in education has already been noted. But here our knowledge stops, and we can only hazard the belief, that, just as it has been demonstrated false that Newport was inhabited only by the "rabble," so also it is erroneous to brand it an intellectual desert. Its eighteenth century culture did not rest on a vacuum.[81]

As the Dutch West India Company's post at Manhattan was primarily a trading enterprise one would not expect to find there evidences of a highly cultured life. Nevertheless, signs of the contemporary intellectual and artistic ferment of the Netherlands existed also at New

[79] *Pa. Mag.*, LVI, 69–79; XVII, 1; Learned, *Pastorius*, 190; *Narratives of Pennsylvania*, 300–304.

[80] Hildeburn (*Issues of the Pennsylvania Press*, I, 1–17) lists twenty-five titles printed by Bradford, eleven on religious subjects, a like number on secular topics, and two containing a smattering of each.

[81] Wright, *Literary Culture*, 70 n.; *Journal of William Jefferay*, 27, 31; R. I. Hist. Soc. *Colls.*, XVI, 41; R. I. Hist. Soc. *Pubs.*, VI, 104; Updyke, *Narragansett Church*, I, 61.

Amsterdam. Portraits painted in Holland often hung on the walls of Dutch homes, and some genre painting was attempted at Manhattan. Jacobus Gerritsen Strycker, well-versed in the early and middle styles of Rembrandt, executed some good portraits, but the decadent work of Henri Couturier and the low level of Gerret Duycinck's accomplishment left much to be desired. An inventory of 1643 of the possessions of Jonas Bronck, an ordinary burgher, reveals his ownership of eleven pictures, "big and little," twenty books in Dutch, Danish and German, eighteen "old printed pamphlets," and "seventeen manuscript books which are old." Such polyglot libraries were not unusual among the burghers, but their collections never rivalled those of the Bostonians. The Dutch were, however, more musical than their northern neighbors, and many spinets and virginals were in use at the time of the English conquest. New Amsterdam also produced three poetasters whose effusions equal those of the Puritans at the Bay village. Nicasius de Sille essayed both poetry and prose, and Dominie Selyns could easily have claimed the seventeenth century colonial record for sheer bulk, with his two hundred odd Latin and Greek epitaphs, epithalamiums and other occasional verses. His *chef d'oeuvre* was a long narrative poem on the Esopus Wars. By far the best of the Manhattan school was Jacob Steendam, whose *Klaght van Nieu Amsterdam* (1659) and *'T Lof van Nieu Nederland* (1661), based on native themes, possess some real merit and deserve to be better known.[82]

The coming of the English dealt a death blow to this nascent Dutch culture, although it lingered on beneath the surface for many years. The conflict of cultures characterized, while greatly retarding, intellectual development at Manhattan in the latter half of the century. The unique cultural achievement of New Yorkers was their linguistic ability. In 1670 the three daughters of Anthony de Milt demonstrated such prowess as Latin scholars as to put to shame the Holland-trained clergy. In keeping with the heterogeneous character of the village population most of the upper classes, women as well as men, conversed equally well in Dutch, English or French, — and they always followed French fashions. Through efforts of Governor Lovelace a "Club" was made up of six English and ten Dutch and French families in 1668. Meetings were held at the homes of members twice a week in winter and once in summer from six to nine o'clock in the evening. The Governor was a frequent guest at these entertainments, which consisted of food, wines, and conversation in three languages.[83]

Clearly, by 1690, there were favorable portents of a vigorous in-

[82] Weigle, *Pageant of American Art*, 6; Morgan, *Early American Painters*, 15-17; Van Rensselaer, *New York*, I, 186; *Recs. N. Am.*, IV, 46; V, 90; Wilson, *Memorial History of New York*, IV, 165; Murphy, *Anthology of New Netherland*.
[83] Wilson, *Memorial History of New York*, I, 349.

tellectual life at Boston and Philadelphia. Boston was the second largest printing and bookselling center of the British Empire.[84] In its first decade Philadelphia gave ample indications of a promising future, and nothing is further from the truth than the charge that Quaker domination in the village proved a stultifying influence in these early years. In all of the towns cultivated minds could experience communion with their kind, and the interchange of ideas necessary to any intellectual activity. Each village had its intellectual leaders, nor were they drawn away, as from English provincial towns, by the physical nearness of the metropolis. Throughout the period the villages served as both intellectual and commercial capitals of their provinces. In fact, the two went hand in hand, and these little seaports, with their direct connections with Europe, functioned as the necessary distributing points for the spiritual and intellectual as well as the commercial products of the Old World.[85]

Because American villages escaped the terrific political and social upheaval of seventeenth century England they did not share in the quickening of intellectual activity which these events brought to the Mother Country. We find in the villages no great power and originality in the political and philosophic thought, no vigorous development in the prose, no elevated inspiration in the poetry. Yet this is not to say that culture in the colonial towns either stood still or declined during this period. It was derivative, as colonial cultures usually are, but it followed developments of the age, and adopted more readily than we are prone to suppose new ideas in science and learning that were agitating the western world. Probably people in these emerging towns lived an intellectual existence less removed from contact with London than were provincial cities like Norwich, Bristol, Exeter or Gloucester. They were also by 1690, save in the case of Charles Town, already removed from the frontier, toward which their relation was more like that of London to the provinces. Their outlook was more eastward than westward. They were not shut in upon themselves or isolated from world currents. Intellectually as well as physically life in the villages was moving ahead. Colonial culture was still adolescent, still taking and not giving, still absorbing what the Old World had to offer, not contributing anything of its own. But the village intellect, embryonic as it was in 1690, constituted another of the forces at work for the producing of an urban society.

[84] As late as 1667 Bristol had only three or four booksellers, whose chief trade was in stationery. Printing was introduced at Glasgow only in 1639 (the same year as Cambridge), at Exeter in 1668. No newspaper was published outside of London before 1690. Latimer, *Bristol in the Seventeenth Century*, 72, 342; Wright, *Literary Culture*, 80.

[85] Virtually no evidence is available for a cultural study of early Charles Town; what intellectual leaders Carolina possessed probably resided there.

IX

Village society in the seventeenth century had already begun to take on certain characteristics of urban existence. In the villages representatives of different Old World nationalities lived in close proximity, at New York in sufficient numbers to produce a varied and conflicting culture, and at Boston and Charles Town to encourage a sense of superiority in the dominant group. Distinctions between rich and poor, later to crystallize into real barriers, had also appeared. Society in the villages was no longer in 1690 a simple democracy of small property holders, but a definite hierarchy of commercial, clerical or official aristocracy, tradesmen, artisans, common laborers and slaves. In the realm of the intellect, village society already demonstrated some of the activity and restlessness characteristic of town life. Religious uniformity was giving way before the appearance of sectarianism or of complete unbelief, and the discipline exercised by an established or quasi-established church was having to meet the challenge of a more attractive secular life. The joys of the market place or tavern contested with the church for the soul of the town-dweller. Educational facilities were becoming a matter of public concern in the northern villages, where also vocational instruction or training in polite accomplishments could be privately obtained. Science was talked about and literature and politics discussed in groups like Governor Lovelace's "Club" or Mather's philosophical society. In Boston two coffee houses encouraged leisurely conversation. Printing in two of the towns disseminated new ideas, and in one of them society was ripe for a newspaper. In general, the close associations and sociability of town life, and the contacts of the seaports with the thought and manners of Europe made for an awareness of new ideas, a willingness to consider innovations, and an opportunity to indulge individual tastes, unfound elsewhere in the colonies at this time. The mental gulf between the societies of town and country had already appeared.

————

THE PLANTING OF THE VILLAGES — CONCLUSION

For the study of the beginnings of our urban society, today become so large a part in the life of the American people as a whole, the years 1625 to 1690 are fundamental. By the latter date all five of the important colonial towns had been planted and had solved the first stubborn problems of pioneering and colonization. Conditioned by the factors of their geographic location, on good harbors or at river mouths, and by the nature of the commercial urge that conceived them, the direction of their economic life was by 1690 definitely determined. By this time, too, the villages had learned by experience that for the general good certain problems of the life of the group within them must in some measure be met by common effort. Finally, also, by the end of the period, they were creating a society peculiar to themselves, and already differentiated from the rural farming life or the roving frontier existence of the rest of colonial America.

Conceivably, the villages in this period might have progressed farther, both economically and socially, had their financial resources been greater. At the outset, the actual building of towns where no towns were required heavy investments of capital from the homeland, and it was many years before these settlements began to be profitable to individual backers, to home governments, or to the inhabitants themselves. With the establishment of trade and industry wealth began to accumulate, it is true, but it could not keep pace with the increasing demands of growing communities for public improvements and public services. The building and care of streets, for instance, continued to be a too heavy drain on town exchequers throughout the colonial era. Consequently we see in this period the achievement by private capital of many projects of public benefit which the community as a whole was too poor to afford. Wharves and bridges, highway construction and improvement, projects of drainage and land reclamation, where need was great enough, were undertaken by individuals with civic permission, and with or without civic encouragement. The villages, too, because of lack of money, were unable fully to perform many of the public functions they assigned themselves, and enlightened programs for police protection, fire prevention, and the care of criminal and dependent classes, which would have made these new communities among the most advanced of their age, had often to be abandoned before completely tried.

Town governments were further hampered in this period by the fact that the powers and functions of municipal corporations were but imperfectly conceived and hazily defined. They were limited by the medieval conception of a charter which conveyed only the barest powers and privileges necessary for the management of corporate property. The full potentialities of the corporation were not yet realized or suspected, and there resulted frequent clashes between civic prerogatives and private liberties. Moreover, the civic power being as yet feeble, it was frequently forced to call on private aid to supplement it in many cases where today it is all-sufficient. The answer to these uncertainties was not found in the seventeenth century; indeed, the search for it still goes on. Fortunately, the conception of public office as a piece of private property, which made members of many municipal corporations in older countries mere greedy and selfish suckers at the public purse, does not seem to have crossed the Atlantic in its most vicious form. As time went on the governments of New York and Philadelphia, it is true, became more and more the private preserve of a limited few, but even here public demands had in large measure to be satisfied, and a smaller percentage of city funds were consumed at corporation banquets. The Selectmen of New England towns tended to be chosen from a few prominent families, and in a later period the immense power of the Moderator developed to control the Town Meeting, yet this institution continued to afford townspeople opportunity for the expression of their demands. One must beware of pushing this point too far, for these new communities were without many of the problems that harassed their older neighbors across the sea, but it does seem, from the evidence now available, that public spirit, which was not an outstanding virtue of the seventeenth century, and which in English provincial towns at this time was very nearly extinct, prevailed to a greater extent in America. Burghers of the New World simply would not put up with some of the abuses English townsmen suffered passively, and in many respects these new towns with their feeble resources were better served than any English municipality save London. Protection against fire in Boston and police provisions at New York illustrate this point.

These years saw the creation of the five towns from the raw materials of a new continent, the actual physical building of the villages. In a period of at most sixty-five years there were developed in the five localities we are considering groups of streets, dwellings, shops, markets and public buildings which bore already the promise of their greater future. Many of the appurtenances of true cities had been added: wharves, warehouses, homes of industry, places of business. Physically in this period no town completely outgrew its village aspects, although Boston and New York developed relatively congested areas, which made it necessary for authorities to deal with problems of traffic and crowding, and to enact regulations designed to prevent fire, free transportation, and insure public health. The growth of this period had been rapid and the accomplishments considerable. All of the villages save Philadelphia had known the crudities, dangers and discomforts of frontier outposts, and all save Charles Town had left them far behind by 1690. Life in the villages had become stabilized, comfortable and settled, but for the most part ample room remained for growth, and open spaces, gardens, orchards and commons preserved the rural appearances of these communities.

In describing the economic organization of the villages, however, one must beware of over-simplification. Janus-like, they faced two ways. From the mother towns whence they sprang they inherited the functions of the medieval manor and a system of rigid control of all trade, industry and labor within their bounds. Yet, with their long struggle with mercantilism still before them, American villages had already discovered some of the formulae for modern wealth. They knew the value of free, if illicit, trade, and had, in the case of Boston at least, some faint foretaste of the profits to be gained by becoming a center of distribution, finance and industry, whose far-flung foreign and penetrating domestic commerce, together with its own industry and production, should make of it the keystone on which to rest the entire arch of the surrounding countryside. Moreover, these embryo capitalists were not blind to the advantages of selling by the small measure, and while increasing "Cent per Cent" in ambitious foreign ventures, they engaged either directly or through others in authentic retail trade. The complete differentiation of the retail merchant, as well as his specialization in one line of goods, was not to come for many years, but its seeds were present in the economy of the colonial towns from the beginning.

In this period, too, the towns faced in embryo most of the social problems incident to their growth into cities. The way in which these problems were met demonstrates the fundamental conservatism of colonial movements. In almost every case the Motherland furnished the model, and the fact that the similarities of treatment in different localities are more striking than the divergencies may be traced to the common English backgrounds of the townsfolk. The Dutch of New Amsterdam contributed little that was unique; Dutch and English communal institutions were fundamentally the same, and the ease with which the transition was effected from burgher to Mayor and Council government is merely an illustration of the case. Colonists drew heavily on English precedent in their market and trade regulations, their dealings with criminals, their care of the poor. English experience guided them in their struggles against fire and their encounters with the liquor problem. Divergencies from English practice were fewer than might be supposed, — criminal codes in the colonies were less strict, the apprenticeship system broke down in part, — but as likenesses between town and town were more evident than differences, so was the likeness of all towns to Old World cities. The colonists came to America with little idea of social experimentation. They wished rather to build towns like those they had known at home, and the remarkable thing is how quickly they succeeded. The first generation had hardly passed before colonial villages were strikingly like those of the Mother Country.

Finally, existence in the villages had by the end of this period become relatively urbanized in most respects. Intellectually, the distance of Boston or Philadelphia from London was less than that between any town and its respective frontier. Life in the villages possessed many elements of urban sophistication; here fashions changed as rapidly as they could be introduced from abroad; here class distinctions were crystallizing and ruling castes establishing themselves economically and politically; here opportunities for education, amusement, medical service and the like were sufficiently numerous and available to seem to contradict the facts of the towns' recent emergence from unsettled wilderness. The intellectual horizon was broader in the villages; new and exciting ideas from across the seas circulated with ease among certain cultured groups in each town. The towns were already developing a unique society which differentiated them from less settled regions of the country, and of which the characteristics were those we associate with city life. Already they had become "oases of endeavor, dignity and enjoyment" in the too-often arid desert of pioneer existence. Physically, economically, socially and culturally, the towns by 1690 constituted a distinct element in American society. Their further progress along the lines already charted is a vital chapter in the country's history.

PART II

THE AWAKENING OF CIVIC
CONSCIOUSNESS, 1690–1720

V

THE EXPANDING SCENE

I

In the three decades, 1690–1720, the five colonial communities put away forever their village aspects and took on the appearance of sizable towns. Their social and economic problems multiplied, and the events of town life were enacted on a constantly widening stage. Although urban development in the New World continued to be ordered by the same factors as in the seventeenth century, the existence of abnormal conditions throughout much of this period is of utmost significance. During nineteen of these thirty years England and France were at war, and the American colonies now assumed their historic role as pawns on the chessboard of European diplomacy. The wars both stimulated and retarded town development. Common danger made for increased communication between settlements and with the Mother Country; opportunities arose for the sale of military supplies, privateering, smuggling, and clandestine trade with the enemy; and in general the social and cultural activities of the towns expanded. On the other hand, the inevitable demoralizing effects of conflict, — financial depression, moral decline, social unrest, and the increased burden of the poor, — shook the economic structure of the towns and severely strained the resources of their inhabitants.

Notwithstanding the ravages of war, urban population generally increased, with the result that only a few English provincial cities, like Bristol and Norwich with about twenty-five thousand inhabitants, exceeded Boston or Philadelphia in these years. Boston maintained its early lead, but Charles Town and Philadelphia showed remarkable gains, the former trebling its population, and the latter nearly equalling the Bay town by the close of the period.[1] Despite their growth, how-

[1] Estimates of population growth in this period appear in the following table:

Populations of Colonial Towns: 1690–1720

	Boston	Philadelphia	New York	Newport	Charles Town
1690	7,000	4,000	3,900	2,600	1,100
1700	6,700	5,000	5,000	2,600	2,000
1710	9,000	6,500	5,700	2,800	3,000
1720	12,000	10,000	7,000	3,800	3,500

These estimates are based upon data in Greene and Harrington, *American Population,* and other sources; see also, Latimer, *Bristol in the Eighteenth Century,* 6, and Bayne, *Norwich,* 268.

ever, the increase in the towns did not keep pace with that of rural regions, and in 1720 dwellers in the five towns constituted only eight per cent of the colonial population.

II

Town expansion and its attendant problems intensified the activity and importance of municipal governments, and public pressure for more efficiency on the part of local authorities, especially in matters of taxation and expenditure, necessitated an extension of their powers. There is noticeable in this period in the northern provinces a distinct tendency to broaden the capacities of local political bodies, either by special acts of assemblies or by charters of incorporation.

At Boston, undoubtedly the best governed town in the colonies, the Town Meeting rarely failed to secure a desired grant of privileges from the General Court. In 1708, however, a group of leading citizens, among them Samuel Sewall, met to discuss the failure of county justices to enforce town laws, which they attributed to "the want of a proper head or Town Officer, or officers impowred for that purpose." At their instigation the Selectmen proposed the appointment of a committee to draft a charter of incorporation. The names of the thirty members of this committee read like a social directory of the Boston of that day, but when they presented their report in March, 1708/9, the Meeting voted it down.[2] Elisha Cooke, political boss of Boston, headed the committee on incorporation, and it may have been that the rank and file feared for their liberties should a close corporation be formed by the group he represented. This small clique had already established a fairly continuous control of the Board of Selectmen and the office of Moderator. Popular resentment against its exclusiveness found expression in a sermon by the Reverend Thomas Bridges of the First Church on April 9, 1709, wherein he spoke of "covetous officeholders . . . intent on gain." The great need of the town, declared the minister, was for honest and unselfish public servants; "There are indeed divers offices in the Town, which qualified men ought to attend out of pure regard to the Public Good . . . without expecting a salary."[3] The attitude of Mr. Bridges and the Town Meeting had its effect, and from 1710 to 1720 the Selectmen displayed commendable activity in municipal affairs. Elisha Cooke and his clique still ran the town, but the "machine" had to clean house.

The town government of Newport secured almost complete autonomy in 1705 through an act of the Rhode Island Assembly authorizing it to "regulate its own prudential affairs." This law endowed the Town

[2] 8 Bos. Rec. Com., 55, 56, 58, 61; Col. Soc. Mass. Trans., X, 345, 350.
[3] Drake, Antiquities of Boston, 535 n.

Meeting with power to levy taxes for all town concerns, — a privilege which would have aroused the greatest official envy at Philadelphia or New York.[4]

These two Middle Colony capitals were governed after the manner of English cities by civic corporations. The Commonalty of New York continued throughout the period under the Dongan Charter, with powers augmented only by a ferry monopoly granted by Lord Cornbury in 1708. The Mayor and Common Council, a corporation existing independently of the community, regarded itself and was looked upon by the people as an exclusive and privileged body; hence its sluggish attitude toward certain municipal needs, and its reluctance to spend even the meager funds at its disposal for public improvements.[5]

Philadelphia received a charter providing for a similar government by Mayor and Common Council in 1691, but this arrangement apparently lapsed when Penn lost control of his colony the following year. In 1700 "Sundry Freemen and Inhabitants" petitioned the Assembly for an act "strengthening and confirming the City Charter and enabling the Mayor and Commonalty to make By-laws." The result was the charter of 1701, granted by William Penn. This document, framed on the familiar English municipal model, created a close corporation consisting of a mayor and common council and endowed with the usual municipal powers. The two greatest defects in the instrument were the lack of adequate powers of taxation and the highly aristocratic nature of the corporation, the members of which were responsible to no one but themselves. As early as 1706 the Corporation felt the need to remedy the first evil, and in 1712 finally secured the passage of a law granting it some small measure of authority to tax "for the Public Use and Benefit." [6] In keeping with the spirit of English municipalities, the corporations of both Philadelphia and New York jealously maintained their exclusiveness. There will be ample occasion to note their indifference to public needs in succeeding chapters.

With all its defects the corporation form of government far surpassed the inadequate provisions for the administration of Charles Town by the South Carolina Assembly. The southern port continued throughout the period to be governed, or misgoverned, by groups of "commissioners" who executed the infrequent acts passed by the Assembly for regulating the necessities of the town. In 1712 the care of the city's poor was entrusted to the vestry of St. Philip's Parish, created by an act of 1706, but this departure unfortunately failed to es-

[4] R. I. Col. Recs., III, 525.
[5] Peterson, New York, chapter I.
[6] Pa. Mag., XVIII, 504; Votes Pa. Assembly, I, ii, 98, iv-viii, 100; II, 49, 84, 109; P. M. C. C., 77; Pa. Statutes, II, 414.

tablish a precedent for the management of town affairs. As the planter group increased in power and prestige, country leaders sought to keep the town with its mercantile activities subordinated to their own interests. Although in 1720 the people of Charles Town constituted over half the population of the province, they were allowed only four representatives out of thirty in the Commons House.[7] Small wonder that the municipal needs of the southern capital were so seldom cared for.

III

In each of the towns increased population created a demand for a program of building expansion; empty spaces gradually disappeared, and new sections opened up beyond original bounds. The erection of large public buildings further emphasized the urban appearance of most of these communities. Boston, Philadelphia, New York and Charles Town doubled the number of their buildings, and Newport witnessed an increase of at least one third. While all this construction meant enlarging the area of each town, signs of congestion began to appear in the older, more settled parts of some of them.

The greatest building activity occurred at Boston. Here the earlier expansion into the North End continued apace until by 1720 the entire section had been built up. At the same time the town was moving rapidly out toward the Neck, and the South End was in the process of becoming a residential district. Recently erected dwellings stretched along Orange Street almost to the town gate. To the westward construction began at Barton's Point, where in 1719 John Staniford advertised a new real estate development, "laid out in House Lotts with two Streets Cross, that have a very fine Prospect upon the River and Charlestown and a great part of Boston." [8]

About the Dock and waterfront, in the business center of Boston, shops and warehouses began to encroach upon the older dwelling houses. Many of the latter were now rented by their former occupants for sums averaging £20 per year to craftsmen and shopkeepers. Newer business establishments were usually built of brick, and the presence of "Mr. Cook's Brick Warehouse in King Street," which checked the spread of a slaughterhouse fire in 1718, probably saved the business district from another general conflagration.[9]

In the newer residential sections, the North and South Ends, brick and frame dwellings multiplied rapidly after 1700. As early as 1692 one third of all houses in Boston were of brick or stone construction.

[7] S. C. Statutes, II, 606; Schaper, "Sectionalism in South Carolina," 345. That the Proprietors were not averse to creating a corporate government for Charles Town may be seen in Documents in the Public Records Office Relating to South Carolina, 140, 217; Pub. Recs. S. C., VIII, 55.
[8] Bonner's Map of Boston, 1722; News Letter, July 7, 1707; July 12, 1719.
[9] Me. Hist. Soc. Colls., VI; News Letter, Feb. 24, 1718; Sept. 10, 1705; Feb. 18, 1706; 6 MHS Colls., I, 423; II, 4.

In 1693 Mr. Samson Waters built a "great house," and Sewall moved his family to a handsome brick residence containing a "Stove-Chamber," which he was proud to have built without any serious accident befalling the workmen. Poorer folk continued to live in little frame houses crowded together upon the older streets. Such dwellings usually consisted of a "Seller, Rome over, a Chamber, and Garret," or might, like a large structure near Scarlet's Wharf, contain "three Tenements, with three Shops and other accomodations."[10] From all accounts, the population of Boston in this period seems to have been adequately housed; certainly the frequency with which real estate advertisements appeared in the *News Letter* from 1715 to 1720 indicates no lack of available houses.

The lottery, later to become a favorite means for disposing of real estate, now made its appearance in Boston. In 1719 Joseph Marion advertised for sale in this fashion two brick houses situated on large lots in the North End. For one of them he issued one hundred tickets to cost £5 apiece, the house going to the holder of the lucky ticket.[11]

The erection of public buildings stood witness to the growing maturity of the town. The old Town House perished in the fire of 1711, and three years later was replaced by an "elegant" brick structure at the head of King Street, where General Court and Town Meeting assembled for many years.[12] Several new church edifices belonging to this period, though still of frame construction, were rather more imposing than the earlier meeting houses. Sewall was particularly enthusiastic about the raising of "Mr. Coleman's New Steeple" in 1717. In 1720 the visitor to Boston would have received the impression of substantial homes for the well-to-do and neat houses for artisans, compactly arranged, and all dominated by the spires of a few well-built churches. The show place of the town was unquestionably the new Town House.

The fact that the Dongan Charter of 1686 had vested all unappropriated lands on the island of Manhattan in the Corporation of New York greatly retarded expansion there prior to 1720. Occasional sales occurred when funds were needed, as in 1691 for the building of a new ferry house and market, but after 1700 the city government made it a policy to lease desirable land rather than sell it. Thus New York, as compared with other towns, tended to become congested. As early as 1694 the Corporation petitioned Lieutenant-Governor Nanfan concerning "Incroachment of Buildings" on the "former line of fortifications . . . Along the Wall Street," and the need to demolish the old wall to make room for expansion. Madam Knight reported the town "well

10 5 MHS *Colls.*, V, 381, 385; VI, 178, 232; *News Letter*, Oct. 21, 1706; Aug. 11, 1707; *Bos. Gaz.*, Jan. 18, 1719/20.
11 *News Letter*, Aug. 31, Sept. 21, 1719.
12 11 *Bos. Rec. Com.*, 149, 180, 207.

compacted. The Buildings Brick Generaly, very stately and high, though not altogether like ours in Boston. The Bricks in some of the Houses are of divers Coulers and laid in Checkers, being glazed [they] look very agreeable." [13]

Despite considerable construction, which produced expansion beyond the wall and congestion within, housing accommodations at New York fell far short of its needs. In 1701 an harassed official informed the Board of Trade, "I have eight in family and know not yet where to fix them, houses are so scarce and dear, and lodgings worst in this place." A census taken in 1703 revealed a mere seven hundred and fifty houses available at Manhattan, and by 1710 there were only a few scattered buildings above Fulton Street.[14] Throughout the period the housing situation at New York remained much the same.

Indifferent to housing needs, the Corporation of New York did provide for its own comfort and that of the Assembly by the erection in 1700 of a fine city hall at the corner of Broad and Wall Streets, on a piece of ground donated by Abraham De Peyster. The addition of "Eighteen Rush bottom Chairs" to its Council Chamber in 1711, and the installation of "a publick Clock" of local manufacture in its tower in 1716 enhanced the magnificence of this brick structure about which revolved the municipal life of the town throughout the remainder of the colonial period.[15]

Philadelphia, unrestricted by geographical situation or by a wall erected for defense in earlier days, had more room for expansion than either Boston or New York. In this period inhabitants erected about six hundred dwellings and other buildings, most of them of brick, since clay and limestone abounded in eastern Pennsylvania. As early as 1704 Thomas Masters built a three-story brick house at the corner of Front and King Streets, and many fine residences followed, some of them designed by James Porteus, the only professional architect practising in any of the towns. George Haworth described Philadelphia in 1715 as "very large, about a mile long, with a great breadth," rapidly filling up with two- and three-story houses. By 1720 the town had spread westward from the Delaware to Seventh Street, and land which in 1685 "sold for ten Pound . . . will fetch above three hundred now." [16]

There seem to have been dwelling houses available in ample number at Philadelphia. From its first appearance the *American Weekly Mer-*

[13] *N. Y. M. C. C.,* I, 259, 357; II, 82, 122, 264; Peterson, *New York,* 82–88; *Journal of Madam Knight,* 52.
[14] *N. Y. Col. Docs.,* IV, 914; Wilson, *Memorial History of New York,* II, 41, 106; *N. Y. Col. Laws.,* I, 425.
[15] *N. Y. M. C. C.,* II, 108, 115, 122, 440.
[16] Hart, *Contemporaries,* II, 76; *Pa. Mag.,* LIII, 6; XXXVII, 339; Scharf and Westcott, *Philadelphia,* I, 187; Jackson, *Early Philadelphia Architects,* 32.

cury carried many advertisements like the following: "A large Brick House in Third Street Philadelphia two Story High and Garrets, with one lot of ground on the back thereof one hundred foot Deep." Real estate and building materials were here generally cheaper than at Boston or New York, and many tradesmen and artificers could thus own their own homes. As in Boston the lottery was coming into use for the selling of houses. John Read and Henry Frogly advertised in 1720 the disposal "by way of Lottery" of a large new brick house in Third Street, as well as good building lots in the same vicinity.[17]

In these years also the Quaker town began to acquire public buildings. In 1710 the Corporation built a combination market and "Courthouse" at a cost of £620, in the center of High Street between Second and Third. Very like a medieval English market house, it differed sharply from more modern structures in New York and Boston, where were exhibited the already forming trends of American colonial architecture. But this newest of the towns was more fortunate in its houses of worship. Swedes in the district in 1698 erected the famous "Gloria Dei," probably the loveliest church edifice to be found in any of the towns at this time, and in 1711 the Anglicans reconstructed and enlarged the first Christ Church, originally built of brick in 1695.[18]

Building activity at Newport lagged behind that of the other towns. Of the possible two hundred varied structures erected between 1690 and 1720 not one appears to have been of brick or stone construction, — all were frame. With the turn of the century the village began to expand "on ye north end," and pressure of population after 1706 led the town proprietors to make a division of common lands into small plots for newcomers. By 1711 the land around the cove towards Easton's Point was added to "ye compact part of ye Town of Newport," necessitating connection with the shipping district by means of a bridge and new highways. Several buildings and warehouses were erected in this section at about this time. Notwithstanding this construction, which considering the size of the village was extensive, some poor families still remained homeless. In 1715 the Town Council had to appropriate thirty shillings for one Adair and his family "To get him a place to live in." The public edifices of Newport, including its churches, were far from imposing, and showed none of that grace and beauty for which the town was later to become famous. In comparison with neighbor towns this village still retained much of its earlier rural aspect.[19]

[17] *Mercury,* Aug. 18, Sept. 22, 1720.
[18] Scharf and Westcott, *Philadelphia,* I, 187; *Pa. Mag.,* LIII, 6.
[19] *Newport T. M. Recs.,* 90, 118; *Newport T. M. Procs.,* April 25, 1711; *Newport T. C. Recs.,* Dec. 15, 1715; *Historic Newport,* 24; Bull, *Memoir of Rhode Island,* III, 3–4.

Expansion in each northern town followed more or less the same trends, being determined by the demands of a naturally increasing population. At Charles Town the problem was somewhat different. To hasten the peopling of their principal town Carolina Proprietors in 1694 instructed Governor Archdale to fortify and "encourage building in Charlestown." Construction progressed rapidly, and in 1700 the town was reported to have "several fine streets" of homes within the fortifications, which Archdale had pushed to completion. A map of 1704 reveals Charles Town completely surrounded by this line of fortifications, within which several fine houses, belonging to such eminent citizens as Thomas Smith, Joseph Pendarvis, Colonel William Rhett and George Logan, contributed to its urban appearance. Other more modest dwellings, and a few warehouses and shops along the waterfront, completed the setting of this southern community. Four churches constituted the only public structures within the walls, while beyond the pale was located a Quaker meeting house. Governor Johnson and his Council held their meetings in the home of Mr. William Gibbon. There was as yet ample room for many buildings within the fortifications, but the cost of living was high at Charles Town, and expansion slow. In 1709 Nathaniel Sale, receiver general, wrote to the Proprietors that "indeed things are so dear here yt. it costs me £46. 10s. a yeare onely lodging and dyet." [20]

The destructive fire of 1698 and the great hurricane of 1713 greatly intensified the housing problem at Charles Town. The latter disaster demolished many buildings just at the time when the housing facilities of the little town were about to be subjected to unusual strain by the influx of refugees from the Indian wars. To guard against such calamities in the future the Assembly ordered all houses to be built of brick, and some such structures were probably added to the few raised between 1690 and 1700. Most rebuilt dwellings, however, continued to be constructed of cypress and mahogany, the materials most easily available, and with tiled roofs after the Barbados fashion. The town barely recovered in this period from its succession of natural disasters, and by 1720 settlement had only just begun to expand beyond the walls which had been demolished three years before.[21]

As a result of building activity in these years each of the five towns

[20] But rents were lower than in the north, an average house bringing £10 to £15 per year. *Cal. St. Pap., 1693-1696,* 341, 475; *S. C. Hist. & Gen. Mag.,* X, 12-14; *S. C. Commons Journal* (1703), 76.

[21] Charlestonians imitated the architecture of Barbados where timber houses with balconies on the west side, high ceilings and large windows to admit fresh air were found to be coolest in summer. Shortage of building stone and brick also encouraged use of timber, although some construction was of Bermuda stone. Smith, *Dwelling Houses of Charleston,* 18, 24, 337-345; *S. C. Statutes,* VII, 58; *Cal. St. Pap., 1719-1720,* 161, 301.

extended its area and at the same time assumed a more urban appearance. Evidences of the growing compactness of Boston, Philadelphia and Charles Town may be seen in ordinances allowing half of a party wall to be set on the neighboring lot, provided a "toothing" were made in the corners whereon the next building might be joined.[22] By 1720 also each town exhibited a marked individuality. Charles Town, compact within its walls, with its West Indian architecture, compared oddly with rural Newport, sprawling for a mile or more along two streets. New York, congested and still largely Dutch in appearance, offered a sharp contrast with Philadelphia, whose brick houses were widely spread out in orderly arrangement. Boston, the largest of the towns, embraced a motley array of houses large and small, of wood, brick and stone, set against a background of church spires and encircling hills.

As towns grew in size and population and forests receded the problem of procuring adequate supplies of firewood became increasingly perplexing. At Boston the shortage of fuel in winter had from the first been a matter of paramount importance, and well before the period closed most of the towns were facing the need of official regulation for the sale of firewood.

As in the past Boston received most of its fuel supply by water, in little craft known as "Wood boats," coming sometimes from regions as distant as Cape Ann. They discharged their cargoes at the Town Dock, or at private landing places like Gill's Wharf where Samuel Sewall purchased his fuel. Sledges still brought wood from inland districts during the winter season. Official "Corders of Wood," too often not above suspicion in the exercise of their duty, measured all firewood for sale in the town. The price of fuel soared in winter time, and poor people had often to do without. In 1706 Sewall advocated the capture of Nova Scotia in order to procure a supply of "coals," and in 1718 the situation became so serious that the town chose a committee to investigate and encourage the "bringing of Sea Coals into this Town." As early as 1714 Ambrose Vincent of Boston advertised for sale "ten Chaldron of the best new Castle coal," and Jonathan Belcher commenced a fairly regular importation of "New Castle Sea Coal" in the next year. Some of the more prosperous denizens found this new form of fuel superior to wood, and John Campbell offered in 1720 to sell a "Large, Strong Iron Kitchen Grate for Burning Coal." [23]

All of the towns save Charles Town found it necessary to regulate

[22] Mass. Acts and Resolves, I, 42; P. M. C. C., 79; S. C. Statutes, VII, 58; 11 Bos. Rec. Com., 123.
[23] N. Y. Col. Docs., IV, 792; 6 MHS Colls., I, 124, 339; 5 MHS Colls., VI, 330; News Letter, April 26, 1714; April 25, 1715; Nov. 14, 1720.

the sale of firewood. New York continued to require official cording of all fuel brought to the wood wharves. To insure fair dealing at Newport the Town Meeting hired John Herries as its first woodcorder in 1697, and ordered him the next year to seize all logs that did not measure four feet in length. In 1703 the clerk of the market took over the cording of wood. The forests surrounding Newport were so rapidly denuded that by 1713 fuel was being brought by boat from New Shoreham and the Narragansett country. Wood vendors seem to have been an unscrupulous lot, who abused "many poor people" by selling short faggots. The same held true of the "Carters of Wood" who delivered it about town, and authorities found it necessary to set a fine of twenty shillings a cord on all firewood that failed to conform to the official measure. Philadelphia was well supplied with wood from the shores of the Delaware. In 1706 the new city government appointed an official woodcorder to "view" all firewood brought to the Blue Anchor landing. It also resolved to benefit from the large quantities of fuel arriving at city docks, and laid "a Small duty vpon wood, etc. land[ed] upon the public Wharfs." [24]

IV

With the multiplication of population in the five towns, and the large amount of building undertaken in each, it became necessary for authorities to lay out, open and pave new streets, improve old thoroughfares, and regulate the traffic daily increasing in their highways. No business required so much time and energy of corporations and town meetings as the provision of highways to meet their expanding needs, and no activity proved so great a strain on the public finances of colonial towns. In the three older seaports extension of streets usually resulted from pressure of growing demands, and was characterized by lack of system, in contrast with the more orderly plans of Philadelphia and Charles Town.

The large amount of land opened up for the erection of new houses and other buildings at Boston necessitated a considerable extension of old highways and the construction of many new ones. In addition, the fifth and sixth "great" fires of 1690 and 1691 provided opportunity for the resurvey of streets, lanes and alleys in the devastated areas at the center of the town. In October, 1692, the General Court empowered the Selectmen and County Justices to lay out new or enlarge old streets in this district. As a consequence the proceedings of the Selectmen are crowded with accounts of highway construction, and by

[24] Fox, *Caleb Heathcote*, 82; *Newport T. M. Recs.*, 46, 163; *R. I. Acts* (*1744*), 27; *P. M. C. C.*, 34, 43.

1710 the streets and lanes of the North End had assumed the pattern they were to follow for over a century. In the South End a similar development was under way. In all cases the Selectmen carefully specified the width and course of the new thoroughfares, and to render their arrangement permanent they ordered in 1708 that "the Streets, Lanes, and Alleys of this Town as they are now . . . bounded, be accordingly recorded in the Town Book." [25]

Another "great" fire swept across Boston in 1711, and for several years thereafter the authorities busied themselves with running new street lines and holding hearings concerning the town's use of its right of eminent domain. In several localities, especially in the burned area on Cornhill Street, the Selectmen wisely improved the disaster by widening all highways. This extensive construction in thickly settled districts so strained the slender resources of the town that outlying sections suffered much neglect, and Boston was presented for "insufficiency of Highways" by the Salt Ponds on the road to Roxbury. The building program also presented itself as a golden opportunity to many townsmen, and so numerous were the applications for special privileges in respect to new roads that the Town Meeting finally voted in 1715 that "the Town will not be att the Charge of Turning the High way to pass through the Lotts of perticuler Persons." By 1720 Boston had evolved an excellent network of highways, although Captain Nathaniel Uring's declaration that "the streets are broad and regular" can be considered true only by comparison with some older English city like Bristol. [26]

Newport heralded the new century with an activity in road building which exceeded in extent all the construction of its previous history. On July 31, 1700, a committee of the Town Meeting was chosen to superintend the laying out of new streets, for which the demand became especially urgent with the division of common lands after 1706. By 1710 the town was expanding around the Cove, where new lanes were being laid out, and in 1714 a highway two rods wide was cut through to this section from Marlborough Street. The next year, probably as a result of pressure from Newporters, the Rhode Island Assembly empowered all towns to exercise the right of eminent domain when land was needed for highways, and ordered the selection of a jury to evaluate property so preempted. As laid out in 1713 on the town plat the streets of Newport might have been termed "broad and regular" in comparison with those of Boston, while its highway system, with

[25] *Mass. Acts and Resolves,* I, 42; 11 *Bos. Rec. Com.,* 30, 67, 68, 72, 133, 191; 8 *Bos. Rec. Com.,* 24, 112; Bonner's Map of Boston.
[26] The highways of Bristol in 1700 averaged "under twenty feet" in width. 11 *Bos. Rec. Com.,* 119, 121, 151, 153, 158, 161; 8 *Bos. Rec. Com.,* 112; N. H. Hist. Soc. *Colls.,* III, 141; Latimer, *Bristol in the Eighteenth Century,* 3.

streets radiating from the business center, provided more variety than the checkerboard plan of Philadelphia or Charles Town.[27]

In 1691 the New York Assembly resolved that for the "Encouragement of Trade and Commerce . . . it is very necessary . . . that buildings streets lanes wharfs docks and alleys . . . be conveniently regulated," and empowered the Corporation of its principal town to lay out all streets and highways within its precincts. New lanes and streets were promptly opened up through lands successively sold by the Corporation in 1691, 1694 and 1700. Most of the road building in this period took place in the section below the Wall, although several new streets were built in the Out Ward after 1707.[28] But as compared with Boston, Newport and Philadelphia, the street system of New York did not greatly expand before 1720; rather did the city become more crowded at the lower tip of Manhattan Island.

The prior planning of Philadelphia and Charles Town characterized the highway systems of these towns. At Philadelphia there was little problem about the position of new streets, since the entire area between the Delaware and the Schuylkill Rivers had been laid out by Holme in 1682. Streets had already been cleared as far as the city was to expand by 1720. The charter of 1701 provided that highways should "forever" continue according to the original plan, and the Corporation, possessing no authority to alter them, was thus spared much of the work of similar bodies in the other towns. Not until December 4, 1719, did the city government find it necessary to employ Jacob Taylor "to Run out ye Severall Streets of this City, . . . to Prevent any Incroachmt that may happen in Building for ye Want" of definite markings. As Charles Town was a walled city, its lines, like those of the Quaker town, had been laid out at the beginning; no fundamental change occurred in the plan of the town prior to 1720.[29]

In 1712 the town of Newport somewhat pompously resolved that since "It is a universal and orderly custom for all towns and places throughout the world when grown to Some considerable maturity by Some generall order to name the Streets, lanes and alleys thereof," it were a great reproach to such a town if there be no addresses to which "Letters of Commerce" might be sent. In 1690 Newport and Philadelphia were the only villages that had officially assigned names to all their thoroughfares, but by the end of the period the other towns had adopted this sign of their "considerable maturity." In 1701 the Boston Town Meeting authorized the Selectmen to assign names to all streets

---

[27] *Newport T. M. Recs.*, 90, 149, 168, 170; *Newport T. M. Procs.*, April 25, 1711; *R. I. Col. Recs.*, III, 384; *R. I. Acts (1744)*, 52; Mumford's Map of Newport, 1713.
[28] *N. Y. Col. Laws*, II, 269; Stokes, *Iconography*, IV, 457; *N. Y. M. C. C.*, II, 322, 342, 364.
[29] *P. M. C. C.*, 170; Crisp's Map of Charles Town, 1704.

in the town. These officers did not complete their work until May 3, 1708, when they presented for the town's ratification the names of one hundred and nine streets, lanes and alleys. Newport had so expanded by 1712 that the authorities reported that "persons at a distance are not capable to demonstrate when occasions require in what street in this Town they dwell." Consequently Mr. John Mumford, surveyor, was employed to make a map of the town, and the Town Council directed to give names to all thoroughfares opened up since 1679.[30]

The other towns made no such orderly arrangement for the naming of their streets. At New York many of the Dutch designations were retained by the English, and the Corporation christened new highways as they were opened up. No thoroughfare in Charles Town had any official label in 1698, but by 1701 familiar street names began to appear, — such as The Bay, Broad and Tradd, — and by 1720 all ways within the lines seem to have acquired their present designations.[31]

Not only did the towns construct many new streets from 1690 to 1720, but they made great efforts to pave them and in other ways to make them passable and adequate for traffic. The advances in highway engineering and care of the streets made in this period were noteworthy, and but for the poverty of the towns might have been carried much farther.

With the turn of the century Boston embarked upon an ambitious program of street paving and repairing, which by 1720 provided it with a highway system the finest in the colonies, and greatly surpassing that of most English cities. In the first years of this period sporadic efforts had been made to surface one or two Boston streets, as when Francis Thrasher agreed in 1703 with the Selectmen to pave "the way on this side the Fortification on ye Neck [Orange Street], . . . Twenty four foot wide," at a cost of £3 per rod. Commencing in 1704, when the Selectmen were authorized to lay out £100 "in paving such Places of the Streets as they shall judg needfull," the town began to make yearly appropriations for street paving. By 1720 Boston had expended, at the least, the large sum of £3,275 for the improvement of its public ways. This money was spent chiefly for "paveing the Townes part or middle of the Street," and the "abutters," who paved the remainder at their own expense, probably laid out an even larger amount. In newly developed districts the town usually met half the cost of paving, — its "accustomed proportion." On May 3, 1708, the Selectmen hired two men to pave "the Street to wards the South end of the Town, to ye value of two hundred pounds," and ordered them

[30] *Newport T. M. Recs.*, 159; *The Names of the Streets . . . of Boston*; 8 *Bos. Rec. Com.*, 17, 49; 11 *Bos. Rec. Com.*, 72, 78, 163.
[31] *N. Y. M. C. C.*, I, 314; II, 144, 257, 265, 282; *S. C. Commons Journal* (1696), 18; *S. C. Hist. & Gen. Mag.*, XI, 52.

first to grade the way. Many wealthy and public-spirited townsmen bore the whole charge of surfacing their streets by means of subscriptions, and in such cases a committee appointed by the Selectmen supervised the work. In 1710 Mrs. Priscilla Gardener notified the Selectmen that if anyone would pave the lane before her property, she would defray the cost by "Next Spring or Sooner." [32]

Main streets were generally paved down the middle for a space twenty-four feet in width, while pavement in the lanes was eight feet wide. Although gravel was in frequent use, the usual surfacing material consisted of stone blocks, and occasionally one reads in the *News Letter* of "A Parcel of Paving Stones" for sale. [33]

Once these costly pavements had been laid, the Selectmen were at great pains to have them kept in repair. They also devised "Effectual Means" to make "abbutters" keep their privately paved sidewalks in good condition. The greatest damage to new pavements came from the wheels of heavy carts, and in 1720 a decree forbade two-horse carts measuring over eighteen feet in width or trucks whose loads exceeded one ton, to pass through the streets of Boston, under penalty of a very large fine. [34]

Lack of funds, or unwillingness to spend them, prevented other towns from undertaking extensive paving projects in this period. Very little attempt to pave the thoroughfares of New York was made prior to 1693. In that year the Common Council, realizing that streets had been "much neglected" and trade hindered thereby, ordered every burgher at his own cost immediately to pave the street before his lot with "good & sufficient peeble Stones." Accordingly, under supervision by the alderman and assistant of each ward, many streets were paved six feet on each side, leaving an unpaved strip running down the center. Jarvis Marshall failed to comply with the new regulations, and when fined in 1696 petitioned for remission. After 1700 a twenty shilling fine for non-compliance aided enforcement of the paving rules, and most of the important thoroughfares, including the Dock, had been paved with cobble stones by 1707. [35]

After 1690 Newport made some provision for surfacing its streets, but so little was accomplished that in 1705 the Town Meeting appointed a committee to "inspect into irregularities & breeches made by some persons in not paving ye streets of ye town." A report of 1707, that a "great part" of the streets in the "compact part" of the town

[32] 11 *Bos. Rec. Com.*, 30, 33, 48, 58, 59, 60, 72, 113, 129, 190; 8 *Bos. Rec. Com.*, 101, 110.

[33] 11 *Bos. Rec. Com.*, 33, 87, 209; *News Letter*, Aug. 13, 1716.

[34] 11 *Bos. Rec. Com.*, 9, 13, 41, 49, 110, 111; 8 *Bos. Rec. Com.*, 144.

[35] *N. Y. M. C. C.*, I, 151, 179, 314, 316, 401; II, 103, 193, 265, 282, 320, 325, 355; III, 224.

had been paved after a fashion,[36] indicated some improvement. But despite ambitious proposals, keen public interest, and the best of intentions, the condition of the streets declined rapidly, chiefly because the little town lacked sufficient funds for extensive surfacing.

Probably in anticipation of an "investigation" by the Assembly, the town in June, 1715, agreed with "pavers to get the Streets paved and . . . for getting Stones." These eleventh hour measures did not prevent the Assembly, when it convened the next month, from complaining that their "metropolitan town . . . hath very miry streets, especially that leading to the ferry or landing place, up to the colony house [Queen Street], so that the members of the courts are very much discommoded therewith, and is a great hindrance to the transporting of provisions, &c., in and out of the said town." Sensible of the reason for this situation, the Assembly voted a grant of £289. 17. 3. from the duty on slaves imported into Newport for the paving of Queen Street from ferry landing to colony house. Having provided that its members might now arrive at its sessions dry-shod, it proceeded to the secondary consideration, the facilitating of transportation within the town, and voted half the income from slave duties for the next seven years for improving the streets of the metropolis. Assured now of ample funds, the Newport Town Council applied itself immediately to the problem, with the result that before the year was out Queen and Thames Streets had been paved down the middle with stone, and property owners required to improve their sides of these two main thoroughfares. A colony law enabling the surveyors of the highways to recover charges against those delinquents who failed to assume their duty in this respect fostered the surfacing of the town's remaining lanes and highways. As at Boston, the new pavements were protected by an ordinance of 1715, requiring all cart wheels to be at least six inches wide.[37]

As long as provincial and county authorities jointly governed Philadelphia, its streets remained a "Detriment & reproach of the Town in Generall." The charter of 1701 provided a remedy for this unsatisfactory state of affairs, and one of the first acts of the new corporation was to pave the market place with gravel. Increasing demand for improvements led the Commonalty in 1706 to advertise for loans to be expended in mending the "breaches in the Streets," but until 1712, when the city government secured power to raise money by taxation,

[36] "Some of them pretty decently and well, other[s] some very slightly, some that have been pav'd ye Ground is Raised over it so that it is of no benefit, and all of the Streets and Lanes that pavement there is very irregular some high and some low and we find several that have not been paved but part, and some not any part and ye Generality not full four feet wide." *Newport T. M. Procs.*, Jan. 30, 1707; *Newport T. M. Recs.*, 116, 122, 129.
[37] *Newport T. M. Recs.*, 179, 180, 181, 200; *R. I. Col. Recs.*, IV, 191.

the public ways of Philadelphia received very little attention. In July, 1712, the Magistrates pressed the overseers of the highways "Strictly" to enforce all highway ordinances, and sometime later endeavored to compel landowners to pave before their properties.[38]

All good intentions notwithstanding, the streets of Philadelphia continued a civic disgrace for many years. The Corporation bestirred itself slightly in 1711, and provided for a small amount of paving. But by this time some exasperated inhabitants had "Voluntarily" paved their portions of the streets with pebble stones, and "many others . . . [were] Levelling to follow their Example." Private initiative thus made up for municipal incompetence, so successfully that at the expiration of his mayoralty in 1719 Jonathan Dickinson was able to assume credit for considerable progress. "We have been upon regulating the pavements of our streets," he reported, "the footways with bricks, and the cartway with stone." Some repairing also went on, so that in 1720 the Grand Jury could find only two bad spots in the entire town. Philadelphia had made a fair beginning; it had a few paved streets, and the only brick sidewalks in the colonies.[39]

The lack of any efficient municipal authority at Charles Town made the absence of paved streets there almost a certainty. The Assembly did find time in 1698 to order inhabitants "to mend and raise the breadth of the fronting part of that lot that belongs to the house they live in . . . with broken oyster shells, six feet upon a direct line into the street, lane or alley, so that it be adjudged sufficient by the Commissioners." Yet even this small improvement remained uncared for, and agitation in 1706 for a law to protect pavements from the "Rowling of tar barrels up and down," met with no results.[40] All of the five towns had by 1720 recognized the need of providing hard surfaces for their principal thoroughfares, though only at Boston had they achieved any notable progress in dealing with the problem. However, this was not an age of macadam and concrete, and colonial highways at their worst had little to fear from comparison with those of most English and European cities.

When the towns embarked upon the extension of their highway systems, they encountered two formidable engineering problems. First, to protect new thoroughfares from erosion by water a system of drainage had to be devised; also, the unevenness of the terrain, the presence of creeks, inlets and other obstructions, necessitated the construction of bridges over which streets could pass. The doggedness and ingenuity displayed in the solution of these problems command the respect of the historian as they inspired the admiration of contemporary observers.

[38] Logan Papers, III, 9; P. M. C. C., 20, 37, 44, 80; Votes Pa. Assembly, II, 22.
[39] P. M. C. C., 115, 136, 137, 150, 155, 163, 172, 180; Court Papers, Phila. Cty., July 7, 1720; Westcott, Philadelphia, chapter LXVI.
[40] S. C. Statutes, VII, 12; S. C. Commons Journals, 1706.

At Boston the Selectmen supervised the grading of all streets for proper drainage. After 1713 most newly paved streets were provided with a crown in the middle and gutters at the side, although in some instances, as in Spring Lane, a gutter varying from six to nine feet in width ran down the center. With the placing of each new pump in the highway, the owners or the town promptly installed a paved gutter to carry away waste water. The road along Boston Neck suffered continual erosion from lying under water during frequent storms, and after it had been many times repaired the town decided in 1712 to lay out £150 for thirty-six rods of sea-wall on the west side.[41]

Perhaps the most noteworthy accomplishment of this period was the introduction of subsurface drainage at a time when it was but little used in Europe. During the seventeenth century inhabitants of Boston had often employed wooden drains to rid their cellars of waste water. In 1704 Francis Thrasher, "at his own proper Cost and charge . . . Layd a large Stone drain in the Street . . . leading to the Neck . . . which . . . [was] not only a Generall good and Benefit by freeing the Street from the Usual annoyance with Water & mire by the Often Stoppage & breaking of the Small wooden Truncks or drains hereto for Layd there, but a more perticuler benefit to ye Neighbourhood as a Comon Shore [sewer] for draining of their Cellars and Conveying away their waste water." In view of the usefulness of this public-spirited undertaking, the Selectmen required all householders who connected their drains with this sewer to reimburse Mr. Thrasher for a portion of his expenditure. This underground sewer proved so useful that many more followed, and the newly paved streets, constantly torn up for this purpose, were seldom properly repaired. To enable the Selectmen to protect these surfaces upon which they had lavished so much time and care, the General Court passed an "act for regulating of Drains and Common Shores" in 1708, which laid penalties upon those who dug open the streets without permission from the authorities. One of the Selectmen's most frequent duties thereafter was the granting of permits for digging up the public ways to individuals or groups who wished to construct sewers. In 1710 they licensed "Mr. Thomas Banister and Compa" to open the street for a sewer, "Provided they lay the Sd draine wth Brick or Stone [as] the law directs, and that they Lay the Same not less than five foot deep under the Ground, . . . and . . . effect the Sd work with Speed, So as to Obstruck the way as little as may be."[42]

These Boston sewers were all constructed by private initiative, and

[41] 11 *Bos. Rec. Com.*, 28, 74, 76, 190, 209, 210; 8 *Bos. Rec. Com.*, 91.
[42] The exact construction of the sewers is not clear. They may have been square like the drain at the Palace in Williamsburg, Va., or they may have been round; both types were in use in European cities. 11 *Bos. Rec. Com.*, 38, 117; *Mass. Acts and Resolves,* I, 643; 8 *Bos. Rec. Com.*, 12.

persons wishing to connect with one were required by law to assume their proportion of the cost of the project. In June, 1711, Obadiah Hull and Samuel Hood presented "an accot of ye charge they have been at in makeing wth Stone [a] comon Shore of fifty four pounds five Shillings and Six pence, wth the names of Such persons who receive benefit by haveing their Cellars drained thereby. Praying the . . . Sel. men to judg and award each particular persons Proportion . . . as the Law directs." The Selectmen decided the partners' share to be £5. 8., and apportioned the remainder among the twenty-seven other residents of Prince Street. From 1708 to 1720 over four hundred and twenty sections of sewer with connecting house drains were laid at Boston.[43]

No other town, in America or England, possessed so fine a system of draining as did Boston. The inadequacy of Philadelphia's drainage greatly annoyed its citizens before the granting of the charter of 1701. In July, 1693, the Grand Jury presented "the want of a Channell to Convey ye water . . . along the Front Street." A week later nine of the residents there expressed their willingness to construct one, and asked the Council to apportion the cost "Equallie & proportionable upon the freeholders on each side of the way." So many complaints poured in upon the Provincial Council that in 1700 it procured the passage of a law for "Regulating of Streets and Water Courses in Cities and Towns." By this act all underground drains had to be laid with brick or stone, and the Governor was empowered to appoint inspectors to see that all such drains were kept in good condition. Six prominent Philadelphians were selected to view the streets and authorized to levy a tax of £400 to further their work. Through the private initiative of townsmen, sporadically encouraged by advice from Mayor and Common Council, a good beginning had been made by 1720 at underdraining Philadelphia, but the greatest advance was to come in the next period, when the paving of streets provided an additional incentive for the construction of drains and sewers.[44]

Even less sewer construction took place at New York. Residents of Broad Street petitioned the Common Council for a "Common Sewer through the same" in 1696. The Corporation, after estimating that such an improvement would cost the town £865. 10., dropped the matter with alacrity. Some sort of a "Common Sewer in the Broad Street" and a "Common Sewer Next the Dock" had been built by 1703. New York was slow to provide underground drainage for its streets and houses, contenting itself with channels through the center of the roadway, even though these became constantly clogged with dirt and refuse. Yet even these rudimentary facilities surpassed

[43] 11 Bos. Rec. Com., 135, 175, 200; 13 Bos. Rec. Com., 19, 21, 30, 62, 71.
[44] Pa. Col. Recs., I, 381, 559; Pa. Statutes, II, 65.

those of Newport and Charles Town, where no adequate arrangements for drainage existed in this period.[45]

The bridge building activities of townsfolk provided the necessary complement to their expanding highways. Such conveniences continued for the most part, as in the past, the work of private capital, but their maintenance and efficiency depended upon the vigilance of public authorities. The geographical location of Boston, together with its growing population and trade, made the need for bridges there imperative. In 1704 the Selectmen sought to eliminate the "Hazzard of the lives of Passengers" over the drawbridge across the Mill Creek at Ann Street by filing complaints against the bridge proprietors with the County Court. The next year they forbade the undertakers of another drawbridge across the Mill Creek at Middle Street to complete their draw, ordering them instead to repair the existing bridge, making it fast and wide enough for the "passage of Horse and Cart." In 1708 the Selectmen forced the proprietors of this structure to rebuild it as a wider bridge with a safe draw. Within a year it was again out of repair, and had to be fastened down, because, as the Selectmen said, "if any person Should Lose their Life or Limb . . . the Town by law is answerable for the damages, and not the persons who receive benefit by the Same as a drawbridge." [46]

Sometime after 1690 a drawbridge was thrown across the creek or inlet at Oliver's Dock. By 1708 this, too, had become "dangerous" and the Selectmen agreed with "the principall owners" to remove the "Timber worke overhanging ye Same." Two years later the board made a contract with Zachary Triscot to build a "Substantiall fast Bridg of twelve foot wide over the Creek in Mackerill lane," for the sum of twelve pounds. This public bridge venture proved far more satisfactory than the privately managed structures over Mill Creek. On August 27, 1720, the Town Meeting instructed its representatives to the General Court "to promote the building a Bridge over the Charles River at the place where the Ferry to [Charlestown] hath Usually been kept, vizt. between mr. Gees and Hudsons point, and at no other place." [47] Provincial authorities willingly encouraged this ambitious project, but, lacking the necessary funds, suggested that a group of proprietors undertake the construction. Regulations concerning tolls were actually drawn up, and compensation provided to Harvard College for the loss of its ferry income, but such a large

---

[45] *N. Y. M. C. C.*, I, 405; II, 83, 322, 378; *N. Y. Col. Laws*, I, 907. In 1706 Governor Nathaniel Johnson blamed a recent sickness at Charles Town on poor drainage, and urged the Assembly in vain to provide for "making common Shores." S. C. Commons Journal, Nov. 20, 1706.

[46] 11 *Bos. Rec. Com.*, 40, 45, 76, 87, 105, 110, 124, 128; Bonner's Map, 1722.

[47] 8 *Bos. Rec. Com.*, 145; Drake, *Antiquities of Boston*, 560.

public work proved beyond the financial capacity of the inhabitants in this period, and came to naught.

Similar activity in bridge building went on at Philadelphia. A drawbridge to carry Front Street over Dock Creek was erected there in 1700. In 1714 the Corporation ordered a "Causway" built "with all Expedition" from the south end of this bridge "leading to Society Hill." This project was still incomplete in August, 1716, and rain had already "washt away some part of the Causeway." The Common Council found the road dangerous in its present state, and if "not Speedily ffinisht will create a much Greater Charge." Consequently, since funds were low, they borrowed on the security of anticipated taxes to finish the causeway. The work was completed the next year, but within two years' time the Grand Jury found that the drawbridge "wants repairing & not passable." Another bridge was built over Dock Creek at Second Street in 1720. This structure, the same width as the street, was constructed of stone at a cost of £160 to the city and £35 more to residents of Second Street. The brick arch, or bridge, at Front and Mulberry Streets, built in 1690, had been repaired in 1704, but in 1719 the Grand Jury found it again in dangerous condition. It was pulled down at this time and rebuilt by the proprietors at considerable expense.[48]

"For the conveniency of people that goeth and cometh to and from Ashley River" at Charles Town, a bridge over Vanderhorst's Creek at Granville's Bastion was constructed by Colonel William Rhett at the province charge in 1704. In 1714 the Assembly erected a brick bridge "capable of bearing any carriage over it" across a creek through Colonel Robert Daniel's land "for the better communication of Charles Town." At Newport, when the new section of land at the Point was opened up in 1714 and a highway pushed through, Thomas Lillibridge raised a "subscription" to build a bridge from the foot of Marlborough Street out to Easton's Point. This bridge was two rods wide, and equipped with a draw to allow small vessels to enter the Cove.[49]

In most of the towns either the inhabitants or some one hired by them made up the labor force necessary for the construction and repair of highways and bridges. The inherited English practice of requiring from each inhabitant a certain number of days each year for work on the roads survived to a considerable extent in colonial towns. At Philadelphia, for instance, the law stated that "the Inhabitants are Obliged to send Able Labourers to do the Work." In

[48] Westcott, *Philadelphia*, chapter LXII; *P. M. C. C.*, 8, 97, 111, 137, 173, 175; Court Papers, Phila. Cty., I (1719); *Votes Pa. Assembly*, II, 291, 307, 312.
[49] *S. C. Statutes*, VII, 37, 63; S. C. Commons Journals, 1713–1716, 278; *Newport T. M. Recs.*, 168, 170.

1712 the Corporation accepted a money payment of one shilling six-pence for each day in lieu of actual labor, and the Assembly ordered "common carters . . . to assist with their carts and teams four days in every year (if thereunto required by the mayor) in repairing the streets." In 1719 people living in the "Woods part" of Newport were directed to bring their carts and serve three days a year in mending roads under the superintendence of one of the surveyors of the highways. Boston, with its ambitious street building program, was forced to hire white labor at relatively high wages. The General Court rendered timely assistance to the town by its law of 1707 requiring all Negroes and mulattoes, since they were forbidden to serve with the watch or train-bands, to perform a proportionable amount of free public labor in some other capacity. The Selectmen improved this opportunity to "assigne each free negro & molatto man of this Towne, . . . to attend and perform four dayes Labour, abt repaireing the Streets or Highwayes." In 1708 the Selectmen made this highway work a regular yearly duty of the free blacks, and twenty-four of them, superintended by Constable Samuel Slater, spent from four to eight days each on the roads. Throughout this period a goodly share of Boston's highway labor, especially the repairing, was performed by these Negroes.[50]

The demands of growing populations and increasing traffic in the towns wrought great advances in highway engineering during these years. Provision of necessary means of communication and transportation heavily taxed the meager treasuries of the towns, but in most cases they nobly met the costs of their constant expansion. In Boston, the amount of money expended by the town and the time and care of the Selectmen are alike worthy of admiration. When the state of town treasuries did not permit of public undertakings, improvements were often performed by individuals or groups of citizens, although sometimes, as in the case of New York's drainage system or the Charles River Bridge at Boston, facilities that were really needed had to be foregone. In general, however, highway conditions in the colonial towns were distinctly superior to those prevailing in England, as may be seen by comparison with the second city of the British Isles. In 1720 Bristol was a wealthy city of about twenty-five thousand inhabitants. The leading streets of the town, which averaged "under twenty feet" in width, were paved on the sides with large cobble stones, and an unpaved trough or gutter, running down the center, was the only means of drainage which the town enjoyed. There were no sewers, and most of the lanes and alleys

[50] P. M. C. C., 80; Pa. Statutes, II, 419; Newport T. M. Recs., 205; 11 Bos. Rec. Com., 60, 72, 158, 166; Mass. Acts and Resolves, I, 606.

were totally unpaved.[51] New York, Boston and Newport, with smaller populations and fewer resources, had highways far more creditable to their civic pride; Philadelphia was beginning to awake to its public duties in this respect, and Charles Town, in spite of a clumsy form of government and a series of natural disasters, showed progress which might well have furnished an example to cities of the Old World.

Some advance was made in this period in the maintenance and protection as well as in the construction and repair of town streets. Two tasks confronted town authorities: the keeping the ways free from obstruction; and the provision of some system of street cleaning. The tendency of citizens to encroach upon the highways of each town continued as much of a public nuisance as ever it had been in the seventeenth century, and strict ordinances, reinforced by heavy fines, were enacted to prevent it. The absence of such regulations at New York and Philadelphia provides an exception to the general rule. Either these corporations were little bothered with encroachments, or they ignored the presence of such nuisances; at any rate, during this period they seemed to feel no need to employ their powers to deal with such abuses.

In 1698 the town of Boston secured a province act enabling the Selectmen to guard its rights against encroachments on its highways, and three years later set a twenty shilling fine as penalty for the erection of fences, buildings, or the removal of landmarks without official permission. At the same time all persons were forbidden to "incumber or annoy any Street" with building materials, firewood, or other obstructions, "above the space of forty-eight hours." Under authority from these ordinances the Selectmen had continually to deal with offenders. In 1701 Josiah Sanders was presented to the Grand Jury for erecting a "portch on the Highway," and in 1704 the Selectmen proceeded against "Sundry p'sons who have made Encroachments on the Lower Side of the Highway" near the drawbridge. Encroachments could be easily settled, but not so the problem of encumbering the streets. In 1705 the Selectmen ordered Edward Mortemore to stop work at the house of James Lablond, because of "his Laying Timber" in the street, and five years later they warned seven builders about cluttering the public ways with stones, earth and lumber. Obadiah Russel was actually fined five shillings for a similar offense in 1711. By far the worst offenders on this score were "the Several Ship wrights," who continually "Transgressed the Town Order by incumbering the High way with Laying Timber there." The streets

[51] Latimer, *Bristol in the Eighteenth Century, passim.* Conditions were even worse at Liverpool; see Picton, *Municipal Archives and Records,* 57, 62, 63.

of Boston were kept clear for the passage of traffic only by the constant heroic efforts of its board of Selectmen.[52]

Newport also suffered frequent annoyance from persons who regarded the public ways as their private preserves, and in 1700 a special committee received authority to deal with cases of encroachment and to remove illegal fences. The surveyors of the highways had to be empowered in 1712 to proceed against persons whose "steps of doores, Shops & Cellars & Cellar doors or shop windows" protruded into the streets, and an additional committee was chosen to aid them in 1715. The principal obstacles to passing traffic at Newport were lumber and lime kilns in the streets, and strict orders to prevent such encumbrances were issued in 1707 and 1712.[53]

The towns were also hard put to it to preserve some measure of cleanliness in their streets, cluttered as they were with increasing business and constant building. Here again, Charles Town proves exceptional, and to the lack of a city government may be ascribed the fact that no provision at all was made for cleaning its thoroughfares. It was the more developed civic pride of Boston that led to the most determined efforts in this direction.

The four scavengers provided by the Boston law of 1684 could not cope with the street cleaning problem of the growing seaport. In spite of occasional attempts to better the situation nothing was accomplished until the accumulation of "Dirt and Trash" on the streets, caused by the fire of 1711 and the building that followed it, goaded the town fathers into action. In May, 1713, the Town Meeting resolved to choose eight scavengers annually, one for each ward; they were to be authorized "to Hire or furnish at the Cheapest Rates they Can" men with horses and carts to carry away the dirt "raked up in all paved Streets Lanes or Highways." All charges for this service were to be born by the town. To facilitate the work of the cleaners an order of 1714 obliged all householders to "Sweep or Rake up the Dirt into Heaps" before their residences, and empowered scavengers to impress any carter to carry it away at one shilling a load. With this arrangement Boston enjoyed well cleaned streets, but by 1720 it had been found "by Experience, Inconvenient for the Town to pay the charge in Common of carrying away the Dirt," and the inhabitants voted that until further notice such costs should be born by the residents of each street.[54] Thus, an excellent street cleaning system broke down because of lack of funds for its support.

[52] *Mass Acts and Resolves*, I, 311; 11 *Bos. Rec. Com.*, 8, 29, 31, 39, 46, 97, 122, 149, 226.
[53] *Newport T. M. Recs.*, 92, 157; *Newport T. M. Procs.*, July 29, 1712; April 27, 1715; Jan. 30, 1707.
[54] 7 *Bos. Rec. Com.*, 200, 218; 8 *Bos. Rec. Com.*, 11, 81, 97, 100, 105, 141; 11 *Bos. Rec. Com.*, 182, 191.

No other town made adequate provision for cleaning its streets in these years, though all took some cognizance of the problem. At New York the early system of requiring city carters for a fixed price to collect street refuse heaped up by householders placed such an intolerable burden upon these functionaries as to be superseded by another method in 1695 when Councilman John Vandespiegel agreed with the Corporation to supervise the cleaning of the streets for one year for a salary of £30. In spite of manifest inadequacies, the authorities employed this contract system for many years.[55] In 1708 and 1712 the salary of the scavenger was cut to £12 and £10; at the same time the area to be cleaned according to the contract was reduced till the then scavenger, the Widow Douw, had only to care for a small section of "the broad Street." Beyond this very limited district it is probable that carmen still hauled away refuse at the stated price of sixpence a load.[56] The Corporation of New York was either too poor to spend much money for cleaning the streets of the town, or wofully lacking in that municipal pride increasingly demonstrated by the Bostonians.

Not until 1710 did the Mayor and Common Council require Philadelphians to "sweep the Streets clean before their respective Houses," and even then their ordinance proved so ineffectual that two years later the Assembly had to decree that "no person shall obstruct or annoy the streets of the said city with rubbish, filth or otherwise," upon penalty of five shillings, unless the obstruction be removed within twenty-four hours after warning by the constable. Inhabitants consistently ignored these wholesome rules, and the streets of Philadelphia remained totally neglected throughout the period. Indeed, the only real effort of the Corporation to improve conditions was probably for its own comfort, when for £8 a year in 1719 it hired Edward Howell to clear the "Dirtt about ye Court House as far as belongs to ye Court House." That the Mayor and Common Council were aware of the existence of the problem is all that can be said for them.[57]

At Charles Town authorities blamed the prevalence of sickness on the "nasty keeping of the Streets," but no action was taken until 1710, when the Clerk of the Market was made scavenger with authority to fine persons who failed to keep their portion of the public ways swept and clean. But Newport's wretched streets more closely

[55] In 1701, for instance, Mayor de Riemer had to obtain a treasurer's order for £3. 19. to reimburse himself for money "by him paid to severall Carmen for Cleaning the Streets on the Buriall of the Earle of Bellomont." *N. Y. M. C. C.*, II, 154–155.
[56] *N. Y. M. C. C.*, I, 219, 224, 245, 376; II, 195, 197, 345; III, 4; Peterson, *New York*, 101, 103.
[57] *P. M. C. C.*, 70, 167, 170; *Pa. Statutes*, II, 419.

reproduced conditions in European cities than did those of any other town. In 1707 a committee of the Town Meeting reported that they found,

> many Nucences which is very Grievous & Noisom to ye Inhabitants as well as to Strangers as several Privy Houses sett against ye Streets which empty themselves upon ye cosways or pavement when people pass, several sinks (some breast high) casts out of ye houses and yards upon ye Pavements, which keeps the Streets thereabouts continually Dirty and Mire, and ye Stincks that issueth out of ye houses is not only noisom but is dangerous to ye Spoiling & Damnifying people's apparill should they happen to be neare when ye filth comes out of ye sd. Sincks. Especially in ye Night when people cannot see to shunn them.

Apparently there was no New World equivalent for that familiar warning in ancient Edinburgh, "Gardyloo!" [58]

The problem of stray animals continued and grew in this period. Extension of highways provided new worlds to conquer for the hardy town hogs, and offered a larger stage for their incessant warfare with village dogs. "Noisome swine" troubled inhabitants of every town, and were everywhere the subject of perennial legislation, generally with small effect. At Boston active hog-reeves and large fines reduced the problem to a minimum, but at Newport in 1703 so many porkers were running loose that several children were "in danger of being destroyed by them." [59]

A great increase in the number of roaming dogs resulted in ordinances similar to the hog laws. In 1697 Boston forbade any person with an annual income of less than £20 to own a dog, and allowed only one such pet to those who could afford the luxury. All dogs were forbidden to run at large upon penalty of the enormous fine of £20 for each week they were so allowed, and inhabitants were permitted to kill all strays. Twelve years later, however, the Selectmen had to proceed against the owners of fourteen "curst & unruly doggs & bitches . . . Suffered to go at Large, wch doggs have been offencive . . . by worrying & Seizing of Cattle or otherwise doing damage." At Philadelphia in 1702 people complained about the "Multitudes of doggees" which caused "great loss of their sleepe and other damages," but no action was taken until 1712, when the authorities prohibited the keeping of "great Dogs" within the city limits. In 1716 Newport required all owners of "great Bitches that is kept within this Township" to chain them up and pay a fee for the privilege of ownership.

---

[58] S. C. Commons Journal, Nov. 20, 1706; Trott's Laws (MS.), part II, 31; Newport T. M. Procs., Jan. 30, 1707.
[59] 8 Bos. Rec. Com., 15; Newport T. M. Recs., 105, 118; N. Y. M. C. C., I, 382; Votes Pa. Assembly, I, i, 75; Pa. Statutes, II, 93, 165; S. C. Statutes, VII, 5, 9.

Philadelphia and Charles Town also suffered much from unruly goats.[60]

The casual British traveler visiting Newport during these years would certainly have had ample opportunity to study American animal life at close range from his tavern window. He himself would probably have been one of the "many strangers" who turned "their horses out into the street" to graze. All thoroughfares were well populated with swine and "great bitches." In addition, he would have seen numerous wandering sheep and cattle, under whose hoofs waddled those itinerant geese, which periodically left their home on the Common to swim in "ye river & pond of water where Cattle should drink," and which they "pudled and made noysome to [other] Creatures." There was no doubt that poor Thomas Peckham, the pound keeper, earned his meager salary.[61]

The volume of traffic coursing through the streets of the five towns mounted with considerable rapidity in this period and became a serious problem to town authorities. At Boston, for example, pedestrians found it increasingly difficult to walk along or across streets jammed with horsemen, carts, Hackney and private coaches, stray animals, wheelbarrows and boys playing football. When Samuel Sewall and Major Walley set out by coach for Charlestown they found it very slow going until they had cleared the business district. Returning with a friend from Brookline one December day in 1711 the diarist noted: "We had much ado to get along for the multitude of Sleds coming to Town with wood, and returning." [62]

As early as 1662 Boston had made ordinances against galloping horsemen and carters who did not lead their horses through the streets; in 1701 the town reenacted these rules and further strengthened them in 1720 by the imposition of larger fines. Because Tremont Street was "steep and hence dangerous for carts and children," the Selectmen had it widened to twenty feet in 1711. Pedestrians and residents were further protected after 1717 when the Selectmen granted to several persons the privilege of setting up a row of posts "eight feet distant from their Respective Buildings . . . So as to defend [them] . . . from damage by Carts." Newporters employed a similar method to protect their houses from carts and drays.[63]

In Philadelphia, wrote Captain Thomas Markham in 1695, "We have very good horses and men ride madly on them." The careless

[60] 7 *Bos. Rec. Com.*, 227; 11 *Bos. Rec. Com.*, 92; *P. M. C. C.*, 37; *Votes Pa. Assembly*, II, 114; *Newport T. M. Recs.*, 159, 191; *Pa. Statutes*, III, 24.

[61] *Newport T. M. Recs.*, 74, 90, 148; *Newport T. C. Recs.*, Aug., 1716.

[62] 5 MHS *Colls.*, VI, 59, 66, 179, 223, 330; *News Letter*, Nov. 3, 1713.

[63] 8 *Bos. Rec. Com.*, 12, 144; 11 *Bos. Rec. Com.*, 64, 121, 134; *Newport T. M. Recs.*, 122.

driving of carters caused much annoyance also, and in 1704 the Corporation called all carmen before the Board to warn them to take "Care how they drive their Carts within this City." An effort was made to restrain by law "Galloping Horses, & also Carters Riding in their Carts & Drays, and excessive . . . driving in any of the Streets," and by an act of the Assembly in 1712 the Corporation was empowered to levy a fine of ten shillings for speeding.[64]

At night streets became especially dangerous for pedestrians. The townsman who ventured forth in the dark faced the twofold threat of being run down by galloping horses, or held up and robbed by footpads. It was safest to go in pairs, as did Sewall when he had occasion to go down to the wharves one dark night, "Benj: Larnell lighting me." At New York the magistrates occasionally ordered lights "hung out on a Pole" from the upper windows of houses "in the Darke time of the Moon." This was done by private persons, "without expense to the Corporation." In 1697, "the great Inconveniency that Attends this Citty, being A trading place for want of Lights" led the authorities to order lanterns or lights put in the windows nightly, under penalty of a fine for neglect. Within a month, however, they changed this rule, and ordered "A Lanthorn & Candle" to be suspended during winter before "Every Seaventh House in the Severall Wards," the cost to be defrayed "in Equall proportion by the Inhabitants of the Said Seaven Houses." A light was hung out at the Post Office in Boston on nights when the mail was expected, and in 1719 Eliakim Hutchinson, Esq., gave the town a "lanthorn," which was lighted outside the Town House on "all dark or Stormy Nights." These meager provisions were the only attempts made by the towns to illuminate their streets in this period.[65]

Under the impulse of new highway and paving projects, the towns sought in various ways to beautify their thoroughfares. Philadelphia led the way in 1700 by ordering each inhabitant to plant one or more trees, "viz., pines, unbearing mulberries, water poplars, lime or other shady and wholesome trees," before his door, that the town "may be well shaded from the violence of the sun in the heat of the summer and thereby be rendered more healthy." The Corporation's order of 1705 that all land between Broad Street and the Delaware River "be Grub'd & Clear'd from all its Rubish in order to p'duce English Grass," further enhanced the appearance of the town. So well were these ordinances

[64] Scharf and Westcott, *Philadelphia*, I, 129; *P. M. C. C.*, 6, 57, 59; *Pa. Statutes*, II, 419.

[65] At that, they were not far behind their English contemporaries. Bristol in 1700 placed the burden of lighting streets on the parishes, and some five hundred house- holders were induced to hang out lanterns; they were, however, extinguished by nine o'clock. Liverpool did the same in 1704. *N. Y. M. C. C.*, II, 21; *News Letter*, Mar. 22, 1707/8; 13 *Bos. Rec. Com.*, 60; Latimer, *Bristol in the Eighteenth Century*, 5; Picton, *Municipal Archives*, 83.

obeyed that within the span of a generation Philadelphia had become noted for its fine turf and shady trees.[66]

The period saw similar improvements in all other towns save Newport. Between 1692 and 1701 all "the Stinking Weeds" were removed from cleared lots at Charles Town. Pine, cedar and cypress trees were planted on the main road leading "out of Charles-Town, for three or four Miles, called the Broadway," which Governor Archdale asserted to be so "delightful a Road and walk of great breadth, so pleasantly green, that . . . no Prince[s] in Europe, by all their Art, can make so pleasant a Sight for the Whole Year." In 1708 the Corporation of New York required inhabitants to pull up "poysonous and Stincking Weeds . . . before Every ones doores," and ordered residents in Broadway to plant trees in front of their houses. Bostonians followed this example in 1711.[67]

Several communities devoted increased attention to the care of their town lands. The five public squares reserved to the people of Philadelphia by the foresight of William Penn were cleared off and planted with English grass. On these plots townsmen might graze their cattle upon payment of an annual fee of twelvepence, used for "Buying & Keeping of the Town Bulls." A "parade" or common at Newport had been carefully set apart as a permanent park and cow pasture by 1713. Boston Common served a similar purpose, becoming the private property of village kine, save on training days, when the whole town assembled there in martial splendor. The town appointed a cowkeeper to watch the herd and paid him two shillings a head. In 1701 Deacon John Marion was asked to provide bulls for the town, and "to give out tickets for Cows going on the Common to Such persons as have Property therein." The joys of the common pasture were thus denied the poor Bossy whose owner could not "show forth a ticket" from the Deacon, and the newly appointed cowkeepers had orders to impound all such animals.[68]

v

Just as increasing population and expanding trade led to the building of new highways and bridges in the five towns, so also did they demand a multiplication of waterfront facilities. The number of wharves and docks varied greatly in each seaport, but in all there was evident a growing public interest in the erection and maintenance of adequate conveniences for shipping.

[66] *Pa. Statutes*, II, 65; *P. M. C. C.*, 18.
[67] *S. C. Statutes*, VII, 5, 9, 18; Carroll, *Historical Collections*, II, 95; *N. Y. M. C. C.*, I, 230; II, 253; 11 *Bos. Rec. Com.*, 118, 154.
[68] *P. M. C. C.*, 18, 20, 38; Mumford's Map of Newport; 11 *Bos. Rec. Com.*, 35, 37, 43, 59, 132, 161.

The town of Boston had naturally a vital interest in maintaining good wharves and docks, since so much of its livelihood depended upon its ocean commerce. Care of the Town Dock absorbed much of the Selectmen's time; it was the haven for the fishing, market and wood boats of the inhabitants, and its use by vessels of other ports required the payment of harbor dues. In 1708 one Captain Flint skipped town without paying docking fees, and the irate Selectmen departed from the tradition of their forefathers by instructing the Treasurer "to retaine a Lawyer" to recover the debt. As he succeeded in collecting £15, the town probably ceased to regard this particular barrister as "vermin." To avoid such difficulties in the future the town appointed wharfingers to collect dock fees and in general to superintend the care of public waterfronts. For the convenience of inhabitants in the North End the town in 1706 built another dock and some wharves at Merry's Point, at a cost of about £1,000, raised by taxes. In 1711 the old Dock had become so encumbered by "dirt or Trash" swept from the streets, and from coopers watering their hoops there, that the authorities sought to remedy the situation by levying heavy fines for such misdemeanors. The next year they hired Josiah Byles to remove "out of ye Dock So much Mudd as he can." Some small wharves and a privy had been built at the Dock at the town's expense by 1716.[69]

With a view to prevent the washing away of land, as well as to protect the town from illegal encroachments, the Selectmen carefully regulated the construction of private wharves. In 1708 Mr. Edward Budd, wishing to enlarge his wharf and slip, was permitted to encroach upon town land because of the obvious improvement resulting from his enterprise. Boston merchants were most active in this period, replacing their old wharves with new and larger structures, or building extensions to accommodate augmented shipping. Prior to 1710 Clarke's Wharf was the largest on the harbor, but at that of Eliakim Hutchinson, on which were located several large warehouses, a great volume of business was transacted.[70]

In December, 1709, Dr. Oliver Noyes and "Some other Gentlemen" proposed to the Town Meeting the erection of a large wharf at the foot of King Street, and submitted elaborate specifications for the new structure. The following January the Selectmen held four public hearings on consecutive Mondays at the Town House, to listen to objections, after which they granted the desired franchise. King Street was resurveyed, and the construction of a sixteen hundred foot pier begun. By July, 1713, the Long Wharf, as it was now called, had

<hr/>

[69] This was the first time Boston had ever retained legal counsel. 11 *Bos. Rec. Com.*, 63, 78, 85, 102, 136, 172; 8 *Bos. Rec. Com.*, 41, 60, 76; 13 *Bos. Rec. Com.*, 9, 14.
[70] 11 *Bos. Rec. Com.*, 82; *News Letter*, Dec. 22, 1707.

progressed sufficiently to be in use, and warehouses were already rising rapidly upon it. A few years later Daniel Neal described the Long Wharf as "a noble Pier, . . . with a Row of Warehouses on the North Side for the Use of the Merchants. The Pier runs so far into the Bay that Ships of the greatest Burthen may unlade without the Help of Boats or Lighters." According to Captain Uring, more than thirty vessels could lie at Long Wharf "at the same time with great conveniency." This enterprise, however, did not forestall the erection of other private wharves by Boston merchants. By 1720 the town's waterfront was crowded with the fifty-eight wharves, large and small, that jutted out into the Bay. The larger ones, like Clarke's, Hutchinson's, Oliver's, Pool's and Belcher's, were all well equipped with fine warehouses.[71]

Agitation for a lighthouse at the entrance to Boston harbor began in 1713. The Town Meeting voted to share the expense with the Colony if such an improvement were undertaken, provided it might also share in the income from lighthouse dues. After continual pressure from the town, the General Court passed an act for the building of Boston Light in 1715, and in September of the next year the first lighthouse in the New World began operation. On January 13, 1720, this lighthouse burned down, and a temporary light had to be employed until a new structure could be erected.[72]

Although the docking facilities of Boston were more elaborate, Philadelphia enjoyed the use of more public wharves than any other town. In 1698 four "common wharves" lined the Delaware, at the foot of Chestnut, High, Mulberry (Arch), and Vine Streets, with two flights of stairs leading down to them from Front Street. To these were later added public wharves at Walnut and Sassafras Streets. In 1691 Proprietory Land Commissioners made a grant of the Blue Anchor Landing at Dock Creek to Dr. Griffith Owen. The Blue Anchor had been deeded in perpetuity to the city by William Penn, and supplied a most important link in the economic life of the community. This flagrant reversal of policy produced forceful remonstrances from the citizenry led by Mayor Humphrey Morrey, and the eventual confirmation of the town's title by the charter of 1701.[73]

The Corporation spent considerable sums to keep the public wharves in repair. The Overseers of Wharves were directed in 1710 to see that "fforeigners & others" who used the public wharves paid "reasonable wharfage." Yet the wharves yielded disappointingly little income, and

[71] 8 Bos. Rec. Com., 63, 66; 11 Bos. Rec. Com., 100, 105, 117, 188; Neal, History of New England, II, 225; N. H. Hist. Soc. Colls., III, 141; Bonner's Map of Boston.
[72] Mass. Acts and Resolves, II, 7; News Letter, Sept. 17, 1716; Jan. 18, Feb. 22, 1720.
[73] Narratives of Pennsylvania, 330; P. M. C. C., 8; Logan Papers, III, 6, 10; Pa. Col. Recs., II, 3, 9; Westcott, Philadelphia, chapter XXVIII.

the Corporation decided in 1720 to lease the Walnut and Chestnut Street piers to Mayor William Fishbourn for a yearly rental of £6 each, "The Same to be Kept . . . in good & Sufficient repair." Naturally, few new wharves appeared in this period, when those provided by the city so well sufficed to handle the port's shipping. Samuel Carpenter's "great wharf" or quay, with its crane, storehouses and granaries, continued, however, to be the busiest landing place at Philadelphia.[74]

A town wharf was erected at Newport some time after 1690, but proved too costly for the town to maintain. Consequently, in 1720 the authorities advertised that "those persons in company that shall after the date hereof repair the said wharf and keep it in repair shall have the power to chuse a Wharfinger and take the usual custom of Wharfage both for Wood or any other things landed thereon." A group of proprietors soon organized to take over the wharf, shares in which sold at forty shillings each. The spurt in the town's trade, brought about by the first two intercolonial wars, caused the construction of numerous other private wharves, all under the superintendency of the Town Council. Smaller wharves began to appear around the Cove with the opening up of land on the Point after 1710. Of the numerous Newport landing places, Carr's, Steven's and Peleg Sanford's were the most important.[75]

Although the commerce of New York expanded rapidly during this period, the Town Dock seems to have been regarded as adequate for the shipping of the port. Apparently only one private wharf was built before 1720, though the Corporation evinced more interest in the construction of quays, which ran the length of the East River Front. Doubtless most ships dropped anchor before the town and were unladed and laded by means of lighters. The great Dock was enlarged in 1697 by the construction of a forty-five foot extension of the bridge. Mayor and Common Council continued to experience difficulties with their haven-masters. Constant complaints of the "foulness" of the Dock and its need of repairs were coupled with loss of revenue from "elusive skippers." In 1716 the Corporation purchased in Holland at a cost of £13. 16. 6. a machine by means of which it hoped to keep the Dock clean, but by July, 1720, it was again disbursing £83 for "Carrying sixty Scow loads of Mudd out of the said Dock," and making provision for the removal of forty loads more. Such tribulations could be expected so long as a large sewer emptied into the landing place.[76]

[74] P. M. C. C., 8, 23, 70, 109, 173, 143; Mercury, May 19, 1720; Narratives of Pennsylvania, 331; Hart, Contemporaries, II, 75.
[75] Newport T. M. Recs., 97, 99, 149; R. I. Col. Recs., IV, 24; Newport T. M. Procs., April 25, 1711; April 27, 1715; Bull, Memoir of Rhode Island, II, 72.
[76] "Journal of John Fontaine," 297; N. Y. Col. Docs., IX, 548; N. Y. M. C. C., I, 393, 432; II, 9, 80, 97, 101; Peterson, New York, 117–123.

The port of Charles Town had fewer facilities for handling its growing traffic than any other town, because an indifferent Assembly failed to make sufficient provision for new wharves. A storm in 1700 washed away nearly all existing landing places, and to protect those that remained the government ordered all persons whose land fronted on the Cooper River to construct brick retaining walls along their banks. All owners of brick houses two stories high were permitted to extend their "piazzas" for six feet onto the abutments and thence to build steps up to their doors. The quay thus provided formed the beginning of the famous Charles Town "sea wall." Two public landing places, twenty feet wide, were ordered built from provincial funds in 1701, to replace wharves destroyed the year before. This construction appears to have been all that was undertaken along the waterfront before the end of the period. Ships of any size would thus have had to be served with lighters, and the very "good pylots" that Charles Town boasted at this time.[77]

VI

In these various ways dwellers in the five nascent cities of the New World continued the task, begun in the seventeenth century, of constructing the setting for urban life in colonial America. Boundaries encroached further upon the countryside as in several of the towns new sections began to be opened up for residence and business, while at the same time, in the older hearts of these communities living became crowded and increasing traffic jammed the thoroughfares. The town-dweller in this period had to provide housing and facilities for growing populations and increasing business activities. New and better streets, bridges and drainage, docks and wharves, shops and warehouses, appeared in answer to his growing demands. Further to signalize his coming of age he gave names to his streets, set aside parks and commons, and erected public buildings differentiated according to the purposes for which they were intended. Yet, urban as they had become, and so different in appearance from rural regions, these towns, like contemporary cities of old England, were still very close to the countryside they were in the process of transforming. Gardens, orchards and open lots, grass in some streets sufficient for pasturage, cattle grazing within sight of stately public buildings, and a steady succession of barnyard life down highways newly paved and drained by the most up-to-date of sewers and gutters, revealed how town had not yet obliterated country, but rather had embraced and enclosed it. The process of urbanization was still far from complete.

[77] *S. C. Statutes*, VII, 16, 21, 28; II, 609; S. C. Commons Journal, 1712–1716, 251; *Cal. St. Pap., 1719–1720*, 303.

VI

THE ECONOMIC PATTERN

I

The three decades following 1690, years of great commercial expansion in the New World, constituted a hothouse period in the growth of the five little ports. Nineteen years of war stimulated general trade, both legal and illegal, and gave rise to the sister activities, privateering and piracy. But in some respects the effects of conflict could not but seriously retard commercial development in the towns, as the inevitable period of depression followed hard on the heels of feverish war prosperity. However, the five years following 1715 saw a gradual recovery from this temporary setback, and by the end of the period all five towns were facing a long era of peace and thriving trade.

The outstanding feature in the economic life of the towns at this time was the rapid growth of the trade of Philadelphia, New York, Newport and Charles Town. As later entrants in the field these towns had originally been hampered in their commercial activities by the economic power of Boston. But now their merchants sought by every means to carve a niche for themselves in the commercial system of the Empire, and to acquire a money supply sufficient to pay for the great importation of English goods now needed to meet the demands of an ever rising standard of living. By 1720 these merchants had largely succeeded in establishing the avenues of trade that their successors followed throughout the colonial period.

The developments of these years promised to Philadelphia a brilliant commercial future, and no town, not even Boston, enjoyed so rapid an extension of its seaborne trade. A "great and extended Traffique" in grain, provisions, lumber, tobacco, horses, livestock, meats, pipe staves and wool with other colonies, especially the Caribbean islands, made wealthy men of Quaker merchants and provided employment for countless artisans. The need of Pennsylvanians for hardware, clothing, and other manufactured goods led to direct connections with Bristol and London, while a flourishing wine trade developed with Lisbon and Madeira. In addition, Quaker principles failed to restrain many Friends from cultivating piratical connections and engaging in illegal trade throughout the intercolonial wars. Under such favoring circumstances Philadelphia grew like a mushroom. In

1696 Governor Fletcher told the Board of Trade that "Philadelphia in fourteen years time is become equal to the City of New York in trade and riches." James Logan reported an increase in customs receipts from £1,500 in 1699 to £8,000 in 1702, while "New York [had] not the half of it." By 1720 the Quaker town, so "full of all Country business and Sea affairs," had outdistanced all rivals save Boston.[1]

The "Citty of New York" also drove a thriving trade overseas to the West Indies and other continental colonies. "The Trade . . . ," wrote Lord Cornbury, "consists cheifly of flower, and Biskett, which is sent to the Islands." Two other important articles of commerce were furs and whale oil. Part of the West India trade was illegal, and Manhattan merchants maintained an even more suspicious connection with pirates than did Philadelphians. New York mariners also invaded the coastal carrying trade, and pursued an increasing traffic with Pennsylvania, Maryland and the southern colonies. The expanding needs and extravagant tastes of aristocratic burghers called for a growing yearly importation of English manufactures, which now arrived less often by way of Boston than directly from Bristol or London. But, although in 1699 Lord Bellomont believed New York to be "the growingest town in America," and its trade continued to increase, Manhattan traffic in this period did not equal that of Philadelphia.[2]

Commercially, Newport benefited in large measure from the Anglo-French conflicts. Not a little of its maritime prosperity derived from successful privateering ventures of Captain Thomas Paine, John and William Wanton, and Captain Benjamin Ellery, and from illicit traffic with the Dutch and the Caribbean buccaneers. In 1708 Colonel Robert Quary told the Board of Trade that Rhode Island's "cheife trade is to ye West Indies, but more especially they have a great trade to Curaco and Surinam, ye chief town is called New Port, wch is grown in few years to a great town, mainly by illegal trade to those places, nor is it possible to prevent it." Newporters, however, attributed their mounting good fortune to "the inclination the youth on Road Island have to the sea," and to the fact that, unlike Boston, the town had lost only two or three vessels to French privateersmen during the war.[3]

Confining their trade largely to the West Indies and Surinam, Newport merchants continued to purchase manufactured goods from Boston. Horses, lumber, beef, pork, candles, garden and dairy produce

[1] *Narratives of Pennsylvania*, 202, 325; *Pa. Statutes*, II, 90; "Journal of John Fontaine," 301; Nettels, *Money Supply*, 120; *Colden Papers*, I, 35; *Mercury*, May 12, 19, April 28, June 9, 1720; *Pa. Mag.*, XXXVII, 339; *N. Y. Col. Docs.*, IV, 159.
[2] Nettels, *Money Supply*, 114, 115, 118; *N. Y. M. C. C.*, II, 38; *Cal. St. Pap.*, 1699, 59; *N. Y. Col. Docs.*, V, 577, 703; IX, 548; *News Letter*, April 26, 1708.
[3] In 1696 Newport was reported "a free port for pirates. Thomas Tew, a pirate, brought £100,000 there from the Red Sea in 1694." *Cal. St. Pap.*, 1696–1697, 74; 1706–1708, 637; 1708–1709, 175; *R. I. Col. Recs.*, III, 385, 391, 400; 2 MHS *Procs.*, IV, 152.

formed their export cargoes. By 1718 over a hundred thousand pounds of wool were being exported annually. In return for these products they imported "English Goods," rum, molasses, sugar, spices and bullion. With rum secured through the molasses trade with the Caribbean for an article of exchange, Newport mariners early entered the African slave trade, though this traffic did not recover from the interruptions of wartime until after 1720. The West India trade provided the town with a supply of specie with which to purchase European articles from Boston, and rudimentary commercial connections with Lisbon and Madeira had been established by 1710. Newporters also at this time commenced to encroach on Boston's monopoly of the coasting trade with Connecticut, New York and Pennsylvania. The little town prospered during the wars, and its business spurted ahead when they closed. There was no doubt that by 1720 Newport had become the "Metropolitan" of southern New England.[4]

Charlestonians had by 1710 extended their provision trade from the West Indies to the Dutch settlements in South America. Though continuing to mount in volume this traffic soon yielded to naval stores in export importance. A flourishing business sprang up with Barbados, Antigua, Nevis, St. Christopher, Montserrat and the Bahamas, whither Carolina merchants sent staves, hoops and shingles, pitch, tar, beef, pork, rice, greenwax candles, tallow, butter and peas in exchange for rum, sugar, molasses, cotton, fustic, tortoise-shell, salt and logwood. From Barbados and Jamaica they also imported Negro slaves. Edward Randolph reported in 1696 a "Trade to Curacao, from which Holland manufactures are brought into Carolina and carried by illegal traders to Boston, Pennsylvania, etc., the return trade in plantation commodities being passed through the same channels." Another observer noted a considerable traffic with Madeira, "from whence wee receive most of our wine." Increasing consumption of manufactured goods, imported directly from London and Bristol firms, which "very nearly drained . . . all our silver and gold coine," spurred merchants to greater activity in order to meet their payments. In 1709 it was reported that "the Trade of the Province, which all passes through Charles Town, is certainly increased of late years." Prior to 1710 this commerce was still widely diversified; the emergence of rice as the staple to transform the economy of the colony within a few decades was only just beginning.[5]

The outbreak of the Yamassee War in 1715 dealt a severe blow to the nascent prosperity of the little port. Inhabitants of the back

[4] *Cal. St. Pap., 1708–1709,* 173; *1717–1718,* 312; Donnan, *Slave Trade,* III, 110 n.; Bigelow, Commerce of Rhode Island, Part I, chapter II; *Newport T. M. Recs.,* 159; *R. I. Col. Recs.,* IV, 258; *Lloyd Papers,* I, 186.

[5] *Cal. St. Pap., 1699,* 106; *1696–1697,* 73; *1702,* 69; *1706–1708,* 120; *1708–1709,* 466; *Colden Papers,* I, 6, 7; Nairne, *Letter from South Carolina,* 15.

country abandoned their homes in large numbers and fled to the town for refuge. Production of provisions and naval stores ceased; savages cut off the deerskin trade and butchered farmers' cattle. At Charles Town prices and taxes soared. For over two years people were plunged in debt, and the colony in desperate straits. But the Southerners exhibited great recuperative powers, and by 1718 some measure of improvement was evident from the fact that the colonists felt able to import £150,000 worth of goods, chiefly woolens, from England. At the close of the period Charles Town faced a hopeful future, based upon its two principal products, deerskins and the new staple, rice. In 1720 "nearly 200 sail of all sorts" were freighted behind Sullivan's Island for the export trade.[6]

Meanwhile, the pathways of ocean commerce explored by Boston mariners in the seventeenth century became increasingly crowded with their ships in the eighteenth. The country back of Boston failed to produce any important staple suitable for export, and Bay merchants consequently engaged more and more in the importation and distribution of foreign articles. Aided by their fine fleet and by the control they had early established over the coastal trade, Bostonians saw their traffic mount steadily in volume. The Bay port suffered more from the wars than any other town, both from military and naval efforts put forth by the Province of Massachusetts, and from losses sustained by the capture of many vessels at sea. Colonel Quary found in 1708 that "Boston hath been a place of great trade, but the warr hath extreamly impoverish'd them, so that trade is not now one third of what it was." Samuel Sewall told a similar tale, — "though some at the same time have made an Estate." [7]

Notwithstanding the restraining effects of war, Boston's commerce made steady progress; in the very year of the above report over two hundred ships were coasting the Atlantic seaboard to southern and island colonies, and shipbuilding flourished. A busy trade in provisions with Caribbean buccaneers, and successful evasion of the Acts of Trade by running in illicit merchandise from off Cape Ann in "Wood boats," served in some measure to offset the depredations of French privateers. In all events trade was fully recovered by 1720, and Boston was still unquestionably the commercial metropolis of English America.[8]

Bostonians imported the major portion of European goods consumed in America, and distributed them by means of their coasting

[6] Before the Indian War the wealth of South Carolina was placed at £709,163, and it was believed to have decreased one-third by 1716. Debts mounted from £44,000 to £100,000; *Cal. St. Pap., 1714–1715,* 236; *1716–1717,* 133, 226, 290; *1717–1718,* 217; *1719–1720,* 322; S. C. Pub. Recs., VII, 246, 267; VIII, 61.
[7] 5 MHS *Colls.,* V, 350; 6 MHS *Colls.,* I, 191, 385; *Cal. St. Pap., 1706–1708,* 637.
[8] *Cal. St. Pap., 1708–1709,* 111; *1716–1717,* 338; *1719–1720,* 91, 360; *N. Y. Col. Docs.,* IV, 792; N. H. Hist. Soc. *Colls.,* III, 143.

fleet to every colony except South Carolina. Despite their entrance into direct trade with England and Portugal, both Philadelphia and New York still obtained many of their manufactured articles by way of Boston. So keen was the rivalry between Boston and New York for the business of Long Island and the provision trade to the West Indies that during the administrations of Dongan and Hunter the New York Assembly levied a heavy duty on goods imported into New York from other colonies. Similar complaints against Bay traders were made at Philadelphia. As Bostonians everywhere took the profits of middleman and carrier, their town maintained a favorable balance of trade against its competitors; gold and silver from other colonies flowed into the coffers of Massachusetts merchants, who in turn used it to redress adverse balances with English creditors. The Bay town was by 1720 the "coin center of the continental colonies," and Philadelphia and New York, despite the unprecedented expansion of their commerce, still remained "tributary" to Boston.[9]

The primary commercial service of Boston was as a marketing and distributing center, which, while it extended throughout the colonies, was particularly important in New England. As earlier, Boston drained coastal and inland towns of their surplus produce, and sent them in return the manufactured goods they needed.[10] Most of the lumber of New Hampshire went to Boston, whence the mast fleet annually departed, while the New Hampshire naval stores industry was financed from King Street. Newport successfully competed with Bay merchants in the West India trade, but was completely dependent upon Boston for its English manufactures. "We are linked to the Province of Massachusetts (perticularly to the Towne of Boston)," wrote Governor Cranston of Rhode Island in 1708. "As to our Traffick and dealings together, wee cannot, without great inconveniency and prejudice differ from them in the valuation and rates of foreigne coine." Indeed not, for Newport annually redressed its adverse balance with Boston by payment of £40,000 "cash." The farm produce of Connecticut likewise came to Boston, for that colony had no merchants sufficiently wealthy to import stores of European goods or West India products. In 1697 Samuel Sewall sent bedding, curtains, blankets, and other cloth worth £24. 4., which he had imported from Bristol, England, to Israel Chauncy at Stratford, Connecticut, and in 1705 he shipped a "trunk" of similar goods to John Lydius at distant Albany.[11]

[9] Boston merchants dealt in New York bills of exchange drawn on England. *News Letter*, April 26, 1708; 6 MHS *Colls.*, I, 349; V, 69, 165; Nettels, *Money Supply*, 99–127.
[10] "All the country of New-England takes off great quantities of British manufactures," wrote Captain Uring in 1720. N. H. Hist. Soc. *Colls.*, III, 143.
[11] "What commodities any [of Rhode Island] . . . have had to export for England, hath been exported by way of Boston, . . . from whence we are chiefly supplied with

Improved roads greatly facilitated this inland traffic. By about 1700 most of the modern roads out of Boston had been laid out, and carts came into general use. The post rider covered the distance from the "mart town" to New York in one week in summer, and in 1710 Madam Sarah Knight undertook her famous journey over that route on horseback. The great eastern road, running from Winnisimet ferry eastward through Salem and Newbury, was improved for the post as far as Portsmouth, and travel over it made easier by the opening up of more ferries. Highways across the province to Connecticut also were made passable for carts and calashes at this time. When the wretched state of English roads, especially those of the West Country near Bristol, is considered, one can the more easily understand the statement of Captain Nathaniel Uring at the end of this period, that he preferred traveling in the colonies to coaching in England, France or Italy: "They have very good roads all through the Country." [12]

Along these roads passed the carts of "Merchants and Inland Traders," with loads of "Mens wearing Apparel, viz. Coats, Breeches, Shoes, Buckles, Shirts, Neckcloaths, and Gloves, . . . also Salt, Nutmegs, Mace, Olives, Cinamon, and several other sort of Goods," to stock the shelves of country stores like that of James Corbin at Woodstock, Connecticut. The itinerant Yankee peddler or country chapman with his mysterious pack became an institution in these years, and drove a profitable trade throughout the countryside. James Gray, "That used to go up and down the Country Selling of Books," died at Boston in 1705, leaving an estate of £700 which he had accumulated from peddling various almanacs, Mather's sermons, and *The Husband-man's Guide in four parts.* So large became this inland traffic, conducted by "pedlars, petty Chapmen and Hawkers," that Boston merchants and country shopkeepers began by 1713 to complain of competition and the consequent decay of trade. Among other things they accused hawkers and walkers of selling large quantities of goods stolen during the great fire of 1711. The General Court, ever sensitive to mercantile demands, promptly passed a law forbidding the traffic, and laying a fine of twenty shillings on violators. But in 1716 the law had to be reenacted, and from all indications the illicit traffic continued to thrive under cover.[13]

---

the manufactory of England." *Cal. St. Pap., 1709,* 172, 173; Nettels, *Money Supply,* 106; 6 MHS *Colls.,* I, 312; V, 51; Neal, *New England,* II, 245.

[12] In 1720 a regular stage service to Bristol Ferry, R. I., commenced operation. Weeden, *Economic and Social History,* I, 410; II, 440, 508; *News Letter,* Dec. 4, 1704; April 4, 1720; 6 MHS *Colls.,* V, 232; N. H. Hist. Soc. *Colls.,* III, 144.

[13] In 1708 there were over a hundred towns in Massachusetts alone; the population of New England was perhaps eighty-five thousand to a hundred thousand. *News Letter,* April 16, 1705; June 30, 1712; *Cal. St. Pap., 1708–1709,* 110; 7 MHS *Colls.,* VIII, 204; *Mass. Acts and Resolves,* I, 720; II, 27.

During these years Philadelphia, too, began to develop a hinterland traffic. By 1720 the Pennsylvania frontier line had moved about forty miles west of the Delaware, and Scotch-Irish and Palatine refugees were rapidly pouring into this back country. Philadelphia thus added a new sphere of influence to the Southern Counties, Maryland and West New Jersey, which had been under its commercial dominance since about 1700. With these regions Quaker merchants exchanged European goods for export produce. The whole trade of West Jersey and the Lower Counties passed through Penn's town, and country-men frequently resented their loss of "Coyne" to the metropolis. As early as 1694 Marylanders complained that Pennsylvania traders had taken £1500 in sterling out of the province in the past two years. As a result the Maryland Assembly enacted discriminatory duties and laws against export of specie to Pennsylvania in 1694, 1695, and 1704.[14]

In 1695 the Pennsylvania Assembly moved to better the "Cart-ways" leading to the back country of the Schuylkill region and to Chester County, and by 1710 Chester County farmers were able to haul their produce regularly to town by cart. "The roads are good here," reported a traveler from Europe in 1716. In 1706 Lord Cornbury granted a monopoly for a stage line between Amboy and Burlington in New Jersey, and another for a ferry from Burlington to Philadelphia, to complete a through line of communication between Philadelphia and New York, for "the transportation of goods and passengers" in "coaches and Waggons," and doubtless for country chapmen as well.[15]

New York's inland traffic did not attain the proportions of that of Philadelphia, and of course could not compare with the trade centering around Boston. To the territory up the Hudson as far as Albany, the settlements of eastern Long Island and lower Connecticut, the New Yorkers after 1690 added East New Jersey as a part of their economic sphere. They did not achieve this without a struggle with the Jerseymen, who made Perth Amboy a port of entry in hope of forestalling the draining off of their trade and specie by Manhattan merchants. New York's traffic was carried on largely by water, although some "very bad and stony" roads were extended into Westchester in this period. A large share of upcountry trade fell into the hands of hawkers and peddlers, who were required in 1714 to take out licenses from the Governor, before they could "trade from town to town" or cry their wares.[16]

[14] Nettels, *Money Supply*, 121–124.
[15] *Votes Pa. Assembly*, I, i, 92; Myers, *Irish Quakers*, 199; *Mercury*, Mar. 17, 1720; *Pa. Mag.*, IX, 442; "Journal of John Fontaine," 301.
[16] Nettels, *Money Supply*, 117; *N. Y. Col. Laws*, I, 805; II, 6.

Settlement in South Carolina advanced very slowly, and by 1720 only a few scattered hamlets and trading posts could be found more than thirty miles distant from Charles Town. Thus the little southern port did not serve a very large area. On the other hand, it continued the center of the southern fur trade, which had by 1700 penetrated nearly a thousand miles into the interior of the continent. By 1720 Charles Town had begun the development of an inland trade which in the next two decades, when roads displaced forest paths, was to grow with great rapidity.[17]

Newport was sadly handicapped in her efforts to create a dependent countryside, for both to north and south of Rhode Island lay the commercial domains of Boston. The only opportunity for inland traffic open to Newport merchants was in the Narragansett country and the region of Windham County, Connecticut. This latter section already enjoyed wagon road connection with Boston. In 1720 all the produce of the Naragansett plantations was coming over the Jamestown ferry to Newport, and a small beginning had been made in northeastern Connecticut, but the town remained largely tributary to Boston. Even so, Massachusetts peddlers after 1714 often found it hard going in Rhode Island.[18]

Although in the year 1720 the commercial hegemony of Boston over the North American continent was still virtually complete, it was no longer undisputed, and there were ample signs of incipient competition from the four other towns. Philadelphia's growth promised great things for the future, when its almost limitless back country should become settled, and New York, too, was expanding at a rapid rate. In its chosen fields, the slave and West India trades, Newport was a potential rebel within the New England empire, and Charles Town was staking out a claim that would eventually be closed to Yankee traders.

II

Town industries auxiliary to the export trade enjoyed a growth parallel to that of colonial commerce. In every town the principal industries were those that had to do with shipping and the preparation of provisions or naval stores for export. Thus more and more demand

[17] In 1712 the Assembly learned that "the path from the Town so far as Goose Creek, is much too Narrow for the passage of Carts & Coaches." Carroll, *Historical Collections*, II, 97; Crane, *Southern Frontier;* Gray, *History of Agriculture*, I, 328; S. C. Commons Journal, 1712–1716, 20, 226.

[18] "Pedlars" opening "packs of any sort of dry goods" in a Rhode Island town were subject to forty shillings fine. *Newport T. M. Recs.*, 174; Peterson, *Rhode Island*, 61; Bidwell and Falconer, *History of Agriculture*, 28, 109; Kimball, *Providence*, 147, 153; *R. I. Col. Recs.*, IV, 62; *R. I. Acts* (1719), 69.

arose for the services of millers, bakers, butchers, packers, bolters, shipwrights, sawyers and coopers.[19]

New York continued to lead in milling, largely as a result of valuable privileges conferred by the "Bolting Act" of 1684. Rural communities, however, became increasingly vociferous in their opposition to the town's monopoly. After an unsuccessful lawsuit against the Corporation in 1691 William Nicoll, Esq., acting as counsel for Jacob Rutsen of Ulster County, petitioned Governor Fletcher for abolition of the monopoly. £400 and other suitable "gifts" are believed to have changed hands, Fletcher, as was to be expected, faring particularly well in the transaction. The struggle reached a climax in 1694 with the passage of a law declaring all measures taken by the city to enforce its privileges to be null and void. New York merchants and tradesmen protested vigorously at this defeat, which they asserted would "Make Every Planter's hutt throughout this Province a Markett for wheate, for wheate Flour and Biskett, whereby the Principalls of Trade are reduced to Confusion." The Corporation maintained that out of 983 houses in New York in 1698 six hundred depended upon the bolting trade, and that since the repeal of the act "The People Desert . . . [and] the Buildings . . . fall to Decay." For the sake of some thirty bolters in rural districts the livelihood of two thirds of the town, which paid from twenty to thirty per cent of provincial taxes, was practically swept away by this "libertisme of Trade." Moreover, the poor quality of the colony's flour since repeal of the monopoly was enabling Pennsylvania to supplant New York in West Indian markets. In 1700 the Corporation passed a retaliatory ordinance levying an "Imposition" on all flour and "harde bread" brought into the city; country Assemblymen countered by refusing all grants of money to Bellomont till he had secured its repeal. The incident has considerable significance as an indication of the widespread mercantilist views of New York merchants, and of growing bad feeling between country and town.[20]

Newport was the only town besides New York where much flour was milled. In 1690 Rhode Islanders had begun to erect those graceful windmills, which today we find so picturesque, for grinding their corn and wheat. Most Pennsylvania flour was milled outside of Phila-

[19] In 1717 the Corporation of Philadelphia granted 434 freedoms, eighty-eight of which were to persons directly connected with the preparation of food for market. At New York from 1694 to 1706, of 319 freedoms granted, there were fourteen butchers, thirty-three bakers, twenty-five victuallers, ten bolters, and six tallow chandlers. The proportion at Newport was about the same. *P. M. C. C.; N. Y. Hist. Soc. Colls.,* 1885; Richardson Collection, 982.

[20] *N. Y. Col. Laws,* I, 326, 449; *N. Y. M. C. C.,* II, 38, 111, 114, 120; *Pol. Sci. Quarterly,* XXX, 80; Osgood, *Colonies in the Eighteenth Century,* I, 263.

delphia, brought into town to be bolted or baked, and then shipped away to the islands in the sloops of Quaker merchants.[21]

The "mistery of cooperage" was one of the largest trades in each town, and the leather industry, especially tanning, saddlery, and the manufacture of shoes, increased in importance. The growth of these two industries was particularly remarkable in Philadelphia, where both cooperage and cordwaining had become crafts large enough to warrant incorporation in 1718. The two trades likewise attained considerable importance at Boston and Charles Town.[22]

In shipbuilding Boston led all towns in this period. Provincial authorities carefully watched the quality of their products, and forbade the building of ships over thirty tons "unless under the direct supervision of a competant shipwright." Bostonians were now turning out really large ships, as tonnage went at the time. In 1693 Sewall witnessed the launching of "The Ship at Brill's Wharf of Four Hundred Tuns, named the Lese-Frigot." By 1720 Boston's fourteen shipyards were producing annually about two hundred ships, ranging from twenty to four hundred tons burthen. A big launching was the occasion of general interest and celebration throughout the town, although the "foolish and profane custom of a Mock-Baptism, in the launching of a Vessel" greatly grieved that keeper of the Boston conscience, Cotton Mather.[23]

The building of ships was an important industry in most other ports. In 1712 more than a dozen Newport shipbuilders furnished vessels for colonial trade. Among leading shipwrights, who met almost daily at the King's Head Tavern to discuss latest developments in their craft, were Ralph Chapman, Benjamin Belcher, James Easton, Stephen Hoockey, and Daniel Lambert. Many of their vessels were sold at Boston; in 1716 Hoockey advertised in the *Boston News Letter* a "Snow very near ready to be Launched and built with choice Timber and Plank." The industry also expanded rapidly at Philadelphia, so that by 1718 at least ten shipyards lined the banks of the Delaware. New Yorkers were slower to engage in shipbuilding, but had made some progress by 1720. In that year Charles Town merchants possessed only twenty vessels, "generally small," most of which had been built in the north, and George Duckett's shipyard on the Cooper River seems to have been used more for refitting than for building ships. These shipyards everywhere created employment for many smiths,

---

[21] Over forty bolters and coopers engaged in the Philadelphia flour trade in 1704; brewing also occupied many persons. Accounts of millers, coopers, etc. (MS); Hart, *Contemporaries,* II, 75; *Newport T. M. Recs.,* 72.

[22] *P. M. C. C.,* 145; *News Letter,* May 16, 1715; S. C. Commons Journal, 1703, 95.

[23] Over five hundred and fifty ships were launched at Boston, 1696–1713. Bonner's Map; *Cal. St. Pap., 1708–1709,* 111; Nettels, *Money Supply,* 69; 7 MHS *Colls.,* VIII, 473.

braziers, sail and ropemakers, and in each town cordage merchants enjoyed a thriving business.[24]

III

New names and new faces appeared in the merchant group of each town in this period. If the uncertainties and vicissitudes of the first two intercolonial wars led to the impoverishment of some of the older merchants, they also provided opportunities for the enrichment and success of many younger and more venturesome spirits. At Boston the merchant class expanded considerably, while only a few seventeenth century magnates, like Sewall, Clark, the Olivers and the Hutchinsons remained active in trade. Business leaders like Stephen Minot, Andrew Belcher, who moved in from Cambridge, the Huguenot Andrew Faneuil, and Thomas Amory, the last newly arrived from Charles Town, became the new mercantile nobility of the metropolis. These men owned, either wholly or in shares, the vessels that unladed at Long Wharf or at their own piers, whereon they erected capacious warehouses for the storage of their merchandise. Here they disposed of European goods wholesale to inland traders and country storekeepers, or to town shopkeepers and citizens. Alongside each wharf lay numbers of their sloops and other small craft, loading or unloading articles for the coastwise trade.

Boston merchants remained throughout this period general importers, trying all ports and commodities to reap a profit. A tendency to specialization in one or two lines of goods was, however, already noticeable. Samuel Sewall's principal exports were "Barrels of Mackerell" and fish or whale oil, which he usually exchanged for cotton-wool or sugar, but he also handled ten other items for export and imported over fifty different commodities. John Mico specialized in "good Cordage of all size," and William Clark in the "best Jamaica Sole-leather"; Isaac Lopez generally sold sugar or "New York Flower," although customers went frequently to his warehouse at the end of Merchant's Row for "Sundry Sorts of European Goods." The more usual offerings of Boston merchants were varied as those sold by Andrew Faneuil at his "Store" in King Street, — "flowered Venetian Silks of the newest Fashion, in Pieces that contain enough for a Suit for a Woman, Cordages of all Sizes, from a Spun-yarn to an Eight Inch Cable; Codlines of the best Sort, and sundry other Sorts of European Goods, as also French Salt." [25]

[24] *Cal. St. Pap., 1708–1709*, 175; *Newport Hist. Mag.*, II, 423; *Lloyd Papers*, I, 155; West and Reynell Account Books (MS); *Pa. Mag.*, LVI, 158; S. C. Pub. Recs., V, 206; VI, 148; VII, 249; *News Letter*, July 3, 1704; April 23, Sept. 3, 1716.
[25] 6 MHS *Colls.*, I, 4 n.; *News Letter*, Aug. 21, 1704; Oct. 8, 1705; Dec. 10, 1705; Aug. 25, 1707; *Bos. Gaz.*, Feb. 15, April 25, 1720.

At Philadelphia the number of merchants mounted so rapidly as to form a distinct class by 1720. The wealth which they accumulated in commerce and their control of the town's economic life made possible the foundations of several large fortunes. Prominent among these merchants were the now familiar names of Edward Shippen, Thomas Lloyd, Jr., Thomas Masters, Richard Willing, Cadwallader Colden, William Fishbourn and Jonathan Dickinson. One of the most enterprising was John Copson, who offered to the public from his warehouse in High Street such variegated importations as decorated maps, guns and fowling pieces, and "a Neat Pocket-Piece, or Medal, struck upon a new and fine Metal and beautiful even as Gold . . . Price 3s." In addition to his activities as importer of European goods, Copson in 1717 acted as private insurance broker for shipowners of the town, and in 1719 backed William Bradford in founding the *American Weekly Mercury*.[26] Samuel Carpenter and William Fishbourn ranked high among the substantial merchants of this period, since besides conducting large ventures in importing and exporting, they owned and operated the principal wharves and warehouses at Philadelphia.

The rewards of trade appealed to many at New York; "Nearly everyone who counted, except a few officials sent from England, was a merchant . . . and seemingly they were all speculators in the narrower meaning of the word." Abraham de Peyster, Caleb Heathcote, William Morris, Jacob Franks, Benjamin Faneuil, Louis Gomez and Richard Willet constituted the foremost of this group. Cadwallader Colden moved to New York late in the period, and his transactions there are typical of the Manhattan merchant. He imported manufactured goods, especially drugs and stockings, on consignment from Richard Hill of London, and sold them chiefly to shopkeepers. Occasionally Mrs. Colden, to make a little pin money, undertook to market some of his merchandise at retail. Many New York merchants, like Colden, Heathcote, Faneuil and Willet, lent money at interest, although more usually such men invested their surplus in western lands.[27]

Despite retarding effects of war, fire and hurricane, Charles Town in this period gained "ye reputation of a wealthy place." Prior to 1720 the bulk of the traffic was in the hands of British merchants who kept factors resident in Carolina. But by their activity in foreign commerce and Indian trade natives like Samuel Eveleigh, Samuel Wragg, Arthur Middleton, Edward Laughton, Jonathan Amory and Madam

[26] *Colden Papers*, I, 11, 24, 35, 40; *Mercury*, April 28, July 21, 28, 1720; May 25, 1721; Westcott, *Philadelphia*, chapter LXVII.
[27] Fox, *Caleb Heathcote*, 19, 66; N. Y. Hist. Soc. *Colls.*, 1885; *Colden Papers*, I, 48.

Sarah Rhett laid the foundations of fortunes later to be invested in plantations. These merchants imported large quantities of English goods which they disposed of at their warehouses to Indian traders, planters and Charles Town shopkeepers. Arthur Middleton was one of the first to realize the aspiration of every Charles Town business man, — the combination of planting with commerce. Probably no southern merchant trafficked more widely than Samuel Eveleigh. Engaging in the fur, West India, coastwise and English trades, he also served as Charles Town representative for several Philadelphia houses, as did Jonathan Amory for those at Boston.[28] Very little distinction existed between the mercantile group at Charles Town and that of any northern town.

Unlike the case in other towns, the well known names among Newport merchants remained fairly steady throughout the seventeenth and eighteenth centuries. In the period we are now considering Arnold Collings, Augustus Lucas, Benjamin Ellery, Jahleel Brenton, Caleb Carr, Henry Lloyd, Walter Clarke and Captain John Brown, daily attendants at the Exchange on the first floor of the town schoolhouse, engaged in West India trade and made a beginning in the slave traffic. Collings ran a fulling mill in addition to his shipping ventures. John and William Wanton maintained shipyards, warehouses and wharves, took a chance at privateering and perhaps trade with the enemy as auxiliaries to their West India business, while John Easton operated a brewery to prepare beer and malt for the Island traffic.[29]

An interesting development of this period was the system of interlocking mercantile connections between merchants of different towns, maintained usually through relatives. Edward Shippen of Philadelphia had lived at both Boston and Newport, and thus had friends in both places with whom he did business. Thomas Amory settled at Boston, and conducted a considerable trade through his father Jonathan and his brother-in-law, Arthur Middleton, at Charles Town. The Sanfords of Newport and Barbados, and the Hutchinsons of Boston were related by marriage, and Samuel Sewall dealt with London through his connection, Edward Hull. The Faneuils, Peter of New York and Andrew of Boston, negotiated the transfer of moneys due Boston merchants by means of London bills of exchange. The Jews, who located in Boston, New York and Philadelphia, used their race in lieu of the usual family connection; so, too, did many

[28] *S. C. Commons Journal, 1696*, 16; S. C. Pub. Recs., VIII, 62; Wallace, *South Carolina*, I, 253 n.; McCrady, *South Carolina under the Proprietary Government*, 399, 481.

[29] *R. I. Hist. Tracts*, III, 12; *Lloyd Papers*, I, 138, 158, 179; Weeden, *Economic and Social History*, I, 369; Chapin, *Privateer Ships and Sailors*, 76, 175, 187; *Newport T. M. Recs.*, 136.

Huguenots.[30] But the chief importance of the colonial merchants in 1720 lay in their growing wealth, which would enable them in the coming years of peace to expand their activities beyond anything yet known, and to invest much of their saved capital in land.

IV

Expanding population, increasing wealth, and a rising standard of living in the towns led naturally to multiplication and elaboration of agencies for the marketing and distribution of goods to town-dwellers. More retail shops for those not wealthy enough to buy in bulk became a prime necessity. In addition, retailing, one of the most developed forms of merchandising, began in this period to realize some of the possibilities from numerous small sales and from specialization in one or two lines of goods.

The increase in the number of Boston shops, even during the war years, was remarkable. Probably the majority were small retail groceries from which townsfolk bought their sugar, tea, coffee, spices and molasses. Another important group carried a general line of dry goods and seamen's clothing. A few shopkeepers conducted specialty shops with a definite line of goods for sale. Numerous booksellers' and stationers' shops clustered about the Town House, and in Sudbury Street was located the musical instrument shop of Lewis Enstone. Mirrors and lanterns might be had at the "Glass-Shop in King Street," which also advertised to silver "old Looking-Glasses." Innkeepers, like Sarah Cross, often maintained small shops in their public rooms, and frequently some returned mariner, who had made a modest venture of his own, rented a corner of a tap-room for the display of his wares.[31]

There was a good deal of life in and about the Boston shops. Their keepers were shrewd enough to resist invitations to extend doubtful credit. In 1696, when a customer named Lewis tried to defer payment on purchases at the fashionable shop of Mr. Thomas Banister, the owner's reply was, "Pay the old debt first before you run of a new," — (Lewis already owed Banister £50). He next tried to run up a bill of £30 for cloth at the shop of Hannah Cowell, but the canny widow informed him that "being a Woman [she] was not able to ride up and down to get in debts." Two of the town's first citizens created a considerable disturbance in Wilkins' book shop one day in 1701. Cotton Mather encountered Samuel Sewall there, and in a

[30] Weeden, *Economic and Social History*, II, 566, 569; *Letter Book of Peleg Sanford*, 12; 6 MHS *Colls.*, I–II; *News Letter*, April 26, 1708; N. Y. Hist. Soc. *Colls.*, 1885, 87, 90, 93.

[31] *News Letter*, April 4, 1716; April 24, 1719; Jan. 25, June 20, 1720; 6 MHS *Colls.*, I, 112; IV, 108.

voice "so loud that people in the street might hear him," accused the merchant of treating his father, the Reverend Increase Mather, "worse than a Neger." [32]

The twenty-nine retail shops existing in Philadelphia in 1690 multiplied yearly. By 1720 retail trade was flourishing, and observers reported that "Tradesmen's Shops and Streets are well frequented." Business slackened at times, to be sure, when shops became overstocked and prices fell. "Markets . . . wer never worse for dry goods," wrote the dour Colden to Samuel Eveleigh in 1712. "I am oblidged in a manner to retail for ye shop-keepers will hardly look at goods." [33] But stable conditions returned after the Peace of Utrecht, and in May and June, 1717, twenty-eight shopkeepers took out freedoms from the Corporation. Of these nine were women. One of the most prosperous, Charles Read, found in successful retailing a stepping stone to membership in the merchant class. In 1720 he conducted a grocery shop at the corner of Front and High Streets, while experimenting on the side with "Very good Season'd Pine boards and Shingles." George Mifflin, another wealthy shopkeeper about to become a merchant, had an establishment located near Carpenter's Wharf. The town was served by several grocers, like David Evans, who sold "very good Olives and Capers," and Edward Horne, at whose place one might buy "English Saffron, of the last Year's Growth," and "Good new Caraway seed." [34] There seems to have been less differentiation of stocks in Philadelphia shops than at those of Boston.

Retail shop trade developed more slowly in other towns. Although the number of shops at New York increased after 1710, far more of Manhattan's retailing remained in the hands of merchants and English factors than at Boston or Philadelphia. Governor Hunter could find none but English clothes for sale, and reported that one hundred per cent advance over London prices was "reckoned cheap . . . in the shops" of New York. Gotham shopkeepers learned early and well how to take the middleman's profit. New Yorkers willingly paid high for the latest and best of goods, but they steadfastly refused to buy anything save quality merchandise, as Cadwallader Colden, now removed to New York, found to his sorrow. "The mixture of your mens stockings," he wrote to his business connection,

---

[32] 6 MHS *Colls.*, I, 167, 199; III, 333; 5 MHS *Colls.*, VI, 143.

[33] "The shopkeepers are surprised with glut of goods," Colden wrote again gloomily in 1714; and the failure of the Widow Lee for £3,000 made him and his friends, Trent and Eveleigh of Charles Town, the greatest losers. *Colden Papers*, I, 15, 16, 24; Hart, *Contemporaries*, II, 75; Philadelphia Merchants' Account Book, 1694–1698.

[34] Scharf and Westcott, *Philadelphia*, I, 193; *Mercury*, April 28, May 12, 19, June 9, 1720.

Richard Hill of London, in 1720, "is soe very odd that noe body will Look on them." [35]

There were several retail establishments at Charles Town, among them two milliners' shops, which "shut up for 6 weeks" during the epidemic of 1699, to the inconvenience of townsfolk who had come already to depend on them. Samuel Eveleigh supplied many of them with their stocks. Colden, with his genius for ill luck, arrived in 1711 with a cargo to sell, just at a time when such retail goods had become a drug on the market. The disastrous Indian wars greatly injured retail as well as wholesale business in the town, but by the end of the period this, too, had in a measure recovered. In 1720 an official reported most of the people living in and about Charles Town, "planters, merchants, and shopkeepers," to be "in very good circumstances." [36]

Although Newport in 1708 was rumored to have "a greater plenty of European goods" than any place in New England, it probably possessed fewer shops than any other town, most of its retailing being still in the hands of merchants. Members of the gentry patronized John Rhodes' shoe shop, Elizabeth Huling's millinery shop, and the emporium of Joseph Gardner near Carr's Wharf. A favorite device with young tradesmen of the town was to get a small stock laid by and invest it in a voyage. When the goods arrived, they could be retailed in the public room of some tavern like the King's Arms.[37]

Side by side with shops of those who bought to sell again were the establishments of those who offered for sale the results of their own labor or the product of their particular craft. A very large part of the population of each town consisted of artisans and tradesmen, many of whom possessed "Land and Some Estate." This class fell naturally into two groups: tradesmen occupied in the food and provision business; and craftsmen or artisans who worked at all other trades. By the early eighteenth century every town was fairly well supplied with purveyors of the first class. Butchers, bakers, confectioners, victualers, brewers, distillers, vintners and "cookes" in increasing numbers labored daily to feed the townsfolk or to prepare foods for export.

No less important was the increase in both number and variety of artisans. To necessary crafts like those of the tailors, smiths, carpenters, cordwainers, tanners, and bricklayers were now added many new and more specialized skills. New York became sufficiently populous and sophisticated to support numerous barbers and periwig

[35] ". . . There was nott aboue a pair in a doz. of a colour that any body would wear & the shopkeeper that bought them was forced to dye them black." N. Y. Hist. Soc. Colls., 1885, 52–102; Colden Papers, I, 40, 48, 54; Doc. Hist. N. Y., I, 713; Valentine, Manual, 1858, 516.
[36] 5 MHS Colls., VI, 11; S. C. Pub. Recs., IV, 78; VII, 218; S. C. Hist. & Gen. Mag., XI, 53; Colden Papers, I, 3, 6, 7.
[37] 2 MHS Procs., IV, 152; Lloyd Papers, I, 149, 162 n.; Newport T. M. Recs., 37, 152; Cal. St. Pap., 1708–1709, 175; Newport Hist. Mag., I, 234; III, 29.

makers, seven painters, six gardeners, three paviors, a seamstress, a
watchmaker, and a spectacle maker. Just what services were offered
by "Daniel De Witt, Mathematician," and "Daniel Curtus, Master of
Science," also classified as "artisans," is not quite clear. Boston, Philadelphia, Newport and Charles Town were likewise well served by "all
manner of handicraft trades, but fewest weavers, they making very
little cloth." Tailors and cordwainers grew so numerous at Philadelphia that they applied for incorporation in 1718, and in granting
their request the Mayor and Common Council made provision for the
formation of similar guilds by artisans of other crafts. Gold and
silversmiths prospered in this period; Boston remained the leading
town for members of their craft, but New York also became a center.
By 1720 the latter town could pride itself on the fine work produced
by its thirteen silversmiths, four watchmakers, two goldsmiths, and
one jeweller, and Philadelphia supported several good silversmiths.
William Clagget of Boston and Peter Stretch of Philadelphia were
foremost among colonial clockmakers.[88]

These artisans usually maintained little shops in their homes, which
could be recognized from the street by some sign characteristic of their
craft. As in the seventeenth century these shops were generally tended
by womenfolk or apprentices. When newspapers appeared they were
among the principal advertisers. In 1707 James Batterson, clockmaker, newly arrived from London, notified people of Boston that "if
any person . . . hath any occasion for New Clocks, or to have Old
Ones turn'd into Pendulums: or any other thing either in making or
mending: Let them repair to the Sign of the Clock Dial on the South
Side of the Town House." James Allen of Philadelphia, goldsmith,
maintained a shop on High Street, where he made "Money Scales and
Weights and all sorts of Work in Silver and Gold," and his wife,
Margaret, who tended shop, also sold "best Virginia Tobacco, Cutt."
This tendency to combine retail shopkeeping with craftsmanship also
developed at Boston, where Benjamin Fitch, "Felmonger and Glover,"
in Dock Square, also sold "all sorts of Wool." [39]

[88] Master craftsmen made immediate use of the newspapers in securing workmen:
"This is to give notice, that a Journeyman Pewterer, who is a good workman in
Hollow-ware, may have constant work and good Wages, if they will go to New
York, and apply . . . to Mr. David Lyell." *News Letter*, June 17, 1717; Aug. 20,
1714; Jan. 2, 1715; N. Y. Hist. Soc. *Colls.*, 1885, 52-102; *P. M. C. C.*, 145; Bigelow,
Historic Silver; Mercury, June 9, May 19, 1720; Wallace, *South Carolina*, I, 389.

[39] George Brownell, "Late Schoolmaster" of Hanover Street, Boston, proved a
genius at combining skills. He advertised "all sorts of Millinery Works done; making up Dresses and flowering of Muslin, making of furbelow'd Scarffs, and quilting
and cutting of Gentlewomen's Hair in the newest Fashion; and also young Gentlewomen and Children taught all sorts of Fine Works, as Feather-work, Filigre, and
Painting on Glass, Embroidering in a new Way, Turkey-work and Dancing cheaper
than was ever taught in Boston. Brocaded work for Handkerchiefs and short aprons
upon Muslin; artificial Flowers work'd with a needle." *News Letter*, May 17, 1708;
Aug. 27, 1716; Oct. 13, 1707; *Mercury*, June 9, 1720.

The shops of tradesmen and artisans in this period far outnumbered establishments for retailing dry goods and groceries. The principal features in their development were the diversity of crafts represented and the fact that in a few cases artisans had found it possible to branch out from their own particular trades and venture a little into general retailing. In no town does there appear to have been a serious shortage of skilled craftsmen.[40]

Another form of merchandising popular in the towns in this period was the auction, or, as it was then known, the "publick vendue." Prior to 1690 the vendue was known only in New York. Here as early as 1704 the Corporation received a petition from the burghers asking for an ordinance to prevent the holding of "Retaile and wholesale Vendues" by any but freemen, in order to keep outsiders from carrying off the town's cash. At Newport and Charles Town petitions exhibiting the need for well regulated auctions led to the appointment of public vendue masters in 1709 and 1710. The Governor of Pennsylvania appointed a similar official for Philadelphia about the same time. In 1720 Philadelphia shopkeepers memorialized the Provincial Council "setting forth the loss they sustain" because the vendue master made a practice of retailing "Shop Goods to the value of One Shilling and under." By the close of this period the public auction in all towns had come to require municipal regulation.[41]

At Boston, where the auction became extremely popular, it was apparently so well conducted as to create little need for official supervision. Ships, wines, and "European Goods" constituted favorite articles for disposal in this fashion. In June, 1704, the thirty ton sloop "Tryal" was sold at the Swan Tavern "by Inch of Candle," and on April 8, 1714, Ambrose Vincent ran off a large vendue for "Merchant's Inland Traders or others" at the Crown Coffee House, continuing it several days later at Minot's warehouse on Long Wharf. Daniel Stevens advertised in 1715 "a large Room and other Conveniences fit for such Business" at his Coffee House in Ann Street. By 1719 Joseph Marion was also selling lots of cloth by means of the lottery, a system which was to be increasingly used in New England in the next period.[42]

In view of the growing populations of this period markets became

[40] In addition to the above-mentioned cases, printers and apothecaries, considered elsewhere, usually had a variety of goods for sale.
[41] Madam Knight found New York vendues profitable, "for they treat with good Liquor Liberally, and the Customers Drink so Liberally and . . . they Bidd up Briskly, . . . after the sack hath gone plentifully about." *Journal of Madam Knight*, 55; *N. Y. M. C. C.*, II, 261; *R. I. Col. Recs.*, IV, 49; *Newport T. M. Recs.*, 136; *S. C. Statutes*, II, 348; *S. C. Pub. Recs.*, XVII, 445; *Pa. Col. Recs.*, III, 91; *R. I. Acts (1744)*, 82.
[42] *News Letter*, June 12, 1704; Jan. 28, 1706; April 5, 1714; Jan. 3, 1715; Oct. 12, 1719; May 30, 1720; *Bos. Gaz.*, April 11, Sept. 2, 1719.

increasingly important as sources of food supply for the citizens. The usually lethargic Corporation of New York exhibited rare activity in this department, with the result that during these years the town's market facilities far surpassed those of all other communities. In April, 1691, the authorities opened a "Butcher's Shamble" on the Green, a meat market "under the trees by the Slipp," and a market for fish and vegetables near the City Hall. All markets opened at seven o'clock on Tuesday, Thursday and Saturday mornings at the ringing of a bell. In keeping with English practice no produce could be sold elsewhere, and no persons might buy to sell again until after the markets had been open for two hours. In 1707 a market house was built in Heeregraft Street to serve residents of the Coenties Slip neighborhood. Three other market buildings, at Clarke's Slip, Countess Key, and the Burgher's Path on the East River were opened before 1712. These were not public markets, but constructed by private individuals with the approbation of the Corporation.[43]

Pennsylvania authorities merged the two Philadelphia markets into one in 1693, and erected stalls at Second and High Streets. In appointing Robert Brett clerk of the market Governor Markham instructed him to follow "the Custom of new yorke." Wednesday and Saturday were market days, but perishable provisions might be sold there at any time. With the exception that hucksters did not always observe the two-hour rule, High Street market served the town well, and butchers slaughtered "above Twenty Fat Bullocks [there] every week . . . besides many Sheep, Calves and Hogs." As early as 1707 the Corporation proposed building a market house, and finally in 1710 the Court House, with market stalls underneath, was completed. The stalls were let at nine shillings a year to freemen only; the Shambles at the west side of the market were reserved for selling meat, while vegetables and other provisions could be obtained in the east stalls. By 1720 the town had become so "full of all Country business" on market days as to require the enlarging of the market. Indeed, Philadelphia butchers complained of the large amounts of meat sent into town by Jerseymen.[44]

The act of 1690 establishing a market place in Charles Town for two years was in 1692 made permanent by the South Carolina Assembly. Though in 1706 the governor branded the absence of all market regulations "a living Sin," it was not until 1710 that an act of assembly put into effect the main provisions of English market law and appointed a clerk to enforce them. At Newport the market continued to be open on Wednesdays and Saturdays as earlier, and a clerk was named in

---

[43] N. Y. M. C. C., I, 215, 217, 234, 244; II, 305, 385, 446; III, 302.
[44] Pa. Col. Recs., I, 377, 382, 391, 582; P. M. C. C., 27, 69, 75, 86, 155; Pa. Statutes, II, 420; Votes Pa. Assembly, II, 144, 160, 229, 279.

1706 to see that the market was kept in good order and that fair measure was given. Trafficking at this one market had increased tremendously by 1720.[45]

Although a place under the Town House had been made available to the people of Boston, the custom of holding a regular market there had lapsed. In 1696, in pursuance of provincial law, the Selectmen ordered a market to be open every Tuesday, Thursday and Saturday. On these days no provisions might be sold anywhere else, and, to give townsfolk first opportunity to buy, hucksters were forbidden to purchase before noon. The market operated with little trouble for about five years. Then the evils of forestalling by hucksters became so flagrant as to cause the Town Meeting to vote that no one should go out to buy provisions on the Neck before two o'clock in the afternoon. For many years the Boston market was well supplied with a great variety of country produce, although the growth of settlement round about the town led to frequent scarcity of game. Trouble with hucksters forestalling the market continued, and in 1711 they and "others" were again forbidden to bargain for any sort of provisions coming into town for sale until mid-afternoon.[46]

As a result of the fire of 1711, which destroyed the Town House and most of the section about it, the market ceased to be held, and hucksters and retailers came back into their own. Their complete disregard of the regulation about purchasing provisions before three o'clock led the Town Meeting to direct the Selectmen in 1714 "to take Effectual Care to Prosecute the Town order" against those who sold to hucksters. But as the trouble continued a committee recommended to the Meeting in 1716 that "the best way to prevent that abuse, is for ye Town to come into ye Setting up of a Public Market." Opposition to the project was so stubborn that a consideration of the committee's report was three times deferred, and when finally "read & debated" in March, 1718, it was "Voted disallowed." Instead, the town chose sixteen clerks of the market to enforce existing orders. At the root of this contest over market arrangements lay the growing feeling among country people against the town of Boston. A refutation of rustic grievances appeared in a broadside, *Some Reasons and Arguments offered to the Good People of Boston, and adjacent Places for Setting up of Markets in Boston,* of which no copy exists, but fortunately Captain Uring records the principal reasons for rural opposition.[47]

[45] *S. C. Statutes,* II, 73; S. C. Commons Journal, 1706, 17; 1712–1716, 210; Trott's Laws (MS.), 31; *R. I. Col. Recs.,* IV, 11; *Newport T. M. Recs.,* 174.

[46] *Mass. Acts and Resolves,* I, 237; 7 *Bos. Rec. Com.,* 224; 8 *Bos. Rec. Com.,* 14, 79.

[47] 8 *Bos. Rec. Com.,* 105, 111, 118, 122, 129; 11 *Bos. Rec. Com.,* 164, 193; *Bos. Gaz.,* Mar. 7, 1720; N. H. Hist. Soc. *Colls.,* III, 142.

Though the town is so large and populous, they never could be brought to establish a market in it, notwithstanding several of their governors have taken great pains to convince the inhabitants how useful and beneficial it would be to them; but the country people always opposed it, so that it could not be settled: the reason they give for it is, if market days were appointed, all the country people coming in at the same time would glut it, and the town's people would buy their provisions for what they pleased, so rather choose to send them as they think fit; . . . any man may judge of the stupidity of the country people.

In 1720 Boston alone, of all the towns, lacked adequate market facilities.

Improvements in communication and in retail marketing in this period led to a decline in the importance of fairs everywhere but at New York. There in 1692 the Assembly ordered the holding of two fairs a year for four days each. They followed English custom, the old cattle fair yielding to that for the sale of all kinds of goods. The Massachusetts market law of 1696 provided for two yearly fairs to be held at Boston on the last Tuesday of May and October. Like those of New York the Boston fairs were "markets overts" of the English type, supervised by the Clerks of the Market, who were charged to prevent frauds and abuses. For some reason, however, Boston fairs were never popular, and seem to have died out long before 1720. Newport seems to have enjoyed only the "Fair" kept by Abraham Anthony at rural Portsmouth for three days each May.[48]

The disorder which attended the holding of Philadelphia fairs from their beginning had by 1697 become so great that the Assembly resolved the institution to be "of little Service, but rather of ill Tendency," and requested the Governor and Council "to put the said Fair down." Governor Markham diplomatically passed the buck by leaving the matter to the Justices of the Peace. So the fair continued, for the justices, as county officers, naturally listened to the arguments of the country people, who believed they would have lost much by its discontinuance.[49]

Shops, markets and fairs supplied the towns adequately with foodstuffs and provisions from day to day. But they were designed for normal times, and the intercolonial wars bred extraordinary conditions with which they were not suited to cope. The strains of wartime bore especially heavily on citizens of Boston and Charles Town, where in times of crisis usual means of distribution broke down.

[48] *N. Y. Col. Laws.*, I, 296; *Mass. Acts and Resolves*, I, 237; *News Letter*, April 28, 1707.
[49] *Votes Pa. Assembly*, I, i, 103; *Pa. Col. Recs.*, I, 555; Westcott, *Philadelphia*, chapter CCV.

The gathering of forces at Boston for the abortive Quebec expedition of 1709 created a severe shortage of grain and provisions, the more intense because large quantities of foodstuffs were being "sent to Forraign Markets for Private Advantages." The Selectmen, seriously concerned for the food supply of "this Great Town," sent an unsuccessful petition to the Governor, calling for a temporary embargo on the export of foodstuffs. The situation again became critical in the next year. In February the bakers informed the Selectmen that, although "there were not above fifteen hundred bushells of wheat in town," great quantities were being exported to Europe where a simultaneous shortage made for attractive prices. On April 30, when a ship belonging to Captain Belcher, "Laden with Wheat in this Time when Wheat . . . [was] so dear," was about to drop down the harbor, her rudder was found cut away. The next day, wrote Sewall, about fifty men assembled "to hale Capt. Roses ship ashore: but they were dissuaded by several sober men to desist, which they did." The rioters were to be tried for "unlawful Assembly," but the Grand Jury refused to return an indictment. "To my surprise," continued Sewall, "Capt. Belcher behaves badly at the trial." The Selectmen, alarmed by the prevailing "uneasiness," addressed to the Governor another fruitless petition for an embargo on provisions. Fortunately the supply soon increased, and the town hastened to provide against future shortages by empowering the Selectmen to purchase grain and sell it at low prices to the poor.[50]

Notwithstanding this care, the next crisis seems to have caught the authorities unawares, since no public supply was available when a grain shortage occurred in 1713. Sewall was out of town on May 20, and so missed "the Riot Committed that night in Boston by 200 people in the Comon, thinking to find Corn there; Wounded the Lt. Govr and Mr. Newton's Son; cry'd Whalebone [for a password]. Were provoked by Capt. Belcher's sending Indian Corn to Curasso. The Selectmen desired him not to send it; he told them, The hardest Fend off! If they stopp'd his vessel, he would hinder the coming in of three times as much." Such a bread riot indicated the true extent of the shortage, and this time the town obtained a Governor's proclamation laying an embargo on grain and provisions leaving the port. The General Court passed a law requiring every master of a vessel docking at Boston with fifteen hundred bushels of wheat to sell it to the people in small lots at stated prices. The inhabitants were now thoroughly aroused to the problem of providing cheap food for the poor, and throughout the remainder of the period the Selectmen made regular purchases of

[50] 11 *Bos. Rec. Com.*, 94, 101, 106; 8 *Bos. Rec. Com.*, 84; 5 MHS *Colls.*, VI, 280, 288.

grain, which they sold during the winter months below the market price, from a hired granary.[51]

Philadelphia, Newport and New York were located in grain producing regions, and suffered no lack of supply during the wars. Charles Town, however, experienced a food shortage in 1715, when the Indians began to drive planters into the town. Here miserable refugees, "imprison'd between mud walls, stifl'd with excessive heats, oppress'd with famine [and] sickness," continued to pile into the little port until in 1717 one planter wrote in despair, "We are ready to eat up one another for want of provisions, and what we can get is very bad." Prices soared beyond the capacity of the poor to buy; meat was "excessive dear," and corn brought fifteen pence a bushel, but generally there was "now none to be got." Even after the war distress continued, for Indians had destroyed crops and slaughtered livestock for miles around the town. Prices remained so high that in October, 1719, Governor Johnson requested the Assembly seriously to consider "the very great rates of all provisions in Charles Town," and recommended regulation of prices charged by butchers and the laying of high export duties on foodstuffs. We have no record of the Assembly's action.[52]

Business expansion in the towns enhanced the importance of carters and draymen, who in both New York and Philadelphia became subject to municipal regulation. In 1691 the Common Council of New York appointed two captains of carmen, and increased the number of licensed carters to twenty-four, each of whom had to pay six shillings a year for his license. Twelve of these men were to be "att ye Water Side," and twelve in the town on alternate days, and all drivers were required to take turns carrying away weekly at six pence a load the dirt swept up from the streets by inhabitants. Any carter failing in his duty was subject to a fine, half of which went to the person who informed against him.[53]

At Philadelphia municipal regulation began in 1704, when several of the town's teamsters were admonished by the Mayor "(in view of mischief lately Committed by some of them) to take care how they drive their Carts within this City." The next year the Corporation issued an official schedule of rates for the carting of goods. In 1711 carters and porters banded together to petition the Mayor concerning the smallness of their wages, and after due deliberation their pay was raised. Within a month, however, they came in for more attention, when the Corporation was forced to pass an ordinance to prevent "Carters buying Up & Ingrossing of ffire Wood." The many draymen

[51] 5 MHS *Colls.*, VI, 384; 11 *Bos. Rec. Com.*, 194, 196, 198, 200, 214.
[52] *Cal. St. Pap.*, *1714–1715*, 236; S. C. Commons Journal, *1712–1716*, 327; S. C. Pub. Recs., VII, 19.
[53] *N. Y. M. C. C.*, I, 223, 232; III, 218.

and carters of the other three towns did not in this period create any considerable problems.[54]

Northern towns enjoyed in these years certain improvements in passenger transportation. At New York in 1696 John Clapp announced a Hackney coach at his tavern in the Bouwerie, "for Persons desirous to hire the same," but he failed within a few years for lack of public support. Bostonians had been patronizing Em's coach for many years, and after 1707 one Simson kept a Hackney and a "Slay" for hire, in which Sewall often drove to funerals. A livery stable on Green Lane in the North End opened for business in 1708, and in the *News Letter* of October 13, 1712, appeared the announcement by Jonathan Wardell of another "good Hackney Coach to accommodate Persons on reasonable Terms." Four years later Wardell arranged with James Franklin of Newport to run a stage coach between the two towns once a fortnight, "while the Ways are passable," and in 1720 another stage line commenced operations between John Blake's in Sudbury Street, Boston, and Bristol Ferry, Rhode Island.[55]

V

The transferred economic institutions of the Old World became thoroughly adjusted to their new setting in the thirty years following 1690. There was no change in the theory of the just price, or in the belief that it was the function of town governments to regulate all economic life so as to secure the greatest good to their inhabitants. By 1720 most of the machinery set up to control the economic life of the towns was running smoothly, and in much the same manner as similar institutions at Norwich, Bristol or Exeter in England.

Town authorities everywhere except at Charles Town took continual pains to protect their tradesmen and artisans from outside competition, while at the same time they sought to make their regulations sufficiently flexible to insure infiltration of an adequate supply of craftsmen and laborers. New and more stringent laws appeared concerning the "freedom" to open and conduct business in all the northern towns.

Shortly after the incorporation of Philadelphia the Mayor and Common Council issued an ordinance forbidding non-freemen of the city from keeping "Open Shops, or to be master workmen." So many immigrants piled into the town after 1716, many of them "not qualify'd to Exercise thear Trades," that certain crafts suffered from inferior

---

[54] *P. M. C. C.*, 6, 20, 164; 8 *Bos. Rec. Com.*, 12, 144; Richardson Collection, 982; for Bristol carters, see Latimer, *Bristol in the Eighteenth Century*, 3.

[55] Evan Thomas kept a livery stable in Philadelphia in 1717. Stokes, *Iconography*, IV, 392, 399; 5 MHS *Colls.*, VI, 66, 72, 81; *News Letter*, Oct. 15, 1716; April 4, 1720; Scharf and Westcott, *Philadelphia*, I, 194 n.

workers, and the cordwainers and tailors solicited corporate privileges in order to regulate their mysteries. In granting their petition the Common Council recognized the general need for such extra-municipal regulation, and provided for the chartering of other craft guilds if the artisans concerned desired "the better to serve ye Publick in their respective Capacities."[56] New York, Newport and Boston also suffered in this period from the coming in of unauthorized workmen, and dealt with the problem in much the same manner as did Philadelphia.

Enforcement of these regulations against "foreigners" was not altogether successful. Especially troublesome were "divers transient persons" who drifted into the towns for a little trading and soon departed, carrying with them a goodly share of the inhabitants' ready cash. New York and Boston resented these interlopers because they paid no taxes, and Newporters complained that they undersold local tradesmen. Intruding Jerseymen and peddlers aroused the ire of Philadelphia tradesmen who branded them public nuisances.[57] Everywhere the itinerant tradesman disrupted local business, and strange artisans were unwelcome in towns already well supplied with representatives of the various crafts. But as time went on, especially with the rising tide of immigration after the Peace of Utrecht, the problem became increasingly difficult to handle.

Colonial towns secured adequate numbers of artisans and craftsmen through the English apprentice system, which became well acclimatized after 1690. In 1704 the Mayor's Court at Philadelphia assumed charge of apprenticeships and adopted the usual seven year indenture. The Corporation of New York stipulated four years as the minimum time of apprenticeship in 1695, but finding this unsatisfactory, returned to the seven year period in 1711. Boston and Newport continued the system as set up in the seventeenth century.[58]

A youth or a young girl could serve an apprenticeship in almost any branch of business. Boys in this period were bound out to occupations as varied as merchant, goldsmith, "limner," distiller, wagon maker, printer, bookseller, weaver, hatter, cordwainer and cooper. The most usual crafts for a girl were cooking and sewing, "Needle worke and other matters fitting for a good housewife." In the northern towns, especially, the most respectable families frequently bound out their children, particularly the sons, as apprentices in certain trades.[59]

[56] P. M. C. C., 34, 146.
[57] In 1700 Newport found that some "transient traders, taking up quantities of goods from merchants in Boston, &c., come here and vend them at low rates, and then run away, and never pay the said merchants." N. Y. M. C. C., II, 80; Mass. Acts and Resolves, I, 720; II, 47; R. I. Col. Recs., III, 357, 421; IV, 162; P. M. C. C., 63, 146.
[58] P. M. C. C., 112; Geneal. Soc. Pa., Pubs., VII, 84; N. Y. M. C. C., I, 373; II, 454; McKee, Labor in New York, 16.
[59] N. Y. Hist. Soc. Colls., 1885, 569, 594, 602; 1909, 119; Franklin, Works (Bigelow, ed.), I, 38, 45; Newport T. M. Recs., April 16, 1716; 7 MHS Colls., VII, 199; 5 MHS Colls., V, 397, 452.

The towns drew their apprentices from the country as well as from within their own precincts. New York, Philadelphia and Boston seem to have been well supplied with such novices, but Newport suffered a shortage. Although the scarcity of land on the island of Rhode Island forced many farmers to "put their children to trades," Governor Cranston reported in 1708 that "the inclination the youth . . . have to the sea [leads] the greater part to betake themselves to that imployment" and forsake their crafts. There was also a general scarcity of female labor, for, as Castleman noted at Philadelphia, "even the meanest single Women marry well there, and being above Want are above work." At Boston in 1709 John Winthrop was voicing the perennial lament of urban gentry: "Or maide is gon home, and we have no body, nor can't get help for money." But the newspapers, when they appear, abundantly show that in the northern towns, at least, the lack of skilled labor which one would normally expect in the New World was supplied by steady immigration of English and Scottish craftsmen, coming in either as freemen or as indentured servants.[60]

Such, however, was not the case with ranks of society below the trained artisans, and as the eighteenth century progressed the towns found themselves facing a shortage of "common" or unskilled labor. Some of the "inferior sort" left the towns to take up land on the frontier, and, in Boston at least, those who remained behind became sullen and disrespectful of their superiors. In 1691 Samuel Sewall found Peter Weare to be about the only "reasonable Labourer I know of." In all towns common laborers demanded good wages, and at Charles Town they received as high as two shillings a day in addition to food and lodging.[61]

Two sources of unskilled labor were available to the townsmen, the African Negro and the indentured servant. Prior to 1714, when the close of the wars permitted a resumption of the flow of immigration, Negroes seem to have been much used as laborers and servants in all of the towns. Their numbers in New York increased from seven hundred and fifty in 1700 to over sixteen hundred in 1720. Most of them were slaves, although there was a considerable number of free blacks. So many owners of slaves hired them out by the day or week that in 1711 the Common Council designated Wall Street market as the place where they should stand till their labor should be purchased. At Charles Town slaves performed virtually all menial work. There were four hundred Negro servants living at Boston in 1708, half of whom were native born, and Governor Shute reported that the number

---

[60] *Cal. St. Pap., 1708–1709*, 175; *News Letter*, July 25, 1715; Hart, *Contemporaries*, II, 76; 6 MHS *Colls.*, V, 188.
[61] 5 MHS *Colls.*, V, 150; Carroll, *Historical Collections*, II, 260; *Pa. Mag.*, XXXVII, 335.

had risen to two thousand in 1720. Many of their race also dwelt at Newport and Philadelphia.[62]

Negroes fresh from Africa were far from docile. Because citizens greatly feared "theire turbulent and unruly tempers," they were carefully watched in all the towns, and forbidden to gamble or to frequent taverns. During the wars some Spanish Indians were brought to New York where they were classed as blacks. At midnight on April 6, 1712, under the leadership of a Negro named Cuffee, these slaves set fire to a house as a preliminary to their supposed scheme to murder the white inhabitants and capture the city, but they were surprised and seized before their desperate plan could be carried out. Within a short time thereafter twenty-one slaves were executed before the terror gradually subsided. No other town suffered from a Negro "conspiracy," although Philadelphians became alarmed in 1693 by frequent "tumultuous gatherings" of blacks, and in 1707 began to resent the "Want of Employment, and Lowness of Wages, occasioned by the Number of *Negroes* . . . hired out to work by the Day." The authorities did nothing about the matter at this time.[63]

Inhabitants of northern towns greatly preferred to "imploy servants before slaves," when they could get them. After the Peace of Utrecht hundreds of Palatines and Ulster Scots came to New York and Philadelphia as indentured servants. Newport received only a few Scotch-Irish, but at Boston about three Irish servants to every Negro were coming in by the end of the period. From 1715 on advertisements like the following were frequently to be found in Boston newspapers: "Sundry Servants, . . . lately come from [Ireland, via] England, whose Time is to be Disposed of, Enquire of Mr. Thomas Moffatt, Merchant at his Ware-House on the Dock in Boston." [64] Yet the problem of securing an adequate supply of unskilled labor for the towns became increasingly acute from 1690 to 1720, and the influx of North Europeans after the wars only partially replaced the use of unruly and inefficient Negro slaves.

This period was notable for increased activity of both town and provincial authorities in making regulations to insure that artisans and tradesmen charged a "just" price for their goods, gave fair measure, and maintained a high standard of quality in their products. As bread formed the staple article of diet among townsfolk, the assize was carefully set by town fathers. By 1700 the bakers of every town

[62] *N. Y. M. C. C.*, II, 458; *Cal. St. Pap., 1708–1709*, 110, 171; *1719–1720*, 357; *Pa. Col. Recs.*, I, 308; *S. C. Statutes*, VII, 363.

[63] *News Letter*, April 14, 28, 1712; McKee, *Labor in New York*, 150; *Pa. Col. Recs.*, I, 380; *Votes Pa. Assembly*, I, ii, 132.

[64] *Doc. Hist. N. Y.*, III, 566; Knittle, *Palatine Emigration*, 149; Herrick, *White Servitude*; S. C. Commons Journal, 1712–1716, 270; *Cal. St. Pap., 1719–1720*, 357; *News Letter*, 1715–1720.

except Charles Town had to conform their products in size, weight and price to officially published standards. Fees for services rendered by carters, porters, and many minor functionaries of the town were also carefully stated. For instance, at Boston a grave digger might charge four shillings for digging a grave in the North Burying Ground, but if the interment was to be in the South Burying Ground his fee could be only three shillings. Profiteering continued a cardinal sin. At Charles Town in 1703, the Governor, aroused at shoemakers for "exacting upon ye people of twelve Royall a pair when leather is Sold at a royall a pound," put pressure on profiteers by proposing a bill "Against ye Combination of all Tradesmen." [65]

In the interests of trade and competition with other colonies, the governments of each province made laws to regulate the quality, weight and measure of all commodities. The size of lumber, shingles and casks, as well as the quality of grain, flour, meat and leather exported to the West Indies, was carefully scrutinized by town authorities, who chose officials to inspect these articles regularly. At Boston the size of bricks was specified, Newport chose a "Viewer of Cattle and Horses to be transported," and New York required all butter for export in firkins to be branded with the letters "N. Y." In 1702 English weights and measures became standard at Charles Town, and thereafter Winchester measures were used to the exclusion of all others in each of the five towns. So widespread was the demand for these weights that Caleb Ray of Boston opened a shop in 1708 and advertised himself as the "Chief Skale-Maker of New England." [66]

Some persons there were, as always, who tried to beat the law and their customers, but vigilant authorities usually detected them. Thus, in September, 1713, a surveyor at Boston found ten thousand shingles to be defective, and consigned them to a bonfire at the end of Long Wharf. When in October a countryman was discovered trying to sell a cartload of turnips by a false bushel measure at the Dock, the Justices ordered the measure "to be broke into Pieces, and the Turnips that were unsold to be given to the Poor." Many people who kept sheep on Rhode Island complained bitterly to the Newport Town Meeting in 1715 that town butchers secretly stole and slaughtered their animals at night, with the result that an ordinance was promulgated forbidding anyone to set up a slaughterhouse without a license, and requiring those who engaged in the business to show the ears of all slaughtered beasts to the Clerk of the Market that the marks might be identified. In 1713

[65] S. C. Commons Journal, 1703, 95, 110; Pa. Col. Recs., I, 576; Pa. Statutes, II, 61; R. I. Col. Recs., IV, 11; 11 Bos. Rec. Com., 3, 5, 205.
[66] 11 Bos. Rec. Com., 15, 160; S. C. Statutes, II, 55, 186; S. C. Commons Journal, 1712–1716, 337; R. I. Col. Recs., III, 527; N. Y. M. C. C., II, 218; III, 227; Pa. Statutes, II, 90; News Letter, April 26, 1708.

the strong moral influence of religion was brought to bear upon sharp trading practices at Philadelphia, when the Yearly Meeting "Advised that all Friends be very careful in making and vending all provisions and other commodities for transportation, taking care that the same be of good and due fineness, measure and weight." [67]

VI

Every one of the five towns made rapid commercial progress in this period, and by 1720 the commercial pattern had been evolved that was to prevail until the American Revolution. One of the most significant results of this expansion in colonial trade was the mounting fund of saved capital seeking investment. Almost as soon as the *Boston News Letter* began to be published, advertisements appeared by gentlemen who had £100 or £200 "to lend out at Interest upon good Security." [68] After 1715 considerable sums became available for "interest, or Land Security," for which one could negotiate "at the Post Office in Boston." John Campbell, the Postmaster, regularly sold British newspapers after 1705, from which his customers could glean the latest financial news, and in 1720 the *Boston Gazette* began to print quotations of South Sea, Bank, Africa, India and Mississippi stocks, as well as lottery annuities. At New York, too, these stocks were being regularly quoted in 1720. [69]

Accumulated capital in the towns derived largely of course from the profits made by merchants, but an increasing number of artisans and shopkeepers were at the same time raising their standard of living and laying by small stocks for investment in trading ventures. Many Boston tradesmen acquired "Some Estate" in this period, and an observer found that among Newport artisans who took to the sea those who were industrious and thrifty put by a small sum to buy a share in the cargo, which was regarded as a great "benefit to the town." Philadelphians like George Mifflin and Charles Read, who received their freedoms in 1717, had within three years saved enough money to enable them to begin their transition from shopkeeper to merchant. Another source of wealth, especially at Philadelphia, New York, Newport and Charles Town, derived from successful privateering ventures and the ill-gotten gains of piracy. The Wantons of Newport grew rich upon the quarterdeck, while at New York merchants openly consorted with gentlemen of the black flag. "When Frederick Phillipp's ship and the

[67] *News Letter*, Mar. 30, Sept. 13, Oct. 26, 1713; *Newport T. M. Recs.*, 174; Sharpless, *Quaker Experiment*, 27 n.; *Pa. Col. Recs*, I, 576.
[68] The *News Letter* contained over twenty of these notices, 1705-1708. Borrowers also appeared, but less frequently; see, Sept. 10, Nov. 12, 1705.
[69] *News Letter*, July 30, 1705; July 4, 1715; *Bos. Gaz.*, May 23, 1720; Adams, *Provincial Society*, 84.

other two come from Madagascar," wrote Bellomont to the Board of
Trade, "New York will abound with Gold." In 1698 James Miller and
some of his pirate company "shared £1,000 a man at Charlestown," and
Bellomont learned that in 1701 "4 or 5 very rich Pyrats were come
to Charlestown; . . . there were abt half a dousin Pyrats lately hang'd
in Carolina, but it was because they were poor. . . . These rich ones
appear'd publicly, and were not molested in the least." [70]

The first two intercolonial wars left in their wake periods of depression which blighted the hopes of many a merchant and shopkeeper.
Governor James Moore of South Carolina had, however, little sympathy for the debtors of Charles Town. "We have had of late," he
wrote to Nicholson in 1701, "diverse, idle, extravagant and profuse
run away from their creditors to Virginia, the easiness of the journey
encourages them to run in debt more than they are able or design to
pay." At this same time Philadelphia merchants found great difficulty
in marketing their wheat, and reported that trade was dead. Boston
suffered greatly throughout the period. The worst years were 1708 to
1713; in 1708 Sewall could not get a manuscript printed for his friend
Samuel Danforth, because "Paper is grown so excessive dear," while
to another correspondent he reported, "We are groaning under the
vast expence and Disgrace of the Disappointed Expedition against
Canada." In these years trade at Boston fell off two-thirds, and many
merchants and shopkeepers were "extreamly impoverish'd." Philadelphia felt the pinch of hard times most in the very last years of the
war, when "Markets . . . were never worse," and failures in business
common.[71] The harmful effects of war, however, could only provide
a temporary check to business, which quickly rebounded after the
Peace of Utrecht. Viewed as a whole, the period was one of increasing
prosperity in the five towns, where the commercial spirit of piling
"Cent per Cent" was running too high to be suppressed for more than
a brief time.

One of the most important institutions growing out of the towns'
commercial needs was the colonial post office. Absence of any regular
mails between towns or with Europe had "always been a great
hindrance to the Trade of those parts." In 1692 a court favorite,
Thomas Neale, received a royal patent giving him authority to institute
and operate a post office in the colonies for a period of twenty-one
years. Andrew Hamilton of New Jersey, Neale's deputy in America,
opened the first office at New York, and the first route, from New

[70] N. E. Hist. & Gen. Reg., XVI, 84; Mercury, April 28, May 13, 1720; N. Y.
Col. Docs., IV, 532; Cal. St. Pap., 1697–1698, 24; 1701, 16, 651; Nettels, Money Supply, 95 n.
[71] Cal. St. Pap., 1701, 651; 1707–1708, 637; Adams, Provincial Society, 54; 6
MHS Colls., I, 375, 385; Colden Papers, I, 10, 24.

York to Philadelphia, began in 1693. The Boston office also opened at this time. By 1698 a weekly postal route ran from Portsmouth, New Hampshire, through Boston, Newport, New York, and Philadelphia to Newcastle, Delaware. At Charles Town an unofficial post office to receive and send off West India and European mail was established in 1698, and in 1702 an effort was made to unite Charles Town to the system of the northern towns, but traffic apparently did not warrant it, and the postmaster, Edward Bourne, confined his efforts to mails going and coming by sea. It cannot be said that the colonial post office as yet provided either cheap or regular service, but even the erratic mails afforded were a great improvement over anything the towns had known before.[72]

The expanding activities of the period also emphasized the need for a better medium of exchange. Lack of much ready money, and the heavy demands made on the colonies during the wars, resulted in large issues of paper currency. Massachusetts led the way in 1690, and by 1712 Rhode Island, New York and South Carolina had fallen into line. Undoubtedly a more ample medium of exchange was needed, and the use of bills facilitated the conduct of trade, but the "evils of inflation" soon came upon the colonists. The situation at Boston and Charles Town was particularly significant in that it uncovered violent antagonisms between debtor and creditor classes, and between rural districts and the town.[73]

In 1720 Boston was still the leading seaport, the center of the great shipbuilding industry, and the money capital of the American colonies. Her supremacy was, however, being vigorously contested by her ambitious and somewhat jealous rivals. More remarkable for the period as a whole, and more charged with future import, was the rapid economic development of the other four towns, especially of Philadelphia. These settlements had definitely emerged as the economic centers of their respective provinces, and, with their new commercial maturity, were challenging Boston as serious contenders in a field where for nearly a century the Bay town had enjoyed unquestioned sway.

[72] Castelman reported from Philadelphia in 1710, "There is a Post-Office lately erected, which goes to Boston in New-England, Charlestown in Carolina, and the other neighbouring Places." The Charles Town post must have gone by water on the "Packett Boat." Rich, *United States Post Office*, 14, 17; *N. Y. Col. Laws*, I, 293; *Mass. Acts and Resolves*, I, 115; *S. C. Statutes*, II, 188; Trott's Laws (MS.), Pt. II, 25; *News Letter*, May 31, 1714; *Mercury*, Mar. 8, 1720; Hart, *Contemporaries*, II, 76; S. C. Commons Journal, 1707–1711, 291.

[73] Dewey, *Financial History*, 25; Nettels, *Money Supply*, 13, 250; *Colonial Currency Reprints*, I, 359, 410; Davis, *Currency and Banking in Massachusetts*, Pt. I, 403; S. C. Pub. Recs., VII, 157; Wallace, *South Carolina*, I, 251, 260.

VII

PROBLEMS OF A GROWING SOCIETY

I

At the beginning of the new century it became clearly evident that the social problems which had made their appearance in the towns in earlier years had come to stay. They were the inevitable results of community living, and intensified as the urban characteristics of colonial seaports became more marked. In these three decades they were immensely complicated by the events and consequences of the first two intercolonial wars, and their solutions became increasingly more difficult and more costly to the towns. Little by way of new methods for dealing with the problems of urban society was introduced in this period, but the costs of fire prevention, water supply and police protection, of dealing with crime, disorder, drunkenness and prostitution, and of caring for the poor and for the public health mounted with great rapidity. The ability of the towns to devote such enlarged sums to securing their collective well-being is a considerable indication of their increasing maturity. That they willingly did so is refreshing evidence of an awakening civic consciousness on the part of town leaders.

II

The threat of fire grew rather than diminished in this period. Despite stricter preventive regulations and improved fire fighting equipment, the "joyning and nearness of buildings, being mostly of Timber," frequently transformed a small blaze into general conflagration. Town authorities everywhere sought to lessen the danger by continued precautions and new methods of prevention. They continued to enforce the curfew rules, and in two instances drew up more stringent requirements for the construction of buildings. Following a severe fire at Boston in 1691 the General Court again attempted to forestall future disasters by "An Act for Building with Stone or Brick in the Town of Boston," requiring all new houses to be of stone or brick and covered with slate. Construction of new buildings was to be approved by Justices and Selectmen, and only by license from the Governor and Council could any timber structure henceforth be erected. The intolerable burden of these regulations fell hardest on laborers and tradesmen, who petitioned in 1697 for a relaxation of the law. The Court turned a deaf ear to them, and in 1700 passed an additional act levying a £50 fine upon anyone presented for erecting an unlicensed frame building. Brick came more into favor and fashion after the fire of 1711, but as late as 1713 the Selectmen presented eight persons for ignoring the prohibition against timber construction. The laws against wooden buildings were well intentioned and occasionally well enforced, but not until after 1716 was the town entirely successful in restricting their erection.[1]

Like Boston, Charles Town received its first building legislation as a result of a large fire. In 1698, and again in 1704, the South Carolina Assembly ordered chimneys henceforth to be constructed of brick or stone, and all wooden chimneys to be demolished within a month. In 1713 it forbade the future erection of any timber structure "unless in particular cases," and empowered commissioners of the act to order the destruction of existing frame houses if they considered them "common nusances." This law proved so burdensome that it had to be repealed in 1717, and frame houses were permitted provided chimneys and hearths were built of stone or brick.[2] The fact that a majority of the houses in New York and Philadelphia were of brick or stone, and that Newport had not yet suffered from any serious conflagration probably explains the absence in these towns of building laws specifying the materials of which houses might be constructed.

In all communities, however, the defective chimney was still the most common cause of fire, and required continuous supervision. At New York in 1691 Dirck Vandenburg, bricklayer, headed a committee of four to "goe round the Town and View each fire place and Chimney that they be Sufficient and Clean Swept," and two years later he became sole "Overseer and Viewer" of hearths and chimneys, with power to call in the constables to aid him in his duties of inspection. Probably at Vandenburg's instigation, a new method was tried in 1697, whereby the alderman and assistant were made responsible for the condition of hearths and chimneys in their ward, and were directed to appoint two inspectors to view each house weekly. This arrangement proved so satisfactory as to last for over twenty years. As a result the town of New York seems to have had clean chimneys, a fact which goes far to explain why it suffered so little from fire.[3]

Boston, too, enjoyed considerable success in coping with its chimney problem. Public chimney sweeps performed their duties satisfactorily

---

[1] Mass. Acts and Resolves, I, 42, 404; N. E. Hist. & Gen. Reg., XVI, 84; 29 Bos. Rec. Com., 180–220.
[2] S. C. Statutes, VII, 11, 58; III, 5; S. C. Commons Journal, 1712–1716, 329.
[3] N. Y. M. C. C., I, 255, 391; II, 22.

until about 1708, when the Selectmen had to appoint James Maxwell "to inspect the breachs of the Town order relateing to Chimneys happening to be on fire." This move resulted in thirteen convictions during the next year, and a gain to the town of £6. 10. Among the offenders were Cotton Mather, and the famous traveler, Madam Sarah Knight. Soon, however, inhabitants began to complain of the frequent fires occasioned by the "Careless & negligent performance of the worke of Chimney Sweeping, And that there is no person here who hath Served a time to that Mistery." In 1711, after two years of survey and negotiation, Richard Procter and John Cookson received from the Selectmen a seven year monopoly of chimney sweeping in the town. They were sworn to sweep at a specified rate any chimney within forty-eight hours after notice had been given by a householder, and to pay a ten shilling fine should it flame at the top within fifteen days after cleaning. Procter and Cookson, aided by the terror resulting from the fire of 1711, kept Boston chimneys well swept in the latter years of the period.[4]

Neither Newport nor Charles Town appears to have experienced any great problem with chimney fires in this period. Prior to 1697 the Rhode Island town appointed an official "to looke after . . . sweeping of Chimlies." At Charles Town the five "Fire Commissioners" named in 1698 were directed to levy a twenty shilling fine on any householder whose chimney was found to be "foul." [5]

At Philadelphia, largely because the Corporation failed to enforce the cleaning laws, defective chimneys constituted a real menace. In 1696 an act of the Assembly levied the large fine of forty shillings upon any householder whose flues flamed from lack of proper cleaning. This provision proved difficult to enforce and convictions almost impossible to secure. The forty shilling fine was obviously too large, and in 1713 the Corporation announced that if "the Offender will Pay the fforfeiture without further Trouble, he shall have Ten Shillings abated him." In 1716 Alderman Carter reported that out of twenty-nine persons convicted of having flaming chimneys, only nine had paid the legal penalty. Since the list of delinquents included ex-Mayor Samuel Preston, Isaac Norris, Recorder Robert Assheton, James Logan and five members of the Common Council, it is perhaps unnecessary to observe that no action was taken on this report. Finally in 1720 the city government made an agreement with James Henderson to be the public chimney sweep, and to "keep a Number of Sufficient Hands to Carry on the Same." [6]

[4] 11 *Bos. Rec. Com.*, 52, 57, 63, 66, 68, 97, 121, 140, 156, 208; 8 *Bos. Rec. Com.*, 68, 82; 13 *Bos. Rec. Com.*, 51.
[5] *Newport T. M. Recs.*, 78; *S. C. Statutes*, VII, 10.
[6] *Pa. Col. Recs.*, I, 508; *Pa. Statutes*, II, 67; *P. M. C. C.*, 91, 107, 185, 188.

Hope of preventing fires led the towns to take other precautionary measures. Pennsylvania authorities ordered in 1701 that anyone who "shall presume to smoke tobacco in the streets of Philadelphia either by day or night, shall forfeit . . . twelvepence." In 1704 the Corporation prohibited the boiling of pitch or tar within twenty feet of any building, and ruled against night fires on ships lying at the wharves in 1714. At Charles Town after 1713 no householder could keep hay or straw in kitchens or outhouses "joyning to his dwelling house." Children and servants at Newport were deprived in 1711 of the often dangerous pleasure of "throwing squibs of powder & lighted fire-works on the streets." [7]

The danger of keeping too much gunpowder stored in thickly settled districts was widely recognized. A law of 1701 prohibited Philadelphians from having more than six pounds of this dangerous commodity in their possession unless stored more than forty perches from any building. So much powder was kept at Boston during the war years that in 1706 the General Court, to protect life and limb, as well as to prevent fire, ordered the erection of a storehouse, and in 1719 forbade the keeping of powder on ships at the wharves. Retail shops selling ammunition were permitted to keep in stock twenty-five pounds, provided it was packed in brass or tin "Tunnels." Charlestonians after 1719 were required to deposit all their powder in the public magazine. Throughout the period the New York Corporation debated the erection of a powder house, but no action came of it. [8]

Notwithstanding all efforts made to prevent fire, conflagrations occurred with increasing frequency throughout the period, necessitating on the part of town authorities and private citizens the expenditure of ever greater amounts of both time and money for the acquisition and organization of fire fighting equipment. By 1720 the majority of the towns were employing the best apparatus and methods for the control of fire then known to the western world.

At Boston the possession of the finest available fire defenses had already become a tradition which was continued in the new century. Each large fire produced a renewed demand for better methods and equipment. Following a severe blaze at the Dock on March 10, 1702, which destroyed eight valuable warehouses, the old water engine was repaired and a new one ordered from England. The Selectmen also revived the engine company, which had lapsed in 1686, and placed it under the command of Henry Deering. This company met the last Monday in each month to "Exercise themselves in the use of the Sd.

[7] *Pa. Statutes*, II, 162, 420; *P. M. C. C.*, 9; *S. C. Statutes*, VII, 58; 8 *Bos. Rec. Com.*, 9; *Newport T. C. Recs.*, Nov. 5, 1711.
[8] *Pa. Statutes*, II, 9; 11 *Bos. Rec. Com.*, 18, 23; *Mass. Acts and Resolves*, I, 558; II, 23, 136; *Trott's Laws* (MS.), 736; *N. Y. M. C. C.*, II, 103, 124.

Engine." Another engine, acquired in 1707, was well housed, and a second company of twenty men formed to operate it. The purchase of many new ladders, swabs and buckets from Henry Deering in 1711 completed the town's fire fighting equipment when its greatest disaster took place.[9]

This fire, the most destructive ever known in the colonies, blazed forth in Cornhill Street about eight o'clock in the evening of October second. According to Sewall, it began "in a little House [privy] belonging to Capt. Ephraim Savage, by reason of the Drunkenness of [Mary] Mors." All buildings "on both sides of Cornhill, from School Street to . . . Dock Square, all the upper parts of King Street on the south and north side, together with the Townhouse, were consumed to ashes." Governor Tailer was able to see the leaping flames from "20 Leagues off." They raged for two hours, destroying over a hundred houses, despite heroic efforts by terror-stricken inhabitants to check their progress, and the use of twenty-two barrels of powder for blowing up buildings. Several sailors perished while trying to save the bell of the First Church, and at least eight other persons were killed and many injured by falling timbers or exploding powder. While the fire was on thieves made off with large quantities of goods belonging to the one hundred and ten homeless families. Suffering was widespread, and the citizenry hastened to the aid of the unfortunates, a collection of £700 being taken up at the various churches.[10]

After this disaster the question of prevention again came before the General Court, which thus laid down the principle of community responsibility: "Not only the person in whose house the fire first breaks out, but the neighborhood are concerned to employ their utmost diligence and application to extinguish the fire and prevent the progress thereof." To this end the Court empowered Selectmen and Justices to appoint ten firewards "in the several parts of the town," with authority to direct the people during fires. Ten leading citizens were named for this new office in February, 1712, with instructions to care for the public apparatus, and to "give such necessary orders as may best serve the said Town in Suppressing & Extinguishing of Fire." These forerunners of the public fire department immediately assumed charge of the water engines and their operators, as well as of all other equipment. Through their influence the Selectmen made extensive purchases of ladders, pails, hooks, axes and powder in 1712 and 1714. In the latter year they also acquired three new engines of the Dutch

---

[9] A sixth "great" fire occurred near the Mill Creek in 1691; its extent is unknown. 5 MHS *Colls.*, VI, 54; 7 *Bos. Rec. Com.*, 216; 8 *Bos. Rec. Com.*, 23, 38, 73, 76; 11 *Bos. Rec. Com.*, 25, 41, 56, 59, 86, 131.

[10] 5 MHS *Colls.*, VI, 323; *News Letter*, Oct. 8, 29, 1711; 6 MHS *Colls.*, V, 52; 7 MHS *Colls.*, VIII, 117; 8 *Bos. Rec. Com.*, 89.

suction type, like those being introduced in London at about this time. By 1720 the town had formed an embryo public fire department of twenty capable men and six engines, under the direction of the ten firewards, which could be counted upon, to the best of its ability, "to prevent the Spreading of Fire." [11]

Whenever fire broke out in the towns an attempt was made to save goods within the burning building by carrying them out into the streets. In the confusion of the Boston fire of 1711 the great problem was to protect movable property from thieves and to return it to its proper owners. One of the reasons for the appointment of firewards so soon after was the need then revealed for some responsible persons to superintend the removal of personal effects from burning buildings to some safe place. As late as January 28, 1712, the Justices were advertising for the return of property removed from homes during "the late fire." In the midst of the ensuing discussion a communication to the *News Letter* for February 6, 1715/16, pointed the way to a solution. The writer blamed both the lack of success in extinguishing fires, and the general pilfering which accompanied them, on the "great Croud and Confusion that oftens falls out at a Fire; where no Body Governs, no Body will Obey, very few will Work, and a great many Lookers on . . . only incumber the Ground." Obviously, "some further Good Methods and Orders" were needed, for which the writer proposed the adoption of a system in use in Amsterdam, Holland, to "hinder" the progress of a fire.[12] The publicizing of this Dutch scheme greatly influenced methods of fire fighting at Boston. It resulted in a grant of increased power to the firewards for controlling workers and onlookers during fires, and for a more effective check-up on inhabitants. Even more significant was the fact that it seems to have been the inspiration for a group of public spirited men who sought to remedy the deficiencies of the public fire service by private initiative when they founded the first colonial fire company a year later. This organization was composed of twenty men, each of whom agreed to

[11] 11 *Bos. Rec. Com.,* 154, 179, 186, 214, 219; 8 *Bos. Rec. Com.,* 106; Young, *Fire Brigades,* 78, 80.
[12] The principal points of the Amsterdam system were:

I "The Laws forbid all Crowding to the Place, no Body that is not a Neighbour Inhabitant dares enter into the Street where a Fire is broke out, for he would immediately be clipt into Gaol."
II The men appointed and paid to fight fires are "under a most exact Regulation and Discipline, . . . disposed into Classes, and each Class is governed by a Master."
III "The men are under the same Discipline as Soldiers," and trained for their work.
IV The firemen are held responsible for all movable property, which is placed in bags when removed from burning buildings.
V Organized "Societies for Extinguishing of Fire."

Mass. Acts and Resolves, I, 677; 11 *Bos. Rec. Com.,* 150.

bring two buckets and two large bags to every fire. Members employed their bags in carrying goods out of burning houses to a spot
where one of them designated for the purpose stood guard. The
Boston "Fire Society" of 1717 antedated by nineteen years the famous
Union Fire Company of Philadelphia, and its rules furnished the model
for Benjamin Franklin's organization.[13]

In this period Charles Town and Philadelphia were the only other
towns to make adequate provisions for combatting fire, and even their
arrangements fell far short of those at Boston. On February 24, 1698,
there broke out "a great fire at Charlestown which burnt down a great
part of the town and a few days before the fire ther was an earth
quak." The loss of about fifty dwellings and warehouses in this
disaster led to the first public provision for the protection of the town
against fire. Five Fire Commissioners were appointed with power to
blow up buildings to prevent the spread of fires, and to levy a tax of
£40 on the town for the purchase of "six lathers of several sizes,
fifty leather bucketts and six fire hooks." Just a year later a severe
fire destroyed property valued at £30,000. Despite this "great loss" inhabitants were soon "rebuilding their homes," only to see most of the
town reduced to ashes by a third holocaust in 1700. In 1701 the
Assembly raised £100 by taxes to buy more fire equipment, but by 1713
it had come to the realization that something more was needed. Accordingly, new commissioners were appointed and ordered to assess
the citizens for funds with which to purchase a water engine in England. Charles Town was thus the second American town to acquire
a fire engine.[14]

Although Philadelphia suffered no general conflagration, the authorities there evinced a considerable interest in fire prevention. A
petition from the inhabitants asking for some fire regulation resulted
in the passage of a law in 1696 requiring householders to provide
themselves with ladders and leather buckets. Justices of the Peace
were to provide "six or eight good hooks for the purpose of tearing
down houses," and were given authority to blow up buildings should
the danger become great. These rules were embodied in a complete
fire code for Philadelphia in 1701, but the town was slow to acquire
further equipment. In 1711 Mayor Samuel Preston remarked in a
little speech to the Board of Aldermen that he had "frequently had in
his Consideration the many Providences this City had Mett with in

<hr />

[13] Drake, *Antiquities of Boston*, 557. Cf. *Rules of a Fire Society*, of Boston,
with the "Minutes of the [Union] Fire Company." Hereinafter I shall designate
private agencies like the Boston Fire Society as "fire companies," and refer to public employees who operated water engines as "engine companies."
[14] *Narratives of Carolina*, 200; *Charleston Year Book, 1880*, 302; *S. C. Statutes*,
VII, 10, 20, 58; *Cal. St. Pap., 1699*, 289.

that fires that have so often happened have done so little Damage, and . . . it is our Duty to Use all possible means to prevent & Extinguish ffires for the future by providing of Buckets, Hooks, Engines, etc." The Board reflected upon the matter for nine months, and then authorized the Mayor or Recorder and any two Aldermen "to Manage & Direct att all fires," and the Treasurer to lay out the proceeds from chimney fines for buckets. Nothing was done about an engine until December, 1718, when Alderman Bickley sold the Corporation a fire engine for £50. A year later, after he had been paid, the Alderman delivered the "ffire Engine, . . . with all its Materials," to the Mayor, who placed it in a central location near the Friends' Meeting House in Front Street.[15] After a tardy beginning the Quaker town was now ready to embark on its notable career of fire fighting.

The other two towns were fortunately spared any large losses by fire in this period, and consequently felt less need for fire legislation. Newport, being still a scattered village, lost only an occasional house; the nearest approach to a general fire was a blaze which broke out in a smithy in 1705 and spread to a nearby house, but "by the great industry of our people" it was soon extinguished. At New York in 1714 a fire consumed three houses, but by "Breaking down" several others, the flames were checked.[16] The fact that most structures in New York, like those at Philadelphia, were built of brick or stone greatly reduced the menace of a general conflagration.

III

Town expansion also necessitated a great increase in the number of wells dug and pumps erected, especially those for public use, and more careful attention on the part of authorities to the repair and cleaning of the sources of the public water supply. In 1696 the sixteen wells that had been built at New York before 1690 were placed under the supervision of a man from each ward, paid by the residents, whose duty it was to keep the wells in his district "Sweet Usefull and in Good Repair for ye Common Benefitt of the Citty." From ten to fifteen more public wells were erected in the streets of Manhattan before 1720. The Corporation no longer shared in the costs of building, but resorted instead to the less expensive means of allowing residents of a neighborhood "att their own proper Cost and Charge"

---

[15] Westcott, *Philadelphia,* chapter XLI; *Pa. Col. Recs.,* I, 478; *P. M. C. C.,* 78, 79, 157, 169; *Pa. Statutes,* II, 67, 162.
[16] *Newport T. M. Recs.,* 78; *R. I. Acts* (1744), 26; *N. Y. M. C. C.,* I, 391; II, 309; III, 139; *News Letter,* Oct. 19, 1705; Mar. 19, Nov. 29, 1714; Stokes, *Iconography,* IV, 482.

to dig wells in the streets at such places as the Mayor and the Alderman of their ward might specify.[17]

As in other matters of municipal concern, the Mayor and Common Council of Philadelphia were slow to assume responsibility for the public water supply. The town was well equipped with wells and pumps located on private properties or in the streets in 1714 when the Corporation took the "Great Conveniency of Public Pumps" under consideration, and voted that all existing and future pumps should become the property of "the Persons Erecting the same, Who shall keep them in Repair at their own Cost." In return the proprietors received permission to charge rent for the use of their pumps. To encourage the digging of more "Public Pumps in the Street," a special ordinance of 1715 provided that anyone who would erect a pump might lease the site from the city for twenty-one years at a rent of one shilling per annum.[18] Under this system Philadelphia became noted for the large number of public pumps in its streets; they yielded excellent drinking water, and served a useful purpose in times of fire.

Bostonians continued active in the construction of wells both for private and for public use. Many people, like Obadiah Wakefield and John Farnum, set up pumps in the cellars of their houses, and by 1709 Simon Willard and others had laid pipes from the old Conduit to their homes and were enjoying the luxury of running water. In addition to the many private pumps built in the streets, the town itself erected seven. The Selectmen arranged with Elder Bridgham in 1702 to repair the old cistern at the Governor's Spring, so that a ready supply of water might be available in case of fire, and a special pump was later set up at the Conduit near the Dock for the same purpose. Richard Procter, an appointee of the Selectmen, strictly enforced the ordinance requiring those who used wells and pumps to keep them clean and in constant repair.[19]

Newport acquired its first pumps in this period. In 1698 the Town Council ordered a pump for the town well, and decided "that the Well be cleansed & the Money for the charge payd out of ye Town Treasury." In 1701 they granted liberty to John Scott and others to dig a well and set up a pump in the highway "by the bridge neere his house." After 1714 all Newporters who dug wells and set up pumps on town lands or highways did so at their own expense.[20]

---

[17] N. Y. M. C. C., I, 361, 428; II, 149, 263; III, 57.
[18] P. M. C. C., 97, 105, 148.
[19] News Letter, Dec. 31, 1705; Nov. 9, 1713; 11 Bos. Rec. Com., 26, 33, 47, 86, 188, 223; 8 Bos. Rec. Com., 26.
[20] The town had at least six public wells in 1714. Newport T. M. Recs., 79, 94, 169.

Everywhere the greatest preoccupation with the sources of town water grew out of its importance in time of fire. This was particularly true at Charles Town where numerous conflagrations found the place very inadequately supplied. All wells and pumps, being located on private property, were largely inaccessible in time of need. Consequently the Assembly provided in the Fire Act of 1713 that the Commissioners should cause a number of wells to be sunk and fitted with pumps, in order that the new engine might be conveniently supplied with water.[21]

IV

The abnormal conditions produced by the first two intercolonial wars considerably augmented the problem of keeping the peace in the towns. The frequent result was the failure of local agencies, and the establishment by provincial authority of military control in these communities.

The constable continued, as in the past, to be the principal law enforcement officer. His tasks increased so rapidly as to make *The Constable's Pocket-Book: or, A Dialogue Between an Old Constable & a New,* compiled by Nicholas Boone of Boston in 1709 almost a necessity. In addition to many burdensome court duties and the serving of innumerable warrants, constables had to superintend the night watches and act as policemen during the day. In Boston and New York these officers even had augmented responsibilities on the Sabbath, when they labored chiefly to keep others from laboring.[22]

Growth of business at Newport, Charles Town and Philadelphia necessitated an increase in the number of constables. Newport was divided into four wards in 1704, and a constable assigned to each division. In the same year the Common Council of Philadelphia appointed a constable for each of the ten new wards of the city. Despite this increase, it was still difficult to induce citizens to serve, and in 1712 the Pennsylvania Assembly ordered a fine of £10 to be levied upon any person refusing the doubtful honor of promotion to the constabulary. Daniel Standish paid this fine the next year rather than serve.[23]

Constables were usually recruited from among tradesmen and artificers, and despite numerous fees incidental to the office, its responsibilities so impinged upon their time that their businesses suffered considerably. Wearisome duty was not the worst of the constable's

---

[21] *S. C. Statutes,* VII, 58.

[22] *R. I. Acts (1715),* 47; *Pa. Statutes,* II, 420; *S. C. Statutes,* VII, 7, 9; *News Letter,* Sept. 2, 27, 1705; *N. Y. M. C. C.,* II, 65.

[23] *Newport T. M. Recs.,* 98, 118; *S. C. Commons Journal,* June 6, 1692; *P. M. C. C.,* 8, 97; *Pa. Statutes,* II, 420.

lot; he often found its performance unpleasant and dangerous. At Newport, Constable John Stanton complained of being "much Abused by William Bright with bad Language &c.," while attempting to suppress unlawful gaming, and was given the satisfaction of seeing Bright fined £30 in currency. Philadelphia constables were less fortunate in securing compensation for maltreatment. In 1707, when Solomon Cresson was performing his duty by "bidding a Lewd Tavern-keeper disperse her Company," Governor John Evans arose from his table, beat the poor officer, and "sent him to Prison; where he was kept till the Afternoon of the Day following." In 1713 one William Hill, who had "lately in a heat broke his Bell, & given out that he would Continue no Longer at the Place," came with contrite spirit before the Common Council and expressed "a great Deal of Sorrow for his so doing & humbly" prayed "to be continued." They granted his petition.[24]

On the whole there was little change in the position of the constable in this period. His duties multiplied, but there was no increase in either his prestige or his efficiency. On the other hand, wartime conditions wrought considerable upheaval in the towns' systems of civilian watches. The outbreak of the first intercolonial war in 1689 brought uncertainties and disorders with which the civilian watches of Boston and New York were unable to cope. In 1690 Charles Town and Philadelphia, both unexposed to dangers in the early stages of the Anglo-French struggle, were the only towns maintaining local watches.

Philadelphia managed to retain its civilian watch throughout most of the period. For a short time after 1698 the watch was discarded for a single bellman, who called out the time of night and the state of the weather while going his rounds to look out for fires, but in 1701, under authority of the new charter, the Corporation reestablished a citizen's watch. When Governor Evans three years later sought to raise a militia, he was met by the protest of Mayor Anthony Morris that the military guard would discourage inhabitants from watching at night, since militiamen were to be exempted from taking their turns at that unpleasant duty. The Governor replied that a militia would be more effective, but the Quaker authorities thought otherwise, and to signalize their conviction even built a new brick watchhouse in the market place. The constables presented so many persons for failing to serve their nightly turns that in 1705 the Board passed a more stringent watch ordinance, greatly angering Evans, who construed it as defiance of his militia proclamation. Under this new ordinance the constables summoned twelve townsmen to watch each night. When Evans

[24] *Newport T. C. Recs.*, Feb. 3, 1706/7; *Votes Pa. Assembly*, I, ii, 180; Ancient Recs. Phila., 30; *P. M. C. C.*, 92.

engineered a French scare in 1706, two constables accompanied the watch nightly, with instructions to observe "carefully and duly," and to ring the market bell if any turbulent Gallics should appear. This watch continued throughout the period, though in 1712 the Corporation again strengthened the rules pertaining to those who shirked watch duty.[25]

The four other towns felt more severely the effects of war, and in each civilian protection gave way for a period to some form of military guard. In 1690 both Boston and New York were receiving military protection, which lasted until the close of King William's War in 1697. On May 30, 1698, the town of Boston, resolved to restore the "Select Watch," directed its Selectmen to appoint "10 men of fidelity" to walk the town nightly. They were to be paid from the proceeds of a tax laid on each family and warehouse owner. New rules were issued to the watch in 1701, instructing them to inspect with particular care the warehouses near the Dock, and "to call persons to take care of thier lights" when they saw "Ocation." [26]

With the outbreak of Queen Anne's War the town voted to continue the night watch, "except in such time in the Intrim as a Military watch be keept." A military guard was introduced sometime in 1704, and not until 1707 did the Selectmen request of Governor Dudley liberty to revive and maintain the "Select watch." Permission being granted, the authorities hired twelve men at forty shillings a month each, to serve under the old regulations. In 1709 the appointment of two "Overseers" completed the form taken by the Boston watch before 1718. Yearly appropriations, varying from £250 to £350, were made for its support. A special "Ward" of eight "meet & Sober persons" was selected in 1712 "to Ward on the neck of High way between Boston & Roxbury," to prevent "Loose vain persons negrose &c unnecessarily Travilling or walking to and from Boston . . . on the Lords day." This constituted the first daytime watch established in any town. Additional police regulations had to be made in September, 1712, to meet growing disorders in the town, and the Selectmen and County Justices "agreed to walk by turns by night to Inspect the Order of ye Town for eight Weeks next following," — a custom they observed regularly each year thereafter.[27]

The Corporation of New York revived its civilian watch shortly after the Peace of Ryswick, when it authorized the Mayor to hire as

[25] *Pa. Col. Recs.*, I, 581; Westcott, *Philadelphia,* chapter LV; *P. M. C. C.,* 9, 11, 16, 27, 35, 39, 79, 81; Ancient Recs. Phila., 31.
[26] 7 *Bos. Rec. Com.,* 231, 232, 237, 238, 241; *Mass. Acts and Resolves,* I, 381; 11 *Bos. Rec. Com.,* 3, 5, 7, 171.
[27] 8 *Bos. Rec. Com.,* 24, 43, 131; 11 *Bos. Rec. Com.,* 26, 54, 96, 118, 142, 169, 191, 212, 231, *et passim;* 13 *Bos. Rec. Com.,* 43, 58, 72, 73; *News Letter,* Aug. 27, 1705.

bellmen "four Sober honest men upon Such Reasonable Terms as he shall Judge Needfull." These bellmen made the rounds of the "Citty" once every hour during the night, proclaiming "the season of the weather and the hour of the night," to the ringing of their bells. In regard to thieves, prowlers, and disturbers of the peace, they had instructions to "take the most prudent way they Can to Secure ye said Persons Untill the Next Morning that they may be examined by the Mayor." For a few months in 1713 six men were employed, but the number was reduced in the following year, and from that time on a force of four men constituted the entire police department of the town by night.[28] With only these few bellmen on nocturnal duty in 1720 New York could no longer pride itself on the excellent protection it had enjoyed when forty-five watchmen patrolled the streets each night.

Charles Town's exposed situation on the southern frontier added to its normal problems of fire prevention and public order the constant threat of external attack. Confusion and indecision marked all attempts to provide protection for the little port. In 1696 the "remiss" constable's watch gave way to a tax supported guard of a captain and five armed men, but two years later the citizen's watch was again restored, because of the negligence of the paid patrol, "especially since the fatal and dismal conflagration." Legislation designed to increase its efficiency was enacted in 1701; a brick watchhouse and several sentry boxes were provided, any watchman found sleeping therein to be fined forty shillings or "Tyed neck and Heales, Two Hours ye next Morning."

The inadequacy of this protection during wartime led in 1703 to the substitution of a military watch, consisting of an officer and twelve armed men, and costing the town £550 annually. But again in 1709 the Assembly noted that there had been "for a long time past no regular watch kept in Charles Town, which, if not duly taken care of and in time prevented, now in this time of war and eminent [sic] danger, may be of fatal consequences, and the ruin of this flourishing and thriving town." An armed watch of ten men was ordered to patrol the town nightly, with the provision that in times of danger the Governor might double the number. For the first time, commissioners were appointed to enforce this act, and to their efforts may be attributed the better observance of the law. Outbreak of the Yamassee War again cut short the experiment with civilian protection, and in 1713 a tax of £520 per year was levied to support a new military patrol of twenty-two men, eight of them to make the rounds each night. Nowhere does the

---

[28] N. Y. Hist. Soc. *Colls., 1880,* 403, 416; *N. Y. M. C. C.,* II, 20, 62, 120, 188, 210, 242, 288, 291, 315; III, 20, 217.

absence of effective local authority to superintend the municipal affairs of Charles Town appear so unfortunate as in the case of the watch.[29]

The last town to establish its watch was Newport. In 1700 a provincial law gave all Rhode Island towns permissive power to form night watches, and provided penalties for citizens who refused to take their turns, but Newport felt no need for such a nocturnal guard until 1713. Prior to 1707 the town's sole protection was one bellman, on duty only in winter. Beginning in 1707 a military guard appears to have been kept in the town because of fear of French privateers, but in 1709 the threat had passed, and Newport returned to its solitary bellman who walked the town twice a night, at eleven and four, from November to April. Growth of the town by 1713 led to the creation of a constable's watch of four men. Yet its life was brief, for in the quiet following the almost immediate restoration of peace Newport returned to its earlier arrangement, hiring Thomas Taylor at a salary of £9 to act as bellman for the winter of 1716–17. No watch was again established during this period, despite the passage of a colony law empowering all town councils to maintain one in times of peace.[30]

The duties of the watches varied from town to town, but everywhere they were expected to preserve peace and quiet during the night, announce the time, describe the state of the weather, and keep a sharp lookout for fire. Boston and Charles Town watchmen were especially enjoined to take up all servants and slaves abroad in the streets after dark. Watchmen were expected to be exemplary in their conduct at all times, and were subject to fines if they smoked or fell asleep while on duty, were "disorderly," or neglected their routine in any way. City authorities of today might well revive the order of the Boston Selectmen of 1717, "that the watch men be forbid going abt to beg Money or New years gifts of ye Inhabitants." [31]

Occasionally watchmen came to blows with an offender, or had their troubles in "prudently" suppressing disorders in taverns. The streets of Charles Town were so frequently filled with brawling sailors, whose favorite sport was beating up the watch, that the authorities in 1700 instituted a seven o'clock bell to ring all seamen aboard their ships for the night, and ordered the watch to lock up in the guard house all stray mariners found in town after that hour. The presence of sailors from the royal navy at Boston during the war occasioned frequent broils with the watch. The Selectmen reported in

[29] Archdale's Laws (MS.), 36; *S. C. Statutes*, VII, 7, 17, 22, 47, 54, 57, 60; *S. C. Commons Journal*, *1702*, 47, 64, 66, 72; *1703*, 9, 21; *1704*, 34; Trott's Laws (MS.), Pt. I, 232, 314, 407; Pt. II, 69.

[30] *R. I. Acts* (*1705*), 47; (*1744*), 80; *Newport T. M. Recs.*, 105, 152; *Newport T. C. Recs.*, Nov. 5, 1711; Dec. 6, 1714; May 2, 1715; July 2, Dec. 6, 1716.

[31] *S. C. Statutes*, VII, 7, 17; 8 *Bos. Rec. Com.*, 7; 11 *Bos. Rec. Com.*, 5, 123; *N. Y. M. C. C.*, II, 20.

1709 that seamen from H.M.S. *Reserve* "did lately offer Abuse to Several of the watchmen." More serious were disorders resulting from operations of the press-gang: "A sailor was beaten last night," recorded Sewall on June 27, 1711, "and threatened to be carried on Board the Weymouth; which the Watch prevented." In 1704, when Constable Wood and James Dough, watchman, went to Enoch Story's tavern in Philadelphia late at night to quiet the inmates, they were badly beaten by Governor Evans, William Penn, Jr., Sheriff Finney, and their drunken companions. Some outsiders, coming in with Alderman Wilcox, attacked young Penn whom they failed to recognize. The Grand Jury indicted the assailants, who brought counter charges against the constable and watchman, but the Governor saved his friends by a proclamation forbidding the case to come to trial. The nocturnal guardians of Boston also found a continual source of annoyance in disorderly persons who haunted taverns late at night.[32]

The uncertain events of the war years greatly deranged the police systems of the five towns, and upon several occasions civil watches gave way to military patrols. Once the former had been suspended it was difficult to find money to revive them. By 1720, however, every town save Newport had either formed a new watch or restored the old. The system insured some measure of nocturnal tranquility in the streets, and the advance made by the towns compared favorably, on the whole, with the situation in provincial cities of England.[33] New York alone, at the close of the period, found itself with a watch inferior to that which it had enjoyed in the seventeenth century.

V

Crime, disorder and vice showed a marked increase in every town during this period. With the considerable growth in wealth and population, and the presence of new elements along the waterfronts which accompanied the expansion of trade, such a development was to be expected. But it was accelerated and complicated by the social unrest and moral relaxation which attended the wars and the years immediately following them.

The prevailing offense against society was theft. Boston suffered most from this crime, both because of its size and wealth, and because hundreds of people flocked there during the wars to increase the number of what Sewall called the "disorderly poor." A wave of petty rob-

[32] Ravenel, *Eliza Pinckney*, 78; 11 *Bos. Rec. Com.*, 98; 5 MHS *Colls.*, VI, 93, 317; Logan Letter Books, I, 159.
[33] With a population of about thirty thousand, Bristol, England, was served only by twelve night constables, "farcically called watchmen." Liverpool's "vice-roys of the street" numbered only twelve from 1667 to 1721; Latimer, *Bristol in the Seventeenth Century*, 18, 30; Picton, *Municipal Archives*, 29, 127.

beries occurred in the years 1704–1707. The thieves made a specialty of articles readily convertible into cash, such as silver, linen and silks, and it was generally believed that country peddlers often acted as agents for the disposal of these stolen goods. A similar epidemic broke out in 1712. Among the most active criminals were two shoplifters, who secured introductions to unsuspecting tradesmen and pilfered them of "lace and other goods." A series of housebreaks occurred in 1715; the Selectmen voted a £25 reward for the discovery of any of the robbers, and persuaded the Governor to issue a proclamation promising pardon to any thief who would turn state's evidence against those "that have been guilty of the Notorious Burglaries and thefts late Committed." [34]

Philadelphia experienced some increase in crime after 1700, and in 1720 was also suffering from a wave of robberies. William Smith of Charlestown, Massachusetts, and Hannah Travis, a local girl, "Commonly called *Dancing Hannah*," operated profitably as thieves for some time before they were apprehended and given the death penalty in March of that year. Many dishonest seamen availed themselves of their shore leaves to purloin a few souvenirs from the Quaker town, and in one case four of them were pursued as far as Lewes and brought back to town. In addition to the trouble with lawlessness within Philadelphia, a gang of highwaymen operated on the road to Darby, robbing unprotected travelers. A year of such robberies rendered official nerves strained and touchy. When Ann Husen was sentenced to death for burglary by the Court of Oyer and Terminer, Governor William Keith refused her pardon, because "her Crime was a growing Evil in the City of Philadelphia, which had but very lately been made a Felony of Death, wherefore to make a Proper Example of the Force of the Law would be of Use & Importance." [35]

During the later years of Queen Anne's War New York was much subject to the depredations of burglars. In 1711 Jacob Riemer informed the Mayor's Court that John Mitchell had stolen from his house twenty-four gallons of cider, beer and Madeira. Revealing that even the houses of God were not respected by the gallowsbirds of Manhattan, a gang broke into Trinity Church on February 10, 1714, stealing the communion service and several other articles of value. The Governor's Council rounded up and examined all persons known to have been at public houses on that night, but the culprits remained undetected. This sacrilege so alarmed all churches that their members

[34] 5 MHS *Colls.*, VI, 93, 189; *News Letter*, Dec. 22, 1712; Jan. 17, 31, 1715; 11 *Bos. Rec. Com.*, 221.
[35] This accounts for the severe penal code of 1718 which superseded Penn's humane laws. *Pa. Statutes*, III, 199; *Pa. Hist.*, III, 9; *Mercury*, Feb. 23, Mar. 17, June 23, Oct. 20, 1720; *Pa. Col. Recs.*, III, 109.

united in a petition urging the Governor to take drastic steps to check the growing impiety and immorality of New York.[36]

The criminals of this period seem to have expected poorer pickings in the two smallest towns, for both of them were less afflicted by instances of lawbreaking. Charles Town suffered greatly from the pilfering of Negro slaves "at unreasonable hours of the night," and in 1698 the watch was specifically enjoined to keep a weather eye open for all such dusky prowlers. About the same time, also, a number of women released from Newgate were sent over to Charles Town, where their presence probably did not serve to lessen the problem of petty thefts. Newport's only serious crime of the period occurred in October, 1706, when a gang of intercolonial horse thieves, stopping at William Bright's tavern, filched his handsome sword and tankard, and rode off to New York on horses belonging to Stephen Easton and others.[37]

The presence of pirates in all towns, and the fact that the authorities winked at their crimes, is evidence of ethical laxity among business and professional classes. Many so-called respectable merchants increased their wealth by illicit trade, much to the disgust of Edward Randolph, Lord Bellomont, Jahleel Brenton and Colonel Robert Quary. Pirates even found a haven among the Quakers: "I saw them walking about the streets of Philadelphia," complained Randolph in 1698.[38]

The appearance of paper money gave the signal for the emergence of a group of counterfeiters, many of whom were readily detected. Thomas Odell of Boston counterfeited the £4 bills of Massachusetts in 1705, and tried to pass them in Pennsylvania where he was discovered. Though he made his escape while being taken by boat to Newport, he was later recaptured and sentenced at Boston to pay a fine of £300 and to pass a year in prison. When James Mar, a New York engraver, similarly misapplied his skill he was sentenced to hang, but was granted executive clemency, the Governor finding himself unable to refuse a lachrymose petition from "Most of the Gentlewomen of the City." Less fortunate were Edward and Martha Hunt of Philadelphia, who received sentences of death and life imprisonment respectively for counterfeiting in 1720.[39]

Not only was dishonesty on the increase, but townspeople tended to greater violence in their behavior toward one another. The Mayor's Court at New York had continually to deal with cases of assault and

---

[36] Peterson, *New York*, 22; *Doc. Hist. N. Y.*, III, 444, 455.
[37] *S. C. Statutes*, VII, 7; *S. C. Council Journal, 1692*, 38; *Cal. St. Pap., 1696–1697*, 533; *News Letter*, Oct. 8, Nov. 4, 1706.
[38] *Cal. St. Pap., 1696*, 314; *1697–1698*, 211.
[39] *News Letter*, Aug. 14, 1704; June 18, Nov. 12, 1705; Sept. 21, 1713; *Mercury*, Mar. 17, Oct. 20, 1720.

battery. Mary Wilson accused Hugh Crow in 1704 with attacking her "With his double fist . . . so that of her life it was despaired," noted the Clerk, and the jury award of £10 damages seems lenient. In a fish-wives' scuffle in 1705 Joan Atkins, "with staves swords Clubbs and other weapons, did beat wound and evill treat" Isabelle Maynard, but no indictment was brought. Citizens of Philadelphia seem to have been continually running afoul of drunken sailors and getting themselves beaten up. In 1713 John Hoffin and John Buckley preferred charges of this nature against John Barfield and Daniel Moody. The tars were fined, but the money was later refunded by a lenient Mayor's Court. One wonders who was really punished in 1717 when Nicholas Williams, a minor, brought into Court for beating his father, was fined £50. The fine was afterwards remitted, because the "family was so poor." Charles Town, too, suffered a plague of brawling sailors.[40]

Few aristocrats, save the boy governor of Pennsylvania, indulged in such crude offenses as assault, but on several occasions they resorted to the field of honor. Three duels were fought at Boston in this period. Thomas Lechmere's humorous account of a fight between two officers on the Common, February 15, 1712, contrasts sharply with Sewall's sad reflections on the affair: "On Friday, . . . two of our sparks (officers), Messrs. Douglas and Alexander had a mind to shew their manhood. Alexander (like the Great of old) gave the challenge." When the principals arrived on the scene, "there they bravely gave the word draw, out they pulled spado, to it they went, . . . and like two brave heroes gave each other a mortal wound." Thomas Dongan, nephew of the Governor, killed Dr. John Livingston in an affair at New York in 1715, and was found guilty of manslaughter. The Reverend Francis Philips of the Anglican Church challenged Peter Evans to a combat *"Gladio Cinctus"* at Philadelphia in 1715, for having "basely slandered a gentlewoman," but the Grand Jury prevented the meeting.[41]

In the towns the tendency to mob action noted earlier was intensified. A disgraceful episode, revealing connivance of the highest officials in illicit trade, occurred at Charles Town in 1701, when Chief Justice Trott, on coming out of the trial of the *Cole and Bean* for violation of the Acts of Trade, "in the open street, . . . among a crowd of people, fell upon the informer, and struck him several times," thereby precipi-tating a riot. In 1705 a group of New York privateersmen began a riot before the sheriff's house, assaulting the officers of the law, and wounding several other persons; several fatalities resulted from this

[40] Peterson, *New York*, 22; *Minutes Mayor's Court*, 163, 225, 277, 278; 6 MHS *Colls.*, III, 387; *P. M. C. C.*, 96, 142; Ravenel, *Eliza Pinckney*, 78.
[41] 5 MHS *Colls.*, V, 410; VI, 334; VII, 208; 6 MHS *Colls.*, V, 256; *News Letter*, Sept. 19, 1715; Westcott, *Philadelphia*, chapter LXVII.

affray. Of Boston it was charged in 1720 that its citizens had for a long time been "inclined to Riots & Tumults," such behavior being by no means limited to the sterner sex. As the troops, returning from their abortive Canadian expedition of 1707, debarked at Scarlett's Wharf, a crowd of women shouting "So-ho, souse ye cowards. Salute Port Royal," greeted them with a barrage of chamber pots. The two bread riots have already been noted. Even quiet Newporters could be aroused by danger of possible enforcement of the Navigation Acts. Caleb Heathcote informed the Board of Trade in 1719 of the disposition among the Newport "rabble" to mob the customs officers. In one case the collectors had seized some illegal claret, "yet the town's people had the insolence to rise upon them, and insult both them and the civil officers" by staving in the casks, drinking their fill, and pouring the remainder into the streets. Rioting of slaves too often disturbed the peace of Philadelphia's First Day. So frequent were such outbreaks that in 1715 the Assembly memorialized Governor Gookin, expressing the hope that "those Tumults which frequently happened in this City since the beginning of our Session" might be stopped.[42]

Growing disorder in the towns brought the question of adequate facilities for punishment increasingly before the public. Yet townsmen strangely neglected their gaols and prisons, and only New York can be said to have maintained a "sufficient" place of confinement in this period. The old "Stadt Huys," "made strong and Convenient" in 1698, served as a prison until the completion of the City Hall in 1700, which contained quarters secure enough to "hold felons." A "Cage, Whipping post, pillory, and Stocks" were set up beside the "Ducking Stool" before the City Hall in 1703, and removed seven years later to a location in Broad Street.[43]

Elsewhere town authorities allowed their places of detention to fall into ruinous neglect. The condition of the Boston prison may be judged from the fact that in 1699 the pirates, Joseph Bradish and Tee Witherly, easily made their "escape with the Maid [Kate Price] that helped them out." No steps to improve the building were taken in this period. Minor offenders and "Idle drunken and disorderlie persons" were incarcerated at the Alms House, since there was still no house of correction available. This mingling of moral delinquents with the unfortunate poor in close confinement was an evil which the town could not correct without the concurrence of County Justices. Even as a place of punishment for unruly persons, the Alms House failed of its purpose, and in 1709 the Town Meeting instructed the Selectmen to confer

[42] *Cal. St. Pap., 1701,* 651; *News Letter,* Sept. 24, 1705; 8 *Bos. Rec. Com.,* 155; *R. I. Col. Recs.,* IV, 258; *Votes Pa. Assembly,* II, 183.
[43] Peterson, *New York,* 192; *N. Y. M. C. C.,* I, 238; II, 57, 59, 244, 256, 425; III, 227.

with the Justices, praying "that the House of Correction may be put into Such postture . . . as may Serve the ends for which it was designed." Again in 1712 the town petitioned the Court in vain, and in 1720 offered to donate land if the county would agree to build a separate Bridewell upon it. The sole improvements effected during these thirty years were the erection of three "cages," and the purchase of a whipping post and stocks.[44]

Conditions were even worse at Philadelphia. The pirates, Clinton and Lasells, broke out of prison there in 1698, and two years later Penn called attention to the need for a more secure place of confinement. In 1707 the Grand Jury presented the middle and upper windows of the gaol as insufficient, and in 1713 the Common Council denounced the whole building as "a public nusance, . . . it being too Notorious that Criminalls ffrequently Escape." They ordered the dilapidated structure torn down and a new prison built on a lot already purchased. But not until the Assembly required the erection of this new prison by law was the building begun, and only toward the close of 1721 was it open for use.[45]

Like the other towns, Philadelphia had more adequate provision for the swifter dealing with offenders. William Southbee "& other Inhabitants," who were shocked in 1698 by the drunkenness prevalent at the ordinaries, petitioned the Provincial Council to "Cause stock and Cage [to] be provided" for town drunks. Their petition was granted, and after 1701 the Corporation carefully kept these instruments in repair, along with the "Whipping post & pillory" acquired in 1705.[46]

Newport and Charles Town were no exceptions to the general rule concerning neglect of prisons in this period. Throughout the entire time Newport spent only twenty shillings "towards ye repaire of ye prison." This expenditure barely made the gaol secure enough to hold two of the seven pirates confined there in August, 1710; it was quite insufficient to detain the Negro, Emanuel, who broke out in September and made his getaway on Captain James Clark's best horse. Most offenders were placed in the "Pair of Stocks of Correction" which Thomas Peckham made in 1712, or in the new "Caidge" built after a "Moddle drawn by the Town Council." At Charles Town in 1701 a brick "Watch-house" was set up and used as a place of detention. When Stede Bonnet's pirates escaped from this structure in October, 1717, Governor Johnson urged the Assembly to build a prison in the town, since the repeated jailbreaks by felons and debtors seriously

[44] 5 MHS Colls., V, 498, 503; 8 Bos. Rec. Com., 61, 93, 96, 148; 11 Bos. Rec. Com., 62, 193; 13 Bos. Rec. Com., 76.
[45] Cal. St. Pap., 1697–1698, 214; Pa. Col. Recs., I, 582, 583; P. M. C. C., 87; Scharf and Westcott, Philadelphia, III, 825.
[46] Pa. Col. Recs., I, 531; P. M. C. C., 26, 28.

threatened the safety of citizens. No action being taken, the watch-house remained the only place of confinement.[47]

Standards of morality in the towns underwent a considerable decline in this period from the levels of the seventeenth century. Such a development followed naturally from increasing populations, and the large number of foreigners and mariners who peopled the waterfronts, — factors which made possible a greater anonymity of vice. Moreover, normal town conditions were heightened by the effects of war, and all their morally relaxing and degenerating consequences.

All observers reported an increase in sexual immorality at Boston. Gossipy Ned Ward found illicit relationships, especially among younger people, common in 1699. Lecture days, he wrote, "call'd by some amongst them Whore Fair," were notorious for the "Levity and Wanton Frollicks of the Young People, who, when their Devotion's over, have recourse to the Ordinaries, where they plentifully wash away the remembrance of their Old Sins, and drink down the fear of a Fine, or the dread of a Whipping-post." [48] With the coming of Queen Anne's War, when the town was frequently filled with soldiers and sailors, cases of adultery and bastardy multiplied. Though not confined to any one group, such offenses were most usual among the seafaring population and the large number of widows. "And now, if I begin with Seafaring," confided Cotton Mather to his *Diary* in 1718, "Oh, what an horrible Spectacle have I before me! A wicked, stupid, abominable Generation; every Year growing rather worse." [49]

Numerous prostitutes plied their trade in the town, their victims not solely from the army or the waterfront. Many of the respectable consorted with them, among them Cotton Mather's son, Increase. Especially after 1710 several bawdy houses appeared. Mather learned in 1713 of "Houses in this Town, where there are young Women of a very debauched Character and extreamly Impudent; unto whom there is a great Resort of young men." Although he hoped that "by suitable Admonitions, and some other Methods, this Mischief may be extinguished," the fact was that the social evil had come to stay.[50]

Philadelphia experienced the same problems as did Boston. Penn wrote from England in 1697 of the reports he had from his town "that there is no place more overrun with wickedness, Sins so very Scandal-

---

[47] *Newport T. M. Recs.*, 72, 78; *News Letter*, Aug. 15, Sept. 1, 1710; *Newport T. C. Recs.*, Oct. 2, 1710; *Newport T. M. Procs.*, April 27, 1720; *S. C. Commons Journal, 1698*, 33; *1701*, 19; *1717* (Oct. 29); *S. C. Statutes*, VII, 17.

[48] "The child who learned to spell from the 'New England Primer,' as soon as he was able to master words of five syllables, was taught 'For-ni-ca-ti-on.'" Winship, *Boston in 1682 and 1695*, xxi, xxiii, 41.

[49] 7 MHS *Colls.*, VIII, 65, 239, 242, 451, 528, 531, 538, 555; *News Letter*, Jan. 22, 1704/5.

[50] 11 *Bos. Rec. Com.*, 99, 107; Savage, *Boston Watch*, 23; 7 MHS *Colls.*, VIII. 126, 168, 229, 283, 484.

ous, openly Comitted in defiance of Law and Virtue: the facts so foul, I am forbid by Comon modesty to relate." The reply of the Provincial Council explained the root of the problem in every town: "As to the growth of vice, wee cannot but owne as this place hath growne more populous, & the people increased, Looseness & vice Hath also Creept in, which we lament, altho' endeavours have been used to suppress it, . . . offenders Having Received deserved & exemplary punishments, according to Law." Sexual laxity was in such evidence that in 1700 the Assembly passed its first law "Against Adultery, Fornication, &c," providing terrific penalties. The Mayor's Court had frequently to deal with cases of illegitimacy and adultery. As at Boston many public houses became "nurseries of vice and debaucheries," where sailors and townsfolk made assignations. The greatest scandal of the period occurred in August, 1715. Parson Philips, rector of the Anglican Church, talked too freely of his amorous victories over some of the town's most respected ladies, several of whom were married. His arrest and attempted prosecution produced two riots, much violence and numerous broken windows, followed by his ultimate release. Philips, wrote Logan, "appeared a most vile man, not only in practice but in conversation, and [yet] he still holds the church and a number of hearers." [51]

The state of morals was much the same in the other seaports, although in proportion as they were smaller the problem was less acute. New York harbored many prostitutes, but apparently no bawdy houses, and at Charles Town many women of ill fame, outcasts from Newgate, approached men openly on the streets at night. [52]

Everywhere drunkenness was the besetting vice, and authorities sought constantly for means to suppress it. Each community had its town drunks, like George Robinson, the Philadelphia butcher, whom the Grand Jury presented in 1702 for "euill fame as . . . a comon drunker." Lists of "Reputed drunkards & comon Tiplers" were regularly posted in a public place at Boston. [53]

Gambling, despite numerous laws against it, became more and more popular among all classes. Joseph Jepson of Newport was continually in trouble with the Town Council because he "kept Gaming in his house." The more sober citizens of Philadelphia complained in 1695 of gambling "both at fairs and at all other times," and prevailed upon the Assembly a few years later to pass a law authorizing the Mayor to enter suspected gaming houses. In June, 1699, Samuel Sewall suppressed a card game at Boston, and a few days later found to his disgust "A Pack of Cards . . . strawed over my foreyard, which,

[51] Pa. Col. Recs., I, 527; P. M. C. C., 40, 45, 85, 141; Pa. Statutes, II, 5; Logan Papers (Aug. 18, 1715).
[52] Stokes, Iconography, IV, 464, 478; S. C. Commons Journal, 1702, 47; 1703, 59.
[53] Ancient Recs. Phila., 3; 11 Bos. Rec. Com., 126, 132.

tis supposed, some might throw there to mock me." Cotton Mather
agonized in 1711 over "some Young men of my Flock, who abandon
themselves to the ruinous courses of Gaming: who especially betake
themselves thereto, for the Quieting of their minds, when they meet
with any Thing in the public Sermons that proves troublesome to their
Consciences." An incident bearing the aspect of agelessness occurred
at Charles Town in 1699. A young man named Davis, staggering
ashore from the usual gaieties of an embarkation party, allowed himself to be inveigled into play at the home of a card sharper. To meet
his losses he signed a note for £59, a transaction of which he had no
memory whatsoever when collection was demanded the next morning.
At Charles Town, Boston and New York gaming was also the favorite
diversion of slaves and apprentices. Lotteries, which Sewall and other
Boston leaders regarded as "differing little from Gaming for Money:
and as being really pernicious to Trade," were suppressed by the General Court in 1719 as "common and public nuisances," largely because
they encouraged youths and servants to a "foolish expence of money,"
and led to the impoverishment of many families.[54]

The public behavior of many townsfolk was rude and scandalous.
Well-mannered Philadelphia Quakers complained bitterly in 1695 of
those not in meeting for continually "swearing blaspheming God's
holy name, drawing youth to vanity, [and] makeing such noises and
public hootings" as tended to "blemish Christianity and dishonour the
holy name of God." On two occasions in 1702 the Court fined George
Robinson because, in addition to his already noted weakness for his
bottle, he was a "Comon Swearer"; once he was heard to utter "three
oaths in the market place!" That the aristocrat, when in his cups,
could be no less foul-mouthed and disorderly was demonstrated at
Boston in 1709, when Sewall inquired after "Debaucheries at North's
Exchange Tavern," and had to fine Mr. Thomas Banister twenty
shillings "for Lying," "5s. Curse," and "10s. Breach of the peace for
throwing pots and Scale-box at the maid." Occasionally, too, women
forgot their manners, and loosed scandalous tongues. In October,
1715, Margaret Norton of New York, whose use of language was no
more varied than it was fastidious, was charged with calling Zachariah
Hutchins both a "privateer dog" and "that one-eyed son of a bitch,"
and with describing Henry Fountenay as "that old French son of a
bitch." These "vile and approbrious" epithets cost her £16. It was at
Philadelphia, however, that the good men and true of the Grand Jury
informed the Justices of "the Necessity of a Ducking Stool and house

[54] *Newport T. C. Recs.*, Feb. 6, 1715/16; *Pa. Statutes*, II, 360; 5 MHS *Colls.*, V,
498; 7 MHS *Colls.*, VIII, 50, 187, 199; *Mass. Acts and Resolves*, II, 149; Case of
Robert Davis (MS.).

of Correcon, for that the just punishment of scolding Drunken Women, . . . who are become a Public Nusance & disturbance to this Town in General," and desired provision for "those publick conveniencys" with all possible speed.[55]

We have seen that town authorities were not blind to the many moral delinquencies of their inhabitants. They tried to suppress vice wherever it was detected, and in some measure they succeeded, but the problem of human weaknesses transcended their efforts at solution. In the face of their partial failure, Cotton Mather, always in touch with current English developments, borrowed from London the idea of a private organization to combat the "Leprosy of Sin." In 1702 he formed a "Society for the Suppression of Disorders," consisting of about "fourteen good Men, whereof some are Justices," who agreed to meet when disorders arose in the town, and to endeavor to prevent their occurrence. By 1703 membership had grown "too large, to admitt any more," so Mather organized two similar societies, one in the North and one in the South End. These zealots directed their efforts toward the exposure and suppression of vice, especially the "swearing of oaths" and the patronage of disorderly houses. With a view to early education in virtue they also interested themselves in the schooling of children and the time and place of their play. In 1713 Mather "Gott a Catalogue of Young Men, who visited wicked Houses," which he laid before his society, whence admonitions were sent out to the erring youths. Although one of these watch and ward societies died out in 1711, another had been founded the year before, so that throughout the period there existed three such organizations, through which the people of Boston, in their private capacities, waged a relentless war upon vice and immorality.[56]

The disorders just described were not confined to the six working days of the week; indeed, since the Sabbath was a day of rest people tended to "Meet together to be Merry and Vain," and some were "guilty of more Sin that Night than on any other Night" in the week. Everywhere town authorities sought by more legislation and severer penalties to prevent profanation of the Lord's Day. At Charles Town in 1691 it was ordered that "No work of ordinary calling . . . can be done on Sunday," no slaves might labor, no goods could be sold, and the only travel permitted was that to and from church. The next

[55] Ancient Recs. Phila., 3, 40, 42; 5 MHS *Colls.*, VI, 226; Peterson, *New York*, 21.
[56] In 1703 Mather published his *Methods and Motives for a Society to Suppress Disorders,* which he contrived to send "into all Parts of the Countrey." It contained an account of the "Society for the Reformation of Manners," founded in 1692 to inform against violations of penal laws. By 1699 there were eight such organizations in London, Westminster and Southwark, and the movement was spreading all over England. 7 MHS *Colls.*, VII, 418, 500, 517, 523, 531; VIII, 27, 42, 110, 131, 160, 229, 235, 283; Traill, *Social England,* IV, 592.

year the Grand Council strictly forbade "the haunting of punch houses during the time of divine service." In 1712, after the Anglicans had gained full control, the Charles Town Sabbath was made more strict than that of any other town by the requirement that everyone must attend church on Sunday or pay a five shilling fine. All sports and pastimes were forbidden, and taverns were open only to lodgers. That it was necessary for constables and church wardens to walk the town on Sabbath mornings and afternoons was proof that such rigid observance could be maintained at Charles Town only by a determined show of authority.[57]

The Sabbath was probably not any more profaned at Boston than elsewhere, but more fuss was made about it there. The provincial code of 1692 prohibited travel, labor, sports and play on the Lord's Day, and forbade innkeepers to entertain any save strangers and lodgers. The presence of many outsiders in the town during the wars did not aid in the enforcement of the laws, although Governor Dudley in 1708 "argued hard" before he was able to persuade the Council to grant a license to Captain Treat to work Sunday on his ship which was aground in the harbor. Increase Mather blamed the fire of 1711 on the employment of "bakers, Carpenters and other Tradesmen . . . in Servile Work on the Sabbath Day." [58] The demands of trade, more than anything else, were tending to break down the strict observance of the Sabbath.

Similar conditions existed in other towns. At Philadelphia in 1703 four barbers were haled into Court for "trimming people on the first day," and pious Quakers continually agonized over the disorders of young men and apprentices, who assumed "licenteous liberty in robbing of orchards especially on the first day." The Quakers of Newport must have enjoyed a quiet first day, for no change was made in the law of 1679. The Corporation of New York found it necessary to provide for the "better Observation" of its severe Lord's Day code in 1698, when the constables were directed to see to the stricter enforcement of the laws.[59]

The fortunes of war brought increased prosperity to the five colonial ports, but in its wake came the inevitable moral breakdown that follows war. Still, when the moral status of the colonial towns is compared with that of contemporary English cities, the former appear as oases

---

[57] Winship, *Boston in 1682 and 1699*, xxii; *S. C. Statutes*, II, 68, 396.

[58] *Journal of Madam Knight*, 54; 6 MHS *Colls.*, V, 381; 8 *Bos. Rec. Com.*, 13; 5 MHS *Colls.*, VI, 268; *N. E. Hist. & Gen. Reg.*, XIII, 144.

[59] At Bristol, England, in 1703 strict Sabbath ordinances were enforced by the deputies of each ward who perambulated the city to still disorders. City gates were kept closed on Sunday mornings to prevent excursions into the country. Ancient Recs. Phila., 20; *R. I. Acts* (1744), 18; *N. Y. M. C. C.*, II, 65; Latimer, *Bristol in the Eighteenth Century*, 6, 27.

of virtue in a wicked world. The waterfront society had come to stay, but the major portion of the citizens in every town went soberly about their business, living up to the strict morality of their middle class traditions.

VI

With the exception of Charles Town all towns adhered to the old policy of excluding undesirable strangers from within their limits. As in earlier years this attitude was fostered by considerations of trade and the desire to prevent the towns from being burdened with vagrants and paupers. The indigent or undesirable stranger was the eternal nightmare of the town of Boston. Repercussions of border warfare in the "Eastern partes" in the last decade of the seventeenth century made themselves felt in Boston by 1700, and fugitive poor swarmed in. The "Town being so Populous, and they shifting from place to place so long before they be discouered that the Law makes them Inhabitants," it proved almost impossible to expel such intruders. As many strangers arrived by sea, the General Court in 1704 passed a law containing the usual requirements about listing passengers with the Impost Officer. A special official, whose duty it was to detect and warn away strangers, was regularly appointed by the town after 1702.[60]

The influx subsided somewhat after 1704, but increased again in 1711 and 1712. The Selectmen had no more than got the situation under control in 1714 when the Scotch-Irish began to pour into Boston, many of them going promptly on the rates. The inhabitants, resenting what they viewed as intrusion, dealt severely with the newcomers. When the ship *Elizabeth* arrived from Ireland in November, 1719, its forty-nine miserable passengers were warned to leave town immediately. Though this harsh policy certainly worked hardship on many unfortunate people, it is equally certain that the Bostonians needed some means to free themselves from the growing expense of caring for dependents who were not townsmen.[61]

No more did inhabitants of Newport welcome intruding strangers who might become a burden on the public poor rates. Memory of the trouble during and following the Indian Wars remained fresh in the minds of many. After 1702 no ship captain could disembark passengers without permission, nor could persons landed remain in Newport unless granted liberty by the Town Council. Constables were instructed to take up and jail all suspected strangers until they procured

[60] 7 *Bos. Rec. Com.*, 241; *Mass. Acts and Resolves*, I, 451; 11 *Bos. Rec. Com.*, 25, 60, 100, 205, 220.
[61] From 1701 to 1715 over two hundred and thirty persons were warned out; from 1715 to 1720 over three hundred and thirty, most of whom were Ulster Scots. 11 *Bos. Rec. Com.*, 50, 134, 182.

bonds to secure the town from charges. Thus, in 1704, John Bemit and Joseph Gardner each gave bonds of £20 to guarantee that Samuel Baker and his family would not become a burden upon the town. After 1706 the Overseers of the Poor made annual returns to the Town Council of "What Strangers Comes into ye Town." The vicissitudes of Queen Anne's War, which caused many colonists to change their locations, did not pass Newport by. By 1711 the problem was serious, and the Town Sergeant was instructed to warn all persons who "Come into Town without Giving . . . sufficient security to Endemnify ye Town of Any Charge," to produce immediate security or depart. This order was scrupulously observed; even Elizabeth Hunney of Massachusetts, who was with child, was given only four days in which to leave town in 1715.[62]

The attitude of Philadelphia authorities had originally been, come one, come all, but protests of tradesmen about competition from strangers, and the growing problem of the poor, led to the abandonment of this open door policy early in the century. In 1705 a Corporation ordinance required all strangers to post bonds, "indemnifying the City from Charge . . . During the space of seven years." Shortly afterwards, another order forbade inhabitants of Philadelphia to entertain "Inmates" without first notifying the Mayor. These regulations operated successfully until the tide of immigration began to flow after Utrecht. To enable authorities to protect the town against the hordes of poor Germans and Scotch-Irish, the Assembly provided in 1717 that every ship's captain must lodge a list of his passengers with the Provincial Council, and city magistrates were "strictly" directed to seek out "vagabonds and suspected persons."[63] Just at the close of this period Philadelphia was brought face to face with the immigration problem, which would plague its people throughout the remainder of the colonial era.

Elsewhere the problem was less acute. Few poor from other villages sought refuge in New York, and the earlier regulations proved sufficient for this period. In the case of Charles Town, the desire for colonists was still so great that the authorities tried every means to attract immigration thither.

The widely accepted view that the colonial poor hastened off to the frontier does not hold in the case of these five seaports, for notwithstanding its attempts to exclude persons who might became public charges, each community experienced during this period an increase in its pauper class. As in the seventeenth century the families of

---

[62] R. I. Acts (1705), 53; Newport T. C. Recs., June 5, 1704; Nov. 5, 1711; July 5, 1714; Mar. 7, 1714/15; Newport T. M. Recs., 120.

[63] P. M. C. C., 34, 37; Pa. Col. Recs., III, 29. For the rigid policy against strangers at Bristol, see Latimer, Bristol in the Eighteenth Century, 20, 116.

indigent persons were theoretically expected to look after their support, but actually this burden had more and more to be assumed by public agencies.

Several factors contributed to an alarming increase of poor and indigent persons at Boston after 1690. The first two Anglo-French wars added measurably to the usual multitude of widows and orphans in the town. "The Widows of the Flock are numerous," wrote Cotton Mather early in 1718. "They make about a fifth Part of our Communicants." While many Boston men were lost in the unfortunate Canadian expeditions of 1690 and 1711, the majority of the women, as in most seaports, owed their widowhood to losses "by the Way of the Sea." Furthermore, the depression caused by the "decay of ye Trade," and the losses suffered in the disastrous fires of 1702 and 1711 greatly augmented the number of the town's poor. The authorities had also to care for many more bastard children and free Negroes than in earlier days.[64] And, as we have seen, to these dependents for whom the town was naturally responsible, were added during this period outside groups, immigrants and refugees, of considerable proportions.

The first large influx of the period resulted from Indian depredations on the New England frontier during King William's War. The town succoring these penniless unfortunates and their families, many of them stayed on after the dangers had passed. Because of its greater wealth Boston took better care of its poor than did other Bay towns, and it therefore became the lodestone that attracted many of the shiftless and vagrant from the surrounding countryside. In 1712 a committee chosen to investigate methods to prevent the coming in of the poor of other towns reported that the Province laws were sufficient to protect Boston from the scourge of indigent strangers, "if the Same were duly Attended." Finally, to add to the load already borne by the town, the Peace of Utrecht cleared the way for the beginnings of the Scotch-Irish problem, which became acute by 1718.[65]

It is impossible to determine how many people lived on public charity at Boston in this period. Cotton Mather had the names of eighty destitute persons on his personal list in 1712, and the next year he wrote that "the distressed Families of the Poor to which I dispense, or procure needful Relief, are now so many, and of such daily Occurrence, that it is needless for me here to mention them." One thing is certain, — a very great many persons were living in poverty at Boston. This fact caused taxes to skyrocket beyond all earlier rates. In 1700 the

[64] 11 *Bos. Rec. Com.*, 12, 22, 167; *N. E. Hist. & Gen. Reg.*, XVI, 84; 7 MHS *Colls.*, VII, 516; 7 *Bos. Rec. Com.*, 241.
[65] 8 *Bos. Rec. Com.*, 93, 97; 11 *Bos. Rec. Com.*, 178; 13 *Bos. Rec. Com.*, 46, 52, 61, 63, 64.

sum spent by the town for charity amounted to £500; after 1715 the annual appropriation was generally £2,000 or over. The care of the poor consumed so much of the Selectmen's time that in 1691 they turned over this work to four men who became the town's first "Ouer Seers of the poore." In its task of exercising supervision over the town's dependents, this body possessed authority to draw on the Treasurer for such funds as it needed; in 1703 it was further empowered to bind out as apprentices orphans and children whose parents were unable to take care of them. In 1706 the number of overseers was increased to eight. Administration of public charities was greatly improved in 1715 when the Overseers divided the town into eight wards "in order to their inspecting each respective Ward." At this time standing committees of Selectmen, Justices, Overseers and Constables inaugurated the custom of quarterly visits to each ward for the purpose of determining the needs of the poor living there.[66]

The town employed two methods for supporting its indigent. Those who had relatives were boarded with them at the town expense. For those who had no home there was the town alms house, which, unfortunately, served chiefly as a Bridewell. At the instigation of Cotton Mather an attempt was made in 1702 to improve conditions there, and after 1704 the ministers of the several churches took turns preaching to inmates on the Sabbath. The Alms House clearly could not serve its true purpose so long as the building continued to be used by county authorities as a house of correction. The town, realizing this, ordered in 1713 that delinquents should be separated from "those poor honest people who are Sent there Only as Objects of Charity," until a separate Bridewell should be erected. The next year the Overseers were instructed to receive only paupers at the poor house. The failure of the Suffolk County Justices to build a house of correction during this period, and the consequent dual use of the Alms House thwarted the best efforts of the town of Boston to provide satisfactory housing for its poor.[67]

As idleness was the reason for many of the "disorderly poor" at Boston, the town took steps to put them to work. In 1698 it appropriated £400 for materials and tools "To Sett and keep the poor people and Ill persons at work." Spinning wheels were placed in the Alms House in 1702, and considerable sums of money were spent yearly for materials for the work.[68]

[66] 7 MHS Colls., VIII, 150, 260; 8 Bos. Rec. Com., 37, 122, 127, 133, 138, 145: 7 Bos. Rec. Com., 206; 5 MHS Colls., V, 375; 11 Bos. Rec. Com., 23, 55, 62, 242; Mass. Acts and Resolves, I, 538.
[67] 13 Bos. Rec. Com., 57; 7 Bos. Rec. Com., 213; 7 MHS Colls., VII, 422; 8 Bos. Rec. Com., 29, 96, 101, 111, 148.
[68] 7 Bos. Rec. Com., 231, 241; 11 Bos. Rec. Com., 20, 26, 44, 50; 8 Bos. Rec. Com., 24.

Although the town of Boston expended large amounts in a commendable effort to care for its pauper population, the problem demanded assistance from private agencies as well. The churches greatly aided their destitute members, taking up frequent collections for charitable purposes. At the South Church alone £260 was contributed for the relief of sufferers from the fire of 1711. The frequently maligned Cotton Mather was more active in charitable works than any other colonial of his period. He successfully persuaded wealthy people to donate funds for the poor, and gave generously of his own very meager salary to buy books or make small gifts to unfortunates.[69]

The Scot's Charitable Society continued its excellent work throughout the period. By enlisting the sympathies of numerous philanthropic merchants in Scotland, and enlarging its membership, the stock of the organization was increased fourfold from 1696 to 1719, despite heavy drains on its funds occasioned by the wars. Under the able direction of men like John Campbell, the postmaster, and Dr. William Douglass, a yearly average of fifteen new members was added to the rolls, and the Society performed a notable service in the community.[70]

Philadelphia did not suffer so much as Boston from the effects of the wars, but the number of its poor nevertheless increased, until by 1713 they constituted a serious problem. Foreigners, too, were beginning to swell the ranks of Philadelphia's paupers. Before 1700 the few indigent in the town had been largely cared for by their families or by the Society of Friends, but in that year a poor law, enacted by the Assembly, provided for the election in each county of Overseers of the Poor with power to levy and collect taxes for the poor relief. The Common Council of Philadelphia found it difficult to work with these county officers, and in 1705 secured a grant of similar powers for itself.[71]

Under this law the Overseers used the poor funds to furnish aid to the needy and to board paupers in private homes. By 1712, however, the Corporation found "the Poor of this City Dayly Increasing," and proposed the renting of a workhouse where they might be employed. From the Assembly it procured a special enabling act authorizing it "to employ the poor . . . and to compel vagrants to labor." Before Mayor and Council acted further, the Friends opened an alms house, and the public project promptly lapsed. Further attempts to invigorate public charitable agencies were made in 1717 and 1718, when the Assembly passed laws requiring within three years the erection of a

[69] 5 MHS *Colls.*, VI, 324; 7 MHS *Colls.*, VIII, 260, 266, 271, 388, 525, 546.
[70] *Records of the Scot's Charitable Society*, 63, 75.
[71] The city acquired a Potter's Field in 1707. Sharpless, *Quaker Experiment*, 33; *Pa. Cols. Recs.*, II, 9; *P. M. C. C.*, 13, 17, 29, 37, 45, 46; *Pa. Statutes*, II, 254.

workhouse at Philadelphia, open to the whole colony, and making one year's residence necessary for admission to the poor rates of any town. All poor laws were then brought together in a single code. The provision that they conform "so near as may be, to the Statutes of England" was carefully followed in the clause directing that all "idle, Sturdy and disorderly beggars," going on the rates, should wear the letters P P on their right sleeves. At this time the care of the poor was costing the town £400 a year.[72]

With no relaxation of its charitable zeal, the Society of Friends continued to maintain its own poor even after the enactment of the public code. In 1702 John Martin, a tailor, gave his small house and property on Walnut Street to the Philadelphia Meeting. A few other tiny buildings were joined to this in 1713 and opened as an alms house where the poor of all faiths might find refuge. The unique advantage of this arrangement was that here a family might dwell in some privacy apart from others.[73] It was this project that caused the Corporation to abandon its scheme for a public poor house. Philadelphia's municipal attempts to care for its poor after 1715 were inadequate, but private agencies largely supplied the deficiency, and improvements had been indicated that were to come in the future.

Of the larger towns, New York mainly escaped the curse of pauperism. However, the "Calamitous Distemper" of 1702 greatly increased the "number and necessities of the Poor," as did also the arrival of Governor Hunter's Palatines in 1710, and of some Scotch-Irish after 1713. In the latter year, however, there were only seventeen persons on the city poor list, a situation truly remarkable for a town of its size. After a series of unsuccessful experiments with various agencies by the Corporation, the Assembly passed a law in 1695 placing control of poor relief in the hands of a board of overseers appointed by the Commonalty. This body made estimates for the poor tax, and regularly visited the several wards to inspect the condition of the poor. By order of the Corporation in 1707 all paupers clothed by the city were to wear a badge "with this Mark N. Y. in blew or Red Cloath." At about the same time the Common Council began to discuss the erection of "A poor house and a house of Correction." Although none was built in this period, some sort of a shelter for the poor was being maintained by Elizabeth Burger in 1714, when Andrew Roulson, blacksmith, being "very sick and weak and an Object of Charity," was sent to live under her roof. The majority of the New York poor were farmed out to private families, or given direct relief when needed.

[72] P. M. C. C., 80, 82; Pa. Statutes, II, 420; III, 221; Scharf and Westcott, Philadelphia, I, 191; Votes Pa. Assembly, II, 223.
[73] Scharf and Westcott, Philadelphia, I, 191.

The Dutch Reformed Church cared for its own poor members, housing them after 1701 in a new alms house on Wall Street.[74]

At Charles Town provision was first made for the poor in 1694, and a year later five commissioners of the Assembly were chosen to receive and apply gifts for charity, bind out poor children as apprentices, and draw on the provincial treasury for aid to the extent of £10. So many ship's captains left sick or pauper mariners behind them when they sailed away that from 1698 to 1712 shipmasters were required to post a bond of £50 to secure the maintenance of these men. The burden of the Yamassee War bore heavily on the southern metropolis, and the "number and continual increase of the poor" made it necessary to revise the poor laws in 1712.[75] Henceforth the vestry of each parish nominated yearly two or more overseers of the poor, who with the church wardens distributed relief money, and, although alms were expected to be forthcoming, were permitted to lay a tax of £70 a year on inhabitants of Charles Town. Increased taxes, soaring prices, and the crowding of many country refugees behind the ramparts of the town placed a well nigh intolerable burden on the Overseers during the terrible years, 1715 to 1718, and the Vestry was authorized to raise the annual poor rate to £75. By 1720 conditions had eased somewhat and times were returning to normal, but there remained a permanent indigent population that had henceforth to be cared for.[76]

In comparison, Newport had almost no pauper problem, although a poor rate was regularly levied after 1691. Some widows and orphans, and a few aged poor were supported in private homes at the town's expense, but the yearly charge was very small. In 1714 Thomas Lyllibridge was paid £18 by the Town Council "for his maintaining of the Widow Blore — two years last past." Some persons, like Jacob Mason, were provided with clothing at the town's expense, while others, like "one Adair and his family," were given "Thirty Shillings Tow get him a place to live in." By 1710 need was beginning to be felt for an alms house, and the matter was discussed in leisurely fashion in Town Meeting until in 1716 a small building was erected to shelter the poor and provide work for them. At no town were the poor so few nor so well cared for as at Newport.[77]

[74] Eccles. Recs. N. Y., III, 1460, 1511; Stokes, Iconography, IV, 422, 458, 478; N. Y. M. C. C., I, 258, 387, 396; II, 330; III, 52, 59; N. Y. Col. Laws, I, 328, 348; Mayor's Court Minutes, 67, 68, 71.
[75] In 1711 the commissioners had expended £98. 5. 7½. for relief and charity. S. C. Council Journal, 1692, 7; S. C. Statutes, II, 78, 116, 136; S. C. Commons Journal, 1712–1716, 70.
[76] Main features of Elizabethan Poor Law were applied at Charles Town. S. C. Statutes, II, 593, 606; Trott's Laws (MS.), 610; Cal. St. Pap., 1716–1717, 133, 226, 260, 290, 324.
[77] The charity of Newport was enlightened and personal. When Mason petitioned for shirt, "briches," and stockings in 1715, he was denied aid, "it appearing

Thus, the advancing maturity of the five towns, together with the train of events that followed the wars, saddled each town with a pauper class that was henceforth to be a permanent feature of its life. Nothing is more false than the reports of travelers of the absence of poverty from the colonial towns. Each community attacked its problem with some degree of success, and Boston, especially, achieved a high conception of civic responsibility for the age. The large amounts spent in public poor relief, and the philanthropies of private individuals and associations are evidences of the consciousness of town society of the problem of its poor.

VII

Town residents in general continued to enjoy good health. Gabriel Thomas' description of Philadelphia as "very Peaceable and Healthy" in 1697 held true for every community save Charles Town, where the "country fever" still made its annual appearance. The period witnessed a further attempt on the part of the towns to do away with public nuisances injurious to the general health, and to improve sanitary conditions. In 1702 Philadelphia joined Boston and New York in prohibiting the casting of garbage into its streets. The burning of lime, regarded as malodorous and infectious, also aroused public notice. After a visitation of "distemper" in 1702 New York forbade the burning of lime or oyster shells, and Newport took similar action five years later.[78]

Butchers' shambles and slaughterhouses, where offensive to the townsmen, continued to come under municipal regulation. The Boston Selectmen secured an act from the General Court in 1692 authorizing them to specify the location of slaughter, still, curriers' and tallow-chandlers' houses, "where it may be least offensive." The next year they assigned places for three slaughterhouses, and ordered the town distillers, chandlers and curriers to move to locations where their activities could not annoy the neighborhood. Because the slaughter-house belonging to Richard Sherrine, butcher, was "very Noysom and Offensive to ye Inhabitants," he was forbidden in 1710 to kill cattle there, and directed to remove all filth and garbage from the premises.[79]

to ye Council yt ye sd Mason through his Excessive Drinking & Sottishness is not Qualified to be at his own Disposal he having pawned or sold his Clothing for yt he is full of Vermin." He was sent to Fort Island, where he was "kept at Lbour at his Trade & kept from Strong Liquor." *Newport T. C. Recs.*, July 3, 1710; April 5, 1714; Aug. 1, 1715; Dec. 15, 1715; June 4, 1716; *Newport T. M. Recs.*, 55, 182; Richardson Collection, 972: 63.

[78] *N. Y. M. C. C.*, I, 224; Ancient Recs., Phila., 20; *N. Y. Col. Laws*, I, 538; *Newport T. M. Procs.*, Jan. 30, 1707.

[79] *Mass. Acts and Resolves*, I, 59; 7 *Bos. Rec. Com.*, 107, 213, 215, 216.

Less success accompanied the regulation of slaughtering in the other towns. New York repealed its rules of 1691, but so many complaints against butchers ensued that in 1699 the Corporation again forbade slaughtering within the city. In spite of this slaughterhouses had again become a great "Publick Nuisance" by 1720. Similar conditions prevailed at Philadelphia, where complaints were perennial against the "want of cleaning" at butchers' shambles. Somewhat more fruitful was the law of 1704 prohibiting all butchering within the limits of Charles Town.[80]

Especially perplexing was the problem of privies and the disposal of filth. The streets of Newport must have been unsightly and disagreeable in the extreme, "as several Privy houses sett against ye Streets" emptied therein, and passersby were constantly in danger of "Spoiling & Damnifying" their apparel. Philadelphia seems not to have been afflicted by this nuisance, while the other three towns made effective sanitary ordinances to eliminate the evil. At Charles Town in 1692 all inhabitants were forbidden to maintain any "house of ease . . . to the annoyance of any persons whatsoever," under the large penalty of £5. Failure to observe this wholesome act led to many "very offensive" privies, and in October, 1698, these malodorous houses were ordered filled in within two months. A further provision commanded that all "private tubs" be emptied at least once a week. The town of Boston in 1701 forbade the erection of privies within forty feet of any street, shop or well, "unless the same be vaulted Six foot deep and sufficiently enclosed." A "Necessary House for the Vse of the publicq" was erected on the wharf before the City Hall at New York in 1691, and cleaned daily at the public charge. Private individuals, unfortunately, were not so inclined to sanitation, and in 1700 the Corporation was informed that several "Indisposed" persons were making a common practice of emptying tubs of filth in the city streets. A new ordinance thereupon made this misdemeanor punishable by a forty shilling fine. This order apparently did not apply to the "Dunghills near the Custom house bridge," on which the Corporation "from time to time" spent £4. 13. 9. for "Levelling." [81]

Although the American colonies were blest with a most healthful climate, the same could not be said of the sister settlements in the West Indies, where all sorts of infectious diseases prevailed. As a result, ships coming from the islands more and more frequently acted as carriers of these epidemics to the five seaports on the continent. After 1690 a decade seldom passed without each of the towns being

---

[80] *N. Y. M. C. C.*, I, 217, 244, 408; II, 65, 404; III, 249; *P. M. C. C.*, 34; *Votes Pa. Assembly*, I, ii, 100; Court Papers, Phila. Cty., I; *S. C. Statutes*, VII, 12, 38.

[81] *Newport T. M. Procs.*, Jan. 30, 1707; *S. C. Statutes*, VII, 6, 9, 19; 8 *Bos. Rec. Com.*, 12; *N. Y. M. C. C.*, I, 253; II, 30, 41, 50, 103.

visited by a decimating disease, — generally the smallpox or yellow fever.[82]

Charles Town suffered more from sickness than any other town. The battle with the "country fever" went on every summer, but the years from 1697 to 1706 were a period of horrible visitations. In 1698 the Governor thus described the town's plight to the Proprietors: "We have had the small pox amongst us nine or ten months which hath been very infectious and mortal. We have lost by the distemper 200 or 300 persons." Recovery had hardly set in when the yellow fever appeared in August, 1699. Samuel Sewall learned of this calamity from his friend, the Reverend Hugh Adams, in October: "150 dead in 6 days time; . . . Infection was brought from Providence [W. I.]" The visitation lasted until November, and Adams believed the disaster to be "Worse by far than the great Plague of London, considering the smallness of the Town. Shops shut up for 6 weeks; nothing but carrying medicines, digging graves, carting the dead." But this was not all. The Charlestonians had their cup of suffering filled to the brim by further outbreaks of yellow fever in 1703 and 1706. During the raging of the latter "grievous pestilence" five or six deaths occurred nearly every day. The forbearance shown by the Carolinians during these plagues, and their recuperative powers following them, are indeed remarkable.[83]

Infectious disease appeared frequently, but made less serious inroads, in the northern towns. Boston authorities bravely took the most effective measures to control the smallpox when it smote the town in 1702. In order to prevent the spreading of infection the Town Meeting ordered the bodies of victims to be buried without any elaborate funerals and within an hour after the tolling of a meeting house bell. Whenever a new case broke out, men were hired to watch before the afflicted house and warn all people of the danger, and Daniel Fairfield was appointed as a special officer to inform against all "persons Transgressing ye Town Orders." During the epidemic of 1710 afflicted persons were kept at Fort Hill under the care of nurses, who were strictly enjoined "to Shift & aire theire

[82] *Chart of principal epidemics, 1690 to 1720*

Town	Smallpox	Yellow Fever	Measles	Other Sicknesses
Boston	1702	1693	1713	1702
	1710			1717
Newport	1691	1710		
New York	1690	1702		
Philadelphia		1699		1708
Charles Town	1697/8	1699		1715
	1698	1703		
	1718	1706		
		1711		

[83] 5 MHS *Colls.*, V, 503; VI, 11; *Cal. St. Pap., 1699*, 581; *1706–1708*, 248.

Cloathes, & if they think proper to procure Some Garments for them at the Town Charge, & to use the most proper means to prevent ye Spreading Infection in ye Town." In contrast is the picture given by the behavior of the Common Council of New York of the effect of the yellow fever there in 1702: "Almighty God hath for our Manifold sins Immorality & profaneness been pleased to Visit us att this time with great sickness and Mortality, whereby great Numbers of the Citizens [500] . . . are Dead and Many att this time lye in a Languishing Condition to Avoid which Contagious and Malignant Distemper great Numbers of this Citty have left their usual habitations and Retired to the Country." The sole action taken by the authorities was, as we have seen, the prohibition of the burning of lime and oyster shells, and also of the distilling of rum, which were supposed to cause the spread of the distemper.[84]

A gradual realization that the towns, because of their shipping connections with the Caribbean, were the principal germinating places for contagious disease led to provisions for the prevention of such calamities. Boston, which alone had had quarantine regulations in the seventeenth century, continued and improved upon its earlier rules. In 1702 Massachusetts opened a province pest house on Spectacle Island in Boston harbor, where ships bringing in infected passengers were required to discharge them. The severe penalty of a £50 fine or six months' imprisonment was set for mariners who neglected to observe this regulation. This quarantine station seems to have fallen into disuse by 1715, when the Town Meeting petitioned the General Court for the erection in "some remote place" of a building "for the Lodging of Sick persons . . . from beyond the Sea." Accordingly, the old pest house was reopened and placed under the control of the Boston Selectmen.[85]

Other towns followed the lead of Boston. The South Carolina Assembly in 1698 prohibited all vessels bearing sick passengers from coming to anchor nearer than one mile east of Sullivan's Island, and in 1700 and 1712 Pennsylvania and Rhode Island made similar regulations for their seaports. At Charles Town (1712) and Philadelphia (1719) health officers were appointed to inspect all incoming vessels and license them to land, while at Newport (1712) the Naval Officer was directed to take a doctor with him for the same purpose. A pest house was set up on Sullivan's Island near Charles Town in 1712, where ship passengers and other persons with infectious distempers were required to be isolated and "to maintain themselves." The New-

[84] 8 Bos. Rec. Com., 13; 11 Bos. Rec. Com., 16, 23, 26, 29, 30, 105; N. Y. M. C. C., II, 203; Stokes, Iconography, IV, 440; Eccles. Recs. N. Y., III, 1497.
[85] 8 Bos. Rec. Com., 114, 119, 127; Mass. Acts and Resolves, II, 91; 13 Bos. Rec. Com., 59, 76.

port Town Meeting in 1716 voted to erect a hospital on Coaster's Harbour. The building, which cost £120, was opened within a year for the reception of sickly passengers from West India ships, and in 1717 the Town Council ordered that "if any Inhabitants of this Town shall upon Suspicion of small pox &c. go over to Coasters harbour In Order to prevent the spreading there of that, every Such persons Shall be maintained during their being there out of the town treasury." Two years later further equipment was provided in the hospital for the accommodation of the sick.[86] In 1720 this island hospital was undoubtedly the best equipped isolation and quarantine station at any of the towns.

The period 1690 to 1720 was also marked by an improvement in the medical facilities generally available to the townsmen. An increased number of physicians and "chirurgeons" ministered to the needs of town-dwellers, and apothecary's shops multiplied as each seaport became the medical center of its province. When Dr. William Douglass arrived at Boston in 1720 he found the town to "abound with Practitioners, tho no other graduate than myself," and we know of at least thirteen men who practiced medicine there in this period. In addition, six ministers offered physical as well as spiritual prescriptions to their flocks. Although all attempts to regulate the practice of physic by law had fallen through, some of the native doctors, whose sole source of medical training was by apprenticeship, had, largely by keeping abreast of latest European medical literature, attained to real skill in their art.[87]

The leading Boston surgeon, Dr. Zabdiel Boylston, began practicing shortly after 1700. He sprang into prominence in 1706 when he successfully performed one of the first lithotomies in New England. According to the somewhat lurid account in the *News Letter* of March 10, 1706/7:

> John Kenney Aged about 13 years, Son to Margaret Kenney of Boston, Widow, being in very great torment and pain with the Stone, his Mother and Friends almost despairing of any Cure for him: at last hearing of Dr. Zabdiel Boylston of this Town, Chyrurgeon, they made their application to him, who on the 5th of November last in the sight of several Physitians, Chirurgeons, and Persons of Note, performed the operation very accurately and well, to the good liking of the Beholders; The Stone was a soft spungy stone of the bigness of an Egg, and broke in the taking out, but the young Lad is now and has been for above 2 Months in perfect health, and holds his water.

[86] *S. C. Statutes*, II, 152; VII, 382; Westcott, *Philadelphia*, chapter XLIV; *R. I. Acts* (1719), 65; *Newport T. M. Recs.*, 185; *Newport T. C. Recs.*, July 1, 1717; June 1, 1719.
[87] *Colden Papers*, I, 114; Green, *Medicine in Massachusetts*, 58.

Dr. Boylston performed many operations before 1720, and his patients seemed ever willing to furnish such testimonials to his valued work.[88]

Most of the other Boston practitioners gave medical rather than surgical advice. Sewall employed at least six different bloodletters. When the "sorry, sordid, froward and exceedingly wicked Fellow," who had married Cotton Mather's stepdaughter in 1713, became ill of a "languishing Sickness . . . he successively employ'd no Less than five physicians, before . . . the Glorious GOD putt a Period unto the Grievous Wayes of this Wretch." However, this divine, who entertained such unchristian sentiments towards his relatives by marriage, set out in 1716 to persuade Boston doctors "to bring the *cold Bath* into fashion: Whereby many poor, sick, miserable People may obtain Releef under various Maladies which now remain otherwise Incurable." Boston practitioners also served as dentists and performed tooth drawing operations; Samuel Sewall seems to have been a constant source of income to these early exodontists. Obstetrics, however, remained the prerogative of the midwives, of whom Elizabeth Weeden was the most noted.[89]

The medical profession fared well at Boston. Dr. Peter Bassett had to appeal to the courts against Richard Skinner, mariner, in 1691 for the collection of £2. 11. for forty visits, a bleeding, and some medicines, but, on the other hand, Dr. Leonard Hoar died in 1700 worth about £1,000. In 1720 Dr. Douglass wrote to Cadwallader Colden at New York: "I can live handsomely by the income of my Practice, and save some small matter, . . . I have here practice among four sorts of People: some familys pay me £5 per an. each for advice sick or well, some few fee me as in Britain, but for the Native New Englanders I am oblidged to keep a day book and bring them in a Bill, others of the poorer sort I advise and Visit without any expectation of fees." All of the medical men gave free treatment to the poor, and the Selectmen therefore ceased to pay for medical care except in extraordinary cases.[90]

There were fourteen apothecary shops in Boston in 1720, when Douglass reported superciliously to Colden that "all our Practitioners dispense their own medicines, myself excepted, being the first who hath lived here by Practice without the advantage of advance on

[88] In 1718 Dr. Boylston removed a cancerous breast from a woman "in the presence of several Ministers and others," and in 1720 the grateful husband published a testimonial about the "perfect Cure," having deferred for two years, "least it should break out again." *Bos. Gaz.*, Nov. 28, 1720; 7 MHS *Colls.*, VIII, 197, 202; 7 *Bos. Rec. Com.*, 230.
[89] 5 MHS *Colls.*, V, 351, 427, 444; VI, 68, 178, 290, 349, 421; 7 MHS *Colls.*, VIII, 349; 6 MHS *Colls.*, II, 105; Green, *Medicine in Massachusetts*, 43.
[90] Green, *Medicine in Massachusetts*, 51; 6 MHS *Colls.*, I, 226; *Colden Papers*, I, 114; 7 *Bos. Rec. Com.*, 230. For a Boston quack, see *Bos. Gaz.*, Oct. 10, 1720.

Medicines." One of the best known shops in the earlier years of this period was that of Captain Davis, from which Sewall occasionally "fetched some Trecle Water and Syrop of Saffron." When the newspapers first appeared the patent medicines came into their own. Still a popular remedy in the days of *Vanity Fair*, "Daffy's Elixir Salutis, very good, at four shillings and six pence per half pint Bottle," was sold at the "Sign of the Bible in Cornhill." Perhaps it was here that Sewall purchased those Spirits of Lavender which he joined with "a pound of Figs, that food and Physick might go together." Zabdiel Boylston kept the largest and most complete apothecary's establishment, where he sold both by wholesale and retail. This was also the case with Edward Caine of Pudding Lane, who advertised in 1711 an importation of "Druggs and Apothecary's Ware, done up in some large and others in small boxes, fit for Gentlemens families that live in the Country distant from Doctors." [91]

Many Bostonians, however, could not bring themselves to discard the "kitchen-physick" of their forefathers in favor of the prescriptions of "Galenists" or "Chymists." Little had occurred since the days of Queen Elizabeth to shake their faith in specifics: many still believed that,

> The sovreign'st thing on Earth
> Was parmaceti for an inward bruise.

Common people, and some aristocrats, too, often used Dame Ellis' "Cake of Herbs" for strengthening the stomach. The prescriptions of John Winthrop, Jr., enjoyed lasting fame, and as late as 1719 Cotton Mather wrote to one of Winthrop's sons that he desired to be the dispenser of some of those "noble Remedies" to the sick and miserable. Often humble townsmen and countryfolk who could read obtained their medical aid from such reprints as Dr. Culpepper's *The English Physician: Containing Admirable and Approved Remedies for several of the most usual Diseases: Fitted to the Meanest Capacity.*[92]

Between 1694 and 1720 the Common Council made twenty "Chirurgeons" and two "Barber-Chirurgions" freemen of the "Citty of New Yorke." Of this large number the majority were Dutch and Huguenot physicians who had received their training in Europe. Dr. John Van Burne, who arrived about 1700, was a pupil of the great

[91] *Colden Papers*, I, 114; 5 MHS *Colls.*, V, 408; VI, 223; *News Letter*, Oct. 4, 1708; July 9, 1711. For the extent and variety of Dr. Boylston's stock, see the typical advertisement in *News Letter*, April 7, 1712.

[92] Behnke, *Medical Life*, XLI, 57; Green, *Medicine in Massachusetts*, 19; 7 MHS *Colls.*, VIII, 590. For the credulity of the average man, see a revolting item in *News Letter*, Jan. 14, 1717.

Boerhaave, and a graduate of Leyden, as were also Isaac du Bois and Johannes Kerfbyl. Cadwallader Colden held a degree from Edinburgh, and Dr. John Du Puy had studied in France. In fact, New York was so plentifully supplied with medical men that Colden, when he arrived from Philadelphia in 1718, complained to William Douglass of "the practice of Physick being undervalued" at Manhattan, "and with reason." He was not so fortunate as Dr. Jacob Provoost, who was appointed "Doctor for the Poor" at a salary of £8 per year in 1713.[93]

As at Boston aspiring young men were apprenticed to practitioners for the study of medicine. In 1698 Lewis Peeck came down from Schenectady to New York to serve a four year apprenticeship with Dr. Cornelius Viele, and two years later Gerret Thompson was indentured for five years to the same master. Although no special system of medical licensing existed at New York, the law did require apprentices to serve a stipulated time before they could become freemen, and medical practice came under this regulation. The standards of Manhattan midwives were improved in 1716, when the Corporation passed a very strict and detailed ordinance regarding their practice.[94]

Most New York physicians dispensed medicines and nostrums from their own shops. Dr. Colden opened his shop at New York in 1718 with a supply of drugs sent over by a Mr. Fair of London. On August 6 the dour physician wrote Fair: "I have not sold your elixar I cannott tell when I shall I do all I can to recommend Itt butt Its nott being a bitter makes itt not fashionable." Colden was a good business man, however, and a year later he was able to report to Mr. Fair: "I have sold six dozen of your Elixar at 24s. per dozen the other dozen I made presents of to bring itt in fashion the people here began to be fond of itt butt itt being soon all sold I have heard nothing of itt of Late & I know nott butt the humor has dropt." There were in New York also three apothecaries who did not practice, but who confined their efforts solely to the selling of drugs and medicines.[95]

Newport continued to enjoy the services of the several European trained physicians who had come there in the 1680's. Dr. Norbert Vigneron stood at the head of the medical profession at Rhode Island, and among the various young men who came to serve an apprenticeship under him was William Turner, later the leading practitioner of New Jersey. Doctor Ayrault, the three Rodmans, and Dr. Caleb

[93] N. Y. Hist. Soc. *Colls., 1885,* 54–100; Bosworth, "The Doctor in Old New York," 292, 303, 304; *Colden Papers,* I, 114; *N. Y. M. C. C.,* I, 206; II, 68; Stokes, *Iconography,* IV, 341.
[94] *N. Y. M. C. C.,* III, 121.
[95] Colden also imported many medical treatises. *Colden Papers,* I, 40, 41, 43; N. Y. Hist. Soc. *Colls., 1885,* 54–100.

Arnold all kept apothecary shops in connection with their practices, that of Thomas Rodman being probably the most popular. Dr. John Rodman received a salary from the town treasury for his services as physician to the poor during most of this period. Newport also profited from frequent visits by the famous Jared Eliot, F. R. S., who after 1706 was often consulted in particular cases.[96] The excellent training of this little group of physicians laid the foundations for a splendid medical tradition at Newport.

In 1697 Gabriel Thomas thus paid his respects to the medical profession at Philadelphia: "Of . . . Physicians I shall say nothing, because . . . they, Hang-man like, have a License to Murder and make Mischief." As several excellent doctors with European educations resided there after 1690 this judgment seems somewhat harsh, but for agues and broken bones there was still "no want of empiricks." "Tender Griffith Owen, who both sees and feels," enjoyed a large practice, "in which he was very knowing and eminent," until his death in 1717. After 1700 he was joined by Dr. Cadwallader Colden, Dr. John Kearsley (1711), and Dr. Thomas Graeme (1711), who came over from the British Isles to form a notable group of physicians in the Quaker town. Dr. Owen was regularly employed by the Corporation after 1715 to care for the town's poor. Doctors Graeme and Colden were the favorite training surgeons at Philadelphia, and the famous Dr. Evan Jones, who for years led his profession at New York, served his apprenticeship with the Edinburgh graduate.[97]

When the position of town physician became open after the death of Dr. Owen in 1717, Colden attempted a scheme, which, had it succeeded, would have made Philadelphia the medical center of colonial America. "He came to me one day," James Logan wrote to Penn, "to desire . . . an act of Assembly for an allowance to him as physician to the poor of this place." Logan favoring the project, Colden introduced a bill to which he added the proposals that "a public physical lecture should be held in Philadelphia, to the support of which every unmarried man . . . should pay six shillings, eight pence . . . yearly, and that the corpses of all persons whatever that died here should be visited by an appointed physician. . . . These things I owned very commendable," went on Logan, "but doubted our Assembly would never go into them." He was quite right; it was many years before medical lectures would be held,—and then, at private expense.[98]

[96] Packard, *Medicine in the United States*, 85; Richardson Collection, 968: 85; Austin, *Gen. Dict.*, 166; *Newport T. M. Recs.*, 61; *Newport T. C. Recs.*, May 3, 1714; *Dict. Amer. Biog.*, VI, 78.
[97] *Narratives of Pennsylvania*, 328; Norris, *Medicine in Philadelphia*, 11, 13, 15; Henry, *Medical Profession of Philadelphia*, 24; *P. M. C. C.*, 91.
[98] Bosworth, "The Doctor in Old New York," 306; Col. Soc. Mass. *Trans.*, XIX, 278.

Apothecary shops flourished at Philadelphia. Colden operated one in conjunction with his medical practice, for which he procured his supplies from Lisbon because they were "cheaper than in Britain." He frequently imported over seventy different drugs and medicines. Another prosperous druggist was Francis Knowles, "Over against the Court House," whose specialty, "Right Golden and Plain Spirit of Scurvy Grass," sold at fifteen pence the bottle.[99]

At least fourteen capable doctors, all of them trained in Europe, practiced in Charles Town. Until 1712 Doctors George Frankline and John Thomas received salaries from the Assembly for care of the province poor. The Poor Law of that year specified "Assistance of Physicians and Medicines" for pauper sick, and thereafter the parish vestry provided such services in Charles Town. Probably even more than northern communities did Charles Town become the medical center of its province. In all of them by 1720 as good medical care was available as in most cities of England.[100]

VIII

The continuing problems of urban society in this period stimulated a distinct growth of civic consciousness within the five colonial seaports. Development of this sense of public responsibility tended to maintain a direct ratio to the complexity of the problem to be met and the degree of urbanization attained by the particular community. Thus, in Boston, where town life was by 1720 more developed than elsewhere, there existed throughout these years a serious awareness of the public duty, especially exemplified in constant and expensive attention to the problems of fire protection and poor relief. Philadelphia and New York, with their self-sustaining and parsimonious corporations, Charles Town, bereft of local government, and Newport, where conditions of life were still largely rural, exhibited such civic virtue in varying and lesser degrees, though each of these towns was in this period meeting problems of community living whose necessary public solutions it could neither reject nor ignore. The disruptive effects of years of war, evident to some extent in all of the towns, accelerated in this period the natural growth of urban conditions, and contributed to the necessity for further agencies for dealing with their attendant complexities. So in most of the towns special officers like fire wardens, overseers of the poor, and health officers had to be appointed, and institutions not before required, like poor houses, work houses and public hospitals, made their appearance. Finally, in this period,

[99] *Colden Papers*, I, 35; *Mercury*, Mar. 24, May 5, 1720.
[100] *S. C. Council Journal, 1692*, 49; *S. C. Commons Journal, 1698*, 26; *1703*, 41, 88; *S. C. Hist. & Gen. Mag.*, X–XII; Wallace, *South Carolina*, I, 174.

the supplementary activity of private groups to contribute to the social betterment manifested itself in determined and serious guise. Churches, especially the Society of Friends, continued their private charities; in Boston, the first fire society appeared along with Cotton Mather's Societies for the Suppression of Disorders; and in Philadelphia the premature suggestion was even made that the town support a series of medical lectures. Growing urban problems and increased efforts to meet them characterize the entire period.

VIII

SOCIAL LIFE IN THE TOWNS

I

Despite the upheavals of war years, the energies which in this period enabled colonial town-dwellers to cope with the ever growing problems of their economic and social life permitted also a development in the complexity and sophistication of the society in which they moved. The story of urban existence in America from 1690 to 1720 is one of slow but continual progress along lines which differentiated it from that of farm or frontier.

II

During this period, in every town save Newport, the racial and national composition of the population underwent material changes. Everywhere the most significant alteration in urban populations came from increased importation of Negro slaves. As for non-English whites, their immigration from Europe was considerably checked by the almost constant state of war during the first twenty-five years of the period, but before its close the Peace of Utrecht permitted the beginning of the Scotch-Irish and Palatine folk movements, the consequences of which were eventually to effect real transformation in the racial countenance of these communities.

Most Negroes were to be found at Charles Town, where in 1709 the proportion of blacks to whites was about equal. At New York, African slaves made up twenty-three per cent of the population and constituted a genuine problem. Scarcity of labor, however, led to their steady importation. In 1718, when prime slaves sold for £50 a head at the wharves, over five hundred were brought in. So many Africans had been imported into Boston by 1700 that Samuel Sewall, worried and "dissatisfied with the Trade of fetching Negroes from Guinea," published *The Selling of Joseph* in protest against the traffic. Nor was he alone in his attitude, for the next year the Town Meeting went on record as preferring white servants to black slaves. Labor was scarce, however, and the number of Negroes increased from four hundred in 1708 to two thousand in 1720, when they constituted one-sixth of the total population. The Quakers of Philadelphia and

Newport did not scruple to purchase slaves for house servants, but in
these towns the black inhabitants never reached the numbers attained
elsewhere.[1]

Toward the close of this period non-English immigration from
Europe began to assume considerable proportions. Most numerous
among the newcomers were the Scotch-Irish, who began to arrive at
Boston in 1717. Many of them also sought out Philadelphia and
Charles Town, and a few went to New York. In 1710 Governor
Robert Hunter brought over from England a number of Palatine
families, one hundred and fifty of whom settled at Manhattan where
their children were bound out as indentured servants and apprentices
among artisans of the town. Philadelphia received few accessions to
its German population until 1717, when Palatines began to arrive
with every ship. Thereafter Penn's town became the chief port of
entry for Germans coming to America, not a few of them making the
place their permanent home.[2]

Scattered individuals or small groups of other nationalities found
their way into the various towns. In 1699 there were 195 French
Huguenot families living at Charles Town, while French Protestants
could likewise be found among the most influential inhabitants of
Boston and Newport. In general, however, these refugees soon lost
their identity, and never constituted a distinct national group. The
many Irish Quakers who migrated to Philadelphia after 1690 often assumed an important role in the life of the colony.[3]

For the most part townsmen welcomed the coming of foreigners,
but in two cases trouble arose. Serious religious difficulties developed
between Huguenots and Anglicans at Charles Town in the first decade of the century. The other case of race friction occurred at Boston,
where a nativist feeling had already begun to flourish in the seventeenth century. Late in 1717 Scotch-Irish immigration into the Bay
town began in earnest. In July and August, 1718, from five to seven
hundred Ulsterites entered at the port of Boston, and while most of
them passed through to other places, many again drifted back into the
town. Their numbers were so great at a time when prices were rising rapidly that the authorities feared lest "these confounded Irish"
should eat inhabitants out of house and home. Yet on the whole the

---

[1] *Cal. St. Pap., 1708–1709*, 110, 466; *1719–1720*, 357; S. C. Commons Journal,
1707–1711, 303, 309; *Doc. Hist. N. Y.*, I, 707; 11 *Bos. Rec. Com.*, 5; *Bos. Gaz.*, Jan. 18,
1720; Donnan, *Slave Trade*, III, 408; Ancient Recs. Philadelphia, 11; *R. I. Col. Recs.*,
IV, 59.

[2] 13 *Bos. Rec. Com.*, 29; *News Letter*, Aug. 26, Sept. 16, 30, 1717; Nov. 10, 1718;
Bolton, *Scotch-Irish*, 35, 268; *Mercury*, Oct. 27, 1720; *Doc. Hist. N. Y.*, III, 566;
Pa. Col. Recs., III, 29.

[3] *Cal. St. Pap., 1699*, 107; Baird, *Huguenot Emigration*, II, 208, 316; Myers,
Irish Quakers, 108.

townsfolk received these strangers graciously; Cotton Mather reflected how "the many Families arriving from Ireland, will afford me many Opportunities, for Kindness to the Indigent." That the Selectmen were strict in warning them out of town probably resulted not so much from national antipathies as from the desire to secure the town from increasing pauperism. The real, and only, trouble with the newcomers was that they were poor.[4]

By 1720 all of the towns save Newport exhibited a considerable diversity of population, New York being still the most cosmopolitan. "Our chiefest unhappyness here," wrote Christopher Lodowick, "is too great a mixture of nations." Although he noted an increase among the Huguenots, they formed but a small group when compared with the Dutch, who were the most frugal, laborious and wealthy, or with the growing numbers of English, who were extravagant and showy, "especially the trading part."[5] At New York, Charles Town and Boston materials were present for the creation of anti-foreign feeling which might at any time emerge, while at Philadelphia the elements which were to render her national composition and problems peculiar were already appearing. No longer were these towns to be the home of one national or racial group; they were now beginning to shelter a mixture of peoples, which made for greater cosmopolitanism than was to be found in the average rural village or countryside.

III

The commercial expansion of the towns from 1690 to 1720 naturally brought about a greater accumulation of wealth than had been witnessed by the seventeenth century. During the war years the gap between poor artisan or laborer and rich merchant constantly widened. So sharp was the cleavage between the two classes that it becomes necessary to distinguish a third — the middle class — from which, according to the vagaries of trade, both older groups drew their recruits. The vicissitudes of the war years resulted in the decline of some of the familiar older families, but newcomers, some of them war profiteers, stood ready to add new names to the colonial bead-roll, and many relatively obscure persons emerged to found commercial dynasties of eminence.

In 1690 the Boston aristocracy was in a state of flux, but by 1720 the names of the great pre-revolutionary families were already well established. New faces appeared among the merchants in this period to take their places beside the old. Many substantial Huguenots climbed

[4] Hirsch, *Huguenots*, 103; 6 MHS *Colls.*, V, 387 n.; *News Letter*, July 28, Aug. 4, 1718; 7 MHS *Colls.*, VIII, 548; 13 *Bos. Rec. Com.*, 41, 52, 63.

[5] About ninety Jews came to Newport from Curaçao in 1693. Gutstein, *Jews of Newport*, 46; N. Y. Hist. Soc. *Colls.*, II, 214.

the social ladder along with the Faneuils, Daniel Johonnot and Andrew Sigourney. Andrew Belcher, forsaking his middle class station
as tavern-keeper in Cambridge, moved to Boston, where, as a profiteering and not always scrupulous merchant, he amassed a large fortune.
By his second marriage, to Hannah Frary, and by the marriages of his
three daughters to George Vaughan, Daniel Oliver and Oliver Noyes,
he allied himself with the first families of the colony. In 1730 his
son, Jonathan, became Governor of Massachusetts, and later of New
Jersey. Few traveled so far as Belcher, but many, like Stephen Minot,
Thomas Brinley, Edward Bromfield, Andrew Cunningham, Cornelius Waldo and Thomas Amory, became important personages, marrying and intermarrying into aristocratic circles.[6]

A new and most important group appeared in Boston in this
period to assume leadership on the aristocratic stage. Made up of
royal Governors and other British officials, it lent new tone and color
to Massachusetts society by instituting at Boston many of the courtly
customs and ceremonies of a British viceroyalty. A knight and an
Irish peer were among the Governors who attended Thursday lecture,
clothed in scarlet coat, gold lace, side sword and powdered wig, escorted by a file of "regulars." Those colonials who had "pretensions"
clustered about the Governor's court, seeking the favors he had in his
power to bestow. Samuel Sewall found himself hard put to decide in
1697 whether to condemn or condone the fact that "the Company of
young Merchants Treat the Govr and all of the Council in Boston at
George Monk's." [7]

Despite the overthrow of the theocracy, so-called, and the institution of the royal charter, the Boston clergy still stood high among the
"men of qualitie." No family of colonial times ever commanded, or
deserved, more respect than the Mathers; in religious, political and
public concerns they exerted an enormous influence. We have noted
Cotton Mather's activities in charitable and medical circles; his religious, cultural and political works are too well known to need rehearsal here. A true aristocrat, he was without question the most
public spirited colonial before Benjamin Franklin, who drew much of
his inspiration from the Boston minister. Other clerical members of
the aristocracy were Benjamin Colman, Ebenezer Pemberton, Samuel
Willard, Samuel Myles and Joseph Sewall. These men retained their
leadership in an increasingly complex society by sheer force of their
ability, coupled with the prestige they commanded as churchmen;
wealth was seldom their portion.

[6] Baird, *Huguenot Emigration,* II, 208, 210; 7 *Bos. Rec. Com.,* 192, 230; Winsor,
Memorial History of Boston, II, 534, 545, 548, 557, 559.
[7] Winsor, *Memorial History of Boston,* II, 86; 5 MHS *Colls.,* V, 461.

Like all aristocracies in the formative stage, that of Boston sought to advertise itself and its position by great displays of magnificence. In the fashionable North End merchants built themselves "elegant" three-story brick houses, embellished with sash windows and hand-painted wall papers. Wealthy widows kept calashes, and prosperous business men purchased coaches. Sir Charles Hobby's "Coach drawn with six Horses richly Harnessed," and Captain Andrew Belcher's equipage with its Negro footman were only two of many that drove up to the grand reception given for Governor Dudley in 1702. Boston had never known such a splendid wedding as that performed by the Reverend Cotton Mather for Thomas Hutchinson and Sarah Foster in December, 1703, which was followed by a "very great entertainment," to which Sewall was "not asked." Seasonal changes brought new styles in dress. "It is a great fashion here to wear West India linens," wrote Winthrop in 1706. They are "pretty light, coole," and "Everybody of any Fashion weares them in summer." "There is no fashion in London," declared Neal, "but in three or four Months it is to be seen at Boston." After 1700 the gentlewomen of the town tended more and more to turn their many babies over to the care of wet nurses in order to devote themselves more exclusively to social activities. At the close of the period an English observer, who had been entertained in Boston mansions, remarked: [8]

> that a Gentleman from London would almost think himself at home in Boston, when he observes the Numbers of the People, their Houses, their Furniture, . . . their Dress, and Conversation, which is perhaps as splendid and showy, as that of the most considerable Tradesmen [merchants] in London. . . . In the Concerns of Civil Life, as in their Dress, Tables, and Conversation, they affect to be as much English as possible.

Aristocratic classes in other towns enjoyed a similar growth in wealth and position, although nowhere were their members so numerous or so powerful as at Boston. Quaker aristocrats of Front Street dominated the economic and social life of Philadelphia. In the 1690's many wealthy persons from England joined this group, the most impressive accession being James Logan, who shortly made his influence felt in every sphere of Pennsylvania life. After 1700 there gradually appeared in the entourage of the Governors, who were seldom Quakers, a non-Quaker element of the "better sort," which, by the close of the period, was rapidly acquiring control of the city government and of Philadelphia society. Among these new people were Dr. John Kearsley, the Biddles, Charles Read and Peter Chevalier, the last a direct

[8] Dow, *Everyday Life*, 46; 6 MHS *Colls.*, III, 334; 5 MHS *Colls.*, VI, 59, 91, 150, 223; *Bos. Gaz.*, Sept. 26, 1720; *News Letter*, Feb. 18, 1705/6; Neal, *New England*, II, 253.

descendant of the Duc de Sully. Prominent Quaker families were the Norrises, Shippens, Pembertons, Dickinsons, Hills, Merediths, and Fishbourns.

The Philadelphia gentry built magnificent homes which equalled, and in many cases surpassed, those of the Bostonians. Frequently these were country estates, placed on the outskirts of town. Clark's Hall, near Dock Creek, where James Logan first lived, was such a country seat, and was famed for its elaborate Dutch gardens, while Joshua Carpenter's mansion on Chestnut Street had beautifully landscaped grounds, with fruit trees, a garden, and shrubbery that always attracted the admiration of visitors. These lovely homes required the care of many Negroes and servants for their upkeep. They were elaborately decorated, occasionally perhaps with those "usefull Ornaments for Rooms, . . . & New Beautifull Mapps," sold by John Copson in Market Street.[9]

A notable feature in the development of aristocracies in other towns was the growing tendency to invest new wealth in lands. The accumulation of "treasure by foreign trade," and the presence of the Governor's court assured the prosperity of New York's upper class. In the thirty years after 1690 the Corporation admitted to the freedom of the city sixty-two "Gentlemen" and over a hundred "Merchants." This select group stood in marked contrast to the common people, designated by Bellomont as the scum of the New World. Among the great families the names of Alexander, Bayard, Beekman, van Courtlandt, De Peyster, Nichols, Smith, and Willet were foremost. To these were later added several newcomers, headed by the Honorable Caleb Heathcote and Dr. Cadwallader Colden. As in other towns, this aristocracy was tightly consolidated by intermarriage.[10]

Like their English contemporaries, the New York nabobs, aided often by gubernatorial largess, invested their surplus wealth in land, adding country estate to city mansion. Great families kept from ten to fifteen slaves for personal and house servants, hired English gardeners to care for their grounds, and began to travel the length and breadth of Manhattan in coaches, popularized by Lady Cornbury, and after 1702 made by James White. The quality of New York made itself conspicuous by the "extravagance" of its expenditures for English importations and the elaborateness of its dress and household furnishings.[11]

[9] Scharf and Westcott, *Philadelphia*, I, 181; II, 854; *Mercury*, April 28, 1720; Ancient Recs., Philadelphia, 43; Hart, *Contemporaries*, II, 75.
[10] *N. Y. Col. Docs.*, V, 322; *Doc. Hist. N. Y.*, IV, 1035; N. Y. Hist. Soc. *Colls.*, 1885, 80, 88, 91.
[11] Wilson, *Memorial History of New York*, II, 78 n., 139; *Journal of Madam Knight*, 54; Singleton, *Social New York*, 53.

Newport, too, had its "Gentlemen," and their numbers were on the increase. The fact that in 1700 half the population was still Quaker, and the absence of a royal governor and his retinue made for a less spectacular group of "persons of quality" than at Boston or New York, but here, too, growing wealth supported an aristocratic class. It is notable that at Newport the same old families maintained their ascendancy throughout the colonial period. By 1720 the Huguenots, Gabriel Bernon and Daniel Ayrault, and the Anglican families of Brinley, Ellery, Paine and Vernon were the commercial and social leaders of the town.[12]

Many of the Narragansett planters, like Bernon and Ayrault, who eventually moved to Newport, maintained both town and country houses, combined trade with farming, joined the English church, and lived like true country gentlemen. One sign of increasing wealth was the elaborate funerals held in the town during these years; a total of £55 was spent in 1716 on the interment of Rosewell Lavine. These gentlemen took more and more to black body-servants, and indulged in the same luxuries for their homes and families as the aristocrats of other towns. By 1718 even one who did not approve of Rhode Island condescended to admit that "the Inhabitants begin now to be more civilized." [13]

By 1710 there was a sufficient accumulation of wealth at Charles Town to make possible the rise of an aristocratic class of merchants and nearby planters. Such forceful spirits in trade and politics were Jonathan Amory, the Manigaults and Clapps, Colonel William Rhett and Thomas Pinckney. Conspicuous among proprietary officials, who fraternized with Arthur Middleton, John Barnwell, Ralph Izard and other planters, were the unscrupulous Nicholas Trott, and Governors Nathaniel Johnson and Joseph Boone. The Governor, members of the Assembly, judges, and minor officials nearly all resided at Charles Town, and there developed a proud social set. After discovery that rice made an excellent staple, planters began to grow wealthy and jealous of the merchants, and through their control of the Assembly, the former were able to discriminate against the town. Prior to 1715, however, both classes dwelt together amicably, and on the whole lived a more frugal, less showy existence than did their compeers in the northern towns.[14]

---

[12] Jones, *Quakers in the American Colonies*, xv; *Newport Hist. Mag.*, II, 187; Baird, *Huguenot Emigration*, II, 319, 321; 6 MHS *Colls.*, V, 386.

[13] Miller, "Narragansett Planters," 18, 46; *Newport T. C. Recs.*, Mar. 30, 1716; Sept., 1717; Weeden, *Economic and Social History*, II, 509; Neal, *New England*, II, 195, 233.

[14] In 1717 Charles Town had only four out of thirty members of the Commons House. Schaper, "Sectionalism in South Carolina," 345; Gray, *History of Agriculture*, I, 325; Howe, *Presbyterian Church*, 199; Dalcho, *Episcopal Church*, 23.

The development of artisans and shopkeepers, who made up the colonial middle class, has been discussed in the preceding chapter. Between these people and the "better sort" signs of a tensity of feeling began to appear, which, although of little significance in these years, portended gravely for the future. Some of the new aristocracy were proud and haughty, prone to exact a subservience from "middling" and "inferior" sorts which would have been readily granted in England, but which in the freer air of the colonial towns occasioned some outbursts of resentment. One December day in 1705 Governor Joseph Dudley, meeting with some carters on Boston Neck, ordered them out of the way to give his chariot passage. But the snow was drifted deep, and an argument ensued in which one carter asserted: "I am as good flesh and blood as you, . . . you may goe out of the way." The irate aristocrat drew his side sword and struck at the fellow, who snatched it from him. "You lie, you dog; you lie, you devill," roared Dudley. "Such words don't become a Christian," replied the carter. He received a rejoinder at the end of a horsewhip: "A Christian, you dog! a Christian, you devill! I was a Christian before you were born." Both yeomen were arrested, but later released through the efforts of Judge Sewall. Less of this sort of thing was noticeable at Newport or Philadelphia, where the levelling spirit of Quakerism prevailed, although laborers and mechanics in the latter town bitterly resented having to compete with the slaves of the rich. But it was at New York that class feeling was most open. Here the hauteur and sensitive dignity of the aristocracy on one side, and the dogged prejudices of the poorer folk, especially the Dutch, to whom Leisler appealed, on the other, obtruded an economic and social issue into the already boiling political caldron, which was not to subside for many years. City artisans and laborers in the New World could hardly accept without resentment Bellomont's classification as "the scum of the people, Taylours and other scandalous persons." Another cause of friction was the tendency of town gentry in the northern communities to look down well-bred noses at rustics, "who for want of emprovements Render themselves almost Ridiculous." The country "Bumpkin" and his "Jane Tawdry" who came to town to shop inevitably evoked the derision of urban gentility.[15]

Actually, of course, most members of both middle and lower classes in the towns accepted with cheerful awareness their assigned stations in life. On October 3, 1707, when the Reverend Mr. Pemberton of the South Church, Boston, called a church meeting, he found attend-

---

[15] 5 *MHS Colls.*, VI, 144; 8 *Bos. Rec. Com.*, 131; *Votes Pa. Assembly*, I, ii, 132; Osgood, *Colonies in the Eighteenth Century*, I, 228; *N. Y. Col. Docs.*, V, 322; *Journal of Madam Knight*, 43; 6 MHS *Colls.*, V, 331, 384 n.

ance very slim. "Severall came not," observed Sewall, "because Mr. Pemberton said *Gentlemen* of the Church and Congregation; affirmed they were not Gentlemen and therefore were not warned to come." In this fluid town society some laborers by diligence and good fortune might rise to the middle class, and wealthy shopkeepers like Charles Read and George Mifflin could attain merchant status and so enter the ranks of quality. While these avenues remained open, class antagonisms were kept largely underground. Upon the whole, "all sorts of People, even Servants, Negroes, Aliens, Jews, and common Sailors," (as classified by Joseph Boone of Charles Town) who made up the varied cast of characters on the colonial urban stage, went soberly and industriously about their allotted tasks, content with their way and walk of life, and giving as yet little thought to the problem of classes in society.[16]

IV

Organized religion continued to bulk large in the lives of many townspeople, as earlier, but its supremacy was in this period threatened by the appearance of two important factors, — the breakdown of religious unity occasioned by the growth of rival sects, each offering a different avenue to salvation, and the increasing secularization of town life, enticing people to other considerations than the health of their souls. A diversity of new sects flourished in each town, their existence materially impairing the social control which it had been possible for a united clergy to exercise in the days when it had represented one single establishment or predominant faith. Above all, the rapid growth of the Church of England altered the religious complexion of the northern towns. Waxing strong under royal and official patronage, Anglicanism introduced a religious atmosphere more warm, colorful and latitudinarian than the narrow severity of early Congregationalism or the austere plainness of the Friends. The new age, to which its stately ritual was so well suited, had also its effect upon the older churches. Breathless absorption with tremendous theological speculations occupied the minds of very few burghers in the eighteenth century; the "holy heat" of earlier days had cooled; and nearly every one of the churches exhibited a tendency toward that formalism which inevitably saps the vitality of established institutions.

Simultaneously with this formalizing of religious observance there developed in town life a new complexity, occasioned largely by the

[16] 5 MHS *Colls.,* VI, 195; *Mercury,* April 28, 1720; AHA *Ann. Rept., 1892,* 28; Neal, *New England,* II, 251. Colonial gentry compared more than favorably, however, with that of an English provincial city; see Latimer, *Bristol in the Eighteenth Century,* 16, 30.

expansion of trade and commerce, and by the effects of intercolonial wars. New, and often more attractive, agencies for amusement began to compete with the monopoly formerly exercised by the church over social town life. The growing secular spirit caused a falling off in the power of the clergy as keepers of the morals of their flocks, and practically brought to an end their control over any not in full communion with the churches over which they ministered. The singleness of purpose that had inspired the early saints was largely gone, and the attractions of the world of business and action lured young and old from the narrow bounds of theological restraint and ministerial control. All these influences combined to reduce the importance of the church as an agency for social control in the towns, a situation of which the clergy themselves were not unaware. In contrast with the towns, the older spirit lingered longer in rural districts, and a very obvious difference in attitude between the two begins to be discernible.[17]

The effect of these new forces in religion was most marked at Boston. Here in 1699 a group of progressives gathered the Brattle Street Church, designed on more liberal lines as regards both service and policy of admission than the three existing Congregational societies. Conservative churchmen, especially the Mathers, greeted with a storm of abuse this "presbyterian brat" with its yearnings after "Episcopalian gentility." Town wits enjoyed the fray in a fashion that would have been impossible in days when church squabbles were no occasions for levity, and blithely circulated verses with such doggerel lines as "The old strait Gate is now out of Date," and "Relations are Rattle with Brattle & Brattle." The coolness of Benjamin Colman, young minister to the new society, and his determination to avoid controversy brought him the support of many laymen like Judge Sewall, and friction quickly subsided, so that by 1700 even the Mathers were reconciled. The more liberal position of the Brattle Church attracted many aristocrats of the younger generation to its table.[18]

The admission policy of Congregational churches in Boston resulted in exclusion of many artisans and tradesmen from membership, although not from attendance at services. In the words of a contemporary ballad,

> Our Merchants cum Mico do stand Sacco Vico;
> Our Churches turn genteel:
> Parsons grow trim and trig with wealth wine & wigg
> And their crowns are covered with meal.

---

[17] Cf. for example, the Congregationalism of rural Connecticut with that of urban Boston. Walker, "Why did not Massachusetts have a Saybrook Platform?" 68–86.
[18] 5 MHS *Colls.*, V, 509; Shipton, *Biographical Sketches*, IV, 122, 199; 6 MHS *Colls.*, I, 255; 7 MHS *Colls.*, VII, 325.

We have seen how the South Church was controlled by "Gentlemen." To remedy this situation, "seventeen substantial mechanics" gathered the New North Church in October, 1714, "without the assistance of the more wealthy part of the community, excepting what they derived from their prayers and good wishes." [19]

The Andros troubles dealt what was almost a death blow to the Church of England at Boston and many of its members left town. But with the protection of the new charter and the support of the Earl of Bellomont King's Chapel made so rapid a recovery that by 1710 the church edifice had become "too small for the congregation and Strangers that dayly increase," and new ground had to be acquired from the town to enlarge it. Many leaders of Boston society became regular communicants or attendants at King's Chapel. Governors Bellomont, Dudley, Tailer and Shute were all vestrymen, and among its wealthy and aristocratic members were Sir Charles Hobby, Colonel Francis Nicholson, Captain Cyprian Southack, Colonel Francis Brinley, John Valentine, Dr. John Cutler and Thomas Selby. Anglicanism progressed so rapidly that in 1714 it claimed over eight hundred adherents living in and about Boston. During these years tutors at Harvard College, former stronghold of Puritan orthodoxy, "recommended to the Pupils," many of whom were Boston lads, "the reading of Episcopal authors as the best books to form . . . [our] minds in religious matters and preserve us from those narrow Principles that kept us at a Distance from the Church of England." [20] Times were indeed ripe for the founding of Yale!

Throughout the period other sects prospered. Although Thomas Chalkley complained in 1693 that he was unkindly received at Boston, Quakers were no longer molested in their worship. In 1694 William Mumford, a stonecutter, built the first brick meeting house in the town, for the Society of Friends; in 1709 a new lot was purchased for a burial ground, and a second brick building erected for what Samuel Sewall called "Devil Worship." Unlike Quakerism at Newport and Philadelphia, hardly any of the Boston members came from the upper classes, and its total numbers were never large. The Baptist congregation worshipped with Elder John Emblem as leader until his death in 1699, but not until 1708 was its first regular minister, Ellis Callender, installed. Under his guidance Baptists and Congregationalists tended to draw together, and Cotton Mather preached the ordination sermon, "Good men united," at the installation of Elisha Callender in 1718. A small French Calvinist congregation was estab-

[19] The New South Church was formed in 1715. 6 MHS *Colls.,* I, 255; 5 MHS *Colls.,* VII, 22, 61.
[20] Foote, *King's Chapel,* I, 178, 184, 239, 240, 246, 265.

lished at Boston some time before 1690, meeting for years in the town schoolhouse. A little church was built in 1715, but the membership remained small, and the young people were enticed or "driven to other churches." [21]

New York continued to be a town of many faiths. Here the presence of a royal governor and his entourage proved a great impetus to the growth of Anglicanism. By zealous effort Governor Benjamin Fletcher obtained the passage of an act "to settle a fund for a Ministry in the City of New York . . . which never could be obtained before being a mixt people of different Persuasions in Religion." According to this law taxes for the support of a minister could be levied by wardens and vestry, chosen by the freeholders. After an unsuccessful attempt by parish officers to call a dissenting preacher, William Vesey was selected and sent to England for Episcopal ordination. In 1698, a year after his return, he began officiating in the newly built Trinity Church. Although Vesey became embroiled in the Leisler troubles and affronted Governor Bellomont, the powerful backing of such men as Caleb Heathcote and Lewis Morris assured the continued prosperity of his church.[22]

Throughout the period, despite lip-service paid the principle of religious toleration, there seems to have been more restriction of sects at New York than in any other town. The Reformed Dutch Church had been assured of all its rights and privileges at the time of the surrender to the English, but the opposition of its clergy to the Leislerians in 1690, and later obstacles advanced by the Anglicans, despite the Toleration Act, delayed the issue of its charter until 1696. To accommodate its growing congregation a new church was completed in Garden Street in 1695. Though the Reformed Church was by far the most numerous denomination at New York, official favors all went to the Anglican group. Lutherans and Huguenots, being well established, worshipped unmolested, but were officially frowned upon.[23]

Two important new sects appeared at New York in these years. A few Presbyterians met on the Sabbath in a private house after 1700, and in 1706 Francis Makemie and John Hampton came to preach to them, but Makemie was arrested by order of Lord Cornbury for preaching without a license. The little band throve on such persecution, and in 1717 John Nicoll, Patrick McKnight, Gilbert Livingston, Thomas Smith and a few others organized a congregation on the

[21] Winsor, *Memorial History of Boston*, II, 189, 200, 220, 221; Baird, *Huguenot Emigration*, II, 222, 241.
[22] Dix, *Trinity Church*, I, 81, 85, 90, 108, 174.
[23] Quakers erected a small building in 1696; the French enlarged theirs in 1704. *Eccles. Recs. N. Y.*, II, 1123, 1528; Van Rensselaer, *New York*, II, 151; Cox, *Quakerism in New York*, 43.

model of the Scottish National Church. The Presbyterians built a small meeting house on Wall Street near Broadway, but when they applied for a charter in 1720 they found the way to incorporation blocked by the vestry of Trinity Church, — an unfriendly action that resulted in years of bitterness between the two sects. In 1720 Nicholas Eyers, a brewer, hired a house on Broad Street "for an anabaptist meeting house," telling Governor Burnet that he "had been a public preacher to a baptist congregation within this city for four years," and that he could produce "an ample certificate of his good behaviour and innocent conversation." Burnet licensed him to "execute the ministeriall function in New York City." [24]

The Society of Friends not only ceased to be the sole religious denomination at Philadelphia in this period, but suffered serious inroads from the aggressiveness of its rivals. The Quakers erected a third structure, known as the "Great Meeting House," on the corner of Second and Market Streets, just opposite the Court House, in 1695. Many wealthy Friends with liberal sympathies resided in the city, but the Society's Yearly Meeting was controlled by farmers of Philadelphia, Chester and Bucks Counties, who were sober, conservative, and strongly for the old discipline. Primarily for this reason many of the younger city members, impatient under the Meeting's restraint, went over to the more liberal and showy Christ Church, "Contrary to friends advice to them." [25] In 1720 the Quakers were still by far the largest and most influential religious body in the town, but their discipline and control over the affairs of Philadelphia were being seriously threatened by the growing Anglican group.

Intrusion of new sects began in the 1690's. Francis Makemie was not annoyed at Philadelphia when he preached there in 1692, and induced some scattered Presbyterians to come together with a few Baptists for services in the loft of the old "Barbados Store," where the two groups for a time worshipped in harmony. In 1698 the Presbyterians organized a separate church of English dissenters, Huguenots and Welshmen, with Jedediah Andrews (Harvard, 1695) as their leader. At the same time an Episcopal missionary, Thomas Clayton, arrived, and competition between rival shepherds over stray lambs became so intense that a truce had to be called in 1699. Presbyterianism spread rapidly in Pennsylvania, and in 1705 the Philadelphia Presbytery was formed. With the coming of the Scotch-Irish after 1717 its growth was phenomenal. Meanwhile, the Baptists, too, had organized their own church, with quarters in a brew house. Some disillusioned

---

[24] The tiny Jewish congregation Shearith Israel dated back to 1655 but had no place of worship. *Eccles. Recs. N. Y.*, III, 1671, 1672; *Doc. Hist. N. Y.*, III, 480; Stokes, *Iconography*, I, 190; Pool, *The Mill Street Synagogue.*
[25] Myers, *Irish Quakers*, 108, 213; Jones, *Quakers*, 441.

Keithian Quakers joined them in 1701, and after 1707 the little flock struggled along in a small wooden building for many years before it became sufficiently prosperous to erect a church.[26]

The efforts of the Reverend Mr. Thomas Clayton to form an Episcopal church met with gratifying success. A good sized brick edifice was erected and several hundred converts made between 1695 and 1700. In the latter year the Bishop of London sent over Evan Evans, who reported that he frequently read the liturgy before five hundred people, many of whom came in from country districts to hear him. So many prominent persons, some of them apostate Friends, joined Christ Church that the Quakers became very bitter about their "losses." Governor Charles Gookin and Colonel Robert Quary were generous supporters of the church, which had to be enlarged in 1711, and Sir William Keith was an active member of the vestry. Among prominent laymen were Robert Assheton, Charles Reade, and Dr. John Kearsley. Christ Church, by 1720, despite the unsavory reputation of its minister, was fast becoming the place of worship attended by people of wealth and fashion.[27]

At Charles Town, though the coming in of new sects was not forbidden, dissenters could secure only by determined struggle the toleration granted by the Carolina charter. In 1690, under the leadership of Benjamin Pierpont a group of New Englanders joined with the Independents to erect a building since known from its shape as the "Circular Church." By 1699 a Baptist church had been gathered. The Society of Friends acquired a lot in 1699 on which they built a small church, but regular meetings lapsed several years later, not to be revived until about 1716. The largest groups were the Huguenot and Anglican congregations. A law of 1704 provided for the erection of the Parish of St. Philip's at Charles Town, and for the employment of Anglican ministers at public charge. Thus established by law, Episcopacy flourished, and a new brick church, with belfry equipped with bells, was built with public funds in 1701. This building gave way after 1715 to a larger structure for which £500 was contributed by the Proprietors. St. Philip's enjoyed the support of the Governors and of most of the prominent men, such as Colonel Rhett, Alexander Paris, William Gibbon, John Bee and Jacob Satin.[28]

Establishment of the Anglican Church in 1704, and exclusion of dis-

[26] Swedish Lutherans built Gloria Dei at Wicaco in 1696. Shipton, *Biographical Sketches,* 220; Faris, *Old Churches,* 39, 84; Scharf and Westcott, *Philadelphia,* II, 1234, 1263, 1304.
[27] Keith, *Journal,* 43, 49, 50; Sharpless, *Quaker Experiment,* 90; Dorr, *Christ Church,* 13, 27, 37, 49.
[28] Howe, *Presbyterian Church,* 126; *S. C. Hist. & Gen. Mag.,* X, 137; XXVIII, 23; Trans. Chas. Friends (MS.); Townsend, *Baptists,* 9; *S. C. Statutes,* II, 236; VII, 56; *Cal. St. Pap., 1714-1715,* 145.

senters from membership in the Assembly conflicted with the toleration granted by charter. A bitter religious and political struggle ensued, which was carried to England and resulted in the repeal of the objectional laws in 1706. After this the Huguenots tended more and more to go over to the Church of England, with the result that by 1720 more than half the churchgoers of Charles Town professed that faith. The Episcopal clergymen in this period were not of a very high order, and Charles Town was probably the least religious of all the towns.[29]

At the opposite extreme was Newport. Although the Baptist church continued very strong, over half the inhabitants in 1690 belonged to the Society of Friends, and for the next thirty years Quakers dominated the social and religious life of the town. In this period, however, two churches were founded that were soon to challenge Quaker supremacy and eventually to supersede the "plain people." Encouraged by Governor Nicholson of Virginia a little group of Episcopalians gathered there in 1694. When Bellomont visited the place in 1699 he received a petition from Gabriel Bernon, Pierre Ayrault, William Brinley, Thomas Paine, and thirteen others for aid to the church they were about to erect, and accordingly secured assistance for them from the Society for the Propagation of the Gospel. To hasten the coming of a minister, this nascent congregation informed the Society that "the place where we live is one of the Chief Nurseries of Quakerism in all America. . . . Their behaviour to us outwardly is almost as civil as is consistent with their religion. Although slily and underhand, we are sensible they would pinch us in the bud." The Reverend Mr. James Honeyman arrived in 1704 to take over care of the church built two years before. The new chapel, called Trinity Church, enjoyed remarkable growth, drawing into its fold many wealthy merchant families. The lure of this fashionable communion, eminently respectable and "genteel," proved too strong for many well-to-do Quakers and others to resist. Tradition records that when Friend William Wanton and Ruth Bryant, daughter of a "presbyterian bigot," encountered religious objections to their marriage, William said, "Friend Ruth, let us break from this unreasonable bondage — I will give up *my* religion, and *thou* shalt *thine,* and we will go over to the Church of England, and *go to the Devil together.*" [30]

The other denomination appeared in 1695, when Nathaniel Clap, a young Harvard graduate, began work as a Congregational missionary

[29] In 1710 Thomas Nairne estimated the proportions of religious groups as follows: Anglicans, forty-five per cent; Huguenots and Calvinists, forty-five per cent; Anabaptists, nine per cent; Quakers, one per cent. *Letter from South Carolina,* 46; *S. C. Statutes,* II, 232, 236, 282; AHA *Ann. Rept., 1892,* 28.

[30] Baptists erected a new church edifice in 1708. Jones, *Quakers,* xv; Peterson, *Rhode Island,* 207, 335; Keith, *Journal,* 13, 17; Mason, *Trinity Church,* 10, 11, 14, 17, 25, 34; Isham, *Trinity Church,* 6, 9, 16.

at Newport. Though successful in his labors, he would not consent to the organization of a church until 1720. A complacent account in the *Boston News Letter* states that on November 3rd, "the Rev. Mr. Nathaniel Clap was Ordained here [Newport], to the Pastoral Office over a particular Congregational Church . . . , being the first Work of this Nature which was ever managed in this Government." [31]

Religion no longer pervaded the life of the towns as it had done in earlier years. Town churches still provided a sort of Sabbath recreation for their many members. The beauty and pageantry of the Episcopal service appealed to many over the drab austerity of dissenting forms, and even at Boston in 1696, when "Mr. Veisy preach'd at the Ch. of Engl'd; [he] had many Auditors." Moreover, the churches were forced to compete with an ever growing variety of secular amusements. As early as 1697 Sewall noticed a falling off in attendance at Thursday lectures, and Cotton Mather "fear'd twould be an omen of our not enjoying the Lecture long, if [it] did not amend." There were many deeply religious persons in every town, but as in any age the bulk of churchgoers sought at Sabbath services sociability, entertainment, and opportunity to meet their friends.

The moral control of the churches also lessened in this period of commercial expansion and war. While new religious societies were organized in each town, they did not keep pace with growth in population. Whereas in 1690 Boston churches were able to accommodate one quarter of the population, in 1720 they could shelter only about a fifth of the town's inhabitants. At Philadelphia they could seat probably only seventeen hundred out of a population of ten thousand. New York, Newport and Charles Town presented similar conditions. The truth was that the churches were reaching a smaller proportion of townsmen; some failed to hold their communicants, and all appealed to fewer new members, especially among the youth. The tendency of the Society of Friends to stiffen its discipline toward 1720 appears to have been largely a defensive measure. At Wicaco, near Philadelphia, the register of Old Swedes' Church yields evidence that many young Quaker couples were running away to be married by "ye priest," contrary to "ye advice of ye meeting." The Boston clergy tried to meet the problem in 1705, when the Mathers and others issued "Proposals" to strengthen ministerial authority, but the refusal of the civil government under Dudley to support the churches, and the emerging secular spirit of the Massachusetts seaboard hindered this presbyterianizing movement. Cotton Mather described the situation in every town when he observed "the peculiar Spirit and Error of the Time, to be *Indifferency* to *Religion*"; "the two comprehensive Points of our Corruption,

[31] Shipton, *Biographical Sketches*, IV, 36; *News Letter*, Nov. 7, 1720.

are an Ambition of saecular *Grandeurs,* and an Affection for sensual *Pleasures.*" The secular spirit developed among rich and poor alike. While gentlemen and ladies displayed their newly acquired wealth and sought favors in high places, seafaring folk, of whom there were many in every port, were coming less and less under the spiritual guidance of the churches. Although Charles Town was the religious center of South Carolina, and no services were held beyond its limits before 1703, a slackening of zeal was evident among the Huguenots as early as 1693. About the same time an inhabitant of New York wrote, "As to Religion, we run so high in all Opinions, that there is (I fear) but little reall." [32] Important as was the position which the church still held, there had appeared in all towns by 1720 portents of its declining influence as a social force.

V

Of all town institutions, the most flourishing in this period was the tavern. Each town saw a steady increase in the number of strangers and seafaring men for whom such hostelries were primarily designed. With the multiplication of public houses in every town, an improvement in the quality of service and accommodations began to be evident. Moreover, inns, ordinaries and coffee houses became increasingly the resort of all classes seeking recreation and entertainment. This was especially true of the common man, whom perhaps the churches failed to reach, and to whom the more exclusive and sophisticated amusements of the rich were denied. Yet the increase in the number of taverns was not an unmixed blessing, for the liquor problem remained unsolved, and it became ever more difficult to preserve good order in public houses and to safeguard the morals of those who frequented them.

In no town was there a scarcity of public houses. At Boston in 1691 the authorities licensed eleven taverns, fifteen alehouses, and six "retail" dramshops, and by 1710 eighty-one persons were engaging in the inn and tavern business.[33] Although there were known to be several dives and "speak-easies" down by the wharves, close regulation and constant inspection by Selectmen and County Justices kept Boston public houses on the whole very respectable.

The town had several famous hostelries. Especially popular among official and aristocratic sets was the Blue Anchor, where George Monk, "a brisk and jolly man," made a point of catering to quality. The Rose and Crown and the Royal Exchange, both in King Street, were equally fine establishments. Older Bostonians looked upon these inns

[32] Myers, *Irish Quakers,* 213; Walker, "Why did not Massachusetts have a Saybrook Platform?" 68–86; 7 MHS *Colls.,* VIII, 16, 397, 451, 525, 555; Shipton, *Biographical Sketches,* IV, 498; McCrady, *South Carolina under Proprietary Government,* 264, 296; N. Y. Hist. Soc. *Colls.,* II, 244.
[33] 7 *Bos. Rec. Com.,* 207; 11 *Bos. Rec. Com.,* 104.

with misgivings because of the frequent healths there drunk to the King and the free use of playing cards in their tap-rooms. The Royal Exchange was really the social center of Boston. Here was no place for the rabble; the host desired only the most genteel of patrons, and his advertisements told of room and board for "Gentlemen." Sewall was greatly excited at the novelty of dining there with Sir William Phips in 1690, but as time passed it became the usual thing for him to go there for Governor Dudley's Council banquets and other state occasions. The wine list was long and excellent; one might have for the asking "St. Georges and Fayall, . . . as also right Passado's and right Canary," port, Madeira, and good French brandy.[34]

The demands of commerce led to the opening of more coffee houses. By 1720 there were four of these establishments in Boston, each catering to its regular clientele of merchants and ship captains. Nearly all large public auctions were held at Thomas Selby's Crown Coffee House on Long Wharf; here in 1714 Judge Sewall publicly "read the Act against Schism." In 1715 Daniel Stevens opened his Coffee House in Ann Street, which had a "large Room and other conveniencies" for conducting vendues, and offered "Lodging and Dyet" as well. In 1720 public vendues were also being held at Hall's in Queen Street. At all of these places, but especially at "The Coffee House in Queen Street," Captain Hewit and other mariners hung their mail bags, so that the postmaster had to announce in 1718 that so "many Inconveniencies attend the setting up of Bags in coffee and other Public Houses, whereby Letters are lyable to be Opened, Imbezled or Detained," that all masters of vessels bound for Great Britain were henceforth requested to put up their bags only at the post office.[35]

Boston abounded with taverns and victualling houses serving as resorts for the middle and lower classes. Such a place was Bull's Tavern, where "substantiall mechanicks" formed the New South Church in 1719. Thomas Fitch kept the Three Mariners at the head of Long Wharf, where he catered throughout the period to the better class of sailors. In 1709 there were at least twenty-six of these little inns, in each of which the Selectmen billeted from two to five of the soldiers who assembled in the town for the Canadian expedition. In addition, the "poorer sort" had their hostelries and boarding houses, like the "Sign of ye Turkie Cock in Fish Street," where Thomas Lee, a fisherman, kept a rooming house "for the entertainment of Transient persons with Victual & Lodging," but sold no strong drink.[36]

[34] 5 MHS *Colls.*, V, 495; VI, 73; Drake, *Old Boston Taverns*, 107; *News Letter*, Aug. 21, 1704; Oct. 17, 1715; *Bos. Gaz.*, Sept. 19, 1720.
[35] *News Letter*, June 12, 1704; April 5, 1714; Jan. 3, 1715; Feb. 24, 1718; *Bos. Gaz.*, April 11, May 30, June 20, Sept. 12, 1720; 6 MHS *Colls.*, II, 20.
[36] Drake, *Old Boston Taverns*, 122; 11 *Bos. Rec. Com.*, 90, 95.

New York boasted an even greater variety of public houses than did Boston. The increase in the number of taverns kept pace with the growth of the town; fifty-four taverners, victuallers, and vintners were granted "freedoms" between 1694 and 1720. Most important of the new hostelries was John Hutchin's Coffee House at the Sign of the King's Arms on Broadway, which was opened after the London model about 1697. In the tap-room there was a row of "small boxes," screened with green curtains, where his guests could drink their coffee, ale or Madeira in some seclusion. Upstairs were furnished rooms for meeting purposes. This coffee house soon received the patronage of wealthy merchants, and became the meeting-place of the anti-Leislerian faction at Manhattan. The "Coffee House" was opened in 1702 on Pearl Street, and was for years operated by Johannes d'Honour, while in 1709 William Bradford, printer, began serving customers at the "New-Coffee-House." In 1716 John Fontaine often ate a nine o'clock breakfast at the Coffee House, and returned there to dine when the French Club met at six. At these new hostelries writing materials and the latest British newspapers were always to be had. Auctions were conducted in their common rooms, and here a large amount of the town's commercial transactions took place.[37]

There were a number of good inns and taverns at Manhattan. Throughout the period Gabriel Thompson kept an excellent public house, the White Lion, at the corner of William and Wall Streets, where conferences between the two houses of the Assembly frequently took place, because so many of the members boarded there. From 1698 to 1703 the King's House, run by Joseph David, served as head-quarters of the Corporation while the new City Hall was building. Roger Baker's King's Head, Michael Hawdon's and John Parmyter's taverns were all houses well patronized by the gentry. On the out-skirts of town were two taverns much frequented by parties of pleasure. "About two miles from the town on the road to Kingsbridge, . . . at a place called the Bowery," John Clap kept a good tavern, which served as a halting place, "where a parting glass or two of generous Wine,

> If well apply'd, makes the dull Horses feel
> One Spur i' th' head is worth two in the heel."

Here mine host offered "any Gentlemen Travellers that are strangers to the City, . . . good Entertainment, for themselves and Horses." Madam Sarah Knight drove out there in a sleigh in 1704. By 1710 the

---

[37] London coffee houses, unlike those at Boston, kept no lodgers. Bayles, *Old Taverns of New York*, 67, 68, 77; Fontaine, "Journal," 296; N. Y. Hist. Soc. *Colls.*, *1885*, 54–100.

Bowery had become a favorite place for dinner parties. Bass, the new host, found in the Reverend Mr. John Sharpe one of his best patrons. For many years prior to 1701 Richard Sackett kept a brew house and bowling green on the East River shore, called variously "Cherry Garden" or "Sackett's Orchard," and deservedly popular.[38]

There were in addition many middle class public houses, like William Hunt's on Pearl Street, Nathaniel Smith's, Henry Swift's, George Cocke's and John Macloud's. Down by the Dock the Widow Jourdain and others ran sailors' dramshops, which seem to have been better managed than in other towns. John Buford, who kept a "Common Ale-house or tippling house," was deprived of his license for six months in 1711 for having a set of "False weights." At New York there were also many "victualling" houses, of which those operated by James Perot and Elias Chardavoine offered good French cooking, while Thomas Joes and John Lafont had opened "Confectioners" shops by 1702.[39]

Private lodging houses were as popular as taverns, especially with those who proposed to stay a long time in the town. Mr. Sharpe hired lodgings from his friend Bradford in 1704, and his Diary is full of references to visits to the rooms and diggings of his various friends among the merchants and officers.[40]

The coffee houses were headquarters for British officers, aristocrats and public officials. The Assembly frequently used Hawdon's, Thompson's and the Widow Post's taverns, and the Corporation made Mrs. Post's, Parmyter's and Obadiah Hunt's the scenes of their grand banquets. When Lord Cornbury returned from New Jersey in 1704 the Mayor and Common Council tendered him a banquet at Richard Hunt's, which included thirty-one bottles of wine, and cost the city £10. 18. 6. In 1717 the Corporation slightly bettered this record with "32 bottles of wine" at John Parmyter's, when they ate and drank to his majesty's coronation. These were the men of whom, in their youth, de Sille remarked, "they all drink here, from the moment they are able to lick a spoon." [41]

Philadelphia throughout this period was more than adequately supplied with ordinaries and dramshops, licensed and unlicensed, where sailors, apprentices, artisans and laborers regularly tanked up and not infrequently got into brawls. The authorities in 1698 found the principal reason for the rapid multiplication of such houses in the fact that Philadelphia had "become the rode where sailors and others doe frequentlie pass and repass between Virginia and New England."

[38] Stokes, *Iconography*, IV, 422, 424, 427; *Pa. Mag.*, XL, 283.
[39] N. Y. Hist. Soc. *Colls., 1885*, 64, 90, 93; Stokes, *Iconography*, IV, 471.
[40] *Pa. Mag.*, XL, 260.
[41] Bayles, *Old Taverns*, 84, 86; Stokes, *Iconography*, IV, 148.

Perhaps the steady growth of the town had more to do with this increase; at any rate the liquor business must have held out inviting prospects of profit. In the year 1703/4 the Corporation received fifteen petitions for retail licenses, and from 1716 to the close of the period five women and eleven men, who had been fined for operating illegal dramshops, succeeded in having their fines remitted. In addition, of course, were all those who conducted their business regularly under permits. The competition furnished by the many groggeries so affected the trade of respectable houses that the innkeepers successfully petitioned the Assembly in 1720, "setting forth the Mischiefs that happen from many Dram-Shops and Tippling-houses," and desiring that they might be suppressed.[42]

There were in the city many fine public houses and inns, like the White Horse and the popular Blue Anchor, where strangers met with excellent food and accommodations, and where townsfolk could repair for the ordinary, some Madeira, or a sociable smoke with friends, from those "Good long tavern Tobacco Pipes" sold by Richard Warder. On the Delaware bank of Front Street Henry Flower opened a "Coffee House" in 1703, which immediately became the daily rendezvous of merchants and politicians, and served as the Exchange of that day. This coffee house was not a hostelry; Flower followed the London custom of serving only coffee and chocolate. As the host was also province postmaster, he was able to pass on to his patrons the latest intelligences along with English newspapers and mail. Here the Mayor and Common Council usually held their sessions before adjourning to a tavern for dinner, and here most important public notices were posted.[43]

Shops of other types also catered to the local palate. "Here is to be had on any Day in the Week," wrote Gabriel Thomas in 1697, "Tarts, Pies, Cakes, etc. We have also several Cook-shops, both Roasting and Boyling, as in the City of London; Bread, Beer, Beef, and Pork are sold at any time much cheaper than in England." The sojourner in Philadelphia who found the inns too noisy and wished for more seclusion could easily secure pleasant lodgings in the town. The Reverend Andreas Sandel, pastor of Old Swedes', lived in very comfortable quarters at Mr. Honer's, "where the English clergyman also rented rooms with board, at 12 shillings per week." [44]

The growth of Newport in the early eighteenth century meant that the six licensed taverns of 1691 could no longer supply the town's

[42] Ancient Recs. Phila., 27; P. M. C. C., 83, 106, 116, 143, 147, 174, 190; Votes Pa. Assembly, II, 283, 285, 287.
[43] Mercury, May 19, 1719; Wallace, Bradford, 337; P. M. C. C., 5, 6; Votes Pa. Assembly, I, ii, 161; II, 147, 149.
[44] Narratives of Pennsylvania, 331; Pa. Mag., XXX, 289; Keith, Journal, 43.

demands. The number of inns and retailing establishments increased rapidly; after 1717 the Town Council regularly licensed from seventeen to twenty taverns annually. The presence of many mariners and strangers led to a multiplication of victualling houses and grog-shops. In 1692 Stephen Labear, a Huguenot, and one Palmer were each licensed to "keepe [an] ordinary or a victualling house." Sewall went in 1699 to "dine and lodge at Tho. Mallet's," the best public house in town, when he came with a large company from Boston to greet the Earl of Bellomont on his arrival in New England. After 1710 several excellent hostelries afforded good service to strangers and boarders. Sewall frequently went to Newport on business, and generally "lodged at Mr. Melvils." Here in 1711 he ordered up a sumptuous repast, and invited Messrs. Clap and Pemberton to dine with him. The principal resort of the trading element was Timothy Whiting's King's Arms, where prominent merchants and shipbuilders met daily as a sort of trade guild to discuss developments in their industry and prospects for business. Social life tended more to center at the Exchange Tavern, where Mrs. Sarah Bright offered her patrons the use of a "large Garden, a Billiard Table and Nine Pin Alley." Another famous house was that operated on the Newport side of Carr's ferry to accommodate strangers and travelers who arrived too late at night to cross, and in 1719 Carr was granted a license to retail liquor there that his patrons might be "well supplied." The Town Council held its meetings at Mary Nichol's inn in 1713–1714. Many of the public houses were small neighborhood shops, like that of Nathaniel Dunn, who was given a license in 1716 for forty shillings instead of the usual £5, "it being Considered he lives in a Place where he had not much custom," or like the shops of Nathaniel Douglas and Richard Kitchen, where townsmen went for their "gill of Rum." [45]

There is scant record of the inns, ordinaries and "punch-houses" of Charles Town, though there were doubtless many of them, and numerous lodging houses as well. Perhaps the best place of entertainment the town afforded was that of Peter Poinsett where good French cooking and choice Madeira wines awaited the guest. The establishment of Friend Isaac Redwood served good English fare, and many a fur trader doubtless could be found "tyed by the Lipps to a pewter engine" at the house of George Chicken, vintner. Living was more costly at Charles Town than in the northern towns. Nathaniel Sale paid "£46. 10s. a yeare . . . lodging and dyet" in 1709, which was almost a third more than the amount paid by the Reverend Mr. Sandel

[45] Newport T. C. Recs., May 3, 1714; Mar. 30, 1716; April 9, May 6, June 3, Oct. 7, 1717; Jan. 6, April 7, 1718; Newport T. M. Recs., 57; 5 MHS Colls., V, 501; VI, 322; Newport Hist. Mag., II, 423; News Letter, Mar. 17, 1718; R. I. Col. Recs., IV, 194.

in Philadelphia at the same time.[46] Yet Charles Town was probably as well served by public houses as the other communities.

Although the towns profited by the extension of their tavern facilities, most of them also suffered from the spawning of illicit houses and from disorderly grog-shops sometimes conducted by licensed taverners. The situation was worst at Philadelphia. During the 1690's many taverns there became centers of vice and debauchery, with abuses so flagrant as to constitute a public scandal. In 1695 inhabitants of the town sent a petition to the Assembly, showing that many of these tippling houses were "Kept by several as are not well qualified for such undertakings, tending to debauchery and corrupting of youth." Three years later in London the Proprietor, learning of the scandalous conditions in the town of his founding, forbade the granting of licenses to those "not known to be of civil Conversacon," and required the grantees to give "great securitie to keep Civil houses." The Council could only urge in its own defense that the large number of ordinaries rendered "the same more difficult to be supprest and keept under." [47]

In 1700 after much debate a strict tavern law was passed, regulating licensing, and providing heavy fines for illegal sale of liquor and disorderly establishments. Satisfactory enforcement of this law would have made of Philadelphia a much soberer place. Unfortunately a long and bitter quarrel broke out between Governor and Assembly over the question of license fees, the Governor having found the issuance of more licenses than were needed a profitable source of income, and the original need of supervision for public houses was completely lost sight of. In addition, the Common Council, prone to chickenheartedness, remitted more fines than were ever collected from violators of the law. After 1718 it did keep careful watch over prices and quality of liquor sold, but throughout this period the sober citizen and honest innkeeper suffered from the presence of too many legal and illegal drinking establishments.[48] When one surveys the list of wines and liquors imported into Pennsylvania, most of which were consumed in Philadelphia, the truth of the current formula is patent:

> Not drunk is he who from the floor,
> Can rise again and still drink more.
> But drunk is he who prostrate lies,
> Without the power to drink or rise.

[46] *S. C. Council Journal, 1692*, 40; *Pa. Mag.*, LIV, 2; *S. C. Hist. & Gen. Mag.*, XII, 147; S. C. Commons Journal, 1712–1716, 229; Case of James Risbee, *et al.* (MS.); *Cal. St. Pap., 1708–1709*, 475.
[47] Westcott, *Philadelphia*, chapter XL; *Pa. Col. Recs.*, I, 527, 530, 531.
[48] *Pa. Statutes*, II, Cap. 78, pp. 186, 357; III, 198; J. Dickinson, Letter Book, I (1698); *Votes Pa. Assembly*, I, ii, 65, 96, 102; II, 48, 126.

Any town the size of Boston would of course have its liquor problem. "Oh that the Drinking Houses in the Town might be under a
laudable regulation," exclaimed Cotton Mather in 1698. "The Town
hath an enormous number of them. I have seen certain Taverns where
the pictures of horrible devourers were hanged out for signs: [Lion,
Bear, etc.] and thought I, 't were well if such signs were not sometimes
too significant." It would be unjust to a man of Mather's intelligence
to suppose that he referred to the inns and taverns properly licensed
and operated and regularly patronized by the better elements in the
town. There were plenty of disorderly houses needing regulation, and
vigilant Selectmen saw that they got it. From 1701 to 1711 the Board
turned down 163 applications for retail and tavern licenses, and con-
scientiously enforced both town ordinances and province liquor laws.
In denying three applicants for licenses in 1705 the Selectmen declared "it to be their Opinion that there are more than enough of such
Lycensed Houses Already, and that the new granting of more will be
of Ill consequence to this Town," and in 1711 they renewed only thirty
of the eighty-one licenses issued the previous year. Nor did the authorities hesitate to revoke the licenses of publicans like George
Peream, because in 1708 the "watch have often observed his house
to be disorderly in ye night perticulerly." Disorders in taverns were
not to be tolerated, as even the aristocrats found. The Justices investi-
gated "Debaucheries at North's the Exchange Tavern" in June, 1708,
and fined Mr. Thomas Banister for disorderly conduct. Sewall and
two other Justices went to "enquire" about "Disorders" at John Wallis'
on February 6, 1714, at 9:35 P.M. "Found much Company. They
refus'd to go away. Said they were there to drink the Queen's Health,
and they had many other Healths to drink. Call'd for more Drink;
drank to me. I took no Notice of Affront to them." Then Mr. John
Maylem and Mr. Brinley put on their hats "to Affront me." After the
Judge had threatened them with prison, Mr. Thomas Banister "ask'd
them to his house & they went away at 10:25 P.M." They all paid the
costs of their insolence in heavy fines in Court a few days later.[49]
Boston was a larger town than Philadelphia, and its tavern problem
correspondingly greater, but here it was very much better managed by
the authorities, and disorders reduced to a minimum.

Many illegal dramshops infested Newport, and authorities were
hard pressed to secure enforcement of tavern and liquor laws. As

[49] Mr. Naymaker paid an additional fine of five shillings for "profane cursing,
. . . saying to . . . Colson, the Constable's Assistant, God dam ye," when he refused to drink the Queen's health. 11 *Bos. Rec. Com.*, 46, 54, 79, 91, 111, 114, 129,
168; 13 *Bos. Rec. Com.*, 70; *Mass. Acts and Resolves*, I, 56, 223, 327, 679; 5 MHS
Colls., VI, 226, 419.

many innkeepers failed to report the presence of strangers at their houses, the Town Meeting in January, 1694, provided for the selection of men "to Search out for all tippling houses and places that Entertain Slaves Servants or persons that reside or come into ye Town without leave of ye Town Council." Prodding by the Assembly in 1698 produced a more determined drive against Newport's illicit houses. In 1707 William Wheeler and Benjamin Williams informed "Against Sevell for Selling Liqr by R[etail] without a License," and the next year Jireh Bull was warned "to Desist from Entertaining of negro slaves att Unreasonable hours of ye Night." The Assembly in 1709 established the provincial license fee at forty shillings, "but that sum being deemed too small in some towns where such houses have great trade and custom, as the creating of many unnecessary houses, which is rather a nuisance than a benefit," each large town was allowed to increase the fee to £10, and to exact a larger fine for operating without a license. The Newport Town Council set the fee for tavern permits at £5, and proceeded to eliminate many undesirable and illicit groggeries.[50]

Charles Town suffered considerably from disreputable taverns, slaves and sailors complicating the problem here as in other towns. In 1693 Governor Ludwell issued a proclamation requiring all taverners to take out licenses from him, because many "have and still doe Keepe very disorderly houses," enticing poor laborers and mariners to the "neglect of their Trades or services." English tavern practice became the law at Charles Town in 1696, and in 1711 licensing was placed under the control of the Receiver General, and all games and sports at inns on the Lord's Day were forbidden. The duty of inspecting all houses and enforcing these rules rested with Church Wardens and town constables.[51]

New York alone seems to have escaped any serious tavern problem. The wholesome quality of its taverns was the result of careful and continuous enforcement of the liquor laws. By 1691 it had been found that "great Inconveniency doth arise by trusting of Saylors whereby they Neglect thier Attendance on board greatly to the hindrance of Trade," and the Corporation passed an ordinance forbidding any publican to detain a sailor or give him credit beyond six shillings. This law was strictly enforced and promptly renewed whenever it expired. Licenses to sell liquor and keep taverns were issued by the Mayor's Court only to persons presenting certificates that they

[50] *Newport T. M. Procs.,* Jan. 31, 1693/4; *Newport T. M. Recs.,* 67; *R. I. Col. Recs.,* III, 350; IV, 64; *Newport T. C. Recs.,* Feb. 3, 1706/7; Sept. 6, 1708; April 18, 1715.
[51] *S. C. Hist. & Gen. Mag.,* VIII, 200; *S. C. Statutes,* II, 77, 85, 113, 363, 396, 487.

were "of good life & Conversation and fit to keep such a house," and a fee of £5 was charged for all such permits.[52]

Improvement in both number and quality of public houses in all towns is the characteristic of tavern development in this period. As an institution the tavern was assuming an ever more vital role in the lives of townsmen of all classes. Its expansion increased the difficulty of enforcing licensing laws and maintaining order, yet, on the whole, the colonial towns succeeded in developing its conveniences and regulating its abuses in a fashion that might well have excited the admiration of observers from English provincial cities.

VI

The average townsman at the beginning of the eighteenth century still found diversion from the daily tasks of making a living, if he followed in the steps of his fathers, through the church, or, if he were more worldly minded, at a tavern. But the aristocrat of this period was beginning to indulge in more sophisticated forms of amusement, forms which he occasionally shared with members of the middle and lower classes. The elaborate recreations of the few required both wealth and leisure, which only these larger towns afforded to any degree. In this period, therefore, the divergence became greater between rural sports enjoyed in countryside and village and more distinctly urban forms of entertainment.

New York was undoubtedly the gayest of colonial towns. The hard philosophy of inherited religious traditions placed no restraint upon the leisure of Gothamites; indeed, their amusements and pleasures were carefully fostered by the royal governors, who sought in every way to make life there enjoyable and more like that of the homeland. Dutch and English were alike much given to outdoor exercise. In winter skating and sleighriding were freely indulged. Madam Sarah Knight, visiting Manhattan in 1704, drove out one winter day with friends, and noted that they met "50 or 60 sleys." In other seasons fowling and fishing were very popular among gentlemen. The Bowery, three miles from town, was a famous center of recreation, where Madam Knight found they did not "spare for any diversion the place affords, and sociable to a degree." Among all classes, attendance at court trials was a favorite source of entertainment. In October, 1697, the Common Council discussed the coming trials of seven criminals, "to which it is Supposed great numbers of People will Resorte Insomuch that itt is fear'd the City Hall will not be of Sufficient Strength to Containe them." To guard against accident, they called

[52] *N. Y. M. C. C.*, I, 100, 178, 223, 372; III, 87, 91; IV, 207, 314; *N. Y. Col. Laws,* I, 345, 438, 680, 866.

in two carpenters and a bricklayer, who fortified the floor with "six Studds and a Planke." The Queen's birthday, Gunpowder Day, and news of a British victory were always publicly celebrated. The Corporation observed the great victory at Vigo in 1703 by treating the populace to a huge bonfire, and ten gallons of wine and a barrel of beer with which to drink the Queen's health. On such occasions householders were requested to "make a public Illumination . . . as a further demonstration of their Joy." [53]

Life for the gentry was becoming more gay. Race meetings were held regularly twice a year at Hempstead, riding was always popular, and as wealth increased coaching came more into vogue. With the introduction of the coffee house after 1700 several clubs sprang up in imitation of the prevailing London fashion. Among the most active were the "Irish Club" and the "French Club," both of which met almost nightly for dinner at a tavern. In like manner the Fort served as a social club for army and navy officers. Governor Nanfan issued a license in 1699 to an actor, Richard Hunter, who had been at "great expense in providing persons and necessary's in order to the acting of Plays in this Citty." Five years later Tony Aston came up from Charles Town to spend the winter in New York, "acting, writing, courting fighting." These performances were in all probability given at Fort George for the benefit of free-spending British officials and a few merchant aristocrats. The townsfolk as a whole were as yet unready for such innovations, and secured an order from the Council in 1709 forbidding "Play acting and prize fighting." [54]

The Reverend Mr. John Sharpe, chaplain at the Fort from 1704 to 1713, kept a diary intimately recording the social activities of a New York gentleman in these years. He chronicles a continual round of dinners, teas, coach and "Shese" rides, garden parties and receptions. One day he is entertained "very splendidly at Captain Roches"; on another, he and Lord Cornbury are tendered a banquet at George Willis' Tavern by the Church Wardens. In January, 1710, he frequently "rid out" in a "Slay" and "Dined at Bass Bowary" with gentlemen and ladies. Life in summertime was even more delightful. Interspersed between frequent fishing excursions were the occasions when the parson "went a shooting after dinner at the Mayors." Most enjoyable of all was an invitation to dine in "the ffort, at night at the fighting cocks." Life was certainly not boring for the gentlemen of Manhattan. [55]

[53] Journal of Madam Knight, 56, 57; Krout, Annals of American Sport, 13; N. Y. M. C. C., II, 15, 227, 231, 257.
[54] Singleton, Social New York, 267; Stokes, Iconography, IV, 413, 447, 486; Fontaine, "Journal," 296, 298; Cal. Council Mins., 227.
[55] Pa. Mag., XL, 263, 274, 283, 286, 395, 420.

The greater wealth of the Bostonians made available to them a variety of amusements, and the rich especially had considerable leisure to apply to divertisement. Among all classes gunning was popular, and as accidents frequently resulted the General Court in 1710 forbade shooting at marks or pigeons within the town. Outdoor parties and excursions were much in vogue. "I carry my two sons and three daughters in the Coach to Danford, the Turks Head at Dorchester," wrote Sewall in 1699; "eat Cheese, drunk Beer and Cider, and came homeward." Commencement Day at Cambridge always brought the gentry with their coaches and calashes together for a grand outing after the graduates had propounded their "Quaestiones." Boston Common was the scene of a general town revel on annual training days. Humble folk participated in shooting at the mark, foot races and beer, and watched the "many Gentlemen and Gentlewomen dine in Tents." Some time after 1713 a bowling green was opened, "where all Gentlemen, Merchants and others, that have a Mind to Recreate themselves, shall be well accommodated." Horse races were run for handsome prizes at Cambridge and at Rumney Marsh in 1715 and 1717. Fashionable Bostonians shared the passion of their English cousins for "taking the waters," and increasingly resorted to the Lynn Red Spring, especially after its purchase by Dr. Caspar von Crowninscheldt in 1700. Among its eminent patrons was President Leverett of Harvard. Actual cure for disorders could be better obtained in town. Wait Winthrop in 1715 wrote of being "very much relieved by a strong minerall water here, that I think is better than Linn Spring, or any of the rest." [56]

The celebration by the governors and their associates of royal birthdays, victories, and Christmas was a notable departure from the Puritan tradition. Sewall was impressed in spite of himself when the Town House was illuminated on November 4, 1697, to signalize the birthday of King William. At eight in the evening Messrs. Brattle and Newman "let fly their fireworks from Cotton-Hill." But the Judge was thoroughly disgusted at the observance of Queen Anne's anniversary in 1708 at the Town House, where hardly anything was "professedly done . . . but drinking Healths." More somber were the lamentations of Cotton Mather in 1711 when he learned of "a Number of young people, of both Sexes, belonging, many of them, to my Flock, who have had on Christmas-night, this last Week, a Frolick, a revelling Feast, and Ball." [57]

The aristocrats gave large and elaborate dinners. Governor Dud-

[56] 5 MHS *Colls.*, V, 413, 492; VI, 9, 190, 417; 11 *Bos. Rec. Com.*, 111; *News Letter*, May 3, 1714; Aug. 29, 1715; Nov. 8, 1717; Lewis and Newhall, *Lynn*, I, 71; 6 MHS *Colls.*, V, 312 n.
[57] 5 MHS *Colls.*, V, 462; VI, 215; 7 MHS *Colls.*, VIII, 146.

ley often dined the Council and the House of Representatives, and in 1709 gave a banquet for them at the Green Dragon. Wealthy families entertained lavishly, and even the "Four Churches" came around finally to "treat the Ministers and Councillors in the Town at the Exchange Tavern." The finest parties of Boston in this period were those given by Colonel Hutchinson after the marriages of his daughters. Sewall was "not ask'd" to the first of these, but at the second he thoroughly enjoyed himself; "Had Musick, Cake and Cheese to eat there, and bring away." In contrast with these gala occasions were the daily recreations of townspeople. Sewall loved to sit with a friend and "humble him at a game of Checkers," while Governor Dudley called and "smoke[d] a pipe with my wife at night." [58]

Young people would dance, despite the disapproval of their elders, and George Brownell catered to all the needs of Boston youth. At his house in Wing's Lane in 1713 he taught "Dancing, Treble Violin, Flute, Spinnet, &c. Also English Quilting and French Quilting, Imbroidery, . . . and several other works." Mr. Enstone, organist at King's Chapel, failed to conceal his "School of Dancing and Musick" by giving instruction in needlework, and temporarily ran afoul of the Selectmen in February, 1715. Within two years, however, he was advertising dancing lessons "taught by a true and easier method than has been heretofore." [59]

A design to "have a Play acted in the Council Chamber" was frustrated in 1714 by Isaac Addington and Samuel Sewall, and Miles Burroughs, from Newport, had been forbidden in 1711 to expose to the public view "his Art of Legerdermaine or Subtle Craft, and taking money of many young persons and others . . . for the Sight thereof." The next year the Selectmen instructed Boston's representatives to the General Court to procure an act against such shows because of their "Tendency to corrupt Youth," but the attempt failed, and Bostonians were henceforth allowed to view all varieties of traveling mountebanks. The "inferior sort" were fascinated in 1715 by "The Italian Matchean, or Moving Picture, wherein are to be seen, Wind Mills and Water Mills moving round, Ships Sayling on the Sea, and several curious Figures, very delightful to behold," which was exhibited daily during March by Nehemiah Partridge "for Twelve Pence a piece." Country yokels in town on market days in 1720 must have gaped in wonderment at "The Lyon, being the King of Beasts, and

[58] 5 MHS *Colls.*, VI, 126, 203, 241, 266, 385; 6 MHS *Colls.*, I, 417.

[59] Master Richard Hall of Barbados attended dancing school at Boston. In 1718 his grandmother wrote that "Richard minds . . . his Dancing. He is a brisk Child & grows very Cute and wont wear his new coat yt was made for him." The next year his sister Sarah, aged eight, gave a dancing party. *News Letter*, Mar. 1, 1712/13; April 23, 1716; *Bos. Gaz.*, Sept. 19, 1720; 11 *Bos. Rec. Com.*, 221, 236; Earle, *Child Life*, 87, 101.

the only one of his Kind in America," kept at Mrs. Martha Adams' in the South End. "Sinful inhabitants" of all classes began by 1698 to patronize fortune tellers, despite clerical attempts to discourage these "dangerous transgressors." It must certainly have been his own fault that Dr. William Douglass found winter in Boston "a dull dead time of the year." [60]

In the other towns life was more restricted, and facilities for amusement less developed. Philadelphia remained under the control of the Provincial Council and the County Court until 1701, which meant the prevalence of Quaker discipline and the rejection of sports and amusements as sinful and worldly. Throughout the period the Corporation consisted largely of Friends, and while the Quakers never made up more than half of the population, their influence was instrumental in preventing the townsfolk from deriving much pleasure from life other than "going to Meeting." All "rude or riotous" sports were forbidden by an act of 1700, a law so severe as to be disallowed by the Privy Council in 1705. The Assembly passed another in 1711, directed against stage-plays, fireworks and gambling. Occasionally this law was violated by some non-Quaker like John Simes, innkeeper, whom the Grand Jury indicted for keeping a disorderly house which was a "nursery to Deboch ye Inhabitants," because he permitted John Smith and Edward James to enter his place "being Maskt, or Disgis'd in Women's apparell." Masquerading, it seems, was against the "law of God . . . and ye Law of Nature." Similarly, all horse racing was stopped. But just as amusements forbidden in London sprang up at Southwark across the river, so did Society Hill, just south of the Quaker city, harbor gambling and bull baiting after 1712.[61]

Twice a year, at the Fairs, foot racing and games were tolerated. At other times, riding, swimming, skating, fishing and fowling were the recreations lawfully open to men, while ladies devoted themselves to needle- and fancy-work. The Front Street nabobs made of their dinners great state occasions, and lavishly provided delectable dishes and imported wines for their discriminating guests. Moreover, not to be outdone by Bostonians, the Quaker gentry began to frequent mineral springs. "Not two miles from the metropolis," wrote Gabriel Thomas, "are purging waters . . . as good as Epsom." The town's gallants had a pleasant custom of going about the streets on moonlight nights to chat with the maidens as they sat on their porches,—from which they acquired the sobriquet, lunarians. Signs of a turning from prim-

[60] 6 MHS Colls., II, 29; 11 Bos. Rec. Com., 172, 239; News Letter, Mar. 14, 1714/15; Bos. Gaz., Oct. 10, 1720; Mather, Magnalia, I, 99; Colden Papers, I, 114.
[61] Pa. Statutes, II, 4, 360; Ancient Recs. Phila., 9, 15; Pubs. Gen. Soc. Pa., VII, 73.

itive simplicity became noticeable after 1705, and the Yearly Meeting found it necessary to caution young Friends against "going to or being in any way concerned in plays, games, lotteries, music and dancing." The great difficulty was that Anglicans and others condoned such practices. The "facetious Mr. Staples" opened a dancing school at this time, and a fencing academy also flourished under the patronage of Governor Evans. Wicked Sir William Keith wrote to Colden in 1718 that "Mr. Trent & two or three more of your acquaintance . . . meet at the Tavern where we play a sober game of whisk." In 1719 the Meeting again resolved "That such be dealt with as run races, either on horseback or on foot, laying wagers, or use any gaming or needless and vain sports and pastimes for our time passeth swiftly away, and our pleasures and delight ought to be in the law of God." [62]

At Charles Town the common people regaled themselves in their spare time with many of the old English sports and games. In 1712 the Assembly was forced to decree that none of these might be indulged near taverns on Sunday. Perhaps the most popular sport was cockfighting, which brought together men of all classes and afforded opportunities for wagers on the outcome. The tense political situation of the 1700's ushered in America's first women's Club, founded in 1707, shortly after 170 male Dissenters had organized a political club, and while the town's only accused witch was still in prison. "What is most singular," reported a shocked and grieved parson, "the women of the town are turned politicians also and here have a club where they meet weekly among themselves, but not without falling out with one another. . . ." Although some of the wealthy Charlestonians soon purchased plantations and introduced the gay and easy life known in Barbados, the bulk of the townsmen in 1700 lived quiet lives, retiring in winter at seven o'clock at night, and an hour later in summer. On this schedule families dined at noon, and young ladies, receiving their beaux at three, expected them to withdraw by six. Signs of change appeared after 1703. Tony Aston, as he tells us, arrived in that year from Jamaica, "full of Lice, Shame, Poverty, Nakedness and Hunger; turn'd Player and Poet and wrote one Play on the Subject of the Country." But it was to be some years before another player appeared in the Southern metropolis. [63]

At Newport, still less urbanized than the other towns, hunting, fishing, and bowling on the green continued to be popular recreations among middling and inferior sorts. In the summer wealthy

[62] Watson, *Annals of Philadelphia*, I, 489; Scharf and Westcott, *Philadelphia*, I, 153, 156; II, 853, 863; Hart, *Contemporaries*, II, 76; Mulhern, *Education in Pennsylvania*, 59; *Colden Papers*, I, 94.
[63] *S. C. Statutes*, II, 396; Krout, *Annals of American Sport*, 23; Wallace, *South Carolina*, I, 177; Howe, *Presbyterian Church*, 199; Sonneck, *Early Opera*, 5.

merchants were enabled to vary their elaborate dinner entertainments by an occasional "frolic" or picnic on Goat Island, or in the "Woods part of the town." Most recreational activities, however, focused in the inns. At Mrs. Bright's Exchange Tavern one would have found something to do in the "large Garden" or at the "Billiard Table and nine Pin Alley." It was perhaps at this hostelry that in 1712 Miles Burroughs performed his "Art of Legerdermaine," for a crowd of gaping youths, before leaving for Boston on the recommendation of the Town Council.[64]

Life in the colonial towns from 1690 to 1720 was far more pleasant than it had been in former years. Wealth and leisure commanded new forms of entertainment, and although attempts to introduce refinements like the theater were defeated by the prevalent belief of its immorality and frivolity, there were signs that even this prejudice was soon to break down. At Boston and New York society was gay, and the recreations and amusements offered superior to those available in any English city except London. Indeed, one cannot escape the conclusion that for an Englishman residence in one of these colonial capitals could have been no more of an exile than banishment from the metropolis. The Corporation of Bristol advertised in the *London Gazette* for July 2, 1702, that "acting plays, interludes, or exposing poppets," in that city were henceforth forbidden. Cockfights, suburban excursions and revels were the only diversions allowed the common people, and in 1716 the constables of each ward were ordered to enforce the law of 1700 suppressing "all gaming houses, billiard tables, and other unlawful games." Even fencing teachers were jailed as "rogues and vagabonds." Outside of feasting and drinking, the wealthy burghers had only their Assembly-Room, whither they might repair in winter for dancing and "whisk" from five to nine o'clock in the evening.[65]

VII

By 1720 some provision for public education, either secular or religious, had been made in every town, and a real extension of educational facilities had taken place. A notable fact was the large number of private schoolmasters to be found in the little seaports, catering to the cultural needs of that rapidly growing group who could afford the luxury of education. In addition, there is no doubt that provincial English cities were far less adequately equipped to provide elementary education for the humble elements of their citizenry than were these colonial towns.

[64] *News Letter*, Mar. 17, 1718.
[65] Latimer, *Bristol in the Eighteenth Century*, 26, 116.

Boston continued its excellent educational work begun in the seventeenth century. No where else did public schools even approach the high standard maintained in the Bay town. The elementary writing school founded in Queen Street in 1684 was well conducted by its able master, John Cole, until 1714 when Jacob Sheafe assumed charge. In 1700 a writing school was established at the North End, and in 1720 the South Writing School appeared to satisfy the needs of the other side of the town. Expansion of the North End also led to creation of the North Grammar School, which opened with Recompense Wadsworth as master in 1713.[66]

The apex of the system was the Boston Latin School, presided over by Ezekiel Cheever until his death in 1708, and a constant object of pride and care by the town. In 1710 the Selectmen informed the Town Meeting that in some European schools "Scollars p'haps in the compass of one year, have attained to a Competent Proficiency . . . in Latin," while "many hundreds" of Boston youths spend "two, three or four years more at the Latin School" with small benefit. The Meeting generally agreed with their proposal that "some more easie and delightful methodes be there . . . put in practice." Accordingly, Nathaniel Williams, Cheever's successor, bestirred himself to devise a new method, which, though it does not appear to have been either easy or particularly delightful, was so thorough that it is no wonder that students who passed through the school were well grounded in Latin and Greek.[67]

The excellence of the Boston schools may be traced directly to the interest all citizens shared in them. Until 1710 the Selectmen carefully inspected all schools, after which time "five Gentlemen, of Liberal Education," were appointed to make periodic visits. Prior to this the clergy had shared in the work of inspection, and the change seemed to the disappointed Increase Mather like "Contempt upon . . . all the Ministers in Boston."[68] Lay control proved very effective, however, in caring for the five schoolhouses, in maintaining the standards of instruction, and in overseeing the wise expenditure of funds raised by taxation.

While the town provided excellent free schools, many of the aristocrats preferred to have their sons and daughters privately educated. For little tots there were the dame schools. On April 27, 1691, tiny Joseph Sewall, aged three, was sent "To School to Capt. Townsend's

---

[66] 8 *Bos. Rec. Com.*, 90, 91, 110, 118, 132, 139, 143; 11 *Bos. Rec. Com.*, 4, 202; 7 *Bos. Rec. Com.*, 215, 240; *N. E. Hist. & Gen. Reg.*, XIII, 260.

[67] Stiles, *Literary Diary*, I, 228; 8 *Bos. Rec. Com.*, 78; Col. Soc. Mass. *Trans.*, XXVII, 23. Cf. Morison, *Puritan Pronaos*, 101.

[68] *Mass. Acts and Resolves*, I, 681; 8 *Bos. Rec. Com.*, 65; 6 MHS *Colls.*, I, 391: 7 MHS *Colls.*, VII, 304.

Mothers, his Cousin Jane accompanying him, carried his Horn-book."
Three years later he was transferred to the care of Mrs. Anne Kay,
"a good Woman, and a good School-Mistress." Over twenty masters
conducted the many private writing, grammar and Latin schools in
the town. From 1692 to 1699 Peter Burr kept a school to which
came both boys and girls, not only from Boston, but from places
as far distant as Plymouth. Out-of-town children generally boarded
with their teachers. In 1706 Mistress Mary Turfrey announced that
"at the South End of Boston, [she] Intends to board young Gentlewomen: If any Gentlemen desires their Daughters should be under
her Education: They may please agree with her on Terms." Benjamin
Wadsworth, later president of Harvard College, eked out his income
by boarding children attending school in Boston. In his account book
he carefully recorded all their expenditures, even to two pence to one
little fellow for "lickrish." [69]

By 1718 children were coming from as far as the West Indies to
attend the justly famous Boston schools. In that year Richard Hall,
younger brother of the Barbados Admiralty judge, entered the Latin
School. Both master and usher were "desir'd to treat him with the
highest Tenderness." He lived with his grandmother, Madam Colman, who later wrote that "He has grown a good boy and minds his
School and Latin. . . . I delivered Richard's Master, Mr. Williams,
25 lbs. cocoa." No wonder Richard got on! In 1719 his sister Sarah,
aged eight, arrived at Boston with her maid to attend a private school,
and Madam Colman found her less tractable than young Richard.
She raised a fuss because she had to drink water with her meals,
and picked up bag and baggage and went to live at Mr. Bining's, where
her maid might have a separate room. Three months later her suffering grandmother reported, "Sally wont go to school nor to church
and wants a new muff and a great many other things she dont need."
Sally finally gave in to Boston ways, learning to "sew, floure, write,"
and became famous as "ye best Dancer of any in ye town." [70]

These private schools offered instruction in a wide range of special
subjects. John Green boarded youths who wished to learn "Astronomy,
Reading, Writing, Arithmetick, Merchants Accompts, Geometry, Trigonometry, Gauging, and Navigation." George Brownell, the most
versatile of colonial private schoolmasters, was a universal scholar.
At his boarding school he taught writing, ciphering, dancing, violin, spinet, and all sorts of needlework and embroidery. His illus-

[69] About twenty-five per cent of Burr's scholars were girls, some of whom studied
Latin. 5 MHS Colls., V, 344, 411, 436; Burr, Commonplace Book (MS.); Lloyd
Papers, I, 223; Col. Soc. Mass. Trans., XXVII, 130–142; News Letter, Sept. 9,
1706; Wadsworth, Diary (MS.).
[70] Richard used twelve pairs of shoes annually, and lost "12 hankers. His way is
to tie Knottys at one end & beat ye Boys with them." Sally's bill for dancing les
sons was £2 per quarter; Richard's, £7 for five quarters. Earle, Child Life, 86, 101.

trious pupil, Benjamin Franklin, remembered that "Mr. George Brown-ell . . . was a skillful master, and succeeded very well in his profession by employing gentle means only, and such as were calculated to encourage his scholars." [71]

At Philadelphia between 1690 and 1700 the Friends' Meeting developed a public educational system which provided elementary, vocational and cultural instruction. The school enjoyed the able leadership of George Keith until his religious differences with the Quakers led to his resignation and the elevation of his usher, Thomas Makin, to the head-mastership. Makin apparently presided over the department of classical studies, and Pastorius, till his resignation and succession by John Cadwallader in 1701, over the "practical." In 1699 several "mistrisses" were employed to aid in the instruction of girls and very young boys. In 1701, in response to petitions from the Philadelphia Meeting for a "public school . . . , where all children and servants, male and female, whose parents, guardians and masters, be willing to subject them to the rules and orders . . . shall . . . be received and admitted, taught and instructed, the rich at reasonable rates, and the poor to be maintained and schooled for nothing," the school received legal status in the form of a charter from William Penn, authorizing it to give instruction in "good literature," and in "languages, arts & Sciences." After the issuing of this charter the school moved from the Friends' Meeting House to a new and well-equipped building. It was maintained by voluntary subscription and by legacies from Friends, and seems always to have enjoyed the use of sufficient funds.[72]

Little Israel Pemberton attended the Friends' School in 1698, but did not like the severity of Master Pastorius, who, when Master Makin was away, took that "opportunity to thrash" him. His father thereupon withdrew the lad, and sent him to another school, where he was "sett . . . to learn all Arithmetick de novo," Latin, and "ye Rules of Practice (ye only Rules for business)." Israel's new school was doubtless a private institution. Gabriel Thomas reported in 1697 that there were at Philadelphia "several Good Schools of Learning for Youth, in order to the attainment of Arts and Sciences, as also Reading, Writing, etc." The excellent opportunities for schooling of all sorts in the town inspired some more of Judge Thomas Holme's atrocious but informing verse: [73]

> Here are schools of divers sorts,
> To which our youth daily resorts,
> Good women, who do very well
> Bring little ones to read and spell,

---

[71] *News Letter*, Mar. 28, 1709; Mar. 1, 1712/13; Aug. 27, 1716.
[72] Woody, *Quaker Education*, 46, 49, 53; *Pa. Col. Recs.*, I, 449, 499, 529, 531; Mulhern, *Education in Pennsylvania*, 33, 59; Learned, *Pastorius*, 166.
[73] *Pa. Mag.*, XVII, 369; Learned, *Pastorius*, 174, 189 n.

Which fits them for writing, and then,
Here's men to bring them to their pen,
And to instruct and make them quick
In all sorts of Arithmetick.

Other schools, parochial and private, soon sprang up. Anglicans founded a parish school in 1698, conducted by various masters until the Bishop of London sent over William Skinner to have official charge of it in 1707. In 1700 the Reverend Eric Biork of the Swedish church established a school with "an able teacher." Young ladies, in addition to the formal elementary and secondary training provided at the William Penn Charter School, could be privately instructed in the various feminine arts. "We sent our Magdalene," wrote the Reverend Andreas Sandel of Wicaco in 1715, "to the sewing school of Mrs. Andros in Philadelphia, and to board at Benj. Morgan ['s], where we had to pay six shillings per week, and ten pence for the schooling." Two years later Magdalene was withdrawn from Mrs. Andros' and "taken to Dr. Monckton['s wife] to stay there some years to learne serving, &c." What with the Friends' public school and the many private agencies, it is probable that young girls, especially of the lower classes, received a better education at Philadelphia than elsewhere in the colonies.[74]

Through their Town Meeting, the inhabitants of Newport cared actively for the town's educational needs. In 1697 more lands were set apart for support of the town school, and John Yelbrow required, as part of his duties as schoolmaster, to accept "three or four Orphans to be learnt . . . on free cost," before he might receive full income from this new endowment. In 1708 a new schoolhouse was erected at "ye publick charge." Schoolmasters at Newport had to be their own janitors. In addition to his teaching, Thomas Wakeing was instructed in 1711 to "Cause to be Swept and Kept-Clean all the said School House both above and below," and to "take Care of Opening and Sheting the Windows and window shutters." The town seems to have changed masters every two or three years, which might imply either the inadequacy of their teaching or their dissatisfaction with the position. On the other hand, schoolmasters in the early eighteenth century were everywhere a peripatetic lot, and frequently taught only as a filler-in between more lucrative positions.[75]

A distinct advance in education at Newport came in 1700 with the granting of James Galloway's petition to conduct a Latin school "in

[74] Mulhern, *Education in Pennsylvania*, 74; Dorr, *Christ Church*, 37, 47; Westcott, *Philadelphia*, chapter XLVI; *Pa. Mag.*, XXX, 449.
[75] *Newport T. M. Procs.*, April 28, 1697; Jan. 31, 1704/5; May 2, 1709; *Newport T. M. Recs.*, 96, 128, 136, 166; *Newport T. C. Recs.*, Mar. 7, 1710/11; May 3, Sept., 1714; Richardson Coll., 972: 174.

the two small Roomes" in the town schoolhouse. To render his work more comfortable, the Town Council ordered a fireplace built for these rooms at public expense, and at the same time the Meeting chose a committee of four to secure an additional master to "teach the arts of writeing and arithmetick" at the school. Thus Newport provided and supported all branches of education then in vogue. Dr. John Clarke at his death left some real estate to the town, the income to be used to provide schooling for children of the poor. For many years this gift was in the hands of trustees who badly mismanaged it, but in 1720 the Assembly turned it over to the Town Council, with power "to redress and punish all frauds, breaches of trust, and mismanagement." [76]

Throughout this period the Newport Friends sporadically maintained a school of their own in order to avoid sending their children to town schools, "where they are Taught ye corrupt ways, manners, ffashions and Tongue of ye world." In 1711 they bought land for a schoolhouse. There were also in Newport, as in other towns, several private schools. In 1695 Joseph Lloyd attended one of these, paying 2s. 4d. for his mistress' "yearly feast" at the close of the term. John Hammett, later town schoolmaster, was conducting a private school in 1707, and was granted £4 by the Meeting because he had accepted some poor children gratis. [77]

Charles Town was the last of the towns to acquire educational facilities. The South Carolina Assembly made its first move for schools with an act of 1694, and in 1696 passed a second law creating five commissioners to receive gifts for educational purposes and apply them where needed. They could also draw on the provincial treasury up to £10 annually for the support of a schoolmaster. Congregationalists had their own school, taught by Matthew Bee for several years before he succumbed to yellow fever in 1699. Wealthier inhabitants provided for the private education of their children. In 1700 John Lawson reported that "Their cohabiting in a Town has drawn to them People of most Sciences whereby they have Tutors amongst them that educate their Youth a-la-mode." The custom of sending aristocratic young Charlestonians like the Pinckneys to school in London also began in this period. [78]

In 1710 the Assembly again took up the need for a free school at Charles Town, and appointed commissioners "for founding, erect-

[76] Newport T. C. Recs., Oct. 2, Nov. 6, 1710; Newport T. M. Recs., 145; R. I. Col. Recs., IV, 253.

[77] Klain, Educational Acts of New England Quakers, 7, 34, 36; Lloyd Papers, I, 140, 143; Newport T. M. Recs., 131.

[78] S. C. Statutes, II, 78, 116; 5 MHS Colls., VI, 12; Lawson, New Voyage to Carolina, 3; Foster, History of Education in South Carolina, I, 3; Ravenel, Eliza Pinckney, 86.

ing, governing, ordering and visiting a School," whose teachers were to be members of the Church of England and capable of giving instruction in Latin, Greek and mathematics. In spite of several money bequests the school had not been built by 1712, and the Assembly's educational policy was uncertain and vacillating. About this time James Douglas was appointed master of the "Free School in Charles Town" at a salary of £20 a year, and curricular emphasis shifted from the classics to such subjects as mathematics, surveying, navigation and merchants' accounts. This change was perhaps a result of the opening of a Latin School by the Reverend Mr. William Gay, acting under auspices of the Society for the Propagation of the Gospel, in 1711. Though not a free institution, this St. Philip's Parish school educated a limited number of poor students every year without charge. Its chief object being to produce gentlemen, the emphasis was upon manners and a liberal training.[79] If one could afford it, a child could by 1713 receive as good an education at Charles Town as in any northern center, but development of public facilities was here retarded by the absence of local authority and the haphazard attention given by the Assembly to the problem.

Residents of Manhattan exhibited less concern about education than did their contemporaries in other towns. In 1691 no provision existed for any form of public schooling. Mayor and Common Council took no action until 1702, when they secured the introduction in the Assembly of a bill providing for a "Free School" at New York, passage of which was at least partially owing to the interest of Lord Cornbury. It provided for the appointment of a master, licensed by the Bishop of London, to teach children of French and Dutch as well as of English parentage. The Corporation, being "of the Opinion" that they could find in the city no one qualified to teach, urged the Governor to secure from England a "Person of good Learning of pious Life and Vertuous Conversation of English Extraction and mild temper." As one George Muirson was passing through the town on his way to Albany in 1704, he was stopped by Cornbury and induced to teach at New York, "because," wrote the Governor, "when he arrived here there were several youths going to be sent to Boston, wch I thought would be better to prevent." Muirson lasted only a few months, perhaps not being of a sufficiently "mild temper," and the Corporation appointed Andrew Clarke in his place. Though at one time the Latin School contained over thirty scholars, it had died out by 1710. No further efforts towards public education were made

[79] That pupils were ready for this advanced school implies the prior acquisition of elementary education. *S. C. Statutes,* II, 342, 376, 389; Foster, *Education in South Carolina,* I, 25, 32; McCrady, *South Carolina under Proprietary Government,* 702. Cf. *S. C. Hist. & Gen. Mag.,* XXXII, 35.

until 1720. In that year the Corporation paid £10 to a private school-master, William Huddlestone, "as a present . . . for his Teaching Severall poor Children to Read. And ORDERED that this be not brought into President." [80]

The youth of New York learned their letters in these years at church schools, or, if their parents could afford it, at private institutions. The old Dutch elementary school flourished at this time under the leadership of Abraham de Lanoy, who usually gave instruction to a class of about forty-four boys and a dozen girls, averaging ten years of age. Reading and writing were taught, but the primary aim was to train children for participation in the Reformed Church rather than to educate them for life. Sometime before 1702 William Huddlestone conducted a school that was in part supported by Trinity Church and began in 1706 to receive contributions from the S. P. G. In 1709 the Society formally made Huddlestone its schoolmaster at New York, with a salary of £10, "upon condition that he shall teach 40 poor children gratis." This was a free school, and it was said that the master never refused poor children who were sent to him, although in 1717 "moor poor were daily pressing," and in 1719 he had fifty-one pauper youths under his tutelage. Another Episcopal enterprise was the charity school for Negroes, founded by Mr. Vesey in 1703, and conducted for many years in a room at Trinity Church by Elias Neau.[81]

In 1717 the Reverend Robert Jenney opened a grammar school with thirty-five boys, "the chief of the English, Dutch & French," but received slight encouragement because aristocratic families seem to have preferred to send their sons to one of the many fashionable private schools which flourished at New York throughout the period. Between 1690 and 1720 at least sixteen such were being conducted, the majority in the homes of their masters, although David Vilant was allowed in 1696–1697 to "Keep School in the publick City Hall." Among them, they seem to have enjoyed the patronage of most of the "better sort." In 1708 Mr. Huddlestone wrote to the S. P. G. that four of these masters were then teaching seventy-six pupils, and when his school became a free institution he complained of losing nearly all of his sixty-odd students to the private masters, so that in 1710 he had left only "8 paying boys." [82]

Outside of the city there was almost no education available, and children of great landowners had to be sent into town for their school-

<hr/>

[80] *N. Y. Col. Laws.*, I, 516; *N. Y. M. C. C.*, II, 213, 215, 291; III, 63, 225; Kemp, *Support of Schools in New York*, 71.

[81] Kilpatrick, *Dutch Schools*, 147, 150; *Eccles. Recs. N. Y.*, II, 1233; Kemp, *Support of Schools*, 74, 80; Stokes, *Iconography*, IV, 450, 486; Wilson, *Memorial History of New York*, II, 69.

[82] *N. Y. M. C. C.*, II, 21; N. Y. Hist. Soc. *Colls., 1885*, 54–100; Kemp, *Support of Schools*, 77, 81, 83.

ing. This situation led thinking men to advocate the institution of superior schools for New York. The Reverend Mr. John Sharpe, who in intervals between dinners and cockfights was an able observer, thus summed up the educational situation at New York in his "Proposals" of 1713.[83]

> It is usual at this time to send Children from Albany and Esopus 100 & 150 miles distant to New York to be taught English and it would no doubt increase the number of such if they could at the same time have the opportunity of learning Latine &c, . . . The City is so conveniently Situated for Trade and the Genius of the People are so inclined to merchandise, that they generally seek no other Education for their Children than writing and Arithmetick. So that letters must in a manner be forced upon them without their seeking, but against their assent.

Absence of documents in several of the towns makes it difficult to assess with any degree of finality the amount of education actually provided by the apprentice system. In every town boys and girls were still bound out to learn trades, and as such received manual training at the least. Newport indentures generally called for instruction in reading and writing, as did the laws of Massachusetts, and at Charles Town, where English precedents were almost slavishly followed, it seems highly probable that at least the indentures of poor children bound out by the Vestry carried the Elizabethan provisions for reading and writing. At Philadelphia the Friends' School was open to all poor children, servants and apprentices. At Boston in 1720 Samuel Grainger advertised an evening school for children "whose Business won't permit 'em to attend the usual School Hours," where he taught "Grammar, . . . Arithmetick in a precise and practical Method, Merchant's Accompts, and the Mathematicks."[84]

At New York nearly every indenture called for some measure of instruction in reading and writing, and generally where such provisions were omitted the apprentice seems already to have received an elementary education. In 1693 Frances Champion was apprenticed as a house servant to Elizabeth Farmer, who agreed to "Instruct the said Francis to Reade and to teach and Instruct her in Spining, Sewing, Knitting or any other manner of housewifery." John Macgregory, aged twelve, went to learn shoemaking with Robert Mason, who was also to "teach the Sd. apprentice to Read and Write," and in 1700 John Horne was to be instructed to "read and Write perfectly the English

---

[83] A genius for trade, however, was common to all colonial towns. Kemp, *Support of Schools*, 67; N. Y. Hist. Soc. *Colls., 1880*, 333.

[84] *News Letter*, Mar. 28, 1709; Mar. 1, 1713; April 27, 1716; Col. Soc. Mass. *Trans.*, XXVII, 140; *S. C. Statutes*, II, 593; Woody, *Quaker Education*, 47; *Pa. Col. Recs.*, I, 449; *Bos. Gaz.*, Mar. 7, April 4, 1720.

Tongue" by the master to whom he was indentured. Jacob Coursen's father bound him out to William Bogaert in 1701, and paid for his two winters' "Night Scooling and his said Master Shall Allow him two halfe Winters Schooling." Night schools for apprentices became very popular after 1700, and indentures frequently included arrangements for apprentices to attend them after their daily work was done.[85] If New York was typical of colonial towns, and I am inclined to believe that it was, far more children received their elementary education by this system than by any other.

In conclusion, it remains only to point out the advances made by each town in providing educational facilities for its youth in this period. The public schools of Philadelphia and Newport were superior to those of Bristol and Norwich in England, and even Charles Town would have made a favorable showing by comparison. New York, alone, was below the English level at this time, while no town on the Continent or in the British Isles could exhibit so fine a school system as Boston.[86]

VIII

Several factors in the period 1690 to 1720 contributed to a definite intellectual advance in the towns. Most important among these were the new wealth and leisure in the hands of the aristocratic few, better educational facilities in all of the towns, and the increasingly secular attitude towards life in urban communities. The advance was not spectacular, but it was none the less real; it was steady, and fairly well distributed throughout the population.

None of the colonial towns, and no English provincial city, compared with Boston in cultural attainments in this period. Direct contact by sea with Europe kept Bostonians ever alive to the intellectual currents of the age. After the blight of "Doleful Witchcraft" and the loss of their political influence, members of the clergy turned increasingly to social and intellectual pursuits. Cotton Mather produced his *Magnalia Christi Americana* in 1702, dabbled in deism, interested himself in the collection of scientific curiosities, communicated with the Royal Society and was elected to membership in that august body. Mather was only the foremost of an able group. Nothing is more striking than the success of Boston clergy, after their defeat, in adapting themselves to the spirit of the times. The preachers were far in advance of most of their auditors, especially in matters of science. When Cot-

---

[85] N. Y. Hist. Soc. *Colls.*, *1885*, 578, 581, 589, 590, 593, 600; *1909*, 113, 114, 115, 118, 122, 130, 132, 135.
[86] Latimer, *Bristol in the Eighteenth Century;* Bayne, *Norwich;* P. Smith, *History of Modern Culture*, II, 428.

ton Mather preached on the Copernican hypothesis in 1714 Samuel Sewall wrote in his Diary, "I think it inconvenient to assert such Problems." [87]

More significant, perhaps, than the modernity of the ministry was the intellectual activity of many Boston laymen, some of them recent graduates of Harvard College. Fresh from a reading of Morton's *Compendium Physicae,* and stimulated by correspondence with Sir Hans Sloane, John Chamberlyne, and other members of the Royal Society, Thomas and William Brattle, Benjamin Bullivant, Paul Dudley and Thomas Robie became eager and intelligent followers of the new experimental science. This Boston group published in the *Philosophical Transactions* six papers dealing with astronomy and natural history, papers which in both subject and quality compare most favorably with the fourteen scientific contributions from England's ten most important provincial towns in the same years.[88] Samuel Sewall may have eschewed astronomy, but he assiduously kept up his Latin; he also plugged away at Las Casas in the original for his "purpose in getting a Smattering of the Spanish Tongue." Others assayed French, taking lessons from John Rawlins, "French Schoolmaster," or digging it out for themselves from Thomas Blair's *Some Short and Easy Rules. Teaching the True Pronunciation of the French Language.* Teachers there were also ready to instruct those becoming interested in music. Sewall made it a special point on December 1, 1699, to call at "Mr. Hillers, to enquire about my wives virginals." Others sat for their portraits by Jeremiah Dummer, Tom Child, Joseph Allen or Lawrence Brown; still others purchased those rich and beautiful examples of the cartographer's art, advertised as "emblazon'd Maps," for their homes. Neal found the Boston aristocrats in 1719 a cultured group. "The Conversation in this Town is as polite as in most of the Cities and Towns in England; many of their Merchants having travelled into Europe; and those that stay at home having the advantage of a free Conversation with Travellers; so that a Gentleman from London would almost think himself at home in Boston." [89]

Most wealthy Bostonians owned good libraries; Cotton Mather's collection of over three thousand volumes was the largest in America. In addition to these private collections, there was the Boston Public

[87] AAS *Procs.,* XXVI, 18; Morais, *Deism,* 54, 57, 60; *Amer. Hist. Rev.,* XL, 463; 5 MHS *Colls.,* VII, 31.
[88] James Yonge of Plymouth (England) contributed seven papers; two came from York; one each from Norwich, Newcastle, Birmingham, Manchester, and Boston; none from Bristol, Exeter or Liverpool. *Philosophical Transactions,* IV, 267; V, 148, 379; VI, 85, 458, 499.
[89] *News Letter,* Jan. 19, 1708; March 8, 1714; April 23, 1716; 5 MHS *Colls.,* V, 506; Franklin, *Works* (Bigelow, ed.), I, 40; 11 *Bos. Rec. Com.,* 8; *Old-Time New England,* XII, 3; Morgan, *Early Painters,* 13; Neal, *New England,* II, 228.

Library at the Town House, well attended by its librarian, John Barnard, until the fire of 1711 destroyed the building and many of its treasures. Despite some losses, most of the volumes were saved, and the Selectmen carefully collected them again for the use of the public. A library for Anglicans was also established at King's Chapel in 1698, but seems to have been open only to communicants.[90]

The many bookshops located near the Town House in 1690 greatly expanded their trade, and between 1700 and 1711 sixteen new book-sellers appeared. All save one of these shops were destroyed by the fire of 1711, and although many reopened for business, a new form of marketing now came in to supplement their work. This was the book auction, held usually at a coffee house or tavern. In 1716, for instance, an advertisement announced "A Collection of choice Books, Ancient and Modern, in several Languages, upon most of the Arts and Sciences, few of them to be had at the Stationers [booksellers], the Books very neatly Bound, to be sold by way of Auction . . . at Mr. Selby's Coffee-House." The book trade of Boston was second only to that of London among English-speaking peoples. From the port on the Bay books were sent throughout the continental colonies and to the West Indies. In 1700, for example, Sewall imported "a gross of Horn-books" for a Connecticut customer. Peddlers hawked the wares of Boston book merchants up and down the countryside of New England. The clergy stood solidly behind this method of broadcasting culture. Cotton Mather often advised booksellers "what Books they should send to London for; that from their Ships, there may go forth into the Coun-trey, such things as may best serve the Interests of Truth," and in 1713 he assisted the booksellers in addressing the General Court, "that their late Act against Pedlers, may not hinder their Hawkers from carrying Books of Piety about the Country." [91]

Boston was served by many printers in these years, devoting them-selves to the production of reams of almanacs, broadsides, tracts and sermons. Out of this *potpourri* we may salvage two books of particular merit. John Wise's *Vindication of the Government of New England Churches* (1717), phrased in prose as lucid as that of Franklin and occasionally far more beautiful, displays a common-sense approach to religious controversy and a preoccupation with the problems of civil government which indicate that there was already at Boston an audience ripe for the intellectual developments of the eighteenth century. Thomas Fleet's reprint of the *Tales from Mother Goose* (1719), needs

[90] Morison, *Puritan Pronaos*, 138, 141 n.; 7 *Bos. Rec. Com.*, 162; 11 *Bos. Rec. Com.*, 26, 37, 185, 240; 6 MHS *Colls.*, I, 422.
[91] Littlefield, *Early Boston Booksellers*, 119, 230; *News Letter*, April 9, 1705; Oct. 11, 1708; March 30, 1713; Aug. 27, 1716; Wright, *Literary Culture*, 80; 6 MHS *Colls.*, I, 122, 237, 247; 7 MHS *Colls.*, VIII, 204, 283.

no further comment. *The Journal of Madam Knight* (1704), though not published for over a century, is sprightly, humorous, and the best piece of reading yet produced in the colonies. Sarah Knight's frequently allusive style and apt characterizations show her not only to have been a good storyteller but a woman whose reading was based less upon Mr. Mather's sermons than upon current poetry and romance.

The greatest achievement of the Boston press in these years was the successful establishment of two newspapers. On April 24, 1704, there appeared the first issue of the *Boston News Letter,* which was "published by Authority," and thus escaped the fate of its predecessor. This first American newspaper was founded by John Campbell, the postmaster, "printed by B. Green," and sold by Nicholas Boone "at his shop near the old Meeting-house." For fifteen years the *News Letter* monopolized the Boston scene. On December 1, 1719, after Campbell's removal from the post office, William Brooker, the new incumbent, brought out the first number of the *Boston Gazette,* printed by James Franklin. After Brooker's departure from the post office, the *Gazette* was continued by another printer, Samuel Kneeland. Since the bulk of the space in both these news sheets was devoted to tamely copied reprints of old European news, some commentators have dismissed them as of no cultural importance. It must not be overlooked, however, that from the start these little newspapers were the vehicles by which school teachers, dancing and music masters, and others informed the public of their services. Moreover, their audience was much greater than the size of their circulation would indicate, for the three hundred or so copies of each issue were placed not only in the hands of the wealthy, but passed from person to person, were available in taverns and coffee houses, and sent throughout the colonies as well.

All this activity amazed an English visitor of 1719, who reported that "at Boston the Exchange is surrounded with Booksellers Shops, which have a good trade. There are five Printing Presses in Boston, which are generally full of work, by which it appears, that Humanity and Knowledge of Letters flourish more here than in all other English Plantations put together." [92]

At Philadelphia the official indifference of the Friends to cultural advance beyond a sound elementary education, and the fact that non-Quaker elements did not threaten their control until after 1715, precluded any immediate flowering of the creditable planting of the seventeenth century. Yet many men of learning and intellectual attainment lived in the city during this period, their number occasionally augmented by new leaders like James Logan and Cadwallader Colden.

[92] Neal, *New England,* II, 225

These gentlemen possessed excellent libraries, Logan's ranking perhaps next to Cotton Mather's and William Byrd's in all the colonies. Pastorius owned many folio, quarto, and "Great octavo" tomes, covering an amazing range of knowledge in many tongues. His leisure he employed in reading Bede and Chaucer in English, or in composing poetry, essays, and his charming compendium, *The Bee Hive,* all of which place him in the van of literary men of his generation in the colonies.[93]

For those who wished to use it there was a parochial library in Christ Church after 1710. General merchants frequently included books in their importations, and Regnier Jansen, the printer, also engaged in bookselling after 1698. Andrew Bradford's bookstore at the "Bible and Crown" was a busy shop, from which in 1714 orders were filled for customers as far distant as was John Townsend of Barbados. In 1718 John Copson was selling books along with his other merchandise.[94]

In 1693 William Bradford gave up printing at Philadelphia because the Council had censured him for printing a seditious paper during the Keithian controversy. Thereafter there was no printing in the town until 1698, when Regnier Jansen set up a press which he or his sons operated until 1705. Another quiescent period followed. In 1709 Jacob Taylor took charge of printing for the Quakers until the latter called Andrew Bradford, son of William, from New York to be their official printer. Output of the Philadelphia press, of which there are a hundred and forty known issues in these years, was largely theological. George Keith alone was responsible for twenty-two forcefully written tracts and polemics. From a literary point of view Jonathan Dickinson's thrilling account of Robert Barrow's shipwreck and captivity, *God's Protecting Providence* (1699), equals anything published at Boston. Its popularity caused it to go through two London editions in 1720. The remainder of the printed matter consisted of almanacs, official papers and proclamations. The *Primer* of Pastorius found wide use in the schools, while Bradford's reprint of Tate and Brady's *Psalms* in 1713 enjoyed great popularity in the churches. His best paying pamphlet, however, was *A Legacy for Children. Being Some of the Last Expressions, and Dying Sayings of Hannah Hill, Junr. . . . Aged Eleven Years and Near Three Months,* issued in 1714, and reprinted in 1715 and 1717. On December 22, 1719, with the support of John Copson, Andrew Bradford began publishing the *American Weekly Mercury,* the third newspaper in the colonies, of which the first

[93] Learned, *Pastorius,* 275.
[94] Dorr, *Christ Church,* 45; *Colden Papers,* I, 14; Hildeburn, *Pa. Press,* I, 32, 46; *Mercury,* Dec. 22, 1719.

issue appeared just one day after the inauguration of the *Boston Gazette.*[95]

Cultural activity quickened after the turn of the century. Christopher Witt, physician and portrait painter, founded America's first botanical gardens on the banks of the Wissahickon. He was in addition an accomplished musician, and his translations of Kelpius' hymns were well known in the town. Germans and Swedes continued the musical traditions of their homelands. A concert by the Wissahickon hermits, on viols, trumpets and kettledrums, at the consecration of Gloria Dei in 1700 so impressed a visiting cleric that he wrote home for an organ, — "if there were music in the church the young people would consider church-going a recreation." In 1714 Gustavus Hesselius, "the portrait painter," was in Philadelphia commencing his well-known work. The cultural contributions to the life of Philadelphia by these other racial groups aided measurably in the approaching emancipation from Quaker control.[96]

Though New York might be backward in matters of public education, the wealth and leisure of its merchant group were causing a demand for and the appearance of certain cultural agencies in these years. Manhattan aristocrats were not a bookish group, and there were fewer good libraries at New York than in other towns. The first large private library was that of the Reverend John Sharpe, who was so concerned about the want of learning in the town. In 1700 he presented his books to the city, but little use was made of them for many years. In 1698 one of Dr. Thomas Bray's libraries was founded with a gift of two hundred and twenty volumes, mostly on theological subjects, and housed in the vestry at the Fort, where it was kept for the use of the Episcopal clergy. This collection was later moved to Trinity Church, but unlike Episcopal libraries at Charles Town and Newport it remained "wholly parochial in scope." [97]

Printing began here in 1694, when Governor Fletcher prevailed upon William Bradford, then at odds with the Philadelphia Quakers, to remove to New York. He began issuing his almanacs in that year, and in 1696 published *Le Trésor des Consolations Divines et Humaines* for Antoine Pintard. Bradford became city printer in 1695 with the publication of the charter and laws for the Corporation. Of all his issues, the most interesting to the student of belles lettres was *Andro-*

[95] McMurtrie, *History of Printing,* II, 9; *Pa. Mag.,* XLI, 483; Hildeburn, *Pa. Press,* I, 38, 46, 47.
[96] Drummond, *Early German Music,* 8, 9, 11, 12; *Early Church Music in Pennsylvania,* I, 21; *Pa. Mag.,* XXIX, 130.
[97] N. Y. Hist. Soc. *Colls., 1880,* 338; *1892,* 194, 218; Keep, *Library in Colonial New York,* 8, 12, 19, 22.

boros, a three act farce in which Governor Robert Hunter ably lampooned his political opponents. Bradford also operated as a bookseller, as did Thomas Adams, stationer, after 1698. Abraham de Lanoy was selling books in 1702, and at least one other bookseller was doing business at New York by 1719.[98]

The Manhattan gentry had other cultural interests. Notwithstanding the steady growth of the English population, many inhabitants still remained able linguists, and a "French Club" met regularly at one of the taverns. In addition to the plays already mentioned, John Sharpe records that on September 6, 1710, one "Glaser began at night a Consort at Mr. [Sampson] Broughtons." By 1720 it was quite usual for gentlemen and army officers to gather at some home in the evening, "to hear some good Musick, and to take a Tiff of fresh Lime Punch" to mellow their after-dinner Madeira. The gentry also began to patronize home artists, and there seems to have been sufficient work to employ four limners, Evert and Gerret Duycinck, Gerret van Randst, and Nehemiah Partridge, before 1720. Even the dour Cadwallader Colden found things pleasanter at New York than he had dared hope.[99]

Despite mighty obstacles of Indian wars, pestilence, fire and hurricane, an intellectual coterie, based on the growing wealth of merchants and planters, was already developing at Charles Town. Signs of this were the presentation of one or two plays, and the movement for better schools. In 1699 Edmund Bohun was collecting specimens of plants, minerals and shells for Edward Petiver, botanist of the Royal Society. This work, furthered by efforts of Hannah Williams, Joseph Lord and others, was reported in *Philosophical Transactions* for 1705, and resulted in Sir Hans Sloane's support of Mark Catesby's expedition to Charles Town in 1712. As early as 1707 Henrietta Johnston, possibly a pupil of John Riley, was practicing the new and delicate art of painting with pastels. The Lower House of the Assembly appropriated £70 in 1698 for the purchase of books for a public library. The Proprietors also presented the colony with some volumes, and in 1700 the Assembly passed "An Act for Securing the Provincial Library at Charlestown, in Carolina." This first library law for any American town made the Anglican minister librarian, and instructed him to keep a catalogue of the books, which might be borrowed by any inhabitant upon his giving a receipt for them. In January, 1703, through efforts of Dr. Bray, more books, selected especially for a "layman's library," were added to the collection, which was then housed in the rectory. The populace made

[98] McMurtrie, *History of Printing,* II, 135, 137, 140; N. Y. Hist. Soc. *Colls., 1885,* 61, 89; Keep, *Library in Colonial New York,* 101.
[99] *Pa. Mag.,* XL, 294; Wilson, *Memorial History of New York,* II, 160; N. Y. Hist. Soc. *Colls., 1885,* 72, 73, 97; Morgan, *Early Painters,* 17, 20.

such good use of their library that in 1712 the librarian was given "Discretionary power" in making loans, because so many of the borrowed volumes had been lost.[100]

Also at little Newport, growing wealth enabled a few gentlemen with leisure to look beyond the confines of trade. Christopher Lodowick, physician, Quaker schoolteacher, and almanac maker, corresponded with Thomas Brattle of Boston, and in 1694 wrote for him an exposition of "ye Middle-Parallel Sailing" which revealed a knowledge of Mercator's globe and its limitations. Upon occasion, too, he could turn aside from scientific interests to defend his faith in print against Cotton Mather. Good authority has it that Gabriel Bernon wrote excellent prose and "belle poésie," and Governor Cranston's reports to the Board of Trade do credit at least to his skill in casuistry. Many of Newport's young ladies, like Mehitabel Redwood, acquired accomplishments, as well as manners, at Boston private schools.[101]

Several wealthy Newporters possessed relatively large libraries, mainly secular in content, and made frequent and liberal use of them. A library was established in connection with Trinity Church sometime before 1709, when the vestry voted that "ye Books belonging to ye Library of ye Church which have been Lent out be called in & . . . when they are come in a Survey be made." The use of this collection was not confined to church members, but was open to all inhabitants of the town. By 1719 even Daniel Neal, historian of the Puritans, was forced to admit some cultural improvement at Newport.[102]

These are the years that are popularly regarded as utterly barren with regard to culture in the colonies, and indeed, measured in terms of tangible and lasting achievement, they do seem to constitute a fallow period in colonial intellectual development. Yet to admit this is not necessarily to heap reproof upon Americans of the early eighteenth century. In this period colonial culture had to learn to stand on its own feet. The first generation of those whose youth had been spent in the midst of the intellectual movements of the Mother Country was gone, and their sons and grandsons were left in a country which had as yet no long tradition of cultural achievement to inspire them. So the colonial towns turned their energies to providing first of all the mechanics necessary to any cultural advance, and in this

[100] Diary of Edmund Bohun, xxv; S. C. Hist. & Gen. Mag., XXI, 3; Univ. S. C. Bull., Sept., 1918; International Studio, July, 1927, 13; Antiquarian, Sept., 1928, 46; S. C. Commons Journal, 1698, 13; 1702, 27; S. C. Statutes, VII, 13; II, 376.

[101] R. I. Hist. Soc. Colls., XVII, 89; Updyke, Narragansett Church, I, 61, 116, 222.

[102] The authorities sought unsuccessfully in 1709 to secure the services of Andrew Bradford of New York as printer. Newport had one bookshop in 1713. Mason, Redwood Library, 10; Neal, New England, II, 233; R. I. Col. Recs., IV, 65; Leeds, Almanac, 1713.

period they founded schools and libraries, and patronized a variety of private agencies that were laying the foundations for later accomplishments. The American colonists were going to school. The cultural achievements of these years were none the less real because they did not as yet find expression in great works of art and literature.

On the whole, what the metropolis had to offer, the colonies readily seized upon and assimilated. The bigotry of their failure to support a theater is often cited as a count against them, but the absence of great wealth may be urged as an equally valid explanation. Moreover, the provincial theater in England was still struggling for a foothold; throughout this period no stage performance could be presented within the limits of the city of Bristol. The outstanding social development of eighteenth century London, the coffee house and its attendant clubs, appeared in the colonial towns almost as soon as it became popular in England. The questing curiosity of the eighteenth century with regard to scientific matters, its latitudinarian views in religion, and a sprinkling of its deism crossed the Atlantic and invaded the colonies in these years. Late in this period Addison and Steele began their revolution in popular manners through the pages of the *Spectator;* in the colonies the vehicles for such a movement were ready, and its influence was soon to be felt.

Virtually all of the cultural advance of the colonies in this period was made in the towns. Here alone educational and social agencies, public and private, necessary to the flowering of intellectual life, were to be found. Contrary to the accepted view of historians who have thought too much in terms of the frontier, this progress was as great as any achieved in the Mother Country outside the metropolis. By 1720 two colonial capitals published three weekly newspapers; outside of London at the same date, Bristol had only two, and Norwich, one. While Boston kept five printers busy, and New York and Philadelphia each employed one, the Corporation of Bristol allowed William Bonney to set up the first printing office in the town in 1695, because "a printing house would be useful in some respects." Indeed, cultural progress in colonial America compares favorably with developments in provincial cities of any European country in these years. It must never be forgotten that the townsmen looked not so much to the west as to the east, and in this period their growing merchant marine made possible more rapid and steady contacts with Europe. Each town was becoming more and more the intellectual center of its region, and as it acquired a civic personality its leading men began to develop a colonial culture. The real Americanism of a representative colonial like Cotton Mather is explainable only on the basis of a continuous transit of civilization from east to west via the gateway of the colonial towns.

THE AWAKENING OF CIVIC CONSCIOUSNESS
— CONCLUSION

The difficulty in summing up the achievements of these years lies in the fact that they were years neither of actual beginnings nor of great tangible results, but a period of busy activity of which the fruits were to become apparent at a later time. Perhaps the greatest growth was along economic lines, and upon it depended all physical, social and cultural development. As routes of trade became established and staple products developed for exchange, surplus wealth piled up in the towns, to be administered by a few merchants for their own or their community's social and economic betterment. The wars brought temporary depression, but provided as well opportunities for the emergence of a new group of capitalists, many of them war profiteers or the beneficiaries of ventures in privateering and piracy. A tendency to greater complexity in the economic life of the towns is observable in this period. Merchandizing became more important with the development of retailing in all of the towns and the greater ability of the populace at large to buy. The appearance of newspapers brought in advertising in many of its modern aspects. Nascent capitalism, war profiteering, and the emergence of colonial captains of trade consorted oddly with remnants of medieval practices of trade regulation and price fixing. Boston continued to be the commercial and financial capital of colonial America, but the striking fact of these years was the rapid growth of the other towns, Philadelphia and New York especially, — a fact ominous of the Bay town's later comparative decline.

This economic progress made possible considerable physical expansion in the towns. Growth in population and in number of houses in each town has already been noted. Many of these new houses were spacious and elegant, equipped with conveniences distinctly urban. The erection of public buildings and churches is further evidence of the towns' greater financial maturity. Moreover, this accumulated capital enabled the towns to make far greater expenditures for streets, drainage, bridges and landing places. There is no better commentary on the collective wealth of the Bostonians than the large sums spent on their highways, no better indication of the private capital commanded by their merchants than the magnitude of the Long Wharf project. Towards the end of the period the physical growth of the towns was accelerated by the first sizeable influx of non-English elements, a development that was to have interesting effects on all aspects of town life.

In addition, the material prosperity of the towns made possible greater expenditure in caring for their social needs. It was well that this was so, for the events of wartime, which had accelerated the accumulation of wealth in the towns, at the same time intensified their social problems. The unrest which wars engender made more costly the keeping of order, the supervision of morals and the protection of property. The expense and mortality of the wars, and the vicissitudes of the business cycle increased the amount of pauperism with which the towns had to deal. For the most part the towns admirably met the growing expense of community welfare, though they added little new by way of solutions to the methods corporately employed in the seventeenth century. England was still their model, and England, embarking on her exhaustive struggle for empire with France, was in no mood for social experimentation or reform. But as it was manifest in individuals or private groups the sense of civic responsibility made its greatest strides. The Friends' Alms House at Philadelphia, the Scot's Charitable Society, and Cotton Mather's Societies for the Suppression of Disorders reveal how men of substance were devoting thought and money in attempts to correct the ills of a growing society. Similarly, the Boston Fire Society appeared to perform a service where public police and fire departments failed to function adequately. As for public activities, the towns made some of their greatest advances in the field of public health, the appearance of new and dread epidemic diseases producing, especially in the cases of Boston and Newport, quarantine regulations and hospital facilities that were remarkably efficient. In general, this was a period of expansion, when urban problems grew bigger, their solutions costlier, and the public mind, for the most part, more ready to accept its civic responsibilities. If there were no great innovations, there was at the same time little backsliding, — the continued failure of all towns to distinguish between the unfortunate poor and the truly criminal, and the increasing inadequacy of New York's police force being the outstanding examples of the latter.

Socially, too, the accumulation of wealth had its effect. It intensified the social and economic cleavage between rich and poor, and caused a growing stratification of society into the three groups of better, middling and inferior sorts. Wealth tended increasingly to concentrate in the towns, where it invented new forms of pleasure and new facilities for education peculiar to urban communities. Wealth displayed itself in ostentatious finery and ceremonial formalities, patronized the latest fashions and made heavy expenditures for European importations, monopolized certain churches and certain taverns, and in general sought to emphasize everything that differentiated it from the less fortunate. Bitterness on the part of those to whom society had been less kind, and a tendency among them to mob violence against their betters were the corresponding reactions of the development of a cultivated, aristocratic, urban society, wherein a true provincial culture was shortly to flourish. The growing wealth of the colonial towns was also causing the distance between them and Europe to shrink perceptibly every year. Regular and better means of communication facilitated the transit of European civilization to the New World, and effected in its seaport towns the growth of a wider outlook and a more alert intellectual life than was possible in the remote villages of the hinterlands.

PART III

THE TOWNS BECOME CITIES, 1720–1742

IX

THE URBAN SETTING

I

As the towns approached or attained their centuries, two long decades of peace and expanding trade consolidated the gains and intensified the character of the development of preceding years. In physical appearance raw youth was yielding rapidly to settled maturity. Increased age and experience were evident in the firmer handling of growing urban problems and in the deepening of public consciousness concerning its collective responsibilities. Moreover, the peace that permitted unprecedented commercial prosperity and material expansion was also more than ever making of the New World a haven for land-hungry and underprivileged citizens of the Old. These newcomers scattered throughout the colonies, but many of them, remaining in the towns, contributed to the physical and economic growth and left a mark upon the social and cultural complexions of these communities.

Twenty years of peace and continuous immigration greatly increased urban populations in the New World. At the close of the period Boston was still the largest community, but its population had begun to decline, — a phenomenon which continued until after the American Revolution. Philadelphia, on the other hand, rapidly growing, would soon pass the Bay Town in numbers. Even more significant for the development of urban America was the extraordinary expansion of New York, Charles Town and Newport, the more noteworthy when compared with the practically stationary populations of English cities prior to 1760. At the same time, however, colonial population in general expanded so rapidly that the proportion of persons living in the towns declined from 8 per cent in 1720 to 5.4 per cent in 1742.[1]

[1]
Populations of the Colonial Towns, 1720–1742

Town	1720	1730	1740	1742	Increase
Boston	12,000	13,000	17,000*	16,382*	29%
Philadelphia	10,000	11,500		13,000	30%
New York	7,000	8,622*		11,000	57%
Charles Town	3,500	4,500		6,800	94%
Newport	3,800	4,640*		6,200	63%

* indicates actual census; elsewhere figures are estimates.

Greene and Harrington, *American Population*, 19, 97, 117, 177; 22 *Bos. Rec. Com.*, iv; 15 *Bos. Rec. Com.*, 359; *Doc. Hist. N. Y.*, I, 694; *R. I. Hist. Mag.*, V, 84.

II

Although urban growth everywhere bred conditions requiring the assumption of more authority by town governments, very little change in municipal political institutions took place in this period. The one notable exception was the new charter granted the Corporation of New York in 1731. By the discreet disposition of £1,000 the Mayor and Common Council secured from Governor James Montgomerie, who, it was well known, hoped to recoup his fortune in America, a confirmation of former privileges and a grant of additional concessions. But, though the city obtained an extension of its boundaries and a lucrative ferry monopoly, and the Corporation received augmented executive and judicial powers, the governor retained the right of appointing the mayor and other municipal officers. Thus, in spite of increased authority, the aristocratic nature of the Corporation became rather intensified than otherwise.[2]

Elsewhere attempts to alter existing forms of government proved abortive. They are significant, however, in uncovering the three most important municipal needs, — popular control, administrative efficiency, and financial independence. Under the influence of Governor Francis Nicholson, the South Carolina Assembly in June, 1722, passed "An Act for the Good Government of Charles Town," which erected "Charles City and Port" into a municipal corporation modelled after that of New York. Unhappily for the future of the town, a "faction" of planters and merchants, claiming to represent a majority of the citizens, secured the disallowance of this act in England the next year on the grounds that "the town's people were surprised into the Law." Francis Yonge, colonial agent, held that the "whole complaint against the Corporation is only a Cavill stirred up by some designing persons who are angry they were not placed in the Magistracy." It also appears probable that much of the opposition came from the planter group, which did not wish to see the city made independent of the Assembly wherein it enjoyed complete control. All that Charlestonians achieved by way of self-government in these years was the right to elect parish firemasters, workhouse commissioners and measurers in 1737–1738, and road commissioners after 1742. Had the charter been allowed, Charles Town, thus made competent to deal with local problems, might not have remained the community of unrealized projects that it was.[3]

[2] Edwards, New York, 18; N. Y. M. C. C., IV, 5, 8; N. Y. Journal, Oct. 7, 1734.
[3] S. C. Commons Journal, VI, 16, 41, 63, 98, 148; S. C. Council Journal, II, 73; S. C. Pub. Recs., IX, 97; X, 1, 74, 82, 83, 96, 104, 115; S. C. Gaz., April 2, 1737; April 6, 1738; Vestry Mins., 102.

The aristocratic nature of the Philadelphia Corporation, coupled with its financial ineptitude and its failure to cope adequately with the town's problems, aroused widespread popular distrust. In 1740 dissatisfied inhabitants petitioned the Assembly for a law placing the collection of taxes and certain other powers of the Corporation in the hands of elected "Commissioners and Assessors," in accordance with current English practice. The Assembly passed the bill, but the Mayor and Common Council persuaded Governor Thomas to reject it on the grounds that it infringed rights granted by the charter of 1701.[4]

The two New England towns were, on the whole, well governed. Boston's principal problem came from the smaller villages of Suffolk County, which resented economic control by the capital of the nearby countryside. In 1735 these communities made an unsuccessful attempt to have Boston separated from the County, and three years later Rumney Marsh failed in its effort to detach itself from the town. A similar demand came in 1742 from "freeholders of the woods part of Newport," who wanted independence from the "merchants and tradesmen" of the "compact part" of the town, but a committee of the Assembly rejected the petition after a public hearing. In both of these communities the town meetings, while ostensibly democratic, were in reality controlled year after year by the same group of merchant aristocrats, who secured most of the important offices, and it was only natural for inhabitants of rural districts to desire release from this overlordship.[5]

III

The problem of adequate housing for the townsfolk intensified in this period, for despite considerable building in each town construction failed to keep pace with increase in population. Yet the operations of builders were constantly changing the face of each community; new public structures lent an air of distinction and civic maturity, and elaborate mansions for the rich gave evidence of accumulating wealth and taste, while in some of the towns overcrowding caused a subdivision of building lots and the appearance of multi-family houses.

Philadelphia experienced the greatest expansion. The settled area now reached west past Tenth Street, north beyond Vine, and south along the Delaware to Society Hill. In older sections large three-storied brick houses and other buildings began to replace the "mean and low" frame or brick structures of earlier years. A sign of overcrowding in these areas was the gradual appearance of tenement houses; in 1722

---

[4] *P. M. C. C.,* 110, 178, 189; *Votes Pa. Assembly,* II, 253, 379, 381; *Pa. Col. Recs.,* IV, 376, 385, 389; *Mercury,* Feb. 12, 1740; *Johnson's England,* I, 207.
[5] 12 *Bos. Rec. Com.,* 116, 205; *R. I. Col. Recs.,* V, 54, 59.

four of them were erected on Front Street and two on Second. "House rent is high," wrote Christopher Saur two years later, "because the houses are all built of bricks. . . . According to appearances, plainness is vanishing pretty much." Even humble artisans, like Ebenezer Robinson, brazier, lived in brick houses, though many dwellings sheltered two or more families, and some people had to walk "up one Pair of Stairs" to their lodgings.[6]

A large amount of construction took place between 1720 and 1742. With the erection of many new shops and warehouses in the business section real estate there rose in price. Mulberry Street, on the northern side of town, began to be a popular residential area at about this time. Land along the Delaware south of Walnut Street was opened up after 1728, and had by 1740 become a well-peopled residential district.[7]

A unique development in Philadelphia was the appearance of suburbs. South of the town lay Society Hill, where the Shippen brothers owned a large tract of land which they began to sell off in house lots in 1739. Their advertisements made much of the accessibility of the site to a proposed new market. Another suburban development was opened up in the Northern Liberties in 1741, when Ralph Assheton disposed of his eighty-acre estate in small building lots. Fine rural estates, belonging to wealthy merchants who aspired to the life of country gentlemen, still characterized the countryside around Philadelphia. Among those most noted for their splendid architecture and formal Italian gardens were James Logan's lovely home at Stenton, Andrew Hamilton's palatial residence at Bush Hill, and the buildings of the Wharton estate on the road to Moyamensing.[8]

Philadelphia owed the growing beauty of its public architecture to the talent and skill of its master builders and accomplished gentlemen amateurs, who in adapting the classicism of Palladio and Vitruvius improved upon their British contemporaries by their refusal to sacrifice practical comfort on the symmetrical altar of eighteenth century taste. In 1724 James Porteus, Samuel Powel, Ebenezer Thompson, John Harrison and six other master builders formed the Carpenters Company of Philadelphia "for the purpose of obtaining instruction in the science of architecture." Their studies soon bore fruit. Porteus designed the new Christ Church, completed in 1731, the most ambitious and ornate expression of the Georgian style in America. In 1730 the Pennsylvania Assembly, long in need of a suitable meeting place, ap-

[6] *Mercury*, Feb. 7, 1721; Feb. 13, 1722; May 14, 1730; *Pa. Gaz.*, Feb. 11, 1728; Jan. 24, 1738; *Pa. Mag.*, XLV, 252; Hamilton, *Itinerarium*, 20, 24.
[7] Houses were built in blocks because most lots had a narrow frontage, the usual size being 24' x 80'. *Mercury*, Oct. 7, 1731; Sept. 26, 1734; *Pa. Gaz.*, Jan. 17, Mar. 21, 1738.
[8] *Pa. Gaz.*, Feb. 25, 1738; July 5, 1739; June 18, Sept. 2, 1741; *Mercury*, May 4, 1721; Feb. 12, 1740; Scull and Heap, *Map of Philadelphia*.

propriated funds and purchased a lot on Chestnut Street between Fifth and Sixth, and a beautifully proportioned Georgian building, of which the plans had been drawn by the skilled artisan, Edmund Woolley, was ready for use by 1735. The State House, though incomplete in 1742, was the largest and most elaborately formal public building in the colonies, and its lovely interior, with its grand staircase and rich carvings, the work of Gustavus Hesselius, is a monument to the city's artistic coming of age. From the Delaware River in 1742 the pleasing prospect of Philadelphia, with its brick houses, gentlemen's estates and public buildings, revealed a city in most respects full grown, and comparable with similar communities in the Mother Country.[9]

New York and Boston did not greatly extend their bounds, and became in consequence more compact, in places even congested. The Corporation of New York clung tenaciously to its property, seldom leasing or selling save from dire necessity. But the growth of population stimulated building activity and made the subdivision of large properties a profitable business to the original owners. In 1729 the Weems property was broken up and sold for small building lots, as was also land at the Fresh Water belonging to William Janeway. In 1731, to finance the acquisition of the Montgomerie Charter, the Corporation disposed of two large tracts, which thus became available for building. Other dispositions of city lands in this period were the grant of seventy acres to Alderman Rutgers in 1730 and the sale of ten lots to Jacobus Roosevelt in 1734. Nevertheless, the town continued to suffer a shortage of land and houses, and in 1732 the constables received orders to evict certain squatters from city property in the North Ward, and to "Cause their Hutts to be demolished . . . as public Nusances." [10]

When real estate did become available, enthusiastic building often produced a glut of new properties. In 1735 reports circulated at Boston that, "because trade is very dull by reason of heavy Taxes," one hundred and fifty houses were for rent at New York. John Symmense's dwelling in Broadway, with "a small kitchen, a Grass-Plat, Wood Yard, several Fruit Trees and other conveniences," was advertised for many weeks without finding a buyer. But this situation appears to have been only temporary. The market for real estate soon picked up, and building was proceeding apace by 1739. The auction became the popular means of selling many of these newly erected houses.[11]

[9] *Carpenter's Company of Phila.*, 3, 21; Jackson, *Early Philadelphia Architects*, 42, 50, 52, 60, 62; *Cyclopedia of Phila.*, II, 447; *Votes Pa. Assembly*, III, 208, 473, 516.
[10] *N. Y. Gaz.*, July 21, Sept. 15, 22, 1729; Edwards, *New York*, 147; *N. Y. M. C. C.*, IV, 133, 134.
[11] *N. Y. Journal*, Mar. 3, 10, Aug. 26, 1734; *News Letter*, June 17, 1735; *N. Y. Gaz.*, Mar. 11, 1734; Aug. 4, Sept. 15, Dec. 15, 1725; Jan. 31, 1738; Mar. 11, 1739.

New York dwelling houses still followed the Dutch architectural tradition, differing greatly from those of Philadelphia, where the current modes of Wren's London were known and copied. "The houses are . . . compact and regular; . . ." Dr. Alexander Hamilton described them in 1744; "there are a few built of wood, but the greatest number of brick, and a great many covered with pantile and glazed tile with the year of God when built figured out with plates of iron upon the fronts of several of them." The only public edifice to elicit his approval was Trinity Church, a stone building with a fine interior but a "clumsy Steeple." Despite some expansion, and the absence of many civic buildings, New York remained crowded at the southern tip of Manhattan, which explains why Dr. Hamilton thought it made "more of an urban appearance than Philadelphia." [12]

Although much building took place, the limits of Boston were not greatly enlarged in these years. Many frame dwellings were demolished to be replaced by brick, and the central business district about the Town House became thickly populated. Near here the "poorer sort" lived in tiny quarters, and seldom enjoyed the luxury of a brick house unless it were a tenement. Many dwelt, like Edward Grater, carter, in a small "Wooden" two-family house down near the wharves, or in the "end of a house" up in town. Middle class artisans, living in the center of Boston, occupied "convenient" houses having two lower rooms, a kitchen, wood house and back yard. In this district also were several large double houses with pumps, renting at £40 to £50 per year. The North End, too, was becoming more crowded, and fine old residences occasionally had to give way to buildings like Martha Grover's "Brick Tenement" in Fish Street.[13]

The greatest activity in real estate took place at the South End. Here larger lots, sometimes 65' x 120', were available for homes for the well-to-do. Long Lane, in this locality, was a pleasant street, lined with attractive houses renting for around £98 per year. Yet tenements had made their appearance here, too, by 1734. West Boston, toward Barton's Point, also filled up at this time, becoming, like the South End, a region of large and substantial residences. An English gentleman, surveying the town in 1740, concluded that Boston contained "a great many good houses, and several fine streets, little inferior to some of our best in London." [14]

---

[12] Hamilton, *Itinerarium,* 51, 53; *Life of Bampfylde-Moore Carew,* 115.
[13] *Bos. Gaz.,* Jan. 18, Sept. 27, 1725; June 20, 1726; Mar. 18, 1734; Feb. 2, 1736; June 30, 1740; *N. E. Journal.* Sept. 8, 29, 1729; *Post Boy,* Sept. 1, 1740.
[14] *Bos. Gaz.,* Aug. 13, 1722; Nov. 4, 1723; May 18, 1724; Feb. 2, 1736; Dec. 8, 1740; *N. E. Journal,* Aug. 11, 1730; Bennett, History of New England, 124; *Life of Carew,* 186; 6 MHS *Colls.,* VI, 256; Dow, *Everyday Life,* 22.

The building energies of Boston citizens seem to have confined themselves to domestic structures, for, as the town was already well supplied in this respect, no new public buildings appeared in these years. The spires of its fourteen churches still in 1742 dominated the view of the town from the harbor, and the crowding together of all its buildings, domestic and commercial, in the older sections, gave it a distinctly urban aspect. The most "elegant prospect" that the town afforded was still that from the lower end of Long Wharf for half a mile up King Street to the Town House.

After recovering from the shocks of war, hurricane and fire, Charlestonians embarked upon an extended building program, which included the replacing of old structures and the erection of many new ones. The town expanded beyond its walls, and by 1739 had more than doubled in area. Within the old limits, where houses stood close together upon the streets, much of the rebuilding had taken place before 1730. The principal obstacle to adequate housing at Charles Town was shortage of labor. At far-away Boston in 1722 newspapers carried the notice that carpenters and bricklayers going to Charles Town would "find employment enough . . . by reason of the great want of such Artificers there." This scarcity probably accounted for the prevalence of cheaply built timber houses, which were "neither comfortable nor well constructed." Heavy immigration from New England and New York in the 1730's also raised the price of town sites to "four times the Value in 4 or 5 Yeares time." [15]

The prevailing high price of real estate did not, however, prevent people from acquiring new homes, and after 1730 a veritable building boom took place. The marked improvement in construction and design of Charles Town dwellings can be attributed to the advent of trained carpenters and to men like Peter Chassereau, a London architect who arrived in 1735.[16] In addition to such skillful adaptations of West Indian and classical elements as Robert Brewton's home on Tradd Street, there appeared in newer sections show places like Joseph Shute's "Summer Houses" with their beautiful gardens, and Francis Le Brasseur's elegant residence and orange grove, known as Petit Versailles. Several hundred dwellings, kitchens, warehouses, coach houses, and stables were built during this decade in newly opened areas west and south of the old lines. In 1737 choice lots, part of

[15] *Courant*, Feb. 18, 1723; Smith, *Dwelling Houses of Charleston*, 63, 281; Carroll, *Historical Collections*, II, 130.
[16] He "surveys Lands, . . . draws Plans and Elevations of all kinds of Buildings, . . . calculates Estimates for Buildings or Repairs, inspects and measures Artificer's Work, sets out ground for Gardens or Parks in a grand and Rural manner." *S. C. Gaz.*, Feb. 2, 9, 1734; Jan. 4, 1735; Mar. 5, 1741.

"Number 36, situate in Elliott-Street," measuring 28′ x 88′, were being offered for sale. Another popular residential district was "Archdale's Square, near the Presbyterian Church." [17]

As new residential areas opened up, older sections of Charles Town became consigned largely to business and to sheltering non-house-holders and members of the poorer classes. Here signs of congestion appeared, necessitating the erection of multi-family houses. In 1735 John Laurens advertised a house in Market Square, "divided into four commodious Tenements"; soon after James St. Johns offered one "to be let in several Apartments." Here also in 1727 was completed St. Philip's Church, as much the pride of the inhabitants as the present edifice which occupies its site. In the estimation of visitors Charles Town, with its predominance of frame buildings, made "a fine Shew at a Distance in the Sea," and suited the prevailing taste because "very regularly built." [18]

For the first time in its hundred years of existence, Newport began to develop a closely settled area. By 1730 frame buildings, used chiefly for business purposes, crowded one another along Thames Street for half a mile, and homes on Mary, Marlborough and Spring Streets nestled close like those of other towns. For the most part, however, residents owned large plots of ground, and nearly every house had a garden at its back, so that the town still retained much of its earlier rural flavor. As well as shops and warehouses, new buildings included many homes, and the residential district expanded into favorable locations at the Point across the Cove from Thames Street. After the erection of Trinity Church, Spring Street, running parallel with Thames, became a fashionable place to live. The principal real estate operator of these years was "Augustus Lucas, Esq., Merchant," who advertised his ventures in Boston as well as Rhode Island newspapers. He generally built his houses with the proceeds of a lottery, and in 1732 a lucky Bostonian drew first prize of £50 in the lottery for his "new House and Shop over against the Market House in King Street." [19]

In 1720 the Baptist Church and Quaker Meeting House had been the only large buildings at Newport, but during this period the town acquired some of the most beautiful public structures in the colonies. In 1726 Richard Munday completed Trinity Church, adapting plans possibly drawn in England by Christopher Wren. Few colonial

[17] *Iconography of Charles Town; S. C. Gaz.*, May 13, 1732; June 16, 1733; Sept. 17, 1737; Feb. 9, 1740; Dec. 5, 1741.

[18] *S. C. Gaz.*, Mar. 27, 1735; May 15, 1736; Mar. 9, 1738; April 30, 1741; *An Exact Prospect of Charles Town; Journals of Von Reck and Bolzius*, 26.

[19] Stiles, Draught of Highways; *Bos. Gaz.*, Oct. 10, 1726; June 19, 1727; May 23, 1737; *R. I. Gaz.*, Oct. 4, 1732; Jan. 11, 1733; *Rehearsal*, Sept. 11, 1732.

churches can claim such simple beauty and proportion as this lovely edifice. Three years later, in collaboration with Henry Collins, Munday designed and executed the Seventh Day Baptist Church, whose exquisite interior and delicate carvings constitute the supreme monument to the maturity of colonial taste in this period. The carpenter-architect's success with Trinity Church led to his employment by the Assembly as architect and builder of the Colony House in 1739. Standing at the head of Queen Street in a direct line from the end of Long Wharf, and dominating the older section of the town, this handsome brick structure, finished in 1741, was the most complete public building in any of the towns. Munday was also responsible for the building of many fine homes for the wealthy merchant families of Newport. The impression gathered from a tour of the town's streets today is that the painted frame houses of Rhode Island grandees were surpassed by none in any town for classic proportion and exquisite detail.[20]

By 1742 each of the towns presented a distinctly urban appearance. Increasing demand for houses and rising real estate values led to the subdivision of properties and growing compactness of dwelling houses in older sections. Boston, Charles Town and Philadelphia enforced strict regulations concerning construction of party walls. In the last named town special "Regulators of Party Wall and Partition ffences" issued permits for such building, specified thickness of walls, and levied fines for non-compliance with their orders.[21] Every town had further developed an individuality of its own, which found expression in types of architecture and building materials employed, and especially in the nature of its public buildings.

By 1720 the forests adjacent to the towns had everywhere so far receded that firewood had to be transported from distant points at an ever-increasing expense. Fuel prices rose steadily throughout the period, occasioning much real hardship for the poor. The problem was most acute at Boston, where inhabitants yearly consumed enormous amounts of wood, and where the original supply had early shown its insufficiency. In the winter of 1726 it was estimated that "during the uninterrupted sledding" over five hundred loads a day, or twenty-four thousand loads came across Boston Neck into the town; at fifty-one shillings a cord, this represented an outlay of about £17,000. Yet even this amount proved insufficient, and the Town Meeting sought other methods of providing the townspeople with fuel. In summer lighters carrying about twelve cords each brought wood to the wharves

[20] Isham, *Trinity Church*, 37, 38, 55, 57, 58; *Seventh Day Baptist Memorial*, III, 151; *Newport Hist. Mag.*, III, 56; *American Architect*, X, 71; Clark, *Architectural Monograph on Newport*.
[21] *Pa. Statutes*, III, 244; *S. C. Statutes*, III, 56; 13 *Bos. Rec. Com.*, 247.

for measurement and sale. Here those who could afford to lay in an advance supply could purchase it far more cheaply than in winter, but this procedure obviously did not come within the means of the poor. The scarcity and high cost of firewood tempted many corders to perpetrate "frauds," and the authorities repeatedly passed orders to prevent such cheating. They met with scant success, until an elaborate set of regulations and penalties devised in 1740 brought an end to the abuse.[22]

In 1736 and 1737 the Town Meeting chose committees to study plans for improving the fuel supply of Boston, but both times all action was postponed. Consequently, the bitter winter of 1740–41 found the community unprepared. The price of firewood mounted to forty shillings by March, and many of the poor had to go entirely without. Spurred to action by necessity, the Town spent £700 for fuel for the poor, and provided a warehouse where wood given for charity might be stored and dispensed.[23]

After 1730 the use of imported coal by wealthy Bostonians became more general. Frequent advertisements of "choice" Newcastle, Scots', Welsh or Swansea coal appear in all the public prints. In 1735 New England imported seventeen hundred caldrons of English coal, most of which was consumed at Boston; two years later whole ship loads of coal were arriving from Bristol. Though some of the new fuel was used by smiths and braziers, advertisements increasingly stressed its suitability for "Private-Houses." [24]

The poor of New York also suffered greatly from scarcity of firewood in winter, but here the authorities showed less concern over the problem. In 1721 the Corporation did permit gathering of felled timber lying on its common lands. During the winter of 1732 suffering was intense. On February 22 a resident wrote that "Firewood is so very scarce in this City, that it was sold Yesterday for 32 shillings per Cord, and some for 36 Shillings." Again, in 1737, humble folk became desperate, and rather than pay the high prices asked stole at least one boat load of wood from the North River. Every winter came complaints that the rich bought up the available supply of fuel and left the poor to freeze. As at Boston, conditions became intolerable in 1741, when even the Hudson froze over. Cord wood brought fifty shillings in January, and widespread suffering forced the Corporation to act. It distributed a "large Quantity of Coals" to the needy, and took up a collection of £500 for charity. But within a month this

    [22] *Courant*, Feb. 26, 1726; *N. E. Journal*, Nov. 11, 1728; Mar. 10, 1729; 8 *Bos. Rec. Com.*, 206, 222; 12 *Bos. Rec. Com.*, 109, 113, 243, 250.
    [23] 12 *Bos. Rec. Com.*, 158, 172, 278, 282, 294; *News Letter*, Mar. 26, 1741.
    [24] *N. E. Journal*, Aug. 31, 1730; *Rehearsal*, Aug. 14, 1732; *Eve. Post*, Nov. 21, 1737; Gipson, *British Empire*, I, 41 n.

fund was exhausted, and so long as the cold hung on the price of fuel did not drop below forty shillings.[25]

The rapid growth of Newport, and the clearing of Rhode Island and the Narragansett country for farms created a fuel shortage that became acute by 1733. At this time what was probably the first American proposal for conservation appeared in the *Rhode Island Gazette*. "When I consider," said the writer, "how much the Price of Wood for Firing has advanced in this Town for thirty Years past, it puts me to some Apprehensions for Posterity." He proposed a reforestation law requiring every farmer to plant a certain number of trees, and an act to prevent waste in the cutting and selling of firewood. Newport itself took no action until 1738, when the Town Meeting "weighed the deplorable condition the town will be in if the Small pox should prevail," and countrymen refuse to bring wood into town. Provision was then made for a loan to purchase fuel in case of possible emergency. When a genuine crisis occurred in December, 1740, the Town Council spent £40 on firewood, and arranged with the "Principal Gentlemen" of Newport to reimburse Jahleel Brenton for wood which he allowed the poor to cut on his property.[26]

The fuel problem was less perplexing at Philadelphia and Charles Town. The ready access to wooded regions afforded by numerous small creeks and inlets in both localities, quite as much as the gentle climate of the latter town, prevented suffering from shortage in either place.

IV

Town expansion and increasing traffic made the proper care of highways a continuing necessity, and in general the towns met this problem admirably. New streets were opened up, many paving projects undertaken, and further attention paid to street cleaning. In addition, some of the towns made better provision for drainage, and spent large sums for the improvement of their bridges.

The period saw great activity in highway construction in the growing town of Newport. Two thoroughfares were opened west from Thames Street toward Easton's Point and the Cove, where several lanes already ran before recently erected houses. Pelham and King Streets followed in 1722. The Town Council, empowered by the Assembly to lay out all highways in 1725, manifested considerable energy in surveying and building new roads, receiving assistance after 1727 from a "Town Committty for managing & regulating Streets." By

[25] *N. Y. M. C. C.*, III, 247; *N. Y. Gaz.*, May 9, 1726; Jan. 4, 1737; Feb. 20, 1739; *N. Y. Journal*, Jan.–Feb., 1741; *News Letter*, Feb. 12, Mar. 5, 1741.
[26] *Newport T. M. Recs.*, 226, 228, 304, 307; *Newport T. C. Recs.*, Dec. 1, 1740; Feb. 4, April 6, 1741; *R. I. Gaz.*, Mar. 1, 1733; *Eve. Post*, Feb. 21, 1737.

1742 about twenty new streets, or considerable extensions of existing thoroughfares, had been undertaken at Newport.[27]

The doubling of the settled area at Charles Town made it necessary for the first time to plan, lay out, and construct new highways there. The three main streets running west from the Cooper River were pushed across the peninsula to Ashley Swamp. Church and Meeting Streets were extended south across Vanderhorst's Creek to White Point, and new ways soon opened up to the westward. Private capital promoted most of these improvements, though occasionally the Assembly saw fit to intervene in the laying out of more important thoroughfares. In 1734, to settle a dispute, it determined the course of Dock Street and changed its name to Queen. By 1739 there were thirty-three principal streets in Charles Town, as well as many lanes and alleys, the whole conforming to the original gridiron plan.[28]

Few new thoroughfares were needed in the three larger towns. Most of the new Boston streets ran off Green Lane in the West End, and a few more were constructed in the South End near the Neck. In 1729, "to prevent Incroachments on the Town's Intrest," all streets and lanes were marked out on a survey, to which the Selectmen thereafter carefully adhered. In 1731, for example, they refused to allow the building of a "new way" from Queen to School Street, because the advantage gained would "in no way Countervail" the loss of land. The street known as Belcher's Lane, twenty-one feet wide and a quarter of a mile long, was built by private persons at a cost of £1,000 and presented to the town as a public highway in 1741. At the end of the period Boston possessed sixty streets, forty-one lanes, and eighteen alleys, "besides squares, courts, etc.," which, with a few minor exceptions, constituted its final highway pattern for the colonial period.[29]

As the checkerboard highways of Philadelphia had been marked off for years, the pressing need was for their extension to keep pace with increased building. In 1724 the Corporation hired Jacob Tyler as city surveyor, and instructed him to lay out certain new streets. The authorities, however, largely failed in their management of highways, because in 1713 the Province had divided control of such matters between Corporation and Assessors, among whom agreement proved impossible. Although this state of affairs produced many bitter complaints from citizens, the only action taken by the Corporation con-

[27] Stiles, Draught of Highways; *Newport T. M. Recs.*, 217, 328; *Newport T. C. Recs.*, Oct. 7, 1723; *R. I. Acts (1744)*, 52.
[28] *Iconography of Charles Town; S. C. Session Acts*, 1733–1739, 99; *S. C. Statutes*, VII, 74; S. C. Pub. Recs., XVIII, 301.
[29] Bonner's *Map of Boston;* 12 *Bos. Rec. Com.*, 9, 24, 282; 13 *Bos. Rec. Com.*, 205, 299; Bennett, History of New England, 126.

sisted of an order in 1737 to James Parrock and Peter Brown to open up a street in front of their properties.[30]

In the face of this official paralysis, nearly all of Philadelphia's highway construction had to be undertaken by public spirited townsmen at their own expense. In 1739, tired of dealing with indecisive Assessors and indolent Corporation, citizens appealed to the Assembly for a law regulating the town's streets. Though it passed the legislature, the bill perished before a Corporation-inspired veto of the Governor. This action postponed any effective public control of the town's highway system, and greatly increased the widespread distrust in which inhabitants held their city government.[31]

New York built fewer streets in this period than any other town, for most of the thoroughfares where building took place had been opened up before 1720. The authorities resolved in 1729 that "For the better utility of the Trade and Commerce of the City, Increasing New Buildings therein and Improveing the Revenues of the Corporation," two new ways should be laid out along the Hudson River to connect with four slips recently erected there. The granting of water lots along the East River, and construction by the grantees of bulkheads and wharves, made it an easy matter after 1737 to fill in and extend street ends along the waterfront. Occasionally a road, like that "thro the Hill by the Windmill," was undertaken by a "Number of Gents . . . at their own Expense," and with the good wishes of the Corporation.[32]

The principal obstacle to the maintenance of a satisfactory highway system in each town came, not from the absence of public spirit as in former years, but rather from the inability of local authorities to finance these projects. Nevertheless, marked improvements in highway engineering were achieved in some communities, and in all of them provisions for the care of the streets presented a notable advance over those of contemporary English cities.

The best streets were those of the two New England seaports, where town governments possessed power to tax for local improvements. At Boston, between 1720 and 1737, the town spent over £3,250 for surfacing newly constructed streets in the West and South Ends. As in earlier years, this expenditure applied only to the town's share, or middle of the thoroughfares, and residents continued to lay out an equal or larger amount in paving the sides. The advantages of hard surfaces had been so widely demonstrated before 1720 that authorities had seldom to urge abutters to pave before their doors. In most cases

[30] P. M. C. C., 247, 364; Pa. Statutes, II, 414.
[31] P. M. C. C., 368.
[32] N. Y. M. C. C., III, 487; IV, 496; Edwards, New York, 166; Stokes, Iconography, I, 195.

the Selectmen received a request from an individual or group to pave the "Town's share" of a street, accompanied by a promise to care for the sides. In 1727 residents of the lower end of Prince Street were allowed to pave "Nine feet against their own Land," upon completion of which the Town agreed to pay "for the Remainder." Occasionally the Selectmen ordered the surfacing of a street; in 1721 they voted that "Tanners Lane be gravelled for the conveniency of foot Passengers." [33]

From 1728 to 1733 there was a lull in paving activity, the principal concern of the Selectmen being to keep existing streets in repair. By 1735, however, so many petitions had poured in that the Town Meeting appropriated £300 for surfacing and chose a committee to designate the streets upon which it was to be expended. Orange Street, which ran across the Neck and was continually being washed out by tides or storms, constituted a perennial source of worry to the Selectmen. The way became so bad in 1737 that the Suffolk County Court presented it as dangerous and ordered the Selectmen to have it repaired. Another complaint made the next year charged that in several parts of Boston "the Pavements are Pitch'd so steep that People passing . . . often fall down, and are in great danger of breaking their limbs." The Selectmen took immediate action to remedy this nuisance.[34]

Boston authorities exercised constant vigilance to prevent anyone from "Damnifying the Pavement in the Streets." As in former days, the major threat came from heavy vehicles. Orders regulating their size and weight were strictly enforced, and in 1727 a severe ordinance denied the use of the streets to carts more than sixteen feet long or with tires less than four inches wide. No load might exceed a ton, and all two-horse wagons were prohibited. Doubtless these rules aided measurably in protecting the new pavements from "damnification." [35]

The streets of Newport underwent a remarkable transformation in this period. Beginning in 1721, Spring Street was paved "Six foot wyde against each persons land," and residents of the Point were instructed to "do their duty in mending the highways" there. The next year the Vestry completed the pavement in front of Trinity Church. In 1726 the town ordered all newly opened thoroughfares paved six feet wide on each side "as far as the houses are built to the Southward," and the next year some "very narrow and discommodious" lanes were widened at town expense. More funds became available to the town in 1729, when the Rhode Island Assembly voted the proceeds of the

[33] 8 *Bos. Rec. Com.* 214, 217, 222; 12 *Bos. Rec. Com.*, 4, 23; 13 *Bos. Rec. Com.*, 79, 163.
[34] 12 *Bos. Rec. Com.*, 31, 100, 107, 151, 298; 13 *Bos. Rec. Com.*, 241, 299; 15 *Bos. Rec. Com.*, 19, 108, 111, 113.
[35] 8 *Bos. Rec. Com.*, 206, 211.

slave duty "for paving and amending the streets" of Newport. Four years later, when the slave duty was repealed, "the Compact part" of Newport was authorized "to lay a tax on the ratable property . . . for the repairing of the highways." [36] These new financial resources produced in Newport by 1742 streets that were well surfaced and cared for, and surpassed in this respect only by those of Boston.

Most of New York's streets prior to 1720 had been paved with cobblestones, but the Corporation expended little energy and less money on surfaces for new thoroughfares or on repairs for the old. In 1731, under authority of the new charter, the Mayor and Common Council passed an ordinance requiring all inhabitants to pave in front of their houses and to keep their streets in good repair. [37] Although in 1742 most of the public ways had surfaces of rough cobblestones, efforts by the Corporation to maintain Manhattan's street system in this period merit no particular praise.

Despite encouraging activity by private persons just prior to 1720, the Corporation of Philadelphia, like its New York counterpart, achieved little in the field of street-paving in this period. The Grand Jury in 1723 presented Chestnut, Arch and Sassafras Streets as "common nusances," and George Warner found Market Street the only paved thoroughfare when he visited the town in 1726. The next year the Corporation ordered inhabitants to provide walks in front of their properties, and to cease "hanging their horses on the Posts and Shoeing them on the sd. Pavements within the Posts." But these rules were poorly enforced, and not until 1737 did the Mayor and Common Council begin themselves to have streets paved, charging the costs to the delinquents. [38]

A change for the better resulted from the report of the Grand Jury of 1739 that many streets were not only unpaved, but "Impassable" for want of repair. This presentment impelled the citizenry to seek a street act from the Assembly, which, as we have seen, the Corporation thwarted. Nevertheless, fear for their privileges goaded the city fathers into action, and within a short time improvements in the town streets began to appear. High Street was posted and gravelled twenty feet wide with public funds. Private individuals received orders to pave their portions of the streets, and the Grand Jury induced the Corporation to pave Third Street in 1741. At the end of the period those in authority, driven by outraged public sentiment, had finally em-

[36] R. I. Col. Recs., IV, 423; Newport T. C. Recs., May 3, 1731; Newport T. M. Recs., 212, 214, 232, 238; Mason, Trinity Church, 37; Richardson Collection, 972: 174; Bull, Memoir of Rhode Island, II, 179.
[37] N. Y. M. C. C., IV, 105.
[38] Ancient Recs. Phila., 41; P. M. C. C., 251, 272, 364, 368; Westcott, Philadelphia, chapter LXXXII.

barked upon a serious program of highway surfacing which was soon to provide Philadelphia with very presentable streets.[39]

Absence of effective local government resulted in the general neglect of the streets of Charles Town. Broad and Queen Streets were paved with some sort of hard surface by public spirited citizens, and from the scanty evidence one may infer that in these two decades some few others were similarly improved.[40]

The crowding of population into the towns brought demands for better methods of drainage and sewage disposal, as well as for the construction at convenient points of larger and stronger bridges to facilitate the movement of augmented traffic. Public authorities usually found such projects too costly for their undertaking, but they did lend support to private enterprises wherever possible.

Under careful surveillance by the Selectmen the town of Boston greatly expanded its drainage system. Between 1721 and 1736 the authorities issued 234 permits to open the streets for the laying of sewers and drains, always with the requirement that the pavement be carefully replaced. In some instances licenses for the building of drains were refused, as in 1735, when Jacob Parker, who desired to connect his drain with the Prince Street sewer, was forbidden to do so, because his drain was reputed "a Publick Nusance to the Neighbourhood." Few cities anywhere in the world were so well drained as Boston; in 1740 Bennett reported that "the streets are well paved, and lying upon a descent, the Town is, for the generality, as dry and clean as any I remember to have seen." [41]

At Philadelphia, the construction of brick and stone underground drains begun in the last period continued. In 1727 the Corporation also required the streets to be so pitched that surface water, especially from pumps, would run into the "watercourses" in the middle of the streets. Persons like John Key, who failed to keep the watercourses before their properties clean, found the authorities ready and willing to prosecute them. By 1738 many arched culverts and underground sewers had been constructed, and Philadelphia, too, was well underdrained.[42]

Other towns were less progressive in meeting the problem of drainage. Watercourses and "Common Shewers" were built at Charles Town, to be promptly presented by the Grand Jury whenever they became "stopt up." But the absence of properly constituted authority to superintend the laying of drains and sewers according to a definite plan prevented the town from enjoying a satisfactory drainage system.

[39] Court Papers, Phila. Cty., II; *Mercury,* June 15, 1738; *P. M. C. C.,* 395, 414.
[40] *S. C. Statutes,* III, 405, 694; VII, 12; Ravenel, *Eliza Pinckney,* 18.
[41] 13 *Bos. Rec. Com.,* 125, 136, 278, 295; Bennett, History of New England, 126.
[42] *P. M. C. C.,* 272, 368; *Pa. Mag.,* LVIII, 266; Court Papers, Phila. Cty., II; Scharf and Westcott, *Philadelphia,* I, 208.

Many houses had "Drains running under them into the Streets" in such a manner as to interfere with those of other houses. The town acquired its first well regulated sewer in 1735, when the Assembly provided for "sinking a Drain" in Broad Street, at the expense of abutters, who received the privilege of connecting their house drains with this sewer.[43]

It cannot be said that either Newport or New York squarely faced this problem in these years, and conditions in both towns frequently became deplorable. Newport enjoyed good surface drainage by reason of its location on the side of a hill. But when the flat land at Easton's Point began to be built up, it became necessary to lay drains and sewers to carry off waste water, and several were built before 1742. The Corporation of New York made no effort to add to the two sewers constructed before 1720. Some private sewers were laid, however, and in 1737 John Norris and his helper were nearly smothered while "at work in a Shaft to lay a Drain, about 15 foot below [the] Surface of the Earth." Surface water was drained from the highways in open channels, or "kennels," which ran down the middle of the streets and emptied into the Broad Street sewer. Many New York houses were not equipped with privies, and excrement had to be carried in "ordure tubs" to the East River at night.[44]

Little need for additional bridges was felt in the towns, but increasing traffic made necessary the repair, enlargement or replacement of existing structures. The Hanover Street bridge across Mill Creek at Boston badly wanted repair in 1727, and the Selectmen agreed with the Proprietors to bear one third of the expense, because "Something is Necessary to be done at present for the Convenience of Passengers Carts &c." Twelve years later the drawbridge at Ann Street was rebuilt by the town at a cost of £120.[45]

The question of a bridge across the Charles River came up again in March, 1729. The General Court authorized John Staniford of West Boston to collect funds for the erection of such a structure from Boston to the Spencer Phipps farm in Cambridge. Staniford claimed to have the promise of £1,800 from two Cambridge gentlemen if the colony would contribute a like amount. He argued the benefit of such a project to rural districts, and struck a familiar note when he pointed out that "in the building of this Bridge there would be a great Number of People employed," thus encouraging a "Revival of Business." Though the Town Meeting was known to favor the project it took no action at this time. After tenacious devotion to his scheme for over

[43] S. C. Hist. & Gen. Mag., XXV, 194; S. C. Statutes, III, 405.
[44] Newport T. M. Recs., 219; N. Y. Journal, Nov. 21, 1737; Edwards, New York, 168.
[45] 13 Bos. Rec. Com., 182; 15 Bos. Rec. Com., 153.

a decade Staniford finally procured from the Meeting a vote pledging the Town, when the work should actually begin, to build the portion from the Boston shore to low water, "provided" the General Court would loan the town funds and grant it a "proportionable part" of the tolls.[46] With this highly conditional vote John Staniford's dream came to an end. A public work of such magnitude was as yet too much for any existing agency to finance.

Newport authorities saw that the drawbridge "going to the Point" was kept in good condition by residents of the district until 1726, when John, Peter and Edward Easton obtained release from militia duty "on Consideration of their making and keeping the bridge in repair." Growing traffic soon necessitated a better structure, which was erected by the town in 1734 with the aid of a £200 contribution from the Assembly.[47]

The bridges erected at Philadelphia before 1720 would have served the town adequately had they been kept in repair as were those in the New England towns. But the "publick bridge" at Front and Walnut Streets had fallen into such a "decay'd condition" by 1730 that nearby residents petitioned for its repair. The next year they asserted that it had become dangerous for pedestrians as well as for carts, and that their "Rents were thereby greatly reduced, and several of their Houses standing empty." They offered to make "a very considerable subscription" toward rebuilding the structure, if the Corporation would undertake the task. As a result the bridge was shortly in excellent condition. In 1737 the Corporation built an "Arch & Causeway" over High Street, and repaired the draw at Dock Creek with funds raised by a tax assessment. Within two years, however, the Grand Jury presented the drawbridge as "very much decay'd, and . . . Dangerous passing over." Characteristically, the authorities seem to have done nothing to eliminate this "Nusance" at this time.[48]

Labor for engineering projects and for highway construction was secured by a number of methods. Philadelphia and Boston used public funds to employ workmen. In addition, each free Negro of Boston had to labor eight days a year on the roads in lieu of watch or trainband duty. Prior to 1730 as many as sixty of these blacks performed their work under a white foreman, but after that year their numbers so declined that only twenty-one appeared on the list for 1738. Negro slaves probably did most of the work on the streets at Charles Town.[49]

Newport and New York still followed the English custom of re-

[46] *Bos. Gaz.*, Mar. 12, 1729; 12 *Bos. Rec. Com.*, 224, 234, 281.
[47] *Newport T. M. Recs.*, 212, 230; Peterson, *Rhode Island*, 61; *R. I. Col. Recs.* IV, 500.
[48] Court Papers, Phila. Cty., I, II; *P. M. C. C.*, 266, 368.
[49] 13 *Bos. Rec. Com.*, 106, 109, 145; 15 *Bos. Rec. Com.*, 132, 135.

quiring each householder to work a certain number of days on the roads or to furnish a substitute. New streets at Easton's Point, Newport, were built by "those who live on the Point." The Town Council set a fine of three shillings in 1724 for persons refusing or neglecting to perform their share of highway work, and an even larger sum for those who failed to bring their teams. This system of forced labor proved "very prejudicial and injurious" to the common people, "the poorest Man being obliged . . . to doe or suffer as much as the persons whose circumstances is far superior." In 1729, therefore, the town made an experiment with hired labor, but the expense proving too great returned the next year to the old corvée system. A similar practice irked the common folk at New York. In 1734 "Deborah Careful" complained that having to pay for a substitute on the watch was bad enough, but when she was twice summoned to send a man to work on the roads the situation became intolerable. "I told the Constable I could not see that this dry Season there would be so much Occasion to mend the Roads; oh, say he, the Roads are good, but they must be made strait, and we are to dig down Fresh-Water Hill." It is outrageous, quoth the exasperated widow, "this Loading the poor Inhabitants with so heavy a Tax." [50]

Encroachments on public highways annoyed the towns far less than in former years. At Boston in 1723 the Town Meeting urged the Selectmen not to suffer shipbuilders or others "to Incumber the Streets, . . . by Laying Timber or any other materials thereon." But a new problem arose from the erection of sign posts in front of the increasing number of shops, and after 1736 the Selectmen allowed them only by special permit after they had viewed the premises to determine whether such signs would constitute a public nuisance. The Corporation of New York in 1731 found it necessary to pass an ordinance forbidding people to encumber the streets with building materials without license from the Recorder. Throughout the period city officers at Philadelphia rigidly enforced the orders against obstructing the public ways. At Charles Town the first regulation about encroachments appeared in 1740, while at Newport there seems to have been no serious problem of this sort. [51]

In the three larger towns growing civic pride expressed itself in a movement for cleaner streets. New York seems to have enjoyed the greatest success in this matter. Inhabitants continued to rake up dirt and refuse before their homes for carters to carry away at sixpence a load, until 1731, when the charge was raised to seven pence. In this

[50] *Newport T. M. Recs.,* 212, 223, 230, 246, 247; *N. Y. Journal,* Sept. 2, 1734.
[51] 8 *Bos. Rec. Com.,* 169; 13 *Bos. Rec. Com.,* 300, 347; 15 *Bos. Rec. Com.,* 26; *N. Y. M. C. C.,* IV, 102; Court Papers, Phila. Cty., II; S. C. Pub. Recs., XX, 529.

year, also, new and improved cleaning regulations went into effect. The Corporation set heavy fines, ranging from six to thirty shillings, for casting refuse, garbage, or ordure into the public ways, and provided penalties for persons sweeping dirt into the watercourses in anticipation of the arrival of early rainfall to save them their seven pence. After this date the highways of Manhattan presented a vastly improved appearance, save in winter, when they "fill'd with confused Heaps of Snow, so that Lovers of Sled-riding, . . . [could] scarcely use them without Danger." [52]

Every year with the arrival of spring the Boston Selectmen reminded inhabitants of the town order requiring abutters to keep the streets clean before their doors. By 1725, however, complaints began to be heard about the "Nastiness of the Pav'd Streets," which had not been properly cleaned for two years. At least one citizen held the "Opinion that the Town has laid out a great deal of Money to very little Purpose; for in Rainy time a Man must walk almost Ankle deep in mud on the Pavements." The Town Meeting consequently created eight scavengers to warn people to rake up the dirt into heaps before their houses, and empowered them to impress any cart to carry off the piled up trash at fifteen pence per load. The carters complained bitterly of the burden thus imposed upon them, and in 1732 the Selectmen raised their wage to eighteen pence. Five years later, however, the authorities became dissatisfied with the failure of the carmen to carry the dirt out of town, and agreed with some other people to cart it away "without charge." This new method worked well except in winter, when this most northern town was burdened with heavy snowfall. Jonathan Willis stirred up a heated debate in Town Meeting in March, 1741, when he deplored the "Inconvenience of Ice and Snow, lying in the Streets," and the danger thereby incurred by pedestrians. As a result the scavengers the next winter warned every householder to "keep clear a good and Sufficient Path . . . from Ice and Snow," upon penalty of a fifteen shilling fine for neglect. [53]

Philadelphia streets seem to have been kept relatively clean. The province law of 1712 requiring residents to "sweep the streets clean before their respective houses," seldom enforced before 1720, now apparently operated with considerable success, for in none of the caustic and searching reports of the Grand Juries were dirty streets singled out for mention. On the other hand, Charles Town and Newport took no effective action for securing cleaner thoroughfares. Some inkling of conditions in the latter community may be gleaned from the

[52] N. Y. M. C. C., IV, 102; N. Y. Journal, Dec. 22, 1740.
[53] News Letter, Feb. 26, 1722; Courant, Feb. 22, 1725; 8 Bos. Rec. Com., 191; 12 Bos. Rec. Com., 17, 34, 157, 262, 264, 277, 294.

Town Council's order of 1739, "that Robert Bennett get some Persons to bury all the Dead Doggs, and other carrion, That Lye in ye Streets of this Town." [54]

The familiar town swine more or less disappeared from the streets of colonial seaports in this period, but their place was effectively taken by numerous dogs which proved equally bothersome to the inhabitants. Many Bostonians grumbled at the great number of dogs which worried and injured cattle and sheep, forcing butchers to keep "their Sheep Housed in the Night." But, as with the hogs before them, all attempts to restrict the keeping of dogs failed in the Bay town. At Philadelphia, however, the Common Council dealt a blow at the "mischief" in 1722, by permitting citizens to kill on sight the authors of any canine disturbances. Hogs still bothered the New Yorkers, but here, too, the real danger to the interests of butchers and others came from the many "Mischievous Mastiffs Bull Doggs and Other Useless Dogs," which not only ran at "Coaches Horses Chaise and Cattle" in the day time, but roamed the streets at night, frequently "attacking and flying at the Inhabitants." The Corporation tried to prevent such outrages in 1727 by ordering all owners of dogs to keep them chained up in their yards upon pain of a large fine. Rather belatedly in 1741 notice was given at Charles Town that the laws against swine roving about the streets would be enforced.[55]

Newport thoroughfares still resembled a barnyard. Here, too, swine yielded their ascendance to the dogs which, dead or alive, infested the village streets despite the efforts of Nathaniel Dyer and Peleg Rogers, dog-catchers. In 1729, to "Prevent dogs Kiling or doeing damages," the Town Council restricted the keeping of such dangerous pets to those possessing real estate valued at £50. Although Thomas Peckham, the harassed poundkeeper, received an increase in salary at this time, his duties were made no easier when the town permitted one Dublin to graze his blind white horse in the streets.[56]

The growth of the towns naturally intensified the problem of traffic, and called forth more rigid regulations for the restraint of reckless riding and driving. The Rhode Island Assembly voted in 1729 that whenever a cart or a horse killed a person, a coroner's jury should determine the true cause of death, appraise the value of the cart or horse, and require payment of a sum equal to that value to the Overseers of the Poor, — a curious survival of an antique practice. The Town Meeting in 1739 condemned the practice of carters riding on

[54] Pa. Statutes, II, 419; Newport T. C. Recs., July 2, 1739.
[55] 8 Bos. Rec. Com., 223; P. M. C. C., 220; N. Y. Col. Laws, II, 641; N. Y. M. C. C., III, 407; S. C. Gaz., Dec. 21, 1741.
[56] Newport T. M. Recs., 225, 249, 288; R. I. Acts (1744), 127; Newport T. C. Recs., Sept. 1, 1729.

their teams "without having them under proper government," because it placed children "in great danger of being Trampled on, by their Oxen and Horses, and run over by their Cart wheels." Nothing is more indicative of Newport's growth than this increasing traffic, and the town was forced to order all carters to lead their horses at a walk.[57]

At Philadelphia rows of posts set up in 1720 along each side of main thoroughfares separated street from sidewalk and so afforded some protection for pedestrians. To prevent accidents by carts and wagons new and stricter ordinances were enacted in 1722 against "Excessive Galloping, Trotting & paceing of Horses." Yet accidents continued, the "carelessness" of carters resulting in the death of two children in March, 1733. Because of the danger to shoppers during the heavy market day traffic the Corporation in 1742 ordered "proper Iron Chains be provided to Stop the passage . . . through the Market place." [58]

Through the Town Meeting Boston citizens did what they could for the protection of "foot passengers." In 1723 "Throwing, Rolling or flingin of the Bullet, Commonly called . . . putting the Shot," was forbidden in the streets of the town. As at Philadelphia more rows of posts appeared to safeguard pedestrians from riders and carts. Yet notwithstanding careful enforcement of laws against galloping horses and carters riding on their teams, accidents were far too frequent. Contemporary newspapers present many items like the following: Stephen Lamb, "A Child of about Five Years old, at the South End of the Town, was run over by a Cart, and died immediately after." Boston even suffered from the magnitude of its nocturnal traffic. Jonathan Willis, that diligent uncoverer of public nuisances, inquired of the Town Meeting in 1742 "Whether Nothing can be done to prevent the great Disturbances Occasioned by Horses and Chaise in great Numbers Crouding into Town and also out . . . till Nine, Ten, and sometimes Eleven a clock at Night." The Meeting considered the matter, but took no action at this time.[59]

To the highway laws already in force at New York were added in this period safety orders forbidding boys and apprentices to shoot at marks, "or at Random against any Fence," within the city, while for the protection of pedestrians and of children at play no slave was allowed to ride "disorderly or Precipitately . . . thro' any of the Streets" after 1731. The traffic problem, despite commendable efforts to control it, had come to the towns to stay.[60]

[57] R. I. Acts (1744), 118; Newport T. M. Recs., 311.
[58] P. M. C. C., 215, 220, 272, 415; Mercury, Mar. 13, 1733; Pa. Gaz., Mar. 22, 1733.
[59] 8 Bos. Rec. Com., 172; 13 Bos. Rec. Com., 279; News Letter, Sept. 6, Oct. 25, 1733; Rehearsal, Nov. 8, 1731; 12 Bos. Rec. Com., 285, 293.
[60] N. Y. M. C. C., IV, 89, 105. For Bristol's traffic problem, see Latimer, Bristol in the Eighteenth Century, 131, 175; Bayne, Norwich.

In 1733 New York joined the other northern towns in setting aside a tract of land for its first public park. In this year the Corporation leased a piece of property at the lower end of Broadway near the Fort to John Chambers, Peter Bayard, and Peter Jay, to be "Inclosed to make a Bowling Green . . . with Walks therein, for the Beauty & Ornament of the Said Street as well as for the Recreation & delight of the Inhabitants." Between 1728 and 1740 Boston Common was enclosed on two sides by a fence, to prevent the despoiling of its herbage by carts and horses. "Every afternoon, after drinking tea," wrote an English traveler, "the gentlemen and ladies walk the Mall, and from thence adjourn to one another's houses to spend the evening. . . . What they call the Mall is a walk on a fine green common . . . with two rows of young trees planted opposite to each other, with a fine footway between, in imitation of St. James Park; and part of the bay, . . . taking its course along the north-west Side of the Common . . . forms a beautiful canal, in view of the walk." Deacon John Marion continued to pass out tickets which enabled the preferred stock of the town to graze on the Common until 1733, when John Warwick became cow-keeper, and began to issue "certificates" for the same purpose.[61]

v

Between 1720 and 1742 the waterfronts of the five towns assumed the appearance of completion which was to experience few alterations during the remainder of the colonial period. Each port, except New York, made adequate provisions for the effective and rapid handling of its shipping. Boston, with its now famous Long Wharf and its great private landing places, bowed to few cities anywhere in ability to care for a large volume of commerce. Some new piers were built, so that in 1742 there were 166 wharves and docks of all kinds in the town. The Selectmen spent much time on affairs concerning the Town Dock. In 1727 the eighty year grant of the south side of the Dock to Valentine Hill and associates expired, and the Town decided to take it over, together with certain private buildings roundabout. Though free to fishermen after 1729, this Dock now yielded the town a nice revenue. Another harbor problem constantly before the authorities was the "ruenous Condition" of the sea-wall, built in 1676, and "notoriously" neglected for years until it constituted a real danger to shipping. Town orders and threats of legal action proved equally unavailing to force the proprietors to perform necessary repairs, and the sea-wall continued throughout the period to become an increasing hazard to navigation. The Long Wharf proprietors had agreed to keep a high-

[61] N. Y. M. C. C., IV, 174, 179; 12 Bos. Rec. Com., 58, 78, 141; 13 Bos. Rec. Com., 114, 148, 241, 250, 288; 15 Bos. Rec. Com., 206, 225, 254; Bennett, History of New England, 126; Life of Carew, 110.

way thirty feet wide along the wharf to its end, where the town proposed to erect fortifications. In 1736 a committee of the Town Meeting discovered that passage through this way was frequently obstructed, and also that the proprietors "constantly demand and exact Wharfage" from foreign vessels docking at the town's share of the wharf. This being a palpable violation of their contract, the Selectmen forced the grasping proprietors to observe the exact terms of the instrument thereafter.[62]

Newport's wealthier merchants all owned wharves, some of them large and well fitted with warehouses. Ellery's and Wanton's wharves on the Point, Clark's on the Cove, and the Banister and Malbone piers running off Thames Street were among the most important. In 1738 the town permitted Robert Taylor to carry his wharf "nine hundred feet into the harbor from the high water mark," and though he actually built only seven hundred and forty feet his was one of the largest private wharves in the colonies. After 1740 Abraham Redwood's pier, though not so large as Taylor's, became the scene of great shipping activity. Many smaller docks and piers made up the thirty odd landing places at Newport in 1742.[63]

One of the major public improvements of the period was undertaken at Newport in 1739. A group of enterprising merchants sought a grant of the town wharf land and "all the space of land . . . extending from Thames Street westward across the Cove . . . to Eastons point & across the Point eight hundred feet westward into the water towards Goat Island." In this area they proposed to build a wharf 50 feet wide and 2,011 feet long, extending from Thames Street to the western limits of the grant, "leaving a Channel for the passage of boats into the Cove with a good convenient Drawbridge." The petitioners urged that such a wharf would be sufficiently "commodious for the largest vessels," that its construction would "Imploy a vast number of Tradesmen and other Inhabitants," and that when completed it would form a vista one mile long from its tip to the new Colony House, "the beauty and grandeur of which will appear the greatest perhaps in all New England." The Town Meeting, "sensible" of the advantages to Newport, made the necessary grant. The work was almost complete in 1741, when twenty-seven shops and warehouses were erected on "Long Wharf." Even a sailors' boarding house could there be found with the following inviting sign: [64]

[62] 13 *Bos. Rec. Com.*, 160, 162, 183, 267; 15 *Bos. Rec. Com.*, 369; 8 *Bos. Rec. Com.*, 188, 206, 220, 225; 12 *Bos. Rec. Com.*, 25, 32, 143.
[63] Blaskowitz, *Map of Newport*; *Newport Hist. Mag.*, II, 245; *Bos. Gaz.*, April 27, 1741; *R. I. Gaz.*, Oct. 25, 1732.
[64] This pier was 411 feet longer than the great Boston wharf. *Newport T. M. Recs.*, 312, 325; *Newport T. C. Recs.*, Oct., 1739; Plan of Long Wharf, Newport (MS.); Mason, *Newport*, 179.

Come, brother sailor, make a stop,
And lend a hand to strap the block;
And if the work is neatly done,
You shall have a glass of rum.

Newport's Long Wharf not only fulfilled its commercial promise, but the proposed magnificent approach to the Colony House proved indeed to be the finest in all New England.

In 1742 seventeen good wharves and several fine quays adorned the waterfront of Philadelphia. Most of them were the property of the Corporation, which exhibited unwonted activity in keeping them in repair so that the fruitful revenues therefrom might not suffer. The Common Council borrowed £300 to mend its wharves in 1723, and five years later placed the care of all city waterfront property in the hands of Richard Armitage. High Street wharf and quay, where most larger ships docked, was carried out sixty feet, and a new wharf was built at Sassafras Street in 1730. The existence of such satisfactory public facilities made the construction of private piers less important than in the other towns. Richard Anthony built a small wharf shortly after 1720, and George Warner in 1726 mentioned the piers of Anthony Morris and William Allen as the largest on the Delaware. Most of the privately owned wharves were small landing places, equipped with a storehouse, where shallops and schooners might land their cargoes. Samuel Powel and his son constructed a large wharf with a road leading up to it in 1736, and so improved the neighborhood for the "Common Use & Benefit" that the Corporation gave them the right to take wharfage there in 1742. Most frequented of all landing places continued to be Dock Creek, where nearly all market produce, building materials and fuel coming into Philadelphia were unladed.[65]

The greatest relative improvement in waterfronts came at Charles Town. Despite a severe hurricane in August, 1728, which destroyed fifteen vessels and damaged all piers, many large wharves and "Bridges" had been erected by the end of the period. In 1739 there were eight landing places along the Cooper front of the town. Of these, the "Middle Bridge" was the largest, containing eleven warehouses and the "Bay Markets." The principal private wharves were Brenton's bridge with three warehouses, and Rhett's bridge with two. Samuel Eveleigh marked the harbor with buoys in 1731, and in 1734 a Province port act was passed for regulation of its shipping. The devastating fire of November, 1740, which wiped out the whole trading area

[65] *East Prospect of Philadelphia; P. M. C. C.*, 238, 241, 277, 298, 304, 367, 422; *Mercury*, May 10, 1722; Dec. 16, 1736; Westcott, *Philadelphia*, chapter LXXXII; *Life of Carew*, 110.

of the town, also destroyed most of the wharves and their warehouses, and they were still in the process of rebuilding when the period closed. Fortunately for shipping interests, the harbor made a safe anchorage, and vessels could be tended by lighters during the period of reconstruction.[66]

New York authorities still refrained from building any wharves into the East River although by 1730 two excellent quays, Hunter's and Burnet's, had been constructed by groups of proprietors to whom the Assembly granted wharfage privileges. On the North River front four wharves were built out into the Hudson by 1730, to be used chiefly for the landing of fuel and flour. The Corporation Dock on the East River continued to be the center of New York's shipping, and the authorities suffered perennial difficulties in securing an honest dockmaster. They were so "regularly defrauded" by their appointees that in 1725 they again resorted to the system of leasing the Dock. After this, despite the growing commerce of the port, and the demand for better landing facilities, the Dock was allowed to fall into a state of decay, the Corporation refusing to spend one farthing upon its repair unless the funds should come from the income from the lease. This rent was so seldom forthcoming that at one time several merchants paid for necessary repairs out of their own pockets.[67] No town was so poorly equipped to care for its shipping as New York.

VI

The towns had no need to be ashamed of the physical progress of approximately one hundred years. In most respects they had within that time grown up into little cities. They had built beyond their original bounds, and within their older and business sections the erection of tenements and contiguous single houses and shops brought signs of truly urban congestion. They expanded their street systems as their greater populousness crowded the older thoroughfares, and within the limits of their financial or political capacities tried to provide surfaces that would withstand the daily pounding of increasing traffic. To meet the demands of housing large populations within limited areas they devised methods of drainage, street cleaning, and rudimentary traffic control. They expressed their maturing civic pride as municipalities in attempts to beautify their thoroughfares, and in the erection of graceful and dignified public buildings and churches, while their commercial energies fostered the construction of spacious

[66] *Iconography of Charles Town; S. C. Gaz.,* Jan. 15, Mar. 18, 1732; Oct. 27, 1739; *Trott's Laws,* 597; *Post Boy,* Jan. 26, 1741; S. C. Pub. Recs., XXI, 22.
[67] Bradford's *Map of New York; N. Y. Col. Laws,* II, 847; Hamilton, *Itinerarium,* 51; *N. Y. M. C. C.,* III, 441, 487; IV, 57; Edwards, *New York,* 152.

warehouses, wharves, some of them of magnificent proportions, and other waterfront facilities. Before the end of the period both visiting and native engravers began to take views and "prospects" of these New World cities, and the curiosity of the Mother Country led shortly to their reproduction in British periodicals. These prints reveal busy waterfronts, well furnished with wharves and docks, networks of streets, their sides crowded with attractive homes and business establishments, and the whole dominated by the spires of churches and the towers of public buildings. In the light of this pictorial evidence there is no doubt of the real and rapid growth of metropolitan America, — as an early writer had said of Philadelphia, "the most of any settlement in the World for its time." Inhabitants of the five colonial towns were now living for the most part under conditions as truly urban as any known to their age, and their economic and social problems were henceforth to be largely those of city populations.

X

COMMERCIAL RIVALRIES

I

The two decades of peaceful, though fluctuating, prosperity that followed 1720 brought a tremendous expansion of business to the five colonial towns. The mounting demand for manufactured articles and luxuries, created by growing hinterland and wealthier urban markets, led to large importations from Europe, to pay for which American merchants had to push their West India and South European traffic with renewed vigor. Along commercial routes staked out prior to 1720 the volume of colonial trade continuously increased. The outstanding economic development of the period was the climax of Boston's maritime supremacy and the beginnings of that town's decline. Her commerce grew steadily until about 1735, and her merchants waxed rich, but after 1730 competition from rivals cut so heavily into the carrying trade as to render Boston at the close of the period no longer the commercial metropolis of the American colonies. Instead, there were five "mart" towns on the Atlantic seaboard.

Boston merchants, lacking a native staple of trade and a productive back country, had early developed a flourishing traffic based upon priority in the carrying trade and the shipbuilding industry. With the maturing of other ports this advantage was in large measure lost, and with it disappeared valuable sources for the supply of gold and silver coin. In addition, the town found itself "almost entirely Stript" of the cod fishery, because "both Fish and Supply . . . [are] Confined to the Fishing Towns who generally Send it abroad in their own Vessells, Especially Marblehead, Salem and Plymouth." These factors produced the "Great Decay of our Trade in General," which impelled the Town Meeting in 1736 to petition the General Court for a lower tax rate, pointing out that the "whole Trade to the West Indies and back" had suffered curtailment and the Carolina naval stores traffic had fallen off, at the same time that importations from London had increased until they totalled one sixth of all British exports to the plantations. "Yet what we receive chiefly from thence serves in a great measure to expose our Inhabitants to censure and Extraordinary Taxes." Another memorial in 1742 informed the Court that "Trade in general at this Day . . . is not above One half that it was in 1735, and . . . much on the decline." Despite these Macedonian cries from the Town Meeting, conditions were not quite so bad as they appeared. Part of the economic distress arose naturally from the general depression of the mid-thirties; Boston still remained the leading colonial entrepot, but her merchants had henceforth to accustom themselves to more energetic competition from commercial rivals.[1]

West India trade and the slave traffic caused Newport to flourish. Rhode Island merchants made the rum, molasses and sugar business their specialty, so successfully that by 1741 Newport had wrested a large portion of the Caribbean commerce from Boston. The slave trade also proved lucrative, and merchants prospered who, like Peter Bours, sold "Nigros upon Credit with good Security, or cheap for Ready Money." Not so fortunate in developing direct European connections, though a beginning had been made by 1735, Newporters still had to "send their cash" to Boston in exchange for manufactured articles. In an attempt to free themselves from this economic bondage their merchants increased their traffic with New York, where Rhode Island coasting vessels successfully competed with Yankee ships in the carrying trade, and developed a profitable freight business to Perth Amboy and Charles Town. Rhode Island shipping news regularly appeared in the *New York Gazette* after 1726. Still, despite burgeoning activities, Newport's merchant princes had not in 1742 completely accomplished their desire "to Brake their Dependence from Boston."[2]

The three other seaports made heavy inroads into Boston's traffic, and largely succeeded in freeing themselves from New England domination. Intensive shipbuilding provided Philadelphia merchants with a fleet to compete with that of Boston for the carrying trade of the Middle Colonies and to extend their overseas business with England, Ireland, Portugal and Madeira. Shrewd business men like Edward Shippen, Richard Willing and Samuel Powel no longer needed to import from England via Boston, since they could now freight their own vessels with flour and lumber to exchange in Old World ports for servants and manufactured goods.

> Lately imported from Bristol, in the Ship Jane Galley, likely Servants, Men Women and Boys, bred to most sorts of Business; fine white Salt, Glass-Bottles, and most Sorts of European Goods. To be Sold by Willing and Shippen, at very reasonable Rates, at their Store on Carpenter's Wharff.

[1] 14 *Bos. Rec. Com.*, 12; 12 *Bos. Rec. Com.*, 119, 198; Carrier, *Beginnings of Agriculture*, 283; Gipson, *British Empire*, III, 9; 6 MHS *Colls.*, VI, 400, 410; *Eve. Post*, Aug. 11, 1740.
[2] Bigelow, Rhode Island Commerce, Pt. I, chapter II, V; *Bos. Gaz.*, Jan. 27, 1729; *Lloyd Papers*, I, 289; Bennett, History of New England, 120; Stokes, *Iconography*, IV, 518; *Pa. Gaz.*, Jan. 5, 1731; *Eve. Post*, May 11, 1741; *R. I. Col. Recs.*, V, 13.

After 1730 advertisements like the preceding gave ample evidence of the existence of a direct trade with the Mother Country. Pennsylvania had also become the granary from which the West Indies and the Southern colonies were fed, and in this trade, too, Quaker skippers pared down the Boston freight profits. Philadelphia flour, much of it in Delaware-built vessels, was even shipped to Boston, where local merchants kept a close watch on the activities of New England bakers.[3]

Until about 1730 New Yorkers relied heavily upon Boston vessels for shipping off their flour and lumber, and upon Bay traders for their imported goods. At this time, however, a direct trade with Europe began to develop, with the arrival of twelve ships from England. Merrett and Fletcher of Boston still supplied the Knickerbockers with large quantities of groceries; other Yankees brought in most of the town's dyewoods. But, toward the close of the period, efforts of New York merchants to escape from dependence on the northern connection met with increasing success. Samuel Bourdet commenced importing dry goods, haberdashery and hardware direct from Bristol, and Isaac Rodrigue procured a similar line from London. By 1737 the *New York Weekly Journal* carried regular notices of ships lading for English ports. The town's chief articles of commerce were flour and meat, which had, of course, to compete in Caribbean markets with similar and superior produce from Pennsylvania.[4]

South Carolina produced two staples, rice and deerskins, which enabled Charles Town traders to traffic directly with England and southern Europe, and rendered unnecessary the services of Boston ships and merchants. Vessels from the Thames and the Froome sailed directly to the wharves of Beale and Cooper or James Wilmot "on the Bay" with cargoes of furniture, shoes, linens, hardware, haberdashery and toys. By 1742 the commerce of Charles Town with English cities exceeded that with the northern ports by six to one, and its traffic with the West Indies was double that with the northern colonies.[5]

Concentration by South Carolina planters on staple crops necessitated large importations of foodstuffs. Joseph Shute specialized in Pennsylvania flour, bread, corn, bacon and "good Philadelphia Beer." In 1739 Richard Hockley of Philadelphia wrote from Charles Town

[3] Philadelphia's importations from England amounted to £300,000 in 1743. *Pa. Gaz.*, Mar. 4, Nov. 10, 1729; *Mercury*, Feb. 26, 1723; May 20, 1731; Jan. 18, 1732; Bezanson, Gray and Hussey, *Prices in Pennsylvania*, 2, 29, 61, 67; Gipson, *British Empire*, III, 10 n.
[4] Stokes, *Iconography*, IV, 518; *N. Y. Gaz.*, June 28, 1731; April 14, Aug. 4, 1735; June 7, 1736; *N. Y. Journal*, Nov. 17, 1738; *Mercury*, March 15, 1722; *News Letter*, June 17, 1735.
[5] Sellers, *Charleston Business*, 9, 11, 169; Taylor, "Prices at Charleston," 356, 358, 362; Carroll, *Hist. Colls.*, II, 225; *S. C. Gaz.*, May 8, 15, July 3, 1736; Jan. 1, 1742.

that two Manhattan sloops had recently arrived with "Flour sent from New York . . . by order of some Merchants from Holland to their Factors there in order to have Rice shipt them from hence." The provision trade between New York and Charles Town was heavy enough to warrant John Schermmerhorn in establishing a regular packet service between the two towns in 1728. From Newport the southern city received importations of Rhode Island flour and cheese. Yet with all this volume of trade, Charles Town in 1742 had hardly any commercial dealings with Boston.[6]

Further restriction of the Boston sphere followed the creation of separate economic domains by each of the four smaller ports. Bay mariners lost ground in the southern coastwise trade, and gave way before competition from New Yorkers in Connecticut and Long Island. On the other hand, the growing populousness of the back country and its improving roads increased the volume of goods distributed from Boston to the interior of New England. Shrewd merchants turned to "inland Trade of buying and selling in Towne, which is the best and most Certain profitt, with least of risque or hazard." Jonathan Waldo, shopkeeper, made a specialty of "Country Customers," despite their frequent delinquency "in Paying their Just Debts," and John Lubbock advertised in 1727 to serve rural buyers "at a Days warning." Merrett and Fletcher, "Grocers," carried a large line of domestic and imported foodstuffs, selling by wholesale or retail to inland buyers, as well as to more distant places like New York. Dependence of Connecticut on the Boston market for cattle and produce was clearly revealed in 1740, when "Drovers and Inhabitants" bitterly complained of being "Oppress'd" by the hard money attitude of Boston merchants.[7]

Better roads made travel throughout New England relatively safe and easy by 1720, and connections with the south on through highways were developed during this period. In 1732 Daniel Henchman and T. Hancock of Boston issued a guidebook, *The Vade-Mecum for America: Or a Companion for Traders and Travellers*, its principal features being a description of existing roads and taverns from Maine to Virginia, and a directory of Boston streets. Travel was sufficiently heavy to support several livery stables, where one could hire horses, coaches, chaises or chairs "to ride in the Country." Hackney coaches were also available as earlier. Peter Belton began in 1721 to make weekly round trips between Boston and Newport "in order to carry bundles of Goods, Merchandize, Books, Men, Women and Children,

[6] *S. C. Gaz.*, May 8, 1736; Sept. 17, 1737; Aug. 11, 1739; Jan. 1, 1742; *Pa. Mag.*, XXVIII, 305, 308.
[7] *Lloyd Papers*, I, 245; *News Letter*, July 18, 1723; June 3, 1731; Nov. 27, 1740; *N. E. Journal*, Mar. 20, May 29, 1727; *N. Y. Gaz.*, June 28, 1731.

Money, &c." Alexander Thorpe, liveryman, and Isaac Cusno, saddler, introduced a more elaborate service in 1736, when they procured a seven year franchise from the Rhode Island Assembly to operate two coaches on a regular stage route between Boston and Newport.[8]

Newport's continuing position as a commercial dependent of Boston made possible and encouraged these excellent facilities for communication between the two towns. Rhode Islanders usurped much of Boston's West India trade, and cut into the inland traffic in Connecticut and southern Massachusetts, but they still relied upon their rivals for manufactured and European goods. This meant that much of the specie won by them in the Islands eventually found its way to King Street, Boston. Stephen Ayrault of Newport sent cash to John Salter of Boston in 1733, and two years later Samuel Boutineau sold logwood, molasses and Barbados sugar at Boston for Abraham Redwood to cancel £752. 3. 4. of his account against the Newport Quaker. In 1742 James Vernon, leading hardware merchant of Newport, purchased a supply of frying-pans, spoons, chisels, curry combs, "Spring Lox" and other items costing £311. 6. 1½. from William Colineux of Boston, for which he was "to pay in Nine Months Cash." When peddlers were forbidden by Massachusetts authorities to trade in that colony, they overran Rhode Island. In 1728 the Assembly, on being informed that "Trade hath been greatly hurt by Hawkers, Pedlers, and Petty Chapmen passing to and fro," enacted a law forbidding house to house vending and providing for the jailing of all itinerant salesmen.[9]

Geography aided the other towns to a greater success than Newport in the development of a hinterland trade. The great movement of population into the interior of Pennsylvania, which by 1742 had filled the area as far as Tulpehocken and Bethlehem with Scotch-Irish and German settlers, created a market which enabled Philadelphia to grow as a distributing center. Quaker merchants eagerly drew off the produce of this rich agricultural region, and in return supplied the farmers with the manufactured articles they needed. As early as 1724 Christopher Saur reported that "the wholesale trade is very brisk on account of the adjoining counties." So many Germans settled in the province that a newspaper was founded in 1732 to reach them in their own tongue, and town merchants catered to them in advertisements like the following: "Guter rother Kleber-Saamen vor billichen preis zu bekommen bey George Fitzwater in der Marck strass, Philadelphia."

<hr/>

[8] A coach went to Piscataqua in 1726, and three others to Rhode Island by 1740. *News Letter*, May 15, 1721; Jan. 9, 1735; *Bos. Gaz.*, April 25, 1737; *R. I. Col. Recs.*, IV, 527.
[9] Kimball, *Providence*, 227; Dorr, *Providence*, 172, 207; Letters of Boston Merchants. I, 1; *Mass. Acts and Resolves*, II, 385; *R. I. Acts (1744)*, 110.

The Delaware counties, Maryland and West New Jersey became more than ever attached to Philadelphia in commercial matters at this time. Builders at Chestertown, Maryland, had to send to the Pennsylvania capital in 1730 for carpenters and bricklayers. As at Boston, certain Philadelphia business men made a specialty of country trade. In 1731 Job Rawlinson outfitted prospective farmers, and five years later John Goodwin, shopkeeper, kept a complete stock of European and other goods at reasonable prices for "his Country friends." [10]

Under guidance from the Provincial Council country roads became much better, and in 1733 work started on a highway to connect Philadelphia with Harris' Ferry on the Susquehanna. David Evans began operating a "four wheel'd chaise" to Germantown in 1728, soon extending his service to Frankford and Gray's Ferry. Stage lines followed in West New Jersey, and travel out of Philadelphia in all directions greatly improved. By 1742 several thousands of four horse farm wagons, "from time to time" brought their produce into town "from 10 to 100 miles distance." The new roads proved a boon to country hawkers, who found business excellent. In 1722 Philadelphia merchants and shopkeepers complained of the "Ill Practices of Pedlars," and secured the passage of a law requiring the licensing of all chapmen. Similar agitation in 1728 resulted in more rigid regulation.[11]

Scotch-Irish and Germans also opened up the Carolina back country, and the founding of Georgia provided a buffer province to the southward, which aided the building up of intervening districts. Round about Charles Town plantations were rapidly springing up to form an expanding market for the servants, dry goods, earthenware and clothing sold by such town merchants as J. Lambert and James Crokatt. The planters developed an insatiable taste for English goods, purchasing from Charles Town merchants everything from a four wheeled chaise to materials for japanning a tea-caddy.[12]

There were passable cart roads for about twenty miles out of Charles Town, but the presence of many rivers and creeks made canoes and perriaugers the favorite means of transportation. Coastal packets carried freight north to Cape Fear and as far south as Savannah. In 1737 "a certain person" advertised to go once a week from Charles Town to Ashley Ferry, Dorchester, Stono and Ponpon, "to carry any

[10] A ready sale for produce stimulated market gardening and intensive farming near Philadelphia, in contrast to the wasteful, one-crop cultivation of the frontier. The same was true of the vicinity of other northern towns. Bezanson, Gray and Hussey, *Prices in Pennsylvania*, 103, 263, 267; *Phila. Zeitung*, May 6, 1732; *Pa. Gaz.*, Dec. 16, 1736; *Mercury*, April 19, 1732; Dec. 29, 1730; July 22, 1731; Bidwell and Falconer, *Agriculture*, 84, 138.

[11] *Pa. Gaz.*, May 28, 1730; Feb. 7, 1738; *Mercury*, Sept. 26, 1723; July 26, 1733; June 11, 1740; Douglass, *British Settlements*, III, 333; *Votes Pa. Assembly*, II, 303; *Pa. Statutes*, IV, 141.

[12] *S. C. Gaz.*, Jan. 20, 1733; May 15, 1736.

. . . Pacquets up and down." So many petty chapmen traveled through the plantation country that in 1738 tax-paying town and country shopkeepers complained of their cutthroat competition and clandestine traffic with servants and slaves. The Assembly thereupon passed a law setting high fees for hawking licenses, £50 by land and £100 by water, and requiring the posting of a bond not to trade with servants or slaves.[13]

The trading area dominated by New York expanded little, save in lower Connecticut, where Knickerbockers successfully elbowed out the Bostonians. However, increased immigration into the region already served greatly enlarged the market. Firewood, cattle, wheat and other produce came into New York from country districts to be exchanged for manufactured and West India goods. Unpleasant treatment of countrymen by condescending city merchants frequently bred resentment in the hearts of the former. "You have forgot the nature of Trade and Exchange," "Mr. Farmer" told them angrily in 1730, ". . . if you know no more of *Agriculture* than you do of Merchandize you will be once more obliged to Change your Calling." [14]

Most of Manhattan's trade with rural regions went on by water. In New Jersey, however, good roads were built, making lands near Perth Amboy and the Raritan River available to New York speculators. Regular weekly stage service from Amboy to Trenton, Burlington, and Philadelphia began after 1730, thus making the Jerseys a region of economic contest between traders from the two provincial capitals.[15]

Peddlers and hawkers, especially after their expulsion from the city in 1731, swarmed over the New York back country. In 1738 a letter to the *New York Gazette* reported continuance of their activities, "both in City and Country." The writer declared:

> That many Idle and lazy Straglers, who have no Families to maintain, who pay neither Lot nor Scot, nor do any Duty in the Service of their King or Country, yet are suffered to wander from House to House, and from Place to Place, to dispose of all manner of Wares and Merchandize, to the ruin of Trade, and is a great hurt to the Traders and Shopkeepers.

Despite more repressive legislation in 1739 the peddlers continued to prosper, largely because, here as elsewhere, they performed a real service as distributing agents to remoter countrysides.[16]

[13] *S. C. Gaz.*, May 4, Aug. 3, 1734; Sept. 23, 1737; June 8, 1738; *Eve. Post*, Feb. 20, 1738; *S. C. Statutes*, III, 487.
[14] *N. Y. Gaz.*, May 11, 1730.
[15] *N. Y. Gaz.* April 25, 1726; April 8, 1734; *Mercury*, Feb. 25, 1729; Mar. 20, 1733; Feb. 7, 1738; *N. Y. Journal*, May 19, 1740.
[16] *N. Y. Gaz.*, Oct. 24, 1737; April 24, 1738; Mar. 31, 1740; *N. Y. Col. Laws*, II, 60.

II

The industries supporting shipping flourished in most of the towns, and the preparation of goods for export everywhere employed small armies of artisans and workers. Millers, coopers, and bolters had more work than ever at all ports save Charles Town. New York retained its lead in the packing and bolting of flour. The tanning and currying of leather became leading industries at Philadelphia, where the "offensive smell" of tanpits stood out as one of the characteristic odors of the town. Rum distilling centered at Boston and Newport, as did sugar refining at New York, Philadelphia and Boston.[17]

Boston continued first in shipbuilding, but toward the close of the period this industry, suffering along with the rest of the town's business by reason of competition from smaller towns like Newbury, Gloucester and Marblehead, began its decline. In 1740 at least one shipyard had to be sold for lack of business, and in the first three months of 1742 only three orders for vessels had been received at Boston.[18]

On the other hand, shipbuilding prospered at Philadelphia and Newport. Though the former town turned out only seven vessels in 1726, in the next decade and a half over three hundred and eighty ships, many of them ranging from one hundred to two hundred tons burthen, were constructed on the banks of the Delaware. Upon their entry into direct trade with Europe, Rhode Islanders partially redressed their adverse balances by the sale of vessels, and Newport teemed with busy shipyards and ropewalks. Under leadership of men like the Wantons, the shipbuilders of Narragansett Bay constructed virtually all of the one hundred and twenty sail owned by the town in 1741.[19]

William Walton established a shipyard at New York in 1720, and some small success attended his efforts to push the industry. In all, six yards were opened, but in 1738 trade was so dull that there was "but one new Vessel on the Stocks." About all that the Gothamites accomplished was the provision of good facilities for the refitting of ships. Very few new vessels were built there.[20]

In former years town industries had revolved almost exclusively around shipping, and other rudiments of colonial manufacturing

[17] Edwards, *New York*, 65; *Pa. Statutes*, III, 257; *Pa. Gaz.*, Aug. 30, 1739; 12 *Bos. Rec. Com.*, 119; *Newport T. M. Recs.*, 286; *N. Y. Journal*, Jan. 26, 1736; *N. Y. Gaz.*, Aug. 17, 1730; Feb. 19, 1740.
[18] *Rehearsal*, Aug. 28, 1732; *News Letter*, June 19, 1740; 14 *Bos. Rec. Com.*, 15.
[19] *Pa. Mag.*, XXIII, 254, 370, 498; XXIV, 102; XXXVIII, 137; *R. I. Col. Recs.*, V, 12; *R. I. Hist. Soc. Colls.*, XVI, 2; Bigelow, Rhode Island Commerce, Pt. II, chapter I.
[20] Wilson, *Memorial History of New York*, III, 507; *News Letter*, June 17, 1735. Almost no shipbuilding was undertaken at Charles Town. *S. C. Gaz.*, April 27, 1738; July 2, 1741.

enterprise had been located in villages or hamlets near sources of raw materials. After 1720, however, new industries began to appear in the larger towns. The manufacture of hats became sufficiently important in Boston, Newport and New York to frighten Parliament into passage of the Hat Act in 1732. Report had it that ten thousand beaver hats were then being manufactured annually in New York and New England. A smelting furnace was operated at New York in 1730 and ten years later William Branson erected his steel furnace at Philadelphia. Fine furniture was made at Newport and Philadelphia after 1735. At the latter town Robert Barton made "Walnut, Mahogany, Easy, Close-Stool and Slip Chairs, and Stools, Couches and Settees."[21]

III

Fair trade winds favored these years. In every town merchants amassed considerable fortunes, and many a shopkeeper, by dint of shrewd management, attained merchant status. At Philadelphia George Mifflin acquired a fortune, and Charles Read became a prosperous merchant and political leader. Arthur Savage of Boston conducted a small shop in his home prior to 1728, when he branched out as a general trader with a warehouse on Long Wharf. At New York Arnout Schermmerhorn began in 1719 as a cordwainer, and by 1740 had become one of the leading merchants of Charles Town. In every port new recruits stood ready to join the previously established mercantile leaders.[22]

Most colonial merchants continued to traffic in general merchandise, importing and exporting any commodities for which a market could be found. Many traded independently; others sold European goods on credit and commission for London and Bristol exporters. At New York, and especially at Charles Town, factors directly represented British houses. In the southern town, also, "country factors" acted as brokers for marketing planters' crops. Yet despite this catholicity, there was noticeable a drift toward specialization by some merchants. William Colineux and Samuel Boutineau of Boston, Stephen Ayrault of Newport, and Jacob Franks of New York dealt chiefly in hardware. Richard Willing, Israel Pemberton and Anthony Morris of Philadelphia confined their stocks to dry goods. The slave traffic formed the basis of the fortunes of Peter Faneuil of Boston, Peter Bours of

---

[21] *Doc. Hist. N. Y.*, I, 761; *Newport T. M. Recs.*, 308; *Courant*, April 20, 1724; June 4, 1726; Wilson, *Memorial History of New York*, II, 196; Bining, *Colonial Iron Industry*, 86; *Pa. Mag.*, LV, 301; *Pa. Gaz.*, May 5, 1737; Aug. 9, 1739; *N. Y. Journal*, May 23, 1737.

[22] *Mercury*, Mar. 16, 1721; June 17, 1731; *Pa. Gaz.*, April 19, 1739; *N. E. Journal*, July 29, Dec. 30, 1728; *S. C. Gaz.*, Feb. 9, 1740.

Newport, and Joseph Wragg of Charles Town, while sugar enriched the New York Bayards and the Newport Redwoods.[23]

As these men accumulated surplus wealth in commerce, they turned about for new fields of investment. The great merchant was a ship owner, perhaps also a shipbuilder. His vessels lay at his own wharf, where stood his warehouse, from which he sold his goods wholesale or retail. Often, too, he engaged in some form of manufacture, like milling or distilling. The house of William Allen and Joseph Turner of Philadelphia, probably the most important commercial establishment of these years, carried on a large trade, legal and illegal, with the Caribbean and Spanish Main, and operated a distillery that Allen "imagined made much better Rum than New England did." In 1727 the partners joined a syndicate to purchase the Durham tract in Bucks County, where they erected a profitable iron furnace.[24]

Land, the safest form of investment and fondest possession of the English gentleman, proved irresistibly attractive to the merchant princes of colonial towns, who also aspired to the lordship of great domains. Nearly every rich Charlestonian sank his surplus wealth in land and slaves, turning planter as well as business man. Samuel Wragg bought Lord Shaftesbury's thirty thousand acre barony, and the Pinckneys, Manigaults and others followed his lead. Although the Rhetts seem to have abandoned trade and confined themselves to the culture of rice and indigo, very few of the other Charles Town families held in scorn the profits gained in commerce. Trade and planting went hand in hand. At Boston Elisha Cooke and Samuel Waldo not only acquired lands, but became extensive speculators. Edward Shippen and Peter Baynton of Philadelphia maintained country estates and dabbled in western lands and the fur trade. Rare indeed was the Newport merchant who did not own an estate on Rhode Island or in the Narragansett country. But by far the most famous connection between counting house and broad acres existed at New York, where large holdings became notorious.[25]

By means of voluminous correspondence and constant travel the merchants of the various towns developed intimate connections in these decades. They also linked themselves with members of their class in the West Indies, London and Bristol. Representatives of one family might be found in all places. The Quaker Redwoods originated at Bristol, where in the seventeenth century an ancestor founded the

[23] S. C. Gaz., Jan. 20, July 28, 1733; Feb. 20, May 29, 1742; Letters of Boston Merchants, 1; Newport T. C. Recs., Dec. 1, 1740; N. Y. Gaz., Aug. 17, 1730; Oct. 10, 1737; Mercury, Feb. 20, 1722; Bos. Gaz., Jan. 27, 1729; Dec. 24, 1733.
[24] Pa. Hist., I, 170.
[25] S. C. Hist. & Gen. Mag., XI, 86, 91; Wood, William Shirley, 54; Shippen Papers; Savelle, George Morgan, chapter I; Flick, New York, III, 145.

town library. Scions of the house migrated to Antigua, whence they spread to Philadelphia, Charles Town and Newport, thus locating at the most strategic points in the Empire for the conduct of trade. The Amorys of Boston and the Wraggs of Philadelphia maintained trading connections with their kinsmen at Charles Town, and in 1728 Arnout Schermmerhorn settled in the southern port as agent for his New York brother's packet service. Between the Jewish families of Rivera, Franks, Lopez and Hart of Newport, New York and Philadelphia an intimate commercial bond obtained. The closest relationship of all was that existing between merchants of Boston and Newport. Sea captains, traders and supercargoes from all towns furthered these commercial relations, and could be found in Exchanges or coffee houses of every port, discussing with one another world markets and the state of trade.[26]

This commercial intercourse led also to social and cultural interchanges of the greatest importance. By 1742 the continued exchange between merchants of each town and their mutual interest in the traffic of the Empire were slowly and surely welding them together into a distinct social group, — the only one in the colonies with a common outlook. In each province they were the leading political interest, exerting a far-reaching influence on legislation; in each town they managed municipal affairs, whether through Corporation or Town Meeting; and in each community they constituted the cultured, aristocratic circle whose roots lay deep in the structure of the British Empire. Under their leadership the spirit of commerce pervaded the towns, infecting even the womenfolk and children. Cadwallader Colden, enclosing a small sum of money in a letter to one of his London correspondents in 1724, explained, "I send it to please a little Boy & Girl who want to be merchants as soon as they can speak like their play fellows the Dutch Children here." Love of trade extended to merchants' wives and widows. At Newport Freelove Sophia, consort of John Tweedy, "privately endeavour'd to buy sundry Merchandize unknown to him, for which She had no Necessity," and sold goods from his house, forcing her husband to announce publicly that he would "neither Pay nor Answer for Anything She contracts." Rebecca Amory had her own little shop at Boston in 1735, where she sold mourning crepes, velvets, threads, tapes, etc., and Mrs. Faith Waldo conducted both a wholesale and a retail trade in English draper's goods. Just as merchants traded their way to affluence and influence, so did the "Widows" of New York ardently hope to do.

[26] By 1742 every town had a merchants' exchange meeting daily. R. I. Hist. Soc. Colls., IX; Weeden, *Economic and Social History*, II, 566, 568; *Pa. Gaz.*, Mar. 1, 1739; Gutstein, *Jews of Newport*, 134.

They wrote to Peter Zenger in 1733 that most of them paid taxes, and as [27]

> She Merchants, . . . we in some measure contribute to the Support of Government, we ought to be Intituled to some of the Sweets of it; but we find ourselves intirely neglected, while the Husbands that live in our Neighbourhood are daily invited to dine at Court: we have the Vanity to think we can be full as Entertaining, and make as brave a Defense in case of an Invasion, and perhaps not turn Taile so soon as some of them; and tho' we don't understand the Law, we do the Gospel, witness the seven first Verses of the 23rd Chapter of Proverbs lately put up near the Market-Place.

IV

The large number of people living in the towns and the growing populations in surrounding areas provided an expanding market for the goods of retail shops. Well-to-do inhabitants were at the same time bringing more of their patronage to such establishments because of the improvement in both the quality and the variety of their stocks. The bulk of shop trade, however, still came from those classes whose incomes did not permit the purchase of groceries and apparel in large quantities.

Retail shop trade reached its highest development at Boston, where some degree of specialization prevailed. Large and small groceries were to be found all over town, this petty trade apparently constituting the chief means of support for widows. Mrs. Hannah Boydell sold "Grocery Ware" near the Bunch of Grapes Tavern in 1730, and the Widow Bouyot's shop offered an assortment of preserved fruits, jellies, sirups, egg cakes, macaroons, "March pane," almonds and conserves. In 1732 Alexander Forsyth operated a large grocery shop in Prince Street, and in 1742 George Featherstone, "Grocer from London," opened a most complete shop in Marlborough Street.[28]

Since Boston merchants imported "nothing but the Cream of Goods the City of London affords," town shopkeepers could place choice merchandise before their customers. Shops carrying dry and household goods multiplied rapidly. One such emporium advertised in 1725:

> Just Imported from London, To be Sold *up one pair of Stairs,*
> . . . opposite the Exchange in Cornhill, all sorts of Womans Shoes, and Pattoons, fine Macklins, & English Laces & Edgings, Mantua Silks, Paderina, fine Cambricks, Lawns, Hollands, Muslins, Gold & Silver Stomachers, Ribbons, Gloves, &c.

[27] *Colden Papers,* I, 52; *Post Boy,* Feb. 23, 1736; *News Letter,* May 18, 1732; Sept. 19, 1735; *N. Y. Journal,* Jan. 21, 1733.
[28] *News Letter,* June 3, 24, 1731; Dec. 28, 1732; Feb. 22, 1733; April 17, May 1, 1735; Nov. 2, 1738; Nov. 4, 1742; *Bos. Gaz.,* Dec. 24, 1733; Nov. 10, 1741; *Post Boy,* Dec. 28, 1741.

Some shops displayed extensive stocks of the latest English fashions. Richard Waddington, couturier, kept an exclusive ladies' shop in 1737, at which he also made garments after the "neatest and most fashionable Manner, according to the Court of Great Britain." [29]

Numerous specialty shops made their appearance in this period, so that by 1742 Boston retail trade was well on its way to specialization in stocks. Hannah Deering sold only tobacco, and Thomas Dolbear restricted his trade to "very good Corks." A much frequented establishment was that of Thomas Bromfield, where one procured imported gloves, "suitable for Funerals." In 1732 Henrietta-Maria East, from London, announced her fashionable millinery shop, at the "Sign of the Fan," in Marlborough Street. [30]

"Anything may be had at Philadelphia," wrote Christopher Saur in 1724, "but everything is twice as dear" as in Europe. The number of retail shops, most of them located in Market Street, increased rapidly. Good groceries were to be had at Moses Marranda's or at Thomas Clarke's where ladies went to buy their sweets. John Knight sold fine Canary and Sack at his wine shop just six doors down Market Street from that of his chief competitor, David Evans. In Chestnut Street Moses Hewes operated the town's largest grocery, specializing in all kinds of sugar, fruits, sweet oil and spices. [31]

Many shops on Market and Second Streets carried stocks of clothing and dry goods. In the early 'twenties Philadelphia gentlewomen resorted to George Mifflin's for their silks, cambrics, and other materials by the yard. Thomas Hatten sold Dublin linens in 1728, and Thomas Stapleford supplied customers with "Bed-Ticks with Bolsters and Pillow Cases from London, Coverlids, Rugs, . . . and Cutlary Wares" in 1735. [32]

Philadelphia shopkeepers did not confine themselves so much to one line of goods as did Bostonians, but occasionally a specialty shop appeared. George Fitzwater conducted a seed store, frequently advertising his red clover in both English and German, while John Hyatt restricted his stock to hardware. Such items as pins, needles, snuff boxes, flints, and slates could be had at Daniel Cheston's novelty shop. Andrew Bradford, the printer, rented space in his shop for the sale of special articles, most of which he advertised in his newspaper. [33]

In the first decade of the period only eight shopkeepers took out

[29] *Post Boy,* Nov. 8, Dec. 6, 1742; *Bos. Gaz.,* Sept. 13, 1725; *N. E. Journal,* June 15, 1730; *News Letter,* April 27, 1732; Dec. 29, 1737.
[30] *Courant,* Feb. 5, 1736; *News Letter,* June 3, 1736; Dec. 23, 1742; *Bos. Gaz.,* Jan. 27, 1729.
[31] *Pa. Mag.,* XLV, 253; *Mercury,* May 23, 1723; Oct. 17, 1728; July 10, 1729; July 29, 1731; Oct. 4, 1733.
[32] *Mercury,* March 16, 1721; Feb. 4, 1728; Sept. 30, 1730; April 19, 1733; *Pa. Gaz.,* May 28, 1730.
[33] *Mercury,* Sept. 20, 1731; *Phila. Zeitung,* May 6, 1732; *Pa. Gaz.,* Aug. 2, 1739.

freedoms at New York, but after 1730 their numbers more than trebled and retail trade began to flourish. General merchants still supplied most of the groceries and provisions consumed at New York. In 1727 William Bradford sold coffee, Bohea tea, and "Very good oatmeal" at his printing office, and Giles Sylvester, cooper, tried his luck with West India lime juice. The Widow Lebrosses, one of the "She Merchants," advertised Canary wine and olive oil at her shop in Hanover Square in 1734, and in 1740 John Merrett of Boston moved to New York to conduct the first large grocery business in the town.[34]

Although the retail provision trade developed slowly, Manhattan taste for European "creations" led to an expansion of general shops, resembling in embryo the modern department store. In 1733 George Talbot acquired a good location "next Door to the Play-House," where he displayed his stock of "Beds, Chairs, Tables, Chests of Drawers, Looking-Glasses, Andirons and Pictures, as also several sorts of Druggs and Medicines." Imported English goods, the latest in gowns, silk stockings, hats and buckles, were on sale at the Three Pigeons, and to forestall boredom in gentlemen whose wives lingered over her varied stock, Mrs. Samuel Bourdet also carried a line of saws, hinges and firearms. At the "New Store in Hanover Square," in 1736 the shopping center of Manhattan, one might have bought haberdashery, dry goods, laces, pictures, pipes, snuff, juniper berries, cutlery, hardware and glass.[35]

Some few persons at New York sought a profit in one line of goods. John Miller, formerly the governor's gardener, drove a good trade in seeds, roots, and plants in 1734. At least two shops specialized in Scotch snuff, pigtail and cut tobacco. For years the Widow Vanderspiegel and her son supplied Manhattanites with imported window glass. The New York cosmetic industry was inaugurated in 1736, with the announcement by Mrs. Edwards of

> An admirable Beautifying Wash, for Hands Face and Neck, it makes the Skin soft, smooth and plump, it likewise takes away Redness, Freckles, Sun-Burnings, or Pimples, and cures Postules, Itchings, Ring-worms, Tetters: Scurf, Morphew, and other like Deformities of the Face and Skin, (Intirely free from any Corroding Quality) and brings to an exquisite Beauty, with Lip Salve and Tooth Powder, all Sold very Cheap.

With such potions as these did New York gentlewomen, like their sophisticated sisters in all ages, seek to improve on nature.[36]

[34] N. Y. Hist. Soc. *Colls., 1885*, 100; *N. Y. Gaz.*, Mar. 6, Oct. 16, 1727; June 3, 17, 1728; Oct. 28, 1734; Mar. 11, 1740; *N. Y. Journal*, Apr. 20, 1741.
[35] *N. Y. Gaz.*, Oct. 8, 1733; Aug. 4, 1735; June 7, 1736; Mar. 11, 1740.
[36] *N. Y. Journal*, Feb. 24, 1734; April 19, Nov. 29, 1736; Feb. 23, 1737; *N. Y. Gaz.*, April 7, 1735; July 31, 1738.

At Newport much of the merchandising remained in the hands of merchants, who kept retail shops at their wharves or sometimes further up town. Stephen Ayrault operated a retail hardware business, as did also John Banister, who included dry goods in his stock. After 1730 more retail shopkeepers appeared, among them Joseph Tillinghast, Weston Clarke and James Blackfoot. People came all the way from Providence to make purchases at Newport dry goods establishments, like that of Cuthbert Campbell, who made specialties of fine fabrics, stockings and handkerchiefs. On November 8, 1733, thieves broke into this shop and departed with £40 worth of goods. John Smibert and Bishop Berkeley were regular customers at Mrs. Neargrass' book store. On Redwood's and Taylor's wharves were several establishments dealing in West India goods by retail. So many of the inhabitants were either sailors or connected in some way with the town's shipping, venturing their small savings in some stock or other, that it appears that "everyone in Newport had something to sell." [37]

Most of Charles Town's traffic in general commodities with the plantations fell into the hands of "country factors," who marketed planters' crops. As a consequence, retail shopkeepers in the town confined their stocks to imported groceries, hardware, and dry goods for local consumption, or to specialties such as millinery goods or wines for both local and country custom. John Chevilette conducted a retail shop "on the Bay" where he sold Philadelphia and Bristol bottled beer, Rhode Island cheese, and cider, rum, lime juice, butter and spices, while William Joyliffe dealt in imported "dry groceries." The best Rhenish, Madeira and Canary wines were to be had at John Jones', and fishing tackle, tools and nails at Richard Wigg's ironware shop. An attractive display of London creations and "millenary Ware" confronted the gentlewoman shopper at the Broad Street emporium of Sarah and Lucy Weaver. Carolinians paid dearly for their goods; "This place is within a trifle as dear as the West Indies," Mark Catesby complained; "few European goods are sold for less than 300 p. cent and oftener for 400 or 500." This state of affairs may account for the reluctance of Thomas Gates to sell groceries for aught save cash, "without which the Game is up, &c. I Play no more! I am weary!" [38]

By 1742 retail merchandising had made a flourishing beginning in every town, and at Boston and Philadelphia, with their wider and more sophisticated markets, it had reached as high a stage of development

[37] *Bos. Gaz.*, Oct. 2, 1727; June 30, 1740; April 27, 1741; *R. I. Gaz.*, Jan. 25, 1733; *Post Boy*, Dec. 1, 1735; Feb. 16, Mar. 29, 1736; *Eve. Post*, June 27, 1737; June 19, 1738; *Newport Hist. Mag.*, II, 245.
[38] *S. C. Gaz.*, Dec. 9, 1732; Sept. 27, Oct. 4, 1735; Feb. 28, May 8, 15, 1736; Jan. 26, Nov. 6, 1740; Feb. 20, 1742; Dr. Sherrard's Philosophical Letters, II, 165.

as in the second city of England. Only the strictest candor forbids
the application of this rhyming description of Temple Street, Bristol,
to such New World thoroughfares as Cornhill or Market Street.[39]

> The Spacious Street, where London Wares
> Display the tawdry Pageantry of Fairs,
> Here's the whole Wardrobe of the female Dress
> In wealthy folds a standing Camp possess.
> Temptations offered to the Virgins there
> To choose a Marriage-dress of Modish Air.

As in the previous period, much of the retail trade in each town continued to be conducted by artisans, who, while marketing the products
of their own manufacture, frequently sold other items as well. The
most important development among the skilled crafts was the increasing number of highly specialized arts and luxury industries.

Boston silversmiths were preeminent in this period, although those
of Philadelphia and Charles Town attained a high degree of skill in
their art. In 1723 James Boyer, jeweller from London, established
himself in King Street, whence he advertised to "sett all manner of
Stones in Rings, &c.," as well as "everything that belongs to that
trade." A more specialized branch of the craft was developed when
William Goodwin came over from London to set up as a spectacle
maker. John Cowell, goldsmith, followed the trend of his times when
he began selling coffee at his shop in 1728. The wider use of silks by
Boston ladies gave rise to cleaning and dyeing establishments, like that
at which John Kent produced "Blues & Greens, which were never before perform'd in New England." Many townspeople no longer made
their own soap and candles, when they could be had at the shops of
Josiah Franklin or Mary Hamilton, soap boiler and tallow chandler.
Among the most frequented of all artisans' shops were those of the
milliners. Mrs. E. Atkinson, "lately come from London" in 1729,
designed to make "Mantos, and Riding Dresses after the newest
Fashion," and took in all sorts of millinery work. In addition, she
gave instruction to young ladies in the "dressing of Heads & cutting
of Hair," and other aspects of her craft.[40]

In nearly every street or lane of the town there was a barber's shop,
"well custom'd . . . and completely fitted for that Business." One
of the most popular tonsorial establishments was at the sign of the
"Barber Pole" on Long Wharf, the proprietor of which probably inaugurated a familiar American custom when he put in a line of snuff

---

[39] Retail shops were "uncommon" at Bristol as late as 1710. Latimer, *Bristol in
the Eighteenth Century*, 3, 4, 97.
[40] *Courant*, Jan. 7, 1723; Mar. 19, 1726; *N. E. Journal*, July 29, 1728; *News Letter*,
June 8, 1727; April 3, 1729; *Post Boy*, Sept. 28, 1741.

and tobacco in 1731. It was a splendid sight indeed on December 1, 1724, to watch the "Thirty-two Principal Barbers" of Boston parading through the streets to a tavern, attended by a trumpeter, when they met to raise the price of shaves.[41]

At Philadelphia the goldsmith's craft found a growing patronage from wealthy Quakers who derived great satisfaction from sideboards loaded with fine plate. James Allen, Joseph Best, and William Vallent all kept shops on Market Street. Michael Cario of London and New York offered the aristocracy "all sorts of Jewellry Ware, viz. Diamond Rings and other Stone Rings, Crystal Rings, with Hair set under them, Lockets of all Sort, Buttons for Sleeves, Fine Snuff-Boxes," etc. He also bought old gold, and did all kinds of engraving.[42]

Though Quaker matrons may have tended toward more sober apparel after 1720, other ladies of the town provided ample custom for the shops of tradesmen like John Frost, London staymaker and children's coatmaker, who guaranteed in 1730 to "make Stays without Padding, . . . [and] to make Women look Strait that are not so." Nehemiah Boucher made the best men's clothes at his establishment, where "Merchants, Brewers, Silversmiths, Sadlers, . . . Blacksmiths and Hatters" could have their work "done by way of Barter." Use of finery called for the services of cleaners and dyers, several of whom were available after 1735. In 1740 John Atkins announced that "he can and will . . . take out all Spots, Stains and Filth to the greatest Perfection." As all gentlemen subscribed to the fashion of wearing periwigs, perukemakers continually advertised ready money for all sorts of hair. Another sign of its growing wealth was the fact that Philadelphia supported three coachmakers in these years.[43]

New York aristocrats kept ten goldsmiths, six silversmiths, and five watchmakers busy in this period. The principal goldsmiths' shops were operated by Charles and Bartholomew Le Roux and Peter Quintard. Michael Cario sought a better market at Philadelphia after five years' residence at Manhattan. James Munden and Thomas Butwell made "crooked women . . . appear strate" at their stay shop, catering especially to country trade. A competitor, Moses Slaughter, advertised that his imported stays were "for Shape, inferiour to None," and printed the names of two New York gentlewomen as references for his work. The chaises and chairs in which ladies drove out for their shopping were mostly the work of Nicholas Bailey, coachmaker. All sorts of earthenware and pottery were sold by William and Peter Crolius in 1737, and James Foddy, looking-glass maker, dealt in pic-

[41] News Letter, Jan. 21, 1731; May 15, 1740; Courant, Dec. 7, 1724.
[42] Mercury, May 19, Oct. 20, 1720; Aug. 22, 1723; July 8, 1736.
[43] Pa. Gaz., Jan. 20, 1730; May 5, 1737; Mercury, Mar. 30, 1721; Mar. 21, 1723; May 8, 1729; Aug. 17, 1732; July 31, 1740; April 30, 1741.

ture frames, sconces, and fine dressing-table mirrors. Near the Fort John Aus kept a cutlery shop and made "White Smith's work of all Sorts." [44]

Newport attracted many artisans in these years. William Claggett, the famous clockmaker, moved from Boston in 1726, and much of his best work was done at Newport. Gay young bloods and more sober merchants had their suits made by John Taylor, and bought their haberdashery from Joseph Dore, collar maker. Nassau Hastie came all the way from Charles Town in 1741 to join the Newport barbers, and soon became the favorite trimmer of the gentry. One of the town's most accomplished artisans was John Angel, who made "Polished Chimney-Pieces, Tea-Tables, Tomb-Stones, Grave Stones, Morters, and all sorts of carved Work and Architect, in choice white or Green Marble." [45]

After 1730 Charles Town gentry suffered no scarcity of skilled craftsmen to cater to their needs and tastes. Affluent merchants and planters dearly loved jewelry and baubles, and provided large patronage for the shops of M. Aigon and John Ulrich Giessendanner, silversmiths, and Lewis Janvier, goldsmith. By far the most elaborate stock was that of John Paul Grimke, who always had on hand a "fresh assortment of Brilliant and Rose Diamonds, Rubies, Emeralds, Saphirs, Jacints, Topz's, Amethists, . . . and some ready made rings." When John Pennyfeather's shop was robbed in 1738, over £400 worth of gold and precious stones rewarded the burglars. Fine watches could be had at the shop of Peter Morgue, and Joseph Massey, gunsmith, also did engraving, the South Carolina currency being his especial handiwork.[46]

Gentlemen bought their clothes of Hugh Evans, Peter Hunter, and Thomas Conn, Broad Street tailors, or from William Valance, "Taylor from London," who specialized in riding habits and hunting caps, "better than can be had at the publick Stores." When they died they were probably swathed in the Widow Watson's funeral goods, and laid away in Charles Warham's "newest fashion" coffins. Mrs. Bartram or Edward Knight, cleansers and dyers, kept aristocratic apparel fresh and new. Cabinetmakers, upholsterers, perukemakers and barbers existed in considerable numbers, but of the more usual crafts, such as carpenters, masons, coopers, sawyers and smiths, there were few. Skilled slaves, available for hire, performed the bulk of such work.

[44] N. Y. Hist. Soc. *Colls., 1885*, 100, 117; *N. Y. Journal*, Feb. 3, 1735; Mar. 10, 1740; Jan. 11, 1742; *N. Y. Gaz.*, Oct. 13, 1729; Oct. 10, 1737.
[45] R. I. Hist. Soc. *Colls.*, VIII, 92 n.; Stiles, *Diary*, I, 342; *Newport Hist. Mag.*, II, 187; *Newport T. M. Recs.*, 296, 300; *Post Boy*, Aug. 23, 1742; *Life of Carew*, 183.
[46] *S. C. Gaz.*, Dec. 30, 1732; Feb. 28, May 15, 1736; Mar. 12, Nov. 5, 1737; Nov. 16, 1738; Sept. 12, 1740; May 2, 1743.

Indeed, artisans found Charles Town a place of opportunity; as Bolzius reported, "any Body that will work may get his Living." [47]

The auction increased in popularity as a form of merchandising. At Philadelphia nearly every variety of article or property could be disposed of by inch of candle. Whether it were a ship, a house and chattels, or a lot of imported merchandise to be sold, auctions were well attended, and timely passing of the bottle insured brisk bidding. Flagrant abuses, whereby poor people especially suffered loss by enforced sales, led in 1729 to an act of the Assembly giving the Corporation power of regulation. In 1730 this body appointed Patrick Baird sole vendue master, and, to avoid competition with private shopkeepers, forbade him to auction goods under the value of twenty shillings. Yet in 1742 tradesmen again protested the prejudice to their interests caused by the auctioneer's disposing of "merchandize in Small Quantities," and the Corporation had to raise the limit to forty shillings on all items save clothing and second hand goods.[48]

In other towns, too, the auction enjoyed considerable popularity. In December, 1732, William Dyer and Nicholas Easton disposed of the estate of Daniel Seblar by auction at the Newport schoolhouse; at this time the town appointed William Thurston under bond to conduct all vendues fairly. New York, too, had official vendue masters, and at Charles Town regular slave auctions were held after 1733 at the new market house. Boston merchants often auctioned off shipments of merchandise, rather than sell them by usual wholesale or retail channels. Ships and marine equipment were generally disposed of in this fashion. In 1731 Thomas Fleet, printer, announced his newly fitted auction room at the Heart and Crown, as well as his well known "Tallent" at the business. His principal stock turned out to be books, household goods, and wearing apparel.[49]

The gambling spirit of the townsmen showed itself in the prevalence of lotteries. Nowhere was this method of disposing of goods so frequently employed as at Newport. In 1732 John Coddington "sold by Lottery" a large wharf running off Thames Street, twelve lots of land, and a parcel of imported goods, and within a space of two months the *Rhode Island Gazette* carried notices of eight different lotteries. The man behind most of them was Augustus Lucas, and at Boston, where lotteries were forbidden, Elias Boutineau managed the sale of his tickets. The institution also found favor at New York and Phila-

[47] *S. C. Gaz.*, Nov. 16, 1734; Feb. 28, May 8, Aug. 11, Oct. 2, 1736; April 2, 16, July 23, Nov. 14, 1741; May 8, 1742; *Journals of Von Reck and Bolzius*, 27.
[48] *Pa. Gaz.*, Mar. 20, 1729; Oct. 19, 1738; *P. M. C. C.*, 293, 300, 302, 311, 410; *Pa. Statutes*, IV, 141; *Mercury*, Sept. 16, 1731; Feb. 19, 1734.
[49] *R. I. Gaz.*, Dec. 14, 1732; *N. Y. Gaz.*, July 21, 1729; Sept. 10, 1733; Mar. 20, 1739; *S. C. Gaz.*, May 6, 1732; Jan. 13, 1733; *Bos. Gaz.*, May 11, Dec. 27, 1724; *News Letter*, Mar. 11, 25, 1731.

delphia, but in all towns merchants, shopkeepers and auctioneers condemned it as prejudicial to legitimate trade and conducive to fraud. Before the period closed New York, Pennsylvania and Rhode Island had all joined the Bay Colony in outlawing private lotteries. The Rhode Island act of 1733 followed a new Massachusetts law of the previous year in providing a fine of £500 for the conduct of a lottery, and one of £10 for the purchase of a ticket. New York lotteries all promptly moved over to Perth Amboy, New Jersey, and in 1742 Cornelius Gerbraud even dared to operate one at Manhattan, selling tickets for a consignment of dry goods, haberdashery, and a spinet.[50]

As the towns grew into cities, the problem of feeding swelling populations became ever more pressing, producing as a consequence great activity in the establishment and regulation of markets, fairs, and other agencies for the distribution of foodstuffs. Philadelphia's location in the finest agricultural region of the colonies assured its market ample and varied provisions. Although the Corporation had built new stalls for the High Street market in 1720, thirty more had to be erected two years later at a cost of £400. In another eight years twenty additional stalls were put up between the Court House and the Delaware River, "for the accommodation of such as bring provisions from the Jerseys." Further enlargements took place in 1736, when the Corporation also spent £200 for the paving of Market Street and the installation of posts to protect the new movable stalls with their coverings of painted canvas. At this time the market booths and shambles extended down the middle of High (Market) Street from Front to Third, a distance of about a quarter of a mile.[51]

The principal problem in the operation of this splendid plant arose over the collection of rents. Stall lessees continually fell behind in their payments, and in 1721 the gentlemen who financed the new buildings demanded security for their investment from the Corporation. The butchers, as chief delinquents, pleaded the excessiveness of the rents and succeeded in obtaining a reduction. The next year, however, some of them still failed to remit, and the Common Council, with its usual energy in matters pertaining to its income, decided to use "all lawful means" to secure its due.[52]

Cleanliness and good order characterized the Philadelphia market. Slaughtering and the "Smoaking of Tobacco" were strictly forbidden in the market house, and large fines awaited those who cast refuse of any sort in the stalls. "Persons blowing of Meat, Sellin Goods,

[50] R. I. Gaz., Oct. 4, 18, 25, Nov. 8, 1732; News Letter, July 27, 1732; N. Y. Col. Laws, II, 61; Pa. Statutes, IV, 141; R. I. Acts (1744), 170; Mass. Acts & Resolves, II, 663; Mercury, Mar. 23, 1727; N. Y. Journal, Jan. 31, 1743.
[51] P. M. C. C., 187, 242, 293, 295, 363; Votes Pa. Assembly, III, 72.
[52] P. M. C. C., 188. 210, 223; Votes Pa. Assembly, II, 309, 313.

bringing Empty Carts & lying of Horses in the Market place" met with severe treatment from the market committee. Forestalling by hucksters, who met people coming to market "at the end of the Streets" to buy up their provisions, was stopped in 1728.[53]

The excellence of the Philadelphia market aroused envy and admiration everywhere in the colonies. Robert Parke wrote in 1724 that "all sorts of provisions are Extraordinary Plenty in Philadelphia market, where the Country people bring their commodities." At the close of the period William Black of Virginia, while visiting the Quaker town, penned a charming description of this institution: [54]

> The days of the Market are Tuesday and Friday, where you may be Supply'd with every Necessary for the Supply of Life thro'ut the whole year, both Extraordinary Good and reasonably Cheap, it is allow'd by Foreigners to be the best of its bigness in the known World, and undoubtedly the largest in America; I got to this place by 7 [A.M.]; and had no small Satisfaction in seeing the pretty Creatures, the young Ladies, traversing the place from Stall to Stall, where they could make the best Market, some with their Maid behind them with a Basket to carry home the Purchase, Others that were designed to buy trifles, as a little fresh Butter, a dish of Green Peas, or the like, had the Good Nature and Humility enough to be their own Porters.

In contrast to the one large market at Philadelphia, New York had many. Ownership of all was vested in the Corporation, which until 1741 rented stalls in each directly to tradesmen. After this date all market houses with the right to sublet them, were leased at public auction to the highest bidder. The five markets established before 1720 served until 1738, the Countess Key and Clark's Ferry Markets undergoing some enlargement and repair. Residents of the South and Dock Wards built a new market in Broad Street in 1738, which the Corporation generously accepted for the public use. About the same time expansion created a demand for a market in the West Ward, where citizens erected the Oswego Market on Broadway. This structure served as the distributing point for the "great quantities" of provisions frequently brought from Hackensack, Tappan, and "other parts up the North River." No meats were sold here until 1741, when countrymen received permission to sell them "by the Joynt or in Pieces." [55]

Save when epidemics ravaged the city, Manhattan markets offered an ample supply of all varieties of meat and produce. In 1731 the prevalence of smallpox frightened "Country People from Supplying this Place," and the market in consequence grew very slim. Markets

---

[53] *P. M. C. C.*, 222, 279, 298, 341, 360.
[54] *News Letter*, Sept. 26, 1728; *Pa. Mag.*, I, 405; V, 349.
[55] *N. Y. M. C. C.*, IV, 85, 354, 4:3, 423, 426; V, 41, 45; *N. Y. Journal*, Nov. 9, 1741; Edwards, *New York*, 71.

opened every weekday at sunrise, closing at sunset, and no huckster could buy in them before noon. Efficient clerks maintained the high quality of merchandise by levying fines of forty shillings on unscrupulous traders who sold "unwholesome or Stale victuals, . . . Blown meat or Leprous Swine." [56]

Extension of settlement in Newport south along Thames Street made necessary a new market there, and in 1732 the town erected one at the foot of King Street. A year later the Town Meeting voted to build a "mercat House" at the head of the Dock between the Carr and Tillinghast wharves. Close to the ferry slip, this market received most of the produce from the Narragansett country. Fish in plenty were to be had in the Bay, along the shore of which the Reverend Mr. John Comer walked frequently to "see ye sein drawn." The new buildings were large and well equipped; Town Meetings were held in the ferry market house, and both markets appear to have been places of popular resort. In 1739, while draughting "needful rules" to prevent fishermen from leaving the buildings "nasty and dirty," the Town Meeting passed an order forbidding nocturnal disorders by "young persons gathering there and making a rout and noise to the great disturbance of the neighbors." [57]

Charles Town citizens erected the town's first market house in 1722, on the Bay at Tradd Street, but repeal of the incorporation act deprived the southern community of a planned market system, leaving it to struggle along under the inadequate law of 1710 as rarely enforced by deputies of absentee market clerks who owed their appointments to the Duke of Newcastle. The consumer suffered from the fact that Negroes could "buy and sell, and be Hucksters . . . , whereby they wait Night and Day on the several Wharfs and buy up many Articles necessary for the . . . Inhabitants, and make them pay exorbitant Price." Absence of proper market officials encouraged irresponsible hucksters, forestallers and regrators, and the perpetration of scandalous frauds in weights and measures. All this the Grand Jury presented as "intolerable hardship" in 1735, and the inhabitants prodded the Assembly into passage of another inadequate market act. Although a fine building was erected at Broad and Meeting Streets for the daily sale of provisions and meat, Charles Town did not until 1739 have a really well regulated market. The authorities now appointed their own clerk of the market to superintend its business, which began at sunrise, and forbade purchases by any huckster until the ringing of the nine o'clock bell. At the old Market Place on the Middle

[56] *News Letter,* Sept. 2, 1731; *N. Y. M. C. C.,* IV, 56, 108, 291.
[57] *Newport T. M. Recs.,* 256, 261, 309, 388; *R. I. Gaz.,* Oct. 4, 1732; Richardson Collection, 972: 174; Comer, "Diary," VIII, 84.

Bridge a structure was built for the sale of all produce save meats. Under the new law English market practice was closely followed, and Charles Town for the first time enjoyed the benefits of proper regulation of its food supply.[58]

Continued opposition by countryfolk prevented establishment of a market at Boston for many years. "There is not a place in the World of our Standing, Members, and Trade," wrote T. R. in 1725, "that is without their set Place and constant times of Market." Those favoring erection of a market urged the benefit to farmers as well as tradesmen, and pointed to the successful operation of the system at Philadelphia. The town suffered considerably from the buying up of provisions by hucksters, Indians, Negroes and mulatto servants, who resold them at exorbitant prices, but all efforts to prevent the abuse failed, and the question became a football in local politics for several years.[59] After repeated votes in turbulent sessions the Town Meeting decided by a very narrow margin in 1734 to open markets at Eliot's Wharf, the Dock, and the Old North Church. Though the *News Letter* hailed the event with enthusiasm, rural opposition soon revived, securing by a close vote in the Town Meeting of March, 1736, the discontinuance of the clerks of the market. Feeling ran very high, and on the night of March 24, 1737, Boston first displayed its talent for masquerade, when a "Number of Persons Unknown," disguised as clergymen, demolished the Middle Market House and several adjacent shops, and "sawed asunder" the posts of the North Market. The Lieutenant Governor's announcement of a reward for the detection of the culprits was greeted by this warning challenge, nailed to the door of the Town House:

> Those good Fellows that are for pulling down the Market . . . will show you a Hundred men where you can show One. . . . We have about Five Hundred Men in Solemn League and Covenant to Stand by one another, and can procure above Seven Hundred more of the same Mind. . . . It will be the hardest Piece of Work that ever you took in Hand, to Commit any Man for that Night's Work.

The country faction, with its artisan and laborer allies in the town, meant real business, and the market experiment had soon to be abandoned.[60]

[58] S. C. Commons Journal, II, 64, 158; S. C. Pub. Recs., XV, 323; XVII, 304; *S. C. Sessions Acts, 1733–1739*, 82, 137; *S. C. Gaz.*, April 23, 1737; Dec. 15, 1739; April 3, 1742.
[59] *Courant*, Feb. 22, 1725; 8 *Bos. Rec. Com.*, 223, 225; *News Letter*, Sept. 26, 1728; *Bos. Gaz.*, Feb. 19, 26, 1733; *Some Considerations Against the Setting up of a Market* (1733).
[60] 12 *Bos. Rec. Com.*, 40, 44, 46, 49, 54, 64, 164, 170; *News Letter*, June 6, 1734· April 1, 21, 1737; 13 *Bos. Rec. Com.*, 134; MHS *Colls.*, III, 255.

Nevertheless, those in favor of the project did not despair, and in July, 1740, Peter Faneuil came forward with an offer to build the town a market house. On the morning of July 14 so many people attended the Town Meeting called to discuss Faneuil's proposal that it had to be adjourned to the Brattle Street Church, where in anticipation of a stormy session it was first resolved that the Town should be responsible for any damage done to pews or building. When after bitter debate the vote was called for the pro-market group directed the Assessors to bring in their lists, so that "none might be allowed to Vote in the Affair, Excepting . . . such as were Rated in the last Tax Two Shillings and One Penny." Amid "Heat and Vehemence on both Sides" property thus triumphed over numbers, and Boston accepted Faneuil's magnificent gift by a vote of 367 to 360. Work on the building designed by John Smibert began immediately, and on September 24, 1742, Faneuil Hall was opened with appropriate ceremonies. In addition to the market, the donor had arranged for a large second floor room for public meetings, and here the grateful half of the citizenry placed his portrait, "Drawn in full length." Peter's sense of the ironic, if he had one, must have appreciated the tribute of the *Boston Weekly Magazine:* [61]

> Pompey for Plays, a Theatre gave Rome,
> Gresham to London, an Exchange for Wealth,
> Faneuil to Boston, gives a worthier Dome,
> A Hall for LIBERTY, a Change below for Health.

As the century wore on fairs became less important, tending to move out into the country districts where they frequently became the object of excursions by town-dwellers. The only town fair was that held semi-annually at Philadelphia. "They sell no Cattle nor horses nor living Creatures," wrote Robert Parke, "but altogether Merchants Goods . . . & all Sorts of Necessarys fit for our Wooden Country. & here all young men and women that wants wives or husbands may be Supplyed." In fact, countrymen could see almost anything at the fair, from Joseph Stanyard's ox roast to an altercation such as the one in which Jacob Evoulkt broke the neck of Joseph Koster in 1741. [62]

During these years of peace all towns normally enjoyed an adequate grain supply. Boston authorities, however, continued to keep a public granary ready to open when conditions should call for it. In 1729 the town built a permanent timber structure on the Common near the Alms House, and provided another "Grainery" at the North End four

[61] 12 *Bos. Rec. Com.,* 258, 306, 309; *News Letter,* Sept. 11, 1740; Sept. 16, 1742; *Eve. Post,* July 21, 1740.
[62] *Pa. Mag.,* V, 349; *Mercury,* Nov. 4, 1736; April 21, 1737; *Pa. Gaz.,* Nov. 26, 1741.

years later. The keeper, appointed by the town in 1737, had instructions not to deliver more than a half bushel of grain to a person at one time. Notwithstanding these commendable precautions, occasional shortages occurred. Heavy shipments of grain to foreign countries produced a "great scarcity of Bread Corn" in 1725, and the Selectmen tried in vain to persuade the General Court to proclaim a temporary embargo, while in the winter of 1740 they learned that Thomas Green had bought up twelve hundred bushels of wheat "to Ship off," when town bakers did not possess one quarter that amount. In contrast to Boston's concern for its food supply stood Charles Town, where, because nearby planters raised only enough grain for their own use, the townsfolk had to depend on shipments from Pennsylvania and New York. This kept prices continually high, and frequently, as in 1741, the community found itself "entirely without Flour or Bread of any Sort." [63]

Carters and porters in all the towns carried goods to and from wharves and shops. In general, they quietly performed their duties and needed no official regulation. At New York, however, the custom of licensing drivers and regulating their charges survived. In 1731 the Corporation decreed that every carman should have his license number "fairly painted" in red on each side of his cart so that it might "easily" be seen, and that none might refuse to be hired when requested by any inhabitant. At Boston many porters were needed in attendance at wharves, docks, and other parts of the town, "to convey and carry goods," which frequently resulted in the trusting of valuable burdens to the hands of utterly unreliable persons. A province act of 1736 authorized the Selectmen to appoint officially bonded porters and prepare a schedule of their rates, and in 1738 the Board selected twelve "common porters," giving to each a numbered ticket with a pine tree for a device to wear in his hat. They were strictly forbidden to refuse any "jobb," and enjoined to refrain from the disorders "of which the Common Porters have heretofore been too Notoriously Guilty." Their number was increased to eighteen in 1741. These rough and ready characters seem to have conducted themselves better than formerly, although Thomas O'Brien, often suspected of receiving stolen goods, was finally discharged in 1742 for "Profane Cursing & Swearing." Hackney coaches stood for hire in Boston and Philadelphia, while livery stables kept teams or saddle horses available in all towns.[64]

[63] 8 *Bos. Rec. Com.*, 220; 12 *Bos. Rec. Com.*, 7, 15, 53, 63, 153; 15 *Bos. Rec. Com.*, 248, 262; *Rehearsal*, Feb. 5, 1733; *S. C. Gaz.*, April 26, 1739; July 2, 1741.

[64] Bristol, England, acquired its first Hackney-coach in 1722. *N. Y. M. C. C.*, IV, 91, 95; *Mass. Acts and Resolves*, II, 830, 1067; 15 *Bos. Rec. Com.*, 114, 121, 175, 316; *P. M. C. C.*, 165; *Mercury*, June 11, 1730; May 13, 1731; *Pa. Gaz.*, July 10, 1732; *S. C. Gaz.*, Nov. 25, 1732; Nov. 6, 1736; Aug. 25, 1739; Latimer, *Bristol in the Eighteenth Century*, 130.

V

The townsmen never seriously questioned the ideals of their mercantilistic age, in accordance with which authorities in each community rigidly continued to order the economic life of the inhabitants. Although no change was made in the policy of restricting the exercise of trade within the towns to freemen or inhabitants, the coming in of more foreigners made it extremely difficult to enforce. Charles Town welcomed all white immigrants, but every other town made determined efforts to confine the privileges of trading to persons who paid scot and lot. Peddlers and chapmen were everywhere forbidden to hawk their wares from house to house. The Boston Selectmen began in 1727 to keep careful records of freedoms granted to each person to exercise his calling, requiring the posting of a bond of £50. When the effect of declining trade began seriously to be felt in 1741 John Staniford was appointed to "Enquire after Strangers coming into Town and doing Business here, that they may be assessed." [65]

Newport refused after 1730 to admit anyone to the freedom of the town who did not possess property to the value of £200 or a yearly income of £10, unless he were the eldest son of a freeholder. In 1734 the Town Meeting was forced to consider the problem of the many strangers coming to Rhode Island "under pretence of being Workmen." According to the charges made, these intruders undersold inhabitants, drew away their custom, practised frauds "upon people that have not judgment," and often left town after having "got in debt." Newporters, on the other hand, had qualified for their callings by apprenticeship, and paid taxes. The Town therefore voted that henceforth no tradesman should receive license to open shop until the constable had ascertained him to be an inhabitant in good standing.[66]

The influx of Scotch-Irish and Palatines at Philadelphia threatened to derange the entire economic life of the town. The Assembly enacted strict legislation in 1729 and 1735, authorizing the Corporation to judge the fitness of any immigrant to reside in the city, which, with the charter privilege of granting freedoms, enabled the authorities measurably to restrict the business activity of non-residents. The New York Corporation enjoyed the same powers, and was even more successful in enforcing them. Despite great numbers of intruders, colonial town governments seem to have dealt with the problem better than did, for instance, the Corporation of Liverpool, which had to cope with far fewer newcomers.[67]

[65] 13 Bos. Rec. Com., 164; 15 Bos. Rec. Com., 34, 62, 322.
[66] R. I. Acts (1744), 147; Newport T. M. Recs., 273.
[67] Pa. Statutes, IV, 164, 266, 360; N. Y. M. C. C., IV, 96; Picton, Municipal Archives, 54, 120; Bayne, Norwich, 276.

By 1720 all towns had made regulations to insure fair dealing by merchants and tradesmen, and for the use of standard weights and measures. After this date increased business necessitated strict official supervision over the trading practices of inhabitants. Millers, meat-packers, and coopers were constantly in need of surveillance at New York and Philadelphia. Many tended to pack poor quality flour and meat in casks of false size. The Pennsylvania Assembly regulated the "Gauging of Cask" in 1722, and the next year laid an embargo on exportation of unmerchantable flour. Important additions to this act were made in 1725 and 1734. This action resulted from requests from the Corporation and from newspaper publicity given the "disgrace" brought on by unscrupulous packers and bolters, who had secured a bad name for the colony in the West Indies. On one occasion Andrew Bradford published an affidavit from a Jamaica merchant avowing that he could not get planters to purchase his flour, because "the Badness of most of the Flour, imported from Pennsylvania for some time past, has been so evident." After 1723 the quality of Pennsylvania products improved so much that inferior New York goods were rapidly driven out of West Indian markets. Manhattan merchants memorialized their Assembly in vain for cask and packing regulations. Rhode Island passed acts to insure fair practices in the lumber, cooperage, and meat packing industries in 1731.[68]

Charges of sharp practice by Bostonians had some foundation in fact. In 1725 "Peter Bolt" complained in the *Courant* of the town poor being "unmercifully pinch'd by the Bakers, whose Bread very often wants nearly a quarter Part of its due Weight, notwithstanding the extraordinary Diligence of the Bread weighers, who daily seize great Quantities of it." He attributed the evil to the practice of permitting hucksters to sell bread, since the bakers had to give short weight in order to make a profit. Eventually this agitation led to more frequent judicial visitations at the bakeries. Out of seventy thousand shingles coming from Weymouth in 1725, the Surveyors burned sixty thousand on Copp's Hill, "they not being made according to Law," and on another occasion a shipment from Hingham met a similar end. Within the town abuses in the sale of firewood were notorious, and carters and sloopmen were frequently guilty of "guessing" the weight of hay in order to evade the weigh-master's fees.[69] In general, however, town officers successfully reduced such unfair practices to a minimum.

Materials for study of the apprentice system in the towns from

[68] *Pa. Statutes*, III, 257, 380; IV, 73, 184, 248; *P. M. C. C.*, 206, 225, 273; *Mercury*, Aug. 16, 30, 1722; *N. Y. Col. Laws*, III, 77; *R. I. Acts (1744)*, 157, 162; *S. C. Gaz.*, Mar. 23, 1738; Oct. 9, 1741; *S. C. Session Laws, 1739*, 27.

[69] *Courant*, Aug. 7, 21, 1725; 8 *Bos. Rec. Com.*, 216; *News Letter*, Apr. 9, 1742; 15 *Bos. Rec. Com.*, 229.

1720 to 1742 are so meager as to render generalizations inconclusive. At New York until 1731, when the Corporation ceased requiring a seven year term, the system appears to have functioned satisfactorily, all male and female apprentices serving for seven years or until they came of age, and at the expiration of their term receiving the freedom of the city. Despite shortage of craftsmen at Charles Town, the seven year term seems to have prevailed. The Parish Vestry bound out both boys and girls to all trades, all matters of apprenticeship coming under the jurisdiction of the Justices of the Peace. Lewis Timothy, the printer, sold blanks for "Apprentices Indentures," and in 1740 advertised for a boy to learn the printing trade. A South Carolina law of 1740 required all apprentices to serve the full seven years, according to English practice, even though they came of age before expiration of the indenture. At Newport, too, the system apparently flourished under the surveillance of the Town Council. In 1722 Joseph Drew was bound to Thomas Bailey to learn the art of saddlery, "till he attain the Age of Twenty-one Years," and the indenture of George Vernon, who was bound to the "trade of merchant or Shopkeeper," in 1734, specified a seven year service, although he was then fifteen years old.[70]

Many boys and girls continued to be put out as apprentices at both Boston and Philadelphia, but it is impossible to determine whether or not the system was breaking down in these towns.[71] There is no doubt that apprentice training prevailed in the colonial towns in this period. The unsolved problems center about the length of service, and the attitude of authorities toward allowing persons to exercise their callings if they had never served an apprenticeship under a master craftsman.

The towns secured a ready and more important supply of skilled artisans and craftsmen from the immigrants, — English, Welsh, Scotch-Irish and German, — who were arriving in large numbers. There may also be traced in the newspapers a continual shifting of skilled workmen from town to town. This was especially true among highly specialized craftsmen, such as goldsmiths, printers, teachers and dancing-masters. Northern towns experienced no lack of skilled labor. If some artisans were drawn away, immigrants soon took their places. Philadelphia and Boston were actually embarrassed by the presence of too many, and welcomed opportunities to shunt them off. To New York, after 1728, incoming ships brought cargoes of Scotch-

[70] N. Y. M. C. C., IV, 97; N. Y. Hist. Soc. Colls., 1909, 142, 145, 162, 192; Vestry Mins., 71, 73, 75, 94; S. C. Session Laws, 1740, 84; S. C. Gaz., July 28, Aug. 11, 1733; Feb. 9, 1740; Newport T. C. Recs., May 7, Aug. 6, 1722.
[71] News Letter, Dec. 14, 1730; Mass. Acts & Resolves, II, 757; Court Papers, Phila. Cty., II.

Irish blacksmiths, carpenters, weavers, tailors, cordwainers, and other tradesmen, and by 1742 more specialized workers were also coming in. At Charles Town in 1731 John Peter Purry found "Artificers are so very scarce at present, that all sorts of Work is very dear." This stringency was much relieved by immigration, and in 1734 Hutchinson and Grimke could advertise indentured servants, "men and women, of good trades, from North of Ireland," and the *South Carolina Gazette* thereafter carried notices of most sorts of craftsmen.[72]

Some artisans united to further the welfare of their trades. "The Carpenters Company of the City of Philadelphia" was formed in 1724, for "the purpose of obtaining instruction in the science of architecture, and assisting such of their members as should by accident be in need of support, or the widows and minor children of the members." The company also drew up a uniform scale of prices for both employers and workmen, and operated with such success as to encourage the birth of a rival organization within a short time. In 1724 Boston barbers made an agreement to raise the price of shaves from eight to ten shillings per quarter, and added five and ten shillings to the cost of common and tie wigs. They also instituted a £10 fine for any member who shaved a customer on the Sabbath. In 1741 the caulkers united to refuse payment by notes on shops, and the *Boston News Letter* believed many other trades would soon follow their example, because artisans suffered much injustice in being forced to accept these notes in lieu of money payment for their work. Some New York maid servants organized for self-protection in 1734, announcing that "we think it reasonable we should not be beat by our Mistrisses Husband[s], they being too strong, and perhaps may do tender Women Mischief. If any Ladies want Servants, and will engage for their Husbands, they shall be soon supplied." The high price of wheat at Manhattan in 1741 led to a "general Combination of the Bakers not to bake until the Price fell, which Occasioned some Disturbance, and reduced some notwithstanding their Riches to a Want of Bread."[73]

The common laborers of the towns have left only enough traces of themselves to assure us that they existed in large numbers. Indentured servants also formed a growing group; after 1725 advertisements like the following appeared with frequency in every town:[74]

[72] Tailors, shoemakers, smiths and house carpenters were much needed in 1731, commanding from ten to thirty shillings a day. Carroll, *Hist. Colls.*, II, 130; *S. C. Gaz.*, Dec. 7, 1734.

[73] *Act to Incorporate the Carpenters' Company*, 3, 14, 21; *Courant*, Dec. 7, 1724; *News Letter*, Feb. 9, 1741; *N. Y. Journal*, Jan. 28, 1734; April 20, 1741.

[74] *News Letter*, Oct. 25, 1733; *Mercury*, Dec. 18, 1722; Sept. 11, 1735; *N. Y. Gaz.*, Sept. 11, 1732; Nov. 7, 1737; *S. C. Gaz.*, May 8, 1736; McKee, *Labor in New York*, 16, 31, 127.

One hundred Palatines will be disposed of for Five Years each,
[to] any one paying their Passage-Money at ten Pounds per Head;

or,

Just arrived from Great Britain, . . . several likely Welsh and English servant Men, . . . to be seen at Mr. Hazard's in New York.

In each town, but especially at New York and Charles Town, free
Negroes and mulattoes performed both menial and skilled work. The
number of Negroes at Boston somewhat declined in this period; elsewhere, it mounted. Their presence provided competition which white
laborers and tradesmen bitterly resented. At Charles Town there
were many black artisans, like Jack, the ship carpenter, and Prince,
"well known . . . as a Plaisterer and Bricklayer by Trade." In 1734
and 1742 the Grand Jury condemned the "common Practice by Several
Persons in Charles Town" of suffering their slaves to work out by the
week in competition with white labor. Philadelphians also objected to
blacks who underbid them in "Servile Work." Although harsh legislation in every town restricted his movements, especially at night, the
Negro was of too great use and value to be dispensed with as a source
of cheap labor.[75]

VI

In every colonial port this period brought a marked advance in the
methods and extent of trade. The increased sums of money and larger
number of items handled made it necessary for merchants to maintain
staffs of clerks in their counting houses. Bookkeeping by "Double
Entry, Dr. and Cr., the best Method," came into wide use everywhere
except at Newport by 1733, and schools gave instruction in shorthand
and the Italian method of keeping books. Accountants offered their
services in all the larger towns: "Any Gentlemen, Merchants or others,
that want a Book-Keeper, or their Accompts justly Stated, either in
private Trade or Company, may hear of a Person Qualified, by En-
quireing at Mr. Sweetser's, Sales-Man in King Street [Boston]."[76]

The growing wealth of colonial merchants enabled them to go into
the insurance business for themselves, instead of insuring their vessels through London, which was tedious, troublesome, and "even
very precarious." As in Europe, marine insurance was underwritten
by groups of private merchants, but only one year after the incorpora-

[75] S. C. Gaz., Sept. 17, 1737; Feb. 9, 1740; Oct. 18, 1742; S. C. Hist. & Gen. Mag.,
XXV, 193; Donnan, Slave Trade, III, 409.
[76] S. C. Gaz., May 12, 1733; Mercury, Mar. 28, 1734; Feb. 3, 1736; Courant,
Jan. 8, 1726; News Letter, Dec. 14, 1727; Sept. 16, 1726; Jan. 2, 1729; N. Y. Gaz.,
July 21, 1729.

tion of the first "assurance" companies at London came the announcement in the *American Weekly Mercury,* May 25, 1721, of the opening of John Copson's "Office of Publick Insurance on Vessels, Goods and Merchandizes." Copson's function was to act as agent for procuring "Assessors or Underwriters" for those wishing to insure goods or ships. Joseph Marion, notary, opened an insurance office at Boston in 1724, and John Franklin and Benjamin Pollard had "erected" others by 1739. In the latter year Charles Town merchants established a marine insurance business, and in 1740 several "eminent merchants" of New York, under the direction of George Moore, opened an insurance office on the Dock. Newporters probably secured their insurance through Boston.[77]

Free capital seeking investment became a feature of town economy. At Boston money in sums of from £100 to £200 was frequently advertised for loans, and at New York the beginnings of private banking appeared in 1731. Richard Nichols, attorney and postmaster, announced that "Whereas many Persons in this Province have often Occasion to borrow Money at Interest, and others have sums of Money lying by them which they want to put out, Some want to purchase Houses, Lands, and other things, and others frequently want to sell," he would undertake such transactions with the "greatest Secrecy and Integrity." [78]

The increasing volume of business in the towns, and the fact that most available specie went to redress adverse trade balances with the Mother Country placed a tremendous strain on the feeble financial structure of the colonies. In addition, country districts found all their coin filtering into the towns to pay for imported goods. The only known exit from the dilemma was the issue of paper money. Not even the most conservative of merchants denied the need for a currency, which was acutely felt by all classes. The difficulty lay in controlling the amounts of scrip to be printed. New York and Pennsylvania issues were well managed, and on the whole served their purpose. In South Carolina depreciation was rapid, until by 1730 bills of credit were exchanged at seven to one with sterling.[79]

In New England the currency problem contributed an important chapter in urban history by deepening the conscious antagonisms already existing between town- and country-dwellers. The agriculturally minded countryside, denuded of coin and bound in financial dependence to the seaports, demanded a more liberal expansion of the currency

[77] *News Letter,* Dec. 1, 1737; *Eve. Post,* Dec. 24, 1739; Adams, *Provincial Society,* 208; *N. Y. Journal,* Aug. 11, 1740.
[78] *News Letter,* Sept. 7, 1732; *N. Y. Gaz.,* Nov. 22, 1731; *S. C. Gaz.,* July 16, 1741. For Boston stock investments, see *Bos. Gaz.,* Jan. 17, 1737; 6 MHS *Colls.,* VI, 208.
[79] Dewey, *Financial History,* 23; Sellers, *Charleston Business,* 70.

than city merchants with their eyes on world markets dared permit. In Rhode Island, after almost unrestricted issue of province bills during the 'twenties, Newport business interests found their credit impaired and trade with their Boston connections impossible to conduct in depreciated paper. Abraham Redwood, William Ellery, John Freebody, Nathaniel Kay, and Daniel Ayrault constituted the conservative, hard-money group at Newport, who stood solidly behind the opposition of Governor Jenckes to country inflationists when he vetoed the Assembly's issue of yet another "bank" in 1731. Massachusetts managed its paper currency more conservatively, but its inevitable depreciation, coupled with the business depression of the 'thirties, produced bitter complaints of the tightness of money from debtor classes in both town and country, intensifying a social cleavage that had been long a-growing. The "Land Bank" of 1739, a proposal to issue bills of credit backed by real estate and by the personal security of "Artisans and Traders," crystallized antagonisms between agricultural and debtor classes and mercantile and business interests. Steadfast opposition from Boston merchants, Governor and Council, and threat of Parliamentary intervention finally quashed the scheme. But the natural divergence between town and country interests, now conscious and vocal, and the latter's resentment of control by the former, were come to stay. In Rhode Island the show-down between inflationary country and mercantile city parties was not resolved for many years, and in Massachusetts the scars from the Land Bank fracas lasted throughout the colonial era.[80]

Philadelphia experienced a lack of small change in the winter of 1740/41, and English halfpence in large quantities had to be imported to relieve the stringency. Trouble arose over the passing of these coins as pennies, and in January the bakers refused to accept them, ceasing their baking till their value should be changed. After two nights of mob activity, during which numerous merchants suffered broken windows, the frightened Corporation hastened to adjust the difficulty, and in June issued a proclamation setting the rate at fifteen English halfpence to the shilling, and declaring that he who refused to accept them at their legalized value "ought to be deemed a Disturber of the Publick Peace."[81]

Improvements in the postal service in these years greatly facilitated the transaction of interurban business. The route was extended from Philadelphia as far as Annapolis by 1722, and reached Williamsburg, Virginia, in 1732. North Carolina's delinquency created a temporary

[80] Richman, *Rhode Island*, 70; *R. I. Hist. Tracts*, no. 8; Davis, *Currency and Banking*, 130; *News Letter*, Sept. 1, 1740; *Eve. Post*, Aug. 4, Sept. 1, 1740; Osgood, *Colonies*, III, 356.
[81] *Pa. Gaz.*, Jan. 8, June 18, 1741; *P. M. C. C.*, 402.

obstacle to a through route to South Carolina, but Charles Town, too, enjoyed monthly postal connection with the rest of colonial America by 1740. Charlestonians had need of better communication with the southern part of the province and with Georgia, a want partially supplied by private initiative in 1737, when an "Inhabitant" announced a weekly service between Charles Town and Ponpon, for the carrying of "Letters and Pacquets," if the public would subscribe a sufficient sum to warrant its continuance. Doubtless this route received ample support, for there was a large amount of correspondence between town and plantations. Not only was the colonial post extended, but under the management of Governor Spotswood service considerably improved, and north of Virginia regular weekly posts were maintained. An especially important economic and cultural service performed by this agency was the distribution of newspapers throughout the colonies.[82]

Rapid economic development everywhere characterized these years. Fostered by world peace, and undeterred by temporary depression, colonial commerce enjoyed unprecedented expansion, and the appearance of surplus capital, specialized business services, and the beginnings of modern credit revealed how complex had become its needs and organization. Profits from trade sought outlets in speculation in land, and in manufacturing enterprises sufficiently vigorous to inspire panic among industrial interests in the Mother Country. As the period advanced Boston largely lost the great advantage reaped from its priority in the shipbuilding and carrying trades, and the importance of the production of staple crops that could find a place in the economic planning of a mercantile empire, or of a populous, fertile and expanding back country became increasingly evident. The doubled population and growing wealth of Charles Town are instances of the former. To the latter Philadelphia owed the sound commercial prosperity that was soon to make the Quaker town the first city of colonial America, and next only to Bristol and London in the Empire. New York experienced a temporary depression in these years, and was at all times overshadowed in the provision export trade by her younger and vigorous southern rival. But Newport, on the strength of a growing merchant marine, climbed upward on the economic ladder, and seriously threatened Boston interests in the Caribbean. Attacked from all sides, in the local carrying trade by the smaller ports of New England, and on a wider map by the expanding economic orbits of other colonial capitals, the former "mart town," though still the largest on the continent, be-

---

[82] Rich, *United States Post Office*, 27, 31; *Mercury*, Feb. 26, Dec. 5, 1723; Nov. 26, 1730; *N. Y. Gaz.*, July 31, 1732; *S. C. Gaz.*, Sept. 13, 1739; July 12, 1740; Nov. 28, 1741.

gan in the 1730's to experience the decline in population and the contraction of business that were to continue until after the Revolution. Boston had for a time to yield its position to Philadelphia, which "in a few years hence," reported Alexander Hamilton of Maryland, ". . . will be a great and flourishing place, and the chief city in North America."

XI

PERSISTENT PROBLEMS OF AN URBAN SOCIETY

I

In their dealings with the continuing social problems of urban life the towns gave the greatest indications of their advancing civic maturity. Boston's economic decline found no reflection in the town's social conscience, but rather a renewed determination to master the growing difficulties for which it had already furnished models for solution to other towns on the American continent. The Bay town still led in matters concerning the social well-being of its inhabitants, while Philadelphia developed rapidly into a well-regulated community. At the same time, towns which hitherto had not felt the press of social necessity, or had ignored it, began now to follow the example of Boston in providing agencies both public and private to mitigate the inherent problems of urban life. As a result all five colonial capitals could by the end of the period stand forth as communities mature as any of their day in the acceptance of their civic responsibilities and the employment of collective efforts for their fulfillment.

II

Appearance of urban conditions greatly intensified the fire hazard in all towns. Increasing congestion produced dangerous firetraps, and communities, which had until now escaped such disasters, in this period suffered serious conflagrations. Hence much of the progress achieved against this menace was the result of one community's borrowing and imitating the methods that had been tried and found satisfactory by others. Everywhere, however, necessity brought marked improvement in fire defenses.

Both Boston and Charles Town had in earlier years sought by building regulations to lessen the danger of fire. Boston Selectmen so carefully enforced the law forbidding erection of wooden buildings that in this twenty-two year period only seventy-two permits were issued for timber structures. In most cases such warrants referred to stables, sheds, or warehouses. John Coleman and Jonathan Belcher, merchants, received permission in 1722 to rebuild their frame warehouses on Long Wharf, on condition that they "Slate and rough Cast them and . . . carry up a Brick Wall between them." The Charles Town law prohibiting frame construction had been repealed in 1717, and only the requirement retained that chimneys be made of brick or stone. The devastating fire of November 8, 1740, refocused public attention on the problem, and the act for rebuilding the town, passed on December 20, specified that all new structures must be as nearly as possible of fireproof construction. At Newport, New York and Philadelphia the type of building materials used never became the subject of official regulation.[1]

Although the proportion of chimney fires was greatly reduced, crowded conditions in the towns rendered those that did occur far more hazardous than in former years, and New York and Boston remained the sole communities to deal satisfactorily with the problem. Sweeping regulations at Manhattan underwent no change throughout the period. The procuring of trustworthy chimney inspectors proved the greatest difficulty, and in 1721 the Common Council had to set a six shilling fine for those refusing to accept the office. The sweeping monopoly granted at Boston in 1714 operated most successfully for many years, only six defective chimneys being reported between 1715 and 1736. In 1738 the Town Meeting authorized the employment of one or more official chimney sweeps and made violation of their monopoly punishable by fine. William Haislup, who obtained the contract, kept five "hands" regularly at work. The town issued more elaborate rules in 1742, by which the sweepers received a raise in pay and directions to clean any chimney within forty-eight hours of notice given under penalty of a five shilling fine. By reason of constant care on the part of the Selectmen Boston seldom suffered from blazing chimneys.[2]

The other towns were less successful in meeting the chimney problem. James Henderson and his men, who took over chimney cleaning at Philadelphia in 1720, had the backing of a province law forbidding the firing of chimneys to clean them in order to save the cost of sweeping. In 1731 the Assembly ordered all cooperages and bakeries equipped with brick or stone chimneys. But an epidemic of chimney fires shortly after this produced an essay from the pen of Benjamin Franklin protesting the prevalence of shallow hearths and defective flues. Inasmuch as chimneys often blazed "most furiously" immediately after they had been swept, he urged the Mayor to license sweepers subject to fines if any chimney broke out within fifteen days

[1] 29 Bos. Rec. Com., 221, 225; S. C. Gaz., Postscript, Dec. 25, 1740.
[2] N. Y. M. C. C., IV, 82; Courant, Jan. 14, 1723; 12 Bos. Rec. Com., 196, 295; 15 Bos. Rec. Com., 124, 140.

of cleaning, — a device long in use at Boston. Unfortunately, his wise counsel went unheeded, and the town continued to suffer the menace of dirty chimneys.[3]

In 1723 some inhabitants of Newport petitioned the Town Meeting "concerning appointing Chimney Sweepers for the Town," but, probably because of the rarity of fire in the town, no action occurred at this time. The South Carolina Assembly consistently ignored the condition of Charles Town chimneys, cleaned usually, if at all, by slaves, with the result that chimney fires there were frequent.[4]

The four northern communities continued to take all known precautions against the outbreak of fire. At Charles Town, however, the sad consequences of the lack of local government are here most glaringly evident. Had some local authority existed to concern itself with the community's welfare, the town might easily have been spared some of the disasters it suffered in these years.

In the north careful ordinances regulated the storing of explosives. In January, 1739, Boston firewards seized six half barrels of gunpowder, "conceal'd and kept for Sale in a Store." A consequent order required all powder to be carried in covered vessels by water to the town's storehouse. The firewards put on a "drive" in 1740, seizing nine barrels of powder and other combustibles in private houses, whose owners paid heavy fines. The Pennsylvania Assembly, by an act of 1725, following an early precedent of the town of Boston, gave to William Chancellor, in his warehouse on the outskirts of the town, a monopoly of storing gunpowder at a stated charge of twelve shillings per month. No one else might keep powder anywhere within two miles of the city. In 1728 the New York Corporation brought to a conclusion its thirty year discussion of this problem by building a powder house and hiring a keeper for it. Charles Town seems to have had a privately operated powder house by 1731.[5]

The Rhode Island Assembly forbade bonfires at Newport during the annual celebration of Gunpowder Treason Day, and prohibited the use of fireworks at all times. The large increase in the fine for violation in 1737 — from twenty shillings to £10 — suggests a failure to enforce this law. The curfew at Newport rang every night at nine. To supplement fire orders promulgated in 1721 by the Philadelphia Corporation, the Pennsylvania Assembly made penal offenses the keeping of fires on ships, the boiling of tar near the docks, and the use of fireworks. In 1723 the Grand Jury presented William Fishbourn's stable as a fire

[3] P. M. C. C., 188, 266, 272; Pa. Statutes, III, 252; IV, 215; Pa. Gaz., Feb. 4, 1735.
[4] Newport T. M. Recs., 220; S. C. Gaz., Jan. 20, 1733; Jan. 25, 1739.
[5] 15 Bos. Rec. Com., 230, 251, 277; News Letter, Feb. 8, 1729; Pa. Statutes, IV, 31; Court Papers, Phila. Cty., I; N. Y. M. C. C., III, 446, 465; N. Y. Gaz., May 10, 1731.

hazard because filled with hay, and in 1730 the Corporation ordered all joiners and carpenters to cease burning "Combustible Matter" in the streets, unless their bonfires were more than one hundred yards from the nearest building.[6]

Praiseworthy as were these measures, the crowding together of town houses produced more and graver fires, and the acquisition of additional fire fighting equipment and the search for new and better methods continued to engage the activities of town authorities and private citizens alike. In 1721 Boston owned six fire engines which were regularly "tried" on the last Monday of each month by the twenty members of the engine companies under the direction of their masters. The town made important additions to this equipment in 1727, acquiring a "Large wooden water engine" operated by Elias Townsend and twelve men, for the North End, and replacing the wooden engine at the Old North Church with a "Copper Engine," to which ten men were assigned. Jonas Clark sold the Selectmen another engine in 1740, following requests for better fire defenses from the "Westerly Part of the Town." Increases in the membership of the eight engine companies gave Boston a hundred and two firemen in 1742. In 1740 a premium of £5 was offered to the company whose engine "shall first be brought to work" at each fire, and on April 30 the Selectmen made the first awards to Messrs. Underwood and Earle for the promptness of their companies at two recent fires.[7]

There were three fire engine builders in Boston, and several of the town's new machines were products of local manufacture. In 1733 John and Thomas Hill, under the direction of Rowland Haughton, built an engine which threw "a large quantity of Water twelve feet above the ground." James Read advertised in 1736 a copper engine fit for use "in any populous Place." [8]

Activity by private citizens supplemented this excellent public fire equipment. Nearly everyone kept leather buckets and other implements like axes, ropes, hooks and ladders. In 1728 Joseph Marion announced the opening of "an Assurance Office for Houses and Household Goods from Loss and damage by Fire in any Part of the Province, . . . by the name of the *New-England Sun Fire Office*," proposals to be kept on view daily for two months at his marine insurance office. It is not known whether this project succeeded, but the meager evidence is in its favor. The Boston Fire Society had twenty members in 1724, when it first printed its regulations, and in 1742 its most famous mem-

[6] *R. I. Acts* (*1744*), 165, 200; Mason, *Trinity Church*, 60; *Pa. Statutes*, III, 252; *Mercury*, Nov. 23, 1721; Court Papers, Phila. Cty., I; *P. M. C. C.*, 299.
[7] 13 *Bos. Rec. Com.*, 79, 128, 169, 172, 232; 12 *Bos. Rec. Com.*, 249, 258; 15 *Bos. Rec. Com.*, 237, 258, 261, 271, 281, 293, 329.
[8] *News Letter*, Jan. 25, 1733; Feb. 26, 1736; *R. I. Gaz.*, Jan. 25, 1733.

ber, Peter Faneuil, advertised for the return of his "New Fire Bagg," which he had lost at Mr. Deacon's fire.[9]

The alertness of Bostonians in dealing with the problems of fire prevention and protection seems to have produced real results, for the town underwent no "great" fires in this period. A series of small blazes, 1721–1723, were believed the work of incendiaries, and when five "cases of coals" were found beside an inn in April, 1723, public opinion became hysterical. More than twenty men walked the town nightly, hoping to apprehend the "Authors of this repeated Villany, . . . suppos'd to be Negro Servants." Lieutenant Governor Dummer offered a reward of £50 for conviction of the firebugs, and the town made improvements in its night watch. Boston narrowly escaped another general conflagration in 1742, when fire blazed forth at the warehouse of Deacon, the chaisemaker, consuming coaches valued at £1,000. A high wind threatened to spread the flames to nearby dwellings, but "by seasonable Assistance, with the Water Engines and Buckets, a stop was happily put thereto." [10]

The great advances made in the fighting of fire at Philadelphia resulted more from the efforts of public spirited residents than from any genuine concern of the Corporation for the city's welfare. Most inhabitants owned buckets purchased from Abraham Cox. In 1730 the Corporation bought two hundred buckets from England, a hundred more from Thomas Oldham of Philadelphia, and a quantity of fire hooks, ladders and axes, all from funds raised by public pledges. In 1735 the buckets were repaired and painted, and at the same time the authorities purchased a hundred new ones.[11]

With characteristic carelessness the Corporation allowed its only fire engine to stand exposed to all kinds of weather until 1726, when it was repaired and housed. Two years later James Claypoole was hired to care for it and to play it once a month. The need for more engines was emphasized by the outbreak of the town's first large fire at Fishbourn's Wharf in April, 1730. The blaze began in a store, and before it could be mastered had consumed all warehouses on the wharf and ruined many nearby dwellings. The loss was estimated at £5,000, exclusive of looting. "It is thought," wrote Franklin, "that if the People had been provided with good Engines . . . the Fire might easily have been prevented from spreading, as there was but little Wind." A few days later the Corporation, roused at last, levied a

[9] The Sun-Fire Office of London, opened just prior to 1720, and other London companies refused to insure buildings in the colonies. *News Letter,* April 8, 1736; *Post Boy,* Nov. 13, 1738; Feb. 22, 1742; *N. E. Journal,* Nov. 25, 1728; *S. C. Gaz.,* Jan. 22, 1732; *Rules of a Fire Society.*
[10] *Courant,* Jan. 8, 1721; April–July, 1723; 8 *Bos. Rec. Com.,* 175; *News Letter,* Feb. 4, 1742.
[11] *Mercury,* Dec. 18, 1728; *P. M. C. C.,* 288, 296, 305, 308, 340, 343, 357, 409.

tax "to procure Engines, Bucketts, and other Instruments for Extinguishing ffire," and to "Ease the Inhabitants," provided for a public
subscription, to which they individually made large contributions.
Three new engines arrived from London in January, 1731. Each was
housed in a "proper shed" under the care of a hired mechanic. A
Philadelphia-built engine, "which threw the Water much higher than
the largest this City had from London," was rejected by a committee
of the Corporation as too heavy and unwieldy in 1733.[12]

The active mind of Benjamin Franklin continually sought new
ways in which to improve his adopted city. From his efforts in December, 1736, came the formation of the Union Fire Company by
twenty-six of Philadelphia's leading citizens. This organization was
designed more for mutual assistance of members and others against
the theft of their household goods at fires, for, as Franklin said, "We
have at Present got Engines enough in the Town." The detailed
similarity of his articles of association to those of the Boston Fire
Society suggests his familiarity with the rules of the earlier organization. Yet here, as usual, as a popularizer if not an originator, Franklin
rendered real service to the colonies, for the rules of the Union Fire
Company, phrased in his crisp prose and widely publicized in the pages
of his *Pennsylvania Gazette,* became the model for all later associations
of similar purpose. The restricted membership of Franklin's company,
and Andrew Bradford's jealousy of each success of his rival, led to
the founding of the Fellowship Fire Company on January 1, 1738.
Bradford and his associates adopted the Union's rules verbatim, and
conducted an active and spirited company for many years. Another
group formed the Hand-in-Hand Fire Company on much the same
plan in March, 1742. Each member of these companies supplied himself with two buckets and two linen bags, while the companies bought
ladders, hooks and axes from their "common stock." The Union Fire
Company went beyond its original purpose in 1739, when it placed
Franklin in charge of an engine imported from England.[13]

Philadelphia now possessed methods and apparatus for fighting
fire which did credit to its status as a growing city. After acquisition
of its new equipment the town experienced thirteen fires, each of which
was extinguished or prevented from spreading because "the Engines
did great service, and the People were very active." Moreover,
watchful activity by members of the three fire companies practically
brought to an end the theft of household goods.[14]

[12] *Pa. Gaz.,* April 30, 1730; *P. M. C. C.,* 296, 307, 340, 343; *Mercury,* Jan. 13, 1734.
[13] *Pa. Gaz.,* Feb. 4, 1735; *Mercury,* May 26, 1737; Minutes Union Fire Co., I,
41; *Rules of a Fire Society;* Minutes Fellowship Fire Co., I; Westcott, *Philadelphia
Fire Department,* chapter VII.
[14] *Pa. Gaz.,* May 4, Dec. 28, 1732; May 23, 1734; May 20, 1736; Dec. 1, 1737.

At Newport thinking citizens began to realize that with the increasing crowding of frame buildings the immunity from fire hitherto enjoyed could hardly continue. In 1726 a group of prominent men founded a Fire Club, similar to the Boston Fire Society, purchasing buckets and a fire engine. The town took over the care of this equipment sometime before May, 1729, when the members of the Fire Club complained that the engine and buckets "are not so carefully lookt after as they ought to bee." The Town Council decided it would be more "beneficial to the Town" if the Club managers appointed suitable persons to care for the engine "Under Such Regulations as they Shall think Proper." [15]

The Rhode Islanders experienced their first large fire on November 4, 1730, when a blaze breaking out in a cooper's shop on Malbone's Wharf destroyed six warehouses and two dwellings. "Thro' God's wonderful mercy there were no lives lost," wrote John Comer, "and beyond expectation it was prevented from spreading thro' the town." Shortly after this the town acquired an engine which it kept in good repair, and in 1736 Colonel Godfrey Malbone, Newport's richest citizen, generously presented the community with a new suction type engine, "Torrent No. 1," made by Newsham and Ragg of London. Nine "Capable Men" were appointed in July to operate the new machine, and five for the old, with "One particular person to direct the rest, to each engine." The engine companies had orders to "Inspect" and "try" their apparatus regularly, and at any outcry of fire to "bring out ye engines working them according to ye order of their Directors." In 1740 the town had Ezekiel Burroughs build a good engine house at a cost of £16. 16. 1.[16]

In the first decade of the period the Corporation of New York was even more lax than that of Philadelphia in its attitude toward the fire hazard. A Dutchman, writing to the press in 1729, noted with scorn that "the English neither Hear nor See, but Feel only." At a recent fire he had found people only too anxious to be of assistance, but entirely without equipment. He praised the excellent fire fighting apparatus at London; "Nay, the city of Philadelphia (as young as it is) have had two Fire Engines for several years past; and it is a Wonder to Many that this City should so long neglect the getting of one or more of them." Awakened public interest, of which this letter is a sample, caused the Assembly to empower the Corporation in 1730 to levy a direct property tax for several objects, among them the purchase of fire engines. The city fathers thereupon ordered two engines of

[15] *Newport Mercury*, Feb. 26, 1921; *Newport T. C. Recs.*, May 5, 1729; *Newport T. M. Recs.*, 269.
[16] Comer, "Diary," 112; *Pa. Gaz.*, Nov. 19, 1730; *Newport T. M. Recs.*, 289; *Newport T. C. Recs.*, June 2, 1740; *R. I. Acts (1744)*, 199.

"Mr. Newshams New Invention of the fourth and sixth Sizes, with Suctions, Leathern Pipes and Caps and other Materialls." These arrived in May, 1731, and were housed at the City Hall.[17]

Public discussion of the question continued. Two engines are better than none, said one writer, but more are needed, fire drills ought to be held regularly upon militia days, and bucket laws should be enforced. Perhaps this open demand for proper direction inspired the Corporation's purchase of a speaking trumpet for use "in Case of Fire," but it accomplished little else. William Lindsay owned a fire engine in 1737 which he claimed would deliver two hogsheads of water a minute "in a continual stream," but failed to interest the Common Council. In this year the Assembly authorized the Corporation to appoint thirty strong men to "have the Care management working and useing" of the city fire engines.[18]

A number of small fires occurred in the 1730's, but by the "early assistance of the Fire-Engines" they were all "extinguished without any considerable damage." On March 19, 1741, the roof of Fort George took fire, "and the Wind blowing very fresh at the South East, the Governour's House, the Barracks, and Secretarys Office, were in less than two Hours Consumed." The very day of this misfortune the Corporation swung into action, buying a hundred new buckets marked "City of N. Y.," and in June it purchased two more London engines at a cost of £100. Appointment of fourteen more men to the engine companies brought this force up to forty-four. When a severe fire broke out near Burnet's Key in January, 1742, it was readily "suppress'd" by diligent management of "the four Engines." [19] New York, too, had at last brought its fire fighting equipment up to date.

Charles Town's fire defenses were inferior to those of the northern towns, and here, where frame houses predominated, the ravages of the flames were most disastrous. In 1731 a destructive blaze gutted most of the town, with severe property losses, and numerous small fires occurred from time to time. In 1734 the Assembly forbade fires on ships in the harbor after 9 P.M., and prohibited the boiling of tar on the wharves. In this year, too, John Laurens promoted a subscription for a new fire engine from London. Belatedly in 1736 a province law required each householder to possess a ladder and buckets, and provided for the annual election of five firemasters with authority to tax for fire equipment, erect pumps, inspect ladders and buckets, blow up

[17] The writer also proposed a fire insurance company after the London model. *N. Y. Gaz.*, Feb. 11, 1729; *N. Y. Col. Laws*, II, 645; *N. Y. M. C. C.*, III, 55; IV, 122; *Pa. Mag.*, LVI, 436.
[18] *N. Y. Gaz.*, Dec. 21, 1731; May 9, 1737; *N. Y. M. C. C.*, IV, 228, 436; *N. Y. Col. Laws*, II, 1064.
[19] *Mercury*, Jan. 1, 1734; *N. Y. Gaz.*, Dec. 23, 1735; *Post Boy*, Jan. 5, 1736; *N. Y. Journal*, Jan. 10, 1737; April 20, 1741; *N. Y. M. C. C.*, V, 17, 22, 54.

houses during fires, and care for goods brought from burning buildings.[20]

So great was the danger from conflagration that a group of merchants, after a fruitless attempt to insure their buildings in London, formed a "Friendly Society for a mutual insuring their Houses against Fire" in 1735. The Friendly Society prospered, having an estimated fund of £100,000 currency in 1736, and would probably have enjoyed a long existence but for the disaster which struck the town in 1740.[21]

In November of that year the most serious holocaust any town had yet suffered broke out in a hatter's shop on Broad Street, and, before it had burned itself out, consumed all buildings on Broad and Church Streets down to Granville's Bastion on the Cooper. The burned area was "the most valuable Part of the Town," including 334 dwellings alone, to say nothing of shops and warehouses, and Governor Bull estimated the loss at £200,000 sterling. Officers and sailors from vessels in the harbor aided the terror-stricken inhabitants in blowing up or pulling down houses in vain effort to keep the flames from spreading. Miraculously, only one life was lost in the disaster. To prevent looting a militia guard had to patrol the town for several weeks. Other colonial towns generously took up large collections to aid the homeless Charlestonians, and Parliament made the town a grant of £20,000, but years were required to repair the vast damage done.[22]

The South Carolina Assembly tried to forestall a recurrence of such disasters by requiring all new buildings to be constructed of brick or stone, and all frame structures to be eliminated within five years. The seven commissioners designated to enforce this law were empowered to order distillers and coopers to vacate portions of the town where their establishments might constitute fire hazards.[23] Such measures, wofully inadequate as they were, represented all that was accomplished in this period, and bring strikingly home the fundamental misfortune of Charles Town's condition, the absence of any properly constituted local authority.

III

With the increasing use of fire engines better water supply became one of the towns' paramount needs. Shortly after acquisition of the first Newport engine the Town Meeting ordered "that the public

---

[20] Charleston Year Book, 1880, 302; S. C. Gaz., July 13, Sept. 7, 1734; Nov. 27, 1736; Dec. 7, 1738; S. C. Session Acts, 1733-39, 86.
[21] S. C. Gaz., Jan. 22, 1732; Nov. 15, Dec. 13, 20, 27, 1735; Jan. 3, 1736; Jan. 26, 1740.
[22] S. C. Gaz., Nov. 20, 1740; S. C. Pub. Recs., XX, 336, 557; News Letter, Jan. 15, 22, 29, 1741; Post Boy, Jan. 26, 1741.
[23] S. C. Gaz., Dec. 25, 1740; April 3, 1742.

Springs & Wells . . . be put in such repair that they may be of use if a fire Should happen." Describing a Philadelphia fire in his *Gazette* in 1734, Benjamin Franklin told the public that "Where there is no Pumps in the Yards, it is to be wish'd that People would keep Hogsheads of Water always ready for such Occasions, as they are obliged by Law to do in some Cities [i.e., Boston]." When reviewing the condition of the fire engines the next year, he questioned "whether in many Parts of the Town, Water enough can be had to keep them going for half an Hour together. It seems to me some Public Pumps are Wanting." Conditions greatly improved in the next decade, and by 1744 Dr. Hamilton could report "plenty of excellent water in this city, there being a pump at almost every fifty paces" in the streets. New York was even more badly off than Philadelphia, since here public wells had no pumps fitted to them. Not until 1741 did the Assembly pass a law requiring the alderman and assistant in each ward to view the public wells once a year, and authorizing them to install pumps at the expense of neighboring inhabitants. Boston enjoyed a good water supply, and Charles Town seems not to have felt the problem sufficiently to take any action in this period.[24]

Water for household purposes seems to have been abundantly supplied from public or private wells and pumps in all towns by 1720. In 1723 John Headly of Newport had running water in his house, which he brought "underground from the Spring," but most people continued to pump their water for themselves. Mischievous boys often yielded to the temptation of stealing pump handles, and in 1735 a "Gust of Wind" blew the caps off many Philadelphia pumps to the intense annoyance of the inhabitants. After 1732 residents of Boston were able to use pumps designed and built by Rowland Haughton, "erected after a new and easy Method, where they will deliver more Water and with less Strength, . . . nor at all liable to Freeze, tho' fixed in the most Bleak Places." At New York until 1741 water had to be secured from the public wells in buckets lowered by ropes or suspended from balanced poles. This was also the case with many private wells at Philadelphia, and in 1736, when a rope gave way, Mary Coffey "pitch'd" into her well and was drowned.[25]

In 1727 a series of four newspaper articles on "The Natural History of the Well" informed Bostonians how they might avoid "Noxious" water. The writer held that most well water is "clear and Good" until the insertion of pumps produces dangerous gasses; sunlight, too,

[24] *Newport T. M. Recs.*, 235; *Pa. Gaz.*, May 23, 1734; Feb. 4, 1735; Hamilton, *Itinerarium*, 24; *N. Y. Gaz.*, Dec. 21, 1731; *N. Y. Col. Laws*, III, 181; 15 *Bos. Rec. Com.*, 306.
[25] *Newport T. M. Recs.*, 219; *Pa. Gaz.*, May 6, 1736; *Mercury*, Aug. 21, 1735; Nov. 11, 1736; *News Letter*, Sept. 21, 1732; Edwards, *New York*, 137.

should never be allowed to penetrate a well, as it induces "fatal damps," which are always present in summer. Fortunately all attempts to improve the quality of well water were not so theoretical. Newport wells had become "spoil'd" in 1741, and the Town Meeting ordered them cleaned. At Manhattan filth and sewage frequently filtered into the wells, and their water became so brackish by 1730 as to be scarcely fit to drink and to cause real illness in unseasoned visitors. After the Negro conspiracy of 1740, when the blacks were suspected of an attempt to poison the water supply, most New Yorkers bought spring water for their tea and drinking from vendors who peddled it about the streets.[26]

IV

Two decades of freedom from threat of foreign invasion made unnecessary the keeping of military watches in the towns. Indeed, so strong became the sense of security that even civil watches suffered considerable neglect, until mounting disorders called for a strengthening of these law-enforcement agencies and in two cases necessitated the temporary establishment of military guards.

The duties of the overworked constables if possible increased in these years, and the position became more onerous than ever. At Philadelphia and New York in 1722 Andrew Bradford announced "that long expected Book . . . entituled *Conductor Generalis: or the Office, Duty and Authority of Justices of the Peace, High-Sheriffs [constables], Goalers . . . &c.*" collected from "all the Books hitherto written on those Subjects," and five years later, at Boston, Nicholas Boone issued a second edition of *The Constable's Pocket-Book*. Some idea of the extent of these duties may be gained from the instructions given by Mayor William Fishbourn of Philadelphia to Constable Thomas Todd of Mulberry Ward in 1722:

> Thou art principally to weigh and consider anything which may conduce to the glory of God, honour of the King, and benefit of the inhabitants, in having a well-governed city, wherein all just endeavours are used to suppress all manner of vice and debauchery, . . . [and] to exert thyself in a punctual performance and discharge of thy duty.

Then follows "some particular matter" concerning his conduct during the day. He was especially to suppress profanation of the Lord's Day, inspect taverns regularly, taking the names of all tipplers, "endeavour the conservation of the King's peace in all respects," apprehend all persons smoking out-of-doors, and report householders casting filth into

[26] *N. E. Journal*, Aug. 7, Sept. 4, 1727; *Newport T. M. Recs.*, 219; *Pa. Gaz.*, May 6, 1736; *Mercury*, Aug. 21, 1735; Nov. 11, 1736; *News Letter*, Sept. 21, 1732; Edwards, *New York*, 137.

the streets. Probably his most difficult task arose when he saw or heard "any lewd, scolding women, that either are of such disorderly tempers to disgust the neighborhood, or of lewd conversation, by accompanying with men at unseasonable times or places." After these items came ten detailed rules for setting the night watch. One wonders if poor Todd himself ever got any sleep.[27]

Always unpleasant, it was sometimes dangerous also to serve as a constable. At Philadelphia in 1734 Thomas Taunton, butcher, assaulted, beat, wounded, and otherwise "evilly" treated Constable Hunt, "so that of his Life it was Greatly Despaired." The butcher was fined and imprisoned, and upon his release had to post a bond for good behavior, since Peter Hunt, with some justification, was "apprehensive of the sd. Thomas Taunton doing him some bodily harm." More fortunate was Robert Browne of New York, who escaped constabulary duty in 1742 because of his religious tenets, the Superior Court ruling that "no Quaker was Compellable to Serve the Office of Constable itt being an Office of Trust." [28]

Each town was protected, with varying degrees of diligence, by a night watch; some of them also provided special daytime police supervision. The efficiency of these agencies depended largely upon whether or not the watchmen were paid, and the availability of public funds for their support. In 1723 the Boston watch consisted of twelve men distributed among three watch houses, but the wave of incendiarism that swept the town at that time revealed the need for a larger and more efficient organization. Five new watch houses were built, and five "able bodyed men of Sober Conversation" assigned to each. The Selectmen designated the beats of each company, directing them "to walke Silently and Slowly, now and then to Stand Still and Listen in order to make discovery. And no smoking to be on their walking the rounds." In 1728 Thomas Mullings and John Stringer became inspectors with instructions to see that watchmen fully discharged their duties. Those found "faithful in their trust" received salaries of ten shillings a month in 1732, and by 1735 the town was spending £1,200 a year to provide for the nocturnal security of its inhabitants and "Merchandize, . . . as well as all Vessels continually Trading hither from all Ports." In 1736 a considerable saving was effected by reducing the force to sixteen men, distributed among four watch houses. Despite occasional complaints from members of the watch that the town was "Considerably in Arrears for their Wages," the system as now established operated successfully for many years.[29]

---

[27] Westcott, *Philadelphia*, chapter LXVIII; S. C. Pub. Recs., XXII, 406.
[28] Court Papers, Phila. Cty., II; *P. M. C. C.*, 355; *N. Y. M. C. C.*, V, 82.
[29] 13 *Bos. Rec. Com.*, 103, 112, 175, 296, 303; 8 *Bos. Rec. Com.*, 175; *Courant*, April 22, 29, 1723; 12 *Bos. Rec. Com.*, 40, 122, 130, 136, 138; 15 *Bos. Rec. Com.*, 180.

Inability of the town watchmen to prevent robberies led proprietors of Long Wharf to build a private watch house there in 1726, for which they hired one watchman and induced the town to bear the charge of two more. In 1732 James Bowdoin and other merchants persuaded the Selectmen to grant their privately paid watchmen equal authority with the town watches, and the next year Nathaniel Cunningham secured a grant of £50 to support the merchants' watch. Thereafter the town annually appropriated a similar sum to maintain two men on Long Wharf. A regular watch and ward was kept at the gates on Boston Neck on the Sabbath, and Justices and Selectmen continued to inspect each ward of the town at regular intervals.[30]

The Newport Town Council accorded leisurely obedience to the Rhode Island compulsory watch law of 1719 by directing its constables in 1722 to keep a "Regular watch of Six men" on duty from eight o'clock at night until sunrise. The two bellmen then serving were also retained. This watch continued regularly throughout the period, making its headquarters at a watch house near the Ferry Market, and after 1733 the Assembly periodically enacted legislation enabling Newport to levy taxes for its support. Jonathan Chase was "added as a Special constable to suppress disorders on the Sabbath & at nights" in 1732, and in 1739 the seven constables received express orders to prevent disturbances, report taverners, retailers and barbers who opened their shops on the Sabbath, and break up all noisy gatherings of boys and servants.[31] The work of the paid watch at Newport was probably more satisfactory than that of any other town.

The four bellmen who alone guarded New York proved unable to cope with increasing nocturnal disturbances there. A temporary watch of a constable and six men followed commission of "several Felonies and Burglaries" in 1728, and a permanent watch was constituted under the Montgomerie Charter in 1731. All inhabitants living south of the Fresh Water had to serve in turn, but those not willing to do so in person could present a substitute in "his, her or their stead." Thus women became eligible for duty on the watch. In 1734 "Deborah Careful" complained in the press that she had often been summoned to watch, and "forced to pay as much as the richest man in Town [for a substitute], tho' (God knows) I can hardly buy my bread; however I was told, I must do it, till there was an Act of Assembly to remedy the Evil." Each alderman kept a list of residents of his ward, and every night at nine the constable took eight of them on the rounds until

---

[30] 12 *Bos. Rec. Com.*, 52; 13 *Bos. Rec. Com.*, 147, 213, 274; 15 *Bos. Rec. Com.*, 55, 58, 364.

[31] *Newport T. C. Recs.*, June 12, Oct., 1722; Aug., 1729; June 2, 1740; *Newport T. M. Recs.*, 255, 256; *R. I. Col. Recs.*, IV, 490; *R. I. Acts* (1744), 200; *Newport Hist. Mag.*, I, 251.

four in the morning. Robert Crannel, supervisor of the watch, must have cut a pretty figure in his "Cloake of ye Citty Livery . . . blew with an Orange List." The Corporation built a substantial two-story watch house at this time, one chamber containing chairs and tables for the watch, the other, equipment for detaining prisoners over night.[32]

So many protests reached the Corporation from persons like Deborah Careful that in November, 1734, it instituted two paid constable's watches alternately to patrol New York's streets at night. During the winters, 1734–1738, this force of twelve guarded the city, but in May, 1735, their number was reduced to six for the summer period. After this the size of the force varied from year to year; in 1738 it had twelve members, the next year, only three. The outbreak of the Negro Conspiracy in 1741 demonstrated its ineffectiveness, and the Assembly ordered a temporary militia guard to prevent further disorders. This force withdrew when the Corporation formed a new paid watch of thirty-six men, eleven of whom went on duty with an overseer each night from sunset to reveille. In December, 1742, however, the Corporation disbanded this group and restored the old inexpensive citizens' watch, a distinct step backward, and indicative of the general parsimony of New York's city government.[33]

Despite mounting crime and violence at Philadelphia, no change was made in the twelve-man watch during this period. After 1723 two constables patrolled the "built part" of the town on the First Day to "Suppress all disorderly persons, and commit negroes, walking about, to the stocks." In vain did both inhabitants and press urge the Corporation to better the watch. Although the Mayor and Common Council really lacked sufficient funds to maintain an adequate police force and had to rely largely upon contributions from townsmen, still their failure to find the means does not redound to their credit. Not until 1745 did a provincial law force them to provide a "sufficient" watch.[34]

Throughout these two decades an armed watch of some sort sought to protect Charlestonians against "Mischiefs and Insults both from ye Inhabitants and Seafaring people." Mutilated records indicate that for some years prior to 1732 the watch was paid out of import duties, and from tavern fees after 1740. In 1741 the two watch commanders suffered a reduction in salary from £300 to £160 because their subalterns had been performing most of their work. Disorders caused by the growing numbers of Negro slaves led to the establishment in 1734 of slave patrols in St. Philip's Parish. Two mounted squads, each

[32] N. Y. M. C. C., II, 65; III, 451; IV, 65, 122; N. Y. Journal, Sept. 2, 1734; Edwards, New York, 121.
[33] N. Y. M. C. C., IV, 238, 252, 392, 419, 460; V, 35, 43, 77, 163; N. Y. Col. Laws, III, 148, 158.
[34] Westcott, Philadelphia, chapter LXVIII; P. M. C. C., 418.

consisting of a captain and eight men, rode alternately on "Saturday nights, Sundays, Sunday nights and holidays" to take up all slaves abroad without permission. Had the well-planned watch, projected under the bill for Charles City and Port, been allowed to continue after 1723, law and order in the southern city might have been effectively maintained.[35]

Even at Boston, where the watch was better and more efficient than elsewhere, the conduct of colonial Dogberrys was not always all it should have been. In 1724 Joshua Williams was dismissed from the Boston watch "upon complaint of his Disorders," and on numerous occasions members were discharged for "unfaithfulness." Watchmen rarely failed to report, for fear of the five shilling fine, but frequently they soldiered on the job. On May 13, 1734, Inspector Mullings informed the Selectmen "that the Watch men at the Powder House in the Common are very deficient in their Duty, and particularly the last Night, He found only Bridgham there — and he also asleep." The Selectmen thereupon decided to inspect the watches themselves twice a month, "that so the Watch men may be paid as they shall deserve." The climax of police inefficiency came in February, 1742, when the startled citizens of Boston learned that,

> Last Saturday Night some malicious and evil minded Persons took off the Hinges and carried Clear away, the Door of the Watch-House at the Town Dock, while our Guardians were at their Natural Rest, to the great endangering of their Health, if not their Lives, there being nothing more pernicious to Persons Asleep, than Nocturnal Air. There has been a Proposal Made in the Neighbourhood, to raise a Guard for the Defense of the said House, to prevent the like Enormity for the future. But all generous Proposals meet with opposition from contracted Spirits, some object and say, that the Watch-Men ought at least to take Care of their own Lodgings.

When the outrage was repeated a month later Thomas Fleet feared the town would henceforth be unable to induce men to serve on the watch. But it must be remembered that watching was often dangerous work, incidents like that of January 16, 1740, when several of the watch were "assailed and wounded" by a gang of ruffians, being far too common. Actually, the Boston watch, when it captured John Hayes, "a notorious thief," in John Phillip's counting house in 1735, or rescued a victim from footpads near the Bunch of Grapes Tavern, performed valuable services for the inhabitants.[36]

[35] S. C. Pub. Recs., IX, 110; XV, 237; XXII, 406; S. C. Statutes, III, 398; S. C. Gaz., Mar. 26, 1737; S. C. Commons Journal, VI, 172.
[36] 13 Bos. Rec. Com., 132, 140, 253, 271; 15 Bos. Rec. Com., 218, 236, 364; Mercury, Mar. 4, 1742; Eve. Post, Jan. 7, 1740; Feb. 22, April 26, 1742; News Letter, Dec. 18, 1735; Nov. 25, 1736.

V

Nothing is more indicative of the growth of urban conditions in the colonial towns than the increase in robbery and crimes of violence. The crowding of population into each seaport fostered the spreading of disorders until by 1740 instances had occurred of nearly every known offense against society.

Widening social distinctions in the towns bred discontent and resentment whence criminal disorders might easily arise. Laborers and indentured servants were frequently the recipients of treatment from their masters which ignored the simplest dictates of humanity and common sense, and these underprivileged groups constituted a potentially dangerous element in each community. As earlier, the rowdiness of sailors on shore leave produced its share of assaults and burglaries. But the most dangerous threat to law and order in the towns came from Negroes and Indians, slave and free, both of whom more readily adopted the white man's vices than his virtues. At New York the Negro population reached its maximum at the end of the period, totalling one fifth of the inhabitants. Driven by fear of the blacks, townsmen dealt with them with often unreasonable brutality, and the Negro detected in crime usually suffered the death penalty. John van Zandt, in January, 1735, horsewhipped his slave to death for having been found on the streets by the night watch, and the coroner's jury concluded that the "Correction given by the Master was not the Cause of his Death, but that it was by the Visitation of God." A "Negroe Fellow" was burnt alive for violation of a white woman and other instances of attempted rape. Slaves belonging to Mr. Humphrey Scarlet tried in 1735 to poison him and his entire family by putting ratsbane in their chocolate, but fortunately "some skilful Physicians" saved their lives.[37]

Discontent and severe treatment intensified the restlessness of the blacks. The constant fear of Negro uprisings culminated in the wave of hysteria known as the "Negro Conspiracy" of 1741. John Hughson, a white man of evil repute, kept a dramshop much frequented by Negroes, where it was suspected black orgies took place and stolen goods were profitably disposed of. A series of robberies in February, 1741, were ascribed to Hughson's disreputable customers, and with the burning of Fort George a month later, believed to have some connection with the earlier crimes, terror of violence from the Negro population reached panic proportions throughout the town. The sensational disclosures of Mary Burton, a white servant girl, who coined

[37] Edwards, *New York*, 113; *N. Y. Journal*, Jan. 28, 1733; Jan. 5, 1735; *N. Y. Gaz.*, Aug. 18, 1735; July 18, 1737.

"wild and impossible stories" of a Negro conspiracy, further terrified the already hysterical populace. Militia had to be called out, and hundreds of people fled to the Bouwerie and Harlem in fear of a black uprising. Many Negroes were rounded up and jailed, and a harsh judicial purge ensued. Quack and Cuffee, two slaves, were burned at the stake, Hughson and his wife were hanged, and before the frenzy had run its course thirteen blacks had been put to the flames, eight hanged, and seventy-one transported from the colony. Though there certainly were instances of Negro crime and disorder, the whole "conspiracy" probably originated in the terrified imagination of the mob, for even the prosecutor, Daniel Horsmanden, later admitted that there were at the time "some wanton, wrong-headed persons amongst us, who took the Liberty to arraign the Justice of the Proceedings . . . [and] declared that there was no Plot at all." [38]

Harsh treatment of Negroes and Indians in all towns resulted in frequent runaways. In South Carolina, where there were estimated to be twenty-eight thousand Negroes to thirty thousand whites, fear of a black uprising was always present. Panic inspired by a projected servile insurrection near Charles Town in 1738 could be satisfied only with the discovery and severe punishment of its instigators. At Newport in 1737 a mulatto woman was executed for twisting the neck of a child and throwing him down a well, and an Indian girl was hanged for killing a fellow servant. Boston authorities suspected Negroes and Indians of instigating the wave of fires during 1721–1723, and the next year passed a most severe code restricting their freedom of action. Nevertheless, cases of robbery and rape by Indians and slaves continued, and in 1742 inhabitants received a shock when two blacks fought a duel on the Common. "It seems they had got some Notion of the Practice of those Pretenders to Honour who to revenge an Affront challenge and engage in that murderous Action; for each of the Principals had a Second to attend him; and . . . engag'd with two-edg'd Swords, . . . but being discovered, they were separated and seiz'd before any wound was given." Philadelphia courts had frequently to deal with blacks guilty of theft or manslaughter. A citizen declared in the press in 1738 that "the disorders committed by the Slaves, every Night and Sunday, are so notorious, that all the Inhabitants must be convinced that a Reformation is absolutely necessary." They are allowed to indulge their insatiable appetites for drink at even the "most credible" taverns, as well as at the corner dramshops, and go "reeling together in the face of the Sun, with great Tumults and Noise, . . . using Threats, Violence, and Curses to the

[38] Horsmanden, *Journal;* Edwards, *New York,* 114; *N. Y. Gaz., N. Y. Journal, Pa. Gaz., Mercury,* April–July, 1741.

Whites." Nevertheless little was done to curb their insolence at this time.[39]

In all towns the prevailing offense against society was petty larceny, ranging anywhere from the theft of a saddle from a horse standing before the George Inn at Philadelphia, or a "parcel of fowls" from a Boston hen house, to the filching of the key to Mr. Pachelbell's "Parlour Door" at Charles Town. Looting of shops and warehouses went on everywhere. In May, 1731, a gang of thieves broke open several Charles Town shops, and planned the robbery of some warehouses during the confusion created by the blowing up of the powder house, but were fortunately discovered before their design could be carried out. Many "convict Felons" transported from England were apprehended at New York for breaking and entering. Richard Medley, glover, received twenty-one lashes on the bare back for stealing and selling "a great number" of Prayer Books and Bibles from Trinity Church. The Philadelphia newspapers chronicled a steadily growing amount of larceny and burglary throughout the period. The biggest "job" was the theft of £2,000 of the public funds from the office of Mayor William Fishbourn in 1730. At a single Mayor's Court in 1733 five men and eight women received sentences for various thefts. Shoplifters and pickpockets frequently appeared at Boston and Philadelphia. At the latter place in 1736 the constables detected a woman in the act of receiving a silver porringer from her eight-year-old son whom she had taught the trade of Oliver Twist.[40]

The confidence game made its appearance as early as 1730, when Alexander Cummings, "a notorious cheat," issued promissory notes at Charles Town. He paid punctually in gold until his credit rose, then swindled the unsuspecting inhabitants in a "Loan Office," and suddenly left town. At Boston in 1733 John Hill solicited charity by showing to sympathetic persons a parchment describing him as having been captured by the Turks who had cut out his tongue. The suspicious parson of Abington seized him by the throat, telling him to produce his tongue or be choked. The tongue appearing, Hill went to live for a time in the Boston gaol. "Some ill disposed Persons" posed as Freemasons at Philadelphia, swindling innocent people, until they were exposed in 1737 by Thomas Hopkinson, grand master of the true lodge. Despite the fact that Bampfylde Moore-Carew, king of English beggars, spent a period of enforced rustication fleecing citizens of the

[39] *Pa. Gaz.*, Oct. 29, Nov. 5, 1730; *S. C. Gaz.*, Aug. 6, 15, 1741; *N. Y. Journal*, April 11, Nov. 14, 1737; 8 *Bos. Rec. Com.*, 173; *News Letter*, Mar. 18, 1742; *Mercury*, July 13, 1721; Aug. 5, 1736; Aug. 3, 1738.
[40] *Pa. Gaz.*, Dec. 16, 1729; Oct. 29, 1730; June 2, 1737; *News Letter*, Feb. 17, 1726; July 29, 1736; *N. Y. Gaz.*, May 10, 1731; *S. C. Gaz.*, Sept. 17, 1737; Mar. 26, April 23, 1741; *N. Y. Journal*, Aug. 9, 1736; *Mercury*, April 30, 1730; Jan. 8, 1734; Aug. 19, Oct. 21, 1736; *Bos. Gaz.*, Mar. 24, 1729.

three largest colonial towns in 1739, the eighteenth century confidence man par excellence was the "notorious Tom Bell," aged eighteen, who made his entrance on the colonial stage in the same year. He had passed just enough time at Harvard to become acquainted with the important names in each colony, which knowledge he put to practical application by posing as the son of a leading man of one colony while operating in another. He worked his game in several of the towns before being discovered in Barbados under the name of "Gilbert Burnet Son of Governour Burnet." He was "whipp'd and Pillor'd," and sentenced to be branded on the cheeks, but was reprieved by the "Goodness and clemency of his Excellency Governour Byng." Most of Bell's colorful and meteoric career belongs to the years following 1742.[41]

Crimes of violence also increased. Footpads appeared in each town, rendering the streets dangerous at night, — even for the watch. One Saturday evening in 1736 as two young sparks were making their way across Boston Neck to visit their "mistresses," they encountered a "Troop of young Ladies or Female Foot pads, who instantly surrounded them and attacked them." One made good his escape, but the other was left "a sacrifice to their Rage, who immediately seized him, and threw him down to the Ground, and . . . strip't down his Breaches and whip't him most unmercifully." Killings were not frequent, but the nature of the few committed would easily have gained them headlines in a modern tabloid. The number of bastard children murdered increased greatly in these years. From the available evidence it may be concluded that in each town there was a growing criminal element, and that probably as many offenses were committed as in communities of the same size today. More assaults and robberies occurred at Philadelphia than in the other towns, and the mounting violence there explains the ordering of severe penalties that have so frequently been criticized as unbecoming a Quaker society.[42]

Disorder and mob violence were characteristic of the populations in the five towns. Boston acquired such a bad reputation for mob activities that the General Court passed a riot act in 1721. The Town Meeting hotly branded as false the remarks made during the passage of the bill, and asserted that "the people of this Town . . . may Justly Claim the title of being as Loyal, Peaceable and Desirous of good order as any of his Majesties Subjects whatsoever." Yet only a month

[41] *Pa. Gaz.*, July 2, 1730; June 16, 1737; *News Letter*, April 19, 1733; *Life of Carew*, 104, 115; *Eve. Post*, Sept. 10, Dec. 10, 1739.

[42] Fragmentary evidence does not permit a statistical analysis of crime, but to one who reads the records the conclusion is inescapable that lawlessness and disorder were on the increase, especially in the three larger towns. *N. Y. Journal*, Nov. 8, 1736; *Mercury*, Dec. 12, 1721; Aug. 30, 1733; Sept. 8, 1737; *R. I. Gaz.*, Oct. 11, 1732; *Eve. Post*, Sept. 6, 1736; Nov. 7, 1737; *S. C. Gaz.*, Mar. 26, 1741.

later poor Cotton Mather was bewailing the exploits of his "miserable, miserable, miserable son Increase. The Wretch has brought himself under public Infamy and Trouble by bearing a Part in a Night-Riot, with some detestable Rakes in Town." The town was hardly vindicated by the action of "some wicked and evil minded . . . Persons" in 1725, who broke into Governor Dummer's coach house and "maliciously broke to Pieces the Front Glass of his Chariot," or by the mobs which rose in July, 1729, to "prevent ye landing of Irish, and to hinder the merchants from sending away ye corn as they attempted." On October 13, 1741, "Late at Night," Justice Anthony Stoddard and Sheriff Winslow were knocked down and stoned while attempting to disperse a large group of townsmen "being assembled in a riotous manner in King Street . . . and committing great Disorders." [43]

A similar disposition to mob violence developed at Philadelphia. "Some vile Miscreants" broke into Mayor Clement Plumstead's garden in March, 1729, tearing up plants and cutting down fruit trees. The riotous propensities of the lower classes manifested themselves in the latter part of 1726, when the pillory and stocks in the market place were burned by some who "had no good opinion of the law," thus necessitating a riot proclamation by the Governor wherein the perpetrators were condemned like reformers in any age. In 1738 a provincial law forbidding erection of fish weirs and racks in the Schuylkill led to a series of riots by the poor who thus found themselves deprived of their supply of fish. 1741 and 1742 were years of tumult. In January, 1741, a group of sailors were indicted by the Grand Jury for taking up the public pumps and carrying them off, thereby inciting a riot, and a few weeks later a mob rose because the bakers had refused to make bread during the controversy over the use of English halfpence in trade. In August the Common Council decided that in order "Speedily & Effectually" to prevent future riots, the members should immediately "repair to the Mayor's house with all the inhabitants they can raise in event of an outbreak." Their opportunity came on October 1, 1742, when the famous "Bloody Election" took place. Party feeling was running high, and two violent encounters occurred between country people and about thirty sailors, "mostly strangers," on one side, and townsmen on the other. Many citizens were badly hurt, several seamen jailed, and everyone blamed everyone else for the fracas. The Corporation was accused of being strangely in-

---

[43] On the night of Oct. 5, 1736, "some evil minded Persons stole out of the Garden of Nathaniel Wardell, Chaise-Maker, a NECESSARY HOUSE, and carried it away." The distraught owner offered a reward of £10 for their conviction. 8 *Bos. Rec. Com.*, 155; 7 MHS *Colls.*, VIII, 611; *Courant*, July 24, 1725; Comer, "Diary," 78; *News Letter*, Oct. 7, 1736; Nov. 5, 1741; *Eve. Post*, July 27, 1741.

active, (perhaps it was guarding the Mayor at his house as prearranged) but later the Speaker of the Assembly upheld its lack of action on the grounds that it had no authority in cases of riot.[44]

The crime and disorder of these years, though increasing in proportion with growing town populations, was more the natural expression of a rude and lusty populace, as yet unused or unresigned to the restraints of law and society, than an indication of widespread viciousness or brutality. Most crimes were the spontaneous outbreaks of mob excitability, — riots, tavern brawls, temporary uprisings of depressed and underprivileged groups, or the roistering exuberance of sailors on shore leave. Much of the disorder was confined to the rowdy society of the waterfronts. Burglaries and pocket-picking alone indicate real premeditation, and these were the natural resort of the more unfortunate elements of town society. The majority of townsmen still observed the laws necessary for their harmonious dwelling together, and honestly sought solutions for the serious problems thrust upon them by the presence in their midsts of Negro slaves, sailors, and the "disorderly poor."

This prevalence of disorder should by rights have forced upon the townspeople some consideration of their penal systems, but until after 1730, when the problem in most places could no longer be avoided, the towns in general continued to treat their gaols with the happy disregard of earlier years. Save at Philadelphia, town authorities still preferred fines or corporal punishment to the incarceration of offenders. In the Pennsylvania capital, however, an advance in the prison system was effected which testified to the social views, humanity and common sense of the inhabitants.

The new Philadelphia prison ordered by the Assembly in 1718 was completed toward the close of 1722 at the southeast corner of Third and High Streets. A solid, two-story stone structure, consisting of two connecting buildings and a yard enclosed by a high wall, it was the only place of confinement in the colonies where any distinction was made between different classes of prisoners. One building was reserved for debtors, while the other was fitted with cells for criminals. William Biddle, the keeper, was allowed to charge twopence a day for food furnished to the inmates. But though stoutly built, at least fifteen persons succeeded in breaking out of the new prison between 1729 and 1732.[45]

Such as it was, the old Boston prison served Suffolk County until

---

[44] *Pa. Gaz.*, Mar. 20, 1729; Westcott, *Philadelphia*, chapters LXXXI, XCVI; *P. M. C. C.*, 314, 316, 342, 405; Court Papers, Phila. Cty., V; *Pa. Col. Recs.*, IV, 620; *Votes Pa. Assembly*, III, 98; S. C. Pub. Recs., XIII, 44.
[45] Scharf and Westcott, *Philadelphia*, III, 1825; *P. M. C. C.*, 229, 230, 279; *Mercury*, Mar. 7, 1732; *Pa. Gaz.*, Oct. 9, 1729; Aug. 19, 1731; Nov. 16, 1732.

1732. Yet so dilapidated and insecure had it become that four men escaped from it in 1723, and seven in 1726. The "new Goal," opened in 1732, represented small improvement, for in May of that year four prisoners escaped by cutting off the bars of the upper windows and jumping out. Before departing in 1737 James Barnes, a convicted murderer, thoughtfully wrote a billet "acquainting the Keeper of the Prison that he had made his escape about 12 o'clock, that he was in a very great Hurry, and could not stay to pay his fees, but would do it the next time he came there." After years of urging, the Town Meeting finally prevailed upon the County Court to erect a house of correction, so that the Alms House might be restored to its "primitive purposes." A piece of land on the Common was sold to Suffolk County in 1721, and shortly after the Bridewell opened for the housing of unruly servants and minor offenders.[46]

At New York criminals and debtors alike were lodged in the basement of the City Hall. Attemped jail-breaks in 1724 and 1725 resulted in the addition of two bellmen to the watch especially to guard the prison, and in the appointment of four prison guards in 1727. In 1730 the prison was repaired and the watchmen dismissed. By the Charter of 1731 the Corporation received authority to build an almshouse, which was completed in 1735, and thereafter used as both a house of correction and a workhouse for "Beggars, Servants running away or otherwise misbehaving themselves, Trespassers, Rogues, Vagabonds, [and] poor people refusing to work." [47]

Refusal of the South Carolina Assembly to provide a prison at Charles Town, in the face of repeated public demands, constituted a civic disgrace. All prisoners, debtors or criminals, were herded into "stifling Rooms" hired by the provost marshal at his own expense. For want of a prison "not one Writ in five . . . is executed," asserted Governor William Bull in 1729, and escapes were alarmingly frequent. Finally in 1736 the Assembly levied a tax for the erection of a "Work House and Hospital for the reception of the poor . . . & vagrants." This institution opened the next year, but no prison was provided for many years to come.[48]

The Newport prison was reported in such bad condition that "there is no securing any person who is there committed, which may . . . greatly encourage malefactors." So, indeed, it did. Thomas Hammett, a murderer, broke from this building disguised in his wife's cloak in 1732, and on the night of March 23, 1737, sundry prisoners made good

[46] *Courant,* Jan. 21, 1723; *News Letter,* July 21, 1726; Mar. 17, 1733; *Mercury,* April 14, 1737; 8 *Bos. Rec. Com.,* 153.
[47] *N. Y. M. C. C.,* III, 362; IV, 250, 258, 284; *N. Y. Col. Laws,* II, 645.
[48] *S. C. Pub. Recs.,* XIV, 86, 111; XVII, 467; *S. C. Gaz.,* Sept. 27, Oct. 11, 1735; Nov. 5, 1737; Mar. 27, 1742; *S. C. Statutes,* VII, 90.

their escape. "Before they went away they wrote on the Floor of the Prison with Chalk, that the Prison-Keeper might not forget them,

> Fare you well Davis, your Prisoners are fled,
> Your Prison's broke open while you are in Bed."

Much more effective in punishing offenders was the "town whipper," appointed in 1721 to preside over the new whipping post and stocks placed at the Upper Market after 1739.[49]

Imperfect as they were, town prisons seem to have been better kept than those of contemporary English cities, and there is little evidence of either the brutality or the squalor of English or European gaols. Their primary defect was their inefficiency, not their cruelty, for as protection against the growing disorders of the age they were surely frail and inadequate. Yet signs of social advance can be detected in the larger towns. By the end of the period Boston and Charles Town no longer housed "Honest Poor Peoples" in close proximity with real lawbreakers, and Philadelphia, in a spirit of enlightened experimentation, kept debtors and hardened criminals in separate buildings. However, increasing crime in the towns was bound to bring the prison question to the fore before many years.

As the towns approached maturity urban moral standards began to diverge widely from those of the countryside. Within the towns, also, wealthy aristocrats, as in other societies, increasingly pursued a manner of living radically different from that of middle and lower classes. The center of morality was shifting, and wealth and urban conditions brought about new and more elastic codes of conduct. At the Yearly Meeting of the Society of Friends at Philadelphia in 1726 country members frowned on the "extravagance" of the more urbane Quakers of the town, and condemned "That immodest fashion of hooped petticoats." The Meeting also advised that "ffriends be careful to avoid striped shoes, or red or white heeled shoes or dogs; or shoes trimmed with gaudy colors." "Superfluity of furniture," snuff-taking, and the use of fans came under its disapproval, and Quaker ladies were especially admonished not to "accustom themselves to go with breasts or bare necks." Signs of the same spirit appeared among the middle class at Boston. Many persons read with approval James Franklin's Addisonian pamphlet, *Hoop-Petticoats Arraigned and Condemned by the Light of Nature, and the Law of God*. The vogue for dancing led to violent controversy at Philadelphia, where George Whitefield condemned it in 1740, and when an unlettered Charles Town tradesman "saw the publick Advertisement of a Ball . . . it

[49] *R. I. Col. Recs.*, IV, 187; *R. I. Gaz.*, Oct. 11, 1732; *News Letter*. April 1, 1737; *Newport T. M. Recs.*, 212, 308.

touch'd all the Springs of Uneasiness. . . . Good God, said I, what can the Advertiser mean! To make Stoicks and Epicures of us? Does he imagine us lost to all Sense of Misery and reverence of a Deity!" [50]

In every town the profits of peaceful trade led to great display, which seemed to many to be mere wanton extravagance. Aged Samuel Sewall observed with alarm that "Affectation and use of Gayety, Costly Buildings, Stilled and other Strong Liquors, Palatable, though expensive Diet, Rageth with great Impetuosity, and . . . [lead] to Sensuality, Effeminateness, Unrighteousness, and Confusion." Elaborate and costly burials were said to be ruining those who could ill afford the luxury of "gloves, scarfs and scutcheons," and in 1721, 1724 and 1742 the General Court of Massachusetts passed laws prohibiting "Extraordinary Expense at Funerals." Similar complaints against display and declining moral standards emanated from New York and Charles Town.[51]

Increase in wealth brought about a noteworthy change in the status of women. As their interests widened they asserted their individuality and frequently relaxed their morals. Some ladies no longer deemed it necessary to continue living with husbands they found unbearable, and the newspapers are punctuated with advertisements of elopements and runaway wives. Nor were they all of the lower classes, as has been frequently maintained. The new leisure enjoyed by Newport ladies gave them opportunity for sociability and idle gossip at which their husbands professed to be scandalized. The *précieuses* of New York were assailed for their avid interest in politics:

> Politicks is what does not become them; the Governing Kingdoms and Ruling Provinces are Things too Difficult and Knotty for the fair Sex; it will render them grave and serious and take off those agreeable Smiles that should always accompany them.

Others railed against tea drinking, and the "silly Trick of taking Snuff," which was "attended with Such a Coquette Air in some young (as well as older) Gentlewomen and such a sedate Masculine one in others." In 1735 one brazen New York widow even printed a proposal of marriage "to the Dear Man I adore" in a newspaper, while her example was followed en masse by sixty nymphs from the Bahamas who, learning of good game at Charles Town, arrived there in 1736 and seductively advertised for husbands in the public press. At Philadelphia in 1733 a social critic observed that,

[50] Myers, *Irish Quakers*, 204; *Pa. Gaz.*, March, 1740; *S. C. Gaz.*, Jan. 19, 1740.
[51] 6 MHS *Colls.*, II, 235, 237; *Mass. Acts and Resolves*, II, 229, 336, 1086; *Eve. Post*, June 20, 1737.

It is now become the practice of some otherwise discreet women, instead of a draught of beer and toast, or a chunk of bread and cheese, . . . as our good Old English custom is, . . . that they must have their two or three drams [of rum] in the morning.

Many moralists in each town sighed for the good old days, and agreed with the New York printer who observed in 1739 "that the young maidens . . . have not half the good qualities that they were blessed with in the years 1710 and 1711." [52]

Sexual laxity in the towns was now so frequent as to be no longer received with great official distress. Bastard children were born with repeated regularity, and the authorities seem to have been less concerned with the offense than with the problem of supporting the illegitimate offspring. Hannah Dwight of Philadelphia had remitted her fine of £5 for giving birth to a fatherless child on condition that she leave the province, because she had now three to support, and Anne Gordon, guilty of the same offense, went scot-free in 1734. At Newport, when John Woodman "got a Bastard Child on the Body of Ann Crate," both offenders were discharged when the father posted a bond for the child's support. Illicit relations between Negro slaves and white servants, or sometimes with their mistresses, occurred often enough to attract public attention, and in 1723 the Pennsylvania Assembly was petitioned by a group of Philadelphians "concerning the Intermarriages of Negroes and Whites." This condition was at its worst at Charles Town, where moralists warned young men to "frequent less with their black Loves the open Lots" near King Street. In 1735 a young blade and a sea captain even fought a duel over their "pretensions to the Favours of a certain sable Beauty." [53]

The large seafaring population of Boston encouraged a greater extension of vice than at any other town. Prostitutes, many of them mariners' wives, ranged the streets near the waterfront, occasionally to be taken up by the watch. One "Little Prude of Pleasure" kept a house near the Old South Meeting, frequented by "Lawyers, Sea-Officers, Journeymen, Gentlemen, Merchants, Apprentices," and the *Courant* had to caution her not to act her "loose Behaviour . . . at the Window on the Lord's Day in the Time of Divine Service, in the Hearing if not in the Sight of the Minister." One of the town's "houses of ill fame" was demolished by "a new Sort of Reformers,

[52] In 1731 the *Mercury* devoted three and a half columns to "A General Review of Female Fashions." *Mercury*, Sept. 17, 1730; Nov. 25, 1731; *R. I. Gaz.*, Oct. 18, 1732; Singleton, *Social New York*, 380, 383, 389; *N. Y. Gaz.*, May 31, 1731; Dec. 12, 1737; *S. C. Gaz.*, July 10, 24, 1736; *N. Y. Journal*, Feb. 23, 1735; *Pa. Gaz.*, Mar. 15, 1733.
[53] *P. M. C. C.*, 318, 336; *Newport T. C. Recs.*, June 2, 1740; *Mercury*, Aug. 16, 1722; *N. Y. Gaz.*, July 18, 25, Aug. 8, 1737; *Votes Pa. Assembly*, II, 337; *S. C. Gaz.*, Sept. 6, 1735; July 24, 1736; *Eve. Post*, Feb. 14, 1737.

vulgarly call'd the Mob" in 1734, "under the countenance of some
well-meaning Magistrates," and on March 9, 1737, a bawdy house in
Wing's Lane "for harbouring lewd and dissolute Persons, was beset
by a mob which broke all the windows, stove in the doors, and did so
much damage to the place that the Woman who kept the same, . . .
[was] obliged to quit it." Yet one wise observer believed that "there
is more Wickedness in many Taverns, than in any Bawdy House." [54]

Prostitutes plied their trade in every town. One argument urged
against the introduction of Freemasonry at Manhattan was that its
entertainments would lead to the "discouraging of Virtue," at a time
when there was already much "Whoring" in the town. The "general
rendezvous" of Manhattan courtesans was the Battery, where Dr.
Hamilton was told he might find a "good choice of pretty lasses among
them, both Dutch and English," any time after sunset. Newport
gentlemen, he found, met their paramours more discreetly. Philadelphia constables had special orders to take up all street walkers and
to search "suspected lewd houses." The Mayor's Court fined Ruth
Holigan £5 and deprived her of her license in 1738 for having allowed
her tavern to become a place of assignation, and in 1741 the Grand
Jury indicted Margaret Cook for "continually" receiving, entertaining,
and supporting "whores, Vagabonds, [and] diverse Idle Men of a
suspected bad Conversation." [55]

Prostitution was one of the concomitants of urban life, but it
touched only a small proportion of the inhabitants of each colonial
town. The bulk of the people stood for a stricter morality. At Boston
the substantial mechanics who formed the New North Church enforced a rigid discipline, and as late as 1750 members who fell from
grace were forced to stand before the congregation clad in a white
robe while the minister read the accusation. Philadelphians made life
intolerable for persons who, like Alexander Ure, lived with the wife
of another man, "& the People frequently threw Stones on his House
top." Yet society in the eighteenth century was lusty and coarse, in
youthful America as in older Europe, and the Atlantic ocean offered
no insulation against either good influence or bad. [56]

Gambling increased in every town. Among the rich card playing
for stakes became popular, and lower classes hastened to imitate
them. At Boston "Gaming in the Streets for Money" occasioned

[54] Courant, Mar. 5, Sept. 14, 1722; June 1, 1724; Rehearsal, May 28, 1733; Douglass, Summary, I, 238; Eve. Post, Mar. 14, July 4, 1737; June 26, 1738.
[55] N. Y. Gaz., Feb., 1737; N. Y. Journal, May 11, 1741; Hamilton, Itinerarium, 54,
185, 218; Mins. Mayor's Court, 26 n., 746; Westcott, Philadelphia, chapter LXVIII;
Court Papers, Phila. Cty., V; S. C. Gaz., Apr. 3, 1742.
[56] Persons guilty of sexual offenses at Bristol, England, had to stand in the choir
during service and confess their sins. Drake, Antiquities of Boston, 546; Pa. Col. Recs.,
V, 277; Latimer, Bristol in the Eighteenth Century, 94.

"Great Disorders," and at New York the "Multiplicity of gaming houses," where servants and youths spent their money at "Billyard, Truck Tables and Cards," shocked all sober people. In 1737 the *New York Weekly Journal* printed "Cautions against Quadrille, . . . to advise young People, or those who but lately come to town to improve themselves in the *Beau Monde*, . . . against the Conduct of those Harpies" who are set to fleece them.[57]

Drunkenness was the vice most prevailing among all classes, and seems even more widespread than in former years. Rum swilling was to the colonies what the gin evil was to England. Frequent deaths followed excessive tippling at Philadelphia, and in 1741 a child, "about 4 or 5 years of Age, died by drinking a large quantity of Rum." Benjamin Douglass of Newport came to an ignominious end in 1728, when "being in drink and going into a little house [he] fell down from ye seat and broke his neck." Similar excesses occurred at Charles Town. Each community had its laws against immoderate drinking, and Boston still posted lists of drunkards, "as the Law Directs." Moralists flooded the public prints with communications claiming that "the abuse of Strong Drink is becoming Epidemical," and rhymes like the following plea for temperance:[58]

> This town would quickly be reclaimed,
> If drams no more had vent,
> And all the sorts that could be named
> To *Strombolo* were sent.

Changing moral codes and the rising secular spirit could not but result in a decline in Sabbath observance. At Newport, Charles Town, and New York no change occurred in the Lord's Day legislation during this period, although evidence of the need for its enforcement is not wanting. So great had "Licentiousness, and many Disorders committed on the First Day" become at Philadelphia by 1738 that the Common Council "did amongst other things come to a Resolution" to prosecute all barbers who opened their shops on Sundays. In 1741 the Grand Jury presented as a nuisance the unholy conduct of youths, servants and slaves, observing with grave concern that the "Whites in their tumultuous Resorts, . . . most Darringly . . . swear, Curse Lye Abuse & often fight."[59]

The gates on the Neck between Boston and Roxbury were regularly

[57] 8 *Bos. Rec. Com.*, 200, 224; *Bos. Gaz.*, June 6, 1737; *N. Y. M. C. C.*, IV, 311; *N. Y. Journal*, Jan. 17, 1737; *S. C. Gaz.*, Feb. 12, 1732.

[58] *Mercury*, April 19, 1721; Dec. 1, 1737; Nov. 26, 1741; Comer, "Diary," 57; *S. C. Gaz.*, May 8, 1736; 13 *Bos. Rec. Com.*, 171; *Courant*, Feb. 26, 1726; *News Letter*, Feb. 24, 1737; *Pa. Gaz.*, Mar. 21, 1734.

[59] *S. C. Gaz.*, Mar. 26, Nov. 5, 1737; *Pa. Gaz.*, July 6, 1738; Court Papers, Phila. Cty., II.

closed from sunset on Saturday to Monday morning, while within the town a strict Sabbath ward was kept. Despite continued enforcement of the laws, frequent complaints were made of people working on the Sabbath, walking unnecessarily in the streets, and "Swimming in the Water," and in 1736 the officers of the law were enjoined to greater circumspection. When Bennett visited the Bostonians in 1740 he noted that "Their observance of the Sabbath . . . is the strictest kept that ever I yet saw anywhere." [60] Indeed, to a Londoner it might have appeared so, but it was only by the increased use of authority that inhabitants were restrained on Sundays. There seems to be no doubt that throughout the hundred-odd years of American urban growth there was a steady decline in the observance of the Sabbath,—a decline that was far more rapid than in the country districts.

VI

In the north, to avoid excessive strain on town poor rates, the custom still survived of requiring strangers to give bonds before being allowed to settle in a community, but the unparalleled immigration, 1720–1742, created a situation beyond the power of the authorities to control. The two New England towns were most successful in their attempts to exclude undesirable intruders, partly as a result of the efficiency of their warning out systems, but largely because the numbers with which they had to deal were not so great as in the Middle Colonies.

Rhode Island immigration legislation, the most exclusive of all, concerned chiefly Newport, its principal port of entry. In 1727 an act of the Assembly empowered the towns to expel all non-resident vagrants and indigents, and gave town councils authority to accept or reject bonds from strangers. Any person who returned after having been warned out might be whipped with thirty-nine lashes or fined forty shillings. Two years later a special law requiring captains of ships to post bonds of £50 for each passenger landed from any place except England, Ireland, Jersey and Guernsey showed an early American preference for discriminatory treatment of immigrants, being especially directed against Palatines. That these regulations were carefully observed may be seen from the action of the Town Council of Newport in 1741, when it ordered David Carey and his family escorted out of town, "and if he returns to be whipt with 15 lashes." [61]

Hundreds of Scotch-Irish landed at Boston in 1723, many becoming charges on the town. To forestall future trouble all Irish who had

<hr />

[60] 8 *Bos. Rec. Com.*, 213; 13 *Bos. Rec. Com.*, 223; *News Letter*, Aug. 12, 1736; 5 MHS *Procs.*, 115.
[61] *R. I. Acts (1774)*, 102, 127; *Newport T. C. Recs.*, June 12, July 2, 1722; May 20, 1741.

arrived since 1720 were ordered to register with the Town Clerk for purposes of a survey. In 1733 the Selectmen recommended that something be done about the many ship captains who gave bonds for their passengers and then absconded. Boston's success with this problem was largely the result of official vigilance. From 1721 to 1742 over five hundred strangers were warned out of town.[62]

The New York Assembly by a law of 1721 forbade any townsman to entertain a stranger at his house for more than three days without permission from the Mayor, and provided for the return of any who became public charges to the places whence they came. Masters of vessels had to file passenger lists with the Recorder within twenty-four hours of landing, and either post security of £50 for each passenger who might become a public burden, or return him to his port of embarkation. In 1731 the Common Council promulgated an ordinance with similar provisions, directing the constables to seek out all strangers at Manhattan and give their names to the Mayor.[63]

Rising tides of immigration forced Pennsylvania to pass a most rigid immigration and vagrancy act, which heavily taxed all entering foreigners, but which, because of its severity, remained in force only a few months. After this the authorities registered all immigrants, and in 1735 a supplement to the poor law prohibited the legal settlement at Philadelphia of anyone coming directly from Europe except mariners and persons of unquestionable health, unless he gave notice to the Mayor within five days of his arrival. To protect Philadelphians against vagabonds and paupers from other colonies a law of 1729 allowed the Corporation to expel such intruders as were likely to be thrown on the poor rates. Newspapers frequently printed the terms of this law as a warning.[64]

The towns seriously attacked the pauper problem in this period, and although the poor everywhere increased in numbers, each community improved its facilities for caring for them. The town of Boston had so many of its own poor to maintain, and laid out such large sums of money for their aid, that there is no cause for wonderment at its vigorous policy of excluding strangers. As the decline of trade set in more townsmen needed charity, many sources of wealth dried up, and the town's benevolent facilities were strained to the utmost. The noteworthy fact is the readiness with which Boston accepted responsibility for its indigent.

The Overseers of the Poor passed upon all applications for relief and administered the town charity funds. In 1732 they joined with the Selectmen and County Justices in making regular surveys of Boston

[62] 8 Bos. Rec. Com., 177; 13 Bos. Rec. Com., 240, 244, 311; Post Boy, May 11, 1742.
[63] N. Y Col. Laws, II, 56; N. Y. M. C. C., IV, 52.
[64] Pa. Col. Recs., III, 395; Pa. Statutes, IV, 164, 266; Pa. Gaz., Oct. 29, 1741.

to determine the condition of its poor. By a provincial law of 1735 their number was increased from eight to twelve, and each overseer was put in charge of a ward the following year, with power to warn out intruders, apprentice poor children, and issue warrants for poor relief.[65]

The opening of the new Suffolk County Bridewell in 1721 at last gave the Overseers a chance to restore the Alms House to its function as a refuge for the indigent and homeless. The structure had become overcrowded by 1730, but it was not until five years later that a committee on the "Growing Charges of the Town" proposed the erection of a workhouse to employ the poor, which device it was hoped would reduce the poor rates. Necessary funds being raised by public subscription, a large, two-story brick building, containing varied equipment, was built on the Common near the Bridewell, and opened in July, 1739. The experiment was minutely and efficiently regulated. Expenses during the first nineteen months of operation were £2,451, and the income, £1,897, but since food and clothing totalled £1,603 of the cost, the whole was pronounced a success. The inspection committee reported in 1741 that ten men, thirty-eight women, and seven children were being employed at the workhouse.[66]

The Alms House and the workhouse were open to pauper inhabitants of Boston whose families proved unable to support them. Indigent strangers could also be admitted, if some other agency paid their expenses. When John Lashley of St. George's, a recently admitted inhabitant, died at the Alms House in 1738, the Overseers collected his charges from Thomas Fisher, the sea captain who had gone his bond.[67]

Boston spent large sums of money on its poor, among whom were "hundreds" of widows. Annual appropriations rose from £800 in 1727 to £940 in 1729, and by 1735 £2,069 was insufficient to meet the charges. The inhabitants became alarmed at this great increase at a time when business was bad and taxes difficult to collect. In 1736 there were eighty-eight persons in the poor house, "and but One Third Part of them Town born," which meant that £1,379. 13. 4. went to support those "who are crept in amongst us." The next year the poor cost the town £4,000! This unprecedented situation led the Town Meeting to petition unsuccessfully for lower province taxes.[68]

In addition to this admirable public provision for the poor, much private charity was dispensed at Boston. The most active agency was the Scot's Charitable Society, whose records show increased funds and

[65] 13 Bos. Rec. Com., 122, 265; 12 Bos. Rec. Com., 127, 131, 136; Mass. Acts and Resolves, II, 756.
[66] 12 Bos. Rec. Com., 16, 111, 159, 180, 230, 248, 272, 281.
[67] 15 Bos. Rec. Com., 144, 182, 235.
[68] 12 Bos. Rec. Com., 108, 119, 121, 178; Courant, Aug. 13, 1722.

an altogether praiseworthy use of them. In 1737 the stock amounted to £1,990. 4. 2., and an average of fifteen new members joined the society each year. In 1724 fifty-four Boston Anglicans founded the Episcopal Charitable Society of Boston in New England. They built up a stock of £1,000, the interest of which they distributed to the poor by much the same methods as did the Scots, "provided they are of the Church of England." Persons of the "Irish Nation or Extraction" established the Charitable Irish Society of Boston in 1737, which by the close of the period numbered 116 paying members. Many citizens, like Cotton Mather, had their personal charities, but it was largely through the churches that these people made their influence felt. The bitter winter of 1741 caused great suffering among the poor, and the Overseers' proposal that the churches undertake collections in their behalf met with gratifying results. On two Sabbaths a total of £1,240. 19. 0. was collected. No town in Europe or America showed so much concern for its unfortunates as did Boston. Bennett's tribute is well worth quoting: [69]

> They provide very well for their poor, and are very tender of exposing those that have lived in a handsome manner; and therefore give them good relief in so private a manner, that it is seldom known to any of the neighbors. And for the meaner sort they have . . . the Town Alms-House, where they are kept in a decent manner, and are, as I think, taken care of in every respect suitable to their circumstances in life; and, for the generality, there are above a hundred poor in this house; and there is no such thing to be seen . . . as a strolling beggar.

Notwithstanding the province law requiring erection of a workhouse at Philadelphia by 1720, the Corporation found the Friends' poor house and the out system of relief sufficient for all needs. In 1724 Christopher Saur wrote, "There are people who have been living here for 40 years and have not seen a beggar in Philadelphia." Conditions had changed radically, however, by 1729, when the Overseers of the Poor presented a memorial to the Assembly showing the "Hardship they labour under from the great Number of Poor from foreign Parts, and the neighboring Provinces, and likewise from the insolvent Debtors Wives and Children." The Assembly came to the aid of the city by lending the Corporation £1,000 towards the construction of the new Alms House. A fine brick structure, encompassed by a piazza, was erected in 1732 near Society Hill on a plot of ground occupying an entire city square. Besides providing an asylum for the indigent, this building included an infirmary for the sick and apartments for the

[69] *Records of the Scot's Charitable Society,* 63, 105; Episcopal Charitable Society, 1; Bolton, *Scotch-Irish Pioneers,* 175, 333; *News Letter,* Feb. 5, 12, 1741; 5 MHS *Procs.,* 116. Cf. Latimer, *Bristol in the Eighteenth Century;* Bayne, *Norwich,* 269.

insane. As taxes raised for the poor were insufficient to support the Alms House, the Corporation resolved in 1734 to place the establishment under the supervision of an efficient manager. The first appointee "misbehaved himself," and in 1736 Joseph Scull took his place. Under Scull the institution was made to yield a revenue.[70]

In 1735 the Assembly ordered that only legal residents of Philadelphia could receive public charity, and gave the Mayor, Recorder and two Aldermen authority to set the poor rates, which were now raised. The Corporation also received complete control of the Alms House and the right to appoint Overseers of the Poor. This law is significant, because it was a step toward lodging more authority and responsibility in the Corporation. Thereafter Mayor and Common Council performed admirable service in caring for the poor.[71]

Throughout the period all poor Quakers and many paupers of other sects found shelter at the Friends' Alms House, which after 1729 occupied a fine new stone structure on Walnut Street. Much private benevolence came from wealthy citizens, other religious denominations, and organizations like the Carpenters' Company.[72] Considering the strain placed on the town's resources by continued immigration, Philadelphia showed marked improvement in recognizing and meeting the problem of its dependent population.

Newport's expansion increased the number of its poor, and the tiny Alms House soon proved inadequate. In 1723 a special tax of £150 was collected to construct a new "Charity house," which was ready for use by December, under a keeper hired by the town. In 1735 the building had become so overcrowded that the Town Meeting directed the keeper to "allow something to Richard Thomas, a poor man disappointed of going to [the] almshouse after being granted permission to do so." [73]

The Rhode Island Assembly in 1721 gave the Town Council control of "lands Goods and Stocks of Money, heretofore given to Certain Charitable Uses," in order to "redress Misemployment" of these donations. Most of these funds the Council granted to needy persons in the form of out-relief. A sum of money was given to the Widow Drinkwater in 1724, "that Shee may not suffer till Shee may be in a Capacity to be removed to a convenient place." Mehitable Way and Mary England received fuel and clothing in 1739, and in 1741 the Town Council made an interesting arrangement when it granted to Margaret Freeman, "a poor Woman who Came from New York and

[70] Pa. Mag., XLV, 250; Votes Pa. Assembly, III, 73; Pa. Statutes, IV, 79, 164; P. M. C. C., 305, 309, 330, 332, 363; Pa. Gaz., Jan. 16, 1734; May 11, 1738.
[71] Pa. Statutes, IV, 266; P. M. C. C., 358, 396.
[72] Pubs. Gen. Soc. Pa., VIII, 87; Westcott, Philadelphia, chapters LXII, CXVI.
[73] Newport T. M. Recs., 219, 277, 282; Newport T. C. Recs., May 5, Nov. 3, 1729; Dec. 4, 1732; June 2, 1740.

is going to Travell to Boston," thirty shillings "to Carry her Along." Newport suffered severely from the burden of poor sailors who took sick in port and whose captains then left them behind without funds. In 1731 the Assembly ordered all Rhode Island masters to notify the Town Council when they left sick mariners behind, and to deduct six-pence a month from the wages of all Rhode Island sailors to form a fund for the support of needy seamen and their families. The estates of insane persons were placed under the trusteeship of the Town Council in 1742. Here, as elsewhere, the churches were active in charitable affairs. The Reverend John Comer continually aided the poor of his congregation, and Trinity Church had a sizeable fund for benevolent purposes. Mr. Honeyman, its rector, was also president of the "Scotch Society in Newport," which was founded toward the close of the period after the Boston model.[74] As there were fewer poor at Newport than at any other town, the inhabitants were able to give them excellent aid, and there was probably no suffering at this time.

The Parish Vestry, under the act of 1712, continued to care for the poor of Charles Town, employing the out-relief method until 1735. The burden of the poor increased rapidly after 1730, especially when pauper fugitives and discharged soldiers from Georgia poured into the town, and in 1734 the Vestry hired a house and provided "proper Attendance" for "all such as are real Objects of Charity." Annual parish poor rates rose from £625 in 1732 to £1,740 in 1740; additional funds derived from fines for Sabbath breaking and legacies from wealthy inhabitants. The Assembly recognized the community's predicament in 1736, and built a "Workhouse and Hospital" for the poor, to which by 1738 the Vestry transferred the inmates of its alms house and all poor lodged with private families. This new institution was ably administered by the Vestry, and it may well be doubted whether inhabitants of poor houses in other towns had better bedding or enjoyed "good Beife" so often as did those at Charles Town. Considering the almost insurmountable difficulties, one can find nothing but praise for the admirable and effective work of the St. Philip's Vestry.[75]

The poor, and members of the lower classes generally, suffered acutely from the destructive hurricane of 1728, which inundated the streets and drove twenty-three ships ashore. It was perhaps this dis-

[74] *Newport T. C. Recs.,* 1724; Aug., Dec. 3, 1739; Mar. 2, 1741; *Newport T. M. Recs.,* 296; *R. I. Acts (1744),* 87, 150, 249; Comer, "Diary," 84; Mason, *Trinity Church,* 55, 60; Claggett Indenture, 1741.
[75] St. Philip's Vestry Mins., 4, 19, 50, 54, 59, 63, 78, 97, 104, 107; Church Wardens' Accts., 1725–42; *S. C. Gaz.,* Aug. 3, 1735; *S. C. Statutes,* III, 430; VII, 90.

aster, together with the example of the Scot's Charitable Society of Boston and the influence of current English philanthropic ideals, that led to the founding of the St. Andrew's Society on November 30, 1730. Composed of Scots, its principal design was "to assist all People in Distress, of whatsoever Nation or Profession." By 1732 it had disbursed £460 to needy persons, and in time its relief work became outstanding in the colony. Other national groups supplemented the charitable activities of the Scots; Englishmen formed the St. George's Society in 1736, and in 1737 a group of Huguenots transformed the "Two-Bit Club" into the South Carolina Society, whose worthy aim was to relieve "our fellow creatures in distress." [76]

Manhattan poor were "put out" to private families until 1735. In October, 1724, "Mad Sew" received a supply of clothing from the authorities, "She being very old Poor & Non Compos Mentis," and on another occasion the Corporation offered Sarah Meals forty shillings "to Remove herself" out of town. By 1731, however, New York was no longer free from paupers. The Montgomerie Charter specifically provided for construction of an alms house, and the imperative need for it was pointed out by a correspondent to the *New York Gazette* in 1734. This writer stressed the increasing number of non-resident paupers, the doubling of the poor rate, and the prevalence of "Idle, Lewd and Deceitful" beggars on the streets, situations for which the only remedy was to put the poor out to work, as was the practice in other towns. Such agitation finally forced the Corporation to commence work on its poor house, a fine, two-story brick structure near the present City Hall, which was ready for occupancy in 1736. Unfortunately, much of the good work for which the building was designed was vitiated by the fact that the authorities also used it as a house of correction.[77]

Despite opening of the new alms house, and renewed attention to the pauper problem, the lot of the indigent population of Manhattan was a hard one. Furthermore, New York alone, of all the towns, had thus far failed to develop any outstanding town benefactors, whose private munificence might in part have compensated for the failure of public authorities. A communication to Zenger's *New York Journal* exposed the failure of the Corporation to care for the poor children of the town and the deplorable conditions that were thus allowed to arise.[78]

[76] Easterby, *St. Andrew's Society*, 13, 20, 22, 30; *St. George's Society*, 3, 14; S. C. Gaz., Mar. 6, 1736; *Rules South Carolina Society*, iii.
[77] Peterson, *New York*, 191; N. Y. M. C. C., IV, 240, 250, 307; N. Y. Gaz., Feb. 18, 1734; Mar. 2, 17, 1736.
[78] N. Y. Journal, Feb. 14, 1737; N. Y. Gaz., Feb. 20, 1739.

I believe it would be a very shocking Appearance to a moralized Heathen, were he to meet with an Object in Human Shape, half starv'd with Cold, with Cloathes out at the Elbows, Knees through the Breeches, Hair standing on end, Commanding the Almighty to Curse, Damn, Stink, Rot, &c. all and every Thing that seems to offend. . . . Yet this is what we must see and hear every Day with Impunity, even from Children scarce able to utter their Words. From the age of about four to fourteen they spend their Days in the Streets, with Marvels, Tops, Hoops, Farthings, &c — then they are put out as Apprentices, perhaps for four, five, or six Years, so they too often become their own Masters before they know what it is to obey. . . .

By the close of the period every town, with the possible exception of Newport, admitted the existence of a permanent pauper population, demanding public attention, regulation and aid. The vicissitudes of town life, and the growing burden of immigration made the problem of the poor one likely to increase rather than diminish in the years ahead. The greater wealth and civic conscience of the towns enabled them to make noble efforts to meet it, and in several instances their accomplishments were admirable. Boston and Philadelphia, through up-to-date and well-managed public workhouses, and the truly re-markable generosity of private charities, cared efficiently for their poor and succeeded in removing beggary from the streets. Charles Town and Newport, with lesser needs and smaller resources, met their problem in a similar fashion. Only New York lagged in both public and private provision for its poor.

VII

Growing populations crowded into limited areas made even more necessary than in previous years public concern for the general health of each community, and it is consistent with the developing character of town life that such concern was genuinely and almost universally manifested. By 1720 most town authorities had acquired a fund of experience in the control of injurious public nuisances, and their vigi-lance in such matters, together with improved methods for cleaning the streets, made for a comparative absence of conditions which might harmfully affect the health of townsmen, and for the easy removal of such conditions when they did arise. Boston made regulations to secure proper drainage in tombs at the burial grounds in 1729. Rats became a serious pest in the town in 1738, so that by 1741 the General Court was induced to offer a bounty for each rodent killed. Extermi-nation of 8,418 rats in the next year cost the province £139. 16. 4. The Newport Town Meeting abolished Samuel Carr's slaughterhouse on the ferry wharf as "a disservice to the neighborhood" and a public nuisance to persons crossing on the ferry. At Charles Town in 1734 tallow chandlers were presented for the obnoxious conditions of their establishments, and prohibited from setting them up in the "close built parts of the town." Noxious vapors from the brackish contents of the Fresh Water Pond and surrounding marshes annoyed and alarmed New Yorkers in 1732, but despite many complaints the Corporation appeared powerless to act.[79]

Philadelphians petitioned the Pennsylvania Assembly in 1723 for the removal of slaughterhouses, tan and lime pits, "erected on the publick Dock and parts adjacent," and the matter was referred to the Corporation. Against this attack on vested interests the tanners defended themselves by ascribing the nuisance "to the present Disorderly Condition" of the public Dock, which the Corporation had permitted to become a "Receptacle for all kinds of filth from a very great part of the Town." They further argued that, although precedents for placing tanpits outside city limits existed at both London and New York, the public should beware "how far such a Precedent might be made use of in the Destruction of many other Tradesmen." An acrimonious newspaper controversy followed, which finally resulted in complete victory for the interests.[80]

As in earlier years, the general health of the townsfolk continued good. The authorities, as we have seen, took many precautions against disease, but with the existing state of medical knowledge they were comparatively helpless in the face of deadly epidemics brought periodically into the towns by ships from foreign ports. An exception must be made in the case of smallpox, in the treatment and prevention of which great advances were made in this period.[81]

Epidemic disease appeared most frequently at Boston and Charles Town. Smallpox broke out at Boston in 1721, infecting 5,889 persons, 844 of whom died, largely because they refused to undergo the process of inoculation proposed by Cotton Mather and Dr. Zabdiel Boylston. Charles Town was thrice stricken by the yellow fever. In

[79] 12 *Bos. Rec. Com.*, 215; 13 *Bos. Rec. Com.*, 262, 333; *Newport T. M. Recs.*, 242; *S. C. Hist. & Gen. Mag.*, XXV, 194.
[80] *Votes Pa. Assembly*, III, 20, 348; *Mercury*, Aug. 9, Sept. 13, 1739; *Pa. Gaz.*, Aug. 23, 30, 1739.
[81] Epidemics in the towns, 1720–1742

Town	Smallpox	Yellow Fever	Distemper (Diphtheria)	Measles	Colds
Boston	1721–1722 1729 1738		1735	1729	1732
Newport	1739				1732
New York	1731 1738		1741	1728	
Philadelphia	1730 1732 1736	1741			
Charles Town	1733 1738	1728 1732 1739		1729	

1732, at the height of the plague, from eight to twelve white people, in addition to many Negroes, were buried daily. Trade utterly stopped, and many residents fled the town. Over eight hundred deaths resulted from a visitation of smallpox in 1738. According to Richard Hockley, many persons resolved to leave and settle to the northward. "Indeed the Climate is so changeable that . . . so farr from esteeming it a pleasant Winter Country, I think it a very disagreeable one." So general became the impression of Charles Town's unhealthy climate that the press felt called upon to counteract it by publication of every possible account of longevity in the vicinity.[82]

A severe outbreak of smallpox occurred at New York and Philadelphia in 1731–32. Of the former place an observer wrote, "Many Children dye, . . . as well as grown Persons, and the Country People are afraid to come to Town which makes Markets thin, Provisions dear, and deadens all Trade, and it goes very hard with the Poor." In one week seventy-six persons died, and an estimate placed the total deaths for 1731 and 1732 at six percent of the population. Hundreds of wealthy inhabitants fled to Long Island to be inoculated, but this luxury was denied the poor. A similar situation prevailed at Philadelphia at the same time, although mortality there was not so great.[83]

That Newport largely escaped any serious epidemic may be explained by good fortune, less traffic with pestilential regions, and the salubrious climate of Rhode Island. "This Island," wrote Daniel Neal, ". . . is deservedly esteemed the Paradise of New England for the . . . temperateness of the climate; that though it be not above sixty-five miles south of Boston, it is a coat warmer in winter, and being surrounded by the ocean is not so much affected in summer with hot land breezes, as the towns on the continent." After 1729 so many wealthy planters and merchants from Charles Town joined with people from Barbados and Antigua in spending their summers at Newport that the Rhode Island town became popularly known as "the Carolina Hospital." [84]

In an effort to prevent ships from Europe and the West Indies from bringing in passengers with infectious diseases, the authorities of all communities made further quarantine regulations. Physicians appointed by the Governor made regular inspections of incoming vessels at Philadelphia. Patrick Baird served in this capacity until 1728, when Doctors Graeme and Zachary succeeded him. In 1738 the river

[82] News Letter, Feb. 26, 1722; S. C. Gaz., Aug. 30, 1735; May 4, 1738; April 2, 1741; Mercury, Aug. 3, 10, 1738; Pa. Mag., XXVII, 308.
[83] News Letter, Feb. 26, 1722; N. Y. Gaz., Nov. 15, 1731; Nov. 15, 1732; Colden Papers, II, 42; Mercury, April 22, 1731; P. M. C. C., 330.
[84] Inoculation was practiced in 1739. Bridenbaugh, "Colonial Newport as a Summer Resort," 2; Newport Hist. Mag., II, 34; Eve. Post, July 23, 1739.

pilots were instructed not to bring any vessel carrying sick passengers within a mile of Philadelphia until ordered by the port physicians to do so. Governor Thomas urged the Assembly in 1739 to provide a pest house for sick Palatines coming into the town, but the project lagged until 1741, when a visitation of yellow fever, commonly called Palatine fever, demonstrated the imperative need for an isolation hospital. Governor Patrick Gordon sponsored the matter, and after much wrangling, wherein the erection of a pest house became a po-litical issue, the Assembly in 1743 finally set aside 342 acres of land on Province Island for a site for the quarantine station. A group of trustees managed the land and the construction of buildings for housing sick immigrants. They provided that all expenses for inmates should be borne by the owners of the redemptioners or the masters of the vessels that had brought them to Pennsylvania.[85]

Massachusetts authorities passed a three year act in 1721 requiring all vessels from France and the Mediterranean to put into quarantine at Spectacle Island. All persons inoculated for smallpox at Boston in that year were sent to the same place. This hospital was abandoned in 1737, when a grant of £570 from the General Court enabled the town to build a new quarantine station and isolation hospital at Rains-ford's Island. In 1738, however, smallpox victims were moved to a pest house in the West End, which thereafter served this purpose.[86]

Similar regulations were in force at the other towns. At Charles Town in 1721 the harbor pilots, on boarding a ship, inquired after dis-ease, requiring all vessels bearing sick passengers to anchor in quar-antine at Fort Johnson until they received orders to dock. A new pest house was built at Coaster's Harbor in Narragansett Bay in 1721, "to accommodate such persons, who may come in any vessel where is the Small pox or any contagion." All cases of infectious disease at Newport were also removed to Coaster's Harbor. Care-ful inspection of all passengers crossing Bristol Ferry was made whenever pestilence prevailed at Boston. Fear of ships bringing small-pox from Antigua and South Carolina in 1738 led to the establishment of a temporary quarantine station at Bedloe's Island in New York harbor, and during the epidemic of 1739 an isolation hospital within the town was erected next to the poor house.[87]

Town quarantine regulations evince a considerable awareness of the dangers of epidemic disease, and a praiseworthy willingness to utilize public authority for its control. In the then state of medical knowledge they were probably the most effective measures that could

<hr/>

[85] *Pa. Col. Recs.*, IV, 496; *Mercury*, Jan. 28, 1742; *Pa. Statutes*, IV, 382.
[86] *Mass. Acts and Resolves*, II, 228, 943; 13 *Bos. Rec. Com.*, 94, 116, 143, 205, 252; 15 *Bos. Rec. Com.*, 144, 156, 173, 282.
[87] *S. C. Statutes*, III, 127; *Newport T. M. Recs.*, 211, 284; Comer, "Diary," 105.

have been taken. At the same time, colonial medicine itself in the course of these two decades achieved more progress than in all the preceding years of its history. This advance was confined almost solely to the towns, where the medical profession became more respected and its members rose in the social scale. Two of the outstanding medical discoveries of the early eighteenth century came out of Boston. Country practice for the most part lagged far behind.

There were at least fifteen prominent physicians and surgeons at Boston, two of whom, Dr. Zabdiel Boylston, trained in the colony, and Dr. William Douglass, educated in Europe, achieved more than local fame. In addition to these reputable practitioners, there were plenty in town who essayed anything from supplying artificial eyes to a recipe for "driving Buggs from Beds." Despite professional progress, many people probably still had more recourse to quacks, or home doctoring under the guidance of such compendia of medical fact and fiction as the new edition of Culpepper's *The Poor Man's Family Book,* than to treatment by qualified physicians. In obstetrics the midwives continued to reign supreme. Midwife Roberts in 1736 employed the columns of the *News Letter* to inform her clients of her change of address.[88]

The scourge of every colonial town was smallpox, and it was at Boston during the epidemic of 1721 that the first effective measures were taken against it in the western world. Dr. William Douglass had lent Cotton Mather a volume of the *Transactions* of the Royal Society, wherein that universally curious mind had discovered an account of the Turkish method of inoculation. Mather called this "new method" to the attention of Boston physicians in a communication of June 6, 1721. As a whole the profession opposed the innovation. Douglass charged Mather with having made an incorrect summary of the method, but the native practitioner, Zabdiel Boylston, tried it on members of his family with immediate success. The controversy that followed is too well known to require rehearsal here. In July, 1722, Dr. Boylston was able to inform the public that "I have patiently born with abundance of Clamour and Ralary, for beginning a new Practice here (for the Good of the Publick)," and to present a battery of recommendations, both American and European, for the conviction of Dr. Douglass' anti-inoculatory "Club of Physicians." By 1730 the idea of inoculation for smallpox was generally accepted, even Dr. Douglass now giving "Testimony" in its favor, and inhabitants of other towns and of country districts came flocking into Boston for treatment.

[88] *Colden Papers,* II, 198; Hamilton, *Itinerarium,* 160, 167, 175; *N. E. Journal,* May 4, 1730; *Eve. Post,* Mar. 21, 1737; *Bos. Gaz.,* Mar. 14, 1722; *News Letter,* Feb. 12, 1736.

PERSISTENT PROBLEMS OF URBAN SOCIETY 403

Douglass' objections to inoculation were not those of the divine or the bigot, but those of the serious scientist with a sense of social responsibility. Unconvinced of the safety of the practice, he "reckoned it a sin against society to propagate infection by this means and bring on my neighbour a distemper which might prove fatal [and] which he might perhaps escape . . . in the ordinary way." He was himself author of Boston's other great contribution to medical science, *The Practical History of a New England Eruptive Military Fever* (1736), an admirable case history, and the first complete account of the symptoms of scarlet fever. Not until ten years later did Dr. John Fothergill publish the so-called "classic" account of this disease.[89]

There was a considerable growth of the professional spirit among Boston doctors in this period. Local medical apprentices received an opportunity for scientific instruction when the bodies of recently executed criminals were granted them after 1723 for dissection under the supervision of regular practitioners. Failure of the province to regulate the practice of medicine, and desire among doctors for mutual exchange of knowledge and ideas led to the formation of a "Medical Society" at Boston in 1736. Dr. Douglass, its leading spirit, wrote to Cadwallader Colden that "We design from time to time to publish some short pieces," and although the projected volume of *Medical Memoirs* seems never to have been printed, some of the members' writings appeared in the public newspapers, thus spreading medical ideas, and in general giving publicity to the profession. "Philanthropos" argued in the *News Letter* in 1738 for professional regulation. He proposed setting up a board of physicians and surgeons, appointed by the General Court, with power to examine and license all candidates in medicine, in order to eliminate the "Shoemakers, Weavers, and Almanack-Makers, with their virtuous Consorts, who have laid aside the proper Business of their Lives, to turn Quacks."[90]

Many physicians acted as their own apothecaries, although Doctors Douglass, Boylston, and Moffatt limited themselves to their practices. Dr. William Rand, who aided Dr. Boylston in caring for the town poor, and James Penniman, Jr., jointly advertised "all Sorts of Apothecary and Grocery Ware, at a Reasonable Rate, by wholesale or Retail," at their shops in 1733. The shop of Dr. Gardiner in Marlborough Street was one of the most frequented, especially by country people and mariners, who there bought medicine chests fitted out "as they

[89] *Philos. Trans.*, VI, 88; VII, 20; *Colden Papers*, I, 140; 7 MHS *Colls.*, VIII, 624; *Bos. Gaz.*, Oct. 20, 1721; July 17, 1722; *News Letter*, July 31, 1721; Jan. 29, Feb. 26, Mar. 5, 1730; Fitz, "Zabdiel Boylston, Inoculator," 315; *N. E. Journal*, Mar. 23, 1730.
[90] *News Letter*, Mar. 30, 1723; Mar. 28, 1734; Jan. 5, 1738; *Colden Papers*, II, 146; *Eve. Post*, Nov. 9, 1741; *Post Boy*, Feb. 16, 1736.

are for the Royal Navy, at the Apothecary's Hall in London." Thomas Ashton, apothecary, dealt solely in drugs, and did not attempt the practice of medicine. Boston printers regularly sold patent medicines and quack remedies in large quantities, after giving them wide publicity in their newspapers.[91]

While most Boston practitioners were colony trained, a majority of those in the four other towns were graduates of European medical schools. Fourteen physicians dispensed medical advice to inhabitants of Newport from 1720 to 1742, over half of whom had received their medical education in the Old World. The Rodmans were the first great Newport medical family. John, Thomas, Clarke and Walter all practiced in the town, and at least John and Thomas kept apothecary shops. Dr. Walter Rodman was town physician in 1739, when he received £23 for attending three men with "sore Leggs." Most learned among Newport physicians were John Moffatt and John Brett. At least seven different practitioners were in the town's pay for attendance on the poor at one time or another, and all saw service on coroners' juries; six of them sat at one inquest in 1737.[92]

"Here are no Phtisics or Consumptions," wrote a visitor to New York in 1731, "and so very few Physicians and Apothecaries that People live to a very great Age." It is true that longevity was the rule, and the population flourished, but so also did a group of about ten physicians and "Chirurgeons" in 1721, to which at least six more were added before 1742. Several of these men had received their training at the great school at Leyden, and interest in their art led them to maintain close correspondence with members of the profession in other towns. Dr. Colden and some of his colleagues put forth learned arguments against inoculation in 1722, but they later surrendered and employed the new method widely in the epidemic of 1731. James Alexander wrote to Colden in December of the epidemic year that "Inoculation takes mightily upon Long Island." The usual controversies over the practice were raging as late as 1738, but inoculation had definitely found favor with the medical profession at New York.[93]

New York, too, was rich in quacks. Probably many an unsuspecting burgher answered the attractive advertisement of Elias Wollin of Bohemia, who "infallibly and instantly Cures the Tooth-Ache to Admiration, also Bleeds without any Manner of Pain, Cups, &c." Such

[91] 12 *Bos. Rec. Com.*, 36; 15 *Bos. Rec. Com.*, 162; *News Letter*, May 17, 1733; Mar. 10, 1739; *Post Boy*, Feb. 1, Nov. 1, 1742; *Courant*, Dec. 17, 1722; *Bos. Gaz.*, April 21, 1729.

[92] The "sensible" Quakeress, Mrs. Leech, kept an apothecary shop. 6 MHS *Colls.*, VI, 128; R. I. Hist. Soc. Scrap Book, II, 56; Hamilton, *Itinerarium*, 184, 191, 194; Richardson Collection, 972:95; *Newport T. C. Recs.*, Oct. 9, 1729; R. I. *Hist. Mag.*, V, 76.

[93] Stokes, *Iconography*, IV, 518; N. Y. Hist. Soc. *Colls., 1885*, 100; *Colden Papers*, I, 141, 143, 145, 150; II, 12; *N. Y. Gaz.*, Mar. 22, 1731; July–Dec., 1738.

persons would better have gone to the shop near the Old Slip, to have their "Teeth drawn, And old broken Stumps taken out very safely and with much Ease by James Mills, who was instructed in that Art by the late James Reading . . . so fam'd for drawing of Teeth." [94]

For common ailments most people went to one of the four apothecary shops to purchase remedies. During the illness of Mrs. Alexander, her husband informed Colden that "She has not made use of yr. medicine being unwilling to change her apothecary. . . . She purposes to take nothing but Old Womens Receipes." Manhattan babies were brought into the world by midwives, who continued under the excellent regulations drawn up by the Common Council in 1716.[95]

Leading practitioners at Philadelphia in 1721 were John Kearsley, Thomas Graeme and Patrick Baird. Advent in the next two decades of such able men as Lloyd Zachary, a student of Kearsley, William Shippen, John Cadwallader, Thomas Bond and Cadwallader Evans made the town the leading surgical center of the colonies. In 1731 Dr. Cadwallader began giving public lectures on dissection, and in 1741 he performed a purely scientific autopsy in a case of *mollites ossium*. Dr. Bond made "good anatomical preparations of the muscles and blood-vessels injected with wax," and his lithotomies were admired in Europe. Philadelphia physicians corresponded with those of other northern towns, and were perhaps better informed upon current European developments than was any other group. They readily accepted inoculation for smallpox, ignoring those local pundits who followed the lead of the Reverend Mr. Massey of England in branding it "A Diabolical Operation, which usurps an Authority founded neither in the Laws of Nature or Religion, . . . and promotes the Increase of Vice and Immorality." Early in the epidemic of 1731 the *Pennsylvania Gazette* reported that "the practice of Inoculation for the Small-Pox, begins to grow among us," and later published an article on the subject taken from the *Transactions* of the Royal Society. Philadelphia continued, as before, to be infested by quacks, like Hendrick van Bebber, who advertised himself as a "Doctor of Physick," and sold "Sal mirabile, and other select remedies" to credulous townsmen and country yokels.[96]

The wholesale and retail drug trade prospered at Philadelphia. Oliver Galtree specialized in imported medicines and instruments in 1722. By far the most important apothecary shop was the Paracelsus Head in Market Street, where in 1734 Dr. William Shippen "made

[94] *N. Y. Gaz.*, June 20, 1737; *N. Y. Journal*, Jan. 6, 1735; May 25, 1741.
[95] *Colden Papers*, II, 146; *N. Y. Gaz.*, Feb. 15, 1732; for midwife's law, see *N. Y. M. C. C.*, III, 121; IV, 112.
[96] Norris, *Medicine in Philadelphia*, 14, 148, 150; Henry, *Medical Profession of Philadelphia*, 24, 27, 29; Hamilton, *Itinerarium*, 21; *Mercury*, Jan. 15, 1723; Oct. 9, 1735; Mar. 14, 1738; *Pa. Gaz.*, Mar. 4, 11, 1731; May 4, 1732.

and sold Chemical Preparations, Galenical Medicines and Common Oyls." The latest in patent nostrums could be had at Peter Sonman's, whose regular stock included

> Squires grand Elixir, Bateman's Pectoral Drops, Eaton's Stiptick, Lockhart's and Matthew's Pills, Gairaud's best Hungary Water, Stoughton's Bitter, Daffie's Elixir, Bateman's and Blagrave's plain and golden Spirit of Scurvy Grass, Owner's Lozenges, Clifton's and Bannister's golden spirit of Venice Treacle, Turner's Drops and Pills for curing Convulsions, Epilepsies and Falling Sickness, &c.

Such establishments probably drove out of business many of the widows who had formerly enjoyed a monopoly in the marketing of sovereign remedies. The mother-in-law of Benjamin Franklin was more fortunate in this respect, since she undoubtedly had the benefit of free advertising for her "Widow Read's Ointment for the Itch." [97]

More than thirty physicians, almost all of them European trained, and some of them highly skillful, cared for the health of Charlestonians. The active Vestry of St. Philip's annually hired a good doctor to minister to the poor, at a salary ranging from £100 to £150 plus medicines, and after 1736 patients at the new hospital also received his services. Among the most prominent of Carolina practitioners were Dr. John Moultrie, who began practising in 1738, and Dr. James Kilpatrick. Dr. John Lining, a Scot, conducted valuable medical experiments upon himself to account for the spread of "non-infectious epidemic diseases," which he attributed to fluctuations in perspiration. He also began taking regular meteorological observations in 1738, and made careful studies of the yellow fever epidemics of 1732 and 1739. Charles Town physicians frequently practised in partnership, and all seem to have conducted their own apothecary shops. [98]

Use of inoculation for smallpox during the visitation of 1738 produced bitter argument. Lewis Timothy, an ardent anti-inoculator, used the columns of his *Gazette* to fan the fire of controversy. All summer a prosy paper war was waged by the "ancients," Thomas Dale and Commissary Garden, against Doctors Kilpatrick and Mowbray, exponents of modernity, until to the relief of everyone, the historical scholar included, Timothy announced a "fresh supply of Foreign news" for his paper. [99]

Apparently, by 1742 all the colonial towns possessed medical facili-

[97] *Mercury*, Mar. 30, April 6, 1721; May 24, 1722; Feb. 12, Aug. 29, 1734; *Pa. Gaz.*, Feb. 3, 1729; Aug. 19, 1731; Sept. 1, 1737.
[98] St. Philip's Vestry Mins., 1729–1742; *S. C. Gaz.*, Jan. 6, 1733; Sept. 21, 1734; June 25, 1737; Jan. 12, 1738; Nov. 24, 1739; Dec. 5, 1741; Chalmers, *Weather and Diseases of South Carolina*, I, 47; Behnke, *Medical Life*, XLI, 67.
[99] *S. C. Gaz.*, June 1, 15, Sept. 7, Oct. 5, 1738; *S. C. Session Acts*, 1739, 111; *Annals Med. Hist.*, n. s., III, 50.

ties very creditable to cities of their time and age. With the general use of inoculation for smallpox, and the erection of isolation hospitals, the importance of the towns as medical centers for their provinces became more marked, as people from adjacent country regions flocked into town, not only to refit their medicine chests and lay in a supply of their favorite cure-alls, but also to enjoy the benefits of immunity from one of the most dreaded diseases of the age. As civic personalities the towns shouldered responsibility for the general health of their inhabitants, everywhere endeavoring to do away with obnoxious nuisances by legislative action, and save in the case of New York, employing reputable members of the medical profession to look after the illnesses of the poor.

VIII

In these years social problems in all the towns became distinctly those of urban communities. No town escaped the crowding together of buildings which made fire doubly a hazard and water more than ever a necessity. Everywhere the living together of many people, very rich and very poor, master and servant, owner and slave, led to jealousies and unrest, which bore fruit in burglaries, mob disorders, and crimes of violence. Each town had, therefore, to look to its police and prison facilities, and to increase its provisions for the protection of life, order and property. Overcrowding in the towns, and the constant coming in of immigrants, produced a class of permanently unemployed or unemployable, and the towns' greatest efforts were put forth to see that these people were cared for and that their numbers did not increase. Finally, urban conditions, and the dependence of the towns on foreign commerce facilitated the spread of disease, and everywhere the civic power joined with the medical profession in attempts to thwart it. For Newport, Charles Town, and to some extent, New York, these were years of considerable advance in the control of urban problems. In matters social and humanitarian, Philadelphia progressed rapidly. As for Boston, well established traditions of civic responsibility, and several generations of experience in dealing with the problems of urban life enabled that town still to lead in most matters of public concern for the public welfare. But by 1742 the gap between Boston and its neighbors was not so great as formerly, not from any retrogression on the part of the Massachusetts capital, but because of the gradual social maturing of the other four towns. The first century of urban America had brought the social conscience of the towns to a generally high and fairly uniform level of development.

XII

SOCIAL MATURITY

I

As peace permitted the physical growth and commercial expansion of the towns, it also formed and deepened the pattern of their social life. Increased immigration altered the racial complexion of all communities. Accumulation of wealth exalted the position of its owners, and made more socially necessary the existence and labors of servile classes, whose economic status it at the same time further depressed. Religion broadened to meet new complexities in the social order, and with the greater materialism of the eighteenth century its emphasis became more social, rather than doctrinal or theological. More and more it had to share with the tavern and with secular amusements the leisure time of the town-dweller. The former became more than ever important in the social and business life of the towns. Education and entertainment, like religion, grew to meet the diverse demands of a more complicated society, and like literature and the arts began to flourish under patronage from wealth which the fortunes of trade had amassed. The pattern of urban life had become well fixed after a century of development, and like full-grown cities these colonial towns exhibited racial, economic, and religious diversities, while offering social, educational and intellectual opportunities far more varied than were to be found elsewhere in colonial America.

II

The steadily rising tide of Scotch-Irish and German immigration began in the second quarter of the eighteenth century to produce marked changes in the colonies. Natives of Ireland and of northern Europe, arriving at every port, swelled the population of each community, for while the majority of newcomers moved directly on to rural regions or frontier, many of them, artisans especially, remained to practice their trades in the growing capitals. Thus the towns received valuable additions of both skilled and common labor. On the other hand, frequent advent of immigrant paupers caused poor rates to soar, and general fear of further costs produced more restrictive legislation. Cosmopolitanism, with its attendant advantages and problems, now became a permanent characteristic of town life.

The reception accorded to immigrants varied greatly in each community. New York and Charles Town, experiencing grave problems from the increase of Negro slavery, placed virtually no restrictions in the way of newcomers. Shortage of labor at New York between 1720 and 1726 led to the importation of over eight hundred slaves, who brought fancy prices ranging from £45 to £70. After the latter date the steady arrival of ships bearing servants from Ulster provided a far more satisfactory supply of labor, and blacks came to be used chiefly as house and body servants. Charles Town, where continual importation of slaves had made the African population equal to the white, welcomed the influx of Scotch-Irish in the 1720's, and of Germans and Swiss who followed shortly after. Most of these immigrants were indentured servants and trained in skilled trades, so that they provided much needed accessions to the artisan population of the southern city.[1]

Incoming foreigners went principally to Pennsylvania, and it was at Philadelphia that immigration effected its greatest alterations in the constitution of town population. The Pennsylvania capital received large numbers of Scotch-Irish, who, merging easily with the English elements, created no particular problem, but the presence of many Palatines bred a new situation. They came in such quantities during these two decades that the little city could neither assimilate nor care for them. Between 1727 and 1742 at least ninety-five shiploads of Germans arrived at the Quaker town; in 1738 alone about nine thousand immigrants from the Rhineland sought Pennsylvania, all of them entering through the port of Philadelphia. As early as 1730 German signboards appeared over many shops, German began to be spoken in the streets, and advertisements in German were printed in the press. In 1732 the commercial needs of this people caused the founding of the *Philadelphische Zeitung*. Sober and industrious, the Palatines added much to the life of the town, but they were of a different tongue and nation, — a fact that was to have profound significance in its social development.[2]

Immigration was heaviest into the middle colonies, because of the more attractive economic opportunities there afforded. The exclusive attitude of New England towns discouraged the coming in of foreigners, and very few, especially among the Germans, appear to have sought out the more northern locality in this period. Nevertheless, in 1723 Boston authorities found that "great numbers of Persons have lately bin Transported from Ireland into this Province, many of which

[1] *N. Y. Gaz.*, June 10, 1728; *N. Y. Journal*, May 25, 1741; *S. C. Gaz.*, Dec. 7, 1734; April 2, 1737; Mar. 9, 1738; S. C. Pub. Recs., VIII, 25; XII, 180; XVII, 339.
[2] Graydon, *Memoirs*, 6; Diffenderfer, *German Immigration*, 45; *News Letter.* Feb. 8, 1739; *Mercury*, Sept. 30, 1731.

. . . are now Resident in this Town, . . . [and] may become a Town Charge." All persons living in Boston who had come from Ireland since 1720 were therefore required to register within five days, and inhabitants sheltering such newcomers were ordered to report their presence within forty-eight hours. Feeling against "foreigners" became so intense that in July, 1729, "a mob arose to prevent ye landing of Irish," and the watch had to be strengthened to preserve order in the town. With the decline in trade in the 'thirties the Selectmen became even more careful about warning out the Scotch-Irish, and in 1736 forbade Captain Robert Boyd, of the brig *Bootle* from Cork, to land any of his "Transports." [8]

Scotch-Irish in small numbers began arriving at Newport in the early 'twenties, such families as the De Courcys and Scotts soon making important contributions to the life of the colony. A few Germans found their way to Rhode Island, where some of them bore out current fears by becoming public burdens. In 1740 the Newport Town Council granted a temporary tavern license to Jacob Hasay, "upon consideration of his Keeping of Palatines Some Time." Newport continued to import Negroes for servants, and its slave traffic became the largest in the colonies.[4]

Throughout these years immigration from England itself continued to outweigh that from other sources. Not only the gentlefolk, but the bulk of colonial artisans and tradesmen, remained Englishmen by birth or heritage. Yet, by the end of the period, advent of other groups was slowly altering the pattern of population in each town. At Philadelphia a large and unassimilated German element preserved its own language, press and methods of business. At Charles Town there was a predominance of black laborers which even the later arrival of European exiles could not offset. New York sheltered considerable representations of each important non-English group, — German, Scotch-Irish and African. In New England racial heterogeneity was less marked. Boston discouraged the advent of non-English immigrants, and very few of any group voluntarily sought out Newport. With the exception of Boston, where the policy of restricted immigration had its origins in the rising costs of poor relief, nativism is hardly present in this period. The great fear lest Pennsylvania become predominantly German had not yet arisen. The growing towns needed the labor of these foreigners, and several generations of experience had accustomed the townsmen to accept their presence without either resentment or alarm.

[3] 8 *Bos. Rec. Com.*, 177; Comer, "Diary," 78; 13 *Bos. Rec. Com.*, 311; *Courant*, Mar. 5, 1722.
[4] R. I. Hist. Soc. *Colls.*, XXVI, 2; *Newport T. C. Recs.*, June 20, 1740; *N. E. Journal*, Oct. 23, 1729; *News Letter*, Mar. 13, 1740.

III

The social cleavage noted in earlier periods now became more distinct in each town. From the economic gains of peaceful trading merchant grandees accumulated riches so rapidly as to raise their position far above that of other townsmen. Times being on the whole prosperous, industrious laborers could still become artisans and shopkeepers, and thrifty tradesmen might graduate into the merchant class. But the mere possession of wealth no longer constituted the sole and sufficient means of procuring entrance to the ranks of the better sort. After a hundred years this class was becoming well-defined, sure of itself, and arrogant, and more and more it stressed inheritance and breeding as the basis for social position. Benjamin Franklin, for instance, never succeeded in making himself quite "socially acceptable" to the Philadelphia gentry. On the other hand, we have seen that poverty existed. Class lines were tightening, and an undercurrent of resentment began to flow among the lower ranks of city life. This feeling was for the most part still inarticulate, — class consciousness in the eighteenth century had none of the organization or aggressiveness that characterize it today, — yet occasions arose when the "inferiour sort" gave expression to their constant envy and frequent disgust with the conduct of the aristocrats, who now lived, economically, socially, morally, and in many cases religiously, apart from the rest of the community, while continuing to control it in their own interests.

Nothing better indicates the extent of social stratification attained at Boston than the modes of living prevailing among different groups. Rich merchants and their associates dwelt in elaborate town houses, beautifully appointed, and filled with elegant furniture. As early as 1723 Grafton Feveryeare at "The Black Wigg" was supplying the North Enders with Holland stoves, and by 1730 "Stampt Paper in Rolls for to paper Rooms" was in considerable demand for their walls. Such establishments required a corps of servants, black and white, and an income of at least £1,500 a year to maintain, yet some Boston merchants kept country mansions at Roxbury or Muddy River as well. Small wonder that English gentlemen began thus early to prospect here for "a pretty woman worth 5 or 6000 £ str. fortune when minded to marry." [5]

Boston gentlewomen dressed in the latest and most expensive London clothes and bedecked themselves with lavish jewelry. In March, 1734, a quantity of Nassau silks "of the Colour provided for the royal wedding" was dispatched to Boston "early, that . . . Ladys may have

[5] *Eve. Post,* June 13, 1737; *N. E. Journal,* Oct. 26, 1730; *Bos. Gaz.,* Nov. 4, 1723; 6 MHS *Colls.,* VI, 91, 240; VII, 77, 383.

them as soon as some of ours." London merchants well knew by now that Boston provided a ready market for the latest English fashions. These ladies of the aristocracy gave over the care of their many off-spring to "Wet Nurses," and later to nursery governesses, who carefully instructed them in the ways of gentility from such manuals as *The School of Good Manners. Containing . . . Rules for Children's Behaviour.*[6]

Most of the Boston gentry kept coaches, and carriage makers like John Lucas had orders enough to keep them constantly at work. Gentlemen and their "virtuous consorts" reclined on caned seats or sank comfortably into the green plush of their equipages, while Negro coachmen drove them to church or to social gatherings, for all to see and for laborers and tradesmen to envy. Those with pretensions, but without the means to keep carriages of their own, could hire of George Hewes "a Handsome Chair Chaise on Reasonable Terms," while Samuel Bleigh and Alexander Thorpe kept coaches and black horses to rent for funerals.[7]

The wealthy carried their display even to the grave. Members of the upper class were ushered out of life with such expensive ostentation that the General Court passed laws against "extraordinary expenditures for funerals" in 1721 and succeeding years. The object of thus attempting to curtail the mortuary extravagances of the rich was to prevent desire for emulation among the humbler classes. When Andrew Faneuil was "honourably Interr'd" in 1738, over eleven hundred persons accompanied his "generous and expensive" funeral cortege, while crowds of spectators lined the streets. One wonders if Peter Faneuil paid the usual fine for violation of the province law. No law, however, existed against extravagance in laudatory obituaries, cataloguing the virtuous actions, Christian deportment, blameless lives and brilliant accomplishments of deceased gentry. "Mr. C. H." at the Crown Coffee House offered to lighten the burden of bereaved Bostonians by supplying them with engraved sets of ready-made obituary notices, "With Void Spaces for the Name, Age, distinction, and Profession, or such Particular and Eminent Qualities, as do not properly fall under the Notice of General Description."[8]

Middle class tradesmen and artisans of Boston lived comfortably in plain frame houses equipped with serviceable furnishings. Those who prospered owned a few pictures, some glass, plate and china. They also indulged a taste for tea, coffee, chocolate, and occasionally im-

[6] *News Letter*, July 18, 1723; Feb. 15, 22, 1732; May 16, 1734.
[7] *N. E. Journal*, Aug. 25, 1729; *News Letter*, Mar. 12, 1730; June 28, 1733; June 26, 1740; *Post Boy*, April 26, 1742.
[8] *N. E. Quarterly*, V, 800; *News Letter*, Feb. 25, 1731; Feb. 23, 1738; *Eve. Post*, Feb. 4, 1740.

ported fruits and sweetmeats, and "a Variety of other desireable, tho'
expensive, Comforts of humane Life, . . . common in Families of but
a moderate Size and Rank in the World." In 1728 "the Necessary
Expenses in a Family of but middling Figure, and no more than Eight
Persons" were estimated by the *New England Weekly Journal* to be
about £265. 18. 9. per year. Most people of this rank kept one maid-
of-all-work, whose wages generally cost them £10 a year, a sum
slightly more than half the annual expenditure for candles, soap, and
washing.[9]

At the bottom of the social ladder came the laborers, seafarers,
servants and slaves. Their lot was unenviable, and their bare livings
hardly won. Few could rise much above their station, and they had
continually to suffer the contempt of their betters. Lately Gee, a baker,
even managed a sneer at "Common Sailors" in one of his biscuit advertisements in 1722. More condescending still is the account of a
woman sentenced to stand in the pillory for cheating in 1739:[10]

> She is a Fish Monger to her Business, and had begun a Quarrel
> about a Sale of Herrings; for this reason she stood with a String of
> them hung about her Neck; . . . with these low People it's only such
> a Way of punishing (which however some may sneer at) that gains the
> End of Punishing, Reformation.

There is small cause for wonder that the mob occasionally rose at
Boston, or that the lower classes resented the fact that social position
rather than numbers controlled the Town Meeting.

At Newport the merchant aristocracy lived on much the same scale
as at Boston. "Both men and women all agreed in a rage for finery."
Dean Berkeley and his friends daily saw "the men in flaming scarlet
coats and waistcoats, laced and fringed with brightest glaring yellow.
The Sly Quakers, not venturing on these charming coats and waistcoats, yet loving finery, figured away with plate on their sideboards."
One Friend soberly bragged to the Dean that his solid gold tea pot
was such a treasure as even Queen Caroline did not possess. Doubtless,
one of the most elegantly garbed gentlemen was old Edward Pelham,
Harvard graduate and man of leisure, who "had never engaged in any
business, but lived on his inheritance." Friend Abraham Redwood
maintained an imported coach with liveried driver and footman. Newport's gentlemen of "Capacity and Leisure" and their beautiful women-
folk ("generally very airy and frolicksome"), lived in lovely homes
that were a tribute to their artistic taste. Dr. Hamilton found Godfrey
Malbone's mansion, with its great gilded hall, the most magnificent in

[9] *N. E. Quarterly*, V, 800; *Bos. Gaz.*, May 16, 23, 1737; *Eve. Post*, June 20, 1737.
[10] *Courant*, Sept. 17, 1722; *N. Y. Journal*, Jan. 22, 1739; *Bos. Gaz.*, March 28, 1737.

the colonies; "Round it are pretty gardens and terraces with canals and basins for water, from whence you have a delightful view." William Coddington's forty acre estate a mile outside the town was only one of Rhode Island's handsome country seats. Everywhere among the prominent families appeared signs of great wealth. The Collings, Cranstons, Dyers, Eastons, Ellerys, Gouldings, Richardsons, Rodmans and Taylors all lived luxuriously, and through their control of the Town Council ordered the affairs of Newport, commercial and political, to their liking.[11]

Newport had also a substantial middle class, and solid citizens like Latham Thurston amassed as much as £2,000 in a lifetime of diligence and thrift. The many yeomen of the Island who shipped as common sailors, and the men who labored in warehouses and on docks formed the lower strata of town society, envying and cursing their superiors with much the same spirit as their Boston comrades. In the summer of 1730 a quarrel between the "gentlemen's party" and one "not so" led to a mob "insurrection" and attempted gaol delivery.[12]

In New York the aristocracy distinguished itself by greater display and ostentation than in any other town, this surface brilliancy undoubtedly constituting one of the reasons why visiting Englishmen constantly found the city so attractive. In 1731 one of them wrote that "the City of New York hath near as many Inhabitants as Philadelphia, and is a more delightful place. The Gentlemen here are exceeded by none in Kindness and Civility to Strangers." [13] On the other hand, the Manhattan gentry showed little awareness of the obligations of noblesse so evident elsewhere, and signally failed to produce any public benefactors as had their peers in other northern towns.

Evidences of riches at Manhattan increased after 1730. Some fine houses were built in the town, and suburban residences appeared on Greenwich and Bloomendale Roads, but in general they did not equal the show places of other northern towns in either size or architecture. Their interiors, however, wore an air of great wealth. Window hangings of camlet, japanned tables, gold-framed looking-glasses, spinets and massive eight-day clocks were very much in evidence, as were also richly carved furniture, jewels and silver plate. Black house servants were popular, wealthy New Yorkers like Caleb Heathcote often keeping as many as forty. Coaches came into general use among the gentry by 1730, and many Broadway residences had stable and coach houses adjoining them. Governor John Montgomerie's equipage brought £81

[11] Berkeley, *Works*, IV, 157 n.; *Newport Hist. Mag.*, I, 10; III, 56; 7 MHS *Colls.*, IX, 23; Hamilton, *Itinerarium*, 123, 125, 192; *R. I. Gaz.*, Oct. 4, 11, 1732; *Bos. Gaz.*, Sept. 12, 1737; *Eve. Post*, Nov. 23, 1741.
[12] *Newport T. C. Recs.*, 1740; Comer, "Diary," 110.
[13] Hamilton, *Itinerarium*, 106, 108, 228; Stokes, *Iconography*, IV, 518.

when sold at auction in 1731. Lewis Morris had his arms and motto painted on the doors of his coach in the same year, sight of which excited great curiosity in many an "honest tradesman." [14]

The middle class lived comfortably enough, but in a manner far below the rich. "A good Handy Servant Maid that can perform all sorts of House-Work" was the most that any of them could afford. Holding wealth and social position in great respect, they yet bitterly resented social climbers to whom they attributed the decline in morality. One tradesman complained in 1738 of "some of our topping Citizens, who pretend to be reckon'd among the Gentry, of so mean a spirit, as to carry People from the bottom to the top of their Houses, viewing every Room; and boasting of their Riches and Grandure." Another warned the public of "Spungers or Hanger's on, with which most of the great Families are pester'd; they have little to recommend them." The "Poor Jack Tars," laborers, and free blacks eked out meager existences in menial occupations, and passed their few spare hours in little punch houses, where, "Being Easie Merry Fellows," they soon liquidated their small savings. About the only luxuries that all classes possessed in common were rum and tea: [15]

> Bohea is the Favourite thro' this whole Town,
> The mode from the Satten unto the Stuff-Gown.

The class antagonism everywhere present in the towns were nowhere so near the surface as at New York. In large measure this may be attributed to the passions aroused, first by the Leisler affair, and then by the bitter events of Governor Cosby's rule. Never subtle in its ways, the aristocracy became particularly blatant in its advertisement of well-matched weddings. In 1721 occurred the "match so much talked of" in taverns and on street corners, between Governor Burnet and Anna Maria van Horne. The Benjamin Bagnals, Quakers though they might be, celebrated two marriages in their family with much pomp and ceremony in 1737. Bad weather on the wedding day of Benjamin Bagnal, Jr., caused the Governor to favor "the Bridegroom and Bride with his Chariot." The many sententious accounts of fashionable weddings, and the bitter political feeling between members of different classes prompted a partisan tradesman to insert the following notice in a newspaper in 1737:

> This is to give Notice, that on the 11th of November, one *Thomas Bassett*, a Bermudian Black-a-more, was married at Stratford, to *Nancy Cosby*.

[14] Stokes, *Iconography*, I, 195; IV, 253; Wilson, *Memorial History of New York*, II, 161, 245, 251; *N. Y. Gaz.*, Sept. 21, 1730; *N. Y. Journal*, Feb. 23, 1736.
[15] *N. Y. Gaz.*, May 11, 1730; Jan. 21, 1734; Nov. 15, 1736; Dec. 12, 1737; April 24, 1738; *N. Y. Journal*, May 11, 1741.

Though artisans and tradesmen, as freemen, possessed the local franchise, instructions from the gentry usually determined their conduct at election time. During a ward election in 1734 two broadside letters, signed "Timothy Wheelwright" and "John Chisel," expressed the despair of the working classes with prevailing conditions, and called for an assertion of their "ancient liberties." [16]

Religious affiliations naturally divided the Front Street aristocracy of Philadelphia into two groups, Quakers and others. Predominance of the Friends in the early years had made for a less ostentatious upper class than at New York or Boston. Nevertheless, Christopher Saur observed that times were changing by 1724. "The dear old folks, most of whom are dead, may have spoken to their children a good deal about plainness. It is still noticeable in the clothes except that the material is very costly, or is even velvet." And he might further have excepted the "silk-Stockins" sold by Peter Baynton to Quaker maids and matrons. [17]

Plainness certainly vanished from the dwellings of the gentry. No community had finer mansions facing its streets, nor could any equal in magnificence the nearby country estates. About a mile and a half out of town was George McCall's "Plantation called Chevy Chase," one of the most sightly of suburban seats, while at Germantown was located the summer villa of Robert Strettel, a wealthy merchant. When William Black visited the latter in 1744 he found himself divided in appreciation between the estate's fine stables and its "Admirably well Shap'd" mistress. The greatest evidences of luxury were to be found in the homes of this comfort-loving gentry, — furniture of "the newest Fashion" by famed Philadelphia craftsmen, and Mr. Franklin's "new Invented Iron Fire-Places." As in other towns, the pages of the newspapers were constantly enriched by accounts of aristocratic marriages, like the wedding of William Fishbourn, Esq., to Mrs. Jane Roberts, or the nuptials of Robert Charles, Esq., and Miss Philadelphia Gordon, "a lady of great merit." Demises of the "gentility" were likewise noted with fulsome praise for their characters and accomplishments. [18]

The quiet, uneventful, busy and comfortable life of Philadelphia tradesmen in this period is best recorded in the *Autobiography* of Benjamin Franklin. As for the common people, their position was much the same as in other towns. Their dress was plain and sober in con-

[16] *N. Y. Gaz.*, May 11, 1730; July 11, Aug. 22, Dec. 5, 1737; Stokes, *Iconography*, IV, 536.
[17] *Pa. Mag.*, XLV, 252; *Mercury*, March 20, 1729.
[18] *Mercury*, Feb. 18, March 20, Sept. 11, 1729; Oct. 30, 1735; Jan. 16, 1737; Mar. 18, 1742; *Pa. Mag.*, I, 408; *Pa. Gaz.*, Sept. 18, 1729; April 22, 1731; Feb. 12, Dec. 3, 1741.

trast to the elegance of the aristocrats. They bitterly resented the pretensions and haughtiness of the rich and professional classes, as the following bit of almanac verse, dedicated *To Spring,* clearly reveals:

> Now the pleasant time approaches;
> Gentlemen do ride in coaches,
> But poor men they don't regard
> That to maintain them labor hard.

The frequency of advertisements for runaway servants in the newspapers indicates that the servile classes had ample cause to be dissatisfied with their lot. Conditions were not much better for the free laborer. Though constantly made aware of their proper place in society, members of this group sometimes broke the bonds that hemmed them in and aped their betters. Two Hibernian servants "fought a gallant Duel before a Number of Spectators" on Society Hill in February, 1730. Mr. S. B. was thoroughly disgusted with the actions of Negro house slaves: [19]

> What in my Opinion adds to their great and uncommon Impudence, is a Species of Self Conduct they have when they appear Dress'd, which is indeed in a very uncommon Manner, Silk Gloves, and Petticoats, good Holland and Cambricks, lac'd Shoes with Silk Clock'd Stockings, Silver Watches in their Fobs, Five Pounds in their Pockets, going to Taverns, calling for Bottle of Wine, fresh Lime Punch, when six-pence a piece were given for Limes, Pipes and Tobacco, and My Service to you Mr. *Dick,* your Health Mr. *Peter,* your Toast Mr. *John* and your Lady, let her be I pray you. And how I have actually seen them look upon honest Tradesmen, and theirs, with great contempt, and using them with Scurrilous and abusive Language, when Notice had been Taken by them, that their dress did not become them, or upon being called bold impudent *Slaves.*

Charles Town society had become decidedly aristocratic by 1742. Rich merchants, when they had made their fortunes in trade, sought to set up as country gentlemen or planters as soon as possible. In the environs of the town appeared pretty residences like John Robinson's "commodious" dwelling with its gardens and fish pond, or Henry Middleton's fifty thousand acre plantation cultivated by eight hundred slaves. Such families as the Blakes, Broughtons, Colletons, Crokats, Izards, Pinckneys and Wraggs presented the unusual spectacle of a class of culture and leisure living on the very edge of a wilderness a life of refinement much like that of northern aristocrats. As in other towns, this was achieved largely by means of intimate contacts with

[19] Jerman's *Almanack,* May 1, 1727; *Pa. Gaz.,* Feb. 10, 1730; *Mercury,* Aug. 3, 1738.

England.[20] In 1741 Eliza Pinckney found that the ladies and gentlemen of the town were gay in their dress and "liv'd very Gentele," and "upon the whole . . . you will find as many agreeable people of both sexes for the size of the place as almost any where." Carolinians of "the Genteelest manner" traveled to and from their social center in coaches of London manufacture. Observers noted a "gaiety" of dress and deportment scarcely exceeded in the "Court-end of London." This was especially true of widows, who "by foreward carriages do snap up the young men," thereby plunging Charles Town maids into a "Melancholy Disposition of Mind." [21]

In the entire coastal region of the province by 1740 the artisans and tradesmen of Charles Town constituted virtually the only representatives of the middle class. As compared with northern urban centers, their numbers were small. The "poorer sort" had already come under the blight of slave competition; Eliza Pinckney believed them "the most indolent people in the world, or they could never have been wretched in so plentiful a country." As wealth piled up at Charles Town, the affairs of the metropolis came more and more to be operated for the benefit of the aristocratic few, and the remainder of the population found its interests largely overlooked.[22]

IV

Externally, the progress of religion in the towns during these years seemed unimpeded. New churches appeared in each community, and membership mounted in existing religious societies. Some magnificent church edifices were erected, and townsmen supported their respective denominations with generous gifts. On the other hand, the increase in town populations outran the growth of churches, and more people remained beyond the reach of religious teachings than ever before. Especially was this true of the immigrants who not infrequently found but cool welcome in town churches. Religious observance had also by 1730 slipped into a narrow formalism of Sabbath worship and lip service to established and accepted creeds. Spiritually, colonial towns were passing through a state of apathy akin to that which held contemporary Europe in its grip. Such heresies as Arminianism, Socinianism, and especially Deism found in the towns most fertile soil; here too, religious indifference flourished. With its latitudinarian views the Church of England could more nearly comprehend the spirit of the

[20] *S. C. Gaz.*, Sept. 17, 1737; *Journal Board of Trade, 1734–1741*, 422. Charles Town's close relations with London were not unique. New York's were perhaps closest of all, but every town had its roots deeply planted in the British Isles.
[21] Ravenel, *Eliza Pinckney*, 5, 18; *Pa. Mag.*, XXXVI, 162; *S. C. Gaz.*, Mar. 2, 1734; Sept. 17, 1737; Howe, *Presbyterian Church*, 230.
[22] Ravenel, *Eliza Pinckney*, 17; Wallace, *South Carolina*, I, 400.

new age, and thus became solidly entrenched in every town. There were according to the standards of the faithful much backsliding and impiety, and townsfolk, especially the immigrants and "inferior sort," were as ripe as were farmers of the countryside for the tidal wave of religious emotion which inundated the colonies after 1735.

More new religious organizations sprang up in Boston than anywhere else. Congregationalists were especially active, promoting the establishment of four new churches in this period.[23] In 1727 the Reverend John Moorhead arrived from Ireland to minister to Ulsterites in Boston from a little barn on Long Lane. Three years later he became ordained minister at the Church of the Presbyterian Strangers, which grew before long into an important religious society.[24]

Extension of the Anglican communion in these years is most significant. Despite puritan assertions that it inculcated "a lifeless religion & an irreligious life," Episcopalianism flourished under aristocratic patronage and became eminently respectable. The church won a considerable victory when Timothy Cutler, former rector of Yale, forsook Congregationalism and took orders in England, returning in 1722 to assume charge of the new Christ Church. The numbers and influence of the Anglicans steadily grew, until by 1733 they were paying one tenth of the taxes of Boston. In 1727 they began to petition for an American bishop. Growth of the South and West Ends led to the erection of a second place of worship, Trinity Church, "Very neat and Commodious, the Architect[ure] Modern." [25]

Diversity continued to characterize the religious life of Newport. Doctrinal differences within the First Baptist Church led to the withdrawal of a group to form the Six Principle Baptists in 1721, and the Congregationalists gathered a second church in 1728.[26] The growth of Trinity Church in both membership and wealth resulted in the erection of a splendid new edifice with lovely interiors in 1725.

The most noteworthy feature of Newport churches was the extraordinarily high quality of their clergy. Nathaniel Clap, learned and greatly reverenced, impressed George Whitefield in 1740 as "a good old puritan, and gave me an idea of what stamp those men were, who first settled New England." John Comer, who accepted the call to the First Baptist Church in 1725, delivered sermons of the quality he found his Newport listeners demanded, introduced public singing into his services, and generally played an active part in community life.

[23] Hanover Street, 1721; Hollis Street, 1732; West, 1737; Tenth, 1741.
[24] An Irish priest began privately to perform mass in 1732. Winsor, *Memorial History of Boston*, II, 223, 227; Bolton, *Scotch-Irish*, 168; *Bos. Gaz.*, Jan. 10, 1737; *Rehearsal*, March 20, 1732.
[25] Foote, *King's Chapel*, I, 321, 346, 483; Cross, *Anglican Episcopate*, 71, 98; 6 MHS *Colls.*, VII, 214; Douglass, *Summary*, I, 531.
[26] Backus, *New England Baptists*, II, 16; Peterson, *Rhode Island*, 322.

His successor, John Callender, was probably the ablest Baptist divine in America; his *Historical Discourse,* on the occasion of Newport's centennial in 1739, has been justly celebrated for both historical and literary excellence. In it he spoke with the sweet reasonableness that characterized religious sentiment at Newport, when he ascribed the chief cause of civil disorders to [27]

> The unjust, unnatural, and absurd attempt to force all to be of one opinion, or to feign and dissemble that they are; or the cruel and impious punishing those, who cannot change their opinions without light or reason, and will not dissemble against all reason and conscience.

The visit of George Berkeley, Dean of Londonderry, enhanced religious as well as intellectual life at Newport. Arriving in January, 1729, he soon gave over his design of founding a college in the West Indies, and spent three years in the New England town which charmed him completely. His presence provided great stimulus to the growth of Trinity Church, whither people flocked to listen to the Dean's sermons. His tolerance won all hearts; even Mr. Clap could find some comfort in his admission, "Give the Devil his due, John Calvin was a great man." Among his many gifts to Trinity was a handsome organ presented in 1733. Through his influence the Reverend John Honeyman began gathering Negroes into the fold, and in 1742 could report eighty-one blacks regularly attending services. Newport had indeed so large a share of leading American clergymen that Samuel Johnson of Stratford, when he declined to come to Trinity in 1738, gave as his reason "the sense of my own unqualifiedness to answer the ends of a ministry among so large and polished a people as those of Newport." [28]

The development of Baptists, Congregationalists and Anglicans was paralleled by that of the Society of Friends. As the aristocrats passed over to Episcopalianism, Quakerism recruited most of its new adherents from the middle class. Much of the continued success of the plain people could be attributed to the effective work of the great Quaker itinerant, John Fothergill, who visited Newport in 1721, and again in 1736–1738. By the close of the period the Yearly Meeting at Newport was the largest in the world; in 1743 Quakers came from as far as a hundred and fifty miles "to the Eastward," to make up a record attendance of "not less than 5,000." [29]

Newport was probably the most truly religious of the towns. Although the citizens were "not so straight-laced" as those of Boston,

[27] Callender, *Historical Discourse,* 39, 163; Comer, "Diary," 36, 58.
[28] *N. E. Journal,* Feb. 3, 1729; Berkeley, *Works,* IV, 160; *News Letter,* June 26, 1733; Mason, *Trinity Church,* 58, 77; Schneider, *Samuel Johnson,* I, 89.
[29] Jones, *Quakers,* 129 n.

Dr. Hamilton thought them quite genuine in their professions. Berkeley found [30]

> The inhabitants of a mixed kind, consisting of many sorts and subdivisions of sects. Here are four sorts of Anabaptists, besides Presbyterians, Quakers, Independents, and many of no profession at all. Notwithstanding so many differences, . . . and though less orthodox, I cannot say they have less virtue (I am sure they have more regularity) than those I left in Europe. They are indeed a strange medly of different persuasions, which nevertheless do all agree on one point, viz. that the Church of England is the second best.

New York experienced almost no religious change before the arrival of Whitefield in 1740. A new sect officially appeared in 1729, when Hebrews formed a permanent congregation and built a "solid, neat, stone Temple" on Mill Street in the next year. Growth of the Reformed Dutch Church, numerically the strongest denomination still, led to erection of the large Middle Church on Nassau Street in 1729. In both Old and Middle Churches the preaching continued to be in Dutch. Continued opposition of the Anglicans to a charter for the Presbyterians aggravated the bitterness between the two communions until it eventually found expression in politics. To protect their property, the Consistory vested the fee of their ground and buildings in the General Assembly of the Church of Scotland in 1732. The favored church was Trinity, which increasingly enjoyed the attendance and munificence of the aristocracy; its prosperity made possible enlargement of the building in 1735, and its embellishment with an organ made by John Klemm of Philadelphia in 1739. By 1742 as many as a thousand worshippers crowded into Trinity on the Sabbath. [31]

Manhattan religious history during this period was characterized by violent sectarian antagonisms, especially between Anglicans and Presbyterians, and by infusion of the religious issue into political life during the Cosby regime. In general, the Episcopalians and the Dutch formed the conservative, and the Presbyterians the radical faction, both parties having aristocratic leadership. The Jews, many of them wealthy and eminently respectable, had often to suffer the derision of the populace. In 1742 a gentleman attended a Hebrew burial "out of curiosity," and came away ashamed of "those many who dare to Stile themselves Christians." A "Rabble of Christians" very nearly prevented the interment, hurling epithets even at the dead, and worst of all, a "gentleman seemed to head this Mob." [32] Religion was indeed

[30] Hamilton, *Itinerarium*, 191; Berkeley, *Works*, IV, 160; *Hist. MSS. Comm.*, VII, Pt. I, 242; *R. I. Hist. Mag.*, VI, 169.
[31] Pool, *Mill Street Synagogue*; *N. Y. Eccles. Recs.*, IV, 2397, 2496, 2582, 2601, 2699; Dix, *Trinity Church*, I, 214, 233.
[32] *Doc. Hist. N. Y.*, IV, 1043; *N. Y. Journal*, May 16, 1743.

at a low ebb at New York in 1735, formalism and sectarian animosities having very nearly crowded out all true devotion.

The growing heterodoxy of Philadelphia, especially the spread of Anglicanism, made a profound impression upon the Society of Friends. Country Quakers, who controlled the Yearly Meeting, stubbornly refused to make concessions to the spirit of the eighteenth century, directing their efforts instead to enforcement of stricter discipline and more sober living, a program which ill accorded with social trends at Philadelphia. As was to be expected, this concern with outward forms signally failed to reawaken that spirituality for which the sect had formerly been noted. Nor did the exhortations of a succession of able itinerant preachers, like Fothergill and John Bownas, meet with any marked success in the city. When Bownas arrived in 1727 he sadly observed the "great falling off in spirit" he had so admired twenty years before. By 1742 the Friends made up only about one quarter of the city's population, and Quakers were finding it increasingly necessary to censure members for "declining" to attend worship, and to "disown" others for marrying out of meeting.[33]

A sufficient number of the German Reformed and Lutheran faiths were living at Philadelphia by 1732 to form a joint congregation. In 1742 the Lutherans broke away from the Reformed group, and in the same year Count Zinzindorff organized a Moravian congregation. The first permanent Roman Catholic church in any town was formed in 1732, when eleven of that faith founded St. Joseph's Chapel. "New Side" followers of Whitefield gathered a second Presbyterian church in 1740, worshipping in the tabernacle that had been raised for the new leader. As in the other towns, Anglicanism was the most rapidly growing denomination. Christ Church attracted so many worshippers, especially from the socially and politically prominent, — those who had once constituted the backbone of urban Quakerism, — that by 1727 "the present church" was found to be too small. Generous contributions from parishioners and from sympathizers as far distant as Barbados financed the erection of a beautiful new brick building under the direction of Dr. John Kearsley. When finally completed in 1740 the new Christ Church, with its London organ, was easily the finest place of worship in the colonies. Here the Mayor and Common Council maintained a pew, and in this twenty-two year period at least five of the city's mayors were vestrymen.[34]

The many Scotch-Irish who came to Charles Town in this period found the Congregational Church the only religious organization using

---

[33] Scharf and Westcott, *Philadelphia*, II, 1244; *Pubs. Gen. Soc. Pa.*, VIII, 85, 272.
[34] Jackson, *Cyclopedia of Philadelphia*, III, 897; IV, 939, 1044; Dorr, *Christ Church*, 58, 61, 67.

their form of worship. Here they found a welcome, but, desiring ministers of the Westminster Confession, they soon broke away to set up a Presbyterian Church in a small wooden edifice in 1731. Some few German Lutherans gathered for private worship in 1734, but no congregation was organized in this period. As royal governors frowned upon dissent of any kind, the growth of these sects was necessarily slow.[35]

St. Philip's, with the patronage of royal officials and aristocracy, and supported from colony taxes, was virtually an established church. In 1727 a new building was opened, described as "spacious and executed in very handsome taste, exceeding everything of the kind we have." To this church on Sabbath mornings people came from miles around, in long cypress canoes by way of the many rivers and creeks. Passengers on their way to Christian worship were paddled along by Negro slaves to the haunting cadences of heathen African melodies.[36]

Religious practice at Charles Town experienced much the same decline as in northern communities. In 1743 Commissary Garden wrote to a friend that "As to the State of Religion in this Province, it is bad enough, — Rome and the Devil have contriv'd to crucify her between two Thieves, Infedelity and Enthusiasm. The former, alas! too much still prevails; but as to the latter, Thanks to God it is greatly subsided, even to the Point of vanishing away." [37]

In every town there were more stray lambs than ever before. The old religious zeal had died out, and while respectable people regularly attended services on the Sabbath, general apathy and absence of enthusiasm prevailed. Not only did indifference flourish, but backsliding was so common as greatly to alarm the clergy. With the passing of the two Mathers the towns no longer possessed any great religious leaders to warn them of the dangers of secular grandeur and the affectation of sensual pleasures. Boston ministers regarded the thunderstorms and earthquake of 1727 as portents of great hope, but results were disappointing; "all signs failed." [38] The introduction into the colonies of Deism in a virulent form provided another challenge for organized religion. Cotton Mather, always in advance of his times, had flirted with Nature and Nature's God as early as 1715, but now the movement began to make serious headway. Deism found its widest acceptance in the towns, especially at Philadelphia, where men like Sir William Keith and Franklin and his cronies of the Junto eagerly embraced the new

---

[35] Howe, *Presbyterian Church*, 201; *Charleston Year Book*, 1884, 262.
[36] Dalcho, *Episcopal Church*, 115, 120; Ravenel, *Eliza Pinckney*, 18, 43.
[37] *N. Y. Journal*, May 30, 1743; Wallace, *South Carolina*, I, 414.
[38] Boston had seventeen churches, which could serve about thirty per cent of the population, an improvement over the previous period. In other towns the discrepancy was probably greater.

thought. Dr. Douglass and the Reverend Charles Chauncy of Boston became interested in the movement, as did Robert Feke and his friends at Newport, and many prominent New Yorkers and Charlestonians. As in England, the movement found favor mostly with the urban aristocracy, who endeavored, if anything, to keep it from the common man. That these new ideas did seep down, however, at least as far as the newspapers, is revealed by the *South Carolina Gazette* in 1738, where, in discussing the religious scene, Lewis Timothy employed the latest deistic jargon, speaking of his "resignation to the Will of the Supreme Author of the Universe." [39]

The spirit of the age in both Europe and America was not deeply religious. In colonial towns, where large numbers of artisans, laborers and servants lived without much religious restraint or ministration, the decline of spirituality was more rapid and more evident than in rural districts. Also, as we shall see, the growth of secular social agencies was in this period providing for the church competition more challenging than any it had ever before had to meet.

So far had the decay of organized religion progressed by 1730 that times were ripe for a new wave of evangelistic emotion. The phenomenon we call the "Great Awakening" had its European-inspired beginnings in a revival among the Germans of Pennsylvania, and in an evangelical movement in New Jersey led by Theodore Freylinghuysen and John and William Tennent in the 1720's. Prior to 1739 Philadelphia and New York alone of the towns felt the force of the movement. In the former the Tennents made many converts among the Scotch-Irish, and at Manhattan Freylinghuysen aroused the Dutch to a high pitch of religious fervor. At Boston Benjamin Colman and William Cooper became interested in the ideas of Jonathan Edwards of Northampton and in the new spirit infused by him into his congregation after 1734. They distributed some of Edwards' writings among their parishioners, and Colman urged the English evangelist, George Whitefield, then in Georgia, to carry on his work of conversion in New England. [40]

Whitefield arrived in Philadelphia in November of 1739, and during the following year conducted revivals in each of the four other towns. Though he did not scorn the smaller places, contemporaries noted that "he chiefly confines his Labours to populous towns." The reception everywhere accorded him was unprecedented. Countrymen joined town-dwellers in crowding to hear him; audiences of from four to ten

[39] 6 MHS *Colls.*, VI, 8, 52; Franklin, *Works* (Bigelow), I, 138; Morais, *Deism*, 17, 54; Osgood, *Colonies in the Eighteenth Century*, III, 407; *S. C. Gaz.*, June 15, 1738.
[40] Osgood, *Colonies in the Eighteenth Century*, III, 407; Winsor, *Memorial History of Boston*, II, 231.

thousand became usual at his revival services. Save for his own, the Anglicans, and the Society of Friends, most religious denominations received him with open arms. Although the evangelist believed he had done his best work at Boston, where he had "never had so little opposition," the effects of his labors proved more lasting at Philadelphia. "The alteration of the Face of Religion here is altogether surprising," one Philadelphian exclaimed. "Religion is become the subject of most conversations. No books are in request but those of piety and devotion, and instead of idle songs and ballads the people are everywhere entertaining themselves with psalms, hymns and spiritual songs." Here in November, 1740, just one year after Whitefield's arrival, was erected the first temple to the new religion in America, when the Presbyterians built a large tabernacle which their apostle filled to the doors at every service.[41] Indeed, the enthusiasm with which Philadelphians followed the teachings of the new evangelist was not without its stultifying effect upon other aspects of their social and cultural life.

The role of the towns in this "first great and spontaneous movement in the history of the American people" is highly significant. Here dwelt many humble folk — artisans, laborers, servants and slaves — many of whom had not before known the ministrations of religion. To such as they Whitefield spoke in the language of the masses, and for them his broad humanitarianism, popular sympathies, and contempt for aristocratic religions held out a great appeal. The towns were also important as centers for revival services, and served as lodestones to the thousands of country people who gathered to hear the preaching of evangelists. Nowhere else could such large crowds be brought together, and only in the towns could revivalists speak over and over again to shifting audiences. Hence much of their best work was accomplished in an urban setting.

Religious life in this period generally reflected the growing complexities of town society. Increasingly certain churches, especially the Anglican, became given over to fashionable worship by leaders of society and wealthy members of the middle class. For those like the "substantial Mechanicks" who had founded the New North Church of Boston in an earlier period, a variety of religious associations were open, — Baptist, Presbyterian and Quaker. In these years as well, a true "people's religion" was born from the efforts of evangelists who catered to the more emotional elements among older denominations, and also to the drifting masses who had never found a home within the fold of any religious organization.

[41] *Pa. Gaz.*, Nov. 8, 29, 1739; *News Letter*, May 1, Sept. 25, 1740; Disway, *Earliest Churches of New York*, 134; R. I. Hist. Soc. *Colls.*, XVI, 7; *S. C. Gaz.*, Jan. 12, 26, March 22, Nov. 6, 1740; *News Letter*, June 26, 1740; *Eve. Post*, Nov. 10, 1740.

V

As a focus for business, social, and recreational life, the tavern continued a most important town institution. Open as it was to all, it became the great center for middle and lower class activities. More and more the tavern competed with the church, tending to strip it of many of its social and recreational functions. The importance of various public houses as the temporary homes of itinerant shows and exhibitions grew along with their popularity as places for business transactions and fashionable private entertainments. As social life in the towns became more organized, taverns formed the headquarters for the multiplicity of clubs, designed for persons of all classes and interests. The number of public houses increased with the expansion of each community, and a marked improvement in the quality of food and drink, the elegance and convenience of appointments, and the reliability of service took place. With this development, however, the liquor problem more than kept pace, and as might be expected, no satisfactory solution could be found.

New York, where more than anywhere else town life centered about the tavern, maintained throughout the period its reputation for high quality public houses and good order therein. Thirty-three victuallers and vintners secured freedoms from the Corporation, and inns and ordinaries multiplied to meet the demands of the growing population. Coffee houses at New York tended to develop into taverns, offering food and lodging in addition to the usual conveniences of such establishments. Such was the case with the coffee house kept by Johannes D'Honneur, and better known as the Black Horse Tavern. The Exchange Coffee House, opened in 1729 at the corner of Broad and Water Streets, soon became the principal scene of real estate transactions. In 1738 Daniel Bloom, a retired mariner, purchased the Jamaica Pilot Boat from Francis Child, and reopened it as the Merchant's Coffee House. These two latter establishments were conducted on the London model exclusively, and the Merchant's soon became the resort of all people connected with auctions and shipping.[42]

Several New York taverns, like Todd's and the Black Horse, enjoyed wide reputation. Committees of the lower house of the Assembly met regularly at D'Honneur's tavern, which gradually became a sort of social headquarters for members of the popular party. Here Andrew Hamilton lodged during the Zenger trial, and here he attended the magnificent banquet tendered him "as a public Testimony of the glorious Defence he made in the Cause of Liberty." Todd's, on the

[42] Bayles, *Old Taverns*, 91, 128; *N. Y. Gaz.*, June 10, 1728; March 25, 1729; March 8, 1731; June 20, 1737.

other hand, was the favorite resort of Governor Cosby and the court faction. There for many years were celebrated the fashionable balls and elaborate dinners of the aristocracy. At Edward Eastham's Fighting Cocks in 1736 "gentlemen and others" met and wagered on their favorites. The Coach and Horses in Broadway was in 1740 "a well customed House, and well known and used by the Country People and Travellers, to and from Boston and Connecticut." [43]

Good entertainment could also be secured at the many middle class hostelries of New York. Favorite places for seafarers were John Mackleman's Blue Anchor on the Dock, and, until 1738, John Dunk's Jamaica Pilot Boat. Dozens of little dramshops prospered, many of them run by widows, to whom the Corporation granted inexpensive relief in the form of free licenses, in order to help them gain a living. Probably as many transients used lodging houses as taverns, and inhabitants regularly patronized the cook shops of Michael Berthon, Stephen Morris and others, either to have their roasts cooked or to purchase pastries and other prepared foods. The popular tavern district of Manhattan lay in the neighborhood of the Meal Market (Wall and Pearl Streets), although retailers could be found nearly anywhere in the city. [44]

More than ever New York social life focused at the taverns. In 1734 "John Scheme" reported that as "I often frequent the Coffee House, & take a Hitt at Black Gammon, I there, have opportunity of Hearing the various sentiments of the Courtiers." But the example such people set the common folk is bad: "I mean the Luxury and Profuseness, and I am sorry to say it daily creeps in among us. . . . We strive who shall have the most Dishes of Meat at his Table, and in the best Order; who shall drink the richest Wine, who shall wear the most costly apparell." His observations contained much truth, for gay balls were held at Todd's, and sumptuous banquets frequently given at all the larger inns. At the smaller houses cock fights and traveling shows amused the common folk and many of their betters. The Corporation secured passage of the Powder House Bill in 1722 by "treating the Assembly" at the Widow Post's at a cost of £13. 7. 6., and ten years later found the same procedure equally effective in dealings with Governor Cosby. Bowling Green became a popular resort with the upper and middle classes, for here John Mills, gardener, kept an excellent table and elaborate formal gardens. Another such place was the Spring Garden, run by Thomas Scurlot. There in 1729 William Smith, James Alexander, and four other lawyers, formed a

[43] *N. Y. Gaz.*, Aug. 11, 1735; Jan. 29, 1740; *N. Y. M. C. C.*, III, 289; IV, 150; *N. Y. Journal*, Nov. 26, 1733.
[44] *N. Y. Gaz.*, June 10, 1728; Oct. 26, 1730; *N. Y. M. C. C.*, IV, 365, 382, 471; N. Y. Hist. Soc. *Colls., 1885*, 100; Hamilton, *Itinerarium*, 50.

private corporation of members of the legal profession, arranging to meet there on the first Wednesday in each month to discuss matters affecting their group and professional interests.[45]

The Mayor and Common Council seem to have had very little difficulty with the town's public houses. There were, of course, here as elsewhere, illicit and disreputable establishments, like the "Sign of the Dog's Head in the Porridge Pot," kept by Ebenezer Grant in 1736, where the "scum of society" met in "slovenly" surroundings. Occasional brawling occurred: in 1743 a lodger emerged victorious from a scuffle with his landlord and went to bed, but, his host returning armed with a sword, had to make a hurried exit via the window, and badly injured himself by falling into the "pav'd Yard." There was little need for additional tavern regulation in this period; the only new ordinance passed was an abortive measure, never enforced, to prohibit shuffleboard, billiards, truck tables, and other forms of gambling in public houses.[46]

Boston, as the largest colonial town, licensed more inns, taverns, and ordinaries than did any other, and nowhere were these establishments the subject of more careful regulation. Though from twenty to sixty public houses received permits annually, the number was smaller than formerly, and not many new hostelries appeared. The four coffee houses, especially the Crown, on Long Wharf, owned by Governor Belcher, continued popular resorts for members of the mercantile group. Prior to 1735 they were almost the only places for the holding of public auctions, but after that date the Sun Tavern became a favored center for such activities.[47]

The Bunch of Grapes, the Green Dragon, the Royal Exchange, and the Rose and Crown remained the best and most fashionable hostelries at Boston. A quarrel over a card game in the exclusive Royal Exchange in July, 1728, ended in a duel between two aristocratic youths, Henry Phillips and Benjamin Woodbridge, in which the latter was killed. Henry Price, a tailor, organized the first Masonic Lodge at the Bunch of Grapes on July 30, 1733. In 1721 John Brown opened the George Tavern on Boston Neck near the Roxbury line, and his place soon became the scene of gay dinners and a favorite goal of coaching parties. Here in 1733 Brown was beaten with pine boards by William Thompson, "a Person known to be Rude and Vile." The culprit later confessed that he had been bribed to commit the assault by Daniel Collins, who

[45] N. Y. Journal, March 18, 1734; Jan. 26, 1736; N. Y. M. C. C., III, 289; IV, 150; Stokes, Iconography, IV, 513, 556.
[46] N. Y. Journal, March 1, 1736; Jan. 17, 1743; N. Y. Col. Laws, III, 194.
[47] Bos. Gaz., June 20, 1726; Drake, Old Boston Taverns, 63, 162; Post Boy, March 22, April 5, June 12, Oct. 25, 1736; N. E. Journal, June 26, 1727.

"often before" had used the same method in the hope of securing Brown's license.[48]

Boston had many comfortable middle class hostelries. Countrymen and travelers found good entertainment at the Black Horse in the South End, whose proprietor had "Horses to Let, and Sundry Things to be Sold." John Maylem kept another house well patronized by strangers in School Street in 1733, and William Lowder conducted a quiet little inn at the Three Horse Shoes near the Common. Along the waterfront seamen found numerous taverns catering to their tastes. The Dog and Pot near Bartlett's Wharf attracted many ship-builders, and the Widow Day welcomed sailors at her Crown Tavern near Clarke's Wharf. Good food could be had at almost any one of the eight victualling houses which the town supported in 1740.[49]

The authorities kept all-seeing eyes on the conduct of Boston public houses. A province law of 1721 forbade any innkeeper to trust a customer for more than ten shillings, in order "to prevent misspending of money in Taverns." This law did not, however, have the effect of curbing tippling. In 1726 an over-anxious correspondent of the *Courant* reported that "the abuse of strong Drink is becoming Epidemical among us, And it is very justly Suppos'd . . . that the Multiplication of Taverns has Contributed not a little to this Excess of Riot and Debauchery." Not that he would urge abolishing all public houses; taverns were originated by our forefathers, "who had the same Pious Design in appointing Taverns as in Erecting Churches and Colleges among us." But now nearly everyone in Boston frequents these places "to sit Tipling and Sotting in, for whole Evenings, or perhaps for whole Days." This honest citizen was particularly grieved at the turn of social life in the taverns, especially "the CLUBBS, The Set Clubs," where people come and "Sett" almost every night. There was a "Senior Club," composed of "gentlemen of honour," the "Young Club," a gambling "Club of Rakes," and the "Tippling Club," whose members drank "for drinking's sake." For the most part inspectors appointed by the town kept drunkenness to a reasonable minimum, and only seventeen names appeared on the list of inebriates for 1727.[50] Bostonians, like inhabitants of other communities, were finding the tavern the most entertaining place in town, and despite much drinking tavern life there was usually respectable.

[48] Winsor, *Memorial History of Boston*, II, 484; Drake, *Old Boston Taverns*, 34, 62; *News Letter*, April 19, 1733.
[49] *Post Boy*, April 6, 1741; *Rehearsal*, Feb. 5, 1733; Drake, *Old Boston Taverns*, 62; 15 *Bos. Rec. Com.*, 254.
[50] *Mass. Acts and Resolves*, II, 194; *Courant*, Feb. 26, 1726; *News Letter*, Feb. 24, 1737; *Eve. Post*, June 26, 1738; 13 *Bos. Rec. Com.*, 171, 229; 8 *Bos. Rec. Com.*, 185.

Expanding traffic and population at Philadelphia brought about a demand for more public houses than the town had hitherto enjoyed, and during this period a marked improvement in the number, quality and conduct of the town's taverns took place. Henry Flower operated the Coffee House in Front Street until 1732, when the Widow Roberts took it over. John Shubert opened the London Coffee House on Water Street near Carpenter's Wharf in 1734, an establishment which rapidly became one of the principal mercantile and social centers of Philadelphia. Most public vendues were held at the coffee houses, and Friends greatly deplored the free use of liquor at these sales. At such places, too, one agreed with skippers like James Gruchy of the *Charming Polly* for passage or freight to London and other ports, and transacted all manner of commercial business. Shubert's house had become the recognized fashionable center of Philadelphia by 1735, when John Penn "made a very handsome entertainment" for the General Assembly there, and Thomas Lawrence, Esq., dined the Corporation upon retiring from the office of mayor.[51]

Several fine new hostelries appeared at this time, to enjoy long and prosperous existences. In 1729 the Tun Tavern was opened on Water Street, and Owen Owen announced "to all his good Friends and Acquaintances, &c., that he is return'd to his former House, the *Indian King* in Market Street." The Three Tuns in Chestnut Street, kept by William Tidmarsh in 1733, the Sign of the Crown on Market Street, and the George in Second Street were also well-customed inns. Joseph Gray catered to country people at his Horse and Groom in Strawberry Alley until 1742, when he took over the Conestogoe-Waggon in Market Street. At this new inn he advertised the best of wines, rum, molasses, and "other liquors by small Measure," and good treatment for both "Man & Horse." [52]

Retail groggeries and small inns abounded in the Quaker city. They drew a steady income from neighborhood patronage and from countrymen who flocked into town on market days. In sparsely populated sections like the South Ward most public houses existed for retailing only. A tavern was kept at the prison until 1729, when the Corporation, deciding it had become a "great Nusance," ordered it closed. At least thirty-one retail establishments were licensed between 1738 and 1742. Up small alleys and in poorer districts numbers of "low Tippling Houses" sprang up. Richard Hillyard, laborer, and keeper of one of them, was reported by the Grand Jury in 1734 to "maintain a Comon and disordered Ale House," and to allow "divers

[51] *Mercury*, April 19, May 10, 1722; Sept. 26, 1734; Sept. 25, Oct. 9, 1735; *Pa. Gaz.*, Aug. 14, 1734; Oct. 19, 1738; Aug. 2, 1739; *Post Boy*, Oct. 20, 1735.
[52] *Mercury*, April 17, 1729; May 31, 1733; April 17, 1735; July 15, 1742; *Pa. Gaz.*, Nov. 13, 1729.

idle & ill Disposed persons . . . as well by Nights as by Day . . .
to remain tipling Drinking and ill-behaving themselves to the great
Disquiet and disturbance of all the Liege People." During the great
Indian conference of 1736 James Logan learned with alarm that many
of these dramshops were openly violating the law by furnishing thirsty
natives with firewater.[53]

Philadelphians of all classes made constant use of their taverns
for any sort of occasion, from the holding of a grand banquet by the
Society of Ancient Britons at the Tun, to the exhibition of a camel or
of "the Great Hog's portrait" at the Indian Queen. At smaller places
like the Red Lion in Elbow Lane there was generally some activity.
Here in 1736 Thomas Apty, a plasterer, "laid a wager of Half a
Crown that he would drink within the space of one hour and a half, a
Gallon of Cyder Royal: which he had no sooner accomplished, and
said *I have finished,* but he fell down, . . . and then expir'd." In
fact, the amount of heavy drinking at Philadelphia was prodigious. At
election time, October 23, 1728, forty-five hundred gallons of common
beer was "drunk and thrown away." Franklin published in the pages of
his *Gazette* a "surprizing tho' authentick" account of the rum importation for 1728, which totalled 2,124,500 gallons, or £25,000 worth of
liquor. The Friends, alarmed by increasing tippling, began a temperance movement among their members, a cause supported by Andrew
Bradford in the pages of the *Mercury.* But his five sober reasons for
eschewing the bottle only elicited the following response in the *Gazette:*

> There's but one Reason I can Think,
> Why People ever cease to drink,
> Sobriety the Cause is not,
> Nor Fear of being deam'd a Sot,
> But if Liquor can't be got.[54]

Upon the whole, despite more taverns and much immoderate drinking, the authorities managed the public house problem better than in
former years. In 1721 the Assembly passed an act allowing the
Governor to issue licenses, and requiring all innkeepers to post a bond
of £100. They were forbidden to trust customers for more than ten
shillings, or to sell to minors, servants, slaves or Indians. The Corporation received authority to enforce this act within the city limits.

[53] Court Papers, Phila. Cty., I; *P. M. C. C.,* 290; *Pa. Col. Recs.,* IV, 86; *Pa. Gaz.,*
Dec. 29, 1737.
[54] The author could even enumerate five positive reasons for drinking:

> If on my Theme I rightly think,
> There are Five Reasons why Men drink:
> Good Wine, a Friend, because I'm dry,
> Or lest I should be by and by:
> Or any other Reason why.

Mercury, Feb. 3, 1736; *Pa. Gaz.,* Feb. 7, 1728; Sept. 15, 1737.

Another law of 1722 established heavy penalties for the sale of adulterated beer, and made the approbation of county justices a necessary condition of the issuing of licenses at Philadelphia. The latter provision was carefully observed, but the sale of inferior liquor went on. In 1726 some merchants petitioned the Assembly to remedy the "intolerable frauds . . . of large Sediments, with mixtures of Dirt and Filth" in beer made by "Cheats, not fit to commerce with." After 1730 the Justices carefully regulated prices and quality of liquor, and began a serious drive against illicit houses.[55]

With the rapid expansion of Charles Town and Newport, taverns sprang up in increasing numbers, and these towns for the first time faced the need for tavern regulation. Under the lax licensing laws of the South Carolina Assembly inns and punch houses multiplied in Charles Town, and the first coffee house there opened about 1724. Town life revolved about these places, where business and pleasure joined. Henry Gignilliat's tavern on Broad Street was the town's most elegant hostelry, often serving banquets of "about 40 Dishes." In 1734 Charles Shepheard took it over, and opened the Georgia Coffee House in connection therewith. As in other towns, the smaller houses entertained traveling shows, like the exhibition in 1738 of an "Ourangnogang, (or Man of the Woods) tho' this . . . [was] a female of that Species," which looked "much like the Indians." Victualling houses and food shops enjoyed large patronage. In 1736 John Herbert, "Pastry-Cook from London," announced his shop for making all kinds of pastries, dressing meats for dinners, and preparing pickles, located on the Green behind St. Philip's Church. Pleasant lodgings, suited to all purses, were available throughout the town. Visiting merchants stayed with people like the Widow King, who advertised "very good . . . Lodging Rooms to let at her House in Broad Street, near the Bay."[56]

In 1736 Gabriel Manigault, province treasurer, had reported much unlicensed retailing in Charles Town, but not until 1741 did the South Carolina Assembly turn its attention to the need for better tavern legislation. A new act authorized the five Justices of the Peace at Charles Town to issue annual licenses for public houses at £6 each, and made innkeepers who failed to take them out liable to a £20 fine. A unique provision, growing out of the Charles Town labor situation, stated that "no able tradesman shall . . . keep any common tavern," in order that much needed artisans should not be encouraged to forsake their crafts. Taverners were also instructed to forbid their

[55] Pa. Statutes, III, 248, 291; Votes Pa. Assembly, II, 474; P. M. C. C., 190; Pa. Col. Recs., III, 534; Pa. Gaz., Jan. 11, 1739.
[56] S. C. Gaz., Dec. 9, 1732; Feb. 16, March 2, May 11, 1734; May 8, 1736; Aug. 13, 1737; Jan. 12, 1738; Nov. 13, 1740; Mar. 6, 1742.

customers "to play at any billiard table after the sun hath set one hour." [57]

Between 1720 and 1730 the town of Newport annually licensed about twenty public houses; after that time the authorities somewhat reduced the number. Though a coffee house existed in 1721, Timothy Whiting's King's Arms continued to be the center of commercial activity, until Jonathan and Mary Nichols opened the famous White Horse Tavern in 1730. Here the project for the Long Wharf was set on foot in 1739, and here its proprietors regularly met for many years. This building, still standing, was a substantial frame structure, with fine common rooms and neat sleeping chambers. Its excellent cuisine and good service made it the favorite stopping place for members of the Assembly, who regularly held their sessions there until the erection of the Colony House. Francis Gilbert and William Swann also kept good hostelries. Most Newport taverns were houses of public entertainment, whither townsmen regularly repaired for their daily dram of rum or draught of beer. In such places as the Union Flag Tavern they might read in 1732 the "latest Intelligences both Foreign and Domestick" in James Franklin's *Rhode Island Gazette,* and after its demise in the *Boston Weekly Post Boy,* the most popular Boston paper at Newport. A collection was taken up in the taverns in 1740 to honor the privateering successes of Captain Charles Hall, by having "his Statue finely cut on . . . a Block of Marble to Stand upon a Handsome Pedestall with each Foot upon a Spaniard's Neck." [58]

Several victualling and lodging houses offered good service at Newport. The Widow Babcock's ordinary was popular with strangers, and in 1741 she received a liquor license. There were numerous dramshops and sailors' groggeries, where a fair portion of the product of the town's twenty rum distilleries found a market. Many of these were kept by widows like Sarah Rosen and the Widow Moon. The Town Council moved against keepers of many unlicensed establishments in 1722, and when Joseph Bennet and James Atkins refused to take out the necessary licenses, ordered "that their signs be pulled down" and each of them fined. [59]

Respectability and good order prevailed in most Newport public houses. The Assembly passed an act in 1721 for the "Better prevention of Drunkenness," because many persons were wasting "so much of their Time and Money at Taverns." Henceforth a fine of twenty

[57] *S. C. Statutes,* III, 581; *S. C. Gaz.,* April 3, 1742.
[58] *Newport T. C. Recs.,* Oct., 1722; April 7, 1729; May 11, 1741; *News Letter,* June 5, 1721; March 28, Sept. 25, 1740; *R. I. Almanack,* 1728; *Post Boy,* Sept. 28, 1741; *Mercury,* April 12, 1722.
[59] Weeden, *Economic and Social History,* II, 459; *Newport T. C. Recs.,* June 12, Oct., 1722; 1724.

shillings awaited the innkeeper who sold drinks to any whom the
Town Council denominated "Common Tiplers." All taverners had
to post bonds to maintain good order and keep regular houses after
1729. Inhabitants as well as mariners were included in a law of 1732
forbidding innkeepers to give credit for more than twenty shillings,
and denying them redress by law for the same.[60]

The sparsity of new tavern legislation, and its similarity in all towns,
indicate that the problem of public house regulation was fairly well
and generally understood by 1742. The importance of the tavern as
an urban institution grew rapidly throughout the period. The opportunities it offered for relaxation, entertainment, and the transaction of
business were open to all town inhabitants. It contributed to the
organization of social life by fostering the creation of clubs, and bringing together men of all interests. At the same time, it was the one
agency that influenced the social and economic life of every class,
enabling representatives from all walks of life to rub shoulders in a
friendly and growingly democratic fashion.

VI

A widening variety of secular amusements, like the tavern at
least as attractive as church-going, accounted for much of the decline
in the influence of organized religion in the towns. In this era of
economic prosperity wealth and leisure became increasingly available
among the upper classes for the indulgence in elaborate and sophisticated forms of recreation and diversion. Hence the theater, hitherto
without necessary patronage, made its appearance in several of the
towns, and concerts, balls, and assemblies further amused well-to-do
town aristocrats. At the same time, there was a significant increase
in public amusements in which rich and poor alike might participate, —
games, public contests, tavern shows and the like. Entertainment, too,
varied its manifestations with the growing complexities of urban life,
and showed a tendency to become organized in the interests of special
groups; the development of clubs of all kinds and degrees of exclusiveness characterized much of the social life of the period. Finally, the
shifting of moral standards released many types of sophisticated urban
pleasures from the dislike and disapproval with which they had
formerly been regarded, and the gaieties of dancing, cards and games
of chance now became the happy prerogative of all classes of town
inhabitants.

Life among all ranks was gayest at New York, where a long tradition of easy joviality reached back to its earliest founding. Even the

[60] *R. I. Acts* (*1744*), 83, 123, 167; *R. I. Col. Recs.*, IV, 474.

common man here found existence more amusing. On summer evenings Dutch wives still indulged their ancient custom of smoking and gossiping on their front stoops, while their men folk went off to a tavern. The Corporation now observed every holiday, festival or British victory with a bonfire "at the usual Place," and the accustomed "ten Gallons of Good Wine" for the populace. City elections always proved a source of excitement. In 1737 there was "voting all day at City Hall," with dinners and music all the while, and so spirited did the contest become that gentlemen even sent their carriages to bring artisans and laborers to the polls. Occasional exhibitions delighted the townsfolk after 1730. An Arabian camel was to be seen at the Cart and Horse, and an "upright German" exhibited his ingenious horse that could understand several languages. Cock fighting retained its early popularity among New Yorkers of all stations, although some aristocrats felt that the poor had no right to attend the matches when they had to leave their "necessitous Children" in the streets. The turf had also its followers of all ranks. The Hempstead Course was still used, but most townsmen favored the new track at Church Farm on Manhattan.[61]

Wealthy families found new diversions of many sorts. In fine weather riding, hunting and pleasure excursions were much indulged. On the river Captain Rickett's "Pleasure Boat" received the patronage of those not fortunate enough to secure an invitation to cruise on Colonel Lewis Morris' yacht, Fancy, or in Governor Montgomerie's covered barge.[62]

Dancing had been popular for many years, and about 1735 public balls came into vogue. In 1736 the gentry celebrated the birthday of the Prince of Wales at the Black Horse Tavern "in a most elegant and genteel Manner."

> There was a most magnificent Appearance of Gentlemen and Ladies. The Ball began with French dances. And then the Company proceeded to Country Dances, upon which Mrs. Morris led up two Country Dances made upon the Occasion. . . . There was a most sumptuous Entertainment afterward.

Henry Holt, dancing master, arrived from Charles Town the next year, advertising himself as a pupil of Mr. Essex in England. His "Long Room" soon became a favorite resort of pleasure-loving aristocrats. On December 6, 1732, "the new Theatre," owned by Rip

---

[61] N. Y. M. C. C., III, 317, 320, 359; Mercury, March 2, 1721; Sept. 15, 1737; N. Y. Journal, Jan. 5, 1735; March 7, 1737; June 11, 1739; N. Y. Gaz., Nov. 5, 1733; Nov. 26, 1739.
[62] Young people out driving late at night often bundled at Child's Tavern, "a wicked and base custom of these parts." N. Y. Gaz., Aug. 30, 1736; Wilson, Memorial History of New York, II, 161, 458.

van Dam, opened with Farquhar's *Recruiting Officer,* — "the part of Worthy acted by the ingenious Mr. Thomas Heady, Barber and Peruke-Maker to his Honour." Soon, however, Holt's Long Room became the town's principal theater, where "By Permission" during the next three years *The Adventures of Harlequin and Scaramouche, The Busy Body, The Beaux Strategem,* and other pieces were performed with "universal Applause" to crowded houses.[63] New York did not enjoy so many performances in this period as did Charles Town, yet an auspicious beginning had been made for the development of a local theater.

In these years Manhattan gentry became absorbed in club life. A Political Club met at Todd's Tavern to oppose Governor Cosby in 1733, and the following year the Hum Drum Club made its appearance. Later the Hungarian Club was organized. A "New Club, Lodge or Society of Free Masons (as they call themselves)," was established at New York in January, 1738, with David Provoost, Jr., as Grand Master. Many citizens looked upon masonry as subversive, and deplored the elaborate entertainments given by the order at the Black Horse, where, it was charged, ladies of questionable virtue appeared. When this "vile and wicked Society of Hell Cats" paraded in the streets, members "were continually complimented with Snow Balls and Dirt." Yet the order prospered, despite maledictions from its enemies, and soon the most respected gentlemen of the city were donning its regalia.[64]

Greater wealth and numbers made possible the appearance of even more diversions for the common man at Boston. Although still more sober than New York, the town gave little evidence, on weekdays at least, of its former dedication to the "puritanical" way of life. Never before had the "inferior sort" so many forms of entertainment available to them. Children played ball on the Common in summer, and skated on its pond in winter. Their parents found constant enjoyment at the many taverns where shows of all sorts were continually on view. "Ursa Major, or the Great White Bear," was the object of many admiring eyes in 1733, competing for a stray shilling with John Dyer's waxworks, "being a lively Representation of Margaret Countess of Herrinburg, who had 365 Children at one Birth, occasioned by the rash Wish of a poor Beggar Woman, who is represented asking her Charity. Price 6 pence." Although the Selectmen forbade the "Diversion of Rope Dancing, . . . Tumbling and Posturing with Swords," in 1734, they had no objection to animal shows, and granted Benjamin

[63] *Mercury,* Nov. 6, 1735; *N. Y. Journal,* March 18, 1733; Jan. 26, 1736; July 4, 1737; Feb. 2, 1741; *Bos. Gaz.,* Jan. 8, 1733; *N. Y. Gaz.,* Feb. 6, 1739; Jan. 22, 1740.
[64] *N. Y. Journal,* Jan. 7, 1733; Jan. 24, 1738; Hamilton, *Itinerarium,* 49, 106, 215; *N. Y. Gaz.,* Feb. 7, 21, 1738; Jan. 22, 1739.

Clements of New York permission to exhibit his performing dog and horse. Among other curiosities on display at Boston taverns during this period were a black moose from Cape Sable, the peripatetic camel, a lion, and a tame young bear. The bowling green on Cambridge Street still afforded recreation for "Gentlemen and others"; another opened on Fort Hill in 1742. Early in the period one MacDaniell began to operate a public billiard room, and occasionally there was a bear baiting for common folk, and others, to enjoy. Holidays and anniversaries now came in for regular observance with illuminations and salvos of artillery. The vogue for "frolicks, . . . especially among People of the lower or Middling Class," evoked severe condemnation from local Addisons. What must they have thought of the party of North End "debs" who in 1737,[65]

> took Slay and went to a Publick House at Roxbury, where they stay'd till pretty late at Night, having Eat and Drank freely and been extream merey; but when the Reckoning was brought in, (which was not very small) they looked with sorrowful Countenances upon each other, and at last told their Host, that they expected to have been followed by some young Gentlemen, upon whose Credit they relied for the Payment of their Expenses. But this no way satisfying the Landlord, they were forced to *trench their Duds,* as the Phrase is in other Countries, viz. to leave some of their most superfluous Cloaths behind them, as Pledges for the Debt.

Boston gentry seem not to have taken so readily to organized recreation as did their confreres in other towns, especially in New York. A Physical Club met at Withered's Tavern for convivial and medical discussion toward the close of the period, and groups of merchants who walked together "on 'Change" usually met for dinner. Authorities still frowned on the theater, and those with a taste for the drama had to content themselves with reading plays like *George Barnwell,* which was printed in installments in the *New England Weekly Journal* in 1732. Freemasonry made its official debut in 1733, when a lodge was established with Henry Price as Grand Master. When a sort of Masonic convention paraded to the Royal Exchange in 1739, a large crowd turned out to witness their "Appearance, which is generally allow'd to be the most splendid and magnificent that ever was in New England." [66]

Dancing made a great appeal to the gentry. Public balls still evoked official disapproval in the early 'twenties, but many persons went over

[65] *News Letter,* Oct. 17, 1728; Jan. 25, April 19, May 9, Dec. 6, 1733; Dec. 6, 1735; Oct. 9, 1740; 13 *Bos. Rec. Com.,* 259; *Bos. Gaz.,* April 17, May 22, 1721; May 30, 1726; Feb. 26, 1739; *Eve. Post,* Feb. 21, June 20, 1737.
[66] *N. E. Journal,* Feb. 14, 1732; Johnson, *Beginnings of Freemasonry,* 80; *News Letter,* July 5, 1739.

to Charlestown, where the authorities were less severe. After 1725 public dancing became generally acceptable, and it is proof that the perennial tribulations of large social functions had already appeared to learn that in 1727 "a certain person had his Hat exchang'd at the Dancing School on Thursday Night last." In the next decade Peter Pelham conducted many fashionable assemblies at his dancing school. Sober members of the middle class regarded the exercise of the terpsichorean art as sinful, and at least two outbursts occurred in the press after the "Birth of so formidable a Monster in this Part of the World." But sighs for the return of primitive piety availed little, and dancing masters like Pelham, Ephraim Turner, and the ubiquitous George Brownell conducted their academies not only without official interference but with considerable profit.[67]

The change that came over society at Philadelphia in this period is nowhere more evident than in the rapid development of facilities for recreation. All classes shared in the increasing social maturity. Here inhabitants enjoyed more tavern shows and exhibitions than in any other town. Philadelphians were amazed at the "curious and exact Modell of the Czar of Muscovia's Country Seat" in 1723, which was advertised as "absolutely the most ingenious and compleat piece of Workmanship . . . that ever was exposed either in Europe or America." At Owen Owen's tavern in Market Street one might have seen the portrait of a "HOG, bred in America, . . . suppos'd to weigh near Nine Hundred Weight." Those who preferred real life to pictures or ingenious artificiality were satisfied with a sight of the Arabian camel, or the Sheik Sidi, "A Christian Nobleman from Syria," who took in the Governor and Council for an entertainment costing £37 in 1738. Quaker discipline so far relaxed as to permit occasional horse racing, cock fighting, bull baiting, billiards and cards, and to allow the opening of Ellicott's bowling green, where choice drinks might be sipped between strings. William Black tells us that in 1744 he "took a turn to the Center House, where is a Billiard Table and Bowling Green, where we amus'd ourselves in the Afternoon." [68]

The prevalence of dancing still shocked orthodox Friends, but they could no nothing to prevent it. Samuel Pierpont openly advertised in 1729 his school for the "Art of Dancing, . . . where for the Recreation of all Gentlemen and Ladies, There will be Country-Dances every Thursday Evening." So many students attended the academy of Thomas Deering that in 1735 he divided his classes into "young ones

[67] N. E. Journal, Oct. 16, 1727; News Letter, Nov. 23, 1732; April 3, 1740; Bos. Gaz., Feb. 17, 1729; 13 Bos. Rec. Com., 258; 15 Bos. Rec. Com., 91, 159.
[68] Mercury, Aug. 15, 1723; July 24, 1732; May 26, 1737; Pa. Gaz., Aug. 5, 1731; July 24, 1732; Dec. 29, 1737; March 1, 1739; May 22, 1740; Pa. Mag., I, 404.

and advanced Scholars," meeting on alternate days. His Friday night balls, when both groups danced together, were open to the public. George Brownell and Theobald Hackett were also well patronized dancing-masters. To the school of the latter, who prided himself on his acquaintance with the newest styles of London, Dublin and Paris, children were sent from distant places to board and learn "the most graceful Carriage in Dancing, and gentile [sic] Behaviour in Company, on all Occasions that possibly can be had by any Dancing." Little Mary Grafton wrote to her father in Newcastle in 1739:

> Since my coming up here I have entered with Mr. Hackett to improve my Dancing, and hope to make such Progress therein as may answer to the Expence, and enable me to appear well in any Public Company. The great Desire I have of pleasing you will make me the more assiduous in my undertaking, and [if] I arrive at any degree of Perfection it must be Attributed to the Liberal Education you bestow on me.

The Philadelphia gentry formed an exclusive dancing assembly sometime before 1740, but the denunciations of Whitefield brought their parties to a premature conclusion, and Franklin's *Gazette* reported that the "Dancing School, Assembly and Concert Room have been shut up, as inconsistent with the Doctrine of the Gospel." [69]

It also grieved peace-loving Quakers that many of their fellow citizens patronized the fencing academies of Samuel Pierpont and Richard Lyneall, and, though this was allowed to continue, they would have none of the theater. In 1723 a stage was erected on the outskirts of town, which, as it received the patronage of Sir William Keith, Mayor James Logan was helpless to suppress. A "New Booth" on Society Hill opened the next year, but throughout the period no plays were performed within the city. The exhibition of a set of marionettes in 1742 gave Philadelphians their only stage performance in these years. [70]

The environs of Philadelphia became well known for health-giving waters in these years. Dr. Thomas Bond encouraged his patients to picnic and take the waters at Spring Garden, whose chalybeate properties he greatly admired. Even more famous was the "Bath" spring near Bristol, which became the summer resort of genteel valetudinarians.

[69] *Pa. Gaz.*, March 13, 1730; July 13, Aug. 3, 31, 1738; May, 1740; Earle, *Child Life in Colonial Days*, 111; *Mercury*, Nov. 11, 1733.
[70] Opposition by Philadelphia and Boston authorities to the theater resembles that of Bristol, England, where players had to perform outside the city limits, and where the Reverend Mr. Bedford quoted seven thousand passages from plays offensive to fourteen hundred Biblical texts. *Mercury*, Aug. 7, 1729; Jan. 14, 1742; Latimer, *Bristol in the Eighteenth Century*, 60.

Its reputation for cleanliness even induced some Britishers to forego Bath and Tunbridge Wells for Penn's Woods.[71]

Philadelphia developed into a great club town as organizations of all sorts sprang up after 1725. Sometime prior to 1728 a group of unmarried men formed a club which met at Bachelor's Hall. The next year Welshmen organized the "Society of Ancient Britons" to celebrate St. David's Day, and shortly afterwards an English society began festive observation of St. George's Day. Establishment of St. John's Lodge at Philadelphia in 1730 constituted the introduction of Freemasonry into America. The secrecy maintained by the order, and its elaborate entertainments caused humble folk to regard it with suspicion. As if to confirm their fears some "ill disposed Persons," posing as Masons in 1737, swindled several innocent people, and brought about the death of Daniel Rees by burning him with acids during a mock initiation. Benjamin Franklin, secretary of the Lodge, attempted to allay public alarm by exposing the frauds, and declared that his order had "no principles or practices that are inconsistent with religion and good manners." By far the most interesting and exclusive of colonial clubs was the "Colony in Schuylkill," organized on May 1, 1732, by Thomas Stretch, Enoch Flower, Isaac Snowden, and other gentlemen of the city. This convivial society fancifully imagined itself an independent American colony, and annually elected a governor, assembly, sheriff, and other officers. The members built their "Castle" on the banks of the Schuylkill, and each Easter made feudal payment of two fish for their fief. Only the better sort ever crossed its moat, or gained admission to the "Garrison" of its rival, the Society of Fort St. David's.[72]

Social life at Philadelphia traveled far in these years from Quaker conceptions of the value of plainness and the frivolity of many innocent diversions. Unfortunately, the arrival of Whitefield in 1739, just as Philadelphia was becoming the most urbane of the towns, put a blight on public recreation which lasted for several years. As late as 1744 Dr. Hamilton observed that he had never visited "a place so populous where the *goût* for public gay diversions prevailed so little."

As Charles Town and Newport were smaller communities, the development of recreational facilities there was slower and less elaborate. In the Carolina town amusement was largely an aristocratic luxury. The formal social season for the planters began in December, but

[71] Gordon, *Geography Anatomiz'd* (13th ed.), 360; Jackson, *Cyclopedia of Philadelphia*, III, 711; Bache, *Bristol Borough*, 10.
[72] Westcott, *Philadelphia*, chapter CXVI; *Pa. Gaz.*, Feb. 25, 1728; March 4, 1729; June 26, 1732; June 16, 1737; *Mercury*, April 7, 1729; Johnson, *Beginnings of Freemasonry*, 60, 130; *History of the Schuylkill Fishing Company*, I, 339, 356; Hamilton, *Itinerarium*, 25.

many came into town in summer as well to escape the "country fever." Clubs of all sorts abounded. In addition to the social activities of various philanthropic societies mentioned elsewhere, members of such clubs as the Whisk, Fort Jolly Volunteers, Amiable, and Meddlers periodically enjoyed good fellowship, bounteous dinners and choice wines. In 1741 the first American convention of Ubiquarians, that neo-classic order of noble Romans, was founded by several "Gentlemen of Taste and Distinction," enfranchised by the Praetor, Censors and Senators of the Grand Convention in England. Less impressive, but of more lasting consequence, was Masonry's advent in 1735. Most gentlemen indulged in the "Royal Diversion" at the cock pit, and played cards and billiards. High stakes were wagered: tradition has it that Ansonboro was won at a single sitting by Lord George Anson, who lived at Charles Town from 1724 to 1735. The newly formed Jockey Club laid off a race track, called York Course, at the Quarter House near Charles Town in 1735. At regular meetings during February and March one mile races were run for silver tankards or £100 currency.[73]

The coming of the theater marked a great recreational advance at Charles Town. Plays were presented at the "Court Room" in 1734, and on February 21, 1735 the *South Carolina Gazette* announced a performance of Otway's *Orphan* at "the New Theater in Queen Street." *The Recruiting Officer, The Fair Penitent, George Barnwell, Cato,* and other popular London plays were performed at the Queen Street Theater in 1735–1736. Although "Laicus" had exclaimed, "Monstrum Horrendum," upon seeing the advertisement of a public ball, aristocrats dearly loved to dance, and as early as 1735 a grand ball was held in the Court Room under direction of Henry Holt, to which none were "admitted but by printed Ticket." An "Assembly of Dancing and Cards" also met regularly in apartments on Church Street.[74]

With the appearance of more varieties of artificial amusements, social life at Newport began to take on community character. The first town club was formed in 1726, and several more were regularly gathering round tavern punch bowls by 1742. While gentlemen smoked, drank and debated at public houses, their wives visited one another for gossip. Dancing increased in popularity toward the close of the period, and by 1741 young aristocrats met regularly in an assembly to dance minuets and "sett Country dances," or to play cards.[75]

[73] *S. C. Gaz.*, Feb. 5, 12, April 29, May 13, 1732; Feb. 1, June 1, 1734; Aug. 16, 1735; March 19, 1737; March 26, 1741; Harrison, *John's Island Stud*, 101.
[74] *S. C. Gaz.*, March 4, 11, Aug. 5, 1732; Nov. 22, 1735; Feb. 28, May 8, 1736; Jan. 19, 1740; Willis, *Charleston Stage*, 1–33; Johnson, *Beginnings of Freemasonry*, 134.
[75] Peterson, *Rhode Island*, 61; *R. I. Gaz.*, Oct. 18, 1732; Chapin, *Providence Sunday Journal*, Oct. 22, 1929.

One of the most sophisticated developments of the period was that which made Newport our earliest fashionable watering-place. After 1730 the salubrious climate of Rhode Island attracted many visitors from the West Indies and the Carolinas for their health. Here they found life enjoyable indeed. Pleasure excursions on the Bay to New Shoreham or Prudence Island were very popular, as were races by Narragansett pacers for silver tankards on the beach. Town merchants and lodging house keepers made the best of the season, as do their descendants at present day coast resorts. A continuous round of tea and dancing parties, and of grand dinners with a West India turtle as the *pièce de résistance,* made this embryo American Bath a gay, pleasant, and sophisticated, as well as most healthful spot.[76]

VII

With the development of city life education marched forward in every town. A growing realization of the value to the community of good schooling led to increased secularization of institutions of learning and a more secular emphasis in courses of study. Moreover, as the towns matured as commercial and business centers, and the need for education became more widespread, learning ceased to be the monopoly of clerics and gentlemen. Hence there appeared a tendency to stress useful and practical vocational knowledge rather than the more recondite offerings of the classical and theological curriculum. The growth of private schools was even more noteworthy than that of public institutions; such agencies offered instruction in every branch of knowledge, useful or genteel. Towns were now more than ever the educational centers of their respective provinces. Here a young man might fit himself for a career in either business or society, and many outsiders were drawn to town schools which afforded a training the equal or superior of any that might be had in English or Continental cities.

Boston, Newport and Philadelphia ranked foremost among American towns in providing educational facilities for all classes. The two New England towns, especially Boston, developed public education to the highest degree of any contemporary communities in the western world. The five free schools established at Boston before 1720 continued under the town's careful supervision in this period. Able masters and ushers were employed at good salaries, and instruction was in consequence excellent. The town also provided school buildings that were spacious and roomy, and kept them in constant repair. The Selectmen and a committee of important citizens made annual visits

[76] Bridenbaugh, "Colonial Newport as a Summer Resort," 2; *Newport T. C. Recs.,* Aug. 3, 1730; Berkeley, *Works,* IV, 158; Hamilton, *Itinerarium,* 185, 187, 190, 191.

of inspection, reporting in 1738 that nearly six hundred students were regularly receiving instruction in town supported institutions. In these "free" schools, as in all other towns where such institutions were maintained, those children whose parents were able to do so feed the masters. The only really "free" education was that for charity scholars. In the poor law of 1735 the General Court took cognizance of the fact that the children of the town poor had "much increased," and empowered the Overseers to apprentice children of all who could not care for them, and similarly to bind out all children above the age of six who could not read the alphabet, "For a decent and Christian Education." [77] Nowhere, either in Europe or America, was the public interest and care for education so great as at Boston.

The great increase in Boston's poor in these years led to some rather unsuccessful efforts at charity education. Samuel Sewall and others planned a charity school in 1727, but when they sought a building the Judge wrote in disgust to Thomas Fitch, "I was much exercised last night to observe that our Charity School should be liable to be made a May-game to every Landlord." He proposed erection of a school building, but because of the expense the project soon lapsed. A year later James Pigett opened a school "for the Instructions of Negros, in Reading, Catechizing, & Writing," to which for a small fee masters could send their black servants. It greatly grieved the Reverend Timothy Cutler in 1727 that there were no schools in his parish, and also that only one of the town schoolmasters was a Churchman. Shortly afterwards the Society for the Propagation of the Gospel selected Edward Mills to teach "indigent members" of the Anglican Church, a work which he continued until his death in 1733. Samuel Grainger, vestryman of King's Chapel, then gave up private teaching to take over the church school. Within a year he also died, but the Episcopalians, finding Boston "very well supplied . . . with free schools," made no further attempt to revive parochial education. [78]

The private schools of Boston, which offered instruction as good as that in town institutions, received abundant patronage, especially from those desiring vocational or specialized training. Samuel Grainger had usually about one hundred scholars in attendance at his private writing school, and Timothy Cutler praised his "distinguishing capacity for that business." There were private schools of all sorts, but those offering instruction in "practical subjects" were most popular. After his dismissal from the Hollis Professorship of Mathematics and

[77] 8 *Bos. Rec. Com.*, 170, 196; 12 *Bos. Rec. Com.*, 213, 246, 265, 292; *Mass. Acts and Resolves*, II, 756.
[78] 6 MHS *Colls.*, II, 224; *N. E. Journal*, April 8, 1728; Foote, *King's Chapel*, I, 395; *News Letter*, June 21, 28, 1733; Jan. 17, 1734; 12 *Bos. Rec. Com.*, 6, 36, 41.

Natural Philosophy at Harvard in 1738, Isaac Greenwood (Harvard, 1712), author of the popular text, *Arithmetick Vulgar & Decimal: with the Application thereof to a Variety of Cases in Trade and Commerce,* conducted an excellent private school of mathematics in Boston. Caleb Phillips gave instruction in shorthand at his school, and sent corresponding pupils their lessons weekly, guaranteeing them to be "as perfectly Instructed as those that live in Boston." Joseph Kent, M. A., catered to adults at his chamber in King Street, "where Gentlemen, for a reasonable Consideration, may be taught Geometry, plain and spheric; the Doctrine of Triangles, plain and spheric, as also Sailing, Surveying, Heights & Distances, the Projection of the Spheres, . . . Algebra, &c." Samuel Grainger's "evening School for Writing, Accompts, and Mathematicks," opened in 1724, seems to have been the only night school in Boston in this period.[79]

Many private teachers also offered cultural instruction to Boston youth. James Hovey, A. B., opened his school near the Orange Tree in 1742, where he "Taught Latin and Greek (both to young Gentlemen and Ladies), Arithmetick, and diverse Sorts of Writing, viz. English and German texts: the Court, Roman, Secretary, & Italian Hands." Instruction in French could be readily obtained. Most popular of the language masters was Louis Langloiserie, who arrived in Boston in 1730 and received permission from Harvard College to teach "the French Tongue to Such Undergraduates as are desirous to attend his Instruction" outside of "ye College Studying Hours or Exercises." His charges for private lessons in the town were twenty shillings per quarter.[80]

Young girls in Boston in this period had a try at all branches of education. They could begin in some school like that of George Brownell[81] to learn reading, writing, ciphering, dancing, and use of the needle, and at Peter Pelham's they could acquire the "art of Painting on Glass." From thence they might proceed to Ephraim Turner's Dancing School on Tremont Street, study French privately with Monsieur Langloiserie, and from some other master acquire "a knowledge of some agreeable parts of History." For the benefit of female apprentices Samuel Grainger announced in 1727 that "Such Young Women who cannot attend his Day School, may also be taught Writing and Accompts apart in the evening." The young ladies of Boston

---

[79] There were thirty-one schoolmasters in Boston in this period. *Bos. Gaz.,* Sept. 16, 1723; Sept. 7, 1724; Sept. 18, 1727; March 25, 1728; Nov. 9, 1735; April 2, 1739; Sept. 23, 1742; 5 MHS *Colls.,* VII, 245; *News Letter,* May 29, Jan. 17, 1734; Oct. 9, 1735.

[80] *N. E. Journal,* Oct. 26, 1730; July 18, 1738; *Bos. Gaz.,* Oct. 31, 1737; *News Letter,* March 25, 1736.

[81] George Brownell was the great peripatetic. He began at Boston in 1715; taught at New York in 1721, and in 1731–33; at Boston, 1734; Philadelphia, 1736. 13 *Bos. Rec. Com.,* 258; 15 *Bos. Rec. Com.,* 91.

eagerly patronized the several private schools, and, from the extent of its sales, it seems probable that most of them must have progressed at least as far as *Instruction for Children, or the Child's and Youth's Delight. Teaching an easy Way to Spell and Read true English,* which reached its twenty-sixth edition in 1739.[82]

Through their Town Meeting inhabitants of Newport generously supported public education. In 1720 the town school building housed elementary, writing and Latin classes. Two new schools appeared in this period to serve the "Woods part" of Newport, both of them partially supported by income from school lands. In 1727 the town provided for repairs to both these buildings, as well as for the "Great School House," and a year later, when it appeared that the meager fees paid the schoolmasters in the Woods Part of the town hardly warranted keeping a school there, made each master an annual grant of £10 in addition to his fees for tuition. A special tract of school lands at Sachusett Beach was set aside in 1735 to support the Woods schools and their new masters, John Gould and Thomas Cook. John Hammett conducted the "Great School" throughout the period, and sometime after 1738 Edward Scott, uncle of Sir Walter, began his twenty years of service as master of the grammar school. In 1739 the town built a fine new school house with an imposing belfry. Newport's leading citizens, particularly the Coddingtons, Nathaniel Clap and John Callender, were untiringly active in their interest in education, so that the town's three schools, providing elementary and secondary instruction, were offering inhabitants better educational facilities than were available at any other town save Boston.[83]

The various religious denominations of Newport also applied themselves to the promotion of education. The Friends' school continued; a school for Congregationalists was founded by Nathaniel Clap in 1729; and on March 31, 1729, the Reverend Mr. John Comer established a Baptist school with Samuel Maxwell as its teacher. "Strange doings," however, ensued, and Maxwell went over to the Church of England. Comer repaired the loss by himself assuming the teaching, and in March, 1730, he ordered four hundred sets of printed verses from James Franklin. Nathaniel Kay, collector of customs, who died in Newport in 1734, left £400 with which, after the death of his wife, to build a schoolhouse on Trinity Church property for the "benefit and use of a school to teach ten poor boys their grammar and mathematicks gratis: and to appoint a master at all times . . . who shall be Episcopally ordained." The school opened in October, 1741, under Cornelius

[82] 15 *Bos. Rec. Com.,* 159; *Bos. Gaz.,* Sept. 18, 1727; July 15, 29, 1734; *News Letter,* July 5, 1739.
[83] *Newport T. M. Recs.,* 221, 234, 245, 251, 256, 282, 291, 305; *Newport T. C. Recs.,* Jan. 7, 1740.

Bennett, who served as temporary master until an ordained teacher could be procured.[84]

Newport had fewer private schools than any other town, primarily because of the excellence and nearness of private educational facilities at Boston, where many boys and even more young "gentlewomen" attended boarding school. In 1732 a Mr. Beal, who had taught singing at Yale, opened a school of "Vocal Musick" at Newport. He was assisted by his son, who had "good voice and Judgement," and remained in town at least long enough for "his Skill" to become "Well Known." But though Rhode Islanders might patronize voice teachers, in order to better their "public singing" in church, John Owen Jacobi of London, who came to Trinity Church as organist in 1738, had nothing but disgust and vexation for the state of their musical knowledge.[85]

> Newport did not answer my Expectation. . . . The want of Instruments, Together with the Niggardliness of the People of this Place, and their not having a Taste for Musick, render it impossible for any one of my Profession to get a competent Maintenance here.

Although the Mayor and Common Council of Philadelphia made no attempt to set up or maintain city schools in this period, educational facilities in the town were among the best in the colonies, for religious societies and private teachers largely compensated for the public deficiency. The William Penn Charter School received continued bountiful support from the Friends; a "number of branches" of this institution was set up throughout the town, and wealthy Quakers established scholarships for needy children. Thomas Makin continued as headmaster until his death in 1733, and after a succession of teachers Anthony Benezet began a long and fruitful career there in 1742. Christ Church Charity School also enjoyed a prosperous existence. Quakers evinced considerable interest in the welfare of Philadelphia's Negro population. Some were admitted to the Penn Charter School, and in 1723 Samuel Keimer announced his intention to "wash Poor Hagar's Black-moors white" by teaching them to read the Holy Writ "in a very uncommon, expeditious and delightful Manner, without any Manner of Expence to their respective Masters or Mistresses." A group of philanthropic citizens established a charity school in 1741, at which it appears that Negroes received admission.[86]

[84] Klain, *Educational Acts of New England Quakers,* 36; Comer, "Diary," 49, 63, 102; Mason, *Trinity Church,* 28, 75, 88.

[85] *Bos. Gaz.,* May 2, 1726; March 13, 1727; Berkeley, *Works,* IV, 158; *R. I. Gaz.,* Dec. 7, 1732; R. I. Hist. Soc. *Pubs.,* n. s., VII, 235.

[86] Mulhern, *Secondary Education in Pennsylvania,* 44; *Pa. Gaz.,* Nov. 29, 1733; *Mercury,* Feb. 12, 19, 1723; June 11, 1741.

Excellent teaching in its private schools made Philadelphia the Mecca for students from New Jersey, Delaware, and Maryland. A good education, according to the standards of the age, could there be obtained by any one who had the necessary money. Young men and boys, after learning their letters at a dame school, could get their grammar, Latin and Greek, "as also Reading and Writing, Arithmetick Vulgar and Decimal, and several Parts of the Mathematicks," with Master William Robbins, and their French from Daniel Duborn. The increasing tendency toward practical and vocational education found expression in the curricula of many private schools. In 1733 Andrew Lamb advertised his school to "teach Merchants Accompts, after the Italian Manner by Double Entry," as well as practical mathematics and surveying. The next year Theophilous Grew fathered another institution devoted to similar subjects. At least five evening schools, offering vocational instruction, such as bookkeeping and surveying, for working people and apprentices, existed during this period. The drift toward the practical was not unmet by criticism from those who favored the old classical training. But in 1735 a stout defense of the "new education" appeared in the *American Weekly Mercury*. The author, deploring the current emphasis on the study of Latin, advocated the teaching of "the Grounds of Grammar in the English Tongue, . . . Writing and Accompts, . . . Arithmetick, . . . the Excellent Art of Italian Book-keeping," geography, chronology, history, and "above all a Good Narrative Style." "Can there be anything more Rediculous," he demanded, after quoting John Locke on the teaching of Latin, "than that a Father should waste his own Money and his Sons Time, in setting him to learn the Roman Language, when at the same Time he designs him for a Trade?" [87]

Philadelphia had perhaps more and better private schools for girls than were to be found elsewhere in the colonies. Mrs. Rhodes kept a school in 1722 to "teach any Young Ladies or Gentlewomen to read and write French to perfection," and the next year offered to give them instruction in their homes. More fashionable was the establishment of John Salomon, "from Paris," who taught Latin and French, giving "due Attendance" to all gentlemen and ladies. Learning the polite tongue was a luxury enjoyed only by gentlewomen, but at Noel Ledru's "Evening-School in Laetitia Court" young girls of the middle classes could learn the more practical arts of writing, arithmetic, and "Patern-Drawing." That omnipresent pedagogue, George Brownell, at his boarding school in Front Street, as usual offered young ladies

[87] *Mercury*, Dec. 31, 1728; May 13, June 18, 1730; Nov. 7, 1734; Jan. 7, 14, 1735; *Pa. Gaz.*, Feb. 24, May 13, 1730; Nov. 18, 1731; March 31, April 8, 1732.

an all-around education in reading, writing, ciphering, dancing, and "a Variety of Needlework." [88]

The state of education at New York improved somewhat during these years, for though public efforts at establishing schools largely failed, there was a noteworthy multiplication of private educational agencies. Able masters continued to instruct children of both sexes in the Dutch tongue at the elementary school of the Dutch Reformed Church. The Reverend Robert Jenny's grammar school, supported by the S. P. G., died out about 1722, leaving the Dutch school and Thomas Huddlestone's elementary school the only institutions giving charity instruction. Shortly after Huddlestone's death in 1731 the Corporation paid his mother a mere £8, "as Gratification" for the trouble and care she and her son had taken in teaching "several Poor Children" reading, writing, and the principles of religion.[89]

The provincial Assembly resolved in 1732 that, since "The City and Colony . . . abounds with Youths of a Genius not Inferior to other Countries, it must undoubtedly be a Loss to the Public and a Misfortune to such Youths if they are destitute of the opportunity to improve their Capacities, by a Liberal Education." Therefore, it proceeded to found a public school for instruction in Latin, Greek and mathematics, appointed Alexander Malcolm its master, and appropriated funds for the education of twenty boys, ten of whom might come from the city. This school was abandoned in 1738. The only other free institution of this period was a small charity school at Greenwich Village. The town's gross neglect of its poor children called forth the severe condemnation of Zenger's newspaper in 1737 and a demand for "a more regular Education of our Youth, especially of the poorer Sort." Most pauper children simply roamed the streets, the writer maintained, and even apprentices received "but one Quarter's Night-Schooling per annum." [90]

This absence of public facilities allowed private schools to flourish. Alexander Malcolm's school, which he gave up to become master of the Free School in 1732, was well attended by the sons of gentry who wished to study philosophy and the classics. "Grammar, Writing, Arithmetick Vulgar & Decimal" were offered by William Thurston in 1732, and five years later Joshua Ring advertised to teach reading and writing for twelve and a half shillings a quarter, although those who could not afford to pay so much would be "taught for less." John

---

[88] By 1741 Philadelphians were reading Fénelon's *Education of Girls*. *Mercury*, May 23, 1722; May 23, 1723; June 17, 1736; *Pa. Gaz.*, Jan. 22, March 4, 1736; May 4, 1738.

[89] Kilpatrick, *Dutch Schools of New Netherland*, 150, 216; *N. Y. M. C. C.*, IV, 74.

[90] *N. Y. Col. Laws*, II, 813, 973; Kemp, *Support of Schools in New York*, 74; *N. Y. M. C. C.*, IV, 174, 452; *N. Y. Journal*, July 26, 1736; Feb. 14, 1737; Stokes, *Iconography*, IV, 562.

Campbell opened his boarding school for boys in Bridge Street in 1741, and the year following, in Duke Street, Samuel Wilcox, from London, began teaching Latin, French and shorthand, in addition to the usual three R's.[91]

New York had also many private schools for girls. The itinerant George Brownell catered to both sexes in 1731 with a curriculum of elementary subjects, languages, bookkeeping, dancing and needlework. Martha Gazely arrived from London in 1731 to teach young ladies to make artificial fruits and flowers, "Wax-works, Nuns-work, Philligris, and needlework," while psalmody constituted the principal study at Mr. Winter's singing school in Broadway. French and Spanish were "carefully taught after the best Method . . . practised in Great Britain" for twenty shillings a quarter in 1735, and soon after that date several French schools sprang up at Manhattan.[92]

Many families living in the upcountry now found tutors like Edward Gatehouse, who were willing to go to their estates, but by far the larger number still educated their children in the town. Cadwallader Colden wrote on this subject to his Quaker aunt in 1732:

> I was extremely concern'd to find that you was not pleas'd with our sending the children to town. We had no design besides giving them some Education that they cannot have in the Country & rub off some of that country awkwardness which is a great disadvantage to young people that expect some time to be in Company.

On the other hand, Manhattan lads began about 1740 to prepare for entrance to Yale College with the Reverend Mr. Samuel Johnson at Stratford, Connecticut.[93]

Evening schools had their greatest development at New York. They were largely attended by apprentices, whose indentures called for "Night Schooling" sufficient for them to "Learn to Read write and Cypher." John Walton, "late of Yale College," advertised his evening school in 1723, its term lasting from the first of October to the first of March, the period generally specified by indentures of apprenticeship. He offered reading, writing, arithmetic, fractions, and the "Mariner's Art" at reasonable prices. James Lyne also conducted an evening school in the winter for apprentices and others who desired to learn geometry, trigonometry, navigation, surveying, and algebra, while another master offered instruction in bookkeeping. At least

[91] Stokes, *Iconography*, IV, 516; *N. Y. Gaz.*, Sept. 4, Dec. 18, 1732; *N. Y. Journal*, April 4, 1737; March 30, 1741; June 14, 1742.
[92] *N. Y. Gaz.*, June 21, Dec. 21, 1731; July 7, 1735; *N. Y. Journal*, Feb. 11, 1733; June 27, 1737; Jan. 7, 1740.
[93] *Colden Papers*, II, 84; *N. Y. Gaz.*, Oct. 11, 1731; Schneider, *Samuel Johnson*, I, 31.

twenty-four masters taught at New York, either in private or religious schools, between 1720 and 1742, and for people of quality, at least, the instruction offered compared well with that in the other towns.[94]

Educational facilities at Charles Town, especially for children of the elite, improved markedly after 1730. Emphasis on polite learning as a stimulus to the arts and sciences, improved conversation and the social graces resulted in the predominantly classical curriculum of the Free School, and, as early as 1723, in agitation for a local college. It is clearly evident that most of the youth in the southern metropolis, as well as from the country round about, received their schooling in the province; the tradition of education in England has been somewhat overstressed. The Free School was attended not only by Charles Town boys, but by boarders from the plantation country and the Bahamas. Planters who did not maintain tutors in their homes sent their children to boarding schools in Charles Town, a journey which in that rough country exposed them to considerable danger and hardship; in 1737 one youngster was drowned at Ashley Ferry "on his return to the boarding school." George Logan advertised in 1737 that "if any Gentlemen living in the country are disposed to send their Children to Charlestown," he would board them and instruct them in dancing. Likewise, he offered to go into the country if there appeared to be sufficient encouragement for such a venture there. It cost Eliza Pinckney £140 a year, currency, to send her little sister, Polly, to Mrs. Heck's school in Charles Town.[95]

Most Charlestonians received their practical or cultural education in private schools. In 1733 John Miller taught "these sciences: Arithmetic, Algebra, Geometry, Trigonometry, Surveying, Dialling, Navigation, Astronomy, Gauging, Fortification. The Stereographic and Orthographic Projection of the Sphere. The use of the Globe and the Italian Method of Bookkeeping." Two night schools, conducted by Barnabas Flemming and Daniel Thomas, offered instruction in similar subjects. At any time after 1720 instruction could be had in English, Latin and Greek, and in French and music after 1733. In addition, several masters and mistresses taught dancing, drawing, embroidery, and needlework to young women of the town.[96]

Despite emphasis on the training of gentlemen, education of poor children was not neglected at Charles Town. A number of poor scholars was annually chosen to attend the Free School at the expense

[94] N. Y. Hist. Soc. *Colls., 1909; Mercury,* Oct. 24, 1723; *N. Y. Gaz.,* July 21, 1729; Sept. 7, 1730.

[95] *S. C. Gaz.,* April 1, 22, 1732; March 8, 1734; Sept. 17, 1737; Jan. 18, Aug. 4, 1739; June 19, 1740; Feb. 27, 1742; Ravenel, *Eliza Pinckney,* 58; Foster, Education in South Carolina, I, 20, 119, 148; *N. Y. Journal,* March 21, 1737.

[96] *S. C. Gaz.,* March 17, May 12, July 14, 1733; Feb. 19, 1737; June 9, 1739; Jan. 19, 1740; Dec. 12, 1741; May 29, 1742.

of the S. P. G., and after 1730 the St. Andrew's Society provided tuition for twenty more. St. Philip's Vestry cared for the elementary education of such as fell within neither of the above groups. The only attempt to provide schooling for Charles Town's many blacks came in 1740, when a Mr. Boulson, who had formerly kept a "Dancing School, Ball, Assembly, Concert Room, Etc," abandoned his entire way of life after having listened to the exhortations of George White-field, and turned his establishment into a school for Negroes. He soon had fifty-three pupils under his tutelage, and though he was haled into court for violation of the Slave Code by teaching blacks to read, the authorities allowed him to continue.[97]

The educational advance of these two decades wrought visible improvements in every community. Although public education existed only at Boston and Newport, other agencies, private and parochial, somewhat made up for its absence in the remaining towns. Inhabitants of the five towns were far better educated than the generality of country-dwellers, and where a country-born boy or girl was fortunate enough to acquire learning it was usually accomplished by spending several winters in the nearest large town. It also seems probable that a much greater proportion of the American townsmen were literate than was the case in contemporary English and European cities.

VIII

Years of peace and plenty in the early eighteenth century made possible the emergence of a genuine colonial culture. The colonists had devoted one hundred years, more or less, to providing themselves with the physical necessities of life; now, more than ever, they had leisure to cultivate and enjoy its adornments, and wealth to import and develop them. This was as true of their intellectual as of their material luxuries. The same ships that brought them the latest English and European manufactures carried also cargoes of books and ideas, — treatises on architecture and gardening, on science and philosophy, the works of Pope, Addison and Gay, and copies of current London drama. The new wealth of the colonial towns enabled upper and middle class virtuosi to purchase these means of refinement; the rapid spread of urban education permitted their enjoyment and appreciation. Wealth and leisure, too, brought about an improvement in colonial taste, evidences of which appeared in the beautification of homes and gardens, the elaboration of interiors by use of carvings, wallpapers, and hangings, and the creation of truly decorative furni-

[97] St. Philip's Vestry Mins., 75; McCrady, *Royal Government in South Carolina*, 530; *News Letter*, Aug. 21, 1740.

ture and cabinet work by native craftsmen. A sense of beauty was beginning to pervade the towns, transforming their houses, public buildings, and gentle ways of life. Improving taste, and the money to exercise it, were further demonstrated in the public patronage of music and the theater, and the support of local engravers and portrait painters. The culture that grew up in the colonial towns was still strongly derivative and truly provincial, continually nourished by increasingly intimate connections with the Mother Country, which only the wealth, commercial activities, and geographic position of the five seaports made possible.

As in other spheres of urban life, each community developed a cultural individuality of its own. In intellectual matters Boston easily led the rest, though the scepter of its supremacy was soon to pass to Philadelphia. As a center of book publishing and marketing it was surpassed only by London in the Empire. In 1724 the booksellers, following the example of the barbers, formed a sort of trade association to fix prices and make regulations for the conduct of their business. These enterprising merchants supplied the whole of New England and many of the other colonies with reading matter of all sorts, and while theological and religious titles still predominated on their shelves, more secular literature was appearing each year. Richard Fry sold twelve hundred copies of the poems of Stephen Duck of Wiltshire in 1732, and Boston bookshops could supply the works of Aristotle, Virgil, Ovid, Shakespeare, Milton, Swift, De Foe, and Richardson, in addition to copies of the *Guardian* and the *Spectator*. Richard Wilde held a book auction at the Exchange Tavern in 1727, consisting of works on divinity, travel, history, navigation, medicine, mathematics, and poetry, and after 1730 Thomas Hancock in his printed catalogue advertised large importations of books in similar fields "from London in the last Ships." [98]

Boston was likewise the newspaper center of the American colonies. This fact carried more cultural significance than in earlier days, for the conception of the functions of journalism was expanding, and these weekly sheets now had space in their columns for reprints of writings current on the other side of the Atlantic, the efforts of native writers, and discussions of local opinions. The town's third newspaper appeared in 1721, when James Franklin established the *New England Courant,* a peppery sheet of considerable merit, which ran until 1727. In that year the founding of the *New England Weekly Journal* gave Bostonians a paper of somewhat better literary quality than the *Courant.* This was followed by the *Weekly Rehearsal* in 1731,

[98] *Courant,* July 2, 1722; Dec. 7, 1724; *Rehearsal,* May 1, 1732; *N. E. Journal,* May 29, 1727; *News Letter,* May 27, 1731.

and by the *Boston Weekly Post Boy* in 1734. With their columns filled with controversy, religious, literary and scientific efforts, specimens of contemporary English writings, and even local literary criticism, these little American Spectators were of inestimable cultural value not only to Bostonians, but to inhabitants in a wide area of surrounding colonies. As before, they provided in their advertising columns a vehicle by which teachers, booksellers, and artists could inform the public of their presence in the towns. Boston papers enjoyed a large number of readers for the times, and their circulation extended all over New England and the colonies to the southward.[99]

Many Bostonians possessed large libraries. Cotton Mather's collection was rivalled after 1726 by Thomas Prince's great assemblage of books and manuscripts. Presence of flourishing bookshops points to the existence of many smaller libraries. Prince proposed to Samuel Sewall in 1726 a "Schem for a Lending Library" for the clergy. This the Judge deemed "inconvenient" because of the expense, but he did contribute forty shillings toward the purchase of a polyglot Bible for ministerial use. The Town Library enjoyed many accessions during this period, and in 1734 Colonel Thomas Fitch headed a list of subscribers to a considerable donation for the acquisition of additional volumes.[100]

Much of Boston's literary culture still centered in the clergy, and thus continued to exhibit either a theological or an historical turn. The more lasting titles from the Boston press in these years illustrate the tendency, — Penhallow's *History of the Wars of New England with the Eastern Indians* (1726), Mason's *History of the Pequot War* (1736), and Samuel Willard's *Complete Body of Divinity*, issued in 1726, the first folio volume to be published in the colonies. The *Chronological History of New England, in the Form of Annals,* by Thomas Prince, which appeared in 1736, though of little literary value, did show considerable skill in the assembling of materials. But as most of their literary and intellectual fashions the colonists borrowed and imitated from London, the trend away from clerical domination is more significant and in keeping with the times. The newspapers, whose columns provided space for Addisonian essays and feeble attempts at light versification, fostered this tendency, but the rise of a group of self-professed and self-conscious wits in this puritan stronghold is its most interesting manifestation. Mather Byles, whose Christian name reveals his ancestry, later pastor of the Hollis Street Church, began his career with an excursion into journalism by contributing

[99] The *Weekly Rehearsal* became the *Boston Evening Post* in 1735. See especially *Rehearsal*, Jan. 10, March 13, Aug. 28, 1732.
[100] 6 MHS *Colls.,* II, 208; 13 *Bos. Rec. Com.,* 249.

bits of verse to the *New England Weekly Journal,* which he had helped to found. He produced a poem on the death of George I, in the florid obituary manner of the day, which encouraged the belief of his friends that "he bade fair to rise, and sing, and rival Pope." Byles was but one of a group of versifiers and tavern wits, among whom was Joseph Green, but most of their light rhyming and punning controversy belong to a later period. That Pope's influence pervaded religious as well as secular poetry may be seen in the writings of Jane Turrell, daughter of Benjamin Colman. The Bard of Twickenham was slavishly followed and adored in Boston, where whatever was according to Pope was right. During these years Dr. William Douglass headed another group of rebels against the puritan way, but with the demise of the *Courant* they lost their principal vehicle of expression, and thereafter confined themselves largely to acrimonious correspondence and discussions at the Physical Club.[101]

Scientific activity by Boston gentlemen and scholars provided another sign of the times. Isaac Greenwood's success furnishes an early instance of the Boston taste for public lectures; in 1726 he presented a series of lectures and experiments on Newton's fluxions and principles of mechanical philosophy, for which he published an excellent syllabus, and in 1734 conducted a course illustrating "the elements of Astronomy . . . on the Orrery." Dr. Douglass' "Physical Club" disputed almost nightly the latest theories of medical advance or the order of the universe, while its leader occupied himself in the collection of over eleven hundred indigenous plants. But the most impressive testimony to Boston's scientific accomplishments is to be found in the nineteen contributions of Paul Dudley, Henry Newman, Thomas Robie, Zabdiel Boylston, Benjamin Colman and Isaac Greenwood to the *Philosophical Transactions* of the Royal Society, which in quality as well as quantity completely overshadow the twelve offerings of nine English provincial cities from 1720 to 1742.[102]

Bostonians began also to develop a taste for prints and pictures. William Price did a thriving business in prints and maps at his "Picture Store"; in 1722 he sold the Burgis views of New York and Boston, and Captain Bonner's map of Boston, while in 1742 he produced his own view of the Bay town. An artistic event of great importance was the arrival of John Smibert from Newport in 1729.

---

[101] *N. E. Journal,* Sept. 4, 1727; Johnson, *Beginnings of Freemasonry,* 224; Tyler, *American Literature,* 133.

[102] In all the five colonial towns contributed twenty-nine papers (Philadelphia, six; New York, three; Charles Town, one), while English provincial cities (Oxford and Cambridge excepted) and Scotland contributed but twenty-one. Most of the Scottish papers were the work of Colin McLaurin of Edinburgh. *Bos. Gaz.,* Nov. 28, Dec. 5, 1726; *N. E. Journal,* July 10, 1727; *News Letter,* June 13, 1734; Douglass, *Summary,* II, 216 n.; *Phil. Trans.,* VI-VIII.

Within a year he exhibited his portraits of Samuel Sewall, Nathaniel Byfield and Paul Mascarene, together with copies of Van Dyke and Reubens executed by him in Europe. This first American art exhibit attained the dignity of a rhymed notice in the *London Daily Courant* for April 14, 1730. In 1734 Smibert opened a shop on King Street, where he offered for sale "A Collection of Valuable Prints, engrav'd by the Best Hands, after the finest Pictures in Italy, France, Holland, and England, done by Raphael, Michael Angelo, Poussin, and other the greatest Masters, . . . being what Mr. Smibert collected in the above-mentioned Countries." His studio and color-and-print shop became the artistic center of the colonies, and many a gentleman and his consort went thither to sit for portraits during the next decade. Other Boston painters were Nathaniel Emmons, who "minded accuracy more than Profit," and Joseph Badger, a disciple of Smibert. Peter Pelham, the well-known engraver, also painted a few portraits. In the summer of 1741 Robert Feke arrived at Boston to execute his portrait of Isaac Royal and his family, and while there he perhaps made likenesses of other members of the gentry.[103]

The "diversion of musick" received almost as much attention as painting in the Massachusetts capital. The first colonial public "Concert of Musick on Sundry Instruments" was performed in Boston on February 18, 1729. At the "New Concert Room" in Wing's Lane musicians gave two concerts in 1732, and frequent public performances of "Vocal and Instrumental Musick" as "elegant" as in England took place before the close of the period. Bostonians eagerly took up music for themselves, and sent their children to learn harpsichord and spinet under Mr. Charles Theodore Pachelbell and other teachers. Many citizens, like Jonathan Belcher, sought to "Relax" in their chambers "with base viol & flute," and William Price found eager custom for his "Flutes, Hautboys, Violins & Strings, Musick Books and Songs." Even town churches turned genteel, with new organs and singing by note.[104]

It was thus possible by the end of the period for inhabitants of Boston to indulge their tastes in letters, painting and music. Alone among the arts, sculpture, which because of its technical difficulties hardly developed in colonial America, and the theater, which still fell under the ban of clerical disapproval, were unrepresented in the Bay town. But, although Boston could still claim to be the intellectual cap-

[103] *News Letter*, May 21, 1722; May 15, 1735; Sept. 30, 1742; *N. E. Journal*, Feb. 5, 1728; March 27, 1740; *Bos. Gaz.*, March 20, May 1, 1738; Hamilton, *Itinerarium*, 139; Bayley, *Five Colonial Artists*, I, 337; *N. E. Quarterly*, VIII, 14; Foote, *Robert Feke*, 11, 41, 45.

[104] *Bos. Gaz.*, Feb. 10, 1729; Feb. 26, 1733; *News Letter*, Feb. 1, 15, May 3, Dec. 6, 1733; March 4, 1736; Sept. 22, 1743; Hamilton, *Itinerarium*, 178; 6 MHS *Colls.*, VI, 127, 183.

ital of the colonies, Philadelphia showed most promise for the future. As society matured in Penn's city, cultural advance was achieved in all lines save the theater, which here, as at Boston, suffered from the scruples of the dominant religious group. Architecturally, Philadelphia far surpassed the New England town, and the fine taste of its inhabitants encouraged the work of such gifted amateurs as Dr. John Kearsley and Andrew Hamilton. Aristocratic patronage for the arts was always forthcoming in the Quaker city, and cultural life there took a decidedly secular turn, which was absent from the Boston scene.

The publishing activity of Philadelphians produced three new public prints in this period. In 1728 Samuel Keimer established the *Pennsylvania Gazette,* which was soon purchased by Benjamin Franklin, and became under his editorship one of the liveliest and most influential of colonial newspapers. In 1732 the *Philadelphische Zeitung* appeared in an attempt to reach the German population, but the venture proved premature and the paper expired after a few issues. The *American Weekly Mercury* died with its owner, Andrew Bradford, in 1742, but his nephew, William, almost immediately began publication of the *Pennsylvania Journal.* Franklin and the Bradfords maintained a sharp rivalry which enlivened much of Philadelphia's publishing history. It caused Andrew Bradford in February, 1741, to bring out the *American Magazine,* in an attempt to forestall Franklin's projected *General Magazine,* which appeared in March. Both attempts at periodical publication proved abortive, however, the former lasting only three months and the latter, six. Easily the most important issue of the Philadelphia press was *Poor Richard's Almanack,* through which, beginning in 1732, Franklin's wit and wisdom reached all classes in town or country.

The bookshops of Philadelphia, while not so numerous as at Boston, offered after 1730 as wide a selection of titles. Andrew Bradford's shop had catered almost wholly to religious interests, with "most Sorts of Bibles, Common-Prayer Books, Testaments, Psalters, Psalm-Books, with Supplements, and notes by Tate and Brady," but Benjamin Franklin sought the custom of all groups, and in addition to a stock like Bradford's, he offered the best of the classics, like Ovid, Virgil, Horace, Juvenal, and Eutropius, the works of Fénelon, Rabelais, Bacon, Dryden, Otway, Locke, Congreve and others, as well as a "Great Variety of Maps and Prints." At the close of the period William Bradford opened a new bookstore, which, containing the largest stock in the middle colonies, gave Franklin real competition. Another source of books at Philadelphia was the annual fair, at which, as in Germany, large quantities of reading matter were sold "at Reasonable Prices." The six bookshops received good patronage from a growing group of men of secular tastes, who built up excellent libraries. Robert Strettel possessed a large collection of "Greek, Latin and French authors," and Charles Read owned many fine volumes which he lent out with generous frequency. In 1737 he advertised for the return of his many "dispers'd" books, "particularly . . . the Spectator, Tatler, Guardian, Conquest of Mexico, Athenian Oracle, & some whole sets lent out." James Logan's library of three thousand volumes gave evidence of the best and most catholic taste, perhaps, of any provincial collection.[105]

Alexander Hamilton observed that there "was no scarcity of men of learning and good sense" at Philadelphia, and a non-professional interest in belles lettres and the classics prevailed there more than at any other town. Isaac Norris and John Kinsey among the Friends, and Dr. Thomas Cadwallader, Benjamin Franklin and Thomas Makin of the middle class were all men widely read in ancient literature. Schoolmaster Makin composed creditable Latin verse, of which *Encomium Pensylvaniae* (1728) and *In Laudeo* (1729) are the best. The outstanding American intellectual of this period was James Logan, who, amid many public duties, found time to publish *Cato's Distichs englished into Couplets* (1735), and to produce an annotated translation of Cicero's *De Senectute*. His scientific interests led to his defense of Thomas Godfrey's improvement on the quadrant, and his contribution to the *Philosophical Transactions* of three papers, one of which reveals an understanding of sex differentiation in plants. Two other Philadelphians contributed to this journal, Joseph Breintnall, and the Quaker John Bartram, whom Linnaeus called "the greatest natural botanist in the world." At his home on the outskirts of the city, which he built with his own hands, and which is interesting in possessing some of the rare examples of stone carving which colonial America produced, the latter created his botanical gardens, studied medicine and surgery, and carried on a prodigious correspondence with European scientists. Just at the close of the period he embarked on the first of two notable journeys for the collection of North American flora.[106]

Among Philadelphia's artisans and tradesmen were several men of literary ability whose companionship provided stimulus for the intellectual development of the young Franklin. Aquila Rose, James Ralph, Joseph Breintnall, George Webb, Jacob Tyler and Henry Brooke formed a group of wits and poetasters unique in the New World. In 1727 Franklin organized them into the Leather Apron Club, copied

[105] *Mercury*, Jan. 27, 1730; May 1, 1735; June 26, 1742; *Pa. Gaz.*, Aug. 11, 1737; Jan. 13, 1738; Jan. 25, April 12, 1739; Jackson, *Cyclopedia of Philadelphia*, II, 314; Wallace, *William Bradford*, 12.

[106] When Dr. Hamilton attended the Governor's Club, the topic for discussion was Cervantes and other "foreign writers." *Itinerarium*, 23, 33; *Pa. Mag.*, LVI, 68; XXXVII, 369; *Phil. Trans.*, VII, 57, 68, 112, 669; VIII, 409; *Pa. Gaz.*, Oct. 30, 1735.

after one of Cotton Mather's Neighborhood Benefit Societies. The Junto (as it came later to be called) held regular meetings at taverns for the discussion of morals, politics, poetry, and natural philosophy, and for interchange of books. Out of this latter function grew the idea of a subscription library. On July 1, 1731, the instrument of association of the Library Company was signed by twenty-four members of the Junto and other interested persons, and Lewis Timothy made librarian. James Logan and Franklin sent to Peter Collinson in London for their first importation of books in 1732. Among the titles they ordered there is not one on a religious or theological subject; most of them represent literature, history, philosophy, science, medicine, and architecture. Within a short time the Library Company was enlarged to include one hundred subscribers, and in 1739 its books were housed in a room in the new State House. In 1728 a donation of parchment folio volumes by Ludovico Sprogell formed the basis of an excellent parochial library at Christ Church, to which in 1741 the Reverend Mr. Cummings made important additions from his private collection. By the will of Thomas Chalkley his "small library" went to the Friends' Meeting. Under Robert Johnson, who assumed charge of it in 1742, the collection was greatly augmented by purchase and by donations from Peter Collinson, Dr. John Fothergill, and other London Friends.[107]

Wealthy Philadelphia merchants provided encouragement and patronage for colonial portrait painters. Robert Feke visited the town in 1739 or 1740 to make his striking portraits of Mr. and Mrs. Tench Francis. The favorite Pennsylvania artist was Gustavus Hesselius, one of the few at this time to make his living by his brush. In 1740 he and John Winter advertised to do painting "in the Best Manner, . . . viz. Coats of Arms drawn on Coaches, Chaises, &c, or any other kinds of Ornaments, Landskips, Signs, Showboards, Ship and House Painting, Gilding of all Sorts, Writing in Gold or Colour, old Pictures clean'd and Mended." Hesselius painted a number of Philadelphia worthies, but his best work may be seen in the exquisite interiors of the new State House. Perhaps owing to its German population, Philadelphia had always shown itself hospitable to music. Singing, and playing on the spinet, virginal and other instruments now became common, and capable teachers appeared to give instruction. In perhaps the earliest piece of musical criticism in America, a writer on elocution and music remarked in the *Mercury* in 1729, "there is scarce a Soul so

---

[107] *Mercury,* June 19, 1729; Jackson, *Literary History of Pennsylvania,* chapter II; Franklin, *Works* (Bigelow), II, 242; *Pa. Mag.,* XXX, 300; XXIII, 106; XXXIX, 450; Abbott, *Library Company of Philadelphia,* 3; *Pa. Gaz.,* June 5, 1735; Dorr, *Christ Church,* 333; Scharf and Westcott, *Philadelphia,* II, 1189; Allen, *Tides of English Taste.* I, 147, 169.

rustick as not to admire both in their Excellency." In 1730 Franklin published the hymns of Conrad Beissel of Ephrata, which passed through two more editions by 1739. An annual subscription concert begun at the "Concert Room" in 1740 was driven out of existence by the denunciations of Whitefield, but as the "Musick Club," under the leadership of Tench Francis, the group continued to give creditable private concerts on harpsichord and violins.[108]

Newport made relatively the greatest cultural advance of the period, and when Dean Berkeley and John Smibert arrived in 1729 they found there an aristocratic society with developed, cultivated tastes, which charmed them into remaining. James Franklin had come from Boston to set up his press in 1726, and was about to become printer for the colony. At this time the leader of the Newport group was that elegant gentleman of leisure, Peter Pelham, Sr., whom John Comer found "A witty man and a great scholar, but alas too light in his conversation." At his death in 1730 leadership of Newport culture passed to Henry Collins, a wealthy merchant, whose generous patronage of the arts earned him Dr. Waterhouse's tribute of "the Lorenzo de Medici of Rhode Island." For upwards of thirty years he headed every artistic and civic movement in the town. In 1730, with Peter Bours, Daniel Updyke and others, he founded the "Society for the Promotion of Knowledge and Virtue by a Free Conversation." Five years later the group numbered twenty-four members, meeting at their respective homes every Monday night to "converse about and debate some useful question in Divinity, Morality, Philosophy, &c," the exact nature of which they never divulged.[109]

This interchange of thought produced some worthy results. Bishop Berkeley wrote his *Minute Philosopher* while in Newport, and in 1739 John Callender celebrated the town's coming of age in his *Historical Discourse on the Civil and Religious Affairs of the Colony of Rhode Island*. For catholicity of treatment, accuracy, and straightforward literary style, the latter work was the best historical treatise yet produced in the English colonies. The Baptist clergyman also made a collection of materials on the history of his church, and evinced a great interest in education. After 1740 Peter Bours availed himself of the leisure which his profits from the slave trade made possible to pursue the scientific study of the cultivation of flowers and seeds, and to correspond with Cadwallader Colden concerning his results. Most of the members of the philosophical society owned good libraries, and

---

[108] *Mercury*, March 13, Aug. 14, 1729; Sept. 17, 1730; *Pa. Gaz.*, March 22, 1739; May 8, Oct. 16, 1740; *Pa. Mag.*, I, 416; Hamilton, *Itinerarium*, 236; Drummond, *Early German Music*, 9.

[109] R. I. Hist. Soc. *Colls*, XXV, 97; Comer, "Diary," 111; *Seventh Day Baptist Memorial*, III, 150; *R. I. Hist. Mag.*, V, 81; *Newport Hist. Mag.*, IV, 68.

patronized the bookstores of James Franklin, "under the Town School House," or of Mrs. Neargrass, where books of divinity, history, law, medicine and drama, "most of them new and well bound," were on display. The library of Trinity Church, open to all people, received a gift of seventy-five volumes from Bishop Berkeley in 1731.[110]

James Franklin began issuing the *Rhode Island Gazette* on September 29, 1732. This newspaper showed the same attention to literary matters that had characterized his *New England Courant,* its second issue containing a plea for contributions from Newport "Gentlemen of Capacity and Leisure," and a poem of some merit, "To the Scatterwaters," appeared in an early number. Franklin's audience was small but appreciative; a Boston correspondent begged for more "Dogood Essays," declaring his home-town papers dull and "always full of important Events," which crowded good literature from their columns. The urban imperialism of Boston, however, kept circulation small, and Franklin was forced to abandon the enterprise. Boston newspapers had already an established reading public at Rhode Island, where Cuthbert Campbell, postmaster, took subscriptions for the *Weekly Post Boy* for "Customers at Newport and the adjacent towns." [111]

John Smibert, who came to Newport with Berkeley, provided an impulse for the development of the fine arts on Rhode Island. Mrs. Berkeley, whom he had taught to paint during the long Atlantic crossing, made several portraits while at Newport. Smibert remained in the town for about a year, and executed several works there under the patronage of Henry Collins, but the most important result of his Newport stay was his influence on Robert Feke, who was to become "the best colonial portrait painter in America before Copley." Feke was Newport-born and a protégé of Henry Collins, already well known for his collection of paintings. Perhaps his best piece of these years was the imaginative portrait of Pamela Andrews, completed only one year after the publication of Richardson's popular novel. In 1740, under commission from Henry Collins, he painted likenesses of Nathaniel Clap and John Callender. Feke read widely, became interested in Deism, and had by the close of the period attained considerable independence and maturity in his artistic style. Dr. Hamilton found him in 1744 "the most extraordinary genius ever I knew, for he does pictures tolerable well by the force of genius." The other leading artistic figure of the town was Richard Munday, whose public buildings and private residences added much to the charm of Newport at the same time that they placed him foremost among colonial architects. Music, alone of the arts, failed to find favor at Newport in this period, the

[110] Comer, "Diary," 119 n.; R. I. Hist. Soc. *Colls.,* 1889, 23; *Colden Papers,* III, 40; *R. I. Gaz.,* Oct. 4, 1732; Jan. 25, 1733; *Newport Hist. Mag.,* II, 9; IV, 22, 33; *Post Boy,* Dec. 6, 1742; Mason, *Trinity Church,* 10, 49.
[111] *R. I. Gaz.,* Oct. 4, Nov. 16, 1732; *Post Boy,* Sept. 28, 1741.

town being still too small to provide adequate patronage for the drama.[112]

Cultural development at New York and Charles Town was less deeply rooted and more flashy than in the other communities. Moreover, it was confined almost wholly to aristocrats, and was gregarious and sociable rather than deeply scholarly or scientific. While New York made less progress, culturally and artistically, than other northern towns, its advance was none the less marked, and an aristocratic group of intellectuals performed a notable service to the town, endowing its life with certain flavor and distinction. In 1725 William Bradford founded the fifth colonial newspaper, the *New York Gazette,* and in 1734 Peter Zenger established the *New York Weekly Journal,* which soon became the organ of opposition to Governor Cosby, and notorious as the subject of the famous libel trial in which Andrew Hamilton of Philadelphia made his plea for freedom of the press. Though Bradford drew heavily on the *Spectator* for material, his sheet had on the whole little literary appeal. Zenger, on the other hand, printed *Cato's Letters,* selections from Addison, Steele, Pope, Fielding, and many other contemporary English writers. The only important book published at New York in these years was Cadwallader Colden's *History of the Five Indian Nations* (1727), which exhibited none of the charms of the author's private correspondence. Indifferent portraits of Manhattan worthies were made by such "phiz mongers" as Nehemiah Partridge, the Duycincks, and Ralph Goelet. Beyond the visits of Henrietta Johnson and Robert Feke, and the execution of engraved views of New York and Albany, there was little evidence of interest in art at Gotham. Bradford conducted a bookshop where he sold Bibles, Prayer Books, dictionaries, textbooks, and a few works by classic authors. Not until 1739 did he broaden his stock to include the works of Aristotle, Palladio's *Architecture,* and Locke, *On Human Understanding.* Zenger's shop offered much the same selection, as did the new store kept by George Burnet in 1742. Manhattan aristocracy was not bookishly inclined, and the prevalence of two languages still hindered the development of "polite learning" at New York. Toward the close of the period, however, Dutch began to give way to English; "The Dutch tongue declines fast amongst Us, Especially with the Young People," wrote Cornelius van Horne in 1743. "And all Affairs are transact'd in English and that Language prevails Generally Amongst us." [113]

[112] Hamilton, *Itinerarium,* 123; Foote, *Robert Feke,* vii, 38, 41, 45, 63; R. I. Hist. Soc. *Pubs.,* n. s., VII, 235.

[113] *N. Y. Journal,* Aug. 27, 1739; Nov. 25, Dec. 2, 23, 1734; Sept. 27, 1742; Osgood, *Colonies in the Eighteenth Century,* II, 452; *Colden Papers,* I, 271; *N. Y. Gaz.,* Feb. 27, 1727; Dec. 3, 1733; June 25, 1736; Nov. 6, 1738; Aug. 27, 1739; Foote, *Robert Feke,* 37; *Mercury,* Feb. 20, 1722; Morgan, *Early American Painters,* 17, 20.

In 1729 the Reverend Dr. Millington of England bequeathed about a thousand books to the S. P. G., which the Venerable Society "Agreed to fix . . . in the City of New York." The Corporation, after accepting the library, caused the books "to be wiped and Cleaned and an Inventory of them to be taken." In 1730 the authorities fitted up a room in the City Hall as a library, where they placed the Millington and John Sharpe collections under the care of Cornelius Lodge. Unfortunately for the development of general culture at New York, the contents of this public library were largely either theological or controversial.[114]

Music had been popular at Manhattan for many years prior to 1720, and most ladies of proper education played the spinet or harpsichord. Following the introduction of the drama in 1732, public concerts began to be given, one of which, "where there was a great Number of Ladies" present, evoked the following bit of verse:

> Music inchants the list'ning Ear,
> And Beauty charms the Eye.
> What Cruelty these Powers to join:
> These Transports who can bear?
> Oh! let the Sound be less divine,
> Or look ye Nymphs, less fair.

In January, 1736, Mr. Pachelbell, late of Newport and Boston, gave a concert of vocal and instrumental music at Todd's Tavern, "the Harpsichord Part Perform'd by him self. The Songs, Violins, and German Flute by private hands." Success at four shillings a person led to another performance in March, but eight years then elapsed before New York enjoyed another public concert. Though Manhattan in 1742 was awakening to an interest and a desire for literature and the arts, it cannot be said that great actual accomplishments had as yet been made.[115]

The merchant planters of Charles Town were quick to patronize the arts with their newly acquired wealth. Here, however, culture remained too exclusively the possession of the aristocracy, and the middle class, in sharp contrast with conditions in Boston and Philadelphia, had little opportunity to participate in the ornaments of gentle living. The printing press made its initial appearance in Charles Town in 1731, and the next year witnessed the founding of two newspapers, the *South Carolina Weekly Journal* and the *South Carolina Gazette*, the

---

[114] *N. Y. M. C. C.*, III, 474; IV, 10, 25, 145; Keep, *Library in Colonial New York*, 29, 64; Wilson, *Memorial History of New York*, IV, 114.

[115] Governor William Burnet contributed two papers, and James Alexander, one to the Royal Society. *N. Y. Gaz.*, Dec. 31, 1733; Jan. 13, 1736; *N. Y. Journal*, March 8, 1736; *Mercury*, July 25, 1723; *Phil. Trans.*, VII, 49, 142; VIII, 419.

latter established by Thomas Whitmarsh, a "partner" of Franklin, and soon edited by Lewis Timothy, formerly of the Library Company of Philadelphia. Good literature, in small samples, was purveyed in its columns; Timothy printed whole numbers of the *Spectator,* as well as countless imitations thereof, and drew freely upon Pope, Swift and Gay. Booksellers, limners, musicians, teachers and players soon filled its advertising columns. Timothy also kept a bookshop well stocked with Bibles, Prayer Books, Watts' Psalms, histories, plays and primers, where the urbane gentleman might find some modern or ancient author to suit his taste. Book learning, however, was not the forte of the Charlestonians. The town had only a few literary men, like scholarly Chief Justice Trott and Commissary Garden. These and a few others, including Doctors John Lining and Thomas Dale, probably formed the audiences at Mr. Anderson's lectures on Natural Philosophy in 1739.[116]

The several artists who settled in Charles Town found ample patronage from wealthy families. Henrietta Johnson did some of her best work just prior to her death in 1729. B. Roberts arrived in 1735, undertaking landscapes for chimney pieces as well as portraits. Shortly after his death in 1740 his *chef d'œuvre,* the "Prospect and Plan of Charlestown," was placed on sale by his widow, who continued his work of "face painting" and sold pictures and prints. In this year also Jeremiah Theus began his long career as "court painter" of Carolina.[117]

Music and the drama, gregarious arts that may be enjoyed in sociable surroundings, appealed most to the Charlestonians. The drama made its debut in February, 1735, with a performance of Otway's *Orphan,* preceded by a creditable prologue of local composition. Two weeks later the first musical play in America, *Flora, Or Hob in the Well,* was produced at the Courtroom, and six other theatrical performances followed in the course of the winter. The inhabitants built a theater the next summer on Queen Street, where, by subscriptions from wealthy merchants and planters, ten currently popular London plays were produced. The town began its musical career in 1732 with a public concert for the benefit of Mr. Salter at the Council Chamber, and two more such programs rounded out the season. Thereafter subscription concerts, usually followed by elaborate balls, became a regular diversion of the Charles Town gentry. After 1735 a concert of vocal and instrumental music, largely by native talent, was annually held on the twelfth of November, "Being St. Cecilia's

[116] Trott's collections of laws are well known, and he was also a fine Hebrew scholar. Lining corresponded with the Royal Society on physiology and meteorology. *S. C. Gaz.,* April 15, 1732; Sept. 10, 1737; May 19, July 19, 1739; Feb. 2, 1740; Feb. 19, Aug. 22, 1741; *Annals Medical History,* n. s., III, 50; *Phil. Trans.,* VIII, 683.
[117] *Antiquarian,* Sept., 1928, 46; *S. C. Gaz.,* Sept. 2, 1732; Jan. 4, May 17, 1735; July 23, 1737; Feb. 9, Oct. 6, 1740; May 14, 1741.

day." At no other town did music become so popular as in the southern metropolis.[118]

Culturally, the towns added much in these years to the creation of a definitely urban society. The long period of peace afforded opportunities for the development of the arts and graces of gentle living, and all classes shared to some extent in the benefits of this growth. Laboring and artisan classes could now enjoy amusements and educational facilities far beyond the experience of their country brothers. But, as in the days before the proletarian state it is the upper classes who determine the characteristics of any society, it is to their interests and activities that we must look in estimating the cultural achievement of the American towns. The profits of their commercial activities had from the first formed the basis for town cultural life, and in this period their growing wealth brought the arts of "Erudition and Politeness" to their first real flowering in colonial America. Gains from trading enterprises, concentrated in the populousness and sociability of city environments, provided patronage for the theater in Charles Town and New York, and for public musical performances in all towns save Newport. Long time possession of wealth also brought awareness of the good and beautiful things in life, and a desire to cultivate them; so men of "Capacity and Leisure" patronized artists, musicians, and the skilled craftsmen who created the lovely accessories of urban living. These same men began to realize some of the obligations of wealth, endowing libraries, and leaving gifts for civic or educational uses in their wills. Possessors of wealth also sought means to improve, elevate and express themselves, and to that end provided necessary custom for the many teachers of music, painting, languages, dancing, fencing, and polite feminine accomplishments, whose numerous advertisements must have constituted a considerable source of income to the colonial press.

Urban culture, though based largely upon wealth, was also remarkably dependent upon the interchange and companionship of social living. Those arts and amusements especially flourished which could be indulged gregariously, — dancing and dining, music and the theater. Nor were science and speculation mere cloistered scholarship. The Physical Club of Boston, the Philosophical Society of Newport, and Franklin's Junto testify to the contrary. Moreover, the scholarly work of this period was not the product of rural contemplation, but more

---

[118] The first St. Cecilia's Day concert was for the benefit of Charles Theodore Pachelbell, who left Boston to become organist at Trinity Church, Newport, in 1733, and then drifted on via New York to Charles Town, where he both played and taught. *S. C. Gaz.*, April 15, 1732; Feb. 8, 1735; Oct. 23, 1736; Sept. 17, 1737; Oct. 4, 1742; Ravenel, *Eliza Pinckney*, 31; Willis, *Charleston Stage*, 10, 33; Sonneck, *Early Concert Life*, 11, 13.

usually the mature mental recreation of active men of affairs. Retiring from the slave trade, a Newport merchant took up the study of experimental botany; Colden, Logan and Trott produced their scholarly writings during and following active political and business careers. The sociable nature of the intellectual achievement of these years is eloquent evidence of the development of an urban society.

The fact that in these years administrative changes were drawing the colonies closer within the imperial commercial system, and the improved communications which their increasing trade fostered and rendered necessary, intensified the relation with the metropolis and made colonial urban culture provincial in the best sense of the word. Practically every intellectual fashion of the Mother Country found prompt and distinct echoes in the colonies. In religion the freethinking and skepticism of eighteenth century England was coupled with a colonial backwash from the sweeping tides of Wesleyan revivalism. Colonial scientists must have been indeed lonely but for the correspondence and inspiration of their European colleagues. Colonial town-dwellers dressed in London styles, reproduced the taste of fashionable London in their homes, organized clubs after London models, and where the theater appeared presented London plays on colonial boards. Nowhere did Addison, Steele and Pope have more sincere admirers than on the western shores of the Atlantic. It followed that when colonials applied themselves to creation, in literature, in the fine arts, or in the lesser arts of domestic life, the results were highly imitative and unoriginal. Yet this was the inheritance out of which a native art and literature were to spring, and cannot therefore be dismissed merely as the slavish and often weak reflection of a noble model. The towns made possible the inspiration of this close connection with England, and there the first faltering imitations of British fashions took place. There, too, when the colonials should have learned their vocabulary and mastered their tools, the first signs of original accomplishment would appear. In the meantime, in the primary cultural achievement of these years, the inclusion of American society in the stream of world events, the towns played the paramount role.

Cultural interchange between various urban communities constitutes a distinctive development in this period. It too was to some extent dependent upon commercial advance, since only improved roads and better postal service made it possible. In earlier years we have seen how the most skilled artisans constituted a migratory class, drifting from one town to another in search of the greatest demand for their work. Now, with the increasing sophistication of city life, and the appearance of representatives of the fine arts and purveyors of highly specialized services, this tendency becomes more marked. The itinerant George Brownell, with his repertoire of elementary instruction, needlework and dancing, Henry Holt, and Charles Theodore Pachelbell are representatives of that peripatetic group who peddled instruction in the arts and graces of polite society from town to town. The printers had early shown their adventurous spirit in seeking new fields of endeavor, and by 1740 much of the printing and journalism in each of the five towns may be accounted for by members or connections of the Bradford and Franklin families. In this period, too, artists traveled from town to town, seeking commissions where patronage was best. There followed a closer intellectual relationship between the towns, and a greater likeness in their cultural development, which was furthered by increasing contacts between the scholarly men of each town, now very nearly as close as the commercial connections of the merchants. Colden and Douglass were but two of many who sought intellectual companionship despite the obstacle of distance. Much interchange occurred between the various discussion, philanthropic and fraternal societies. As a result, there was now less gap between the cultural status of various towns. Each community contained a group of cultivated, scholarly men, able to speak with and understand one another, whatever their geographical residence. By the end of the period it was possible for an educated gentleman like Dr. Alexander Hamilton to travel the length of the colonies with letters in his pocket to the cultural leaders in each community, to converse and exchange ideas with them, and enter into their discussions, activities and amusements. Nothing better indicates the emergence of a definite urban society.

The towns themselves were aware of their distinctness and proud of their social maturity. The first town on the American continent to observe its centennial did so in this period, and Newport's first hundred years were celebrated by John Callender with a literary memorial of no mean capacity. But these communities also realized that though they had conquered the first physical demands of living in a new world, they had yet to meet the real challenge of intellectual achievement. "In the Rise of States," wrote a Boston correspondent to the *Rhode Island Gazette* of October 25, 1732, "the Arts of War and Peace, Agriculture, and the like, are of necessity more attended to than Erudition and Politeness, that comes on of course afterwards, when the *Golden Age* succeeds the *Iron*. So that instead of wondering why our Country has produced so few good Writers, and why those which have been produced, have not always given a general *Satisfaction,* we may rather admire at the contrary."

ONE HUNDRED YEARS OF URBAN GROWTH

The first hundred years of town history on the American continent witnessed the foundation and gradual development of a truly urban society. The story of American life is customarily regarded as a compound of sectional histories, and in the early colonial period two sections are commonly considered, — the tidewater and the frontier. Yet the tidewater was itself divided, and if we consider the sections as social and psychological rather than as purely geographical entities, it is possible to distinguish three of them, — the rural, agricultural society of the countryside; the restless, advancing society of the frontier; and the urban, commercial society of the larger seaports. Beginning as small specks in the wilderness, the five communities grew from tiny villages into towns, and finally attained the status of small cities. With other village communities of similar interests and out- look which multiplied and grew in the eighteenth century, they emerged as a social and economic "section" extending the length of the Atlantic seaboard, and exhibiting definite urban characteristics in striking contrast to rural farming districts and wilder regions of the frontier. Life in urban areas produced its own peculiar problems to be faced, and the urban viewpoint, based upon continuous close contacts with Europe, derived less from agriculture than from trade. Com- mercially minded town society looked to the East rather than the West, and was destined from the first to serve as the connecting link between colonial America and its Old World parents.

The future of the colonial towns became immediately evident from the conditions surrounding their birth. Designed as trading com- munities, they were established on sites most favorable for the pur- suit of commerce. They were the western outposts of European com- mercial expansion in the seventeenth century. City-dwellers from the Old World formed the larger proportion of early town populations, and from the start commercial relations with England or Holland were maintained. Most significantly, the founding process occurred at a time when western Europe, under Dutch and English leadership, was gradually outgrowing and casting off the limitations of medieval feudal economy. Colonial towns grew to maturity in the era of world ex- pansion attending the emergence of modern capitalism, and being new communities, with few irrevocably established customs or traditions, they frequently adapted themselves to the economic drift with more

467

ease and readiness than did the older cities of England. Moreover, the colonizing movement was itself an expression of early capitalistic activity. It called forth organized rather than individual efforts and resources, created new and wider markets for economic development, and opened up seemingly unlimited territories for imperialistic exploitation. It thus produced a marked effect upon Old World economy, accelerating the breakdown of local units of business, and facilitating the formation of larger and more complex organizations of commerce and finance.

The problems which confronted town-dwellers in America were not only those of urban communities, but of a pioneer society as well. Urban development depends largely upon community wealth, and upon the willingness of the group to devote portions of it to projects for civic betterment, or to consent to taxation for this purpose. To a considerable extent the nature of town governments and the extent of authority vested in them conditioned the expenditure of town wealth for community enterprises. Here the colonists were hampered by the traditional nature of the charters of medieval English municipal corporations, whose limitations ill accorded with circumstances in seventeenth and eighteenth century America, especially with the imperious demands for expansion and immediate activity in the New World. In New England towns a new political organization, the town meeting, developed, which exhibited considerable efficiency in the handling of urban problems. This institution was more immediately susceptible to social wants and requirements than were the aristocratic, self-perpetuating corporations founded in America after the example of English municipal governments. Its greater powers of local taxation, and the fact that it placed the spending of public moneys and the enactment of civic ordinances in the hands of those directly affected by these operations, made it a far more effective form of government for dealing with community problems. These problems were the greater, because in the first century of their history the five colonial seaports enjoyed a much more rapid physical growth than did the cities of contemporary Europe. The individual enterprise of American town-dwellers, and the commercial expansion and prosperity they achieved, aided in the solution of these problems of town living, but much of the efficiency and success which attended their efforts may be attributed to the emergence in the New World of a relatively high sense of civic responsibility in the early eighteenth century, at a time when public consciousness in Europe had receded to an extremely low ebb.

The towns were primarily commercial communities seeking treasure by foreign trade, and their economic vitality and commercial demands led to their early breaking the narrow bonds of medieval eco-

nomic practice to forge ahead on uncharted but highly profitable commercial adventures. All five, during their first century, developed
from simple manorial organizations, completely dependent upon European connections, into full-fledged commercial centers, only partially
tied to England, and in many cases competing with British cities for a
share of imperial traffic. Boston entered early into the West Indian
provision trade, thereby setting an example for other American commercial communities. Soon Massachusetts mariners were seeking to
monopolize the colonial carrying traffic in ships of their own building,
and the profits of carrier and middleman became the basis of the Bay
town's prosperity. Her priority in this field gave her an advantage
which other seaports did not begin to overcome until the fourth
decade of the eighteenth century. A further foundation for urban
economic prosperity lay in the existence of an expanding frontier
society with its great need for manufactured products. This made possible an earlier development of the towns as distributing centers for a
wide hinterland than was the case with English cities like Bristol,
Norwich and Exeter, and became in this first century as important a
factor in the economic growth of New York, Philadelphia and Charles
Town as in that of the New England metropolis. As a producer of
staple goods for exchange in trade, Boston, with its limited back country was at a disadvantage. More fortunate were New York with its
flour and furs, Philadelphia, with its great staples of wheat, meat and
lumber, and Charles Town, which after 1710 found prosperity in
the important South Carolina crops of rice and indigo. Eventually
the communities enjoying this sound economic backing rose to threaten
the supremacy of Boston in colonial trade, while Newport and Philadelphia cut heavily into the Bay town's West India commerce. In the
eighteenth century also Newport attained importance in shipbuilding
and the slave trade. By 1742 Boston merchants were facing a period
of relative decline, while their competitors in other colonial towns
found the volume and profits of their traffic steadily mounting.

Continual increase in the volume of colonial trade and enlargement
of the territory served by the towns led to greater complexity in commercial relations. In the early years merchants performed all types of
business, but toward 1700 their functions began to be more specialized.
Retail merchandising having definitely emerged by 1700, the great
merchant now dealt chiefly with larger operations of exporting, importing and wholesaling, leaving much of the small trade to the shopkeeper. Demands of trade had by 1710 necessitated the issuance of
paper currency in most of the colonies, and the establishment of the
colonial post office to serve intercolonial communication. Growing
business further led to the creation of insurance offices and some ex-

tension of credit facilities. Profits from trade, originally completely absorbed in shipbuilding ventures and industries subsidiary to shipping, now began to create a surplus which sought investment in land, or, in some communities, in the development of certain forms of manufacturing.

Economic prosperity thus made possible the rise of colonial cities. It led to physical expansion of town boundaries, and facilitated dealing with urban problems by corporate effort. Wealth wrung from trade, more than any other single factor, determined the growth of a town society, in which urban amusements and a colonial culture might thrive. This is not, however, to force the history of urban America within the narrow bounds of an exclusively economic interpretation. Social and intellectual development are dependent upon and conditioned by economic progress, but they are not its necessary and inevitable result. They are altered, encouraged or stifled by the action and influence of material forces, but they are not necessarily caused or even initiated solely by economic factors.

When we consider American urban society, apart from its economic aspects, we find it characterized by certain problems affecting it as a unit, and with which as a unit it had to deal. Such problems in general, or collective attempts for their control and regulation, are either absent from or unimportant in rural or frontier societies, but in the case of our urban section they are present, in rudimentary form at least, from its inception. They persist and grow with the maturing of that section, and the means taken for dealing with them further differentiate the urban from other types of society.

Logically, the first of these problems to appear are the physical, and of these the most immediate was housing. As in rural regions this remained for the most part an individual problem, and there are only a few cases on record where even indirectly, by sale or subdivision of land or by encouragement of artisans, the community stepped in to relieve a housing shortage. On the other hand, the laying out and maintaining of a highway system constituted a problem, perhaps the first, which transcended private initiative. Not that the community at any time scorned the assistance of private enterprise; a favorite device, at Boston and elsewhere, throughout the colonial era, was by remission of taxes or grant of other privileges to encourage individuals to open up streets and undertake paving operations for public use at their own charge. But from the beginning public authorities indicated the location of roads, supervised the opening up of new ones, ordered their clearing or partial paving by abutters, and strove to prevent encroachments upon them. At Philadelphia and Charles Town, where some prior power had surveyed and planned the thoroughfares, the first task of local authorities was light; it was more arduous in other communities, where there was no preliminary plan, and where the design had constantly to be expanded and altered to keep pace with town growth. The problems accompanying the mere existence of a highway system, — paving, cleaning and upkeep, — called for full exercise of municipal authority. Sometimes the community exacted from each inhabitant a yearly amount of labor on the streets; in other cases it hired this labor and paid for it outright. In either case it had to levy special taxes, for materials or labor or both. To insure some cleanliness in the streets, it passed mandatory ordinances restricting the conduct of townsmen, impressed the services of carters, and employed public funds for the hire of scavengers. Further to protect the public ways, it restricted and regulated the traffic upon them, especially the weight of cart loads and the width of their wheels. Less necessary but desirable improvements in the highways, like the construction of drains, first came about through private demand and initiative, but as the civic power matured and public funds became available, these too became public functions and responsibilities. In either the municipal or the individual approach to highway problems the towns had good precedent in the Mother Country. In actual execution, especially with regard to refinements like paving and drainage, they seem in some cases to have gone beyond contemporary English cities. With a few exceptions, this generalization does not apply to the corporation governed towns, or to the unfortunately ungoverned metropolis of South Carolina.

Highways may be said to constitute the most rudimentary of public utilities, but there were others, — bridges, wharves, and engineering projects, — of which colonial townsfolk almost immediately felt the need. In the beginning, while municipal authority was politically and financially feeble, these were almost solely the product of private enterprise, but with the gradual tendency of town development they became increasingly matters of public concern. Following Old World precedent, bridges were conceived as parts of the highway system, and hence undoubtedly under public control, but they were usually constructed and operated by private persons or companies, under grant from local or provincial authorities. As the century progressed, in a few cases, notably at Philadelphia and Boston, town governments directly managed the operation and upkeep of bridges. Land reclamation projects, and harbor facilities like lighthouses, pursued a similar history. In the case of wharves, they were either a municipal or a private concern. Most towns maintained a minimum of public docking facilities, while more ambitious wharf projects, like the Long Wharves of Boston and Newport, were only within the capacity of private capital.

At Philadelphia public docking facilities were so excellent as to discourage employment of private capital in their erection; at New York, so poor as to require it. Toward the end of the era, when the demands of trade began to make regular transportation between communities desirable, stage and freight routes, too, were operated by private capital, under license, usually from the provincial government.

Fire constitutes a threat especially dangerous to urban communities, and as buildings in colonial towns were from the beginning placed close together, its imminence was immediately felt. The combatting and prevention of fire called forth more than individual efforts from the start. Municipal ordinances required the keeping of fire fighting equipment by all townsmen, regulated their chimneys, forbade bonfires, fireworks, and the housing of explosives in crowded areas. Public authorities had also to make direct outlays for fire fighting equipment of their own, and hire companies for its care and operation. In Boston, Philadelphia and Newport private societies for the protection of property during fires were organized to supplement public agencies. Similarly, water supply for fire uses was a matter of public concern and regulation. Boston, with its crowded streets and buildings of inflammable construction, and its willingness to spend public money and energy for public welfare, was in general far in the forefront with regard to its fire defenses, but by the end of the first century all towns possessed fire engines of the latest European model, and fire fighting regulations equal or superior to those of the average English town.

A distinctive urban function grew in part out of the fire hazards of crowded sections, — the enactment of building regulations. Only public authority could specify the nature of legal building materials as did Boston after the fire of 1679 and the South Carolina Assembly after the Charles Town fire of 1740. Exercise of municipal powers was also necessary to prevent imperfect construction and dangerous neglect of town chimneys and hearths. In addition, conditions of urban congestion led to party-wall regulations like those of Boston and Philadelphia.

Another, more subtle class of problems, those which involved the personal relationships of inhabitants, affected town society from its inception. Intensified by the peculiar conditions of urban life, they required collective rather than individual efforts and powers for their control. Old World experience had taught town-dwellers the immediate need for means of preserving the public peace in settled communities, and the early appearance of constables in all towns supplied the traditional response to that need. For their security after nightfall the towns appointed bellmen or watchmen of varying degrees of efficiency. New York, after developing a highly effective nocturnal police in the seventeenth century, allowed this institution to languish from unwillingness to devote the necessary public funds thereto; other towns were slower in supplying the need, though somewhat more successful by the end of the first century. Efficiency of the watch was in direct ratio to the availability of public funds for its support, — impressment of a citizen's watch having revealed its inadequacy by the turn of the century, — and here the New England towns, with their powers of local taxation, were at a distinct advantage. There are numerous instances, during periods of unusual danger or disturbance like wars or epidemics, when the towns entirely failed in their efforts to preserve nocturnal peace, and their functions had to be taken over by the military arm of the provincial government.

Existence of crime and disorder early became a community concern in urban settlements. Here invitations to lawbreaking existed in the inequalities of wealth and opportunity, and materials for its perpetration in the diverse and unruly elements of town and seaport society. The concentration of people, many of them hardworked and underprivileged, also made for mob disorders, which increased in violence and frequency with the growth of the towns. Presence of sailors, blacks, foreigners, paupers, unpopular religious sects, interlopers in trade, profiteers, and rival political factions, all provided increasing incentives for disorder and violence as the period progressed. Town society clearly soon passed beyond the stage where individual efforts or the force of public opinion could deal with this problem; rather it required the sanctions of the law. Provincial governments passed legislation, and municipal authorities enacted ordinances outlawing offenses against society. Riot acts were drawn up by colonial assemblies, and the local constabulary did its best to round up and confine the perpetrators of disorder and violence. In general, the towns could do little to remove the causes of criminality, and the solution of this peculiarly vexing problem of city life remained as remote in the seventeenth and eighteenth centuries as today.

For punishments, colonial authorities followed a number of Old World precedents, favoring especially the speediest and least expensive methods, — fines, floggings, public humiliation, restitution of stolen goods, and, occasionally, mutilation. In general, their criminal codes were less brutal than those of contemporary Europe. Efforts to make the whole community a partner in the work of law enforcement appeared in the division with informers of the proceeds from fines. Prisons were still generally places of detention for those awaiting trial, though imprisonment as punishment for crime seems to have become more widespread as the period advanced, and save in the case of debtors was probably somewhat more in use in the colonies than in the Old World. The frequency of jail breaks indicates the inefficiency of all colonial prisons, and their inadequacy suggests the absence of more vicious criminal types that troubled older societies. Yet colonial prisons were probably no more inadequate than those of contemporary England, and certainly far less squalid and brutal. Save in the case of Philadelphia in the eighteenth century, the rudimentary penology of the times made no distinction between various classes of offenders, and absence of prison facilities led to frequent misuse of alms and workhouses, wherein pauper and lawbreaker were housed together.

Offenses against the moral and ethical standards which society imposes appear more flagrant in the comparative populousness and congestion of urban environments, and early forced themselves upon the attention of colonial communities. In addition, the psychology of the times made many aspects of the regulation of conduct, manners and dress a legitimate province for the public authority. Early appearance of prostitution in the towns shocked authorities into decreeing harsh penalties for it and similar offenses. With its increasing prevalence in a society which included growingly diverse and uncontrollable elements, they seem everywhere to have become less concerned with the actual offense than with the fear lest the illegitimate offspring become charges to the community. Drunkenness was a prevailing vice, and in all towns the authorities and the better elements fought to eradicate it. Excellent tavern legislation in several of the towns reduced this offense to a minimum, but illegal sale of liquor, and misuse of the legitimate product, continued to baffle municipal authority throughout the period. Sabbath legislation in every town, — as strict in the Anglican South as in Puritan New England, — attempted to insure the sacred character of the Lord's Day. Gambling, card-playing, loitering, idleness, extravagance in dress and behavior, and evidence of frivolity came under the ban of public regulation, either through colony or municipal authority, or as at Philadelphia through the dominant religious group. Especially at Boston and Philadelphia many seemingly innocent amusements suffered from the disapproval of a stern and narrow religion, which served as a powerful and useful supplement to the civic power.

The existence and effects of crime and immorality are intensified in urban communities; so, too, the problem of pauperism. Reports of travelers as to the absence of poverty from colonial towns can only be regarded as comparatively true, for in each town numbers of those unable to care for themselves soon constituted a problem of which the community had to take cognizance. The generally excellent methods with which the towns met this problem indicate a considerable sense of civic maturity and responsibility. New York and Charles Town

favored the out-relief method through most of the period, but Boston
and Philadelphia had by the end of the century well-regulated and practically self-supporting workhouses, and Newport maintained an adequate almshouse. Considerable direct relief had to be granted, especially at Boston, and in all towns save New York private or religious
organizations supplemented the public work of poor relief. Methods
to forestall the growth of poverty were devised, such as compulsory
apprenticeship of poor children, exclusion of strangers without obvious means of livelihood, and, especially in the New England towns,
restriction of immigration. In times of particular stress special de-
vices had to be resorted to, as the distribution of corn or firewood, or
a temporary embargo on export of necessary commodities. At Boston,
where the problem of poverty became acute in the 1670's and was never
thereafter absent, careful registration of all aliens and dependents prevailed, and a public granary was maintained.

The general health, which in rural regions may be privately cared
for, early became in urban communities a matter for public concern,
and municipal ordinances soon restricted the conduct of inhabitants in
matters which might affect the general well-being. Location of wells
and privies, and of slaughterhouses and tan pits which might become
public nuisances, removal of dumps and disposal of refuse were all
subjects of municipal regulation. Similarly, public authorities directed
inhabitants in their behavior during epidemics, and enacted quarantine regulations in an attempt to prevent visitations of infectious
disease. Toward the end of the century excellent isolation hospitals
appeared in several of the towns, erected and operated by the municipality. Despite failure in this period of all attempts to regulate
the practice of medicine by town or colony, the medical profession in
the towns attained a relatively high development for the times.

In their approach to the physical and social problems of urban life
the towns were imitators, not originators. The townsmen came to
America with a fund of European experience from which they seldom
deviated, and new methods as they employed them had usually first to
cross the Atlantic. Poor relief and tavern legislation were directly
imported from Great Britain, and the towns might conceivably have
done better with their police problem had not Old World precedent
served them so exclusively as a guide. Yet it may be said that in
several cases there are distinct improvements in the thoroughness with
which old methods were employed, and which may usually be traced
to the individual civic pride of townsmen, reflected in their municipal
governments. This is especially true of communities which enjoyed
the town meeting form of government, where, as we have seen, the
direct demands of townspeople could effect greater thoroughness and

efficiency in dealing with town business, but even in the corporation governments of America there is less indifference to the public welfare than may be noted in contemporary England or Europe. Visitors were impressed with the excellence of poor relief at Boston and Philadelphia, and with Philadelphia's model prison. Fire defences in the towns were a combination of English and Dutch examples, and, especially at Boston, probably unsurpassed for their time. Solution of urban problems in colonial towns was continually hampered by lack of public funds or of necessary authority for obtaining them, — the sad decline of New York's excellent watch is an illustration, — but it was assisted, where public power failed, either politically or financially, by an encouraging growth of civic consciousness among private individuals and non-political organizations. Establishment of private agencies for charity, education, fire protection, improvement of morals, and the like, and the appearance of individual benefactors to the public welfare of the community, in an age not distinguished for civic virtue or interest, is a remarkable and significant accomplishment of town society in colonial America.

Having as they all did a common model and experience, colonial towns exhibit a remarkable similarity in the solution of their urban problems. There are many instances of the failure of a community to provide the usual and accepted necessary solution, but, with the possible exception of Philadelphia's eighteenth century prison, hardly a single example of the development by one town of a unique institution. By the time that local divergences from the original plan might have been expected to appear, communication had sufficiently improved to permit of one town's borrowing from the successful experience of another. The same holds true for privately initiated supplements of municipal endeavor. The Scot's Charitable Society and the Fire Society appear in Boston, copied from European models, and at a later date are further copied by other American towns. In the eighteenth century, because of its long experience in dealing with urban problems, the greater efficiency of its form of government, and its willingness to spend public money for the public good, Boston became the great example, with respect to municipal institutions, for other towns on the continent, but it enjoyed no monopoly of this function. New Yorkers had the fire defences of Philadelphia held up to them as a model, Bostonians were shamed by the excellence of Philadelphia's market, while Charlestonians tried to fashion their city government after the example of the corporation of New York. By the end of the period under review this inter-city exchange of experience had resulted in a striking similarity in municipal institutions, as well as a fairly uniform level of their development. Boston, for the reasons enumerated above, was probably still somewhat in advance in matters of social and material concern, though with its humanitarian agencies Philadelphia was running a close second. Charles Town, within the limits of its governmental incapacity, dealt in fairly efficient fashion with its problems; at Newport, a lesser development of these problems had not yet necessitated any great display of urban consciousness. Even at New York, where political factionalism, a selfish corporation, and the difficulty of amalgamating two languages and nationalities prevented a consistent and devoted attempt to solve the problems of urban living, a comparison of its municipal life with that of older provincial cities of the British Empire would not have resulted in discredit to the former.

The accumulation of economic resources and their concentration in urban units, their direction in commercial ventures which attracted and supported large populations within these units, and the problems of providing for the physical and social well-being of those who thus became city-dwellers, all these aspects of urban development succeeded in bringing forth in America a distinctive society. In constitution, spiritual life, recreational activities, and intellectual pursuits it differed from types of society to be found in other sections of the continent. In respect neither to national origins nor to economic status of their inhabitants did the towns long remain homogeneous. Settled originally by people of the same nation, usually of the same locality, they soon came to include children of other European countries and of another race. Early in their history there could be found small groups of Scots in Boston, French Huguenots in Boston, New York and Charles Town, Welsh in Philadelphia, and a few Jews in every town. Many Germans settled in the 1680's in the environs of Philadelphia, and New York from the time of the first English occupation presented the problem of two peoples, each with their own language, schools and churches, living side by side under government by the numerically weaker group. This incipient cosmopolitanism flowered with the renewed immigration of the early eighteenth century, when all towns received numbers of Scotch-Irish, and the middle and southern cities, especially Philadelphia, large accessions of German exiles. For the most part these strangers were allowed to settle peaceably in colonial towns, whose economic expansion enabled them easily to absorb the newcomers, and though recent arrivals seldom attained social recognition or overcame the barrier of language where it existed, still there was little nativism and small emphasis on the superior advantages of Anglo-Saxon nativity. Such bountiful immigration did, however, lead to many restrictions, especially in the north, where the labor market was well supplied and the poor rates overburdened, to establishment of special churches and social organizations, and in Philadelphia, at least, to common use of the German language in business transactions. By far the greater problem was created by the presence of African Negroes in all towns. In Boston and Newport, where they were used mainly as house servants, and where many of them were free, the problem was negligible. They were subject to various discriminatory rules, such as those which required them to work out their obligations to the community in menial labor rather than by watch or militia duty. But at New York and Charles Town their greater numbers kept constantly present the fear of servile insurrection. At the former town they were the unfortunate objects of such waves of hysteria as the Negro Conspiracy of 1741, and at Charles Town, where they at times equalled the white population in numbers, a severe slave code kept them in subjection.

Social stratification further differentiated urban society from the easy democracy of the back country, where any man might own land and all must work with their hands. Distinctions between the well-to-do and the not-so-rich were perhaps relatively unimportant in the beginning, when society was still so fluid that luck or diligence might elevate a man above his fellows in a short time, but with the accumulation of wealth and economic power in the hands of a few, and the coming in of numbers of artisans, indentured servants and immigrant laborers, class lines tightened and society crystallized into easily recognizable categories of better, middling, and poorer sorts. In all towns native aristocracies were commercial in origin, even at Charles Town where they later sought land as a basis for social distinction. They consolidated their position by means of wealth from successful trading ventures, collecting thereby social prestige and political influence. They lived grandly, dressed gaily, kept horses and coaches, and employed the labor of the less fortunate. The commercial, political and social leadership of the towns was in their hands. Later, as urban life became more sophisticated, they contributed to the development of secular amusements and to the relaxation of earlier strict moral codes. They gained further brilliance by alliance with representatives of British officialdom in America. Below them the middle class, professional people, tradesmen and artisans, lived comfortably but more plainly, enjoying in prosperous times many of the good things of life, but in hard times feeling the pinch far more than did their wealthy neighbors. Steady laborers might know periods of prosperity, but many of them could be squeezed out by the vicissitudes of the economic cycle. They performed the menial labor of the towns, enlisted as common seamen, and constituted a group from which much urban poverty and disorder were recruited. Negro and Indian slaves, mere unprivileged pieces of property, rounded out the caste system as it developed itself in metropolitan America.

Save Newport, each of the towns had originally been dedicated to a dominant Protestant religious organization, but after a century of growth diversity, indifference and actual unbelief came to characterize the religious scene. The complexities of town society were in large measure responsible for this development, for different national or social groups soon evolved their favored sects and denominations. When the ministry could no longer speak with one voice to all elements of town populations, it lost much of its influence, both social and clerical, and the appearance of agnosticism and irreverence was rapid. In general, at the end of the first century, Anglicanism was in all towns the religion of officials and aristocrats; Quakerism and Congregationalism, which had once in their own localities enjoyed this favored position, had joined the ranks of middle class religions, which further included Baptists and Presbyterians; while for the common man a religious refuge was just appearing in the enthusiastic, emotional revivalism of Whitefield. Absence of devotion penetrated all classes; the poorer sort were largely indifferent to the attractions of religion, freethinking characterized such middle class groups as Franklin's Junto, and aristocrats indulged a fashionable Deism. In contrast, a stern and uniform religious fundamentalism for a much longer time characterized the rural communities of the countryside.

Much of their power the quasi-established churches had attained in an age when religious concerns so dominated men's thoughts as to exclude many other aspects of life. But the commercial success of colonial towns altered this singleness of outlook by acquainting townsmen with the delights of secular grandeurs and providing money for their enjoyment. As the age advanced the church step by step gave way before the institution of more attractive secular recreations. Most successful of these, appearing very early and appealing to all classes, was the tavern. Instituted originally as a necessary convenience for strangers and travelers, it soon showed itself to be the resort of all classes of townsmen, the place where they conducted much of their business and where much of their social life was passed. In the eighteenth century coffee houses became as in England the rendezvous of business men and the scene of many commercial transactions. Taverns served not only as places of casual conviviality, but as headquarters for the multifarious clubs into which town social life gradually organized itself. They also offered opportunities for cards, billiards and games of chance, and housed the many traveling shows and exhibitions which the better transportation of the eighteenth century made possible.

Games, contests, tavern recreations, and public celebration of holidays constituted the entertainment of the common man, but for the aristocrats mounting wealth and sophistication were creating more elaborate forms of amusement. To the hearty private dinners and occasional excursions of early days succeeded great public banquets, dances and balls, musical entertainments, and finally, in two of the towns, dramatic presentations. Gradually the commercial aristocracy of the towns, combining with royal officials, evolved a society whose entertainments were artificial, costly, sophisticated and exclusive. But for aristocrat or common man, the vicarious amusements that money could buy, and their variety and attractiveness, differentiated town society from that of the countryside with its simpler, spontaneous pleasures, and tended to draw town-dwellers away from a strict and narrow conception of life as a duty and a task. Copied as they were from the recreations of English society, they also tended to make social life in the towns more like that of the metropolis.

A final characteristic of town society was that it offered to its members a wider intellectual opportunity and challenge than was possible to the man whose life was bounded by his fields or by the hard necessity of clearing away the forest. From earliest childhood opportunities for education, free or otherwise, were open to the town-dweller. Especially was this true of the poor, whose educational needs were largely cared for by religious societies, charity schools, or compulsory apprenticeship. This last system enabled youth of the poorer classes to equip themselves for a trade. In other strata of society young men might fit themselves for business at private vocational schools, for a place in society with private masters, or for higher education for a learned profession at public or private Latin schools or with a private tutor. Young women, too, in the towns might purchase instruction in various fields of learning or merely in the polite arts of feminine society. Also, in the northern English towns, Boston, Newport and Philadelphia, there was from the start a tradition of scholarliness and of respect for intellectual achievement. It followed that a society so trained, constantly in contact by ship with Europe, was alive and ready to adopt the intellectual fashions of the age. Hence, in this first century of American life, most of the intellectual activity, in science, literature and the arts, and what intellectual progress there was, took place in the towns. Only there were there material and opportunity for such activity. And rather than regard the results of that progress with condescension, we should, with James Franklin's subscriber, wonder at the contrary. In comparison with the Augustan Age of eighteenth century London, intellectual and social life in the colonies may seem bare and sterile, but in comparison with the intellectual barrenness of provincial life in England itself, its cultivation and sophistication appear revealed. Urban culture in the eighteenth century was provincial culture at its best, nourished during this period of faltering imitation, which had to precede that of native accomplishment, by constant contact with the vital intellectual currents of England and Europe.

In these various ways the developments of a hundred years of life under relatively urban conditions created a society at once distinct from that of rural regions, whether tidewater or back country, and even further removed from that of the westward reaching frontier. The communal attitude toward the solution of the physical and social problems of diversified populations dwelling together in close propinquity, and the constantly widening outlook which material progress, commercial expansion, and contact with the larger world of affairs made possible, were its distinguishing characteristics. In general, this society was more cooperative and social, less individualistic in its outlook toward problems of daily life, far more susceptible to outside influences and examples, less aggressively independent than the society of frontier America. At the same time it was more polished, urbane, and sophisticated, more aware of fashion and change, more sure of itself and proud of its achievements, more able to meet representatives from the outside world as equals without bluster or apology than the rural society of the colonial back country. Because its outlook was eastward rather than westward, it was more nearly a European society in an American setting. It had appropriated various points on the American continent and transformed them as nearly as possible into likenesses of what it had known at home. It was itself less transformed in the process than might have been expected, because the contact with the homeland never ceased, but rather increased with the passage of years. Its importance to American life as a whole was therefore great. Here were centers of the transit of civilization from Old World to New, — five points at the least through which currents of world thought and endeavor might enter, to be like other commodities assimilated and redistributed throughout the countryside. It was well for the future of national America that its society should not remain completely rural and agricultural, isolated and self-sufficient, ignorant of outside developments and distrustful of new ideas from abroad, as it might well have done had there been no cities. Instead, the five towns provided the nucleus for a wider and more gracious living in the New World.

BIBLIOGRAPHY

The materials used in the preparation of this book are, for the most part, well known to students of colonial history; and I do not, therefore, propose to indulge in what a seventeenth century scholar once called a paroxysm of citation. Rather is it my desire to give the curious reader a few sailing directions by which he may make any one or all five of the colonial seaports. Any scrap of evidence, physical or documentary, surviving the period studied is potentially valuable to the social historian, but, as my footnotes abundantly show, town records, province laws and records, precious newspapers, maps, prints and personal materials, such as letters, diaries and journals have yielded the bulk of my information.

The most useful and accessible guides to the manuscript and printed materials for the history of the five towns follow:

1. The *Card Catalogues* of the Massachusetts Historical Society (Boston); the Harvard College Library (Cambridge); the Newport Historical Society; the Rhode Island Historical Society (Providence); the New York Public Library; the New York Historical Society; the Historical Society of Pennsylvania (Philadelphia); the Library Company of Philadelphia; the Library of Congress; and the Charleston Library Society.

2. The *Publications* of the state and local historical societies of Massachusetts, Rhode Island, New York, Pennsylvania, and South Carolina, the best guide to which is still A. P. C. Griffin, "Bibliography of American Historical Societies" (American Historical Association, *Annual Report*, 1905, vol. II).

3. *Special Bibliographies* dealing with materials for the five towns: Clarence S. Brigham, "Bibliography of American Newspapers, 1690–1820" (American Antiquarian Society, *Proceedings*, new series, 1916 ff.), is essential; Clarence S. Brigham, "Report on the Archives of Rhode Island" (American Historical Association, *Annual Report*, 1903, vol. I, pp. 606–609), for the town records of Newport; H. V. Ames and A. E. McKinley, "Report on the Public Archives of the City of Philadelphia" (American Historical Association, *Annual Report*, 1902, II); Charles E. Hammett, *A Contribution to the Bibliography and Literature of Newport* (Newport, 1887); Charles R. Hildeburn, *The Issues of the Pennsylvania Press: 1685–1784* (2 vols., Philadelphia, 1885); *Massachusetts Broadsides, 1639–1800* (Massachusetts Historical Society, *Collections*, vol. 74); Edson L. Whitney, "Bibliography of the Colonial History of South Carolina" (American Historical Association, *Annual Report*, 1894, pp. 563–586).

4. *Town Histories* are only too frequently works of filial piety, narrowly provincial and uncritical, seeking to establish "firsts" for the community in question. The great histories of Boston, New York, and Philadelphia, by Justin Winsor, James Grant Wilson, and Thompson Westcott are exceptions to this statement. Westcott's monumental *History of Philadelphia* calls for special comment. First published serially in the *Philadelphia Sunday Despatch,*

483

1867–1884, it was condensed and issued in book form as J. T. Scharf and T. Westcott, *History of Philadelphia* (3 vols., Philadelphia, 1884). The Historical Society of Pennsylvania has collected two sets of the original: one in 5 vols., unpaged and listed by chapters; the other in 32 vols., illustrated with original documents, pictures, and drawings by David McNeely Stauffer. Unique among works on early American cities is I. N. Phelps Stokes, *The Iconography of Manhattan Island* (6 vols., New York, 1915–1928), which combines cartography, iconography, collections of extracts from a wide range of sources and a running historical account with exquisite bookmaking. There are no histories of Charles Town or Newport worthy of the name. There is little of value in George Champlin Mason's gossipy *Reminiscences of Newport* (Newport, 1884), but the author presented specially bound copies, each containing different sets of original manuscripts and prints, to the Newport Historical Society, the Rhode Island Historical Society, and the New York Public Library.

5. *Prints and Maps* form a primary source which has received too little attention from historians. I. N. Phelps Stokes and D. C. Haskell provide an excellent guide to the admirable Stokes Collection now housed in the New York Public Library in *American Historical Prints, Early Views of American Cities, etc.* (New York, 1932). *The Iconography of Manhattan Island* reproduces virtually all the known maps and views of New Amsterdam and New York. The following list includes the prints and maps used in the preparation of this work:

Prints

Ebenezer Burgis, *A South East View of Ye Great Town of Boston in New England in America* [ca. 1720] (Boston, 1722).
William Price, *A South East View of Ye Great Town of Boston in New England in America* (Boston, 1743).
"View of Newport about 1740," R. I. Hist. Society, *Collections*, XVIII, 1. (Date is doubtful.)
Ebenezer Burgis, *A South Prospect of Ye Flourishing City of New York in the Province of New York in America* [ca. 1740] (Reissue by Thomas Bakewell of a Burgis map of about 1720, New York, 1740).
"The South Prospect of the City of New York in North America," *London Magazine*, 1761. (Based largely on the Burgis view, and probably shows the city, ca. 1750.)
Peter Cooper, *The South East Prospect of the City of Philadelphia* [ca. 1718] (Historical Society of Pennsylvania. Unreliable and idealized).
"The East Prospect of the City of Philadelphia, in the Province of Pennsylvania," *London Magazine*, 1761. (Date, ca. 1754.)
B. Roberts, "An Exact Prospect of Charlestown, the Metropolis of South Carolina," *London Magazine*, 1760. (Based almost wholly on the Roberts' view of 1739.)

Maps

John Bonner, *The Town of Boston in New England* (Boston, 1722).
Charles Blaskowitz, *A Plan of the Town of Newport in Rhode Island* (London, 1777).

John Mumford, *Draught of the Town of Newport. January 3rd, 1712/13.*
(Reduced facsimile.)
Newport, R. I., Draught of Highways, &c., 1713–1760. (Large MS plan in
Massachusetts Historical Society.)
Newport, R. I., Plan of Long Wharf in 1760. (Large MS draft in Massa-
chusetts Historical Society.)
William Bradford, *A Plan of the City of New York from an actual survey
made by James Lyne* (New York, 1730).
Historical Map of Pennsylvania (Philadelphia, 1885).
"Philadelphia as William Penn Knew It," *Pennsylvania Magazine of History
and Biography,* LIX, 208.
Nicholas Scull, *Map of Philadelphia* [1761] (Philadelphia, 1858).
Edward Crisp, "A Plan of Charles Town from a Survey of Edwd. Crisp, Esq.
in 1704," *Charleston Year Book,* 1880, frontispiece.
"Iconography of Charles Town at High Water [1739]," *Charleston Year Book,*
1884, frontispiece.

Valuable as are these maps and prints nothing can take the place of personal
observation of the historical remains of the five communities. Lining the
narrow streets of Newport are probably more seventeenth and eighteenth
century houses than can be found anywhere in America; and the eighteenth
century "atmosphere" of Charleston is proverbial.

Finding List of Manuscripts

Massachusetts Historical Society
Peter Burr, Common-place Book (Accounts of a schoolmaster, *ca.* 1695).
Episcopal Charitable Society in New England (Records, 1724–1790).
Benjamin Wadsworth, Account Book.

Baker Library, Harvard Business School
Journal of a General Store, 1685–1689.
Letters of Boston Merchants, 1732–1766.

Harvard College Library
Joseph Bennett, History of New England, 1740 (Sparks MSS, II).

Rhode Island Historical Society
Freebody Papers, MS Bk., no. 16.
Papers concerning Newport.

Historical Society of Pennsylvania
Accounts of millers, cooper, etc., and the bolting trade, 1704–1705.
Ancient Records of Philadelphia (Wallace Collection).
Court Papers, Philadelphia County. (2 vols.)
Letter Books of James Logan.
Indentures of Apprentices, 1677–1849.
Logan Papers.
Minutes of the Fellowship Fire Company. (2 vols.)
Merchant's Account Book, 1694–1698.

Library Company of Philadelphia
Minutes of the [Union] Fire Company commencing the 7th Day of
December, 1736.

South Carolina Historical Society
    Transactions of the Society of Friends in Charles Town, 1719.
    Case of Robert Davis, 1699.

South Carolina Historical Commission (Columbia)
    Journals of the Commons House of South Carolina (to 1742).
    Public Records of South Carolina (to 1742).
    MSS Laws of Archdale's administration.

Vestry of St. Philip's Church, Charleston
    Church Wardens' Accounts (to 1742).
    Vestry Minutes (to 1742).

INDEX